This book should be returned to any branch of the

SKELMERSDALE

BY MARK MITCHELL AND DAVID LEAVITT

The Penguin Book of Gay Short Stories
Italian Pleasures

PAGES PASSED FROM HAND TO HAND

The Hidden Tradition of
Homosexual Literature in English
from 1748 to 1914

EDITED AND WITH AN INTRODUCTION BY
Mark Mitchell and David Leavitt

VINTAGE

Published by Vintage 1999

2 4 6 8 10 9 7 5 3 1

The editors gratefully acknowledge permission to reprint extracts and excerpts from the following:

The Golden Age by Kenneth Grahame copyright © The University Chest, Oxford, by permission of Curtis Brown, London; *The Challoners* by E. F. Benson by permission of A. P. Watt; *The Hill* by H. A. Vachell by permission of John Murray (Publishers) Ltd; *The Better End* by L. U. Wilkinson by permission of Laurence Pollinger Ltd and the Estate of Louis Wilkinson; *The Complete Short Stories Vol. One* by D. H. Lawrence by permission of Laurence Pollinger Ltd and the Estate of Frieda Lawrence Ravagli; *Maurice* by E. M. Forster by permission of The Provost and Scholars of King's College, Cambridge, and The Society of Authors as the literary representatives of the E. M. Forster Estate.

First published in Great Britain in 1998
by Chatto & Windus

Vintage
Random House, 20 Vauxhall Bridge Road, London SW1V 2SA

Random House Australia (Pty) Limited
20 Alfred Street, Milsons Point, Sydney, New South Wales 2061, Australia

Random House New Zealand Limited
18 Poland Road, Glenfield, Auckland 10, New Zealand

Random House South Africa (Pty) Limited
Endulini, 5A Jubilee Road, Parktown 2193, South Africa

The Random House Group Limited Reg. No. 954009
www.randomhouse.co.uk

A CIP catalogue record for this book is available from the British Library

ISBN 0 09 976871 2

Papers used by Random House are natural, recyclable products made from wood grown in sustainable forests. The manufacturing processes conform to the environmental regulations of the country of origin

Printed and bound in Denmark by
Nørhaven A/S, Viborg

For Ruth Whiddon Alford

and in memory of

Ida Leavitt Leight {1899–1997}

"Two men can defy the world."

— E. M. FORSTER
Maurice {1914}

ACKNOWLEDGMENTS

For their generous assistance in the development and preparation of this book, we would like to thank Robyn Asleson, Hennie Aucamp, Jonathan Burnham, Timothy d'Arch Smith, David Deiss, David Filer, James Gifford, Walter Kaiser, Shusuke Kobayashi, Michael Lee, Graham Mitchell, Peter Parker, Mark Roberts of the British Institute Library, Florence, Dawn Seferian, Randolph Trumbach, Burton Weiss, and Jayne Yaffe.

CONTENTS

Introduction   *xiii*

TOBIAS SMOLLETT   1
1748   from *The Adventures of Roderick Random*

JOHN CLELAND   9
1749   from *Memoirs of a Woman of Pleasure*

CHARLOTTE CIBBER CHARKE   16
1756   from *The History of Henry Dumont, Esq.*

HERMAN MELVILLE   22
1856   "I and My Chimney"

BAYARD TAYLOR   48
1870   from *Joseph and His Friend: A Story of Pennsylvania*

CHARLES WARREN STODDARD   64
1873   from *South Sea Idyls*
       "In a Transport"

WALTER PATER   77
1885   from *Marius the Epicurean*

ALAN DALE (pseudonym of Alfred J. Cohen)   83
1889   *A Marriage Below Zero*

HOWARD OVERING STURGIS   206
1891   from *Tim: A Story of Eton*

AMBROSE BIERCE   214
1891   from *Tales of Soldiers and Civilians*
       "The Mocking-Bird"

HENRY JAMES   220
1891-92 "Collaboration"

Anonymous   240
1893 from *Teleny; or The Reverse of the Medal*

The REVEREND EDWIN EMANUEL BRADFORD   255
1893 "Boris Orloff"

JOHN FRANCIS BLOXAM   263
1894 "The Priest and the Acolyte"

STANISLAUS ERIC, COUNT STENBOCK   275
1894 from *Studies of Death: Romantic Tales*
        "Hylas"
        "Narcissus"
        "The True Story of a Vampire"

KENNETH GRAHAME   296
1895 from *The Golden Age*
        "The Roman Road"

FREDERICK ROLFE, BARON CORVO   304
1897 "In Praise of Billy B."

OWEN WISTER   309
1902 from *The Virginian: A Horseman of the Plains*
        "Em'ly"

EDWARD FREDERIC BENSON   323
1904 from *The Challoners*

JOHN GAMBRIL NICHOLSON   338
1905 from *The Romance of a Choir-Boy*
        "A Catalogue"

WILLA CATHER   351
1905 from *The Troll Garden*
        "The Sculptor's Funeral"

HORACE ANNESLEY VACHELL 364
1905   from *The Hill: A Romance of Friendship*
        "A Revelation"

CHARLES KENNETH SCOTT-MONCRIEFF 375
1908   "Evensong and Morwe Song"

SAKI (pseudonym of Hector Hugh Munro) 381
1911   from *The Chronicles of Clovis*
        "Tobermory"

LOUIS UMFREVILLE WILKINSON 389
c. 1912   "The Better End: Conclusion of a chapter
        from the unpublished novel, What Percy Knew,
        by H*nr* J*m*s"

EDWARD IRENAEUS PRIME-STEVENSON 392
1913   from *Her Enemy, Some Friends — and Other Personages:*
        Stories & Studies Mostly of Human Hearts
        "Out of the Sun"

DAVID HERBERT LAWRENCE 404
1914   "The Prussian Officer"

PATRICK WESTON (pseudonym of Gerald Bernard Francis Hamilton) 424
1914   from *Desert Dreamers*

EDWARD MORGAN FORSTER 438
1914   from *Maurice*

INTRODUCTION

I.

In 1902, Edward Carpenter published what may have been the first English-language anthology with a homosexual theme, *Ioläus: An Anthology of Friendship*, which excerpted works by — among others — Lord Byron, Pindar, Plato, Plutarch, Saint Augustine, and August von Platen. In his preface, Carpenter wrote:

> The degree to which Friendship, in the early history of the world, has been recognized as an institution, and the dignity ascribed to it, are things hardly realised to-day. Yet a very slight examination of the subject shows the important part it has played. In making the following connection I have been struck by the remarkable manner in which the customs of various races and times illustrate each other, and the way in which they point to a solid and enduring body of human sentiment on a subject.

That "Friendship," for Carpenter, meant specifically a bond between two men (or two women) is borne out by the book's epigraph, from Plutarch: "And as to the loves of Hercules it is difficult to record them because of their number. But some who think that Ioläus was one of them do to this day worship and honour him; and make their loved ones swear fidelity at his tomb." Like Damon and Pythias, Achilles and Patroclus, and the Ladies of Llangollen, Hercules and Ioläus represented for Carpenter a high-minded, even exalted ideal of same-sex love, one that his contemporaries might emulate, and that he himself sought to embody in the rural utopia he shared with George Merrill. Yet in order to find such positive models, Carpenter had to ransack world literature; to construct a version of history in which friendship, not marriage, was the defining term. *Ioläus*, in other words, is less a collection of homosexually themed writing than of homosexually themed reading.

II.

Since the eighteenth century, men who were sexually attracted to other men — sodomites, pederasts, urnings, Uranians, similisexualists, queers — have constituted a distinct and numerous reading class. Indeed, long before many bookstores in the English-speaking world sponsored "gay and lesbian studies" sections, such readers displayed an astonishing tenacity in locating those poems, stories, novels, essays, and even individual sentences in which references to homosexual experience might be found. Thus, both Oscar Wilde and Marcel Proust could recognize the signposts to Vautrin's homosexuality in Honoré de Balzac's *Illusions perdues* and *Splendeurs et misères des courtisanes*. (Lucien de Rubempré's death, says Vivian in "The Decay of Lying," is "One of the greatest tragedies of my life," while André Maurois, in his biography of Proust, quotes from one of his subject's memoranda: "Vautrin stopping in order to visit Rastignac's house; *tristesse d'Olympio* of pederasty.") The merest allusion could be enough to clue the reader: to Hadrian and Antinoüs, to David and Jonathan ("thy love to me was wonderful, passing the love of women"). And the works in which such content lay — nascent, unbudded — these readers passed on to one another. Word-of-mouth dissemination: *read this.*

III.

In his 1913 story "Out of the Sun," Edward Irenaeus Prime-Stevenson describes a very particular library:

> Ah, his books! The library of almost every man of like making-up, whose life has been largely solitary . . . is companioned from youth up by innermost literary sympathies of his type. Dayneford stood now before his bookcase, reading over mechanically the titles of a special group of volumes — mostly small ones. They were crowded into a few lower shelves, as if they sought to avoid other literary society, to keep themselves to themselves, to shun all unsympathetic observation. Tibullus, Propertius and the Greek Antologists [*sic*] pressed against Al Nafsewah and Chakani and Hafiz. A little further along stood Shakespeare's Sonnets, and those by Buonarrotti; along with Tennyson's "In Memoriam," Woodberry's "The North-Shore Watch," and Walt Whitman. Back of Platen's bulky "Tagebuch" lay his poems. Next to them came Wilbrandt's "Fridolins Heimliche Ehe," beside Rachilde's "Les Hors Nature;" then Pernauhm's "Die Infamen," Emil Vacano's "Humbug," and a group of psychologic

works by Krafft-Ebbing and Ellis and Moll. There was a thin book in which were bound together, in a richly-decorated arabesque cover, some six or seven stories from Mardrus' French translation of "The Thousand Nights and a Night" — remorsely [*sic*] separated from their original companions. On a lower shelf, rested David Christie Murray's "Val Strange" and one or two other old novels; along with Dickens' "David Copperfield," the anonymous "Tim," and Vachell's "The Hill," companioned by Mayne's "Intersexes," "Imre" and "Sebastian au Plus Bel Age."

It is neither coincidental that Dayneford's library contains some of the same volumes that Carpenter excerpted in *Ioläus,* nor surprising that he "remorsely" (remorselessly?) separates some of the stories in *The Thousand and One Nights* "from their original companions." ("The Third Kalandar's Tale," in Sir Richard Francis Burton's translation, is included in *The Penguin Book of International Gay Writing.*) Dayneford's library, like Carpenter's, has an ideology. For him, the quasi-scholarly excision of literary fragments — taking them literally out of context — is not so much a trick as a necessary, if ruthless, step in the effort to invent, through reading, a *new* context in which homosexual bonds, instead of being vilified, are glorified.

The list-making impulse does not end with Prime-Stevenson. In 1924, a "Student of Boyhood, Youth and Comradeship" published a catalogue of books from his (or — who knows? — her) private library; a total of 454 titles drawn from poetry, drama, belles-lettres, essays, biography, and fiction, including many familiar from both Carpenter and "Dayneford."

IV.

H. Montgomery Hyde, in *The Other Love: An Historical and Contemporary Survey of Homosexuality in Britain* (1970), recounts a seminal episode in the history of pages passed from hand to hand. In 1889, Charles Hirsch (later to become a publisher in Paris) was running the Librairie Parisienne on Coventry Street in London. Among his regular clients was Oscar Wilde, who purchased from him not only books in French (among them novels by Zola and Maupassant), but what Hirsch calls works of a "Socratic" nature. Nor did Wilde usually come alone to the bookstore; often he was accompanied by "distinguished young men" of a literary or artistic appearance who showed him "a familiar deference."

One afternoon Wilde arrived at the bookstore with a small, carefully sealed package, which he asked Hirsch to hold for a friend who would show him Wilde's card. Hirsch agreed, and in due course one of the young men Hirsch had met in Wilde's company came by for the package. Several days later the same young man brought it back, leaving it to be picked up by another young man. Altogether three exchanges of this kind took place, and the last young man, "less discreet" than the other two, brought back the package in a rather "poorly wrapped" condition. When Hirsch opened it, he discovered the manuscript of a novel transcribed in several different handwritings, and full of marginal additions and erasures. He misread the title as *Feleny*. "It was evident," he wrote, "that several writers of unequal merit had collaborated on this anonymous but profoundly interesting work."

One wonders, in this post-Freudian age, at Hirsch's misreading. After all, wouldn't publishing *Teleny* — as Hirsch would later do in a French translation — be to risk, in England, conviction on a *felony* charge? (Curiously, the English edition sets the story in Paris; the French one in London.)

v.

The vast majority of "gay" texts known today were written after the Great War; and the vast majority of these after the Stonewall riots; and, as if literary history were a series of Chinese boxes, the vast majority of these after the advent (in the West) of the human immunodeficiency virus.

Imagine yourself, then, a homosexual reader in the year 1914. You are standing in a vast, shadowy library, and you want to read something . . . well, something about two men, or two women, who form a possibly erotic bond: something that speaks to your experience, or to an experience of which you dream. Where do you begin? There is no catalogue to guide you. Gore Vidal's *The City and the Pillar* has not been written; nor has James Baldwin's *Giovanni's Room*, nor Rita Mae Brown's *Rubyfruit Jungle*, nor Edmund White's *A Boy's Own Story*. Not even Radclyffe Hall's *The Well of Loneliness*. Neither James Merrill nor Dale Peck's parents have been born. *Maurice* will be finished this year — a quiet revolution in Weybridge — but it will not see the light of day until decades after you have died. Perhaps its dog-eared pages will find their way into your hands if you are lucky enough to be part of Forster's intimate circle, which probably you are not.

Maybe you know someone who has suggested a few titles to you. Maybe you are a client of one of the select continental bookstores that stock privately published editions — works like Prime-Stevenson's *Imre: A Memorandum*, printed in Naples in 1906, or the pseudonymous Patrick

Weston's *Desert Dreamers,* or the slim volume of *Songs of Adieu* by the first Uranian poet, Lord Henry Somerset. Perhaps you have heard about *Tim,* with its astonishingly blatant (though repellently sentimental) account of a love between two boys. Maybe someone has told you about Theodore Winthrop's *Cecil Dreeme* (1861), in which the male narrator falls in love with a young man who turns out to be a girl in disguise. If so, you are fortunate. If not, you will have no choice but to scan spines and titles, hoping to find one that makes an allusion to the Greeks.

The surprise — like the surprise Glinda the Good Witch imparts to Dorothy at the end of *The Wizard of Oz* — is that the books were there all along, if only you had known where to look. For even if, like Proust and Wilde, you have supersensitive antennae, a capacity to detect even the faintest stirrings of homosexual longing, the fact is that you are living in a world where the vast majority of readers and critics are so unfamiliar with the signs that they can hurry through an account of a homosexual love affair as uncompromised as that in Bayard Taylor's *Joseph and His Friend* and not ever register what it means. After all, they have probably not read *Ioläus,* nor would they define friendship in quite the manner that Carpenter does. The most astute of all Wilde's aphorisms may be this one: "It is only superficial people who do not judge by appearances."

VI.

Today the study of pre-1914 homosexual literature is still a matter of pages passed from hand to hand. To assemble this anthology, we asked friends. We read photocopies of photocopies that scholars and antiquarians sent to us; books of which only one copy existed in one "special collection." We did our time at the British Library in London and at the Clarke Library in Los Angeles, mentally translated the F-shaped S's in Charlotte Charke's *Henry Dumont,* an edition so old and frail that specially weighted velvet bags had to be used to hold it open.

On what basis did we make our selections? In order to construct a timeline, of sorts, from prose fiction text to text: beginning in the eighteenth century, where inveighings against sodomy sometimes found their way into long novels (and often encoded an unsuspected sympathy), through works of privately printed pornography, to horror stories and children's stories, boys' school novels and Westerns and exemplars of consummate queeny wit, all the way to Forster.

It is often said that the only thing homosexual men have in common is a series of sexual practices. These pages suggest the presence of much more: at the beginning of our literary tradition, a longing for a greenwood (that homage to Arcady) and a cabin where two men might live together peacefully and unbothered, as Carpenter and Merrill did. Only later does the exurban world become the source of repression, the city instead offering freedom to the homosexual — not as part of a utopia-questing dyad, but in community with the fellow members of his tribe.

VII.

Let us return to Carpenter. If he gave *Ioläus* the subtitle *An Anthology of Friendship,* did he do so merely to be euphemistic? No. Friendship was an ideal in which he believed profoundly. It was also a politically savvy strategy. Indeed, to him Wilde's trials were a setback for the "intermediate sex" insofar as they exposed to public scrutiny the cruder aspects of the Victorian homosexual underworld: blackmailing renters, feces-stained sheets, outraged maids. He preferred not to dwell, in his anthology, on "the grosser side of the passion, in such writers as Catullus and Martial." Still, *Maurice* was provoked not by finer sentiments, but by Merrill touching Forster's backside, "gently and just above the buttocks."

> I believe he touched most people's. The sensation was unusual and I still remember it, as I remember the position of a long vanished tooth. It was as much psychological as physical. It seemed to go straight through the small of my back into my ideas, without involving my thoughts. If it really did this, it would have acted in strict accordance with Carpenter's yogified mysticism, and would prove that at that precise moment I had conceived.

Because homosexuality was still a crime in England when Forster wrote *Maurice,* he never published it in his lifetime. And yet for half a century, this deeply subversive novel was passed from hand to hand: he shared the manuscript with such of his friends as J. R. Ackerley, Paul Cadmus (who drew a portrait of the author at the same time), E. J. Dent, Christopher Isherwood, William Plomer, Forrest Reid, and Lytton Strachey (the model for the character Risley, the one who "accented one word violently" in each of his sentences). In the end, probably as many people read *Maurice* in manuscript as would have done so had Forster, like Prime-Stevenson, paid to have a private edition printed.

VIII.

Perhaps because we were born after the greenwood faded, a glamour attaches itself to that cabin, with its faintly erotic closeness: the smell of wood smoke, the bed with its rough blankets, the two men in work clothes that have really been worked in, reading in collapsing chairs. As a visitor, you are welcome to browse through the library. No searching now. One book (or manuscript) after another you pick up, thumb through. And how curious! The shelves are overloaded, buckling. Titles you've never seen. You choose something almost at random, sit down in the third chair that is always waiting, and begin.

PAGES PASSED *from* HAND *to* HAND

TOBIAS SMOLLETT

{1721–1771}

In *The Adventures of Roderick Random* (1748), Tobias Smollett depicts one of the first explicitly homosexual characters in English literature: Earl Strutwell, "notorious for a passion for his own sex," who takes advantage of the young Roderick's naiveté in order to kiss him, fondle him, and steal his watch. Typically for eighteenth-century England, Smollett's attitude toward Strutwell is an indignant one. Nonetheless he also lets the earl have his say in a lengthy and eloquent defense of homosexual love, which contradicts the chapter's official tone of censure, and which the earl presents to Roderick along with a copy of Petronius's *Satyricon*.

As H. Montgomery Hyde points out in *The Other Love*, Strutwell's declaration that sodomy "gains ground apace and in all probability will become in a short time a more fashionable vice than simple fornication" was cited in a pamphlet published in 1749 under the title "Satan's Harvest Home: or the Present State of Whorecraft, Adultery, Fornication, Procuring, Pimping, Sodomy . . . And other Satanic Works, daily propagated in this good Protestant Kingdom." This pamphlet protests the habits of "vile Catamites" and concludes that nothing can be "more shocking, than to see a Couple of Creatures, who wear the shape of Men, Kiss and Slaver each other, to that Degree, as is daily practised even in our most publick places; and (generally speaking) without Reproof; because they plead in Excuse, that is the Fashion. Damn'd Fashion! Imported from Italy amidst a Train of other unnatural Vices."

"Satan's Harvest Home" is one of the earliest documents to identify Italy as "the Mother and Nurse of Sodomy," suggesting one of the reasons why Italy was such a popular destination for homosexual émigrés.

FROM *The Adventures of Roderick Random*

CHAPTER 51

I cultivate an acquaintance with two noblemen — am introduced to Earl Strutwell — his kind promise and invitation — the behavior of his porter and lacquey — he receives me with an appearance of uncommon affection — undertakes to speak in my behalf to the minister — informs me of his success, and wishes me joy — introduces a conversation about Petronius Arbiter — falls in love with my watch, which I press upon him — I make a present of a diamond ring to lord Straddle — impart my good fortune to Strap and Banter, who disabuses me, to my utter mortification

Baffled hitherto in my matrimonial schemes, I began to question my talents for the science of fortune-hunting, and to bend my thoughts towards some employment under the government. — With the view of procuring which, I cultivated the acquaintance of Lords Straddle and Swillpot, whose fathers were men of interest at court. — I found these young noblemen as open to my advances as I could desire: I accompanied them in their midnight rambles, and often dined with them at taverns, where I had the honour of paying the reckoning.

I one day took the opportunity, while I was loaded with protestations of friendship, to disclose my desire of being settled in some sine-cure; and to solicit their influence in my behalf. — Swillpot squeezing my hand, said, I might depend upon his service, by G——d. The other swore that no man would be more proud than he to run my errands. Encouraged by these declarations I ventured to express an inclination to be introduced to their fathers, who were able to do my business at once. Swillpot frankly owned he had not spoke to his father these three years; and Straddle assured me his father having lately disobliged the Minister by subscribing his name to a protest in the house of peers, was thereby rendered incapable of serving his friends at present; but he undertook to make me acquainted with Earl Strutwell, who was hand and glove with a certain person that ruled the roast. This offer I embraced with many acknowledgments, and plied him so closely, in spite of a thousand evasions, that he found himself under a necessity of keeping his word, and actually carried me to the levée of this great man, where he left me in a crowd of fellow-dependants, and was ushered to a particular closet audience; from whence in a few minutes, he returned with his lordship, who took me by the hand, assured me he would do me all the service he could, and desired to see me often. — I was charmed with my reception, and although I had heard that a courtier's promise is not to be depended upon, I thought I discovered so much sweetness of temper and candour in this Earl's countenance, that I did not doubt of profiting by his protection. — I resolved therefore, to avail myself of his permission, and waited on him next audience day, when I was favoured with a particular smile, squeeze of the hand, and a whisper, signifying that he wanted half an hour's conversation with me *tête a tête*, when he should be disengaged, and for that purpose desired me to come and drink a dish of chocolate with him to-morrow morning. — This invitation, which did not a little flatter my vanity and expectation, I took care to observe, and went to his lordship's house at the time appointed. Having rapped at the gate, the porter unbolted and kept it half open, placing himself in the gap, like soldiers in a breach, to dispute my passage. — I demanded to know if his lord was stirring? — He answered with a surly aspect, "No." — "At what hour does he commonly rise? (said I)" — "Sometimes sooner, sometimes later (said he, closing the door upon me by degrees.)" — I then told him I was come by his lordship's own appointment; to which this Cerberus replied, "I have received no orders about the matter;" and was upon the point of shutting me out, when I recollected myself all of a sudden, and slipping a crown into his hand, begged as a favour that he would enquire and let me know whether or not the Earl was up. The grim janitor relented at the touch of my money, which he took with all the indifference of a tax-gatherer, and shewed me into a parlour, where, he said, I might amuse myself till such time as his lord should be awake. — I had not sat ten minutes in this place, when a footman entered, and without speaking, stared at me; I interpreted this piece of his behaviour into "Pray Sir, what is your business?" and asked the same question I had put to the porter, when I accosted him first. The lacquey made the same reply, and disappeared before I could get any further intelligence. — In a little time he returned, on pretence of poking the fire, and looked at me again with great earnestness; upon which I began to perceive his meaning, and tipping him with half a crown, desired he would be so good as to fall upon some method of letting the Earl know that I was in the house. — He made a low bow, said, "Yes, Sir," and vanished. — This bounty was not thrown away, for in an instant he came back, and conducted me to a chamber, where I was received with great kindness and familiarity by his lordship, whom I found just risen, in his morning gown and slippers. — After breakfast, he entered into a particular conversation with me about my travels, the remarks I had made abroad, and examined me to the full extent of my understanding. — My answers seemed to please him very much, he frequently squeezed my hand, and looking at me with a singular complacency in his countenance, bid me depend upon his good offices with the ministry in my behalf. "Young men of your qualifications (said he) ought to be cherished by every administration — For my own part, I see so little merit in the world, that I have laid it down as a maxim, to encourage the least appearance of genius and virtue, to the utmost of my power — You have a great deal of both; and will not fail of making a figure one day, if I am not mistaken; but you must lay your account with mounting by gradual steps to the summit of your fortune. — *Rome was not built in a day.* — As you understand the languages perfectly well, how would you like to cross the sea, as secretary to an embassy?" — I assured his lordship, with great eagerness, that nothing could be more agreeable to my inclination: Upon which he bid me make myself easy, my business was done, for he had a place of that kind in his view. — This piece of generosity affected me so much, that I was unable for some time to express my gratitude, which at length broke out in acknowledgments of my own unworthiness, and encomiums on his benevolence. — I could not even help shedding tears, at the goodness of this noble lord, who no sooner perceived them, than he caught me in his arms, hugged and kissed me with a seemingly paternal affection. — Confounded at this uncommon instance of fondness for a stranger, I remained a few moments silent and ashamed, then got up and took my leave, after he had assured me that he would speak to the Minister in my favour, that very day; and desired that I would not for the future give myself the trouble of attending at his levée, but come at the same hour every day, when he was at leisure, which was three times a week.

Though my hopes were now very sanguine, I determined to conceal my prospect from every body, even from Strap, until I should be more certain of success; and in the mean time, give my patron no respite from my sollicitations. — When I renewed my visit, I found the street door opened to me as if by enchantment; but in my passage towards the presence-room, I was met by the *valet de chambre*, who cast some furious looks at me, the meaning of which I could not comprehend. The Earl saluted me at entrance with a tender embrace, and wished me joy of his success with the Premier, who, he said, had preferred his recommendation to that of two other noblemen very urgent in behalf of their respective friends, and absolutely promised that I should go to a certain foreign court in quality of secretary to an embassador and plenipotentiary, who would set out in a few weeks, on an affair of vast importance to the nation. I was thunderstruck with my good fortune, and could make no other reply, than kneel and attempt to kiss my benefactor's hand, which he would not permit, but raising me up, pressed me to his breast with surprizing emotion, and told

me he had now taken upon himself the care of making my fortune. —
What inhanced the value of the benefit still the more, was his making light
of the favour, and shifting the conversation to another subject: Among
other topicks of discourse, that of the *Belle Lettre* was introduced, upon
which his lordship held forth with great taste and erudition, and discovered an intimate knowledge of the authors of antiquity. — "Here's a book
(said he, taking one from his bosom) written with great elegance and spirit,
and though the subject may give offence to some narrow-minded people,
the author will always be held in esteem by every person of sense and
learning." So saying, he put into my hand Petronius Arbiter, and asked my
opinion of his wit and manner. — I told him, that in my opinion, he wrote
with great ease and vivacity, but was withal so lewd and indecent, that he
ought to find no quarter or protection among people of morals and taste.
— "I own (replied the Earl) that his taste in love is generally decried, and
indeed condemned by our laws; but perhaps that may be more owing to
prejudice and misapprehension, than to true reason and deliberation. —
The best man among the ancients is said to have entertained that passion;
one of the wisest of their legislators has permitted the indulgence of it in his
commonwealth; the most celebrated poets have not scrupled to avow it at
this day; it prevails not only over all the east, but in most parts of Europe;
in our own country it gains ground apace, and in all probability will
become in a short time a more fashionable vice than simple fornication. —
Indeed there is something to be said in vindication of it, for notwithstanding the severity of the law against offenders in this way, it must be confessed that the practice of this passion is unattended with that curse and
burthen upon society, which proceeds from a race of miserable deserted
bastards, who are either murdered by their parents, deserted to the utmost
want and wretchedness, or bred up to prey upon the commonwealth: And
it likewise prevents the debauchery of many a young maiden, and the pros-
titution of honest men's wives; not to mention the consideration of health,
which is much less liable to be impaired in the gratification of this appetite,
than in the exercise of common venery, which by ruining the constitutions
of our young men, has produced a puny progeny that degenerates from
generation to generation: Nay, I have been told, that there is another motive perhaps more powerful than all these, that induces people to cultivate
this inclination; namely, the exquisite pleasure attending its success."

From this discourse, I began to be apprehensive that his lordship finding I had travelled, was afraid I might have been infected with this spuri-
ous and sordid desire abroad, and took this method of sounding my sentiments on the subject. — Fired at this supposed suspicion, I argued against

it with great warmth, as an appetite unnatural, absurd, and of pernicious consequence; and declared my utter detestation and abhorrence of it in these lines of the satyrist:

> "Eternal infamy the wretch confound
> Who planted first, this vice on British ground!
> A vice! that 'spite of sense and nature reigns,
> And poisons genial love, and manhood stains!"

The Earl smiled at my indignation, told me he was glad to find my opinion of the matter so conformable to his own, and that what he had advanced was only to provoke me to an answer, with which he professed himself perfectly well pleased.

After I had enjoyed a long audience, I happened to look at my watch, in order to regulate my motions by it; and his lordship observing the chased case, desired to see the device, and examine the execution, which he approved with some expressions of admiration. — Considering the obligations I lay under to his lordship, I thought there could not be a fitter opportunity than the present to manifest, in some shape, my gratitude; I therefore begged he would do me the honour to accept of the watch as a small testimony of the sense I had of his lordship's generosity; but he refused it in a peremptory manner, and said he was sorry I should entertain such a mercenary opinion of him, observing at the same time, that it was the most beautiful piece of workmanship he had ever seen; and desiring to know where he could have such another. — I begged a thousand pardons for the freedom I had taken, which I hoped he would impute to nothing else than the highest veneration for his person — let him know that as it came to my hand by accident in France, I could give him no information about the maker, for there was no name on the inside; and once more humbly entreated that he would indulge me so far as to use it for my sake. — He was still positive in refusing it; but was pleased to thank me for my generous offer, saying, it was a present that no nobleman needed be ashamed of receiving; though he was resolved to shew his disinterestedness with regard to me, for whom he had conceived a particular friendship; and insisted (if I was willing to part with the watch) upon knowing what it cost, that he might at least indemnify me, by refunding the money. On the other hand, I assured his lordship, that I would look upon it as an uncommon mark of distinction, if he would take it without further question; and rather than disoblige me, he was at last persuaded to put it in his pocket, to my no small satisfaction, who took my leave immediately, after having received a kind squeeze, and an injunction to depend upon his promise.

Buoyed up with my reception, my heart opened, I gave away a guinea among the lacqueys, who escorted me to the door, flew to the lodgings of Lord Straddle, upon whom I forced my diamond ring, as an acknowledgment for the great service he had done me, and from thence hied myself home, with an intent of sharing my happiness with honest Strap. — I determined, however, to heighten his pleasure by depressing his spirits at first, and then bringing in the good news with double relish. — For this purpose, I affected the appearance of disappointment and chagrin, and told him in an abrupt manner, that I had lost the watch and diamond. Poor Hugh, who had been already harrassed into a consumption by intelligence of this sort, no sooner heard these words, than, unable to contain himself, he cried with distraction in his looks, "God in heaven forbid!" — I could carry on the farce no longer, but laughing in his face, told him every thing that had befallen, as above recited. His features were immediately unbended, and the transition so affecting, that he wept with joy, calling my Lord Strutwell by the appellations of Jewel, Phœnix, *Rara avis,* and praising God, that there was still some virtue left among our nobility. — Our mutual congratulations being over, we gave way to our imagination, and anticipated our happiness by prosecuting my success through the different steps of promotion, till I arrived at the rank of a prime minister, and he to that of my first secretary.

Intoxicated with these ideas I went to the ordinary, where, meeting with Banter, I communicated the whole affair in confidence to him, concluding with an assurance that I would do him all the service in my power. — He heard me to an end with great patience, then regarding me a good while with a look of disdain, pronounced, "So, your business is done, you think?" — "As good as done, I believe, (said I.)" — "I'll tell you (replied he) what will do it still more effectually — A halter — 'Sdeath! if I had been such a gull to two such scoundrels as Strutwell and Straddle, I would without any more ado tuck myself up." Shocked at this exclamation, I desired him with some confusion to explain himself: Upon which he gave me to understand, that Straddle was a poor contemptible wretch, who lived by borrowing and pimping to his fellow peers; that in consequence of this last capacity, he had, doubtless, introduced me to Strutwell, who was so notorious for a passion for his own sex, that he was amazed his character had never reached my ears; and that so far from being able to obtain for me the post he had promised, his interest at court was so low, that he could scarce provide for a superannuated footman once a year, in Chelsea-hospital; — that it was a common thing for him to amuse strangers whom his jack-calls run down, with such assurances and caresses as he had bestowed on me, until he had stript them of their cash and every thing valuable about them;

— very often of their chastity, and then leave them a prey to want and infamy; — that he allowed his servants no other wages than that part of the spoil which they could glean by their industry; and that the whole of his conduct towards me was so glaring, that no body who knew any thing of mankind could have been imposed upon by his insinuations.

I leave the reader to judge how I relished this piece of information, which precipitated me from the most exalted pinnacle of hope to the lowest abyss of despondence; and well nigh determined me to take Banter's advice, and finish my chagrin with a halter. — I had no room to suspect the veracity of my friend, because upon recollection, I found every circumstance of Strutwell's behaviour, exactly tallying with the character he had described: His hugs, embraces, squeezes and eager looks, were now no longer a mystery; no more than his defence of Petronius, and the jealous frown of his *valet de chambre*, who, it seems, was at present the favourite pathic of his lord.

{1748}

JOHN CLELAND
{1710–1789}

Educated at Westminster School, as a young man John Cleland worked for the East India Company in Bombay, where he wrote the first draft of *Memoirs of a Woman of Pleasure*, better known today as *Fanny Hill*. In 1741 he returned to England to sit at his father's deathbed, then fell into such severe debt that he ended up in Fleet Prison. It was during his incarceration that he completed, and published, *Memoirs*. After his release, both Cleland and the printer Ralph Griffiths were arrested over the work, which was subsequently banned as obscene. However, it continued to have lively sales in underground editions. (Benjamin Franklin was purported to own a copy.)

In his later years, Cleland became eccentric, contentious, and crotchety. He lived alone in a room that Boswell described as "filled with books in confusion and dust. . . . He told me he had not tasted wine for seven years." According to Josiah Beckwith, this social isolation was the result of Cleland's having passed "under the Censure of being a Sodomite . . . and in Consequence thereof Persons of Character decline visiting him, or cultivating his Acquaintance." Peter Sabor, who cites this observation in his introduction to the Oxford World's Classics edition of *Memoirs*, suggests that the rumor "might have had a factual basis (Cleland appears never to have married) or have evolved because of the homosexual episode in the *Memoirs*, which was usually expurgated even in pirated editions."

This homosexual episode — held to be an interpolation until 1963, when David Foxon proved that it was part of the original text — is a curious amalgam of outrage and lustful voyeurism. Staying at a public house, Fanny stumbles by chance upon a carnal encounter between two teenage boys, which she sees through to the end despite her professed abhorrence of sodomy. Yet when she jumps down from her perch to denounce them, she falls on the floor and is knocked unconscious. As in *Henry Dumont* and *Roderick Random*, Fanny's "accident" results in the lovers escaping with their lives — and suggests that Cleland might have been more sympathetic to their plight than was his heroine. ❧

FROM *Memoirs of a Woman of Pleasure*

LOUISA AND SHE WENT one night to a ball; the first in the habit of a shepherdess, Emily in that of a shepherd: I saw them in their dresses before they went, and nothing in nature could represent a prettier boy than this last did; being so extremely fair and well limb'd. They had kept together for some time, when Louisa meeting with an old acquaintance of hers, very cordially gives her companion the drop, and leaves her under the protection of her boy's habit, which was not much, and of her discretion which was, it seems, yet less. Emily finding herself deserted, saunter'd thoughtlessly about a while, and as much for coolness and air, as any thing else, pull'd off her mask, at length, and went to the side-board, where, eyed and mark'd out by a gentleman in a very handsome domino, she was accosted by, and fell into chat with, him. The domino, after a little discourse, in which Emily doubtless distinguish'd her good nature and easiness more than her wit, began to make violent love to her, and drawing her insensibly to some benches at the lower end of the masquerade-room got her to sit by him, where he squeez'd her hands, pinch'd her cheeks, prais'd and play'd with her fair hair, admir'd her complexion, and all in a style of courtship dash'd with a certain oddity, that not comprehending the mystery of, poor Emily attributed to his falling in with the humour of her disguise, and being naturally not the cruellest of her profession, began to incline to a parley on essentials: but here was the stress of the joke: He took her really for what she appear'd to be, a smock-fac'd boy, and she forgetting her dress, and of course ranging quite wide of his ideas, took all those addresses to be paid to herself as a woman, which she precisely ow'd to his not thinking her one: however this double error was push'd to such a height on both sides, that Emily who saw nothing in him but a gentleman of distinction by those points of dress, to which his disguise did not extend, warm'd too by the wine he had ply'd her with, and the caresses he had lavish'd upon her, suffer'd herself to be perswaded to go to a bagnio with him; and thus loosing sight of Mrs. Cole's cautions, with a blind confidence put herself into his hands to be carried wherever he pleas'd: for his part equally blinded by his wishes, whilst her egregious simplicity favour'd his deception more than the most exquisite art could have done, he suppos'd, no doubt, that he had lighted on some soft simpleton fit for his purpose, or some kept minion broke to his hand, who understood him perfectly well, and enter'd into his designs; but be that as it would, he led her to a coach, went into it with her, and brought her into a very handsome apartment, with a bed in it, but whether it were a bagnio or not, she could not tell, having spoke to nobody but himself. But when they were alone together, and her *enamorato* began to proceed to those extremities which instantly discover the sex, she remark'd that no description could paint up to the life, the mixture of pique, confusion, and disappointment, that appear'd in his countenance, which join'd to the mournful exclamation, "By heavens a woman!" This at once open'd her eyes which had hitherto been shut in downright stupidity. However, as if he had meant to retrieve that escape, he still continu'd to toy with and fondle her, but with so staring an alteration from extreme warmth into a chill and forc'd civility, that even Emily herself could not but take notice of it, and now began to wish she had paid more regard to Mrs. Cole's premonitions against ever engaging with a stranger: and now an excess of timidity succeeded to an excess of confidence, and she thought herself so much at his mercy and discretion, that she stood passive throughout the whole progress of his prelude: for now, whether the impressions of so great a beauty had even made him forgive her, her sex, or whether her appearance or figure in that dress still humour'd his first illusion, he recover'd by degrees a good part of his first warmth, and keeping Emily with her breeches still unbuttoned, stript them down to her knees, and gently impelling her to lean down, with her face against the bedside, placed her so, that the double-way between the double rising behind, presented the choice fair to him, and he was so fiercely set on a mis-direction, as to give the girl no small alarms for fear of loosing a maiden-head she had not dreamt of; however her complaints, and a resistance gentle, but firm, check'd, and brought him to himself again; so that turning his steed's head, he drove him at length in the right road, in which his imagination having probably made the most of those resemblances that flatter'd his taste, he got with much ado whip and spur to his journey's end: after which he led her out himself, and walking with her two or three streets length, got her a chair, when making her a present not any thing inferior to what she could have expected, he left her, well recommended to the chairmen, who on her directions, brought her home.

This she related to Mrs. Cole and me, the same morning, not without the visible remains of the fear and confusion she had been in, still stamp'd on her countenance; Mrs. Cole's remark was, that her indiscretion proceeding from a constitutional facility, there were little hopes of any thing curing her of it, but repeated severe experience. Mine was that I could not conceive how it was possible for mankind to run into a taste, not only universally odious, but absurd, and impossible to gratify, since, according to the notions and experience I had of things, it was not in nature to force such immense disproportions: Mrs. Cole only smil'd at my ignorance, and said nothing towards my undeception, which was not effected but by occular demonstration, some months after, which a most singular accident furnish'd me, and I will here set down, that I may not return again to so disagreeable a subject.

I had on a visit intended to Harriet, who had lodgings at Hampton-Court, hired a chariot to go out thither, Mrs. Cole having promis'd to accompany me: but some indispensible business intervening to detain her, I was obliged to set out alone; and scarce had I got a third of my way, before the axle-tree broke down, and I was well off, to get out safe and unhurt, into a publick-house of a tolerably handsome appearance, on the road. Here the people told me that the stage would come by in a couple of hours at farthest, upon which, determining to wait for it, sooner than loose the jaunt I had got so far forward on, I was carried into a very clean decent room up one pair of stairs, which I took possession of for the time I had to stay, in right of calling for sufficient to do the house justice.

Here, whilst I was amusing myself with looking out of the window, a single horse-chaise stopt at the door, out of which lightly leap'd two young gentlemen, for so they seem'd, who came in as it were only to bait and refresh a little, for they gave their horse to be held in a readiness against they came out: and presently I heard the door of the next room to me open, where they were let in and call'd about them briskly, and as soon as they were serv'd, I could just hear that they shut and fasten'd the door on the inside.

A spirit of curiosity far from sudden, since I do not know when I was without it, prompted me, without any particular suspicion, or other drift, or view, to see who they were, and examine their persons and behaviour. The partition of our rooms was one of those moveable ones that when taken down, serv'd occasionally to lay them into one, for the convenience of a large company; and now my nicest search could not shew me the shadow of a peep-hole, a circumstance which probably had not escap'd the review of the parties on the other side, whom much it stood upon not to be deceiv'd in it; but at length I observ'd a paper-patch of the same colour as the wainscot, which I took to conceal some flaw, but then it was so high, that I was oblig'd to stand on a chair to reach it, which I did as softly as possible, and with the point of a bodkin soon pierc'd it, and open'd myself espial-room sufficient: and now applying my eye close, I commanded the room perfectly, and could see my two young sparks romping, and pulling one another about, entirely to my imagination, in frolic, and innocent play.

The eldest might be, on my nearest guess, towards nineteen, a tall comely young man, in a white fustian frock, with a green velvet cape, and a cut bob-wig.

The youngest could not be above seventeen, fair, ruddy, compleatly well made, and to say the truth, a sweet pretty stripling: He was, I fancy too, a country lad, by his dress, which was a green plush frock, and breeches of the same, white waistcoat and stockings, a jockey cap, with his yellowish hair long, and loose, in natural curls.

But after a look of circumspection which I saw the eldest cast every way round the room, probably in too much hurry and heat not to overlook the very small opening I was posted at, especially at the height it was, whilst my eye too close to it, kept the light from shining through, and betraying it; he said something to his companion that presently chang'd the face of things.

For now the elder began to embrace, to press, to kiss the younger, to put his hands in his bosom, and give such manifest signs of an amorous intention, as made me conclude the other to be a girl in disguise, a mistake that nature kept me in countenance in, for she had certainly made one, when she gave him the male stamp.

In the rashness then of their age, and bent as they were to accomplish their project of preposterous pleasure, at the risque of the very worst of consequences, where a discovery was nothing less than improbable, they now proceeded to such lengths as soon satisfied me, what they were.

For presently the eldest unbotton'd the other's breeches, and removing the linnen barrier, brought out to view a white shaft, middle-siz'd, and scarce fledg'd, when after handling, and playing with it a little, with other dalliance, all receiv'd by the boy without other opposition, than certain wayward coynesses, ten times more alluring than repulsive, he got him to turn round with his face from him, to a chair that stood hard by, when knowing, I suppose, his office, the Ganymede now obsequiously lean'd his head against the back of it, and projecting his body, made a fair mark, still cover'd with his shirt, as he thus stood in a side-view to meet but fronting his companion, who presently unmasking his battery, produc'd an engine, that certainly deserv'd to be put to a better use, and very fit to confirm me in my disbelief of the possibility of things being push'd to odious extremities, which I had built on the disproportion of parts; but this disbelief I was now to be cur'd of, as by my consent all young men should likewise be, that their innocence may not be betray'd into such snares, for want of knowing the extent of their danger, for nothing is more certain than, that ignorance of a vice, is by no means a guard against it.

Slipping then aside the young lad's shirt, and tucking it up under his cloaths behind, he shew'd to the open air, those globular, fleshy eminences that compose the mount-pleasants of Rome, and which now, with all the narrow vale that intersects them, stood display'd, and expos'd to his attack: nor could I, without a shudder, behold the dispositions he made for it. First then, moistening well with spittle his instrument, obviously to render it glib, he pointed, he introduc'd it, as I could plainly discern, not only from its direction, and my losing sight of it; but by the writhing, twisting, and soft murmur'd complaints of the young sufferer; but, at length, the first streights of entrance being pretty well got through, every thing seem'd to move, and go pretty currently on, as in a carpet-road, without much rub, or resistance: and now passing one hand round his minion's hips, he got hold of his red-topt ivory toy, that stood perfectly stiff, and shewed, that if he was like his mother behind, he was like his father before; this he diverted himself with, whilst with the other, he wanton'd with his hair, and leaning forward over his back, drew his face, from which the boy shook the loose curls that fell over it, in the posture he stood him in, and brought him towards his, so as to receive a long-breath'd kiss, after which, renewing his driving, and thus continuing to harrass his rear, the height of the fit came on with its usual symptoms, and dissmiss'd the action.

All this, so criminal a scene, I had the patience to see to an end, purely that I might gather more facts, and certainty against them in my full design to do their deserts instant justice, and accordingly, when they had readjusted themselves, and were preparing to go out, burning as I was with rage, and indignation, I jump'd down from my chair, in order to raise the house upon them, with such an unlucky impetuosity, that some nail or ruggedness in the floor caught my foot, and flung me on my face with such violence, that I fell senseless on the ground, and must have lain there some time e'er any one came to my relief, so that they, alarm'd, I suppose, by the noise of my fall, had more than the necessary time to make a safe retreat, which they affected, as I learnt, with a precipitation no body could account for, till, when come to my self, and compos'd enough to speak, I acquainted those of the house with the transaction I had been evidence to.

When I came home again, and told Mrs. Cole this adventure, she very sensibly observ'd to me, that there was no doubt of due vengeance one time or other overtaking these miscreants, however they might escape for the present; and that, had I been the temporal instrument of it, I should have been, at least, put to a great deal more trouble and confusion than I imagine: that as to the thing itself, the less said of it was the better; but that though she might be suspected of partiality, from its being the common cause of woman-kind, out of whose *mouths* this practice tended to take something more precious than bread, yet she protested against any mixture of passion, with a declaration extorted from her by pure regard to truth, which was, "*that* whatever effect this infamous passion had in other ages, and other countries, it seem'd a peculiar blessing on our air and climate, that there was a plague-spot visibly imprinted on all that are tainted with it, in this nation at least; for that among numbers of that stamp whom she had known, or at least were universally under the scandalous suspicion of it, she could not name an exception hardly of one of them, whose character was not in all other respects the most worthless and despicable that could be, stript of all the manly virtues of their own sex, and fill'd up with only the very worst vices and follies of ours: that, in fine, they were scarce less execrable than ridiculous in their monstrous inconsistency, of loathing and contemning women, and all at the same time, apeing their manners, airs, lisp, skuttle, and, in general, all their little modes of affectation, which become them at least better, than they do these unsex'd male-misses."

{1749}

CHARLOTTE CIBBER CHARKE
{1713–circa 1760}

The tenth child of the British dramatist and poet Colly Cibber, Charlotte Cibber Charke was the author of an autobiography, *A Narrative of the Life of Mrs. Charlotte Charke* (1755), as well as the novel excerpted here. Widowed after an early marriage to a violinist, Charke pursued a varied career as waiter, pastry cook, and actor (often playing male roles on stage), and was notorious for wearing men's clothes, a habit later taken up by such writers as George Sand, Radclyffe Hall, Colette, and Willa Cather. Lillian Faderman, who includes an excerpt of the *Autobiography* in *Chloe Plus Olivia: An Anthology of Lesbian and Bisexual Literature from the Seventeenth Century to the Present* (1994), writes: "the fact that [Charke] was married and had a child or that she does not discuss having had lesbian sexual relations obviously cannot obviate the possibility that she did have such relations . . . women often fell in love with her when she was in male guise, and at least one woman, 'Mrs. Brown,' with whom she lived as 'Mr. Brown,' followed her through good times and bad."

Although Charke condemns the effeminate sodomite Billy Loveman in *Henry Dumont*, the undertone of pity that suffuses chapter 6 mitigates to some degree the timbre of bloodthirsty approval with which she describes his beating and humiliation. Thus when Dumont's anger with Mr. Loveman finally subsides, it is because "the wretch wore a human form (though in principle below a beast)": a use of parentheses that reduces the "principle" to an afterthought. Likewise, Mr. Loveman's decision to go off with his "wife," Mr. Turtle, and live as "sheperdesses [*sic*] together in some remote country" prefigures not only Joseph's dream of an idealized and democratic "valley of bliss" in Bayard Taylor's *Joseph and His Friend*, but the "greenwood" into which Forster's Alec and Maurice enter at novel's end. ⚓

FROM *The History of Henry Dumont, Esq.*

CHAPTER 6

Miss Evelyn *goes to* Tunbridge. *An odd Adventure happens there.*

Young Dumont had by this time finished his studies, which, with all other necessary accomplishments, compleated him a perfect fine gentleman; but not that sort of fine gentlemen which Mr. Woodward so inimitably represents in Mr. Garrick's celebrated dramatick performance call'd Lethe, or Aesop in the shades; for which the town are much obliged to the author, and the player, for having largely contributed to their entertainment so many successive years, and which has rather encreas'd, than pall'd the appetite, notwithstanding they have been so often fed with it.

But to return to Dumont, his grandpapa began to consider him now in a different light; as he, tho' not past his minority, discovered the Man in every thought and action: and that he might be better able to judge of his disposition, entirely took off that restraint which lay upon him, during the time of his education. The first step he took towards making him master of himself, was allowing him a thousand pounds a year; and by the management of that, he could the easier discern what might be expected from him, when possess'd of many thousands more.

Nor were his hopes and expectations unanswer'd; for tho' he suddenly launched into all the pleasures of life without controulment, he used them but as innocent amusements, without becoming their SLAVE; and in every circumstance kept up that noble character, which the example of his grandsire had set before him.

The first grand publick appearance he made was at Tunbridge, accompanied by Mrs. Evelyn and her daughter; Mr. Evelyn was obliged to stay with the Count, who, confined partly by the gout, and an invincible sorrow for his daughter's loss, never stirred above four or five miles for the Air sometimes.

The magnificent appearance they made, attracted every eye, and excited the curiosity of all the company there; they being strangers to all but Lord Worthland, and Sir John Generous, who joined their party. The fortune-hunters of both sexes, were at their wits-ends to engage with young Dumont and Miss Evelyn, tho' it proved to very little purpose. But among the rest that made pretensions, was a strange mortal, who seeing Dumont dance at the ball one night with Miss Evelyn, sent the following fond epistle, directed

To Henry Demount Esq;

Dere Cretor,

I Hop you vont be uffinded at the libarty I tak, in trubling you with thes lins, and that the ardunt pishon I have concef'd for your angelack form, will plede my pardun. When you dans'd last night, you gave the fatal blo, which will be my utter ruen, unless you koindly answer my bondles luf; I know you ar a parson of fortin, so um I, and do asure you, vere not my charmer vorth one fardin in the vorld, sush beuty voud make amends for sush a vant. Permet me lufly objeckt, to meet you this evening at the fish-ponds, vher I may be happy in paeing my rispex to the divine charmur of my soul. Believe me lufly cretor my only vish is to convince you, how mutch I am vith utmurst sincerity,

Your constant adorer,
Billy Loveman.

The extraordinary stile and spelling diverted him exceedingly; but being intirely innocent of such unnatural proceedings, concluded there must be a mistake in the direction, and that the letter must be designed for Miss Evelyn, to whom he directly carried it; apologizing for his having opened it; which error, he told her, she must attribute to the person, who had certainly made a mistake in the superscription, was the reason of its being delivered to him.

Miss Evelyn read the amorous epistle, laughing inwardly to a violent degree during the perusal; then returning the paper, Mr. Dumont, said she, I don't suppose the person who wrote it, would cast his eyes upon an odious Female; and I am positive the letter was meant as directed.

Dear Madam, replied Dumont, 'tis impossible; 'tis true I have heard there are a set of unnatural wretches, who are shamefully addicted to a vice, not proper to be mentioned to so delicate an ear as yours; but my behaviour could not in any degree give the smallest hope to the unnatural passion of such a detestable brute. I therefore think it highly incumbent on me, to make an example of the villain.

Miss Evelyn would fain have dissuaded him from his purpose, but in vain; for young Dumont was apprehensive, that the bare mention of his name from the mouth of such a wretch, might throw an imputation on his character, which he had rather suffer death than deserve.

Mrs. Evelyn was of the young gentleman's mind, and urged him to put his revenge in immediate execution; advising him to consult with Lord Worthland and Sir John Generous, and entreat them to be witnesses; as an affair of that nature must be necessary to prevent any calumny the monster might possibly raise on account of the deserved treatment and disappointment he should meet from Mr. Dumont. And in order to perpetrate the design, advised him to send only a verbal answer, to let the creature know he would attend his summons; and in the mean time, send or go to Sir John Generous, and communicate the affair to him.

Mr. Dumont's valet brought his master word, that the servant who came with the letter, desired an immediate answer. The valet having a kind of restrained laugh on his face, his master asked him the occasion? I beg your honour's pardon, says he, but the sight of the person who waits the answer, put me into such a fit of laughing, I had scarce power to compose myself sufficiently, to bring the message to you Sir. I really take it to be a young wench in boy's cloaths, by the softness of the voice, and the effeminacy of his behaviour. For heaven's sake, says Miss Evelyn, let the creature come up, 'twill divert us.

Mr. Dumont's servant went down, and brought up the moppit; whose hair was curl'd in the form of a fine lady's, and scented the room with perfumes, it set their heads aching from the violent strength of it; his dress was a fine milk-white fustian-frock, with green sattin cape and facings, a white cambrick handkerchief carelessly tied round his neck, and a pair of white gloves; one of which he pulled off, and discovered a beautiful white hand, with a handsome diamond ring on the little finger.

Upon Mr. Dumont's enquiry into what post he held under Mr. Loveman, he answered, Dear sir, I'm a young decay'd geman, but think myself happy now since the loss of my fortin, to be vale de chamber to my deer master Squire Loveman; and a deer indulgent soul he is, for if my fingur do but ake, he's like a crazy cretor; t'other day one of the footmen trod uppon my toe, and brus'd me in a most barbrus manner, I believe indeed the willing owed me a spight, and my master turn'd him of at a minits varning, and sent for two of the most aminent surgins in townd, to insuit about the cure. And indeed a great cure it vas, for every body thought I should have lost my toe-nail, it looked so black under it — then lifting up his eyes, thanked providence, and the care of the surgins the nail was preserved, and he was perfectly recovered of the unhippy iccident.

That's a happiness indeed, said Miss Evelyn, who knows the consequence of your losing your toe-nail! you might not for ought I know, have been able to have run of an errand these six months. Very true, dear lady, answered Mr. Turtle (for that was the soft creature's name) but if that had been the case, 'twould have been in all the newspapers. But vorthy Sir, I believe by this time, my master expects me to dress him, please to give me your honour's orders. My compliments, says Mr. Dumont, and I shall wait on him at the time and place appointed.

The pretty creature had not been gone above a quarter of an hour, before Lord Worthland and Sir John Generous came to pay a visit; who were immediately informed of the affair, and resolved to join with Mr. Dumont in his revenge on the unnatural scoundrel, for daring to make such an attempt upon a very honourable and worthy young gentleman.

About the hour of five after dinner, they went to the fish-ponds, which was the place proposed. Lord Worthland and Sir John went in a little before, and called for a bottle of champaign by themselves in a different room.

Mr. Dumont came in a few minutes after, and was conducted by Mr. Loveman's footman, up one pair of stairs, to the enamoured swain, who had been waiting impatiently for his arrival above an hour.

When he came in he saw an elegant cold collation set forth, the window curtains close drawn and pinn'd; but found no body in the room; when asking for the gentleman, the servant sneered, and told him, his Lady would wait upon him directly; when immediately there appeared from the inner-chamber, this odious creature in a female rich dishabille; who running to Mr. Dumont, cried out, "I come, I fly to my adored Castalio's arms! my wishes lord! — stopping here, with a languishing air, said, Do my angel, call me your Monimia! then with a beastly transport, kissed him with that ardour, which might be expected from a drunken fellow to a common prostitute. Mr. Dumont being now fully convinced of his horrid design, without farther ceremony knocked him down, and disciplined him with his cane; till the monster was almost immoveable.

The noise of his falling brought up Lord Worthland, Sir John, and the landlord, who were surprized to see Mr. Loveman's odd transformation; but he recollected his footman carried up a large bundle, little conceiving what it contained, or to what end it was brought.

Lord Worthland and Sir John would have bestowed their favours on him; but Mr. Dumont desired they would not rob him of the least part of his revenge, nor indeed was there any need; for Dumont who never suffered passion, without just grounds to influence his mind, thought he had so justifiable an excuse for it on this occasion, he gave it full scope, and left the wretch just life enough to confess his crime, and publickly beg pardon.

The history of the affair in a few minutes got wind, sufficient to blow a whole mob together. And when the male-madam was permitted to decamp as he was, leading between two to his chariot, they snatched him from his supporters, and very handsomely ducked him in the fish-pond; nor had he a friend on his side, for even his own coachman and footman, tho' they were not assistant in his punishment, were heartily glad to see him undergo it. Mr. Dumont having had sufficient revenge, his anger began to subside, and as the wretch wore a human form, (tho' in principle below a beast) his pity and good nature resumed their throne, and by dint of a handful of silver thrown to the populace, they suffered the shameful object of their contempt to be hurried as fast as possible to his lodgings, where the news had got before him; and as a farther addition to his misfortune, poor Mr. Turtle, who was sent with the letter, (not knowing the contents of it,) as injured wives are apt to shew violent resentment, when they find their husbands are engaged in intrigues, flew about the house, raving like a distracted thing, menacing bitterest revenge on him and his filty creter; adding, corse me, if I forgive this willingly; this is the second time you have wronged me; if I bear it a third, the fault shall be mine; I desire we may saprate, ungrateful man; I have ever been true to you, and this is my reward.

Mr. Loveman, who was in too miserable a condition to expostulate with his offended fair; begged madam for that time to set aside its anger, and give what assistance he cou'd towards his relief. Surgeons were sent for, under whose hands he remained for above a month, before he could be moved. At the expiration of which time, he was forced to go privately away from Tunbridge, for fear of a second encounter; and the fracea between him and his lady was made up, (as one of the servants informed us, who overheard their discourse) with a faithful promise to retire from the world, and live *sheperdesses together in some remote country*.

Mr. Dumont satisfied the poor landlord, for the preparations made for him by the love-sick squire, and some damages done in the fray. Then the three friends returned home, and gave the history of their adventure to Miss Evelyn and her mama. Mrs. Evelyn tho' she allowed the justice of the thing, could not help pittying the unhappy creature; but Miss said, she could not entertain the least grain of compassion, for that in her opinion, no punishment was sufficiently severe for such unnatural monsters.

{1756}

HERMAN MELVILLE
{1819–1891}

Melville's story "I and My Chimney" was published in *Putnam's Monthly Magazine* in March 1856, making it the earliest work of American fiction included here. Melville once said, "What I feel most moved to write, that is banned — it won't pay. Yet write altogether the other way I cannot. So the product is a final hash; and all my books are botches." "I and My Chimney," *Billy Budd* and *Redburn* (1849), the forty-sixth chapter of which takes place in a male brothel, in London, thoroughly tell what Melville was most moved to write. So, too, does *Moby Dick* (1851). From chapter 94, "A Squeeze of the Hand":

> Squeeze! squeeze! squeeze! all the morning long; I squeezed that sperm till I myself almost melted into it; I squeezed that sperm till a strange sort of insanity came over me; and I found myself unwittingly squeezing my co-laborers' hands in it, mistaking their hands for the gentle globules. Such an abounding, affectionate, friendly, loving feeling did this avocation beget; that at last I was continually squeezing their hands, and looking up into their eyes sentimentally; as much as to say, — Oh! my dear fellow beings, why should we longer cherish any social acerbities, or know the slightest ill-humor or envy! Come; let us squeeze hands all round; nay, let us all squeeze ourselves into each other; let us squeeze ourselves universally into the very milk and sperm of kindness.

This passage, like D. H. Lawrence's description of the Piazza della Signoria in *Aaron's Rod*, renders any comment superfluous.

"I and My Chimney" is the source of "the closet" — and of its integrity. The wife of "I" supposes the chimney to contain a secret closet, and badgers her husband to open it. In the end, however, "I" prevails: "Besides, even if there were a secret closet, secret it should remain, and secret it shall. Yes, wife, here for once I must say my say. Infinite sad mischief has resulted from the profane bursting open of secret recesses."

Although Melville married and fathered four children, he nonetheless formed a deep attachment to Nathaniel Hawthorne. (Melville paid tribute to Hawthorne in a review titled "Hawthorne and His Mosses" published in the New York *Literary World* on August 17 and August 24,

1850.) William Plomer, in an article on Melville, summarized relations between the two with resonant tact: "Nor did his friendship with Hawthorne bring him what he had evidently expected, for Hawthorne could not respond to the offer of Melville's heart, and withdrew." Long before this, while still a young sailor, Melville had discovered a South Seas version of the greenwood that gave its name to his novel *Typee* (1846). 🙣

I and My Chimney

I AND MY CHIMNEY, two grey-headed old smokers, reside in the country. We are, I may say, old settlers here; particularly my old chimney, which settles more and more every day.

Though I always say, *I and my chimney,* as Cardinal Wolsey used to say, *I and my King,* yet this egotistic way of speaking, wherein I take precedence of my chimney, is hardly borne out by the facts; in everything, except the above phrase, my chimney taking precedence of me.

Within thirty feet of the turf-sided road, my chimney — a huge, corpulent old Harry VIII. of a chimney — rises full in front of me and all my possessions. Standing well up a hillside, my chimney, like Lord Rosse's monster telescope, swung vertical to hit the meridian moon, is the first object to greet the approaching traveler's eye, nor is it the last which the sun salutes. My chimney, too, is before me in receiving the first-fruits of the seasons. The snow is on its head ere on my hat; and every spring, as in a hollow beech tree, the first swallows build their nests in it.

But it is within doors that the preëminence of my chimney is most manifest. When in the rear room, set apart for that object, I stand to receive my guests (who, by the way call more, I suspect, to see my chimney than me), I then stand, not so much before, as, strictly speaking, behind my chimney, which is, indeed, the true host. Not that I demur. In the presence of my betters, I hope I know my place.

From this habitual precedence of my chimney over me, some even think that I have got into a sad rearward way altogether; in short, from standing behind my old-fashioned chimney so much, I have got to be quite behind the age too, as well as running behind-hand in everything else. But to tell the truth, I never was a very forward old fellow, nor what my farming neighbors call a forehanded one. Indeed, those rumors about my behindhandedness are so far correct, that I have an odd sauntering way with me sometimes of going about with my hands behind my back. As for my belonging to the rear-guard in general, certain it is, I bring up the rear of my chimney — which, by the way, is this moment before me — and that, too, both in fancy and fact. In brief, my chimney is my superior; my superior by I know not how many heads and shoulders; my superior, too, in that humbly bowing over with shovel and tongs, I much minister to it; yet never does it minister, or incline over to me; but, if any thing, in its settlings, rather leans the other way.

My chimney is grand seignior here — the one great domineering object, not more of the landscape, than of the house; all the rest of which house, in each architectural arrangement, as may shortly appear, is, in the most marked manner, accommodated, not to my wants, but to my chimney's, which, among other things, has the centre of the house to himself, leaving but the odd holes and corners to me.

But I and my chimney must explain; and as we are both rather obese, we may have to expatiate.

In those houses which are strictly double houses — that is, where the hall is in the middle — the fire-places usually are on opposite sides; so that while one member of the household is warming himself at a fire built into a recess of the north wall, say another member, the former's own brother, perhaps, may be holding his feet to the blaze before a hearth in the south wall — the two thus fairly sitting back to back. Is this well? Be it put to any man who has a proper fraternal feeling. Has it not a sort of sulky appearance? But very probably this style of chimney building originated with some architect afflicted with a quarrelsome family.

Then again, almost every modern fire-place has its separate flue — separate throughout, from hearth to chimney-top. At least such an arrangement is deemed desirable. Does not this look egotistical, selfish? But still more, all these separate flues, instead of having independent masonry establishments of their own, or instead of being grouped together in one federal stock in the middle of the house — instead of this, I say, each flue is surreptitiously honeycombed into the walls; so that these last are here and there, or indeed almost anywhere, treacherously hollow, and, in consequence, more or less weak. Of course, the main reason of this style of chimney building is to economize room. In cities, where lots are sold by the inch, small space is to spare for a chimney constructed on magnanimous principles; and, as with most thin men, who are generally tall, so with such houses, what is lacking in breadth must be made up in height. This remark holds true even with regard to many very stylish abodes, built by the most stylish of gentlemen. And yet, when that stylish gentleman, Louis le Grand of France, would build a palace for his lady friend, Madame de Maintenon, he built it but one story high — in fact in the cottage style. But then how uncommonly quadrangular, spacious, and broad — horizontal acres, not vertical ones. Such is the palace, which, in all its one-storied magnificence of Languedoc marble, in the garden of Versailles, still remains to this day. Any man can buy a square foot of land and plant a liberty-pole on it; but it takes a king to set apart whole acres for a grand Trianon.

But nowadays it is different; and furthermore, what originated in a necessity has been mounted into a vaunt. In towns there is large rivalry in building tall houses. If one gentleman builds his house four stories high, and another gentleman comes next door and builds five stories high, then the former, not to be looked down upon that way, immediately sends for his architect and claps a fifth and a sixth story on top of his previous four. And, not till the gentleman has achieved his aspiration, not till he has stolen over the way by twilight and observed how his sixth story soars beyond his neighbor's fifth — not till then does he retire to his rest with satisfaction.

Such folks, it seems to me, need mountains for neighbors, to take this emulous conceit of soaring out of them.

If, considering that mine is a very wide house, and by no means lofty, aught in the above may appear like interested pleading, as if I did but fold myself about in the cloak of a general proposition, cunningly to tickle my individual vanity beneath it, such misconception must vanish upon my frankly conceding, that land adjoining my alder swamp was sold last month for ten dollars an acre, and thought a rash purchase at that; so that for wide houses hereabouts there is plenty of room, and cheap. Indeed so cheap — dirt cheap — is the soil, that our elms thrust out their roots in it, and hang their great boughs over it, in the most lavish and reckless way. Almost all our crops, too, are sown broadcast, even peas and turnips. A farmer among us, who should go about his twenty-acre field, poking his finger into it here and there, and dropping down a mustard seed, would be thought a penurious, narrow-minded husbandman. The dandelions in the river-meadows, and the forget-me-nots along the mountain roads, you see at once they are put to no economy in space. Some seasons, too, our rye comes up, here and there a spear, sole and single like a church-spire. It doesn't care to crowd itself where it knows there is such a deal of room. The world is wide, the world is all before us, says the rye. Weeds, too, it is amazing how they spread. No such thing as arresting them — some of our pastures being a sort of Alsatia for the weeds. As for the grass, every spring it is like Kossuth's rising of what he calls the peoples. Mountains, too, a regular camp-meeting of them. For the same reason, the same all-sufficiency of room, our shadows march and countermarch, going through their various drills and masterly evolutions, like the old imperial guard on the Champs de Mars. As for the hills, especially where the roads cross them, the supervisors of our various towns have given notice to all concerned, that they can come and dig them down and cart them off, and never a cent to pay, no more than for the privilege of picking blackberries. The stranger who is buried here, what liberal-hearted landed proprietor among us grudges him his six feet of rocky pasture?

Nevertheless, cheap, after all, as our land is, and much as it is trodden under foot, I, for one, am proud of it for what it bears; and chiefly for its three great lions — the Great Oak, Ogg Mountain, and my chimney.

Most houses, here, are but one and a half stories high; few exceed two. That in which I and my chimney dwell, is in width nearly twice its height, from sill to eaves — which accounts for the magnitude of its main content — besides, showing that in this house, as in this country at large, there is abundance of space, and to spare, for both of us.

The frame of the old house is of wood — which but the more sets forth the solidity of the chimney, which is of brick. And as the great wrought nails, binding the clapboards, are unknown in these degenerate days, so are the huge bricks in the chimney walls. The architect of the chimney must have had the pyramid of Cheops before him; for, after that famous structure, it seems modeled, only its rate of decrease towards the summit is considerably less, and it is truncated. From the exact middle of the mansion it soars from the cellar, right up through each successive floor, till, four feet square, it breaks water from the ridge-pole of the roof, like an anvil-headed whale, through the crest of a billow. Most people, though, liken it, in that part, to a razeed observatory, masoned up.

The reason for its peculiar appearance above the roof touches upon rather delicate ground. How shall I reveal that, forasmuch as many years ago the original gable roof of the old house had become very leaky, a temporary proprietor hired a band of woodmen, with their huge, cross-cut saws, and went to sawing the old gable roof clean off. Off it went, with all its birds' nests, and dormer windows. It was replaced with a modern roof, more fit for a railway wood-house than an old country gentleman's abode. This operation — razeeing the structure some fifteen feet — was, in effect upon the chimney, something like the falling of the great spring tides. It left uncommon low water all about the chimney — to abate which appearance, the same person now proceeds to slice fifteen feet off the chimney itself, actually beheading my royal old chimney — a regicidal act, which, were it not for the palliating fact, that he was a poulterer by trade, and, therefore, hardened to such neck-wringings, should send that former proprietor down to posterity in the same cart with Cromwell.

Owing to its pyramidal shape, the reduction of the chimney inordinately widened its razed summit. Inordinately, I say, but only in the estimation of such as have no eye to the picturesque. What care I, if, unaware that my chimney, as a free citizen of this free land, stands upon an independent basis of its own, people passing it, wonder how such a brick-kiln, as they call it, is supported upon mere joists and rafters? What care I? I will give a traveler a cup of switchel, if he want it; but am I bound to supply him with a sweet taste? Men of cultivated minds see, in my old house and chimney, a goodly old elephant-and-castle.

All feeling hearts will sympathize with me in what I am now about to add. The surgical operation, above referred to, necessarily brought into the open air a part of the chimney previously under cover, and intended to remain so, and, therefore, not built of what are called weather-bricks. In consequence, the chimney, though of a vigorous constitution, suffered not a little, from so naked an exposure; and, unable to acclimate itself, ere long began to fail — showing blotchy symptoms akin to those in measles. Whereupon travelers, passing my way, would wag their heads, laughing: "See that wax nose — how it melts off!" But what cared I? The same travelers would travel across the sea to view Kenilworth peeling away, and for a very good reason: that of all artists of the picturesque, decay wears the palm — I would say, the ivy. In fact, I've often thought that the proper place for my old chimney is ivied old England.

In vain my wife — with what probable ulterior intent will, ere long, appear — solemnly warned me, that unless something were done, and speedily, we should be burnt to the ground, owing to the holes crumbling through the aforesaid blotchy parts, where the chimney joined the roof. "Wife," said I, "far better that my house should burn down, than that my chimney should be pulled down, though but a few feet. They call it a wax nose; very good; not for me to tweak the nose of my superior." But at last the man who has a mortgage on the house dropped me a note, reminding me that, if my chimney was allowed to stand in that invalid condition, my policy of insurance would be void. This was a sort of hint not to be neglected. All the world over, the picturesque yields to the pocketesque. The mortgagor cared not, but the mortgagee did.

So another operation was performed. The wax nose was taken off, and a new one fitted on. Unfortunately for the expression — being put up by a squint-eyed mason, who, at the time, had a bad stitch in the same side — the new nose stands a little awry, in the same direction.

Of one thing, however, I am proud. The horizontal dimensions of the new part are unreduced.

Large as the chimney appears upon the roof, that is nothing to its spaciousness below. At its base in the cellar, it is precisely twelve feet square; and hence covers precisely one hundred and forty-four superficial feet. What an appropriation of terra firma for a chimney, and what a huge load for this earth! In fact, it was only because I and my chimney formed no part of his ancient burden, that that stout peddler, Atlas of old, was enabled to stand up so bravely under his pack. The dimensions given may, perhaps, seem fabulous. But, like those stones at Gilgal, which Joshua set up for a memorial of having passed over Jordan, does not my chimney remain, even unto this day?

Very often I go down into my cellar, and attentively survey that vast square of masonry. I stand long, and ponder over, and wonder at it. It has a druidical look, away down in the umbrageous cellar there, whose numerous vaulted passages, and far glens of gloom, resemble the dark, damp depths of primeval woods. So strongly did this conceit steal over me, so deeply was I penetrated with wonder at the chimney, that one day — when I was a little out of my mind, I now think — getting a spade from the garden, I set to work, digging round the foundation, especially at the corners thereof, obscurely prompted by dreams of striking upon some old, earthen-worn memorial of that by-gone day, when, into all this gloom, the light of heaven entered, as the masons laid the foundation-stones, peradventure sweltering under an August sun, or pelted by a March storm. Plying my blunted spade, how vexed was I by that ungracious interruption of a neighbor, who, calling to see me upon some business, and being informed that I was below, said I need not be troubled to come up, but he would go down to me; and so, without ceremony, and without my having been forewarned, suddenly discovered me, digging in my cellar.

"Gold digging, sir?"

"Nay, sir," answered I, starting, "I was merely — ahem! — merely — I say I was merely digging — round my chimney."

"Ah, loosening the soil, to make it grow. Your chimney, sir, you regard as too small, I suppose; needing further development, especially at the top?"

"Sir!" said I, throwing down the spade, "do not be personal. I and my chimney —"

"Personal?"

"Sir, I look upon this chimney less as a pile of masonry than as a personage. It is the king of the house. I am but a suffered and inferior subject."

In fact, I would permit no gibes to be cast at either myself or my chimney; and never again did my visitor refer to it in my hearing, without coupling some compliment with the mention. It well deserves a respectful consideration. There it stands, solitary and alone — not a council of ten flues, but, like his sacred majesty of Russia, a unit of an autocrat.

Even to me, its dimensions, at times, seem incredible. It does not look so big — no, not even in the cellar. By the mere eye, its magnitude can be but imperfectly comprehended, because only one side can be received at one time; and said side can only present twelve feet, linear measure. But then, each other side also is twelve feet long; and the whole obviously forms a square; and twelve times twelve is one hundred and forty-four.

And so, an adequate conception of the magnitude of this chimney is only to be got at by a sort of process in the higher mathematics, by a method somewhat akin to those whereby the surprising distances of fixed stars are computed.

It need hardly be said, that the walls of my house are entirely free from fire-places. These all congregate in the middle — in the one grand central chimney, upon all four sides of which are hearths — two tiers of hearths — so that when, in the various chambers, my family and guests are warming themselves of a cold winter's night, just before retiring, then, though at the time they may not be thinking so, all their faces mutually look towards each other, yea, all their feet point to one centre; and, when they go to sleep in their beds, they all sleep round one warm chimney, like so many Iroquois Indians, in the woods, round their one heap of embers. And just as the Indians' fire serves, not only to keep them comfortable, but also to keep off wolves, and other savage monsters, so my chimney, by its obvious smoke at top, keeps off prowling burglars from the towns — for what burglar or murderer would dare break into an abode from whose chimney issues such a continual smoke — betokening that if the inmates are not stirring, at least fires are, and in case of an alarm, candles may readily be lighted, to say nothing of muskets.

But stately as is the chimney — yea, grand high altar as it is, right worthy for the celebration of high mass before the Pope of Rome, and all his cardinals — yet what is there perfect in this world? Caius Julius Cæsar, had he not been so inordinately great, they say that Brutus, Cassius, Antony, and the rest, had been greater. My chimney, were it not so mighty in its magnitude, my chambers had been larger. How often has my wife ruefully told me, that my chimney, like the English aristocracy, casts a contracting shade all round it. She avers that endless domestic inconveniences arise — more particularly from the chimney's stubborn central locality. The grand objection with her is, that it stands midway in the place where a fine entrance-hall ought to be. In truth, there is no hall whatever to the house — nothing but a sort of square landing-place, as you enter from the wide front door. A roomy enough landing-place, I admit, but not attaining to the dignity of a hall. Now, as the front door is precisely in the middle of the front of the house, inwards it faces the chimney. In fact, the opposite wall of the landing-place is formed solely by the chimney; and hence — owing to the gradual tapering of the chimney — is a little less than twelve feet in width. Climbing the chimney in this part, is the principal staircase — which, by three abrupt turns, and three minor landing-places, mounts to the second floor, where, over the front door, runs a sort of narrow gallery, something less than twelve feet long, leading to chambers on either hand. This gallery, of course, is railed; and so, looking down upon the stairs, and all those landing-places together, with the main one at bottom, resembles not a little a balcony for musicians, in some jolly old abode, in times Elizabethan. Shall I tell a weakness? I cherish the cobwebs there, and many a time arrest Biddy in the act of brushing them with her broom, and have many a quarrel with my wife and daughters about it.

Now the ceiling, so to speak, of the place where you enter the house, that ceiling is, in fact, the ceiling of the second floor, not the first. The two floors are made one here; so that ascending this turning stairs, you seem going up into a kind of soaring tower, or light-house. At the second landing, midway up the chimney, is a mysterious door, entering to a mysterious closet; and here I keep mysterious cordials, of a choice, mysterious flavor, made so by the constant nurturing and subtle ripening of the chimney's gentle heat, distilled through that warm mass of masonry. Better for wines is it than voyages to the Indies; my chimney itself a tropic. A chair by my chimney in a November day is as good for an invalid as a long season spent in Cuba. Often I think how grapes might ripen against my chimney. How my wife's geraniums bud there! Bud in December. Her eggs, too — can't keep them near the chimney, on account of hatching. Ah, a warm heart has my chimney.

How often my wife was at me about that projected grand entrance-hall of hers, which was to be knocked clean through the chimney, from one end of the house to the other, and astonish all guests by its generous amplitude. "But, wife," said I, "the chimney — consider the chimney: if you demolish the foundation, what is to support the superstructure?" "Oh, that will rest on the second floor." The truth is, women know next to nothing about the realities of architecture. However, my wife still talked of running her entries and partitions. She spent many long nights elaborating her plans; in imagination building her boasted hall through the chimney, as though its high mightiness were a mere spear of sorrel-top. At last, I gently reminded her that, little as she might fancy it, the chimney was a fact — a sober, substantial fact, which, in all her plannings, it would be well to take into full consideration. But this was not of much avail.

And here, respectfully craving her permission, I must say a few words about this enterprising wife of mine. Though in years nearly old as myself, in spirit she is young as my little sorrel mare, Trigger, that threw me last fall. What is extraordinary, though she comes of a rheumatic family, she is straight as a pine, never has any aches; while for me with the sciatica, I am sometimes as crippled up as any old apple tree. But she has not so much as a toothache. As for her hearing — let me enter the house in my dusty boots, and she away up in the attic. And for her sight — Biddy, the housemaid, tells other people's housemaids, that her mistress will spy a spot on the dresser straight through the pewter platter, put up on purpose to hide it. Her faculties are alert as her limbs and her senses. No danger of my spouse dying of torpor. The longest night in the year I've known her lie awake, planning her campaign for the morrow. She is a natural projector. The maxim, "Whatever is, is right," is not hers. Her maxim is, Whatever is, is wrong; and what is more, must be altered; and what is still more, must be altered right away. Dreadful maxim for the wife of a dozy old dreamer like me, who dote on seventh days as days of rest, and out of a sabbatical horror of industry, will, on a week day, go out of my road a quarter of a mile, to avoid the sight of a man at work.

That matches are made in heaven, may be, but my wife would have been just the wife for Peter the Great, or Peter the Piper. How she would have set in order that huge littered empire of the one, and with indefatigable painstaking picked the peck of pickled peppers for the other.

But the most wonderful thing is, my wife never thinks of her end. Her youthful incredulity, as to the plain theory, and still plainer fact of death, hardly seems Christian. Advanced in years, as she knows she must be, my wife seems to think that she is to teem on, and be inexhaustible forever. She doesn't believe in old age. At that strange promise in the plain of Mamre, my old wife, unlike old Abraham's, would not have jeeringly laughed within herself.

Judge how to me, who, sitting in the comfortable shadow of my chimney, smoking my comfortable pipe, with ashes not unwelcome at my feet, and ashes not unwelcome all but in my mouth; and who am thus in a comfortable sort of not unwelcome, though, indeed, ashy enough way, reminded of the ultimate exhaustion even of the most fiery life; judge how to me this unwarrantable vitality in my wife must come, sometimes, it is true, with a moral and a calm, but oftener with a breeze and a ruffle.

If the doctrine be true, that in wedlock contraries attract, by how cogent a fatality must I have been drawn to my wife! While spicily impatient of present and past, like a glass of ginger-beer she overflows with her schemes; and, with like energy as she puts down her foot, puts down her preserves and her pickles, and lives with them in a continual future; or ever full of expectations both from time and space, is ever restless for newspapers, and ravenous for letters. Content with the years that are gone, taking no thought for the morrow, and looking for no new thing from any person or quarter whatever, I have not a single scheme or expectation on earth, save in unequal resistance of the undue encroachment of hers.

Old myself, I take to oldness in things; for that cause mainly loving old Montaigne, and old cheese, and old wine; and eschewing young people, hot rolls, new books, and early potatoes, and very fond of my old claw-footed chair, and old club-footed Deacon White, my neighbor, and that still nigher old neighbor, my betwisted old grape-vine, that of a summer evening leans in his elbow for cosy company at my windowsill, while I, within doors, lean over mine to meet his; and above all, high above all, am fond of my high-mantled old chimney. But she, out of that infatuate juvenility of hers, takes to nothing but newness; for that cause mainly, loving new cider in autumn, and in spring, as if she were own daughter of Nebuchadnezzar, fairly raving after all sorts of salads and spinages, and more particularly green cucumbers (though all the time nature rebukes such unsuitable young hankerings in so elderly a person, by never permitting such things to agree with her), and has an itch after recently-discovered fine prospects (so no grave-yard be in the background), and also after Swedenborgianism, and the Spirit Rapping philosophy, with other new views, alike in things natural and unnatural; and immortally hopeful, is forever making new flower-beds even on the north side of the house, where the bleak mountain wind would scarce allow the wiry weed called hard-hack to gain a thorough footing; and on the road-side sets out mere pipe-stems of young elms; though there is no hope of any shade from them, except over the ruins of her great granddaughters' grave-stones; and won't wear caps, but plaits her gray hair; and takes the Ladies' Magazine for the fashions; and always buys her new almanac a month before the new year; and rises at dawn; and to the warmest sunset turns a cold shoulder; and still goes on at odd hours with her new course of history, and her French, and her music; and likes young company; and offers to ride young colts; and sets out young suckers in the orchard; and has a spite against my elbowed old grape-vine, and my club-footed old neighbor, and my claw-footed old chair, and above all, high above all, would fain persecute, unto death, my high-mantled old chimney. By what perverse magic, I a thousand times think, does such a very autumnal old lady have such a very vernal young soul? When I would remonstrate at times, she spins round on me with, "Oh, don't you grumble, old man (she always calls me old man), it's I, young I, that keep you from stagnating." Well, I suppose it is so. Yea, after all, these things are well ordered. My wife, as one of her poor relations, good soul, intimates, is the salt of the earth, and none the less the salt of my sea, which otherwise were unwholesome. She is its monsoon, too, blowing a brisk gale over it, in the one steady direction of my chimney.

Not insensible of her superior energies, my wife has frequently made me propositions to take upon herself all the responsibilities of my affairs. She is desirous that, domestically, I should abdicate; that, renouncing further rule, like the venerable Charles V., I should retire into some sort of monastery.

But indeed, the chimney excepted, I have little authority to lay down. By my wife's ingenious application of the principle that certain things belong of right to female jurisdiction, I find myself, through my easy compliances, insensibly stripped by degrees of one masculine prerogative after another. In a dream I go about my fields, a sort of lazy, happy-go-lucky, good-for-nothing, loafing, old Lear. Only by some sudden revelation am I reminded who is over me; as year before last, one day seeing in one corner of the premises fresh deposits of mysterious boards and timbers, the oddity of the incident at length begat serious meditation. "Wife," said I, "whose boards and timbers are those I see near the orchard there? Do you know any thing about them, wife? Who put them there? You know I do not like the neighbors to use my land that way; they should ask permission first."

She regarded me with a pitying smile.

"Why, old man, don't you know I am building a new barn? Didn't you know that, old man?"

This is the poor old lady that was accusing me of tyrannizing over her.

To return now to the chimney. Upon being assured of the futility of her proposed hall, so long as the obstacle remained, for a time my wife was for a modified project. But I could never exactly comprehend it. As far as I could see through it, it seemed to involve the general idea of a sort of irregular archway, or elbowed tunnel, which was to penetrate the chimney at some convenient point under the staircase, and carefully avoiding dangerous contact with the fire-places, and particularly steering clear of the great interior flue, was to conduct the enterprising traveler from the front door all the way into the dining-room in the remote rear of the mansion. Doubtless it was a bold stroke of genius, that plan of hers, and so was Nero's when he schemed his grand canal through the Isthmus of Corinth. Nor will I take oath, that, had her project been accomplished, then, by help of lights hung at judicious intervals through the tunnel, some Belzoni or other might not have succeeded in future ages in penetrating through the masonry, and actually emerging into the dining-room, and once there, it would have been inhospitable treatment of such a traveler to have denied him a recruiting meal.

But my bustling wife did not restrict her objections, nor in the end confine her proposed alterations to the first floor. Her ambition was of the mounting order. She ascended with her schemes to the second floor, and so to the attic. Perhaps there was some small ground for her discontent with things as they were. The truth is, there was no regular passage-way up stairs or down, unless we again except that little orchestra-gallery before mentioned. And all this was owing to the chimney, which my gamesome spouse seemed despitefully to regard as the bully of the house. On all its four sides, nearly all the chambers sidled up to the chimney for the benefit of a fire-place. The chimney would not go to them; they must needs go to it. The consequence was, almost every room, like a philosophical system, was in it-self an entry, or passage-way to other rooms, and systems of rooms — a whole suite of entries, in fact. Going through the house, you seem to be for-ever going somewhere, and getting nowhere. It is like losing one's self in the woods; round and round the chimney you go, and if you arrive at all, it is just where you started, and so you begin again, and again get nowhere. Indeed — though I say it not in the way of fault-finding at all — never was there so labyrinthine an abode. Guests will tarry with me several weeks and every now and then, be anew astonished at some unforeseen apartment.

The puzzling nature of the mansion, resulting from the chimney, is pe-culiarly noticeable in the dining-room, which has no less than nine doors, opening in all directions, and into all sorts of places. A stranger for the first time entering this dining-room, and naturally taking no special heed at what door he entered, will, upon rising to depart, commit the strangest blunders. Such, for instance, as opening the first door that comes handy, and finding himself stealing up stairs by the back passage. Shutting that door, he will proceed to another, and be aghast at the cellar yawning at his feet. Trying a third, he surprises the housemaid at her work. In the end, no more relying on his own unaided efforts, he procures a trusty guide in some passing person, and in good time successfully emerges. Perhaps as curious a blunder as any, was that of a certain stylish young gentleman, a great exquisite, in whose judicious eyes my daughter Anna had found es-pecial favor. He called upon the young lady one evening, and found her alone in the dining-room at her needle-work. He stayed rather late; and af-ter abundance of superfine discourse, all the while retaining his hat and cane, made his profuse adieus, and with repeated graceful bows proceeded to depart, after the fashion of courtiers from the Queen, and by so doing, opening a door at random, with one hand placed behind, very effectually succeeded in backing himself into a dark pantry, where he carefully shut himself up, wondering there was no light in the entry. After several strange noises as of a cat among the crockery, he reappeared through the same door, looking uncommonly crest-fallen, and, with a deeply embarrassed air, requested my daughter to designate at which of the nine he should find exit. When the mischievous Anna told me the story, she said it was surpris-ing how unaffected and matter-of-fact the young gentleman's manner was after his reappearance. He was more candid than ever, to be sure; having inadvertently thrust his white kids into an open drawer of Havana sugar, under the impression, probably, that being what they call "a sweet fellow," his route might possibly lie in that direction.

Another inconvenience resulting from the chimney is, the bewilderment of a guest in gaining his chamber, many strange doors lying between him and it. To direct him by finger-posts would look rather queer; and just as queer in him to be knocking at every door on his route, like London's city guest, the king, at Temple Bar.

Now, of all these things and many, many more, my family continually complained. At last my wife came out with her sweeping proposition — in toto to abolish the chimney.

"What!" said I, "abolish the chimney? To take out the backbone of anything, wife, is a hazardous affair. Spines out of backs, and chimneys out of houses, are not to be taken like frosted lead-pipes from the ground. Besides," added I, "the chimney is the one grand permanence of this abode. If undisturbed by innovators, then in future ages, when all the house shall have crumbled from it, this chimney will still survive — a Bunker Hill monument. No, no, wife, I can't abolish my back-bone."

So said I then. But who is sure of himself, especially an old man, with both wife and daughters ever at his elbow and ear? In time, I was persuaded to think a little better of it; in short, to take the matter into preliminary consideration. At length it came to pass that a master-mason — a rough sort of architect — one Mr. Scribe, was summoned to a conference. I formally introduced him to my chimney. A previous introduction from my wife had introduced him to myself. He had been not a little employed by that lady, in preparing plans and estimates for some of her extensive operations in drainage. Having, with much ado, extorted from my spouse the promise that she would leave us to an unmolested survey, I began by leading Mr. Scribe down to the root of the matter, in the cellar. Lamp in hand, I descended; for though up stairs it was noon, below it was night.

We seemed in the pyramids; and I, with one hand holding my lamp over head, and with the other pointing out, in the obscurity, the hoar mass of the chimney, seemed some Arab guide, showing the cobwebbed mausoleum of the great god Apis.

"This is a most remarkable structure, sir," said the master-mason, after long contemplating it in silence, "a most remarkable structure, sir."

"Yes," said I complacently, "every one says so."

"But large as it appears above the roof, I would not have inferred the magnitude of this foundation, sir," eyeing it critically.

Then taking out his rule, he measured it.

"Twelve feet square; one hundred and forty-four square feet! sir, this house would appear to have been built simply for the accommodation of your chimney."

"Yes, my chimney and me. Tell me candidly, now," I added, "would you have such a famous chimney abolished?"

"I wouldn't have it in a house of mine, sir, for a gift," was the reply. "It's a losing affair altogether, sir. Do you know, sir, that in retaining this chimney, you are losing, not only one hundred and forty-four square feet of good ground, but likewise a considerable interest upon a considerable principal?"

"How?"

"Look, sir," said he, taking a bit of red chalk from his pocket, and figuring against a whitewashed wall, "twenty times eight is so and so; then forty-two times thirty-nine is so and so — aint it, sir? Well, add those together, and subtract this here, then that makes so and so," still chalking away.

To be brief, after no small ciphering, Mr. Scribe informed me that my chimney contained, I am ashamed to say how many thousand and odd valuable bricks.

"No more," said I fidgeting. "Pray now, let us have a look above."

In that upper zone we made two more circumnavigations for the first and second floors. That done, we stood together at the foot of the stairway by the front door; my hand upon the knob, and Mr. Scribe hat in hand.

"Well, sir," said he, a sort of feeling his way, and, to help himself, fumbling with his hat, "well, sir, I think it can be done."

"What, pray, Mr. Scribe; *what* can be done?"

"Your chimney, sir; it can without rashness be removed, I think."

"*I* will think of it, too, Mr. Scribe," said I, turning the knob, and bowing him towards the open space without, "I will *think* of it, sir; it demands consideration; much obliged to ye; good morning, Mr. Scribe."

"It is all arranged, then," cried my wife with great glee, bursting from the nighest room.

"When will they begin?" demanded my daughter Julia.

"To-morrow?" asked Anna.

"Patience, patience, my dears," said I, "such a big chimney is not to be abolished in a minute."

Next morning it began again.

"You remember the chimney," said my wife.

"Wife," said I, "it is never out of my house, and never out of my mind."

"But when is Mr. Scribe to begin to pull it down?" asked Anna.

"Not to-day, Anna," said I.

"*When*, then?" demanded Julia, in alarm.

Now, if this chimney of mine was, for size, a sort of belfry, for ding-donging at me about it, my wife and daughters were a sort of bells, always chiming together, or taking up each other's melodies at every pause, my wife the key-clapper of all. A very sweet ringing, and pealing, and chiming, I confess; but then, the most silvery of bells may, sometimes, dismally toll, as well as merrily play. And as touching the subject in question, it became so now. Perceiving a strange relapse of opposition in me, wife and daughters began a soft and dirgelike, melancholy tolling over it.

At length my wife, getting much excited, declared to me, with pointed finger, that so long as that chimney stood, she should regard it as the monument of what she called my broken pledge. But finding this did not answer, the next day, she gave me to understand that either she or the chimney must quit the house.

Finding matters coming to such a pass, I and my pipe philosophized over them awhile, and finally concluded between us, that little as our hearts went with the plan, yet for peace' sake, I might write out the chimney's death-warrant, and, while my hand was in, scratch a note to Mr. Scribe.

Considering that I, and my chimney, and my pipe, from having been so much together, were three great cronies, the facility with which my pipe consented to a project so fatal to the goodliest of our trio; or rather, the way in which I and my pipe, in secret, conspired together, as it were, against our unsuspicious old comrade — this may seem rather strange, if not suggestive of sad reflections upon us two. But, indeed, we, sons of clay, that is my pipe and I, are no whit better than the rest. Far from us, indeed, to have volunteered the betrayal of our crony. We are of a peaceable nature, too. But that love of peace it was which made us false to a mutual friend, as soon as his cause demanded a vigorous vindication. But I rejoice to add, that better and braver thoughts soon returned, as will now briefly be set forth.

To my note, Mr. Scribe replied in person.

Once more we made a survey, mainly now with a view to a pecuniary estimate.

"I will do it for five hundred dollars," said Mr. Scribe at last, again hat in hand.

"Very well, Mr. Scribe, I will think of it," replied I, again bowing him to the door.

Not unvexed by this, for the second time, unexpected response, again he withdrew, and from my wife and daughters again burst the old exclamations.

The truth is, resolve how I would, at the last pinch I and my chimney could not be parted.

"So Holofernes will have his way, never mind whose heart breaks for it," said my wife next morning, at breakfast, in that half-didactic, half-reproachful way of hers, which is harder to bear than her most energetic assault. Holofernes, too, is with her a pet name for any fell domestic despot. So, whenever, against her most ambitious innovations, those which saw me quite across the grain, I, as in the present instance, stand with however little steadfastness on the defence, she is sure to call me Holofernes, and ten to one takes the first opportunity to read aloud, with a suppressed emphasis, of an evening, the first newspaper paragraph about some tyrannic day-laborer, who, after being for many years the Caligula of his family, ends by beating his long-suffering spouse to death, with a garret door wrenched off its hinges, and then, pitching his little innocents out of the window, suicidally turns inward towards the broken wall scored with the butcher's and baker's bills, and so rushes headlong to his dreadful account.

Nevertheless, for a few days, not a little to my surprise, I heard no further reproaches. An intense calm pervaded my wife, but beneath which, as in the sea, there was no knowing what portentous movements might be going on. She frequently went abroad, and in a direction which I thought not unsuspicious; namely, in the direction of New Petra, a griffin-like house of wood and stucco, in the highest style of ornamental art, graced with four chimneys in the form of erect dragons spouting smoke from their nostrils; the elegant modern residence of Mr. Scribe, which he had built for the purpose of a standing advertisement, not more of his taste as an architect, than his solidity as a master-mason.

At last, smoking my pipe one morning, I heard a rap at the door, and my wife, with an air unusually quiet for her, brought me a note. As I have no correspondents except Solomon, with whom, in his sentiments, at least, I entirely correspond, the note occasioned me some little surprise, which was not diminished upon reading the following: —

"NEW PETRA, April 1st.

"SIR: — During my last examination of your chimney, possibly you may have noted that I frequently applied my rule to it in a manner apparently unnecessary. Possibly also, at the same time, you might have observed in me more or less of perplexity, to which, however, I refrained from giving any verbal expression.

"I now feel it obligatory upon me to inform you of what was then but a dim suspicion, and as such would have been unwise to give utterance to, but which now, from various subsequent calculations assuming no little probability, it may be important that you should not remain in further ignorance of.

"It is my solemn duty to warn you, sir, that there is architectural cause to conjecture that somewhere concealed in your chimney is a reserved space, hermetically closed, in short, a secret chamber, or rather closet. How long it has been there, it is for me impossible to say. What it contains is hid, with itself, in darkness. But probably a secret closet would not have been contrived except for some extraordinary object, whether for the concealment of treasure, or what other purpose, may be left to those better acquainted with the history of the house to guess.

"But enough: in making this disclosure, sir, my conscience is eased. Whatever step you choose to take upon it, is of course a matter of indifference to me; though, I confess, as respects the character of the closet, I cannot but share in a natural curiosity.

"Trusting that you may be guided aright, in determining whether it is Christian-like knowingly to reside in a house, hidden in which is a secret closet,

"I remain,
"With much respect,
"Yours very humbly,
"Hiram Scribe."

My first thought upon reading this note was, not of the alleged mystery of manner to which, at the outset, it alluded — for none such had I at all observed in the master mason during his surveys — but of my late kinsman, Captain Julian Dacres, long a ship-master and merchant in the Indian trade, who, about thirty years ago, and at the ripe age of ninety, died a bachelor, and in this very house, which he had built. He was supposed to have retired into this country with a large fortune. But to the general surprise, after being at great cost in building himself this mansion, he settled down into a sedate, reserved, and inexpensive old age, which by the neighbors was thought all the better for his heirs: but lo! upon opening the will, his property was found to consist but of the house and grounds, and some ten thousand dollars in stocks; but the place, being found heavily mortgaged, was in consequence sold. Gossip had its day, and left the grass quietly to creep over the captain's grave, where he still slumbers in a privacy as unmolested as if the billows of the Indian Ocean, instead of the billows of inland verdure, rolled over him. Still, I remembered long ago, hearing strange solutions whispered by the country people for the mystery involving his will, and, by reflex, himself; and that, too, as well in conscience as purse. But people who could circulate the report (which they did), that Captain Julian Dacres had, in his day, been a Borneo pirate, surely were not worthy of credence in their collateral notions. It is queer what wild whimsies of rumors will, like toadstools, spring up about any eccentric stranger, who, settling down among a rustic population, keeps quietly to himself. With some, inoffensiveness would seem a prime cause of offense. But what chiefly had led me to scout at these rumors, particularly as referring to concealed treasure, was the circumstance, that the stranger (the same who razeed the roof and the chimney) into whose hands the estate had passed on my kinsman's death, was of that sort of character, that had there been the least ground for those reports, he would speedily have tested them, by tearing down and rummaging the walls.

Nevertheless, the note of Mr. Scribe, so strangely recalling the memory of my kinsman, very naturally chimed in with what had been mysterious, or at least unexplained, about him; vague flashings of ingots united in my mind with vague gleamings of skulls. But the first cool thought soon dismissed such chimeras; and, with a calm smile, I turned towards my wife, who, meantime, had been sitting near by, impatient enough, I dare say, to know who could have taken it into his head to write me a letter.

"Well, old man," said she, "who is it from, and what is it about?"

"Read it, wife," said I, handing it.

Read it she did, and then — such an explosion! I will not pretend to describe her emotions, or repeat her expressions. Enough that my daughters were quickly called in to share the excitement. Although they had never before dreamed of such a revelation as Mr. Scribe's; yet upon the first suggestion they instinctively saw the extreme likelihood of it. In corroboration, they cited first my kinsman, and second, my chimney; alleging that the profound mystery involving the former, and the equally profound masonry involving the latter, though both acknowledged facts, were alike preposterous on any other supposition than the secret closet.

But all this time I was quietly thinking to myself: Could it be hidden from me that my credulity in this instance would operate very favorably to a certain plan of theirs? How to get to the secret closet, or how to have any certainty about it at all, without making such fell work with the chimney as to render its set destruction superfluous? That my wife wished to get rid of the chimney, it needed no reflection to show; and that Mr. Scribe, for all his pretended disinterestedness, was not opposed to pocketing five hundred dollars by the operation, seemed equally evident. That my wife had, in secret, laid heads together with Mr. Scribe, I at present refrain from affirming. But when I consider her enmity against my chimney, and the steadiness with which at the last she is wont to carry out her schemes, if by hook or by crook she can, especially after having been once baffled, why, I scarcely knew at what step of hers to be surprised.

Of one thing only was I resolved, that I and my chimney should not budge.

In vain all protests. Next morning I went out into the road, where I had noticed a diabolical-looking old gander, that, for its doughty exploits in the way of scratching into forbidden inclosures, had been rewarded by its master with a portentous, four-pronged, wooden decoration, in the shape of a collar of the Order of the Garotte. This gander I cornered, and rummaging out its stiffest quill, plucked it, took it home, and making a stiff pen, inscribed the following stiff note:

"CHIMNEY SIDE, April 2.

"Mr. SCRIBE.

"Sir: — For your conjecture, we return you our joint thanks and compliments, and beg leave to assure you, that

"We shall remain,

"Very faithfully,

"The same,

"I and my Chimney."

Of course, for this epistle we had to endure some pretty sharp raps. But having at last explicitly understood from me that Mr. Scribe's note had not altered my mind one jot, my wife, to move me, among other things said, that if she remembered aright, there was a statute placing the keeping in private houses of secret closets on the same unlawful footing with the keeping of gunpowder. But it had no effect.

A few days after, my spouse changed her key.

It was nearly midnight, and all were in bed but ourselves, who sat up, one in each chimney-corner; she, needles in hand, indefatigably knitting a sock; I, pipe in mouth, indolently weaving my vapors.

It was one of the first of the chill nights in autumn. There was a fire on the hearth, burning low. The air without was torpid and heavy; the wood, by an oversight, of the sort called soggy.

"Do look at the chimney," she began; "can't you see that something must be in it?"

"Yes, wife. Truly there is smoke in the chimney, as in Mr. Scribe's note."

"Smoke? Yes, indeed, and in my eyes, too. How you two wicked old sinners do smoke! — this wicked old chimney and you."

"Wife," said I, "I and my chimney like to have a quiet smoke together, it is true, but we don't like to be called names."

"Now, dear old man," said she, softening down, and a little shifting the subject, "when you think of that old kinsman of yours, you *know* there must be a secret closet in this chimney."

"Secret ash-hole, wife, why don't you have it? Yes, I dare say there is a secret ash-hole in the chimney; for where do all the ashes go to that we drop down the queer hole yonder?"

"I know where they go to; I've been there almost as many times as the cat."

"What devil, wife, prompted you to crawl into the ash-hole! Don't you know that St. Dunstan's devil emerged from the ash-hole? You will get your death one of these days, exploring all about as you do. But supposing there be a secret closet, what then?"

"What, then? why what should be in a secret closet but —"

"Dry bones, wife," broke in I with a puff, while the sociable old chimney broke in with another.

"There again! Oh, how this wretched old chimney smokes," wiping her eyes with her handkerchief. "I've no doubt the reason it smokes so is, because that secret closet interferes with the flue. Do see, too, how the jams here keep settling; and it's down hill all the way from the door to this hearth. This horrid old chimney will fall on our heads yet; depend upon it, old man."

"Yes, wife, I do depend on it; yes, indeed, I place every dependence on my chimney. As for its settling, I like it. I, too, am settling, you know, in my gait. I and my chimney are settling together, and shall keep settling, too, till, as in a great feather-bed, we shall both have settled away clean out of sight. But this secret oven; I mean, secret closet of yours, wife; where exactly do you suppose that secret closet is?"

"That is for Mr. Scribe to say."

"But suppose he cannot say exactly; what, then?"

"Why then he can prove, I am sure, that it must be somewhere or other in this horrid old chimney."

"And if he can't prove that; what, then?"

"Why then, old man," with a stately air, "I shall say little more about it."

"Agreed, wife," returned I, knocking my pipe-bowl against the jam, "and now, to-morrow, I will a third time send for Mr. Scribe. Wife, the sciatica takes me; be so good as to put this pipe on the mantel."

"If you get the step ladder for me, I will. This shocking old chimney, this abominable old-fashioned old chimney's mantels are so high, I can't reach them."

No opportunity, however trivial, was overlooked for a subordinate fling at the pile.

Here, by way of introduction, it should be mentioned, that besides the fire-places all round it, the chimney was, in the most hap-hazard way, excavated on each floor for certain curious out-of-the-way cupboards and closets, of all sorts and sizes, clinging here and there, like nests in the crotches of some old oak. On the second floor these closets were by far the most irregular and numerous. And yet this should hardly have been so, since the theory of the chimney was, that it pyramidically diminished as it ascended. The abridgment of its square on the roof was obvious enough; and it was supposed that the reduction must be methodically graduated from bottom to top.

"Mr. Scribe," said I when, the next day, with an eager aspect, that individual again came, "my object in sending for you this morning is, not to arrange for the demolition of my chimney, nor to have any particular conversation about it, but simply to allow you every reasonable facility for verifying, if you can, the conjecture communicated in your note."

Though in secret not a little crestfallen, it may be, by my phlegmatic reception, so different from what he had looked for; with much apparent alacrity he commenced the survey; throwing open the cupboards on the first floor, and peering into the closets on the second; measuring one within, and then comparing that measurement with the measurement without. Removing the fire-boards, he would gaze up the flues. But no sign of the hidden work yet.

Now, on the second floor the rooms were the most rambling conceivable. They, as it were, dovetailed into each other. They were of all shapes; not one mathematically square room among them all — a peculiarity which by the master-mason had not been unobserved. With a significant, not to say portentous expression, he took a circuit of the chimney, measuring the area of each room around it; then going down stairs, and out of doors, he measured the entire ground area; then compared the sum total of all the areas of all the rooms on the second floor with the ground area; then, returning to me in no small excitement, announced that there was a difference of no less than two hundred and odd square feet — room enough, in all conscience, for a secret closet.

"But, Mr. Scribe," said I stroking my chin, "have you allowed for the walls, both main and sectional? They take up some space, you know."

"Ah, I had forgotten that," tapping his forehead; "but," still ciphering on his paper, "that will not make up the deficiency."

"But, Mr. Scribe, have you allowed for the recesses of so many fireplaces on a floor, and for the fire-walls, and the flues; in short, Mr. Scribe, have you allowed for the legitimate chimney itself — some one hundred and forty-four square feet or thereabouts, Mr. Scribe?"

"How unaccountable. That slipped my mind, too."

"Did it, indeed, Mr. Scribe?"

He faltered a little, and burst forth with, "But we must not allow one hundred and forty-four square feet for the legitimate chimney. My position is, that within those undue limits the secret closet is contained."

I eyed him in silence a moment; then spoke:

"Your survey is concluded, Mr. Scribe; be so good now as to lay your finger upon the exact part of the chimney wall where you believe this secret closet to be; or would a witch-hazel wand assist you, Mr. Scribe?"

"No, sir, but a crow-bar would," he, with temper, rejoined.

Here, now, thought I to myself, the cat leaps out of the bag. I looked at him with a calm glance, under which he seemed somewhat uneasy. More than ever now I suspected a plot. I remembered what my wife had said about abiding by the decision of Mr. Scribe. In a bland way, I resolved to buy up the decision of Mr. Scribe.

"Sir," said I, "really, I am much obliged to you for this survey. It has quite set my mind at rest. And no doubt you, too, Mr. Scribe, must feel much relieved. Sir," I added, "you have made three visits to the chimney. With a business man, time is money. Here are fifty dollars, Mr. Scribe. Nay, take it. You have earned it. Your opinion is worth it. And by the way," — as he modestly received the money — "have you any objections to give me a — a — little certificate — something, say, like a steam-boat certificate, certifying that you, a competent surveyor, have surveyed my chimney, and found no reason to believe any unsoundness; in short, any — any secret closet in it. Would you be so kind, Mr. Scribe?"

"But, but, sir," stammered he with honest hesitation.

"Here, here are pen and paper," said I, with entire assurance.

Enough.

That evening I had the certificate framed and hung over the dining-room fire-place, trusting that the continual sight of it would forever put at rest at once the dreams and stratagems of my household.

But, no. Inveterately bent upon the extirpation of that noble old chimney, still to this day my wife goes about it, with my daughter Anna's geological hammer, tapping the wall all over, and then holding her ear against it, as I have seen the physicians of life insurance companies tap a man's chest, and then incline over for the echo. Sometimes of nights she almost frightens one, going about on this phantom errand, and still following the sepulchral response of the chimney, round and round, as if it were leading her to the threshold of the secret closet.

"How hollow it sounds," she will hollowly cry. "Yes, I declare," with an emphatic tap, "there is a secret closet here. Here, in this very spot. Hark! How hollow!"

"Psha! wife, of course it is hollow. Who ever heard of a solid chimney?"

But nothing avails. And my daughters take after, not me, but their mother.

Sometimes all three abandon the theory of the secret closet, and return to the genuine ground of attack — the unsightliness of so cumbrous a pile, with comments upon the great addition of room to be gained by its demolition, and the fine effect of the projected grand hall, and the convenience resulting from the collateral running in one direction and another of their various partitions. Not more ruthlessly did the Three Powers partition away poor Poland, than my wife and daughters would fain partition away my chimney.

But seeing that, despite all, I and my chimney still smoke our pipes, my wife reoccupies the ground of the secret closet, enlarging upon what wonders are there, and what a shame it is, not to seek it out and explore it.

"Wife," said I, upon one of these occasions, "why speak more of that secret closet, when there before you hangs contrary testimony of a master mason, elected by yourself to decide. Besides, even if there were a secret closet, secret it should remain, and secret it shall. Yes, wife, here for once I must say my say. Infinite sad mischief has resulted from the profane bursting open of secret recesses. Though standing in the heart of this house, though hitherto we have all nestled about it, unsuspicious of aught hidden within, this chimney may or may not have a secret closet. But if it have, it is my kinsman's. To break into that wall, would be to break into his breast. And that wall-breaking wish of Momus I account the wish of a church-robbing gossip and knave. Yes, wife, a vile eaves-dropping varlet was Momus."

"Moses? — Mumps? Stuff with your mumps and your Moses!"

The truth is, my wife, like all the rest of the world, cares not a fig for my philosophical jabber. In dearth of other philosophical companionship, I and my chimney have to smoke and philosophize together. And sitting up so late as we do at it, a mighty smoke it is that we two smoky old philosophers make.

But my spouse, who likes the smoke of my tobacco as little as she does that of the soot, carries on her war against both. I live in continual dread lest, like the golden bowl, the pipes of me and my chimney shall yet be broken. To stay that mad project of my wife's, naught answers. Or, rather, she herself is incessantly answering, incessantly besetting me with her terrible alacrity for improvement, which is a softer name for destruction. Scarce a day I do not find her with her tape-measure, measuring for her grand hall, while Anna holds a yard-stick on one side, and Julia looks approvingly on from the other. Mysterious intimations appear in the nearest village paper, signed "Claude," to the effect that a certain structure, standing on a certain hill, is a sad blemish to an otherwise lovely landscape. Anonymous letters arrive, threatening me with I know not what, unless I remove my chimney. Is it my wife, too, or who, that sets up the neighbors to badgering me on the same subject, and hinting to me that my chimney, like a huge elm, absorbs all moisture from my garden? At night, also, my wife will start as from sleep, professing to hear ghostly noises from the secret closet. Assailed on all sides, and in all ways, small peace have I and my chimney.

Were it not for the baggage, we would together pack up, and remove from the country.

What narrow escapes have been ours! Once I found in a drawer a whole portfolio of plans and estimates. Another time, upon returning after a day's absence, I discovered my wife standing before the chimney in earnest conversation with a person whom I at once recognized as a meddlesome architectural reformer, who, because he had no gift for putting up anything, was ever intent upon pulling down; in various parts of the country having prevailed upon half-witted old folks to destroy their old-fashioned houses, particularly the chimneys.

But worst of all was, that time I unexpectedly returned at early morning from a visit to the city, and upon approaching the house, narrowly escaped three brickbats which fell, from high aloft, at my feet. Glancing up, what was my horror to see three savages, in blue jean overalls, in the very act of commencing the long-threatened attack. Aye, indeed, thinking of those three brickbats, I and my chimney have had narrow escapes.

It is now some seven years since I have stirred from home. My city friends all wonder why I don't come to see them, as in former times. They think I am getting sour and unsocial. Some say that I have become a sort of mossy old misanthrope, while all the time the fact is, I am simply standing guard over my mossy old chimney; for it is resolved between me and my chimney, that I and my chimney will never surrender.

{1856}

BAYARD TAYLOR
{1825–1878}

Bayard Taylor grew up in Quaker Pennsylvania — the setting of his novel *Joseph and His Friend* (1870) — and was as famous a latter-day Marco Polo as he was an author, traveling and writing his way through nearly the whole of Europe, Mexico, Egypt, Palestine, Abyssinia, Syria, Turkey, Russia, India, Japan, and China: he is the traveler in John Greenleaf Whittier's poem "The Tent on the Beach." In 1850, Taylor married his childhood love, Mary Agnew, while she was dying; in 1857, he married Marie Hansen, daughter of the Danish astronomer Peter Andreas Hansen. An astonishingly prolific writer, he was also the first to translate Goethe's *Faust* into English.

In *Joseph and His Friend* — dedicated to those "who believe in the truth and tenderness of man's love for man, as of man's love for woman" (a dedication omitted from the British edition) — Taylor makes an intense plea for "a valley of bliss . . . a new world where men might love each other without fear of conventional society."

> "I know such a spot," Philip cried, interrupting him, — "a great valley, bounded by a hundred miles of snowy peaks; lakes in its bed; enormous hillsides, dotted with groves of ilex and pine; orchards of orange and olive; a perfect climate, where it is bliss enough just to breathe, and freedom from the distorted laws of men, for none are near enough to enforce them! If there is no legal way of escape for you, here, at least, there is no force which can drag you back, once you are there: I will go with you, and perhaps — perhaps —"

While the novel suggests a Western American locale for this "valley of bliss," Taylor's Shangri-La is more reminiscent of Italy; as famous at that time for its adherence to the Code Napoléon, which promised freedom from persecution to homosexuals, as for its landscape.

Joseph and His Friend was published by G. P. Putnam's Sons — one of the few works excerpted here (chapters 9 and 10) to be brought out by a major commercial press. ❦

FROM *Joseph and His Friend: A Story of Pennsylvania*

JOSEPH AND HIS FRIEND

The train moved slowly along through the straggling and shabby suburbs, increasing its speed as the city melted gradually into the country; and Joseph, after a vain attempt to fix his mind upon one of the volumes he had procured for his slender library at home, leaned back in his seat and took note of his fellow-travellers. Since he began to approach the usual destiny of men, they had a new interest for him. Hitherto he had looked upon strange faces very much as on a strange language, without a thought of interpreting them but now their hieroglyphics seemed to suggest a meaning. The figures around him were so many sitting, silent histories, so many locked-up records of struggle, loss, gain, and all the other forces which give shape and color to human life. Most of them were strangers to each other, and as reticent (in their railway conventionality) as himself; yet, he reflected, the whole range of passion, pleasure, and suffering was probably illustrated in that collection of existences. His own troublesome individuality grew fainter, so much of it seemed to be merged in the common experience of men.

There was the portly gentleman of fifty, still ruddy and full of unwasted force. The keenness and coolness of his eyes, the few firmly marked lines on his face, and the color and hardness of his lips, proclaimed to everybody: "I am bold, shrewd, successful in business, scrupulous in the performance of my religious duties (on the Sabbath), voting with my party, and not likely to be fooled by any kind of sentimental nonsense." The thin, not very well-dressed man beside him, with the irregular features and uncertain expression, announced as clearly, to any who could read: "I am weak, like others, but I never consciously did any harm. I just manage to get along in the world, but if I only had a chance, I might make something better of myself." The fresh, healthy fellow, in whose lap a child was sleeping, while his wife nursed a younger one, — the man with ample mouth, large nostrils, and the hands of a mechanic, — also told his story: "On the whole, I find life a comfortable thing. I don't know much about it, but I take it as it comes, and never worry over what I can't understand."

The faces of the younger men, however, were not so easy to decipher. On them life was only beginning its plastic task, and it required an older eye to detect the delicate touches of awakening passions and hopes. But Joseph consoled himself with the thought that his own secret was as little to be discovered as any they might have. If they were still ignorant of the sweet experience of love, he was already their superior; if they were sharers in it, though strangers, they were near to him. Had he not left the foot of the class, after all?

All at once his eye was attracted by a new face, three or four seats from his own. The stranger had shifted his position, so that he was no longer seen in profile. He was apparently a few years older than Joseph, but still bright with all the charm of early manhood. His fair complexion was bronzed from exposure, and his hands, graceful without being effeminate, were not those of the idle gentleman. His hair, golden in tint, thrust its short locks as it pleased about a smooth, frank forehead; the eyes were dark gray, and the mouth, partly hidden by a mustache, at once firm and full. He was moderately handsome, yet it was not of that which Joseph thought; he felt that there was more of developed character and a richer past history expressed in those features than in any other face there. He felt sure — and smiled at himself, notwithstanding, for the impression — that at least some of his own doubts and difficulties had found their solution in the stranger's nature. The more he studied the face, the more he was conscious of its attraction, and his instinct of reliance, though utterly without grounds, justified itself to his mind in some mysterious way.

It was not long before the unknown felt his gaze, and, turning slowly in his seat, answered it. Joseph dropped his eyes in some confusion, but not until he had caught the full, warm, intense expression of those that met them. He fancied that he read in them, in that momentary flash, what he had never before found in the eyes of strangers, — a simple, human interest, above curiosity and above mistrust. The usual reply to such a gaze is an unconscious defiance: the unknown nature is on its guard: but the look which seems to answer, "We are men, let us know each other!" is, alas! too rare in this world.

While Joseph was fighting the irresistible temptation to look again, there was a sudden thud of the car-wheels. Many of the passengers started from their seats, only to be thrown into them again by a quick succession of violent jolts. Joseph saw the stranger springing towards the bell-rope; then he and all others seemed to be whirling over each other; there was a crash, a horrible grinding and splintering sound, and the end of all was a shock, in which his consciousness left him before he could guess its violence.

After a while, out of some blank, haunted by a single lost, wandering sense of existence, he began to awaken slowly to life. Flames were still dancing in his eyeballs, and waters and whirlwinds roaring in his ears; but it was only a passive sensation, without the will to know more. Then he felt himself partly lifted and his head supported, and presently a soft warmth fell upon the region of his heart. There were noises all about him, but he did not listen to them; his effort to regain his consciousness fixed itself on that point alone, and grew stronger as the warmth calmed the confusion of his nerves.

"Dip this in water!" said a voice, and the hand (as he now knew it to be) was removed from his heart.

Something cold came over his forehead, and at the same time warm drops fell upon his cheek.

"Look out for yourself: your head is cut!" exclaimed another voice.

"Only a scratch. Take the handkerchief out of my pocket and tie it up; but first ask yon gentleman for his flask!"

Joseph opened his eyes, knew the face that bent over his, and then closed them again. Gentle and strong hands raised him, a flask was set to his lips, and he drank mechanically, but a full sense of life followed the draught. He looked wistfully in the stranger's face.

"Wait a moment," said the latter; "I must feel your bones before you try to move. Arms and legs all right, — impossible to tell about the ribs. There! now put your arm around my neck, and lean on me as much as you like, while I lift you."

Joseph did as he was bidden, but he was still weak and giddy, and after a few steps, they both sat down together upon a bank. The splintered car lay near them upside down; the passengers had been extricated from it, and were now busy in aiding the few who were injured. The train had stopped and was waiting on the track above. Some were very pale and grave, feeling that Death had touched without taking them; but the greater part were concerned only about the delay to the train.

"How did it happen?" asked Joseph: "where was I? how did you find me?"

"The usual story, — a broken rail," said the stranger. "I had just caught the rope when the car went over, and was swung off my feet so luckily that I somehow escaped the hardest shock. I don't think I lost my senses for a moment. When we came to the bottom you were lying just before me; I thought you dead until I felt your heart. It is a severe shock, but I hope nothing more."

"But you, — are you not badly hurt?"

The stranger pushed up the handkerchief which was tied around his head, felt his temple, and said: "It must have been one of the splinters; I know nothing about it. But there is no harm in a little blood-letting except" — he added, smiling — "except the spots on your face."

By this time the other injured passengers had been conveyed to the train; the whistle sounded a warning of departure.

"I think we can get up the embankment now," said the stranger. "You must let me take care of you still: I am travelling alone."

When they were seated side by side, and Joseph leaned his head back on the supporting arm, while the train moved away with them, he felt that a new power, a new support, had come to his life. The face upon which he looked was no longer strange; the hand which had rested on his heart was warm with kindred blood. Involuntarily he extended his own; it was taken and held, and the dark-gray, courageous eyes turned to him with a silent assurance which he felt needed no words.

"It is a rough introduction," he then said: "my name is Philip Held. I was on my way to Oakland Station; but if you are going farther —"

"Why, that is my station also!" Joseph exclaimed, giving his name in return.

"Then we should have probably met, sooner or later, in any case. I am bound for the forge and furnace at Coventry, which is for sale. If the company who employ me decide to buy it, — according to the report I shall make, — the works will be placed in my charge."

"It is but six miles from my farm," said Joseph, "and the road up the valley is the most beautiful in our neighborhood. I hope you can make a favorable report."

"It is only too much to my own interest to do so. I have been mining and geologizing in Nevada and the Rocky Mountains for three or four years, and long for a quiet, ordered life. It is a good omen that I have found a neighbor in advance of my settlement. I have often ridden fifty miles to meet a friend who cared for something else than horse-racing or *monte*; and your six miles, — it is but a step!"

"How much you have seen!" said Joseph. "I know very little of the world. It must be easy for you to take your own place in life."

A shade passed over Philip Held's face. "It is only easy to a certain class of men," he replied, — "a class to which I should not care to belong. I begin to think that nothing is very valuable, the right to which a man don't earn, — except human love, and that seems to come by the grace of God."

"I am younger than you are, — not yet twenty-three," Joseph remarked. "You will find that I am very ignorant."

"And I am twenty-eight, and just beginning to get my eyes open, like a nine-days' kitten. If I had been frank enough to confess my ignorance, five years ago, as you do now, it would have been better for me. But don't let us measure ourselves or our experience against each other. That is one good thing we learn in Rocky Mountain life; there is no high or low, knowledge or ignorance, except what applies to the needs of men who come together.

So there are needs which most men have, and go all their lives hungering for, because they expect them to be supplied in a particular form. There is something," Philip concluded, "deeper than that in human nature."

Joseph longed to open his heart to this man, every one of whose words struck home to something in himself. But the lassitude which the shock left behind gradually overcame him. He suffered his head to be drawn upon Philip Held's shoulder, and slept until the train reached Oakland Station. When the two got upon the platform, they found Dennis waiting for Joseph, with a light country vehicle. The news of the accident had reached the station, and his dismay was great when he saw the two bloody faces. A physician had already been summoned from the neighboring village, but they had little need of his services. A prescription of quiet and sedatives for Joseph, and a strip of plaster for his companion, were speedily furnished, and they set out together for the Asten place.

It is unnecessary to describe Rachel Miller's agitation when the party arrived; or the parting of the two men who had been so swiftly brought near to each other; or Philip Held's farther journey to the forge that evening. He resisted all entreaty to remain at the farm until morning, on the ground of an appointment made with the present proprietor of the forge. After his departure Joseph was sent to bed, where he remained for a day or two, very sore and a little feverish. He had plenty of time for thought, — not precisely of the kind which his aunt suspected, for out of pure, honest interest in his welfare, she took a step which proved to be of doubtful benefit. If he had not been so innocent, — if he had not been quite as unconscious of his inner nature as he was over-conscious of his external self, — he would have perceived that his thoughts dwelt much more on Philip Held than on Julia Blessing. His mind seemed to run through a swift, involuntary chain of reasoning, to account to himself for his feeling towards her, and her inevitable share in his future; but towards Philip his heart sprang with an instinct beyond his control. It was impossible to imagine that the latter also would not be shot, like a bright thread, through the web of his coming days.

On the third morning, when he had exchanged the bed for an arm-chair, a letter from the city was brought to him. "Dearest Joseph," it ran, "what a fright and anxiety we have had! When pa brought the paper home, last night, and I read the report of the accident, where it said, 'J. Asten, severe contusions,' my heart stopped beating for a minute, and I can only write now (as you see) with a trembling hand. My first thought was to go directly to you; but ma said we had better wait for intelligence. Unless our engagement were generally known, it would give rise to remarks, — in short, I need not repeat to you all the *worldly* reasons with which she opposed me; but, oh, how I longed for *the right* to be at your side, and assure myself that the dreadful, dreadful danger has passed! Pa was quite shaken with the news: he felt hardly able to go to the Custom-House this morning. But he sides with ma about my going, and now, when my time as a daughter with them is growing so short, I dare not disobey. I know you will understand my position, yet, dear and true as you are, you cannot guess the anxiety with which I await a line from your hand, the hand that was so nearly taken from me forever!"

Joseph read the letter twice and was about to commence it for the third time, when a visitor was announced. He had barely time to thrust the scented sheet into his pocket; and the bright eyes and flushed face with which he met the Rev. Mr. Chaffinch convinced both that gentleman and his aunt, as she ushered the latter into the room, that the visit was accepted as an honor and a joy.

On Mr. Chaffinch's face the air of authority which he had been led to believe belonged to his calling had not quite succeeded in impressing itself; but melancholy, the next best thing, was strongly marked. His dark complexion and his white cravat intensified each other; and his eyes, so long uplifted above the concerns of this world, had ceased to vary their expression materially for the sake of any human interest. All this had been expected of him, and he had simply done his best to meet the requirements of the flock over which he was placed. Any of the latter might have easily been shrewd enough to guess, in advance, very nearly what the pastor would say, upon a given occasion; but each and all of them would have been both disappointed and disturbed if he had not said it.

After appropriate and sympathetic inquiries concerning Joseph's bodily condition, he proceeded to probe him spiritually.

"It was a merciful preservation. I hope you feel that it is a solemn thing to look Death in the face."

"I am not afraid of death," Joseph replied.

"You mean the physical pang. But death includes what comes after it, — judgment. That is a very awful thought."

"It may be to evil men; but I have done nothing to make me fear it."

"You have never made an open profession of faith; yet it may be that grace has reached you," said Mr. Chaffinch. "Have you found your Saviour?"

"I believe in him with all my soul!" Joseph exclaimed; "but you mean something else by 'finding' him. I will be candid with you, Mr. Chaffinch. The last sermon I heard you preach, a month ago, was upon the nullity of all good works, all Christian deeds; you called them 'rags, dust, and ashes,' and declared that man is saved by faith alone. I *have* faith, but I can't accept a doctrine which denies merit to works; and you, unless I accept it, will you admit that I have 'found' Christ?"

"There is but One Truth!" exclaimed Mr. Chaffinch, very severely.

"Yes," Joseph answered, reverently, "and that is only perfectly known to God."

The clergyman was more deeply annoyed than he cared to exhibit. His experience had been confined chiefly to the encouragement of ignorant souls, willing to accept *his* message, if they could only be made to comprehend it, or to the conflict with downright doubt and denial. A nature so seemingly open to the influences of the Spirit, yet inflexibly closed to certain points of doctrine, was something of a problem to him. He belonged to a class now happily becoming scarce, who, having been taught to pace a reasoned theological round, can only efficiently meet those antagonists who voluntarily come inside of their own ring.

His habit of control, however, enabled him to say, with a moderately friendly manner, as he took leave: "We will talk again when you are stronger. It is my duty to give spiritual help to those who seek it."

To Rachel Miller he said: "I cannot say that he is dark. His mind is cloudy, but we find that the vanities of youth often obscure the true light for a time."

Joseph leaned back in his arm-chair, closed his eyes, and meditated earnestly for half an hour. Rachel Miller, uncertain whether to be hopeful or discouraged by Mr. Chaffinch's words, stole into the room, but went about on tiptoe, supposing him to be asleep. Joseph was fully conscious of all her movements, and at last startled her by the sudden question: —

"Aunt, why do you suppose I went to the city?"

"Goodness, Joseph! I thought you were sound asleep. I suppose to see about the fall prices for grain and cattle."

"No, aunt," said he, speaking with determination, though the foolish blood ran rosily over his face, "I went to get a wife!"

She stood pale and speechless, staring at him. But for the rosy sign on his cheeks and temples she could not have believed his words.

"Miss Blessing?" she finally uttered, almost in a whisper.

Joseph nodded his head. She dropped into the nearest chair, drew two or three long breaths, and in an indescribable tone ejaculated, "Well!"

"I knew you would be surprised," said he; "because it is almost a surprise to myself. But you and she seemed to fall so easily into each other's ways, that I hope —"

"Why, you're hardly acquainted with her!" Rachel exclaimed. "It is so hasty! And you are so young!"

"No younger than father was when he married mother; and I have learned to know her well in a short time. Isn't it so with you, too, aunt? — you certainly liked her?"

"I'll not deny that, nor say the reverse now: but a farmer's wife should be a farmer's daughter."

"But suppose, aunt, that the farmer doesn't happen to love any farmer's daughter, and *does* love a bright, amiable, very intelligent girl, who is delighted with country life, eager and willing to learn, and very fond of the farmer's aunt (who can teach her everything)?"

"Still, it seems to me a risk," said Rachel; but she was evidently relenting.

"There is none to you," he answered, "and I am not afraid of mine. You will be with us, for Julia couldn't do without you, if she wished. If she were a farmer's daughter, with different ideas of housekeeping, it might bring trouble to both of us. But now you will have the management in your own hands until you have taught Julia, and afterwards she will carry it on in your way."

She did not reply; but Joseph could see that she was becoming reconciled to the prospect. After awhile she came across the room, leaned over him, kissed him upon the forehead, and then silently went away.

APPROACHING FATE

Only two months intervened until the time appointed for the marriage, and the days rolled swiftly away. A few lines came to Joseph from Philip Held, announcing that he was satisfied with the forge and furnace, and the sale would doubtless be consummated in a short time. He did not, however, expect to take charge of the works before March, and therefore gave Joseph his address in the city, with the hope that the latter would either visit or write to him.

On the Sunday after the accident Elwood Withers came to the farm. He seemed to have grown older in the short time which had elapsed since they had last met; after his first hearty rejoicing over Joseph's escape and recovery, he relapsed into a silent but not unfriendly mood. The two young men climbed the long hill behind the house and seated themselves under a noble pin-oak on the height, whence there was a lovely view of the valley for many miles to the southward.

They talked mechanically, for a while, of the season, and the crops, and the other usual subjects which farmers never get to the end of discussing; but both felt the impendence of more important themes, and, nevertheless, were slow to approach them. At last Elwood said: "Your fate is settled by this time, I suppose?"

"It is arranged, at least," Joseph replied. "But I can't yet make clear to myself that I shall be a married man in two months from now."

"Does the time seem long to you?"

"No," Joseph innocently answered; "it is very short."

Elwood turned away his head to conceal a melancholy smile; it was a few minutes before he spoke again.

"Joseph," he then said, "are you sure, quite sure, you love her?"

"I am to marry her."

"I meant nothing unfriendly," Elwood remarked, in a gentle tone. "My thought was this, — if you should ever find a still stronger love growing upon you, — something that would make the warmth you feel now seem like ice compared to it, — how would you be able to fight it? I asked the question of myself for you. I don't think I'm much different from most soft-hearted men, — except that I keep the softness so well stowed away that few persons know of it, — but if I were in your place, within two months of marriage to the girl I love, I should be miserable!"

Joseph turned towards him with wide, astonished eyes.

"Miserable from hope and fear," Elwood went on; "I should be afraid of fever, fire, murder, thunderbolts! Every hour of the day I should dread lest something might come between us; I should prowl around her house day after day, to be sure that she was alive! I should lengthen out the time into years; and all because I'm a great, disappointed, soft-hearted fool!"

The sad, yearning expression of his eyes touched Joseph to the heart. "Elwood," he said, "I see that it is not in my power to comfort you; if I give you pain unknowingly, tell me how to avoid it! I meant to ask you to stand beside me when I am married; but now you must consider your own feelings in answering, not mine. Lucy is not likely to be there."

"That would make no difference," Elwood answered. "Do you suppose it is a pain for me to see her, because she seems lost to me? No; I'm always a little encouraged when I have a chance to measure myself with her, and to guess — sometimes this and sometimes that — what it is that she needs to find in me. Force of will is of no use; as to faithfulness, — why, what it's worth can't be shown unless something turns up to try it. But you had better not ask me to be your groomsman. Neither Miss Blessing nor her sister would be overly pleased."

"Why so?" Joseph asked; "Julia and you are quite well acquainted, and she was always friendly towards you."

Elwood was silent and embarrassed. Then, reflecting that silence, at that moment, might express even more than speech, he said: "I've got the notion in my head; maybe it's foolish, but there it is. I talked a good deal with Miss Blessing, it's true, and yet I don't feel the least bit acquainted. Her manner to me was very friendly, and yet I don't think she likes me."

"Well!" exclaimed Joseph, forcing a laugh, though he was much annoyed, "I never gave you credit for such a lively imagination. Why not be candid, and admit that the dislike is on your side? I am sorry for it, since Julia will so soon be in the house there as my wife. There is no one else whom I can ask, unless it were Philip Held —"

"Held! To be sure, he took care of you. I was at Coventry the day after, and saw something of him." With these words, Elwood turned towards Joseph and looked him squarely in the face. "He'll have charge there in a few months, I hear," he then said, "and I reckon it as a piece of good luck for you. I've found that there are men, all, maybe, as honest and outspoken as they need be; yet two of 'em will talk at different marks and never fully understand each other, and other two will naturally talk right straight at the same mark and never miss. Now, Held is the sort that can hit the thing in the mind of the man they're talking to; it's a gift that comes o' being knocked about the world among all classes of people. What we learn here, always among the same folks, isn't a circumstance."

"Then you think I might ask him?" said Joseph, not fully comprehending all that Elwood meant to express.

"He's one of those men that you're safe in asking to do anything. Make him spokesman of a committee to wait on the President, arbitrator in a crooked lawsuit, overseer of a railroad gang, leader in a prayer-meeting (if he'd consent), or whatever else you choose, and he'll do the business as if he was used to it! It's enough for you that I don't know the town ways, and he does; it's considered worse, I've heard, to make a blunder in society than to commit a real sin."

He rose, and they loitered down the hill together. The subject was quietly dropped, but the minds of both were none the less busy. They felt the stir and pressure of new experiences, which had come to one through disappointment and to the other through success. Not three months had passed since they rode together through the twilight to Warriner's, and already life was opening to them, — but how differently! Joseph endeavored to make the most kindly allowance for his friend's mood, and to persuade himself that his feelings were unchanged. Elwood, however, knew that a shadow had fallen between them. It was nothing beside the cloud of his greater trouble: he also knew the cost of his own justification to Joseph, and prayed that it might never come.

That evening, on taking leave, he said: "I don't know whether you meant to have the news of your engagement circulated; but I guess Anna Warriner has heard, and that amounts to —"

"To telling it to the whole neighborhood, doesn't it?" Joseph answered. "Then the mischief is already done, if it is a mischief. It is well, therefore, that the day is set: the neighborhood will have little time for gossip."

He smiled so frankly and cheerfully, that Elwood seized his hand, and with tears in his eyes, said: "Don't remember anything against me, Joseph. I've always been honestly your friend, and mean to stay so."

He went that evening to a homestead where he knew he should find Lucy Henderson. She looked pale and fatigued, he thought; possibly his presence had become a restraint. If so, she must bear his unkindness: it was the only sacrifice he could not make, for he felt sure that his intercourse with her must either terminate in hate or love. The one thing of which he was certain was, that there could be no calm, complacent friendship between them.

It was not long before one of the family asked him whether he had heard the news; it seemed that they had already discussed it, and his arrival revived the flow of expression. In spite of his determination, he found it impossible to watch Lucy while he said, as simply as possible, that Joseph Asten seemed very happy over the prospect of the marriage; that he was old enough to take a wife; and if Miss Blessing could adapt herself to country habits, they might get on very well together. But later in the evening he took a chance of saying to her: "In spite of what I said, Lucy, I don't feel quite easy about Joseph's marriage. What do you think of it?"

She smiled faintly, as she replied: "Some say that people are attracted by mutual unlikeness. This seems to me to be a case of the kind; but they are free choosers of their own fates."

"Is there no possible way of persuading him — them — to delay?"

"No!" she exclaimed, with unusual energy; "none whatever!"

Elwood sighed, and yet felt relieved.

Joseph lost no time in writing to Philip Held, announcing his approaching marriage, and begging him — with many apologies for asking such a mark of confidence on so short an acquaintance — to act the part of nearest friend, if there were no other private reasons to prevent him.

Four or five days later the following answer arrived: —

MY DEAR ASTEN: — Do you remember that curious whirling, falling sensation, when the car pitched over the edge of the embankment? I felt a return of it on reading your letter; for you have surprised me beyond measure. Not by your request, for that is just what

I should have expected of you; and as well now, as if we had known each other for twenty years; so the apology is the only thing objectionable — But I am tangling my sentences; I want to say how heartily I return the feeling which prompted you to ask me, and yet how embarrassed I am that I cannot unconditionally say, "Yes, with all my heart!" My great, astounding surprise is, to find you about to be married to Miss Julia Blessing, — a young lady whom I once knew. And the embarrassment is this: I knew her under circumstances (in which she was not personally concerned, however) which might possibly render my presence now, as your groomsman, unwelcome to the family: at least, it is my duty — and yours, if you still desire me to stand beside you — to let Miss Blessing and her family decide the question. The circumstances to which I refer concern them rather than myself. I think your best plan will be simply to inform them of your request and my reply, and add that I am entirely ready to accept whatever course they may prefer.

Pray don't consider that I have treated your first letter to me ungraciously. I am more grieved than you can imagine that it happens so. You will probably come to the city a day before the wedding, and I insist that you shall share my bachelor quarters, in any case.

Always your friend,
PHILIP HELD.

This letter threw Joseph into a new perplexity. Philip a former acquaintance of the Blessings! Formerly, but not now; and what could those mysterious "circumstances" have been, which had so seriously interrupted their intercourse? It was quite useless to conjecture; but he could not resist the feeling that another shadow hung over the aspects of his future. Perhaps he had exaggerated Elwood's unaccountable dislike to Julia, which had only been implied, not spoken; but here was a positive estrangement on the part of the man who was so suddenly near and dear to him. He never thought of suspecting Philip of blame; the candor and cheery warmth of the letter rejoiced his heart. There was evidently nothing better to do than to follow the advice contained in it, and leave the question to the decision of Julia and her parents.

Her reply did not come by the return mail, nor until nearly a week afterwards; during which time he tormented himself by imagining the wildest reasons for her silence. When the letter at last arrived, he had some difficulty in comprehending its import.

"Dearest Joseph," she said, "you must *really* forgive me this long trial of your patience. Your letter was *so* unexpected, — I mean its contents, — and it seems as if ma and pa and Clementina would never agree what was best to be done. For that matter, I cannot say that they agree now; we had *no idea* that you were an intimate friend of Mr. Held, (I can't think how ever you should have become acquainted!) and it seems to break open old wounds, — none of mine, fortunately, for I have none. As Mr. Held leaves the question in our hands, there is, you will understand, all the more necessity that we should be careful. Ma thinks he has said nothing to you about the unfortunate occurrence, or you would have expressed an opinion. You never can know how happy your fidelity makes me; but I felt that, the first moment we met.

"Ma says that at *very private* (what pa calls informal) weddings there need not be bridesmaids or groomsmen. Miss Morrisey was married that way, not long ago; it is true that she is not of our circle, nor strictly a *first* family (this is ma's view, not mine, for I understand the hollowness of society); but we could very well do the same. Pa would be satisfied with a reception afterwards; he wants to ask the Collector, and the Surveyor, and the Appraiser. Clementina won't say anything now, but I know what she thinks, and so does ma; however, Mr. Held has so dropped out of city life that it is not important. I suppose everything must be dim in his memory now; you do not write to me much that he related. How strange that he should be your friend! They say my dress is lovely, but I am sure I should like a plain muslin just as well. I shall only breathe freely when I get back to the quiet of the country, (and your — *our* charming home, and dear, good Aunt Rachel!) and away from all these conventional forms. Ma says if there is one groomsman there ought to be two; either very simple, or according to custom. In a matter so delicate, perhaps, Mr. Held would be as competent to decide as we are; at least *I* am quite willing to leave it to *his* judgment. But how trifling is all this discussion, compared with the importance of the day to us! It is now drawing very near, but I have no misgivings, for I confide in you wholly and forever!"

After reading the letter with as much coolness as was then possible to him, Joseph inferred three things: that his acquaintance with Philip Held was not entirely agreeable to the Blessing family; that they would prefer the simplest style of a wedding, and this was in consonance with his own tastes; and that Julia clung to him as a deliverer from conditions with which her nature had little sympathy. Her incoherence, he fancied, arose from an agitation which he could very well understand, and his answer was intended to soothe and encourage her. It was difficult to let Philip know that his services would not be required, without implying the existence of an unfriendly feeling towards him; and Joseph, therefore, all the more readily accepted his invitation. He was assured that the mysterious difficulty did not concern Julia; even if it were so, he was not called upon to do violence, without cause, to so welcome a friendship.

The September days sped by, not with the lingering, passionate uncertainty of which Elwood Withers spoke, but almost too swiftly. In the hurry of preparation, Joseph had scarcely time to look beyond the coming event and estimate its consequences. He was too ignorant of himself to doubt: his conscience was too pure and perfect to admit the possibility of changing the course of his destiny. Whatever the gossip of the neighborhood might have been, he heard nothing of it that was not agreeable. His aunt was entirely reconciled to a wife who would not immediately, and probably not for a long time, interfere with her authority; and the shadows raised by the two men whom he loved best seemed, at last, to be accidentally thrown from clouds beyond the horizon of his life. This was the thought to which he clung, in spite of a vague, utterly formless apprehension, which he felt lurking somewhere in the very bottom of his heart.

Philip met him on his arrival in the city, and after taking him to his pleasant quarters, in a house looking on one of the leafy squares, good-naturedly sent him to the Blessing mansion, with a warning to return before the evening was quite spent. The family was in a flutter of preparation, and though he was cordially welcomed, he felt that, to all except Julia, he was subordinate in interest to the men who came every quarter of an hour, bringing bouquets, and silver spoons with cards attached, and pasteboard boxes containing frosted cakes. Even Julia's society he was only allowed to enjoy by scanty instalments; she was perpetually summoned by her mother or Clementina, to consult about some indescribable figment of dress. Mr. Blessing was occupied in the basement, with the inspection of various hampers. He came to the drawing-room to greet Joseph, whom he shook by both hands, with such incoherent phrases that Julia presently interposed. "You must not forget, pa," she said, "that the man is waiting: Joseph will excuse you, I know." She followed him to the basement, and he returned no more.

Joseph left early in the evening, cheered by Julia's words: "We can't complain of all this confusion, when it's for our sakes; but we'll be happier when it's over, won't we?"

He gave her an affirmative kiss, and returned to Philip's room. That gentleman was comfortably disposed in an arm-chair, with a book and a cigar. "Ah!" he exclaimed, "you find that a house is more agreeable any evening than that before the wedding?"

"There is one compensation," said Joseph; "it gives me two or three hours with you."

"Then take that other arm-chair, and tell me how this came to pass. You see I have the curiosity of a neighbor, already."

He listened earnestly while Joseph related the story of his love, occasionally asking a question or making a suggestive remark, but so gently that it seemed to come as an assistance. When all had been told, he rose and commenced walking slowly up and down the room. Joseph longed to ask, in turn, for an explanation of the circumstances mentioned in Philip's letter; but a doubt checked his tongue.

As if in response to his thought, Philip stopped before him and said: "I owe you my story, and you shall have it after a while, when I can tell you more. I was a young fellow of twenty when I knew the Blessings, and I don't attach the slightest importance, now, to anything that happened. Even if I did, Miss Julia had no share in it. I remember her distinctly; she was then about my age, or a year or two older; but hers is a face that would not change in a long while."

Joseph stared at his friend in silence. He recalled the latter's age, and was startled by the involuntary arithmetic which revealed Julia's to him. It was unexpected, unwelcome, yet inevitable.

"Her father had been lucky in some of his 'operations,'" Philip continued, "but I don't think he kept it long. I hardly wonder that she should come to prefer a quiet country life to such ups and downs as the family has known. Generally, a woman don't adapt herself so readily to a change of surroundings as a man: where there is love, however, everything is possible."

"There is! there is!" Joseph exclaimed, certifying the fact to himself as much as to his friend. He rose and stood beside him.

Philip looked at him with grave, tender eyes.

"What can I do?" he said.

"What should you do?" Joseph asked.

"This!" Philip exclaimed, laying his hands on Joseph's shoulders, — "this, Joseph! I can be nearer than a brother. I know that I am in your heart as you are in mine. There is no faith between us that need be limited, there is no truth too secret to be veiled. A man's perfect friendship is rarer than a woman's love, and most hearts are content with one or the other: not so with yours and mine! I read it in your eyes, when you opened them on my knee: I see it in your face now. Don't speak: let us clasp hands."

But Joseph could not speak.

{1870}

CHARLES WARREN STODDARD
{1843–1909}

Like Melville, Robert Louis Stevenson, and Paul Gauguin, the American novelist and short story writer Charles Warren Stoddard spent much of his life touring the South Seas. Notorious for writing exclusively with purple ink, he recorded his adventures on the islands in the frothy collections *South-Sea Idyls* (1873) — published in England in 1874 as *Summer Cruising in the South Seas*, with twenty-five drawings by Wallis MacKay — and *The Island of Tranquil Delights* (1904). A sexual tourist, he writes prose that is dense with base wordplay and suggestive, if oblique, language. Thus Stoddard dresses Kaná-aná, the sixteen-year-old protagonist of "Chumming with a Savage," in "a snow-white garment, rather short all around, low in the neck, and with no sleeves whatsoever. There was no sex to that garment; it was the spontaneous offering of a scant material and a large necessity." Later the boy "mesmerizes" the narrator "into a most refreshing sleep with a prolonged and pleasing manipulation." And in "Taboo. — A Fête Day in Tahiti," Stoddard peels a banana as if he were undressing it: "I poised aloft, with satisfaction, the rare-ripe banana, beautiful to the eye as a nugget of purest gold. The pliant petals were pouting at the top of the fruit. I readily turned them back, forming a unique and convenient gilded salver for the column of flaky manna that was, as yet, swathed in lace-like folds. These gauzy ribbons fell from it almost of their own accord, and hung in fleecy festoons about it."

Although Stoddard does, occasionally, write in a more serious vein — "Why should we return to the world and its cares, when the sea invites us to its isles?" — he seems finally skittish and jumpy in his Pacific paradise: his hopping from island to island reveals a restlessness, an incapacity to maintain a love affair without growing bored. Appositely, he was also the author of an urban novel, *For the Pleasure of His Company: An Affair of the Misty City* (1903), perhaps the first work of American fiction by a homosexual writer to be set in San Francisco.

Roger Austen's *Genteel Pagan: The Double Life of Charles Warren Stoddard* (1991), edited by John Crowley, is the chief study of this author. ⚓

FROM *South-Sea Idyls*

In a Transport

A LITTLE FRENCH *aspirant de marine*, with an incipient moustache, said to me, confidentially, "Where you see the French flag, you see France!" We were pacing to and fro on the deck of a transport that swung at anchor off San Francisco, and, as I looked shoreward for almost the last time, — we were to sail at daybreak for a southern cruise, — I hugged my Ollendorf in despair as I dreamed of "French in six easy lessons," without a master, or a tolerable accent, or anything, save a suggestion of Babel and a confusion of tongues at sea.

Thanaron, the aspirant in question, embraced me when I boarded the transport with my baggage, treated me like a long-lost brother all that afternoon, and again embraced me when I went ashore towards evening to take leave of my household. There was something so impulsive and boyish in his manner that I immediately returned his salute, and with considerable fervour, feeling that kind Heaven had thrown me into the arms of the exceptional foreigner who would, to a certain extent, console me for the loss of my whole family. The mystery that hangs over the departure of any craft that goes by wind is calculated to appal the landsman; and when the date of sailing is fixed, the best thing he can do is to go aboard in season and compose his soul in peace. To be sure, he may swing at anchor for a day or two, in full sight of the domestic circle that he has shattered, but he is spared the repetition of those last agonies, and cuts short the unravelling hours just prior to a separation, which are probably the most unsatisfactory in life.

Under cover of darkness a fellow can do almost anything, and I concluded to go on board. There was a late dinner and a parting toast at home, and those ominous silences in the midst of a conversation that was as spasmodic and disconnected and unnatural as possible. There was something on our minds, and we relapsed in turn and forgot ourselves in the fathomless abysses of speculation. Some one saw me off that night, — some one who will never again follow me to the sea, and welcome me on my return to earth after my wandering. We sauntered down the dark streets along the city front, and tried to disguise our motives, but it was hard work. Presently we heard the slow swing of the tide under us, and the musty odour of the docks regaled us; one or two shadows seemed to be groping about in the neighbourhood, making more noise than a shadow has any right to make.

Then came the myriad-masted shipping, the twinkling lights in the harbour, and a sense of ceaseless motion in waters that never can be still. We did not tarry there long. The boat was bumping her bow against a pair of slippery stairs that led down to the water, and I entered the tottering thing that half sunk under me, dropped into my seat in the stern, and tried to call out something or other as we shot away from the place, with a cloud over my eyes that was darker than night itself, and a cloud over my heart that was as heavy as lead. After that there was nothing to do but to climb up one watery swell and slide down on the other side of it, to count the shadow-ships that shaped themselves out of chaos as we drew near them, and dissolved again when we had passed; while the oars seemed to grunt in the rowlocks, and the two jolly tars in uniform — they might have been mutes, for all I know — swung to and fro, to and fro, dragging me over the water to my "ocean bride," — I think that is what they call a ship, when the mood is on them!

She did look pretty as we swam up under her. She looked like a great *silhouette* against the steel-grey sky; but within was the sound of revelry, and I hastened on board to find our little cabin blue with smoke, which, however, was scarcely dense enough to muffle the martial strains of the *Marseillaise*, as shouted by the whole mess.

Thanaron — my Thanaron — was in the centre of the table, with his curly head out of the transom, — not that he was by any means a giant, but we were all a little cramped between-decks, — and he was leading the chorus with a sabre in one hand and the head of the Doctor in the other. Without the support of the faculty, he would probably not have ended his song of triumph as successfully as he ultimately did, when Nature herself had fainted from exhaustion. It was the last night in port, a few friends from shore had come to dine, and black coffee and cognac at a late hour had finished the business.

If there is one thing in this world that astonishes me more than another, it is the rapidity with which some people talk in French. Thanaron's French, when he once got started, sounded to me like the well-executed trill of a *prima-donna*, and quite as intelligible. The joke of it was, that Frenchmen seemed to find no difficulty in understanding him at his highest speed. On the whole, perhaps, this fact astonishes me more than the other.

Dinner was as far over as it could get without beginning again and calling itself breakfast; so the party broke up in a whirlwind of patriotic songs, and, one by one, we dropped our guests over the side of the vessel until there was none left, and then we waved them a thousand adieus, and kept up the last words as long as we could catch the faintest syllable of a reply. There were streaks of dull red in the east by this time, and the outlines of the city were again becoming visible. This I dreaded a little; and, when our boat had returned and everything was put in shipshape, I deliberately dropped a tear in the presence of my messmates, who were overcome with emotion at the spectacle; and, having all embraced, we went below, where I threw myself, with some caution, into my hammock, and slept until broad daylight.

I did not venture on deck again until after our first breakfast, — an informal one, that set uneasily on the table, and seemed inclined to make its escape from one side or the other. Of course, we were well under way by this time. I was assured of the fact by the reckless rolling of the vessel and the strange and unfamiliar feeling in my stomach, as though it were some other fellow's stomach, and not my own. My legs were a trifle uncertain; my head was queer. Everybody was rushing everywhere, and doing things that had to be undone or done over again in the course of the next ten minutes. I resolved to pace the deck, which is probably the best thing for a man to do when he goes down to the sea in ships, and does business — you could hardly call it pleasure — on great waters.

I went up the steep companion-way, and found a deck-load of ropes, and the entire crew — dressed in blue flannel, with broad collars — skipping about in the most fantastic manner. It was like a ballet scene in *L'Africaine*, and highly diverting — for a few minutes! From my stronghold on the top stair of the companion-way, I cast my eye shoreward. The long coast ran down the horizon under a broadside of breakers that threatened to engulf the continent; the air was grey with scattering mist; the sea was much disturbed, and of that ugly yellowish-green tint that signifies soundings. Overhead, a few sea-birds whirled in disorder, shrieking as though their hearts would break. It looked ominous, yet I felt it my duty, as an American under the shadow of the tricolour, to keep a stiff upper lip, — and I flatter myself that I did so. Figuratively speaking, I balanced myself in the mouth of the companion-way, with a bottle of claret in one pocket and a French roll in the other, while I brushed the fog from my eyes with the sleeve of my monkey-jacket, and exclaimed with the bard, "My native land, good-night."

It was morning at the time, but I did not seem to care much. In fact, time is not of the slightest consequence on shipboard. So I withdrew to my hammock, and having climbed into it in safety ended the day after a miserable fashion that I have deplored a thousand times since, during the prouder moments of my life.

A week passed by — I suppose it was a week, for I could reckon only seven days, and seven nights of about twice the length of the days — during that interval; yet I should, in the innocence of my heart, have called it a month, without a moment's hesitation. We arose late in the morning, — those of us who had a watch below; ate a delightfully long and narrow breakfast, consisting of an interminable procession of dishes in single file; paced the deck and canvassed the weather; went below to read, but talked instead; dined as we had breakfasted, only in a far more elaborate and protracted manner, while a gentle undercurrent of side-dishes lent interest to the occasion. There was a perpetual stream of conversation playing over the table, from the moment that heralded the soup until the last drop of black coffee was sopped up with a bit of dry bread. By the time we had come to cheese, everybody felt called upon to say his say, in the face of everybody else. I alone kept my place, and held it because the heaviest English I knew fell feebly to the floor before the thunders of those five prime Frenchmen, who were flushed with enthusiasm and good wine. I dreamed of home over my cigarette, and tried to look as though I were still interested in life, when, Heaven knows, my face was more like a half-obliterated cameo of despair than anything human. Thanaron, my foreign affinity, now and then threw me a semi-English nut to crack, but by the time I had recovered myself, — it is rather embarrassing to be assaulted even in the most friendly manner with a batch of broken English, — by the time I had framed an intelligible response, Thanaron was in the heat of a fresh argument, and keeping up a running fire of small shot that nearly floored the mess.

But there is an end even to a French dinner, and we ultimately adjourned to the deck, where, about sunset, everybody took his station while the *Angelus* was said. Then twilight, with a subdued kind of skylarking in the forecastle, and genteel merriment amidships, while *Monsieur le Capitaine* paced the high quarter-deck with the shadow of a smile crouching between the fierce jungles of his intensely black side-whiskers. Ah, sir, it was something to be at sea in a French transport with the tricolour flaunting at the peak; to have four guns with their mouths gagged, and oilcloth capes lashed snugly over them; to see everybody in uniform, each having the profoundest respect for those who ranked a notch above him, and having, also, an ill-disguised contempt for the unlucky fellow beneath him! This spirit was observable from one end of the ship to the other, and, sirs, we had a little world of our own revolving on a wabbling axis between the staunch ribs of the old transport "Chevert."

We were bound for Tahiti, God willing and the winds favourable; and the common hope of ultimately finding port in that paradise was all that held us together through thick and thin. We might wrangle at dinner, and come to breakfast next morning with bitterness in our hearts; we might sink into the bottomless pit of despond; we might revile *Monsieur le Capitaine* and *Monsieur le Cuisinier*, including in our anathemas the elements and some other things; they (the Frenchmen) might laugh to scorn the great American people, — and they did it, two or three times — and I, in my turn, might feel a secret contempt for Paris, without having the power to express the same in tolerable French, so I felt it, and held my tongue. Even Thanaron gave me a French shrug now and then that sent the cold shivers through me; but there was sure to come a sunset like a sea of fire, at which golden hour we were marshalled amidships, and stood with uncovered heads and the soft light playing over us, while the littlest French boy in the crew said the evening prayer with exceeding sweetness, — being the youngest, he was the most worthy of saying it, — and then we all crossed ourselves, and our hearts melted within us.

There was something in the delicious atmosphere, growing warmer every day, and something in the delicious sea, that was beginning to rock her floating gardens of blooming weed under our bows, and something in the aspect of *Monsieur le Capitaine*, with his cap off and a shadow of prayer softening his hard, proud face, that unmanned us; so we rushed to our own little cabin and hugged one another, lest we should forget how when we were restored to our sisters and our sweethearts, and everything was forgiven and forgotten in one intense moment of French remorse.

Who took me in his arms and carried me the length of the cabin in three paces, at the imminent peril of my life? Thanaron! Who admired Thanaron's gush of nature, and nearly squeezed the life out of him in the vain hope of making their joy known to him? Everybody else in the mess! Who looked on in bewilderment, and was half glad and half sorry, though more glad than sorry by half, and wondered all the while what was coming next? Bless you, it was I! And we kept doing that sort of thing until I got very used to it, and by the time we sighted the green summits of Tahiti, my range of experience was so great that nothing could touch me further. It may not be that we were governed by the laws of ordinary seafarers. The "Chevert" was shaped a little like a bath-tub, with a bow like a duck's breast, and a high, old-fashioned quarter-deck, resembling a Chinese junk with a reef in her stern. Forty bold sailor-boys, who looked as though they had been built on precisely the same model and dealt out to the government by the dozen, managed to keep the decks very clean and tidy, and the brass-work in a state of dazzling brightness. The ship was wonderfully well-ordered. I could tell you by the sounds on deck, while I swung in the comfortable seclusion of my hammock, just the hour of the day or night, but that was after I had once learned the order of events. There was the Sunday morning inspection, the Wednesday sham naval battle, the prayers night and morning, and the order to shorten sail each evening. Between times the decks were scrubbed and the whole ship renovated; sometimes the rigging was darkened with drying clothes, and sometimes we felt like ancient mariners, the sea was so oily, and the air so hot and still. There was nothing stirring save the sea-birds, who paddled about like tame ducks, and the faint, thin thread of smoke that ascended noiselessly from the dainty rolls of tobacco in the fingers of the entire ship's crew. In fact, when we moved at all in these calm waters, we seemed to be propelled by forty-cigarette power, for there was not a breath of air stirring.

It was at such times that we fought our bloodless battles. The hours were ominous; breakfast did not seem half a breakfast, because we hurried through it with the dreadful knowledge that a conflict was pending, and possibly — though not probably — we might never gather at that board again, for a naval engagement is something terrible, and life is uncertain in the fairest weather. Breakfast is scarcely over when the alarm is given, and with the utmost speed every Frenchman flies to his post. Already the horizon is darkened with the Prussian navy, yet our confidence in the staunch old "Chevert," in each particular soul on board, and in our undaunted leader, — *Monsieur le Capitaine*, who is even now scouring the sea with an enormous marine glass that of itself is enough to strike terror to the Prussian heart, — our implicit confidence in ourselves is such that we smilingly await the approach of the doomed fleet. At last they come within range of our guns, and the conflict begins. I am unfortunately compelled to stay beneath the hatches. A sham battle is no sight for an inexperienced landsman to witness, and, moreover, I should doubtless get in the way of the frantic crew, who seem resolved to shed the last drop of French blood in behalf of *la belle France*.

Marine engagements are, as a general thing, a great bore. The noise is something terrific; ammunition is continually passed up through the transom over our dinner-table, and a thousand feet are rushing over the deck with a noise as of theatrical thunder. The engagement lasts for an hour or two. Once or twice we are enveloped in sheets of flame. We are speedily deluged with water, and the conflict is renewed with the greatest enthusiasm. Again, and again, and again, we pour a broadside into the enemy's fleet, and always with terrific effect. We invariably do ourselves the greatest credit, for, by the time our supplies are about exhausted, not a vestige of the once glorious navy of Prussia remains to tell the tale. The sea is, of course, blood-stained for miles around. The few persistent Prussians who attempt to board us are speedily despatched, and allowed to drop back into the remorseless waves. A shout of triumph rings up from our triumphant crew, and the play is over.

Once more the hatches are removed; once more I breathe the sweet air of heaven, for not a grain of powder has been burned through all this fearful conflict; once more my messmates rush into our little cabin and regale themselves with copious draughts of absinthe, and I am pressed to the proud bosom of Thanaron, who is restored to me without a scar to disfigure his handsome little body. I grew used to these weekly wars, and before we came in sight of our green haven, there was not a Prussian left in the Pacific. It is impossible that any nation, though they be schooled to hardships, could hope to survive such a succession of disastrous conflicts. On the whole, I like sham battles; they are deuced exciting, and they don't hurt.

How different, how very different those sleepy days when we were drifting on towards the Marquesas Islands! The silvery phaetons darted overhead like day-stars shooting from their spheres. The seaweed grew denser, and a thousand floating things, — broken branches with a few small leaves attached, the husk of a cocoa-nut, or straws such as any dove from any ark would be glad to seize upon, — these gave us ample food for speculation. "Piloted by the slow, unwilling winds," we came close to the star-lit Nouka Hiva, and shortened sail right under its fragrant shadow. It was a glorious night. There was the subtle odour of earth in the warm, faint air, and before us that impenetrable shadow that we knew to be an island, yet whose outlines were traceable only by the obliterated stars.

At sunrise we were on deck, and, looking westward, saw the mists melt away like a veil swept from before the face of a dusky Venus just rising from the waves. The island seemed to give out a kind of magnetic heat that made our blood tingle. We gravitated toward it with an almost irresistible impulse. Something had to be done before we yielded to the fascinations of this savage enchantress. Our course lay to the windward of the southeastern point of the land; but, finding that we could not weather it, we went off before the light wind and drifted down the northern coast, swinging an hour or more under the lee of some parched rocks, eyeing the "Needles," — the slender and symmetrical peaks so called, — and then we managed to work our way out into the open sea again, and were saved.

Valleys lay here and there, running back from the shore with green and inviting vistas; slim waterfalls made one desperate leap from the clouds and buried themselves in the forests hundreds of feet below, where they were lost for ever. Rain-clouds hung over the mountains, throwing deep shadows across the slopes that but for this relief would have been too bright for the sentimental beauty that usually identifies a tropical island.

I happened to know something about the place, and marked every inch of the scorching soil as we floated past groves of rosewood, sandalwood, and a hundred sorts of new and strange trees, looking dark and velvety in the distance; past strips of beach that shone like brass, while beyond them the cocoa-palms that towered above the low, brown huts of the natives seemed to reel and nod in the intense meridian heat. A moist cloud, far up the mountain, hung above a serene and sacred haunt, and under its shelter was hidden a deep valley, whose secret has been carried to the ends of the earth; for Herman Melville has plucked out the heart of its mystery, and beautiful and barbarous Typee lies naked and forsaken.

I was rather glad we could not get any nearer to it, for fear of dispelling the ideal that has so long charmed me. Catching the wind again, late in the afternoon, we lost the last outline of Nouka Hiva in the soft twilight, and said our prayers that evening as much at sea as ever. Back we dropped into the solemn round of uneventful days. Even the sham battles no longer thrilled us. In fact, the whole affair was a little too theatrical to bear frequent repetition. There was but one of our mess who could muster an episode whenever we became too stagnant for our health's good, and this was our first officer, — a tall, slim fellow, with a warlike beard, and very soft, dark eyes, whose pupils seemed to be floating aimlessly about under the shelter of long lashes. His face was in a perpetual dispute with itself, and I never knew which was the right or the wrong side of him. B—— was the happy possessor of a tight little African, known as Nero, although I always looked upon him as so much Jamaica ginger. Nero was as handsome a specimen of tangible darkness as you will sight in a summer's cruise. B—— loved with the ardour of his vacillating eyes, yet governed with the rigour of his beard. Nero was consequently prepared for any change in the weather, no matter how sudden or uncalled for. In the equatorial seas, while we sailed to the measure of the Ancient Mariner, B—— summoned Nero to the sacrifice, and, having tortured him to the extent of his wits, there was a reconciliation more ludicrous than any other scene in the farce. It was at such moments that B——'s eyes literally swam, when even his beard wilted, while he told of the thousand pathetic eras in Nero's life, when he might have had his liberty, but found the service of his master more beguiling; of the adventures by flood and field, where B—— was distinguishing himself, yet at his side, through thick and thin, struggled the faithful Nero. Thus B—— warmed himself at the fire his own enthusiasm had kindled on the altar of self-love, and every moment added to his fervour. It was the yellow fever, and the cholera, and the smallpox, that were powerless to separate that faithful slave from the agonizing bedside of his master. It was shipwreck, and famine, and the smallest visible salary, that seemed only to strengthen the ties that bound them the one to the other. Death — cruel death — alone could separate them; and B—— took Nero by the throat and kissed him passionately upon his sooty cheek, and the floating eyes came to a standstill with an expression of virtuous defiance that was calculated to put all conventionalities to the blush. We were awed by the magnanimity of such conduct, until we got thoroughly used to it, and then we were simply entertained. We kept looking forward to the conclusion of the scene, which usually followed in the course of half an hour. B—— having fondled Nero to his heart's content, and Nero having become somewhat bored, there was sure to arise some mild disturbance, aggravated by both parties, and B——, believing he had endured as much as any Frenchman and first officer is expected to endure without resentment, suddenly rises, and seizing Nero by the short, wiry moss of his scalp, kicks him deliberately from the cabin, and returns to us bursting with indignation. This domestic equinox we soon grew fond of, and, having become familiar with all its signals of approach, we watched with agreeable interest the inevitable climax. It was well for Nero that Nature had provided against any change of colour in his skin, for he must have borne the sensation of his chastisement for some hours, though he was unable to give visible expression of it. By-and-by came B——'s own private birthday. Nothing had been said of it at table, and, in fact, nothing elsewhere, that I remember; but Nero, who had survived several of those anniversaries, bore it in mind, and our dinner was something gorgeous — to look at! Unhappily, certain necessary ingredients had been unavoidably omitted in the concocting of the dessert, ornamental pastry not being set down in our regular bill of fare; but B—— ate of pies that were built of chips, and of puddings that were stuffed with sawdust, until I feared we should be called upon to mourn the loss of a first officer before morning.

Moreover, B—— insisted that everything was unsurpassed; and, heaven be thanked! I believe the pastry could easily lay claim to that distinction. At any rate, never before or since have I laid teeth to such a Dead Sea dessert. At this point, B—— naturally called Nero to him and thanked him, with moist and truthful eyes, and the ingenuous little Jamaican dropped a couple of colourless tears that would easily have passed for anybody's anywhere. For this mutual exhibition of sentiment every one of us was duly grateful, and we never afterward scorned B—— for his eccentricities, since we knew him to be capable of genuine feeling. Moreover, he nearly died of his birthday feast, yet did not once complain of the unsuspecting cause of all his woe, who was at his side night and day, anticipating all his wishes, and deploring the unaccountable misfortunes of his master.

So the winds blew us into the warm south latitudes. I was getting restless. Perhaps we had talked ourselves out of legitimate topics of conversation, and were forcing the social element. It was tedious beyond expression, passing day after day within sound of the same voices, and being utterly unable to flee into never so small a solitude, for there was not an inch of it on board. Swinging at night in my hammock between decks, wakefully dreaming of the future and of the past, again and again I have stolen up on deck, where the watch lay in the moonlight, droning their interminable yarns and smoking their perpetual cigarettes, — for French sailors have privileges, and improve them with considerable grace.

It was at such times that the wind sung in the rigging, with a sound as of a thousand swaying branches full of quivering leaves, — just as the soft gale in the garden groves suggests pleasant nights at sea, the vibration of the taut stays, and the rush of waters along the smooth sides of the vessel. A ship's rigging is a kind of sea-harp, played upon by the four winds of heaven.

The sails were half in moonlight and half in shadow. Every object was well defined, and on the high quarter-deck paced Thanaron, his boyish figure looking strangely picturesque, for he showed in every motion how deeply he felt the responsibility of his office. There was usually a faint light in the apartments of *Monsieur le Capitaine*, and I thought of him in his gold lace and dignity, poring over a French novel, or cursing the light winds. I used to sit upon the neck of a gun, — one of our four dummies, that were never known to speak louder than a whisper, — lay my head against the moist bulwarks, and listen to the half-savage chants of the Tahitian sailors who helped to swell our crew. As we drew down toward the enchanted islands they seemed fairly bewitched, and it was with the utmost difficulty that they could keep their mouths shut until evening, when they were sure to begin intoning an epic that usually lasted through the watch. Sometimes a fish leaped into the moonlight, and came down with a splash; or a whale heaved a great sigh close to us, and as I looked over the bulwarks, I would catch a glimpse of the old fellow just going down, like a submerged island. Occasionally a flying-fish — a kind of tangible moonbeam — fell upon deck, and was secured by one of the sailors; or a bird, sailing about with an eye to roosting on one of our yards, gave a plaintive, ominous cry, that was echoed in falsetto by two or three voices, and rung in with the Tahitian cantata of island delights. Even this sort of thing lost its charm after a little. Thanaron could not speak to me, because Thanaron was officer of the deck at that moment, and Thanaron himself had said to me, "Order, Monsieur, order is the first law of France!" I had always supposed that

Heaven had a finger in the making of that law, — but it is all the same to a Frenchman.

Most sea-days have a tedious family resemblance, their chief characteristic being the almost total absence of any distinguishing feature. Fair weather and foul; sunlight, moonlight, and starlight; moments of confidence; oaths of eternal fidelity; plans for the future long enough to crowd a century uncomfortably; relapses, rows, recoveries; then, after many days, the water subsided, and we saw land at last.

Land, God bless it! Long, low coral reefs, with a strip of garden glorifying them; rocks towering out of the sea, palm-crowned, foam-fringed; wreaths of verdure cast upon the bosom of the ocean, for ever fragrant in their imperishable beauty; and, beyond and above them all, gorgeous and glorious Tahiti.

On the morning of the thirty-third day out, there came a revelation to the whole ship's company. A faint blue peak was seen struggling with the billows; presently it seemed to get the better of them, growing broader and taller, but taking hours to do so. The wind was stiff, and the sea covered with foam; we rolled frightfully all day. Our French dinner lost its identity. Soup was out of the question; we had hard work to keep meat and vegetables from total wreck, while we hung on to the legs of the table with all our strength. How the old "Chevert" "bucked," that day, as though conscious that for months to come she would swing in still waters by the edge of green pastures, where any such conduct would be highly inappropriate.

Every hour the island grew more and more beautiful, as though it were some lovely fruit or flower, swiftly and magically coming to maturity. A central peak, with a tiara of rocky points, crowns it with majesty, and a neighbouring island of great beauty seems its faithful attendant. I do not wonder that the crew of the "Bounty" mutinied when they were ordered to make sail and turn their backs on Tahiti; nor am I surprised that they put the captain and one or two other objectionable features into a small boat, and advised them to continue their voyage if they were anxious to do so: but as for them, give them Tahiti, or give them worse than death, — and, if convenient, give them Tahiti straight, and keep all the rest for the next party that came along.

As soon as we were within hailing distance, the pilot came out and took us under his wing. We kissed the hand of a citizen of the new world, and, for the first time since losing sight of the dear California coast, dismissed it from our minds. There was very little wind right under the great green mountains, so the frigate "Astrea" sent a dozen boats to tow us through the opening in the reef to our most welcome anchorage. No Doge of Venice ever cruised more majestically than we, and our sea-pageant was the sensation of the day.

"Click-click" went the anchor-chains through the hawse-holes, down into a deep, sheltered bowl of the sea, whose waters have never yet been ruffled by the storms that beat upon the coral wall around it. Along the crescent shores trees dropped their yellow leaves into the water, and tried their best to bury the slim canoes drawn up among their roots. Beyond this barricade of verdure the eye caught glimpses of every sort of tropical habitation imaginable, together with the high roofs and ponderous white walls of the French government buildings. The foliage broke over the little town like a green sea, and every possibility of a good view of it was lost in the inundation. Above it towered the sublime crest of the mountain, with a strip of cloud above its middle in true savage fashion. Perpetual harvest lay in its lap, and it basked in the smile of God.

Twilight, fragrant and cool; a fruity flavour in the air, a flower-like tint in sea and sky, the ship's boat waiting to convey us shoreward. . . . O Thanaron, my Thanaron, with your arms about my neck, and B——'s arms about you, and Nero clinging to his master's knees, — in fact, with everybody felicitating every other body, because it was such an evening as descends only upon the chosen places of the earth, and because, having completed our voyage in safety, we were all literally in a transport!

{1873}

WALTER PATER
{1839–1894}

From the start, it must be said that Pater was not outfitted to be a novelist: it is for *The Renaissance*, and the almost inconceivable influence that it exerted, that he is most remembered. *Marius the Epicurean* is represented here by Chapter 7 insofar as it is one of the earliest — if not the earliest — (proto-)homosexual "nursing scenes" in literature: a scene that, with the advent of AIDS, has become a fixture of homosexual fiction. Among other such notable pre-AIDS scenes: Wilde's *De Profundis*, when Lord Alfred Douglas abandons him in Brighton, and writes, *"When you are not on your pedestal you are not interesting. The next time you are ill I will go away at once"*; and Forster's *Maurice*, where Clive Durham has a relapse of influenza at the Hallses the night he tells Maurice of his determination to travel to Greece.

Among the most fascinating of books on Pater is Denis Donoghue's *Walter Pater: Lover of Strange Souls* (1995).

FROM *Marius the Epicurean*

A PAGAN END

For the fantastical colleague of the philosophic emperor Marcus Aurelius, returning in triumph from the East, had brought in his train, among the enemies of Rome, one by no means a captive. People actually sickened at a sudden touch of the unsuspected foe, as they watched in dense crowds the pathetic or grotesque imagery of failure or success in the triumphal procession. And, as usual, the plague brought with it a power to develop all pre-existent germs of superstition. It was by dishonour done to Apollo himself, said popular rumour — to Apollo, the old titular divinity of pestilence, that the poisonous thing had come abroad. Pent up in a golden coffer consecrated to the god, it had escaped in the sacrilegious plundering of his temple at Seleucia by the soldiers of Lucius Verus, after a traitorous surprise of that town and a cruel massacre. Certainly there was something which baffled all imaginable precautions and all medical science, in the suddenness with which the disease broke out simultaneously, here and there, among both soldiers and citizens, even in places far remote from the main line of its march in the rear of the victorious army. It seemed to have invaded the whole empire, and some have even thought that, in a mitigated form, it permanently remained there. In Rome itself many thousands perished; and old authorities tell of farmsteads, whole towns, and even entire neighbourhoods, which from that time continued without inhabitants and lapsed into wildness or ruin.

Flavian lay at the open window of his lodging, with a fiery pang in the brain, fancying no covering thin or light enough to be applied to his body. His head being relieved after a while, there was distress at the chest. It was but the fatal course of the strange new sickness, under many disguises; travelling from the brain to the feet, like a material resident, weakening one after another of the organic centres; often, when it did not kill, depositing various degrees of lifelong infirmity in this member or that; and after such descent, returning upwards again, now as a mortal coldness, leaving the entrenchments of the fortress of life overturned, one by one, behind it.

Flavian lay there, with the enemy at his breast now in a painful cough, but relieved from that burning fever in the head, amid the rich-scented flowers·— rare Paestum roses, and the like — procured by Marius for his solace, in a fancied convalescence; and would, at intervals, return to labour at his verses, with a great eagerness to complete and transcribe the work, while Marius sat and wrote at his dictation, one of the latest but not the poorest specimens of genuine Latin poetry.

It was in fact a kind of nuptial hymn, which, taking its start from the thought of nature as the universal mother, celebrated the preliminary pairing and mating together of all fresh things, in the hot and genial springtime — the immemorial nuptials of the soul of spring itself and the brown earth; and was full of a delighted, mystic sense of what passed between them in that fantastic marriage. That mystic burden was relieved, at intervals, by the familiar playfulness of the Latin verse-writer in dealing with mythology, which, though coming at so late a day, had still a wonderful freshness in its old age. — "*Amor* has put his weapons by and will keep holiday. He was bidden go without apparel, that none might be wounded by his bow and arrows. But take care! In truth he is none the less armed than usual, though he be all unclad."

In the expression of all this Flavian seemed, while making it his chief aim to retain the opulent, many-syllabled vocabulary of the Latin genius, at some points even to have advanced beyond it, in anticipation of wholly new laws of taste as regards sound, a new range of sound itself. The peculiar resultant note, associating itself with certain other experiences of his, was to Marius like the foretaste of an entirely novel world of poetic beauty to come. Flavian had caught, indeed, something of the rhyming cadence, the sonorous organ-music of the medieval Latin, and therewithal something of its unction and mysticity of spirit. There was in his work, along with the last splendour of the classical language, a touch, almost prophetic, of that transformed life it was to have in the rhyming middle age, just about to dawn. The impression thus forced upon Marius connected itself with a feeling, the exact inverse of that, known to every one, which seems to say, *You have been just here, just thus, before!* — a feeling, in his case, not reminiscent but prescient of the future, which passed over him afterwards many times, as he came across certain places and people. It was as if he detected there the process of actual change to a wholly undreamed-of and renewed condition of human body and soul: as if he saw the heavy yet decrepit old Roman architecture about him, rebuilding on an intrinsically better pattern. — Could it have been actually on a new musical instrument that Flavian had first heard the novel accents of his verse? And still Marius noticed there, amid all its richness of expression and imagery, that firmness of outline he had always relished so much in the composition of Flavian. Yes! a firmness like that of some master of noble metal-work, manipulating tenacious bronze or gold. Even now that haunting refrain, with its *impromptu* variations, from the throats of those strong young men, came floating through the window.

> Cras amet qui nunquam amavit,
> Quique amavit cras amet!

— repeated Flavian, tremulously, dictating yet one stanza more.

What he was losing, his freehold of a soul and body so fortunately endowed, the mere liberty of life above-ground, "those sunny mornings in the
cornfields by the sea", as he recollected them one day, when the window
was thrown open upon the early freshness — his sense of all this, was from
the first singularly near and distinct, yet rather as of something he was but
debarred the use of for a time than finally bidding farewell to. That was
while he was still with no very grave misgivings as to the issue of his sickness,
and felt the sources of life still springing essentially unadulterate within him.
From time to time, indeed, Marius, labouring eagerly at the poem from his
dictation, was haunted by a feeling of the triviality of such work just then.
The recurrent sense of some obscure danger beyond the mere danger of
death, vaguer than that and by so much the more terrible, like the menace
of some shadowy adversary in the dark with whose mode of attack they had
no acquaintance, disturbed him now and again through those hours of excited attention to his manuscript, and to the purely physical wants of Flavian. Still, during these three days there was much hope and cheerfulness,
and even jesting. Half-consciously Marius tried to prolong one or another
relieving circumstance of the day, the preparations for rest and morning refreshment, for instance; sadly making the most of the little luxury of this or
that, with something of the feigned cheer of the mother who sets her last
morsels before her famished child as for a feast, but really that he "may eat
it and die".

On the afternoon of the seventh day he allowed Marius finally to put
aside the unfinished manuscript. For the enemy, leaving the chest quiet at
length though much exhausted, had made itself felt with full power again
in a painful vomiting, which seemed to shake his body asunder, with great
consequent prostration. From that time the distress increased rapidly
downwards. *Omnia tum vero vitai claustra lababant;* and soon the cold was
mounting with sure pace from the dead feet to the head.

And now Marius began more than to suspect what the issue must be,
and henceforward could but watch with a sort of agonized fascination the
rapid but systematic work of the destroyer, faintly relieving a little the mere
accidents of the sharper forms of suffering. Flavian himself appeared, in
full consciousness at last — in clear-sighted, deliberate estimate of the actual crisis — to be doing battle with his adversary. His mind surveyed,
with great distinctness, the various suggested modes of relief. He must
without fail get better, he would fancy, might he be removed to a certain

place on the hills where as a child he had once recovered from sickness, but found that he could scarcely raise his head from the pillow without giddiness. As if now surely foreseeing the end, he would set himself, with an eager effort, and with that eager and angry look, which is noted as one of the premonitions of death in this disease, to fashion out, without formal dictation, still a few more broken verses of his unfinished work, in hard-set determination, defiant of pain, to arrest this or that little drop at least from the river of sensuous imagery rushing so quickly past him.

But at length *delirium* — symptom that the work of the plague was done, and the last resort of life yielding to the enemy — broke the coherent order of words and thoughts; and Marius, intent on the coming agony, found his best hope in the increasing dimness of the patient's mind. In intervals of clearer consciousness the visible signs of cold, of sorrow and desolation, were very painful. No longer battling with the disease, he seemed as it were to place himself at the disposal of the victorious foe, dying passively, like some dumb creature, in hopeless acquiescence at last. That old, half-pleading petulance, unamiable, yet, as it might seem, only needing conditions of life a little happier than they had actually been, to become refinement of affection, a delicate grace in its demand on the sympathy of others, had changed in those moments of full intelligence to a clinging and tremulous gentleness, as he lay — "on the very threshold of death" — with a sharply contracted hand in the hand of Marius, to his almost surprised joy, winning him now to an absolutely self-forgetful devotion. There was a new sort of pleading in the misty eyes, just because they took such unsteady note of him, which made Marius feel as if *guilty*; anticipating thus a form of self-reproach with which even the tenderest ministrant may be sometimes surprised, when, at death, affectionate labour suddenly ceasing leaves room for the suspicion of some failure of love perhaps, at one or another minute point in it. Marius almost longed to take his share in the suffering, that he might understand so the better how to relieve it.

It seemed that the light of the lamp distressed the patient, and Marius extinguished it. The thunder which had sounded all day among the hills, with a heat not unwelcome to Flavian, had given way at nightfall to steady rain; and in the darkness Marius lay down beside him, faintly shivering now in the sudden cold, to lend him his own warmth, undeterred by the fear of contagion which had kept other people from passing near the house. At length about daybreak he perceived that the last effort had come with a revival of mental clearness, as Marius understood by the contact, light as it was, in recognition of him there. "Is it a comfort," he whispered then, "that I shall often come and weep over you?" — "Not unless I be aware, and hear you weeping!"

The sun shone out on the people going to work for a long hot day, and Marius was standing by the dead, watching, with deliberate purpose to fix in his memory every detail, that he might have this picture in reserve, should any hour of forgetfulness hereafter come to him with the temptation to feel completely happy again. A feeling of outrage, of resentment against nature itself, mingled with an agony of pity, as he noted on the now placid features a certain look of humility, almost abject, like the expression of a smitten child or animal, as of one, fallen at last, after bewildering struggle, wholly under the power of a merciless adversary. From mere tenderness of soul he would not forget one circumstance in all that; as a man might piously stamp on his memory the death-scene of a brother wrongfully condemned to die, against a time that may come.

The fear of the corpse, which surprised him in his effort to watch by it through the darkness, was a hint of his own failing strength, just in time. The first night after the washing of the body, he bore stoutly enough the tax which affection seemed to demand, throwing the incense from time to time on the little altar placed beside the bier. It was the recurrence of the thing — that unchanged outline below the coverlet, amid a silence in which the faintest rustle seemed to speak — that finally overcame his determination. Surely, here, in this alienation, this sense of distance between them, which had come over him before though in minor degree when the mind of Flavian had wandered in his sickness, was another of the pains of death. Yet he was able to make all due preparations, and go through the ceremonies, shortened a little because of the infection, when, on a cloudless evening, the funeral procession went forth; himself, the flames of the pyre having done their work, carrying away the urn of the deceased, in the folds of his toga, to its last resting-place in the cemetery beside the highway, and so turning home to sleep in his own desolate lodging.

> Quis desiderio sit pudor aut modus
> Tam cari capitis? —

What thought of others' thoughts about one could there be with the regret for "so dear a head" fresh at one's heart?

{1885}

ALAN DALE

(pseudonym of Alfred J. Cohen)

{1861–1928}

Alfred J. Cohen, who was born in Birmingham, England, and went to Oxford, served as the music and drama critic for the *New York Evening World* from 1887 to 1895, and subsequently for the *Journal* and the *American*. As "Alan Dale," he was the author of *Familiar Chats with Queens of the Stage* (1890) and *The Great Wet Way* (1910), as well as novels — in addition to *A Marriage Below Zero*, which was brought out by Dillingham in 1889 as a fifty-cent paperback (an uncustomary practice for that publisher), the marvelously titled *An Eerie He and She, His Own Image* (1899), *A Girl Who Wrote* (1902), and *When a Man Commutes* (1918). As "Allen Dale," he was responsible for *Ned Bachman, the New Orleans Detective*.

A Marriage Below Zero attracted the attention of Edward Irenaeus Prime-Stevenson, who wrote of it in *The Intersexes*: "The story, not one of any artistic development, narrates (in the person of a neglected wife) her marriage with an uranian, apparently a passivist, who cannot shake off his sexual bondage to an older and coarser man, an officer. The story ends in the young husband's suicide in Paris, after an homosexual scandal has ostracised him." Other critical responses were frighteningly banal considering the novel's content: the *New York Graphic*, having first identified the author as "that well-known man about town and flaneur, who writes under the name of Alan Dale," went on to describe the book as "extremely moral in its teachings," while the *Cincinnati Enquirer* called *A Marriage Below Zero* "very bright and pleasing . . . the writer has a delightful way of telling his story."

The few contemporary readers of *A Marriage Below Zero* have tended to see it as merely homophobic. Noel I. Garde, writing in the July 1958 issue of *The Mattachine Review* (the magazine of the homophilic Mattachine Society), observed that the novel's unhappy ending established "the accepted standard for homosexual novels in the years to follow." (Forster echoed this sentiment in the "terminal note" to *Maurice*: "Happiness is its keynote — which by the way . . . has made the book more difficult to publish.") More recently Roger Austen, in *Playing the Game: The Homosexual Novel in America* (1977), identified *A Marriage Below Zero* as perhaps the first novel to sketch "homosexuality in the darker colors of evil" and concluded that Dale "certainly wrote a melodramatically anti-gay novel." Such a criticism is misguided, however, because it equates the author's

viewpoint with that of his heroine, whose perspective counts; how often
have the Constance Wildes of the world had the chance to tell their stories? (Apropos Wilde, it is worth noting that the homosexual scandal at
the end of *A Marriage Below Zero* does not echo, but instead anticipates, the
one that brought down the playwright six years later.)

A *Marriage Below Zero* is a cruel book, yet its cruelty is the cruelty of
truth. 🙟

A Marriage Below Zero

"I seek no sympathies, nor need;
The thorns which I have reaped are of the tree
I planted, — they have torn me. — and I bleed:
I should have known what fruit would spring from such a seed."

— BYRON

"Soft love, spontaneous tree, its parted root
Must from two hearts with equal vigour shoot;
While each delighted and delighting gives
The pleasing ecstacy which each receives:
Cherish'd with hope, and fed with joy it grows;
Its cheerful buds their opening bloom disclose,
And round the happy soil diffusive odour flows.
If angry fate that mutual care denies,
The fading plant bewails its due supplies;
Wild with despair, or sick with grief, it dies."

— PRIOR

INTRODUCTION

I suppose I am rather frivolous. I believe in the voice of the majority, to a certain extent; and it has announced my giddiness and superficiality so frequently, that there is nothing left for me to do but succumb to this view as pleasantly as possible. I never listen to the minority in any of the social questions with which I am confronted. It would therefore be inconsistent to pay much attention to its estimate of myself.

Butterfly like I flutter about in society, living in the all sufficient present, reckless of the future, and absolutely declining to recollect the past.

I have a mother who loves me a great deal more than she did some time ago, when I seemed to tacitly insist that she should grow old decently and gracefully. Now I do my best to assist her in her vigorous struggle for perpetual youth, and she is thankful to me; she appreciates my efforts. Ah! it is good to be appreciated, sometimes.

"I really don't know what I should do without you, Elsie," she says, in an occasional outburst of good nature. "You are such a comfort to me; you make me feel as though I were your sister. Sometimes I think I am."

So you see that her affection for me is by no means maternal. I call her "mother" from force of habit, though, accustomed as I am to the word, it often sounds rather ludicrous in my ears.

Conventionality forbids me to use her Christian name. People have always had pronounced prejudices in favor of what they call filial respect, and a quarrel with conventionality is generally fatal, as I have learned. So we trot around to receptions, and kettledrums, and dinners and dances as mother and daughter. I would willingly pass for the former if it were possible to do so, but it is out of the question, unfortunately for dear mamma.

I shall never leave my mother. We shall continue our trot about the social world, until one of us is obliged to give in. I hope I shall be the first to fall, because, like the little boy in the song, I could not play alone. I am convinced that my mother also hopes that she will be the bereaved one. She enjoys life so much, that I cannot blame her.

My demise would necessitate her withdrawal from society for a year or so, but Madame Pauline, in Regent Street, really furnishes such delightful mourning, that, as Mrs. Snooksley Smith said to me the other day: "it is positively a pleasant change to wear it." Mr. Snooksley Smith had been gathered to his fathers a few months previously, so that I know she spoke from experience, poor lonely widow.

I wear a wedding ring. It is concealed beneath a scintillating cluster of diamonds which I have purposely placed on the third finger of my left hand, but it is there. I hate it. It is in the way. If I thought I should ever marry again, I would make it a point of insisting that the lucky man should despise those little golden badges as much as I do.

I must wear mine until I die, I suppose. You see everybody knows that I am Mrs. Ravener; all my friends seem to take an ill-natured delight in emphatically using my married name. I may be as frivolous as I choose, as recklessly flippant as I possibly can, but my wedding ring must remain. It does not upbraid me for my conduct. Not a bit of it. I have a perfect right to do everything in my power to forget it. I would fling my ring to the bottom of the Thames, and still maintain my unquestioned right to do so, but, — ah! there is always one of those detestable little conjunctions in the way.

I hope I am making you wonder what all this means, dear reader, because I intend tearing myself away from mamma for a little and devoting some time to you. You say you would not like to inconvenience mamma? Oh, you need not hesitate. I shall tell her that I need a little rest, and shall interpret her surprised "What nonsense, Elsie!" into a motherly injunction to take it. She is still a little afraid of me, you see. She remembers that, like Mr. Bunthorne, I am very terrible when I am thwarted. Though nothing in my behavior nowadays indicates that I have the faintest suspicion of a will of my own, mamma knows better. Perhaps in the solitude of her chamber she wishes that dear Elsie were the sweet little gushing nonentity she appears to be. In time I may make her forget that I have ever been anything else. Perhaps as she grows old (if she ever does) her memory may be dulled. It is just possible that she may pass away in the fond conviction that her only daughter has never crossed her will. Who shall say that I am not charitable?

I am going to write the story of my married life. I intend to open old wounds by confession which, it is popularly said, is good for the soul. The task may do me good. A little taste of bitter recollection can but enhance the value of the sweet vapidity of my present life. I can pause while I am writing, if I feel at all overwhelmed by the flood of reminiscence, which will pour in upon me by the gates which I voluntarily open, to congratulate myself that it is all over forever.

Like the little girl who used to get out of her nice warm bed, and make her sister call out, "There are mice on the floor," so that she might have the pleasure of rushing back again and huddling up under the clothes in an ecstacy of comfort, I will recall the past, in order that I may enjoy the present all the more.

Perhaps that present palls upon me sometimes, though no one guesses it, and I hardly suspect it myself. Possibly it needs all the contrast with the past that I can give it, to render it endurable. I say "possibly" you know. I wish to be consistently frivolous.

You will be able to remember these remarks when you have read the record of the events which I am about to chronicle, and when you close the book, say with a sigh of relief: "Well, in spite of all, she is living happily ever afterwards."

CHAPTER I

No, I shall not weary you with a long account of my childhood, and all that sort of thing. When I read a story, I always skip the pages devoted to a description of the juvenile days of the hero or heroine. They are generally insufferably uninteresting, or interesting only to the writer, and I can find no excuse for selfishness, with such a weapon as a pen in one's hand.

My mother was left a widow when I was a baby. There is a mournful sound about that piece of intelligence, which is absolutely deceptive. In reality it was a most satisfactory outcome of what I was always told was an extremely unhappy marriage. I heard that my father was a charming man, well read, intellectual, courteous and refined. His death was a happy release for both. Poor papa could not tolerate the shallowness of his spouse's hopes and aspirations; while mamma looked upon her husband as an encumbrance, and an obstacle in the way of her social ambition. A husband is very often unnecessary when you are once in the swim of society. When he has given you the protection of his honorable name, and endowed you liberally with the goods of this world, why, the most delicate thing he can then do, is to cease reminding you of these facts, by taking himself off. At least that is the way a great many people look at the matter, I am told.

I was a year old when papa died. What I was there for, I cannot imagine. There was absolutely no reason for my existence. My mother despised children from the bottom of her heart — or, I might more aptly say, the place where her heart was supposed to be. But I thrived on my bottle. I grew disgracefully fat, and outrageously healthy, and it soon became apparent that there would be no difficulty in rearing me. The only person who could have felt any satisfaction at this was my nurse, who, without me to take care of, would have lost a good situation.

I have promised to say little about my childhood, and I will respect my promise.

I was packed off very young to an extremely aristocratic school, where for years dear mamma left me to myself, pursuing her own sweet course in the labyrinthine mazes of society. She paid my bills regularly, and they were pretty big ones, for nothing that could make me subsequently interesting among mamma's dear friends, was neglected. I was to go into society very young. I think she wanted a little excitement, and imagined that she might get some entertainment from a nice, accomplished daughter. Everybody was aware of the fact that she had one, you see, and also cruelly remembered her real age; so why not use the girl to as much advantage as possible? So, I presume she reasoned.

I was "finished" in the most approved manner. I was taught to play the piano with the most provoking persistence, and made day and night hideous with my frenzied interpretations of things in variations, of pyrotechnical morceaux, and of drawing room "selections."

I sang songs with *roulades* which would have frightened Patti, and effective little *chansons*, with plenty of tra-la-la and tremulo about them. Creatures on whom the education I received would be likely to take effect, ought to be caged up, as dangerous to the community, in my opinion. I spoke villainous French, in order that I might vulgarly interlard my sentences with an occasional Gallic expression. I have done so above. You have Mme. Bobichon, instigated by mamma, to thank for it. A long haired, beery German was going the rounds of the drawing-rooms at this time (I ought to say *salons*, I suppose), and talking the gullible Londoners into the belief that he was a musical prodigy. I was taught German, I presume, in order that I might be able to tell him, in his own language, how much I adored him. I was very accomplished, in a word — desperately so.

I will say this, however: I despised my education. I could see through its superficiality even then.

I enjoyed my school days thoroughly. I liked the society of the merry, laughing, giddy girls I met. Towards the end of my "finishing" period, I went home for a holiday, and the return to school was simply delightful. I dreaded the idea of leaving it for a home which I knew I should detest, and for a mother in whom I had not the faintest interest. At seventeen, however, I was taken into the bosom of my family, and the happiest period of my life came to an abrupt end.

I remained quietly at home for three months before I became that silliest of human beings, a blushing *debutante*. (She doesn't blush long, poor thing.) I had one dear friend whom I regarded as a sister. Letty Bishop had left school two years before I emerged, so that when I was ready to burst upon the social world, she was already a full-fledged society girl.

I shall always remember the ball mamma gave to introduce me to the world. It was a great event for me, an absolute and utter revelation. I rejoiced at the idea of meeting my old school friends, and of resuming the pleasant relations we had enjoyed, without restriction. I was also particularly anxious to become acquainted with members of the male sex, of whom I had heard so much from my friend. I knew none, except John, the butler, who I cannot say impressed me very favorably.

I supposed that men were nice, sensible, jolly beings, immeasurably superior to girls, and with so many more privileges. They could marry whom and when they chose — I thought it, at least — and had unlimited power over creation in general. I hoped in my heart of hearts, that I should soon be chosen, and that some young man would carry me away from mamma to a life which would be more endurable.

As I just said, that ball was an utter revelation to me. I was going to rush at the dear girls I knew, gushingly glad to meet them again after such a long separation, and burningly anxious to take them off to indulge in those nice long talks we had at school.

But when I saw them in my mother's house I hardly recognized them. Could it be possible that these affected, fragile creations, were really the same girls who, only a few months ago, had surreptitiously purchased indigestible cakes, openly read sentimental novels, and enthusiastically sworn eternal friendship the one for the other? Why, they had no eyes for anything female now; all their attentions seemed turned in the direction of the men.

They greeted me with chilling politeness, and turned from me with ill-concealed haste to salute members of the other sex. Of course I had no doubt that they were as eager to meet men as I was. Still, I was not prepared to be treated in this way.

If the behavior of my feminine friends surprised me, I was completely astounded, before the evening was over, at that of the other sex. Why, it was impossible to talk sensibly to these men. They made silly speeches, and showered compliments upon me in a manner that simply caused me consternation and hurt my self respect. I could not imagine what they meant by being so personal. It would have only been after years of familiar intercourse that a girl would have ventured to talk to me as did these men, whom I had never seen before, and with the utmost assurance. It seemed to me that when strangers gave utterance to such ridiculous remarks, they were guilty of nothing less than impertinence.

When they were not unpleasantly self-satisfied, they were absurdly bashful. No girl is ever so contemptuously ill at ease as a bashful man, for whom I have never been able to feel any compassion.

One of our young hereditary legislators asked me to dance, and willing to put him at his ease, for his arms seemed to embarrass him, and his blushes amounted to a positive infirmity, I consented. He seemed to me to be a foolish young peacock, one of those men who Carlyle says attain their maximum of detestability at twenty-five, and ought to be put in a glass case until that period, after which they are supposed to improve. He danced well. I have since learned that most social peacocks do. The poetry of motion seems to accompany lack of brains. When once my lord had disposed of his arm around my waist, he was another being, oh, so much improved!

When the dance was over, he led me into the refreshment room, and brought me an ice. I needed it. I had danced boisterously because I was young enough to enjoy the exercise for itself alone. I could have passed a much pleasanter time, however, had my partner been my one friend and *confidante*, Letty Bishop, than I had done with the gawky arms of young my lord encircling my waist.

"What a delightful waltz," sighed my lord, as he watched me greedily eating my ice. He was no longer embarrassed, my efforts had been successful.

"Yes," I replied, "I love dancing, and I think you waltz nearly as well as even Miss Bishop, that pretty girl sitting over there."

I pointed to a chair where Letty was reclining, surrounded by, I believe I counted seventeen young men. I thought I had paid him a great compliment. I had enjoyed my dance, and felt in a better humor. My lord did not seem at all elated, however. He became silent, and eyed me sentimentally.

"Why don't you have an ice?" I asked, presently, feeling annoyed at his stupidity. "This pineapple is very good — there are real pieces of fruit in it."

"Ah, Miss Bouverie," said he, "I am not in an ice humor."

"Ha, Ha! what a good pun!" I laughed flippantly, wishing he would remove his eyes. "You ought to keep me in countenance, though. I always think people look so gluttonous eating by themselves."

My lord took a chair and an ice at the same time, and sat down beside me. He spoke very little, which I ascribed to the fact that he was enjoying his ice. When he had finished, he asked me if I had any more dances to give him. I looked at my programme. I had none. My lord scowled.

"Miss Bouverie," he said, "you are the only girl here I care about dancing with. All these belles of sixteen seasons weary me," languidly, "and you give me only one meagre waltz."

"I think you are very rude to my guests," I answered, vexed. "They are nearly all young girls, and most of them are nice ones, too. I would as soon dance with you as with anybody, but as this is my mother's party, I believe I am not allowed to choose. I must take everybody who asks me, I suppose. Not that it matters much, however," I added indifferently. "I can't see that a partner makes much difference as long as he dances well. One has no time to talk."

My lord looked surprised. "You are too young," he said, with what I considered unpardonable frankness. Then in a low tone, "Miss Bouverie, I am so glad you are now 'out.' I shan't refuse any more invitations. I've been sending refusals to everybody lately, you know."

Lucky people, I thought. I rose in disgust, and left him. I felt sick at heart. I had been dancing all the evening, and all my partners annoyed me. They appeared to imagine that I was a doll, and condescended to play with me. Was that the way men always treated girls, I asked myself? A long time has elapsed since that evening, but though I have since learned that a man who never says a pretty thing, is an abnormal being who will ultimately sink into obscurity, I wonder that it should be so.

I was completely disappointed. Even Letty Bishop seemed to view me with less interest, while the men were around. She had known me longer than she had known them, and surely I ought to have been considered first.

I felt that I could never like the other sex if it were composed exclusively of creatures like those with whom I had danced, under the most favorable circumstances too, namely, in my mother's house. From what I had seen, I judged that in the social world, women must be the sworn enemies of women, and men the everlasting foes of men. Girls I had heard declare themselves to be eternal friends, never spoke to each other during the evening, and I failed to notice a man address a word to one of his own sex, which would indicate any friendly interest in it.

I wept bitterly as I cast aside my fine feathers that night. My self-respect was wounded. Men had treated me as though I were a silly toy, and I had expected so much from them, and had thought they would be even more companionable than women.

Companionable! Great goodness!

You will probably have arrived at the conclusion by this time, dear readers, that I was a fool. If, however, I possessed no peculiarities, I should not venture to be sitting here. Indeed, I suppose I should be a respectable British matron, with half-a-dozen sturdy children, and — let me see, it is ten o'clock — I might now be ordering a boiled leg of mutton with caper sauce for my little olive-branches' dinner.

CHAPTER 2

Miss Bishop lived in that terribly respectable quarter of London known as Colville Gardens, where the rows of houses look as though they are pining to be allowed a little architectural license, or an escape of some kind from the exhausting restrictions of the prudery in which they have been designed.

Letty was a strange girl, a curious combination of extreme frivolity, shrewd common sense and warm-heartedness. I liked her, because she was the first girl who had ever shown me any kindness. She would listen to my ideas of things with the utmost good temper, point out where she thought I was mistaken, and allow me the luxury of differing from her; which you will admit is a favor usually hard to obtain from friends. Letty Bishop's father was by no means rich. He had been left a widower many years before, and to Letty was assigned the duty of tending his latter years. This she did with a devotion which I admired. I might have emulated her example, but my mother would have shuddered at, and repudiated, the idea of "latter years."

After my miserable failure as a "blushing *debutante*," I was not long in seeking Letty's society. Early the next morning I was in Colville Gardens. I found Letty in the breakfast-room, reading a parliamentary debate in one of the morning papers, so that she could discuss it with her father when he returned from his office. She was attired in the wrapper which women affect nowadays. She threw down her paper when she saw me, and advancing toward me, gave me an effusive kiss on each cheek.

"So glad to see you, dear," she said, "I expected you would be round this morning. Elsie, let me congratulate you on your great success. I'm really proud of you."

I looked what I felt — surprised. That I had been successful, was something I had never contemplated. "I don't know what you mean, Letty," I murmured. "I never spent such a mournfully wretched evening in my life. But," I added, "put on your things and let us go for a nice walk, and I will tell you all about it."

"Now you know, dear," said Letty, sinking into her comfortable chair, "that if there is one thing on the face of this earth which I cordially detest, it is a 'nice walk.' It makes one look so dreadfully healthy, and I abhor dairymaid beauty. No, dear, if you have anything to tell me, say it here, in this cosy room. I'm all ears."

This was not strictly true; Miss Bishop's ears were of the style which our imaginative novelists liken to "dainty pink shells." But I knew what she meant, and was not in a particularly humorous mood, so I took off my things and sat down. "Letty," I said, quietly, "tell me why I was a success."

I felt and looked rather dejected, but she did not appear to notice this. "Why you were a success," she replied energetically, "because you had more partners than you wanted; because you looked lovely in that dear little white silk dress; because all the men noticed you and asked numerous questions about you, and because — well, my dear, I can't give any more reasons; they are obvious. You must know them as well as I do."

I was disappointed. "Tell me, Letty," I asked, "was this a representative party? Was it an average affair?"

"Far above the average, my dear," was Letty's prompt response. "There was at least a man to every two girls, which is unusual, there being generally about seventeen times as many women as men. Then the men were really very nice. Mrs. Bouverie deserves great credit for her selection. The wallflowers were composed of those who deserved to be wallflowers, which is worth noting. The supper was excellent, the floor good, the music admirable, and the arrangements perfect."

Miss Bishop folded her hands after these dogmatic utterances, and half closing her eyes looked at me through her heavy eyelashes. I fidgetted and was uncomfortable.

"If the selection of men were really good," I said thoughtfully and grammatically, "I never want to see a bad selection. Letty, every one of my partners made fun of me. What I have done I don't know, but a man must think very little of a girl to be constantly telling her that her cheeks are like roses, her eyes like stars, her lips — Ah; I sicken when I think of it. Do you mean to say that men talk like that to girls whom they really like and respect?" I was half crying.

Letty rose and kissed me. "You are an innocent little thing," she said, with plaintive condescension, "and my dear," — quite cheerfully — "I am afraid you are going to have plenty of trouble. Why, I assure you, that a man who doesn't say pretty things to girls is looked upon as a man who can't say them — that is, a boor. Men who talk sense — and there are very, very few of them, — are considered egotistical nuisances. Once I had a partner who had traveled considerably, and he would insist upon describing his travels. He used to carry me off to the Red Sea, lead me gently to the desert of Sahara, or row me tenderly over the lakes of Switzerland. He was very wearisome. I hated him. Yes, Elsie, dear," she went on, seeming positively to enjoy my look of disgust, "I would sooner any day hear something about my pretty eyes and my peach-like cheeks, than a graphic description of the Saharan desert, in a ball-room."

My best friend was leaving me alone and a feeling of desolation came over me. "Can't men talk with girls as they would with men?" I asked. "It seems to me that they must take us for very inferior beings. Men surely don't pay each other idiotic compliments, do they?"

Letty grew serious, and a faint blush deepened the "peach-like" color to which she had already referred. "What men say to one another," she remarked, "I am afraid our ears would hardly tolerate. When my brother Ralph was at home — before he went to China — we always used to have the house full of young fellows. I used frequently to come upon them, when they were laughing heartily, and evidently enjoying themselves. I wanted to laugh as well, but they invariably stopped when they saw me, as though I were a wet blanket. Once or twice I asked them to tell me what was amusing them. The youngest of the party blushed, while the oldest adroitly changed the subject. I presume," said Letty, with charming resignation, "that they were afraid of shocking me. I didn't think so then, but I do now. Men like their little jokes, but — I am afraid we shouldn't."

"I wish mamma would let society alone," I pouted sullenly, feeling thoroughly ill-tempered. "I know I shall be forced to flutter about drawing-rooms until one of these men wants my star-like eyes and my satin complexion for his own. I don't look forward to much happiness. I'd sooner be a governess, or a shorthand writer, or — or — anything." I ended in a burst of indignation.

Miss Bishop laughed, and then became thoughtful. "Elsie," she said presently, "have you ever met Arthur Ravener and Captain Jack Dillington?"

"No," I said shortly, "and I'm not particularly anxious to do so."

"Arthur Ravener and Captain Jack Dillington," pursued Letty, disdaining to notice my petulance, "are known in society as Damon and Pythias. They are inseparable. Such a case of friendship I have never seen. I half expected they would be at your mother's party, but I presume they were not invited. I have never met one without the other. They always enter a ball-room together and leave together. Of course they can't dance with each other, but I'm sure they regret that fact. They are together between the dances, conversing with as much zest as though they had not met for a month. Girls don't like them because they talk downright, painful sense. Men seem to despise them. You might appreciate them, however," with a smile.

"I'm sure I should," I said, enthusiastically. "Men who are capable of feeling deep friendship cannot be fools. I should like to know them, Letty. As long as I have to be a society butterfly, I may as well make myself as comfortable as I can under the circumstances."

"You're a strange girl," remarked Letty, with a sigh, "but," reflectively, "I suppose you can't help it. The next opportunity I have I will introduce you to Arthur Ravener. I can promise you he will pay you no compliments. He'll talk books or politics or — anything unseasonable."

"Or Captain Jack Dillington?" I suggested.

"They rarely speak of one another," said Miss Bishop. "Why, I don't know. Some people call them mysteries, because they can't understand them; but — you shall judge for yourself."

"Thank you, Letty," I said, gratefully, and I brought my visit to a close.

Perhaps as I walked home slowly, I may have indulged in a little complacent recognition of my own superiority. I had a soul above social shallowness, I told myself, and it was hardly likely that I should ever be happy in my home surroundings. I know now that it is one of the laws of nature that a budding woman should rejoice in the admiration of the other sex, should court its favor, and should be plunged into dire misery if she find it not. I must have been a peculiar girl, I suppose. Peculiarities do not always bring undiluted happiness to their owners. I paid dearly for mine, and the debt is not yet liquidated.

CHAPTER 3

Four weeks later, after a weary round of festivities (so called), I was sitting discontentedly in Lady Burlington's tawdry drawing-room, wondering why it was that the time passed so slowly. Miss Angelina Fotheringay was singing "*Voi che sapete*," with a hideous Italian accent, and in a gratingly harsh voice. When she began I was anxious to see how she would conduct herself with regard to the high notes in the song, and was prepared to respect her if she would calmly and delicately evade them. Such a proceeding, however, was evidently far from her intentions. She went over them neck and crop, landing in the midst of a heart-rending shriek, but placidly pursuing her course uninjured. My nerves were shocked. I had an ear for music and was therefore clearly out of place.

I wonder why girls will sing Italian and French songs which they cannot pronounce, when there are so many pretty English ballads which are within their scope. French people laugh at our rendering of their songs, and make most unflattering allusions to our efforts. They have a right to make these allusions. You will very rarely, if ever, hear a Frenchwoman attack an English song. She prefers a field in which she knows she will be at home.

"Thanks, so much, dear," I heard Lady Burlington bleat as the songstress concluded amid a volley of applause. I applauded, too, because I was glad the song was at an end.

"I know I am dreadfully importunate," continued my hostess, "but won't you give us one more song? It is such a treat to hear you. Do, dear," pursued Lady Burlington, as Angelina became coy. "There's that pretty little thing you sing so sweetly, let me see — what is it? Ah, I remember 'Angels ever bright and fair.' "

"Angels ever bright and fair," a pretty little thing! Ye gods!

Miss Fotheringay sat down at the piano again, and having hooked a vapid-looking youth to turn over the pages for her, proceeded to request those unhappy angels to take, oh, take her to their care. She concluded with an operatic flourish, and then without being asked favored the company with a little something in variations, of which I shall never know the name.

I felt positively ill, and when Lady Burlington requested me to play, pettishly declined. As I have already said I had a stock of drawing-room pieces which my fashionable professor had selected; but I hated them. I was thoroughly cross, and longed for something or somebody to distract my mind.

No sooner had I expressed this longing to myself than I noticed two young men enter the drawing-room. They attracted my attention at once. The younger was a tall, slightly built man, about twenty-five years of age. His features were so regular, and his complexion so perfect, that if you had shaven off the small golden moustache which adorned his upper lip, and dressed him in my garments, I felt that he would have done them much more credit than I could ever hope to do. He was extremely pretty. His clothes were faultless, his light hair was carefully brushed, and his appearance altogether irreproachable.

I cannot say as much for his companion, who must have been some ten years his senior. This gentleman had a puffy face, with thick red lips, and beady black eyes, something like those of a canary, but not as clear. He had the most unpleasant looking mouth I have ever seen, and as he wore no moustache whatever, it was very visible.

The two new arrivals sat down together during the progress of a song. Then they made their greetings in a quietly dignified manner, and were soon separated in the crowd. I noticed that the younger man looked continually after his friend when the latter went his way. I was still wondering who the two gentlemen were, when I saw Letty Bishop energetically steering her way in my direction, followed closely by the younger.

"Ah, I've been looking for you, Elsie," she said impulsively, regardless of etiquette. "I want to introduce you to Mr. Arthur Ravener. My friend, Miss Bouverie, Mr. Ravener."

Mr. Ravener took the vacant seat beside me, and on closer inspection I found his complexion quite as perfect and his features quite as regular as they had seemed when there was distance between us.

"You do not appear to be enjoying yourself, Miss Bouverie," he said in soft, musical tones.

"I am not indeed," I answered, vexed that he had been able to read my feelings so easily. "I think musical evenings are detestable."

"Query: Is this a musical evening?" Mr. Ravener sank his voice to a whisper, and I laughed outright. The ice was broken.

We entered upon a conversation which was thoroughly delightful, to me at any rate. I found that Arthur Ravener was fond of music, and understood it thoroughly. He asked who were my favorite composers. I told him that I had never been allowed to have any favorites. I had been dosed with Brinley Richards, Sydney Smith and Kuhe, and the effect had been extremely injurious. I liked to hear classical music. It did not weary me in the least; in fact, if I had been properly educated, I might have proved a fairly competent musician.

He was drawing me out, actually. I had not said as much since I left school to any new acquaintance. Here I was talking to a man with as much ease as though he were one of my beloved feminine school-friends. Mr. Ravener listened to me very attentively. He interposed soft "Oh, indeeds," and "Ah's" in a very pleasant manner, and appeared to be interested. He was very serious and extremely deferential. His face showed none of the changes that steal involuntarily over the features of most men when they speak to young girls. He talked to me as unconcernedly as though I were a man. I became as confidential as though he were a woman. I said presently, "if you are so fond of music, how is it you come to evenings like this?"

"May I address the same question to you?" he asked.

"Oh, that's another thing," I replied. "Girls can't do as they like, you know. They have to follow in the paths their fathers and mothers make for them. But I should have thought it would have been different with men."

"It is not, however," said Mr. Ravener, quietly, and I suppose he thought that settled it, as he dropped the subject. I noticed that he seemed to be eagerly searching for some one in the crowd, and at last I saw his eyes rest upon his unprepossessing friend.

"Are you afraid your friend is not enjoying himself?" I asked, rather cheekily I admit.

He reddened slightly. "Captain Dillington always enjoys himself," he said quietly. "He is very happy in society."

I remembered Letty's story of Damon and Pythias, and longed to know something of these two young men, one of whom at least was different from the ordinary drawing-room specimen. Arthur Ravener was certainly attractive, and I felt I was going to be interested in him, so I must be excused if I showed too much curiosity.

"How rarely you find two really sincere friends," I remarked, rather sentimentally. "The present time seems to be wonderfully unsuited to such a tie."

"That is true" — very laconically.

"I think there is nothing so beautiful as friendship," I went on, with persistence.

"You have heard of Damon and Pythias," he said quickly, reading me like a book. I blushed deeply and was then furiously angry with myself. "I don't mind," he went on. "Make all the fun of us you like."

"Mr. Ravener," I protested, "I assure you that when I heard of the friendship existing between you and Captain Dillington, I became interested in you." (A pretty little declaration to make.) "I don't see where any fun comes in. I am tired of the stupid men I meet at such gatherings as these. They have not enough feeling about their composition to allow them to make friends. Far from feeling amused at Damon and Pythias, I am deeply interested in them."

Arthur Ravener looked pleased. I went on gushing like the school-girl I was. "I can think a great deal better of a young man who is capable of being sincerely attached to a companion, than I can of those foolish chatterboxes over there, who are forever telling me I have pretty eyes, pretty hair and a pretty figure, as though I had not been intimately acquainted with myself for the last seventeen years. Don't think I laugh at you, Mr. Ravener, I am very much interested." Then, so ingenuously that it could hardly be considered rude, "I should like to hear all about Captain Dillington, and how you came to know him?"

"There surely can be nothing to tell," he said in strained tones. "What is the friendship between two young men that you should deem it worth discussing?"

"It is worth discussing," I impulsively asserted. "What are we going to talk about? You are not going to tell me about my sylph-like form, or compare my charms with those of my less fortunate friends?"

"No," he replied gravely, "you will find that is not my style when you know me better. I trust we shall know each other better, Miss Bouverie," he remarked quietly.

"Yes." I blushed in my prettiest manner, and cast my eyes down. I was determined to impress Arthur Ravener favorably. I looked extremely well when my long fringed lids could be seen advantageously. Picture my disgust and annoyance when, looking up again, I found I was alone, and just in time to see Arthur Ravener vanishing from the room with Captain Dillington. Even my acquiescence in his wish for our better acquaintance had not been sufficiently interesting to keep him at my side.

He was gone. "Well," I said to myself, "the claims of friendship are great. He is not very polite, but let him go" — which was extremely kind of me, as he had already gone.

Later in the evening I saw the two young men again. Arthur Ravener did not approach me, but bowed in an astonishingly friendly manner, and I, anxious not to seem piqued, returned the nod, accompanied by a smile.

I was subsequently made acquainted with Captain Dillington, for whom, after I had been in his society five minutes, I felt an overwhelming dislike. I cannot say what it was that induced the impression, but Captain Dillington reminded me of a toad, from his beady little eyes, to his sleek, smooth shaven face. He was conspicuously and effusively polite, which I always consider an unpleasant feature in any man's behavior. Though he paid me no compliments, I was uneasy in his society; again I say I do not know why. We discussed various subjects; he in his oily, complacent manner, I in my superficial, gushing way. I was delighted when he left me, but I could not recover my previous serenity.

It was now the hour when departures were expected with resignation; in fact, Lady Burlington was yawning most openly — if I were in a flippant mood, I should consider that a tolerably decent pun — and I could see the poor thing thought she had entertained us sufficiently.

"Good-night, dear Lady Burlington," I said affectionately, with a smile which mamma would have given six years of her life to see; "I have spent a delightful evening."

May I be forgiven that sin, and the thousands of others of a like nature which I have committed, rebelling as I have rebelled against their absurdity. May all who sin in a like manner be forgiven. May only society that knows these words are mostly sins, and that yet accepts them, be unforgiven! That is what I wish.

"How did you like them?" asked Letty Bishop, as I stood in the hall being cloaked, while I silently vowed to myself that I would tell no more lies to my hostesses.

"Who's them?" I inquired ungrammatically and peevishly, for I was tired.

"Arthur Ravener and Captain Dillington."

"I don't know," I answered. "Mr. Ravener was away from me before I could make up my mind whether I liked him or not. I forgive him freely."

"Ah!" said Letty, with such detestable unction that, friend though I was, I could have enjoyed boxing her ears, "he doesn't pay you compliments. I expect the amiability was all on your side."

I made no answer, but with a hasty "good-night," I jumped into the carriage which was awaiting me and was borne homewards.

CHAPTER 4

Arthur Ravener called to "see mamma" a few days later, at least that was the nominal object of his visit, I believe. There is a great deal of humbug about us Londoners. In America young men when they are slightly smitten call upon a girl openly and without beating about the bush; here they ask to see the papas, and the mammas, and the brothers, and the duennas, and everybody but the person they really want.

The idea of any young man deliberately calling to see mamma was so ludicrous, that when I heard of it I laughed. I knew he had come to see me, and I should have thought all the more of him if he had admitted the fact like a man. I was studying hard when I heard him go into the library. I was not puzzling over mathematics, or physics, but was extremely engrossed in a cook-book. I had made a tart, the crust of which was so hideously and irrepressibly solid, that when I had tried to insert a knife in it, the contents of the plate had flown ceilingwards, and cook had looked at me sardonically happy. I hated the woman for that look. I went into the library with a little dab of jam on my cheek, and I was too lazy to worry about it. It was a big room, filled with exquisitely bound books. Dear mamma was very anxious that every volume should be beautifully leather-covered. The contents of the covers were a secondary consideration. It was the correct thing to have a library. It was a good place into which to usher people.

"I thought I would just run in to see if you had recovered from your fatigue of the other night," he said, after we had exchanged salutations.

"Is that why you wished to see mamma?" I asked demurely.

"Of course," he answered. "Mrs. Bouverie might prefer to give me the information herself."

"She couldn't," I declared rather boisterously, "for the simple reason that she never knew that I was fatigued. As a matter of fact I was not. I was bored. The only pleasant part of the evening was furnished by you. There is a compliment for you, before you have been in the house five minutes."

I was very lively indeed, but the arrival of mamma dampened my ardor. She sailed into the room, and seemed extremely pleased to see Mr. Ravener. She liked young men, and always treated them graciously. She did not stay long, however, but begged to be excused. Some girls might have considered this a delicate and motherly piece of consideration. I did not. I had nothing to say to Arthur Ravener or any other young man that might not have been published in the daily papers if the editors had seen fit to inflict it upon their readers. He took one arm chair and I sat opposite. I did not feel at all called upon to talk about the weather and other pleasantly conventional topics. Mr. Ravener had certainly made a most favorable impression upon my maidenly heart.

"You are all over jam, Miss Bouverie," he remarked, as I sat down.

"Don't remind me of my troubles," said I, "I have been cooking very unsuccessfully, and I feel miserable. By the bye, pardon my rudeness in forgetting to ask after the health of Captain Dillington."

There had been a smile on his face as I began my speech. It froze at once — as they say in the novels. A pained blush spread itself slowly over his face. "Captain Dillington," he said deliberately, "is well. Why are you so interested in him?"

"Only because you are," I replied flippantly. "It is the mutual attachment of you two young men that interests me. I think I told you so before, Mr. Ravener."

There was silence for a long time. It was not an eloquent silence. I employed a few leisure moments in removing the jam from my face. He bit his small moustache, as young men often do, more I believe to show that they have one to bite, than because they like it.

"Miss Bouverie," said Arthur Ravener, "you say you were interested in me because you found that I did not pay you silly compliments and talk nonsense. Now don't think me impertinent, if I tell you that I rejoice in the fact that I have met somebody who does not care for such nonsense. Perhaps you will like it better when you are older" — regretfully.

"Never," said I. All the jam was now removed, and though I felt sticky, no one could guess that fact.

"Do you think a young man and woman ought to converse as though they were brother and sister — platonically, I mean?"

"Mr. Ravener," said I, pettishly, "I do not intend to talk metaphysics with you. I have ideas of my own. I like a man, if I have to meet him often, to talk sense."

"Suppose you fell in love?" — tentatively.

"Yes," said I, trying hard to blush a little and failing in a most abject manner. "You are rather impertinent, Mr. Ravener, but no matter. If I ever fell in love, I should see no necessity for discussing it with my 'loved one.' I should not like him any better if he deared and darlinged me. I think I should despise him. I know some people must be demonstrative. Letty Bishop kisses her father about sixteen times in the course of an evening. I suppose she likes it, but it always seems to me very unnecessary. I cannot imagine myself kissing mamma, even if — even if —" I hesitated.

"Even if what?" he asked, unpardonably interested.

"Never mind," sharply. "I was going to reveal family matters to a stranger. You are a stranger, you know. I was going to say — don't think me awful — that I cannot imagine myself kissing mamma even if she did not powder."

He looked rather shocked at my frankness, and I respected him for it. He did not smile, and I went back to my theme. "I could not be demonstrative," I declared. "It seems to me so dreadfully coarse. I flatter myself that I am extremely matter-of-fact."

"I thought so," he said, "and so did —" He stopped in some slight confusion, and reddened in that most provoking manner that people have.

"So did who?" I asked.

"I was merely going to say —"

"Mr. Ravener," I said deliberately. "I want to know who else thought as you did about me."

I suppose he saw I was somewhat determined. "Captain Dillington," he answered in a low tone.

I was thoroughly displeased, and most unreasonably so. Only a few moments previously there was I declaring that the intense friendship of these two young men was something I admired. Now I felt vexed because these boon companions should discuss a girl in whom one of them confessed that he was interested. Men are right when they say one should never expect logic from a woman. I place myself at the head of the unreasonable list.

"You are vexed?" he asked, really troubled.

"Not a bit," promptly. Women cannot reason, but no one can beat them at fibbing. (Fibbing is a polite word for it.)

He seemed relieved. "Do you know, Miss Bouverie," he said as he rose to go, "I can talk to you, as I can to no other girl. That is a positive fact. I don't feel that the instant I leave you, you will run to some feminine bosom and dissect me."

"I shouldn't care enough about you to do that," I said rudely. Could anything have been more impolite? If he could have done anything to increase the good impression he had made upon me, he did it then by simply laughing in a hearty, boyish manner, without an atom of vexation apparent. I had used words of the same purport to partners at some of the hateful parties I had attended, and had been greeted with "Cruel Miss Bouverie"; "Oh, Miss Bouverie, you do not mean it"; "You treat me very badly, Miss Bouverie."

How they annoyed me, those men. I must confess that Arthur Ravener was rapidly becoming more than interesting. Frankness is one of my characteristics.

CHAPTER 5

I firmly believe that if I had told mamma that the Grand Mogul was coming to dinner, and that the Mikado of Japan intended dropping in during the evening in a friendly way, she would simply have remarked, "I am pleased to hear it; we must entertain them." Arthur Ravener's frequent appearance at our house caused not the least surprise, and interested her but slightly. "He is a nice young fellow, Elsie," she said on one occasion. "He is very attentive to you, of course, but there is something about him I don't quite understand. He is cold and undemonstrative, and yet I can tell that he likes you. He seems to have something on his mind."

"Well, that is better than not possessing a mind to have anything on," I retorted in my unpleasantly pert way, "as is the case with the usual nonentities of society."

"Elsie," said my mother, "I dislike to hear a young girl like yourself belittle the people you are accustomed to meet. You may be far superior to them, but — excuse me — I doubt it."

I was snubbed and subsided.

One afternoon as I was walking down Oxford Street, I saw Arthur Ravener and Captain Dillington approaching. Only the latter noticed me at first. He nudged Arthur and, with an indescribably ugly smile on his face, said something to him. I longed to know what it was, woman-like, because I instinctively felt it was not for my ears. Arthur reddened in a most uncomfortable way, and Captain Dillington laughed. I felt annoyed. I resolved that they should stop and speak to me, though I am sure they had no intention of so doing. Accordingly when they raised their hats, by a dainty little feminine manœuvre, I contrived to make them stop. Captain Dillington greeted me boldly. Arthur Ravener seemed tongue-tied.

"Why do you never come to see us, Captain Dillington?" I asked in my airy way, as they turned and walked back with me.

"Would you care to have us both, Miss Bouverie?"

"I don't see why not. There is plenty of room for you."

"I wonder if you will always be as accommodating, Miss Bouverie?" There was something so insolent in his tone, that I became scarlet in the face. I cannot explain what there was offensive in his speech. You who read it will say that I made a mountain out of a molehill. It impressed Arthur Ravener as it impressed me.

"Take care, Dillington," I heard him say in a low voice, as I turned towards a shop window to cool down.

"If you care to come, Captain Dillington," I said haughtily, "we shall be pleased. If you do not care to come —" I shrugged my shoulders; that is very expressive.

The Captain looked alarmed. "I assure you, Miss Bouverie," he said, "you misunderstood me. I should be delighted to call. I am not at all bashful. I feel convinced that we shall meet a great deal" — he made a marked pause — "later."

I cannot describe the look on Arthur Ravener's face. I feel that novelists would call it "the look of the hunted antelope brought to bay." I have no doubt their simile is a good one, though I have never seen an antelope hunted or otherwise.

"Captain Dillington pays very few visits," said Arthur Ravener, lamely. "He sees very little society, indeed."

"Except yours," remarked the Captain.

"Except mine," echoed Arthur, slowly. "But, Captain," appealingly, "I should like you to call one day this week upon Mrs. Bouverie; I think you could manage it if you tried, couldn't you?"

Captain Dillington nodded, and I, not at all anxious to prolong the scene, skipped into a shop with a hasty "good afternoon."

I confess I was puzzled. What Arthur Ravener could see to admire in Captain Dillington it was utterly impossible for me to divine. That the tie which held them together was strong and binding, I could not for a moment doubt. I have always heard that dissimilar spirits form friendships of long duration, but I could not realize that this would hold good in the case of Arthur Ravener and Captain Dillington, one an apparently frank young man who could only just have "begun to live," the other a repulsive being, with no particularly redeeming feature.

I had already seen them often together, and I knew Arthur Ravener was a different man when removed from his friend. It was not true that Captain Dillington saw but little society. He accompanied Arthur on all occasions. In fact, I had never met the one without the other, except at home. Captain Dillington was the chaperon, or at least I looked upon him in that light. However, excuses will never stand analysis.

"What are you doing in here, Elsie?"

I turned round, and beheld Letty Bishop laden with parcels.

"I came in here to look at some —" I began to stammer hopelessly. I never could fib successfully when taken by surprise, which shows that I was an amateur in the art.

Miss Bishop opened the door and looked down the street. Of course she saw the retreating forms of Damon and Pythias, as she called them.

"No, dear," she said calmly, "you came in here to look at nothing at all. You wanted to avoid a certain couple I see fading in the distance. Are you going home, Elsie?"

Yes, I was going home. I admitted the fact. We stepped out into the noise of Oxford Street.

"Elsie," said Letty, suddenly, "I want to talk to you seriously on a subject upon which — pardon me, my dear — I am afraid your mother will have but little to say. You and I have always been great friends, have we not, dear?"

I hate any one to be affecting, especially in the street. I had an awful idea that there was pathos in Miss Bishop's voice, but I made a vow that nothing should induce me to weep and redden my nose, no matter how harrowing she became.

"Yes," I said, "we've been great friends, Letty, and as neither of us intend shuffling off just yet, I vote that we go on being friends, and say nothing about it."

"You can be as flippant as you like," said Miss Bishop severely, "but I am going to talk to you just the same. You remember, Elsie, at the beginning of the season, how miserable you were at all the festivities, and how you dreaded the silly men, as you called them, whom you were obliged to meet. I told you of Damon and Pythias. I introduced you to Arthur Ravener."

"Well?" — impatiently.

"I never imagined that the introduction would lead to anything."

"No?" I was really boiling over with rage, but I tried to conceal that fact.

"No. But it has. People are coupling your name with that of Arthur Ravener. No, don't interrupt me. If I did not care for you, I should say nothing. Look here, Elsie. I am quite certain that you will never be happy, if you do anything rashly. Arthur Ravener is very unpopular. The men won't look at him. I was speaking to my cousin Ned about him the other day, since I have noticed how you encouraged him."

"I —"

"— and Ned told me to warn any friend of mine against him. Why? I asked. He would give me no reason, but, my dear, Ned is a conservative old fellow, and you so rarely hear him say a bad word against anybody, that if he does make an attack it carries weight with it. Personally, I like Ravener; but, my dear, I cannot help listening to what people say. Why I heard the remark the other day that the only reason Ravener and Dillington went into society at all, was to borrow its cloak of respectability."

"Perhaps you think they are highway robbers in disguise, or forgers, or playful assassins?"

"I think nothing, my dear. I only tell you what people say. I do that merely because it was I who introduced you. I had no more idea that you and Arthur Ravener would ever care for one another —"

"Did I say I cared for Arthur Ravener?"

"No, but you do, and my prophetic soul tells me that you will throw yourself away upon him."

"Don't listen to what people say, my child," I remarked loftily, "and you will be a great deal happier. Since you have been talking I have come to the conclusion that I like Arthur Ravener immensely. When I marry it will not be for the sake of my lovely society friends — but for my own. You have done your duty, my dear. You have warned me against a young man of whom you know positively nothing. Thanks. If I can return the compliment at any time, command me."

Then, thinking I could not improve upon this cutting rejoinder, I tripped away.

CHAPTER 6

No one who has followed me thus far can accuse me of having tried to make myself attractive to my readers. My later experiences have taught me that girls who despise what are generally acknowledged to be the pleasures of girlhood, will get but little sympathy in this world. Perhaps that is as it should be. I must have been eccentric.

I remember that I once heard a young man who had been dancing with a corsetless maiden, a believer in the laws of health, declare that such girls ought not to be allowed in a ball-room. To be accepted by society, you must follow the laws it prescribes. The right to be eccentric must be earned — and it takes time to earn it. What right had a chit like myself to declare that I found the young men whom I was called upon to meet, undesirable and uninteresting? Who put such ideas into my head? I cannot lay the blame upon anybody. The ideas were there. Topsy-like, I suspect "they growed."

The subject I now have to deal with is my engagement. I had grown to like Arthur Ravener very much. I thought we had a great deal in common. I never felt that a woman was a silly chattering doll when I was with him. He would talk upon any subject with me, and never once in all our intercourse did he pay me a single compliment. He never showed that he admired me. All he ever said was that he liked talking to a sensible girl who looked upon the world very much as he did himself.

One evening as I was sitting alone at a detestable "musicale and dance," and wondering as usual why girls wasted their best years in training themselves to shine at such entertainments, I noticed Arthur Ravener and Captain Dillington enter the room. The former looked anxiously around — for me, of course, I knew that; the latter remained standing at the door, where he could see all that was going on. The reception accorded Damon and Pythias was always polite, but never cordial. The men seemed to avoid Captain Dillington, and he usually tacked himself to the skirts of some plump old matron, who talked of nothing more exciting than servants and other domestic relaxations. I imagine that Arthur Ravener must have pursued a similar course before he met me — but then my imagination always did go a long way.

"How do you do, Miss Bouverie?" Arthur Ravener in evening dress was extremely comely, but I could have found it in my heart to wish that he were not so pretty.

"I am so glad you have come, Mr. Ravener, to raise me from the Slough of Despond. I was going gradually down — down — down."

He smiled. I wondered if the little curl in his moustache were natural, or, if not, how he managed to bring it to such perfection. He did not seem to be in a talkative humor, so I felt called upon to make a little conversation. I looked around the room. Of course I knew I could say it was very warm. That is always a safe remark of an evening. It would also not have been out of the way to suggest that there were a great many present.

Ah, there was a good subject for conversation in the young couple oppo-site, a bride and bridegroom, a couple three months old — matrimonially old, I mean. They were evidently very much enamored and they sickened me. It was very rude of me to take them all in; but they had no idea I was staring at them, so it was all right. I saw him take up her dance programme, and scan the names with a frown, she all the time glancing at him with pride and admiration. Then he whispered something in her ear, taking care to brush it with his moustache, and she put one dainty gloved finger on his lip. He sat down beside her and for five minutes they talked so earnestly that I am quite convinced they forgot the fact that they were "in society." I am ashamed to say I listened to them. It was not an edifying conversation. He declared that an evening spent away from her was a terrible ordeal. She asserted that it was a good thing to dance with other men, as the contrast between them and her own dear husband showed her how immeasurably superior he was.

And all this time I forgot I was to amuse my companion. I looked at him. He was listening to the bride and bridegroom also. Shame upon us both.

"Does that interest you?" he asked.

"It disgusts me," I answered emphatically.

"Ah!" — I fancied he had awaited my answer a little anxiously. He looked satisfied.

"I do not believe in such demonstrative devotion," I went on. "There is nothing beautiful in it to me."

"No," he said. "It will never last. In two years it will take a very great effort on her part to keep him at her side. She will by that time probably think the effort not worth making."

I was silent. Perhaps at that moment something told me that my ideas were morbid. It is possible that quick as a flash of lightning my woman-hood asserted itself. I say it is possible, and that is all.

"Elsie."

It was the first time he had uttered my Christian name. There was noth-ing at all tender in the way he pronounced it. I blushed slightly and looked a little conscious. Of course I could make no answer. I sat silent and eyed my gloves (which were rather soiled, by the bye, and not worth eyeing).

"Elsie," he said, "you criticise the conversation of that young couple opposite. But put yourself in her place. Would you prefer your husband to sit calmly by your side, and talk, — perhaps as you and I have talked so often, — quietly, undemonstratively, and sensibly. Would you be satisfied to marry a man who absolutely declined to be the conventional lover, writing ballads to your eyebrows, and extolling your virtues, real and imaginary, while the love fever lasted?"

His face was very pale, and his hands nervously clutched the side of my chair, as he leaned slightly towards me.

"Yes, I would be satisfied," I said.

At that moment I felt acutely happy. Of course I knew to what he was coming. I always laugh when I read novels in which the heroines "look up with large surprised eyes," or "innocently wonder" what a proposing lover means. A girl always knows when a man is asking her to marry him. If he expressed himself in Chinese or Hindostanee she would understand him just as well.

I felt I could be happy with Arthur Ravener. He was entirely different to any other man I had met, and the difference seemed to me, then, to be in his favor.

"Elsie," he said, in very agitated tones, "you have remarked very often that you despised these demonstrative beings. When we first met, you told me frequently that I was different — that you found pleasure in my company. I have seen your face brighten when I approached, and, Elsie, I am emboldened by these signs of your esteem, to ask you to be my wife."

I put my hand quietly in his. You, readers, who have perhaps disapproved of my flippancy, will be astonished to hear that for the moment it left me completely. I was deeply moved by Arthur Ravener's proposal. I was delighted. I really believe I felt as an engaged girl ought to feel, — full of admiration for the man who had honored her, and keenly alive to the fact that this world was after all a good place in which to be.

I looked at Arthur. His face was livid. Its startling pallor gave me a shock. I forgot everything for the moment in my anxiety for his present welfare.

"You are ill?" I said.

He looked at me in surprise.

"No," he replied in a low tone. "I am well. Should I not be well" — with a great effort and a strained smile — "when you have just accepted my — my suit?"

Have you ever experienced the unpleasant sensation of knowing that somebody was staring at you, and been impelled to look in their direction? Of course you have. So you will not be surprised if I tell you that I turned from Arthur Ravener and glanced toward the door. Captain Dillington had been staring at me. He looked confused, I am glad to say, when I returned his stare with interest. In fact he turned immediately away, and began an animated conversation with one of his favorite plump matrons.

"Arthur," I said, impulsively, "I know you and Captain Dillington are such great friends that I want to ask you if he likes me?"

There was no coquetry veiled in this question. I sincerely wished to know how I stood (to use a commercial expression) with the bosom friend of my affianced husband.

Arthur Ravener positively started at my question. For a few seconds he seemed unable to answer.

"I — I am sure he does," he stammered at last. "Yes, Elsie, Captain Dillington does like you. I — I am sure of it. Set your mind at rest."

"Pooh!" said I, inelegantly, feeling that Richard was himself again. "My mind is quite at rest. I'm not going to marry you both, you know" — a remark that was neither pretty nor funny, but vulgar. My carriage had been announced and Arthur was fastening my "*sortie de bal*" around me. In the hall stood Captain Dillington. He bowed and then extended his hand to me.

"May I congratulate you, Miss Bouverie?" he asked.

"You may," I answered blushingly. Then it occurred to me that it was rather strange Captain Dillington should know anything about my engagement. Arthur had not left my side since I had accepted him as my future husband. Then I reflected that Arthur and the Captain were great friends; that the Captain probably knew that Arthur intended asking me to be his wife; that he had seen us in earnest conversation, noticed my "happy expression," and put two and two together — an arithmetical process practiced by many. Still, I was not quite satisfied, although I decided that it would be better to appear so.

"I trust we shall see a great deal of each other" — after a pause — "later."

He had made this identical speech the other day, I remembered.

"I hope so," said I. I would try and like him for Arthur's sake, though I was perfectly convinced I should not succeed. The hall door was open. Arthur came down the steps with me. He was still pale.

"Good-night, Arthur," I said, extending my hand.

"Good-night."

His fingers scarcely closed around mine. I had shaken hands with him a dozen times during our acquaintance, and had always told him he ought to take lessons in the art. But his salutation had never been so coldly inexpressive as to-night it seemed to me. I shivered slightly, then drew myself into the obscurity of the carriage and rolled home.

CHAPTER 7

Arthur was very anxious that our engagement should be a short one. My mother would have been perfectly satisfied to have escorted me to the altar on the day following our betrothal, if fashion had established any precedent for such a course. But no, she could not remember any respectable folks marrying after an engagement of less than three months.

"People might talk," she said, and I knew that settled it. There was no more awful possibility. An earthquake would have been pleasant, and a conflagration merely an episode in comparison.

"I don't see why Arthur is in such a hurry," she went on. "Really, you have given him no cause for jealousy; your conduct is always irreproachable. In fact if I were a man I should run a mile to avoid you. I have often thought that your manners must be far from attractive to the other sex."

"Thanks, mother."

"I am sure I am very pleased that it is all going to end so happily, but I cannot consent to your marriage in less than three months. No such case can I remember, except, of course, that of Lady Stitzleton's daughter, which is too shocking for me to discuss with you. Tell Arthur he must wait for three months. I can't for the life of me understand his hurry. You will excuse me for saying it, Elsie, but I confess he does not seem to be particularly —"

"Tender, do you mean, mother?"

"*Épris* is an excellent word to use in this case," said my parent. "If you cannot understand it, however, you can substitute tender. Of course I know that it is very bad form to make any demonstrations in society, but when alone, a little effusiveness is entirely pardonable. You and Arthur were in the library together for a few minutes the other night — perfectly proper of course. As I happened to pass the room, I looked in, prompted of course by my motherly interest. You were at one end of the room, he at the other, and I —"

"Never mind," I said hastily, reddening with vexation. "It shall be as you say — three months."

I stalked from the room thoroughly annoyed. I did not dare to ask myself the cause of my ill temper. Demonstrations of affection I had frequently declared disgusted me, and I had engaged myself to a man who confessed that he thought as I did. I had no reason to complain of Arthur. His behavior toward me had not changed in the slightest since our engagement. He had not attempted to avail himself of the privileges which books on etiquette (I had glanced through them) accord to engaged couples. He had never kissed me, nor hinted at the slightest inclination to do so.

I loved Arthur Ravener, I was proud of the prospect of becoming his wife; but — lest my future history be considered inconsistent with that which I have already related — I will frankly admit, at the risk of being called a contemptible humbug, that I should not have objected in the least if Arthur had been just a trifle less glacial. I admit that now; I made no such admission at the time. I only felt a little discontented, and mentally changed the subject when there was any probability of my discovering the reason of my dissatisfaction.

The news of our engagement soon spread. Shall I be considered egotistical if I say that the men who had previously — so it seemed to me — looked down upon Arthur Ravener, now appeared anxious to know him, and apologetically anxious, too? They had evidently more respect for Elsie Bouverie's affianced husband, than for Captain Dillington's bosom friend. It was rather inexplicable to me, but I was pleased nevertheless.

Arthur was a constant visitor at our house. He never brought Captain Dillington with him. Indeed he always seemed to be so embarrassed when I asked him to do so, that I at last desisted. It was no desire to know the Captain better that prompted me to invite him to join us. He repelled me as no one either before or since has done. But I knew he was my future husband's boon companion, so was perfectly willing to sink my prejudices. I also thought as there was nobody but a blind old bat of a housekeeper in the flat which they had furnished, and in which they lived, that Captain Dillington must feel rather lonely when Arthur was away. Arthur was a very thoughtful young man. He never stayed very late at our house. Although he did not say so, I was convinced that he did not care to leave his friend alone too long. Such consideration for another pleased me. Had I not every right to reason, by analogy, that when I was his wife, he would show me the same devotion?

I thoroughly dreaded the day when I had to tell Letty Bishop of my engagement. I felt that she would be a wet blanket of the most distressing type, and — somehow or other — I wanted to steer as clear of wet blankets as possible. I was agreeably surprised to find that Letty gave my "news" very little attention, for the simple reason that she had similar information to impart. Yes, Letty was engaged. I had known her betrothed for some time, and had included him in the ranks of the men I despised. He was a butterfly. He admired every girl he met, or seemed to do so. However, if Letty was satisfied with him, why, so was I. I was glad to listen to all she had to say about him, as by doing so, I gave her no opportunity to make unpleasant remarks concerning Arthur Ravener. She hoped I would be happy, and laughingly begged me not to hold her responsible for the match. She talked a great deal of nonsense about her Reginald, and I could not get interested. They were evidently a conventionally gushing couple.

"Arthur," said I, that night, adopting my favorite would-be jaunty air, "what will become of Captain Dillington while we are on our honeymoon; there are such a number of places I want to visit, and I'm not going to be hurried." Arthur reddened painfully, and then averted his face. "I was thinking, Elsie," he said with a sickly smile, "that we would abolish that old-fashioned notion of honeymooning, and go immediately after the wedding to your house in Kew."

My mother had presented me with a delightful little villa near Kew Gardens, and it was settled that we were to live there during the first year of our wedded life at any rate. But I could not believe that we were to domesticate ourselves on our wedding day.

"You are joking, Arthur," I said weakly.

"I don't see why," shuffling uneasily on his chair. "I think traveling is an abomination, and, really, you know, honeymoons are not fashionable. Are you — are you" (very anxiously) "very desirous of going out of town?"

"I don't care particularly," I said with magnanimity. "I took it for granted that we should make a trip. I would have preferred it; but, of course, if you would sooner not —"

"What is that, Elsie?"

Enter my maternal parent at an inopportune moment, as usual. She saw we were engaged in discussion and I felt she was anxious to assist us.

"Arthur does not want to take a wedding trip, mother," I said, "and I was telling him that I had been reckoning upon one."

"It is out of fashion, Mrs. Bouverie," remarked Mr. Ravener, looking with appealing eyes at the arbitrator. "I am sure you will agree with me that it is. No one is better acquainted with the usages of society than you are" (deferentially).

Oh, the hypocrite! I knew she would succumb to that, and so did he. If it had not been for that disgustingly polite speech, I felt that she would have decided in favor of the trip, as she had already confided to my care a list of commissions which I was to execute for her in Paris.

"You are right, Arthur," she said, promptly. "Honeymoons are becoming obsolete in the best society. There is something extremely *bourgeois* about them to my mind." There was not the faintest remembrance of the commissions in her tone. Her foible had been touched. Arthur was triumphant, but he looked rather doubtfully at me. He evidently did not want me to think that he was positively averse to a honeymoon.

"Where do you propose going after the wedding?" asked mamma.

"To Tavistock Villa, Kew," was his rejoinder.

"Of course you will not receive for several months?"

"Oh, no — no —," impatiently, "we shall remain in retirement, and see none but — but the immediate family, and — and intimate friends."

Well, I must let Arthur settle such matters, I thought. After all, perhaps he was right. Honeymoons must have distinctly unpleasant features. Traveling was a nuisance, and with the best of intentions, and the largest purse, it was impossible to obtain home comforts at continental hotels, I had heard. When I told Letty Bishop that we had decided to abolish the honeymoon, she opened her eyes in surprise. Was such a thing possible? Surely Arthur Ravener was even more eccentric than she had originally supposed, and she had given him credit for a considerable portion of eccentricity. What! Settle down to common-place matrimony, and receive the butcher, the baker and the greengrocer in the first week of married life! What could he mean?

"Don't be absurd, Letty" I said fretfully, in reply to this outburst. "It was my idea and not his." (There was a whopper, but I felt I must do something desperate.) "I dislike traveling, and I am convinced that we should quarrel before we reached Paris. And then, my dear," faintly "I should not care for my husband to see me — seasick." (That was an inspiration.)

"Well, Elsie, I suppose you know best what you like. It looks queer, though. Honeymoons may not be fashionable in the very, very highest society; but, my dear, you don't belong to the very, very highest society."

"Don't dare to say that to my mother," I cried, "or she would kill you in her frenzied indignation."

I tried to believe that I was satisfied, but I was not. With all my superiority, I was disappointed.

CHAPTER 8

My marriage was not a particularly interesting event from an anecdotal standpoint. My mother was far too precisely conventional to allow anything to interfere in the slightest with the rule laid down by that terrible tyrant in petticoats, Mrs. Grundy.

I was rather surprised that Arthur cared for the amount of publicity which I saw would attend the event, but he positively gloried in it. He seemed anxious to have his marriage recorded in the four corners of the globe. The feminine newspaper correspondents, who called to ask for the particulars of Miss Bouverie's bridal dress, Miss Bouverie's trousseau, and Miss Bouverie herself, I had strict injunctions from my betrothed to satisfy as far as possible.

My wedding morning was one in which novelists delight — plenty of sun, and a delightfully invigorating atmosphere. I was as happy as a bird. The prospect of freedom from the hateful society chains, which I felt would in a few years deprive me of my much prized liberty, added to the love which I felt for Arthur Ravener, were the causes of my bliss.

I was a dainty little bride in my white robes, but I still had the horrible feeling that I was not nearly as pretty as Arthur. The flush on his cheek, his full red lips, long eyelashes, and splendid complexion far surpassed my efforts in those directions. He was more noticed in the church than I was — by which you will perceive that my excitement did not prevent my powers of observation from having full play. Perhaps it was his beauty after all that gained for him the contempt of men. The sterner sex have their weaknesses, and we do not monopolize, — as they are so fond of asserting, — all the petty envy and spite in this world.

I saw all my old friends in the church. My "belongings" certainly out-numbered Arthur's. Two hideous old maiden aunts, one dilapidated uncle, and three lachrymose cousins constituted his force of relatives. I feel it is awful of me to allude in such terms to people who could now claim relationship with myself, but I do not intend to conceal anything from my readers.

A drowsy old minister, so well known that I suppose he thought that any exertion on his part was unnecessary, made us man and wife, and kept his gaze rivetted all the time on the bridesmaids, who imagined they were not paying proper attention on that account, and seemed at a loss to know what to do to get rid of his eyes.

How I should have enjoyed the wedding if it had been somebody else's. Letty and I, in a corner of the church, could have picked everybody to pieces and amused ourselves generally. I can even imagine what I should have said about myself, and I know I should have sworn that Arthur was rouged. My bridesmaids I should have revelled in criticising, because I thoroughly disliked every one of them. My mother had selected them, and I had nothing to do in the matter but submit.

Arthur seemed to be in a dream, from which he only awoke when the reverend gentleman put those extremely leading questions to him. His voice was hoarse as he answered. His hand trembled as he placed the wedding ring on my finger. His fingers were icily cold. Only once did he look at me. I fancied then that there was just a faint tinge of compassion in the glance. I met it with a proud smile. Ah! he little knew what a lucky girl I thought myself.

After the ceremony came a reception and breakfast, at which everybody I had ever seen seemed to be present. In the evening there was to be a ball, at which, of course, we were not to be present. I was glad for once to follow fashion's dictates. Early in the afternoon Arthur and I said good-bye to a few hundred people, and stepping into the carriage which was waiting for us, set out for Tavistock Villa.

As we rolled away from the metropolis towards our country home, I tried hard to direct my thoughts into those channels through which I felt they ought to flow. Here was I, a bride of a few hours, leaving home without a regret and without a reflection of "childhood's associations," the new life, and other pathetic subjects over which nineteenth century brides are popularly supposed to become sentimental. I must put it all down to the flippancy of my nature.

Arthur made no attempt to break the silence. If I was an unusual bride, certainly he was the most utterly unconventional bridegroom it was possible to imagine. His eyes were fixed dreamily upon two little fleecy clouds which were floating about artlessly above us. He could not have looked more hopelessly subdued if he had been sitting in a funeral coach, and going to bury a friend. I suppose my glance aroused him.

"Are you enjoying this ride, Elsie?" he asked, kindly.

"Yes," I answered, noting his effort to amuse me, and feeling grateful to him for it. "I suppose," I said, laughing, "that all these people would be staring at us if they knew we were bride and bridegroom. They take us for brother and sister, undoubtedly."

"Or an old married couple," he added, smiling.

"I wonder if we ever shall be old commonplace people," I went on happily. "Imagine us fifty years from now, Arthur — you a nice reminiscent old man with white hair (you see I decline to think of you as cross and crotchety), sitting on one side of the fire, and I, a talkative old body, having outlived every weakness but that furnished by the tongue, which no woman could outlive if she were a female Methuselah."

Arthur laughed, and seemed for the first time since I had known him to be perfectly at his ease. I put my hand ("my little gloved hand," as my friends the novelists would say) on his arm. He might have squeezed it if he had chosen. I am quite sure I should not have objected, except perhaps by a little maidenly coyness, which does not amount to very much. Arthur, however, took no notice whatever of my innocent little hand. Indeed, by a movement he made as if to look out of the carriage window, he contrived to shake it off. This I did not notice at the time, but as I have since become accustomed to think and brood over every little incident of those days, I have remembered it.

After that we talked merrily for the remainder of the ride. I was determined that I would start my married life with mirth. Men hate miserable, doleful women. Nine out of ten of them would sooner have an ugly wife who laughed than a pretty one who cried. Now I resolved that Arthur Ravener should have a wife who was both pretty and jolly. So I was as lively as I could be.

Tavistock Villa came into sight all too soon. It was a pretty red brick house, which I shall not attempt to describe. I am an utter failure from an architectural standpoint, and only know two things in that line: that some houses are Gothic and some are not. The house had been the gift of my mother, and it had been furnished by my husband. We went in.

I was loud in my admiration of his taste as soon as we had passed the front door. Every article of furniture seemed to have been selected with excellent judgment. I will not weary my readers with a description of tables and chairs and carpets, which have nothing to do with my story.

"Here are your rooms, Elsie," said Arthur, opening the door of an exquisite little boudoir, "and you can be as completely alone here as though you were Robinson Crusoe on the desert island."

"I shall not want to be alone very often, dear," I said, gushingly.

"I have a couple of rooms on the other side of the house fitted up for myself, to smoke and write in," he went on, rather hesitatingly, paying no attention to my pretty little speech. "You see I do a little literary work, and I — I — do not want to be disturbed."

"You shall not be disturbed, Arthur," I said, dutifully. "Let me go and inspect your rooms, please."

He looked annoyed. "They are in great disorder, Elsie," he said, "and I don't think you had better venture into them."

"I feel a wifely interest in them, dear," I pleaded with a smile.

"Not now," he said hastily.

"I believe you're a Bluebeard, Arthur, and that the bodies of a dozen preceding Mrs. Ravener's lie festering in that room. I shall wait until you go out, like the last and surviving Mrs. Bluebeard did, and then make a voyage of exploration."

"You will not be repaid for your trouble," he said, smiling. But he was vexed. I could see it.

"I don't see why your rooms are at one side of the house and mine at the other, Arthur," I said. "It's very unsociable, I am sure."

"Nonsense," was my husband's testy response. "Every man ought to have a den of his own, in which he can smoke, or read, or write."

"I know it," was my prompt rejoinder, "but, though it is an odious thing to say, I could have permitted you to smoke in my boudoir."

"You are not your mother's daughter," he said, laughing rather uneasily.

Arthur then introduced me to a young French girl, whom he had engaged as my maid. Marie was certainly a pretty woman, not a bit Gallic to
look at. She had honest gray eyes, an excellent complexion, and brown
hair. I liked her appearance and thanked Arthur for his thoughtfulness.
Since I had entered Tavistock Villa I had seen nothing but evidences of his
earnest desire to make my life there pleasant. When we had finished in-
specting our new home, or rather, when I had come to the end of my gushing superlatives, and his services as guide were no longer required, we decided to take a stroll through the pretty Kew roads, and return in time for
dinner. He led the way and I followed. Down the dusty, charming little
lanes we went, talking all the time, and laughing frequently. I had never
known Arthur so entertaining as he was that afternoon. He told me stories
of his school days, of his dead father and mother, of his musical studies,
and of all his old friends. I was not obliged to catechize him. He talked
freely and seemed to enjoy it.

That was a delightful afternoon. I shall always remember it. I can see
the delicious little town as I saw it before it became hateful to me. I can
recollect my first impressions of the sunny thoroughfares, the lovely gardens, and the comfortable, unpretentious houses.

It was dark when we turned back. I was rather tired. The day had
been somewhat fatiguing. It is rather an unusual event in one's life to be
married. Arthur might have offered me his arm, I thought. But he made
no attempt to do so, as I walked by his side. We found dinner awaiting us.
It was a very elaborate meal, with I don't know how many courses. I
seemed to have come to the end of my good spirits. I did not feel inclined
to talk, and as Arthur appeared to be wrapped in his own thoughts (not
agreeable ones, either, if I can judge from his face) silence prevailed. It
seemed strange to be sitting there at dinner with him. I felt rather sorry
that he had objected to the honeymoon; I really began to wonder, now
that I had seen Kew, how we could possibly amuse ourselves there for any
length of time. I wondered more for his sake than for my own, as I know
that to men variety is always charming.

"Elsie," said Arthur, breaking the silence at last, "do you think, dear,
that you could get along without me this evening. You have Marie — and
— and I must run up to town?"

My husband was very intently regarding the walnuts on his plate as he
asked this question — very intently indeed.

"Of course, Arthur," I replied, quickly, "if you must leave me, go by
all means. I would not like to interfere with any of your business arrangements, or —"

"You are a good little woman," he said, but he did not look into my face and thank me for what I really considered a sacrifice. I thought it was rather strange that he should be obliged to go up to London so soon. Surely he could have transacted any business he might have had before we started, though as Arthur was "a gentleman" (in the language of the directory) I was at a loss to imagine what business could call him away, and surely the poorest commercial drudge took a holiday and devoted the first week at least of his married life, exclusively to his wife. However, there might be a hundred reasons for his departure, and I had no doubt that when I had earned the right to know what they were, he would permit me to do so.

"I may be rather late, Elsie," he said hastily, "but do not worry." He left the room a few moments later, and returned overcoated and ready to start.

"Amuse yourself, Elsie," he said. "Do anything you like, and try not to be homesick. Good-bye, dear."

He was leaving without kissing me. Though I had protested so often that I would not tolerate a demonstrative husband, Arthur's conduct seemed so strange, that a feeling of resentment came over me. I did not look up.

"Good-bye, Elsie," repeated my husband, uneasily approaching me. "What is the matter?"

"Nothing."

"Well, good-bye."

"Good-bye."

He started for the door, and the next instant I was after him. "Arthur," I cried impulsively, "you shall not go from me in that way, even if you intend being away only half-an-hour. Kiss me."

He bent forward and touched my lips with his, so coldly and undemonstratively, that I shrank back, and looked at him in surprise. I felt chilled. "Come back early," I said, returning to the room hastily, anxious to be away from him. I decided that I would go to my boudoir, so calling Marie to keep me company, we went upstairs to that cosy little apartment.

I had a long evening before me and the prospect was not a lively one. I could not feel at home in Tavistock Villa, which a few hours ago I had never even seen. It seemed to me that Arthur ought to have stayed with me, no matter what sacrifice he made. I knew very little about brides and bridegrooms beyond what I had read in novels, nine-tenths of which either ended with a couples' engagement, or began, in early married life.

I went to the drawing-room and tried the piano, but somehow I could derive no amusement from it. I glanced at a couple of books, but their unreality disgusted me. The heroine in one of them was sentimental to idiocy, with a flower-like face and violet eyes, while the principal character in the other was a hoyden with whom I could find no sympathy. I went back to my boudoir. It was delightfully comfortable. I installed myself in an easy-chair, made Marie sit opposite, poor girl, and then closed my eyes.

"Is it that Madame is recently married?" asked Marie presently, more, I felt convinced, to break a silence that was becoming oppressive than from any real interest in me or my belongings.

"Did you not know that we were married this morning, Marie?" I demanded rather sharply.

"*Comment!*" She was interested now to such an extent that the exclamation she uttered was in her own language. "You were married this morning — to-day?" — with incredulity.

"Certainly," said I. "When my husband engaged you did he not tell you that he was about to be married?"

"No, Madame," replied Marie. "When I called regarding the advertisement he told me I was to be maid to his wife. In consequence I thought you were long married. But, Madame, pardon me, if you were married to-day, why is it that Monsieur leaves you so soon alone?"

"Why not?" I was furious with her and would have given a sovereign for the privilege of administering a sharp slap. I could not answer her question. I knew of no answer. It was evident, however, from her unfeigned surprise that Arthur had done a very unusual thing when he left me alone on my wedding-day. My instinct told me that he was entirely in the wrong. Marie, however, had confirmed this hardly admitted view. She sat with her mouth slightly open, staring at me in such unpleasant surprise that I was forced to turn my face away.

"You are very rude, Marie," I said at last, desperately angry at the girl's stupidly apparent astonishment. "Don't you know that it is the height of impoliteness to stare at anybody like that? I am surprised at you, a Frenchwoman, behaving in such a manner."

It did me good to manifest a little surprise on my own account. I saw no reason why she should be permitted to monopolize it all.

"Madame will excuse me," said the girl quickly. "I am not yet entirely used to English customs. It seemed so droll to me that a bridegroom should leave his bride — Madame will pardon me."

I rose and paced up and down the room. What a fool I was to worry myself about such trifles. Arthur had shown nothing but the most delicate consideration for me up to the present, and yet because he asked my permission to absent himself for a few hours on our wedding-day, I worked myself up into a state of nervous excitement on the ground that the proceeding happened to be a little unusual. Pshaw! what nonsense. Had we not a whole lifetime to spend together? How could I be so ridiculous? "Ha! Ha! Ha!" I burst out laughing. Poor Marie must have experienced another surprise concerning English customs. She looked up, her gray eyes round as saucers.

"Is Madame ill?"

"Fiddlesticks!" I exclaimed, with unpardonable inelegance. "Let us come into the drawing-room, and I will teach you how we waltz over here."

Alas! with all the efforts I made, the time dragged horribly. It was now midnight, and there had been nothing to break the monotony of the evening. I wondered what they were doing at home. Dancing, of course, for my sake. The ball was now at its height, and my mother was in a state of dignified ecstasy. Marie sat in a low armchair, yawning. She tried to yawn gracefully, I am sure, but it was quite impossible.

"Go to bed, Marie," I said, peremptorily, at one o'clock.

"I will wait with Madame," was the reply.

And again we sat down to the contemplation of each other's charms. How lonely it was! We made a round of the house and saw that everything had been properly secured for the night, simply because I felt so nervous that I could not sit there inactive. I will not attempt to describe all the weird noises we heard, because everybody who has sat up in the early hours of the morning knows exactly what they are. At three o'clock I started violently. I think I must have been asleep. The striking of the clock in the hall aroused me.

"Marie," I said a few minutes later, "I am going to bed. My husband will not be back to-night, that is very sure. I will wait no longer. Good-night."

To my surprise Marie kissed me. I remember hoping that she did not intend to do so every night. I hated affectionate people as I have already said often enough. I was almost dead with fatigue. I went to my room, undressed quickly, and was soon in a deep, dreamless sleep, from which I awoke when my watch told me it was ten o'clock, and the sun was dancing merrily over the daintily carpeted floor.

CHAPTER 9

I felt thoroughly good-natured, and was determined to be as smilingly gracious as I possibly could when I met my eccentric husband. Of course I should not even allude to his most unaccountable behavior, but I had no doubt at all that he would be utterly repentant, and that his remorse would even go so far as to melt the ice of his manners.

I selected one of the nattiest little morning dresses that my trousseau contained. It was one of those charmingly devised costumes that would render the most hideous woman acceptable. Now, I was not hideous by any means, and when I took a final look at myself before descending, I had never appeared more comely, I thought. In spite of my early morning vigil, the roses bloomed becomingly on my cheeks, and my eyes sparkled with health.

Down the broad staircase I sailed. I was Mrs. Arthur Ravener now, so it would not do to "trip." Matrons sail. That term has a very dignified sound in my ears. Before entering the breakfast-room, I peeped coyly in. Yes, there sat my husband, deep in a newspaper. He had already begun breakfast, and must have poured out his coffee, and buttered his toast with his own manly fingers. I walked in.

"Good-morning, Arthur," I said, coquettishly, taking my seat at the head of the table. Perhaps I had better confess that I felt a little nervous.

"You are late, Elsie," remarked my husband, laying down his paper. "I thought I would take the initiative and begin breakfast. I hope you do not think it impolite on my part?"

"Not a bit, I shall soon catch you up. I'm as hungry as a hunter. This Kew air seems to be invigorating."

In reality I had no appetite at all. The thought of breakfast sickened me, but I was determined, with all the perversity of my sex, that he should not know it.

"I am glad of that, Elsie," said Arthur, smiling at me kindly. He rose, poured me out a cup of coffee, buttered a slice of toast for me, helped me to some cold partridge, and went back to his seat. He had looked just a trifle uneasy, I fancied, when I entered, but he had now completely recovered. The awful idea occurred to me that he would make no comments whatever on his absence last night. As I had always heard that between husband and wife there should be complete confidence, I resolved that I would do violence to my feelings and broach the subject, as a matter of principle, if for no other reason. I did not want abject apologies, but I was not going to be treated with such sublime disrespect.

"Will you have half my newspaper, Elsie?" asked Arthur, as I sat silently devouring my partridge, with all my good temper rapidly vanishing.

"Thank you." He handed me a couple of sheets.

"They have given a splendid account of the wedding," he said, "and I suppose that all England knows about it now."

"Why are you so anxious for all England to be informed that you are a Benedict?" I enquired scornfully.

He reddened and made no reply. I glanced carelessly through the half column of silly gush, learned that I had made a very interesting bride, and noticed some very flattering allusions to my husband. "After the reception," I read aloud, "the bride and bridegroom left for Kew, where they will spend the honeymoon in their handsome home, Tavistock Villa." "They might have added," I said, laying down the paper and trying to speak indifferently, "that the bridegroom returned to London early in the evening, and was back in Kew again in time for breakfast."

I leaned forward in my chair to enjoy the effect of my sarcasm.

"Don't be foolish, Elsie," said my husband, from behind his newspaper, "I told you I was obliged to go up to London, and I know you are too sensible a little woman to stand in my way in a case like that."

"Stand in your way!" My cheeks were the color of peonies. I was horribly indignant.

"Elsie," said Arthur, "I don't want you to be vexed. You are very young, and — and — well, I am older. There was really no cause for you to worry last night. This house is as safe as a — a bank. Kew is a very quiet, respectable sort of place, and such things as burglars are almost unknown. I — I — was going to telegraph you that I was unable to return, but — but —"

"But what?" — sharply.

"I was afraid a telegram might alarm you. Now, Elsie, there is not a soul who knows anything about this — this — this affair, and I would not talk about it."

"Talk about it?" I exclaimed in angry surprise. "With whom?"

"W-with anybody. With your mother, for example."

"Oh, no," I laughed satirically. "It would not interest her. I am not a gossip, Arthur. Our affairs can interest nobody but ourselves."

"You are a thoroughly sensible girl, Elsie," said Arthur, with what sounded like a little sigh of relief. "Now, hurry with your breakfast, dear, and I'll take you for a nice long drive, and we'll have luncheon out."

That restored my drooping spirits more than anything else could have done. I forgot all about my grievances. After all they were not very formidable. If I never had anything more to contend with during my life, I might think myself fortunate.

It was a glorious day and I was determined to enjoy myself. Arthur had a neat little phaeton waiting at the door, and into it we stepped. Arthur took the whip, and off we went at a delightful rate. How keenly invigorating the air was! I thought of Letty Bishop and remembered how she hated such drives. The bane of her life was a red nose, and she would have had an extremely conspicuous one had she been with us today. After a delicious drive of a couple of hours, we "put up" at a little hotel, and Arthur ordered a most tempting luncheon. What a blessing an appetite is! We were both hungry. The last vestige of my woes vanished as I found myself opposite to a plate of succulent natives. My good spirits must have been contagious. Arthur caught them, and was his own amiable, amusing self. He talked and laughed and told some excellent stories. I had never found myself with so agreeable a companion — and to think that he was my husband! What a senseless girl I had been to worry. I promised myself that for the future I would indulge in no more idiocy.

"Just think, Arthur," I said, as he dallied with some cheese (dallying with cheese is my own idea) and I made a combination of almonds and raisins, "Marie imagined we were old married people. You never told her that we were just married — you sly boy."

"Did you?" It was really very strange why Arthur should get so uncomfortable at my little innocent remarks.

"Of course I did. I don't propose to sail under false colors, as an antiquated dowager."

"What did Marie say?" with eagerness.

"She was very, very surprised. She thought you were so droll to go off to the City as you did. I was angry with her, and she said she was not accustomed to English habits." I spoke cheerfully; I had quite forgiven him.

My husband did not look pleased. "I do wish you would not chatter about me and my business, Elsie," he said with marked vexation. "If Marie makes any more impertinent remarks, send her away."

I said nothing. Arthur was an oddity — *voilà tout,* as my mother loved to remark. I must give way to him in a proper, wifely manner. I was resolved that "amiability, amiability, always amiability," should be my motto. So I cracked him three most inviting filberts and laid them as a peace offering on his plate.

"By-the-bye, Elsie," said my husband presently, as we were thinking about departing, "Captain Dillington is coming to dinner tonight."

If he had given me a sound box on the ears I could not have been more disagreeably surprised. I lost all idea of keeping to the text of my motto. What did he mean by asking this man to our house, the day following our marriage? Why, my mother had told me that as we were not going on a wedding trip, we must live in retirement for a month. I had Fashion on my side, thank goodness.

"To-night!" I exclaimed aghast.

"Why not?"

"It is not usual, Arthur. Why c-can't we have a nice l-little dinner alone?"

"Nonsense. It is perfectly proper to ask one's parents and most intimate friends to the house, I am sure. Elsie, I cannot put Captain Dillington off. You — you do not want me to do so."

He appealed to me. What could I say? I felt that an untruth would be the only thing that would please him. If I told the truth it would be to the effect that I hated Captain Dillington at all times, and my hatred was, if possible, intensified, just now.

"No, no," I said, choking down a little sob, "don't put him off. When d-did you invite him, Arthur?"

"When?"

"Yes, when?"

"Last night."

"Oh, you saw him last night. D-did you meet him accidentally?"

"Elsie!" exclaimed Arthur fretfully, "don't catechize me. What makes you so cross? I want to amuse you. I am doing all I can to prevent you feeling in the least homesick. I am very, very anxious for you to be happy, and you look miserable because I ask my greatest friend to the house. Why you yourself said that our great friendship was a source of admiration to you. It first attracted your attention."

He spoke the truth. I had said all that and more. Of course I meant it. I did admire sincere friendship — but surely there was a limit to all things. His affection for Captain Dillington certainly need not interfere with his love for me. I was his wife after all. I would not argue, however. Captain Dillington was to come to dinner. So be it. I would reserve a careful analysis of my statements for a future occasion.

"I am foolish, Arthur," I said, rising. "Come, let us go home, and see that at any rate Captain Dillington will have something to eat."

He took my hand and pressed it lightly. His eyes looked into mine with gratitude clearly expressed in their depths. Yes, my self-sacrifice had its reward. I jumped at the crumbs he threw to me, and swallowed them ravenously. I could have digested more with perfect facility. We went back to Tavistock Villa. The drive home, however, was not very pleasant. The atmosphere seemed to be less invigorating. There were clouds in the sky. The horses were tired, and the dust, which the wheels of the phaeton sent up in columns, almost blinded me.

There were but few arrangements to make for the accommodation of our guest. I made myself charming in a dress of pale blue silk, and went down to the drawing-room. Captain Dillington was already there. He and Arthur stood with their backs to the door as I appeared. They were in earnest conversation, and did not even hear me enter.

"Good evening, Captain Dillington," I said affably, extending my hand.

"Ah, Mrs. Ravener — delighted I am sure." There was horrible unction in his greeting. Was I so blinded by prejudice that everything this man did simply nauseated my soul?

"I do sincerely hope that I am not intruding," he went on blandly. "I told Arthur —"

"Not at all," I said in the tones which a refrigerator would use if it could speak. "How are things in London?"

"You were there but yesterday," with a smile, as though he were determined that I should not forget this. "There is positively nothing new — positively nothing."

The announcement of dinner was a welcome sound in my ears. How heartily I wished before commencing it that it was over. It was not a very trying ordeal, however. My husband and Captain Dillington talked on a variety of subjects, and I did not feel it at all necessary, under the circumstances, to include myself in the conversation. I did not absolutely wish Captain Dillington to feel that his presence was unpleasant, but I likewise did not wish him to congratulate himself on the fact that it was pleasant.

After dinner I rose, and, leaving them to their own resources, went into the drawing-room. I played some of my beautiful "*morceaux de salon,*" not because I liked them, but because it passed away the time and made a noise. I was not happy enough to indulge in any of the dainty little pieces in which I generally delighted when alone.

It was ten o'clock before they joined me. Captain Dillington congratulated me upon my "exquisite touch" and said a few conventional things, after which the two men sat down to a game of chess.

What a wearisome parody of amusement chess is, in my opinion; I suppose I am not intellectual enough to appreciate it. I remember I once tried to learn it, but I never could remember how to move the pawns, and always called out "check" at the most ridiculously inopportune moments.

I sat in a low rocking chair and yawned desperately. I made no pretense of occupying myself with fancy work, which I despised most cordially.

I took up the *Times* and tried to get interested in the agony column. I wondered what it was that A. B. would hear of to his advantage if he communicated with Mr. Snipper of Lincoln's Inn Fields. I tried to imagine what a weight of woe would be lifted from the heart of Lottie L. when she read that all would be forgiven if she would only return to Jack D.

"You are tired, Elsie," said Arthur at last, pausing in an interesting move as I yawned in an ultra-outrageous manner.

"Very," I said.

Then he forgot that I was there.

At midnight they were still hard at it. My eyelids were closing with fatigue. I was raging inwardly (which ought to have kept me awake, but it did not).

At one o'clock I could stand it no longer. I rose from my chair and went towards the door.

"Good-night," I said, looking straight in front of me. If they replied, I did not hear them. I fled to my room.

CHAPTER 10

I could not sleep. I tried my hardest to woo the old humbug Morpheus, who is always on hand when not wanted, but fails to respond to urgent appeals. I was as wide awake as I had been in the early morning, with the sole difference that I was now feverish and oppressed. I rang the bell that communicated with Marie's room. She responded to the call, looking horribly sleepy and unlovely, poor girl.

"Marie," I said, "I cannot sleep. Would you mind sitting with me until morning? I don't know what is the matter with me, but I am too wide awake even to doze."

I threw open the window of my room and let the cool night breezes blow through my refractory tresses. It was a glorious moonlight night, and as I looked at the pretty little gardens in the lovely blue-white illumination, I felt less ill at ease.

"Madame will take cold," Marie ventured to remark.

"Madame is not so fragile as she looks," was my reply. A crunching sound below made me start and look down. Surely I could not be mistaken. My husband and Captain Dillington were in the garden, slowly walking up and down, arm-in-arm. They were smoking placidly, and conversing in low, earnest tones, between puffs. I sent Marie to bed with a promptitude which must have caused her considerable astonishment. Truly by this time her ideas of English customs must have been of the Munchausen order. I did not know Arthur was so fond of nocturnal rambles. How glad I should have been had he asked me to join him. Perhaps he supposed that I was a delicate little reared-in-the-lap-of-luxury maiden, and felt that my wifely duties consisted in looking pretty and sitting at the head of the dinner-table. What a mistake he made!

I could see the two men distinctly, though they could not detect me behind the pretty plants that adorned my windows. I could hear them talking, though it was impossible to distinguish what they said while they were at a distance. They were approaching me, however, and as they came nearer their words fell distinctly on my ears. "She is a dear little thing, Dill," said Arthur nervously.

"What of that?" came quickly from the lips of the Captain.

"She deserves a better husband. I am beginning —"

"Don't begin then," angrily, "your wife is a mere child. Give her a comfortable home, handsome dresses, and the thousand little comforts that women love, and she will be your devoted admirer for many years to come. Don't let her read trashy books, and when you go into society, monopolize her yourself."

"Perhaps you are right, Dill," sighed Arthur, "you always are, old man, but — poor Elsie!"

I could hear no more. They were already far away, and I had strained my ears — if that be possible — to understand this much of their conversation. I am not sentimental, as I think I have already proved. It may have been the strange influences of the hour that unnerved me. The tears coursed slowly down my cheeks. The garden was blotted from my sight.

The conversation between my husband and Captain Dillington had been couched in the language to which I had been accustomed all my life, and yet I could not have understood its meaning less, if it had been spoken in Greek. Why did I deserve a better husband? Arthur was as good as I was, I loyally believed. He might have a few eccentricities, but I had more faults. For each of his eccentricities I had two faults. I was flippant, childish, emotional. Perhaps, too, I myself was eccentric. Letty Bishop had always said so; my mother had ever declared it. It was Arthur who merited a better wife, not I who deserved a better husband. He had been rather inattentive to me during these early days of our married life. The only reason could be that I was not sufficiently attractive to him. I had not yet studied him enough to conform to his views. It surely was a wife's duty to conform to her husband's views, and not a husband's obligation to regulate himself to his wife's ideas. You see what a dutiful little lady I was inclined to be.

I kept my eyes fixed upon the garden, and longed for an opportunity to go to Arthur and settle any little difficulties before they widened into an impassable gulf.

The opportunity came. With joy I saw Captain Dillington leave Arthur, throw aside his cigarette, and go into the house. I presumed that he intended to continue as our guest. I had made no preparation for him, however.

I dressed quicker than I had ever done before in my life, and throwing

a long cloak over me, rushed down the stairs, pell mell, forgetting my previous views upon the matronly "sail." It was very dark in the hall. The
lights had been diminished to a glimmer. I stumbled on my way to the
door, and should have fallen if some one had not come to my aid.

"Mrs. Ravener!" exclaimed Captain Dillington — for he it was — in
great surprise, "what are you doing about at this hour?"

"Have I not as much right to be about, as you call it, as you and my
husband?"

He made no answer. I could not see his face. "You were not going out,
surely, Mrs. Ravener?" he asked, a few seconds later.

"I was going out, and I am going out," said I with beautiful redun-
dancy.

"You will take cold," he suggested, quickly; "the night air is very
chilly, you know."

"Good-night, Captain Dillington," — preparing to join Arthur. "I
presume you intend remaining with us. You do not think of going up to
town at this hour?" Sweetly hospitable, but I could not help it.

"Oh, no."

"*Au revoir*, then."

"Let me take you to your husband, Mrs. Ravener; you may stumble
again, you know."

"Thank you, Captain Dillington, I can find my way."

"Let me accompany you; I am in no hurry to retire."

"No," I said sharply. "I should make no more ceremony with you
than you do with me, if I wanted you. I wish to see Arthur, alone — alone,
Captain Dillington."

"As you wish." He shrugged his shoulders, and with his unctuous
smile, left me. I went forthwith into the gardens.

Arthur had taken possession of a rustic seat. His delicate profile was
clearly defined in the moonlight. He was evidently deep in thought — and
I suppose he had no idea that his reflections were about to be interrupted.
I walked quickly across the damp, dewy grass, and before he knew it, I was
seated beside him.

"Arthur."

He started violently, and almost jumped from his seat.

"Elsie!" he exclaimed. "You here, and at this time. Why did you
come? You will take a severe cold. You should not have ventured out."

"Would you mind very much if I did take a severe cold?"

"How can you be so foolish, Elsie?" he asked testily. "Of course, I
should mind. Have I not charge of your future life? What is putting such
strange ideas into your head, dear?"

"Arthur," I said slowly, "I was at my open window just now, and I heard you talking with Captain Dillington. Oh, I did not distinguish much of what you said," I went on, as I noticed he looked disconcerted. "You declared that I deserved a better husband, and Captain Dillington thought that I was a mere child, and that as long as I had a comfortable home, I should be happy. Am I a mere child, Arthur?"

"Are you?" he asked slowly, not meeting my eyes. "If you are, Elsie — and I believe it now, as I believed it when I first met you — try and remain so. Elsie, dear, be innocent and good as you now are as long as you can, for your own sake, and —" there were tears in his eyes — "for mine. If you only knew, dear, how anxious I am that your life should be a happy one — that through no fault of mine you should suffer —" he was agitated as I had never seen any man before. "Why did you come out to me here, Elsie. Why — why did you come?" this in feverish, excited tones.

"Because I love you, Arthur," I exclaimed vehemently, throwing my arms around his neck, all my theories as to the absurdity of demonstrative behavior gone to the winds.

"Don't, Elsie," he said, unclasping my arms.

"I will," I said, "I am your wife; you have no right to repulse me. Arthur," noticing with surprise his look of alarm, "you prefer Captain Dillington's company to mine. You selected him for your midnight stroll. You — you — you think n-n-nothing of me. Oh, Arthur, you are unkind, cruel, heartless."

I burst into a passion of tears, which were as much a surprise to me as they were to Arthur. It must have been years since I had wept, and now I was succumbing to a regular storm. I became hysterical. I remember feeling that I was making a fool of myself, and trying to laugh with the most ridiculous result.

"I may be a child," I sobbed, "but I don't want to be slighted; you — you are slighting me. You — do not care for me. You do not, — no — no — you do not. You hate me, I know it. You — wish — you were n-not married. Let me go home. I — I don't want to go, but — if — y-you think it would be better — Why don't you speak? Speak, Arthur, speak."

By this time I was beside myself. I was wrought up to a state of extreme excitement. Arthur said nothing. He took my hands quickly in his. I looked at him; his face was ghastly in its whiteness. His lips were as bloodless as his cheeks. His fingers were icy. I shrank back from him. My excitement disappeared as rapidly as it had come. I sat beside him limp and subdued.

"Elsie," said Arthur, presently, in a broken voice. "I — I must be an awful wretch."

He put his hand before his eyes; I could see the tears trickling through his slender, white fingers. My heart reproached me. Why, oh, why was I born emotional? A plague upon emotional women, one and all, say I.

"You are not — you are not," I murmured, "I am to blame after all. Don't mind what I said, dear. It is this scene, and this — this hour which have affected me. I — I could not sleep — I —"

Arthur again took my hands in his. In his eyes, as he fixed them upon my face, I saw "a something" that sent a thrill of ecstatic bliss through my heart. He leaned forward, and pressed a kiss — warm and tender — upon my lips — the first he had ever voluntarily given me. I looked up.

A cold shudder ran through my frame, a feeling of intense disgust seemed to permeate my soul. Before us stood Captain Dillington, coldly statuesque and hatefully conspicuous. Arthur dropped my hands. The flush upon his face, which I could see in the moonlight, faded. His eyes still fixed upon mine — he had not looked at the captain — grew coldly and studiously friendly as ever. The change was startling.

"I trust you do not object to my cigar, Mrs. Ravener?" asked the intruder politely.

I would rather have inhaled the smoke of ten thousand cigars lighted at one time, than listened to one word from the repulsive lips of this man.

I could not answer him. "Good-night, Arthur," I said, and rising sped across the lawn to the house, and regained my chamber. I slept.

CHAPTER II

For eight days Captain Dillington remained with us, a most unwelcome guest as far as I was concerned. He knew it, too, I suppose. I was too young to be able to dissemble. I disliked the man so thoroughly, that I made the fact only too apparent.

My interview with Arthur in the garden, however, had eased my mind considerably. I felt now that I could soon win my way to his heart, if I could only succeed in gaining his confidence. This, I reflected, must not be forced, but carefully and studiously worked for.

Captain Dillington's visit was a source of horrible discomfort to me. To be sure, while he was in the city during the daytime, Arthur took me for a "constitutional," but after dinner I was left entirely to my own resources and those of my faithful Marie, whom I was now beginning to appreciate more than I could have thought possible. The men sat down to their detestable game of chess, and long after midnight, at which time I left them,

Marie informed me that they remained at the table. When I met them at breakfast, they were polite, amiable, talkative; they seemed to think that as long as they were satisfied, all was well.

How delighted I was when Captain Dillington at last informed me that he must return to London. I was so happy that I believe I favored him with a radiant smile, and oh, deceit! oh, hypocrisy! — hoped he would come again. I imagine he fully understood the frame of mind which induced the utterance of such a flagrantly improbable wish. I fancied I saw him bite his lips, though he merely bowed and thanked me.

"Arthur," I said, clasping my hands, while a flush of pleasure mantled my cheeks as Captain Dillington, with his valise and smile disappeared from our sight, "he has gone — at last."

Now, generally speaking, a fact that is so self-evident as the one which I had just mentioned, would need no further comment. Of course he had gone. We had seen him go. But under the circumstances it seemed to me that Arthur might have said something. He stood with his eyes fixed upon the ground, making little circles in the smooth gravel with the point of his shoe.

"Arthur, dear," I continued, laying my hand with its conspicuous gold circletted finger on his arm, "I am so glad."

My husband did not look up. "What is your objection to Captain Dillington?" he asked. "I am sure he always treated you kindly — and no one could have been more polite."

"I am jealous of him, Arthur."

I got no further in my playful remark. "How dare you talk such nonsense?" he asked, passionately, turning upon me furiously and positively glaring at me. "Women are all the same, inconsistent, foolish, unstable as water. They do not know their own minds from one moment to another. I was wrong to believe you when you declared that you would never discountenance our friendship — that you admired it — that — pshaw! what a fool I was! Great heavens! that I should have been so deceived."

"Stop!" I exclaimed, my voice ringing out so loudly that it astonished me, though I was too indignant and alarmed to pay any attention to it. "You have no right to talk in that manner to me, and I will not permit it. Captain Dillington's presence in this house was an affront to me, and he knows it if you do not. I still say I admire friendship, but when it causes a man to treat his wife with complete indifference and as a necessary incumbrance in his house, I retract and declare that I despise it — despise it from the bottom of my heart."

I turned my back upon him in silent disgust — silent, because in my

bitter indignation I could say no more. Heaven knows that these angry words were called forth by himself. I would willingly have forgiven the first week of neglect and indifference, if with Captain Dillington's departure, he had shown the least sympathy for me. But to champion the cause of that intruder and disregard mine — I was no saint. He had slapped one cheek, but I would take good care that he should not slap the other.

"Have I treated you with neglect?" The anger was gone from his voice. I had frightened it away.

"Have you?" I asked scornfully. "You have treated me with such marked coldness, that even my maid, Marie, has been gossiping with the other servants about it."

Ah, I had made a mistake. I knew it the moment the words were out of my mouth.

"She has, has she?" he exclaimed in a towering rage. "She shall leave the house to-night. I will not pay a pack of drones to gossip about me. She shall go, and this minute, too."

"She shall not. If she leaves your house" (I was beside myself with rage and excitement, and was hardly accountable for what I said) "I will go too."

"Elsie!" There was actual fear in his voice. He looked so handsome as these varied emotions stirred him, that — alas! that I should say it — I felt that my indignation could not last much longer. As he uttered my name, he looked at me earnestly, and with a pained, wearied gaze. I began to feel sorry for him. Despise me, readers, and mentally declare that you would have acted far differently.

Women so often start in as plaintiffs and end as defendants in their controversies with the other sex.

"I mean it," I managed to say in a low voice.

"You would ruin my reputation," he began in a grieved tone. Unpardonably selfish as the remark was, it made just the impression upon me that he probably intended it should do.

"How can you say it?" I asked. "Arthur, listen to me. I love you, and I begin to think that I love you too well. If I did not care for you, I should be glad when you absented yourself from me, but — but — as it is — it — breaks m-my heart."

I was going to give way. I felt quite sure of that.

"Don't, Elsie," said Arthur, hastily. "Don't. I cannot stand scenes. I want you to be happy. I would not for the world see you in such distress, but —"

"But, what —"

"Nothing. Elsie, let us go for a long walk and drop these painful subjects." Painful subjects! He said it, I assure you.

"No," I said, sadly. I would not make myself cheap. He did not want me, I felt sure. I must try another policy.

"What are you going to do to pass away the morning?"

"Oh, I have a wealth of amusement," I said, smiling through my tears. "Do — do not trouble any more about me. You probably have some w-writing to do. Do not let me disturb you. Good-bye," and I ran away to my room.

Yes, I must try another policy. Perhaps I was letting him see too plainly that his neglect caused me pain. It might be that, like some men of whom I have since heard, he disliked to know that a woman was running after him. If I treated him as he treated me, perhaps I might teach him a little respect. Men do not like weak, clinging beings — at least some of them don't, and perhaps my husband belonged to that class. At any rate I would change my policy. Why do I say "change my policy"? I had none before. I was simply acting as my heart told me to act. Now I would follow the course prescribed by my reason. I could lose nothing by so doing, and I might gain my husband's love.

I congratulated myself that I had refused to accompany him on that walk. I was really dying to go, but I would deny myself the pleasure for the sake of possible results. He had not insisted — it would have been no use if he had — I told myself. Perhaps he was annoyed at my refusal. I sincerely hoped that he was. I trusted that he was even seriously angry and would resent my non-compliance with his request.

I must confess that the afternoon passed away most tediously for me. I called in Marie, and made her talk herself tired. I tried to be amused at her chatter, but I found it insufferably uninteresting. She would tell me all about Paris, and her own dull life in that city. The poor girl was the daughter of an honest little Rue du Temple *fabricant*, and her history was not exciting. If she had only been the daughter of a dishonest little *fabricant*, she would have been far more entertaining, I thought. I felt that she was supplying me with conversational gruel, and I was in a condition of mind when I wanted curry. As the hour for dinner drew nigh, I dressed myself carefully. Everything I could do to make myself look pretty — I did. I was determined that Arthur should admire me.

I recovered my spirits sufficiently to be able to "sail" downstairs, and as I reached the dining-room, the flush of excitement came to my cheeks. I wondered how it would all end. Arthur was not in the dining-room, so I threw myself into an armchair to await him. I was rather impatient. I suppose it was natural that I should be. I took up a newspaper and tried to read. I did not have to try very long.

"Mrs. Ravener." It was James, the butler. I suppose he was not sure that I was in the chair, as I was covered with newspaper.

"Yes, James."

"Master told me to give you this note."

I snatched it from the man's hands, and read it hastily. "Dear Elsie," it ran, "I have just received a telegram that calls me up to town immediately. Do not wait dinner for me, and pray do not be angry. Your affectionate husband, Arthur Ravener."

Oh, this was cruel. I waved my hand to James to dismiss him, and then flung myself upon the sofa in an agony of weeping. For twenty minutes I gave my grief full play, and then, when anger came peeping in, I let it enter and take possession of my soul. I rang the bell. James, with suspicious promptness answered the call.

"James, did any telegram come here for your master this afternoon?"

"Not to my knowledge, madame."

"Are you sure?"

"Quite."

"Go ask the servants, and find out if anybody brought a telegram for Mr. Ravener to the house to-day."

He soon returned. "No one has received any telegram. If one had come to the house," he added with the officiousness of his class, "I should have known it."

"You may go."

My blood was boiling. I would not be set aside. Perhaps Arthur Ravener thought I was a milk and water maiden. He made a great mistake. "I gave him the option between peace and war," I said to myself, "and he has chosen war. So be it."

I tried to be lively, but it was a failure. I was changed. I was no longer a flippant girl, but a jealous woman. Does any one know what a jealous woman really is? I think not. Perhaps a volcano always on the eve of eruption is about the best simile I can suggest.

CHAPTER 12

I am not going to weary my readers by describing in detail the ensuing days of my married life. I adopted the new policy I had mapped out. I became apparently indifferent to my husband's presence, uninterested in his nightly outgoings and his matutinal incomings, while at the same time I treated him with studied politeness and friendly affability. We talked and laughed at the dinner-table. We discussed politics — I made it a point of disagreeing with him, for the sake of permitting him to try and win me over to his way of thinking. Of course I let him finally convince me, and then declared how foolish I must have been ever to have thought otherwise. Then we talked books — I in my superficial way, he in his earnest, well read manner. I knew the names of the authors of nearly all the popular works of the day; I was one of those airy beings who examine the covers of books, dip into catalogues, and taste literature, as it were, from the outside.

He was really so entertaining that at times I forgot I was only playing a part. I could not help thinking that he would have enjoyed the conversation just as much if it had taken place with somebody else. I suppose I seemed rather bright — some women as shallow as I was often manage to appear so. I do not believe he appreciated this brightness because it belonged to his wife, but merely — bah; I hate analysis. After all, what I believed on this subject is neither here nor there.

I made not the slightest impression upon Arthur Ravener. A month had flown by since I had stood in my dollish finery at the hymeneal altar. Our walks had been dropped. That was one of the effects of my policy. He seemed perfectly satisfied. He had evidently thought that these "constitutionals" were necessary for my happiness. If I chose to discontinue them — well, then, they were not necessary for my happiness. It was very simple after all.

At breakfast, at luncheon, and at dinner, here I was — there he was. He was as platonically kind as any man could be. He always made enquiries as to my health, my wishes, my plans. I had but to suggest a thing, and I had his acquiescence almost before I had made the suggestion. And all this time, I was eating my heart out for love of this iceberg.

Women must be contemptible things. If I were a man I suppose I could not give utterance to such an ungallant remark, but no one can find fault with me when my sex is taken into consideration, and I am quite sure I shall find plenty of sisters to agree with me.

The old adage about the woman, the dog and the hickory tree, which nicely explains that the more you beat 'em the better they'll be, seems to me wonderfully true. Why should I care for this man? I was very young, of course, but I knew perfectly well that this utter neglect was simply outrageous. I remembered my horror at the compliments and pretty speeches with which my partners in the ball-rooms of my friends had overwhelmed me. I had hated them for their silly, tinsel-bound sentiments; their ill-expressed admiration. I still did so. I should have been just as disgusted if I had heard them at the present time. But there was a happy medium to all things.

Between the conspicuously ridiculous adulation of comparative strangers, and the brotherly indifference of the man I had married, there must be a middle path of warm yet not necessarily demonstrative affection. I thought of the bride and bridegroom whom Arthur and I had criticised one night. "It disgusts me," I recollected saying, when Arthur had asked me if their conversation, to which we had listened, interested me. Well, I had no cause for such disgust in my own home. Arthur's indifference seemed to be unaffected by any policy I might adopt. I even tried to make him jealous. There was a bashful youth, who wore glasses and a perpetual smile, living close to Tavistock Villa, with an adoring mamma and two prim sisters, to whom Hector was as the apple of their eye. He had frequently cast admiringly modest glances in my direction when he had stumbled across Marie and me in our daily walks.

"*Il a l'air joliment bête,*" Marie said to me once in the loud security of the French language as we passed the gallant youth. He must have thought the remark was a flattering one, because he looked even more seraphically pleasant than usual. Dasy was his surname. He lacked the *i* which would have given him some claim upon the dainty characteristics of that little flower.

Mr. Dasy amused me. The delectable idea occurred to me to use him. I would cultivate his society. I would make Arthur desperately jealous. I had always heard that those bashful, rose-colored youths were the most dangerous, and if I had heard it, surely my husband had. Who could possibly introduce us? Of course I could smile at him and encourage him that way, but I was not inclined to have recourse to the methods of an unscrupulous flirt, when I was very far from being one. How I wished that flirting came as naturally to me as it did to some women.

I could call on Mamma Dasy if I liked. Neighborly courtesy would surely sanction that, but I felt I could not do it. I had an awful idea that this mamma might patronize me. I had a hideous presentiment that she would come and see us and wonder why we were not more affectionate. I could tell by her face that she was one of those women who think it the duty of a young married couple to do a little billing and cooing *pro bono publico*. I could not possibly introduce prying eyes into my strange household. I think I should have dreaded any eyes at all, at that time. I was growing morbid. Even Marie was too many for me occasionally.

Fortune favored me. One afternoon, feeling more wretched than usual, and knowing that my husband was safely shut up in his sanctum and that I should not see him until dinner time, I took up a book and strolled towards the gardens. I selected a shady spot, opened my volume, and was soon engrossed in its contents.

When I looked up I found that I was not alone. There, sure enough, as large as life, and equally ugly, sat the Misses Dasy — sister Euphemia and sister Sophronia. They were knitting. If they had been reading I should have looked up in surprise; if they had been drawing, my hair would have stood on end; if they had been indulging in small talk, it would have seemed indecent; — but they were knitting. It looked so natural. They belonged to the knitting class of females. As I said, I looked up. I smiled. Sister Sophronia smiled. Sister Euphemia smiled. We all smiled.

"How strange we do not meet more frequently, Mrs. Ravener," quoth sister Euphemia. "Hector says he often comes across you and your maid." "Yes," chirped sister Sophronia, "we wondered why we so rarely met you."

I thanked the stars — mentally, of course — that I had not been inflicted before. Now, however, I was rather glad to see them, as by them I might find access to dear Hector. So I told no fib when I remarked that I was charmed, though I am afraid that I should not have permitted a fib or two to stand in my way if they could have done me any good.

"Mr. Ravener does not believe in country walks, I suppose," remarked Euphemia presently, "like most men," she added.

Hateful sister Euphemia! I am convinced that her acquaintance with men must have been limited to dear Hector, and — as Portia says — God made him, so let him pass as a man.

"Hush, Euphemia," said Sophronia in an audible aside, and in a virtuous tone. She could not have made any remark less calculated to please me. It was evident they had been discussing us.

"My husband is a literary man and writes all day long," said I, with one of the serenest, most child-like and fancy-picture smiles I had ever conjured up. "I dislike to disturb him, you know. Men are such queer things, are they not?"

"Yes," laughed Sophronia girlishly.

"Indeed they are," simpered Euphemia, dropping a stitch as a punishment for her giddiness.

"Is your brother a literary man?" I asked boldly.

"Oh, no," said Sophronia, scornfully, "dear Hector is nicely established in the hop business — malt and hops, you know." (Evidently imagining that I might think he was a dancing master). "He is taking a holiday just now. He has been working so hard. Dear Hector!"

"He admires you, Mrs. Ravener," quoth Euphemia. "He says you have a face like a woman in — in — some painting, I can't remember the name."

Great goodness! Perhaps he referred to one of the paintings given away with a pound of tea. She was so vague, that fond sister.

"Mr. Dasy compliments me," I said artlessly. "Do you know I think he is a very interesting looking young man. Hector you said his name was? Ah, it is not a misnomer." I sighed just a little.

I felt they always told Hector everything. I was convinced that my utterances would be repeated unembellished. We chatted on pleasantly for half an hour. I made myself as nice as I possibly could, and I think I succeeded in impressing them favorably. I reserved my master-stroke for my departure.

"Good-bye, dear Miss Sophronia — good-bye, dear Miss Euphemia," I said gushingly, as I rose to go. "I am so delighted to have met you. You must call upon me" (I had to say it). "I have enjoyed this afternoon hugely. The gardens are certainly charming. I really think I shall come every day this week, beginning with to-morrow —" this with a little affected chirrup which might signify that I did not really mean it.

Ah, they would tell Hector, and he would accompany them to-morrow. For a beginner in the fashionable art of diplomacy, I was not so bad after all. They looked admiringly after me as I went, and I felt that they would gaze in my direction long after I could see them.

I was formally introduced to Mr. Dasy the following day. The modest hop merchant was completely overwhelmed. He grew purple in the face at everything I said for the first quarter of an hour, which means that his countenance was tinged with that royal hue during the entire fifteen minutes, for he allowed me to do all the talking. I did not flirt. I tried to do so, but could not succeed. I spoke sensibly, flattered Mr. Dasy a little — if that does not give discredit to my statement that I spoke sensibly — and simply allowed him to see that I liked talking to him. Hector certainly was not given to flattery.

He told me all about hops, the magnificent prospects for next year, how last year's crop had been anything but a good one; how terribly small the profits were in these times of cut-throat competition, and similar edifying facts. His talk was hoppy in the extreme. I felt that if only I could have talked malt the combination would have lulled us into beery intoxication.

For a week I cultivated the society of Hector Dasy. I should have been bored to death if I had not kept my object in view. I walked him up and down the Branston Road, in front of the windows of Tavistock Villa. I knew Arthur saw us at least twice, but he said nothing at all.

He was just as amiably indifferent when I met him at dinner; he spoke just as entertainly; not by the faintest indication on his part, was I hurting him. Branston Road only possessed about half a dozen extremely detached houses, so I was not at all afraid of the neighbors. If the thoroughfare, however, had been densely lined with tenements, I do not think it would have made the least difference in my course of action.

At last I resolved upon a final stroke. If it did not succeed I would drop Mr. Dasy, perfectly convinced that I could never make Arthur jealous. It was rather a risky thing to do. I asked Hector Dasy to bring me a book that I particularly wanted, and kept him during the entire afternoon, my willing slave. Before this, I told James to give Mr. Ravener's letters into my possession and to inform his master, as soon as he came in, that I had them. I did this merely in order that Arthur should be forced to enter the drawing-room and see how nicely Hector Dasy and I agreed.

Never had any afternoon passed so slowly for me. The presence of this young man annoyed me intensely and all the more because in order to keep him, I was forced to talk prettily and incessantly. Mr. Dasy was something of a coxcomb with all his bashfulness. I saw with alarm that he really imagined I liked him. I wondered what he would have said if I had told him the true facts of the case. Just before six o'clock, which was my husband's time for returning from town, when he passed the day there, I completed my Macchiavellianism. I had purchased a quantity of wool, which I wanted wound. I was determined that Mr. Dasy should hold it for me. I made him kneel on the rug before me, and at six o'clock I was winding for dear life, and he was smiling beatifically.

Ah! I heard Arthur's step at last. I could always recognize it. James was telling him that I had his letters. James had told. He was coming in my direction. The door opened. He entered.

Now for my *rôle*. "Arthur," I said with affected hesitation, "let me introduce you to my friend, Mr. Dasy — Mr. Dasy, my husband, Mr. Ravener."

I watched Arthur's face. I did not dare to look at poor Mr. Dasy. My husband's countenance showed positively no change. "I am glad to meet you, Mr. Dasy," he began, "I see you are making yourself useful. Isn't it rather too much to ask visitors to assist in such a laborious operation as wool winding, Elsie?" he said, smiling at me in all good fellowship, perfectly satisfied as though Hector had been Marie or — not to libel my French maid by comparison — a dummy from a tailor's shop.

"Mr. Dasy has been here idling away the afternoon," I said as lightly as I could, "and I thought I would utilize his services."

"Delighted, I'm sure," put in poor Hector, who had been looking for his tongue and had only just found it.

"You have my letters, have you not, Elsie?" asked Arthur, coming at once to business.

"Yes," I said coldly, "I took them because I thought they — er — looked — er — important," lamely.

Hector Dasy soon found an opportunity to go. Of course he knew I had a husband, but I presume he had not reckoned upon an introduction while wool-winding. Poor Hector! I felt a little guilty, or should have done if I had given myself the time.

"Dasy seems a nice young fellow, Elsie," said Arthur coolly, at dinner that night. "His family have lived in Kew for years. Eminently respectable. Old Dasy left them well off. I am glad you have discovered congenial society among our neighbors, Elsie," looking at me in such a friendly, disinterested fashion, that I shuddered. "You are mistress here, dear, and you can ask as many people to Tavistock Villa as you like. I shall never interfere."

Of that I now felt certain. Well, my plot had been an utter and a dismal failure. All my time had been spent for nothing. I had cultivated this nonentity with an object in view. The nonentity was there in all his cultivation, and the object had disappeared. I could never make my husband jealous.

What could I do? Tavistock Villa was becoming disgusting to me. I could not endure its atmosphere much longer. I would go up to London to-morrow, make a confidant of my mother — a thing I had never yet done — and hear what she thought about the situation.

CHAPTER 13

You, my fair young readers, will imagine that nothing could be easier than to go to your mother, and tell her — well, anything on earth. That is because you have the right kind of a mother. I had the wrong kind. I am well aware that such a sentiment is not pretty from anybody's lips, but as you already know, I am one of those candid beings who conceal nothing, even when concealment might be beneficial.

There had never been any confidence between my mother and me. She had always considered me uninteresting, and I — well, I could never realize that she really existed out of society. Her ambition never extended beyond the "set" in which she moved; her ideas were suggested invariably by those immediately above her in rank; worldliness reigned rampant within her.

I had been glad to leave her house, and rejoiced to escape from society's prospective thraldom. And now I was going to consult my mother on a question of vital importance. I was about to appeal to the very worldliness which I condemned, to assist me in my dilemma.

I had no difficulty in leaving Tavistock Villa for London. I do not suppose that if I had set out for Timbuctoo, any very unconquerable obstacles would have presented themselves.

My journey to town was without incident; my arrival at Grosvenor Square, stupid. The butler was far too well bred to express any surprise when he beheld me; the maids whom I met *en route* to my mother's morning-room, were too well drilled in fashionable idiocy to look either pleased or interested when I burst upon them.

My mother had only just risen. She had been at an ultra-swell reception the night before, and was to be present at another that evening, so that the interval between the two was to be spent in a lounge-chair with a novel and a few newspapers — those that chronicled in detail the events of society.

She pressed a farcical kiss upon my brow, said she was charmed to see me — though she wasn't — wondered why I had come in such an informal manner and so disgracefully soon, hoped dear Arthur was well, and — well, would I not sit down, and take off my cloak?

I unbosomed myself without any delay. I did not attempt to shield Arthur's neglect. I felt that he deserved everything I could say — and more. I did not tell my mother that I was miserable, because my ideas of misery and happiness did not coincide with hers. I simply laid the situation before her, and asked her superior knowledge of the world what it all meant.

Her languor disappeared as I proceeded; she even sat up straight in her lounge-chair, and when I came to an end she deliberately closed her novel — a tacit recognition of the fact that I was more entertaining than her author.

"Well, my dear," she said blandly, when I paused, "this story is strange indeed, but — but singularly interesting."

"Interesting?" I asked, horrified.

"Yes, my dear, certainly interesting. Though I always thought Arthur Ravener a peculiar young man — you remember when I saw you two in the library that day — I never supposed that he suffered from anything but bashfulness. Bashfulness, though a grievous fault in these enlightened days when young men are supposed to have overcome any little *gaucheries* long before they attain their majority, is not an unsurmountable objection. You see what I mean? I always thought — you know, Elsie, I do a great deal of thinking in my quiet way — that you and he would settle down into a commonplace, everyday couple. Not for one instant did any idea to the contrary enter my head."

She was gratified. I could see it. With disgust in my soul, and no very filial reverence written upon my unpleasantly mobile features, I was obliged to realize the fact that this society mother was entertained by the story of her daughter's marital misfortunes.

"It was only the other day," she went on, "that I heard that Lady Erminow's daughter who was recently married to that young scapegrace, Erickson — you remember her, Elsie, that pretty golden-haired girl — was living so unhappily with her husband. He is a slave to alcohol, my dear. Nothing could be worse than that. It is the lowest, most degrading passion. Lady Erminow has my heartfelt sympathy. By-the-bye, Elsie, Arthur, you omitted to tell me — is he abstemious?"

"Yes — as far as I know," I answered, bitterly.

"I thought it," said my mother, triumphantly. "The cause of his neglect must be found elsewhere. Do not worry yourself at all, Elsie."

"What do you mean?" I asked excitedly. "Do you think you know why he neglects me?"

My mother looked at me with intense scorn. "Of course I do. Do you suppose I have lived so long in the world without being able to diagnose this simple case of domestic infelicity. My dear Elsie, another girl of your age would not need aid in this matter. The case is absolutely transparent. Husband indifferent, always away from home, uninterested in wife — why, my dear child, it is all as plain as a pikestaff."

I listened eagerly. If I only understood the situation I had no doubt but that I could grapple with it. How glad I felt that I had come. If I knew the malady, surely I could find the remedy.

"One thing — before I proceed, Elsie," continued my mother, now so interested that her novel fell to the ground unheeded. "Your case would not be considered at all strange in society, and rest assured, dear, that you would not suffer in the least. Society is a kind friend — my best, — as I have told you so often. Still for the present I do not think I would ventilate my grievances, if I were you —"

"What do you mean?" I interrupted indignantly.

"Hear me, Elsie, and do not be so impulsive, please. As I was saying, for the present I would not ventilate my grievances, as in such a very young married couple, they might — remember I say 'might' — cause a little comment. If you had been married twelve months, or even six — yes, I think six," she added, reflectively, "I would not caution you thus. You see —"

"Nothing," I exclaimed, angrily, "you explain nothing."

"If you do not understand the case," continued my mother, looking rather keenly at me, "perhaps it would be better for your interests — and mine, for I am your mother, Elsie — that you should not do so. Live quietly for a few months more, and then —"

"I will not!" I cried, rising energetically from my seat. "I will not endure such a home, unless there be some very excellent reason why I should do so. I love my husband — I may as well tell you that; but when I see myself neglected in such a shameful way, through nothing that I have done, I will not submit blindly to it. Tell me what the cause of this trouble is, if you know, and I will try to remedy it. If I can do so, and can gain Arthur's love, no one will be happier than I. If I cannot, I will leave him, before the — the — whole affair k-kills me."

I burst into tears.

"You are unreasonably excited," said my mother, sternly, "or you would not dare to talk to me of leaving your husband. Why, girl, your position would be gone — and mine too. You talk of suffering through no fault of your own, but you seem extremely willing to let me suffer through no fault of mine. If you left your husband, I might as well close my establishment. All London would talk, and I — I pride myself upon furnishing no food for idle and detrimental gossip."

She rose from her seat and walked up and down the room, thoroughly and selfishly roused.

"Why will you not take my advice?" she asked. "Go home and stay there quietly for a few months. Then I will tell you what to do."

"I will not!" I exclaimed passionately.

My mother reflected. She saw that I was determined. I was. As I sat in that room I resolved that if I could not discover the cause of my husband's coldness — and discovering, vanquish it — I would leave my married life forever.

"If you will not," said my mother, after a good two minutes of complete silence, and in a wisely calculating tone, "something must be done. Of course, Elsie, there's a woman in the case."

A woman in the case! What woman? What did my mother mean?

"The expression is not a pretty one," resumed my parent, taking my surprise for ladylike wonder at the construction of her phrase. "But it means everything. You know, Elsie, that the French in every catastrophe that happens, declare that '*cherchez la femme*' will explain everything."

"I do not understand you," I said in a dazed way. "Why there is not a soul in our house but the servants and my maid, Marie."

"Perhaps not," said Mrs. Bouverie. "But there are plenty of souls out of your house, my dear, and — according to your story — that is where your husband spends the greater part of his time. His neglect of you is only too clear. He is interested in some other woman, and with her he spends his time. Have I made myself clear?"

She had. I started up, surprised at my own obtuseness and burning to settle this question once and forever. But — no, I could not understand fully.

"If he is interested in some other woman," I asked helplessly, "why did he marry me? He asked me to be his wife. Nobody forced him to do it. I didn't suggest it."

My mother laughed harshly. "I suppose not," she said. "Perhaps he wanted you to be his wife on account of the superior social advantages a married man enjoys. Perhaps as a married man his *liaison* could be carried on more favorably. Perhaps — there are a hundred suggestions I could make. Don't let us forget the fact, also, that you were dowered handsomely."

"Nonsense; he did not want my money, be quite sure of that. Mother," I said, putting on my cloak and buttoning it all wrong, "you are right, there is a woman in the case, and I was blind not to have seen it."

"No doubt your husband's friend, the Captain, is the go-between. That might explain his intimacy with your husband, might it not?"

Of course it might.

"Yes," I said. "What would you advise me to do?"

"I suppose you ask that," said mamma, severely, "in order that you may do something else. You are too obstinate, too self-willed to ask advice. Still," seeing that I looked threatening — I must have done so for I am sure I felt it — "perhaps I had better make a suggestion or two. Go home to your husband and tax him with his infidelity; you will easily see by his manner if the shot strikes home. Don't be impulsive and — ridiculous — as you generally are. Try a little diplomacy. If your husband denies everything — come to me, and I'll help you with a detective or two."

"I will," I said promptly.

"And now, go, Elsie," sinking wearily into her chair, "I declare you have fatigued me. I shall never be able to get through the reception — all this on top of my fatigues of last night."

She waved me away. I did not offer her my brow to freeze. I could not.

Her words rang in my ears all the way home. "A woman in the case." Yes, of course there must be. What a bat I must have been not to have suspected it before. I was eccentric. There was no doubt about it. I ought to have waited a few years before I had married, and gained a little experience in the world. But no! If the price of such experience was the forfeit of my self-respect, I did not want it.

A woman in the case! Who could she be? I wondered if she were more attractive than I was. What a fool I had been to imagine that he would notice me, as I strutted before my glass in the silly pride of a peacock! He was all the time thinking of some one else. I wondered why I could not picture this "some one else." I seemed utterly unable to realize the fact that Arthur Ravener could love another woman.

However, my future should soon be decided. I was excited, earnest, and eager to begin my self-imposed task.

CHAPTER 14

The strength of my resolution to arrive at a definite comprehension of the situation in which I found myself, acted in a sort of sedative manner upon my unstrung nerves. Though I raged during the ride from Grosvenor Square to Kew, at the end of my journey I was calm; desperately calm.

I dressed for dinner with just as much care as usual, and though I did not "frivol" before the glass, and think what an attractive little lady I was, I omitted nothing in my *toilette* that could render me more comely.

I found Arthur in the dining-room when I entered that gloomy apartment, and we greeted each other in just the same friendly, platonic manner that had ever marked our demeanor towards one another. We sat opposite to one another at the long table, and I prepared myself for my usual hour of small talk upon the theatres, the latest pictures, the political situation, and a variety of other topics.

I could feel no interest in anything, however. Horrible visions of Arthur, my husband, *tête-à-tête* with another woman, would fill my brain to the exclusion of everything else; disgust at my husband's deceit; contempt for my own inability to please him; wonder as to how it would all end, and a bewildering attempt to remember everything I had planned to say, played havoc with my conversational powers.

Yes, I was outrageously jealous — blindly, hatefully jealous, with the jealousy which Sardou loves to imagine and Bernhardt to portray, and though I was by no means dramatically inclined, I felt that my situation was unusual. I tried to prolong the meal. I was determined to "have it out," as the saying is, and yet I dreaded the process, because I felt that Arthur must be guilty. I knew I should feel sorry for him. He was one of those few men who could make you pity him at the same time that he cut your throat, and I was one of those many women in whom unnatural compassion exists in all its power.

Dinner was over. I could not prolong it any further if I tried. He had risen from the table. He was about to leave me — "Arthur." I swallowed a lump. My voice sounded choked.

"Elsie," he said, turning at once, and coming back to me. He stood and looked in my face with the cool, un-ardent friendship which I hated to see there. "What is it?"

He waited patiently while I gulped again and strove to be cool.

"May I speak to you, Arthur?"

He laughed.

"Why, Elsie, have you not been speaking to me for the last hour. I always like to hear you, dear. You are one of the most thoroughly sensible little women I have ever met. I —".

"Don't!" I cried, with a gesture of disgust. "Spare me. I do not want to discuss the newspapers, or talk pretty nothings, I wish to speak with you — quietly, you know — on a — a serious matter, con-connected only with ours-selves. Will you come into my sitting-room. Don't — be — afraid. I — I — will not k-keep you l-long."

My teeth chattered in my head with nervousness. I felt cold. My husband looked more uncomfortable than I did. He fidgetted with his feet. His lips twitched slightly. Oh, he knew what was coming as well as I did.

"Will you come?" I repeated as he stood mute and uneasy before me.

"Of course," with an effort, "if you wish it."

If I wished it? I bore him off to my sitting-room. He had never entered the apartment before with me, except when he first introduced me to it. I closed the door. He waited until I took an arm-chair by the window. Then he quietly sat down at the other end of the room and picked up a book. His evident fear that I was about to become demonstrative, while it cut me to the quick, was not without its ridiculous side.

"Ha! Ha!" I laughed hysterically, "you need not be afraid. I won't kiss you. I've not brought you here to tell you how I love you; that would not be original enough to please you — or me. Ha! Ha! Ha!"

I threw myself back in my chair and laughed until the tears rolled down my face. I felt the acutest anguish — and still I laughed. My heart was harrowed by this man's neglect and contempt — and still I laughed. I could not help it. I suppose it was a physiological peculiarity.

Finally I covered my face in my hands and sobbed convulsively.

"Elsie," cried Arthur in the greatest alarm, "you are ill. What is the matter? I" (rising) "will go for Dr. White."

He wanted to get out of the room. If he did, I should see him no more that day. He reckoned without his host.

"I want no doctor," I declared, rising and standing with my back to the door, all hysteria vanished. "If I do, James shall go, and you can re-main here with me. I — I know you will like that."

Again I laughed long and passionately. I was becoming exhausted by this most exhausting emotion. Great goodness! I must make an effort. Here the minutes were slipping quickly by and I had not accomplished a thing. My rival was yet unknown to me.

"Excuse me, Arthur," I said quietly, after a long pause in which he paced the floor uneasily, "your experience with women," I looked him keenly in the face, "will tell you that I — I — am — am — out of sorts."

"What do you mean, Elsie?"

No one could have better feigned surprise I told myself. Arthur Ravener must be an accomplished actor. There was the genuine astonish-ment, caused by a revelation, upon his face.

"You know what I mean," I answered.

"I do not. I swear it."

"You do," I cried, trying unsuccessfully not to ruin my cause by bitter denunciation. "You do" — more quietly. I walked over to him, grasped his arm, and looked into his face. "Now," I said, "tell me honestly, and as a man, that you do not know what I mean."

He shook me off. He was growing angry. "I will tell you nothing," he said, not glancing at me, "until you have explained yourself."

"Very well. Listen. When a young girl marries a man who a few hours after the wedding leaves her alone in a strange house; who makes a lame excuse for his action and subsequently increases his offense against respect and affection by permitting her to pass her time in absolute solitude; who for love substitutes the coldest and most indifferent friendship; who spends a large part of his time in town, leaving her in the country, and attempts no sort of explanation — when he does all this, what is she to suspect?"

He had been growing paler while I put the questions, but as I con-cluded he started up in undisguised fear — yes, it was fear.

"Suspect?" he asked, hoarsely. "What right have you to suspect any-thing? All shame upon the education of girls to-day, if a child like you dares to suspect."

He was as white as a sheet and unreasonably angry.

"You are an excellent diplomat," I said satirically. "You knew too well what a child I was when you married me. The extent of my knowledge of good and evil had been very well gauged by you. I have suspected nothing, and you know it. But, thank Heaven, my blindness has been cured. I can see it all now."

"You have been gossiping," he exclaimed, glaring at me.

"I have done nothing of the kind. I have been neglected and humiliated. I knew no reason why this state of things should exist, so — I asked my mother's advice."

The shot struck home. Arthur Ravener gasped for breath. He seemed absolutely unable to speak.

"You — asked — your — mother's — advice," he managed to articulate, presently. "And — what — did — she — tell — you?"

"She told me this, and I confront you with it: that there was undeniable proof in your neglect that you cared nothing for me, except as a sort of respectable cloak, but that there must be another woman whom you loved, and whom you visited when you were not at Tavistock Villa."

"Ah!"

If I had not known that such a thing must be impossible I should have imagined that Arthur's exclamation was one of relief. The expression of his face changed at once from one of intense alarm to comparative composure. He took a seat, leaned his elbows on his knees, covered his face with his hand, and remained silent.

"Why do you not speak?" I asked impatiently.

"Listen, Elsie," drawing closer to me. "I will be brief. Years ago I vowed I would never marry; you may think that was a boyish resolve. It was not; I thoroughly meant it, as a man. The reason was that women were too exacting, though a house without a woman in it was and still is to me a terribly lonely, uninteresting place. I resolved never to marry. I met you. As you say very justly, I studied you carefully. I came to the conclusion that you were unlike other girls — that we would live quietly and happily together as friends — you going your way and I going mine. I say I firmly believed that this could be done when I married you. I esteemed you greatly, and, Elsie," he paused for a moment, "my esteem has been increased tenfold. Lately, however, it has seemed to me that our life was becoming distasteful to you. At first I thought nothing of the symptoms, but I was unable to think thus lightly of them, later. Elsie," his voice quivering with emotion, "suppose we have made a great mistake?"

For a few moments I was bewildered. His argument was made in such a pathetic tone, that I felt unnatural compassion for him at the expense of my own womanliness would ruin the situation, if I were not on my guard.

"I do not understand you," I said. "You have not answered my mother's suggestions. If — if you love another woman, make a clean breast of it to me — your wife, and oh, Arthur," melting in spite of myself, "I — I will try to — to forgive you the wrong you have done me."

I seized his hand in a frenzy of grief. If only he would tell me all, everything could be remedied, I felt sure.

"Who is the woman?" I asked boldly.

He made no answer.

"Tell me who she is and all shall be set right."

He smiled at me pitifully. "She does not exist," he said. "Elsie, you are the only woman in the world to me."

I recoiled from him in disgust. "You are equivocating," I said sternly. "Be frank while there is still time."

"I am frank," he said in a choked voice.

"Swear that you are telling me the truth."

"I swear it."

I arose. The numbness of despair was upon me. My suffering was deadened, my nerves were lulled into temporary quietude. There was nothing further needed. He had lied to me. I knew that. I had been so blind, that the light shed upon me by my mother's revelation seemed twenty times more powerful to me than if it had not come upon me so suddenly.

"Thank you," I said, opening the door. "Let me apologize for having detained you so long. Good-night."

He had nothing more to say. He passed out of the room, without one glance in my direction.

CHAPTER 15

The months dragged themselves slowly away as though they hated to go, but would infinitely prefer to remain and gloat over my misery. I could not make up my mind to confer with my mother again. Although she had told me she would aid me, I seemed unable to pluck up the courage to know the worst.

My life at Tavistock Villa was unchanged. My relations with my husband were colder than ever. Though never once did he allude to the subject of the conversation recorded in the last chapter, I could see that it had made an impression upon him. He looked at me wistfully; our conversation was strained; a horrible form had stepped in between us, assuming shape as definitely as did the geni in the Arabian Nights story, from a mere shadow.

You would think that his course of action would have been changed. Not a bit of it. We met as before at breakfast and at dinner, after which he would leave the house. He never attempted any explanation, and I, always on the eve of desperate measures, maintained an equally guarded silence.

Of course I was in Grosvenor Square frequently during those wretched days, but as I did not allude to my misfortunes, my mother, selfishly afraid of a scandal which might endanger her eminently respectable position in the society which she loved a great deal better than she did her soul, made no effort to ascertain the situation of affairs.

I suppose my husband and I might have lived together pleasantly. There are women in this world — I have met a few of them — who have occupied similar positions with a smile on their faces. I could not do it. I was not a humbug, I was sorry to say. If only young girls were forced to study the elements of humbuggery as a part of an academic curriculum, what a quantity of subsequent suffering some of them would be spared! The study might be absolutely necessary to only a few, but it would be of benefit to all.

My cup of anguish was full when I met Letty Bishop — married and wonderfully happy. Dear me! How she loved that husband of hers. I compared her affection for dear Reginald to mine for Arthur Ravener, and then stopped. Her husband returned her love with interest. There never was a better mated couple.

I met them at my mother's house one evening. Arthur was with me for the sake of appearances, I suppose. How he ever managed to tear himself away from HER I could not imagine. I did not ask him for any information on the subject.

"What a happy couple!" I said with a sigh. I could not help the remark. Arthur was beside me. I was sitting, like an antique, faded wallflower in the drawing-room, while the others talked and chatted and laughed and gossiped at the other end of the room. He followed my eyes and saw Reginald talking in a whisper to Letty, while a pink-faced maiden executed a *morceau* on the piano.

"They are very impolite to talk while Miss Lancaster is playing," he said coldly.

"They have so much to say," I suggested.

"Doubtless."

"We shall never be troubled with such a burning desire to speak," I went on scornfully.

"That is your fault. I am always willing to talk with you. I enjoy talking with you, Elsie. You are unhappy, and it grieves me sorely to know it — because — because — I am helpless. Our marriage was a — a — mistake. You will not make the best of it. You are eating your heart away with worry. I would give all I possess to have it otherwise."

"You must imagine," I said sternly, "that I am either a lunatic or an idiot, otherwise you would not talk to me so senselessly."

"I imagine nothing of the kind."

"Then you did when you married me?"

"I did not. I thought, as we said so often, that you were in earnest when you declared you would be satisfied with quiet friendship instead of impetuous passion —"

"Then, as you imagine you were mistaken, you propose allowing matters to remain as they are."

"I do not see what else to do. Elsie, why need we quarrel? I esteem you. I admire you. I am sorry —"

"Thank you very much," I said bitterly. "You are very kind. You do me a great honor. You esteem me. You admire me. Oh, that is charming of you. Could you not have esteemed me and admired me without this nonsense?" pointing to my wedding ring. I would have flung it from the open window before us, only I, too, had appearances to keep up.

He made no answer, and I left him, going over to my friend Letty, and permitting her to pour her rhapsodies into my ears. She enjoyed the process immensely, and — well, I could just stand it, and that is about all.

Before I left my mother's house my mind was made up. I would dilly-dally no longer. I would accept my mother's aid, and settle matters finally. I was, as Arthur said, eating out my heart, and it would be better to act while there was still something left of it. I would see my mother on the following morning, and before I returned to Kew I would know that my "case" was in hands that would dispose of it satisfactorily.

I did not sleep at all that night, but with the ever faithful Marie by my side "killed time" as best I could. Marie was a good girl, but like most of her class, officious. She thought it quite correct to openly sympathize with me, and declare that *monsieur* treated his wife shamefully. This irritated me, and, if anything, made me still more fretfully anxious.

I was in Grosvenor Square early the following morning, and burst into my mother's room while she was putting a little suspicion of something rosy upon her face.

"Good gracious me, Elsie!" she exclaimed in amazed vexation, as I threw myself into a chair, "you should indeed cultivate a little repose. You really alarm me with your impulsive movements."

I made no answer. I was not in a humor for repartee of any kind. I waited as quietly as I could while mamma hurried a little china dish containing red out of sight, fondly imagining, I suppose, that I had not seen it. Then she sat down with a hectic flush on one side of her face.

"Domestic troubles, of course," she said, satirically.

"Of course," I replied, with equal satire.

"Well?"

"You said you would help me when I needed your services. I need them now," I replied.

My mother meditated. I could see that she was unwilling to assist me.

She dreaded anything happening which might give the matter publicity. In a word, she was afraid of me, and I admit, not without reason.

"I do not like interfering between man and wife," she began tentatively.

But I was equal to the occasion. The avalanche had started on its course, and nothing could now stop it.

"Very well," I said with palpably assumed indifference, "if you will not aid me in a matter concerning my happiness, I shall leave my husband at once."

As I said, my indifference was palpably assumed, but my mother was one of those who cannot see a pin's point below the surface. The random shot took effect.

"You will do nothing of the kind," she said, severely. "I beg of you, Elsie, to do nothing rash. You will bring my gray hairs with sorrow to the grave," tearfully.

She had employed that expression ever since I could remember, and its dramatic force was impaired by old age. When I used to spoil my frocks at school, when I said rude things, when I insulted my governess, or when I overdrew my weekly allowance — errors with which she was always made acquainted — I was ever threatened with bringing her gray hairs in sorrow to the grave.

She walked to her *secretaire*, and sat down. Then, taking a sheet of note paper with a crest and monogram of enormous proportions, she scribbled a few lines in a bold, back-hand. Folding the sheet, she placed it in a heavily monogrammed envelope, which she left open as she handed it to me. It was addressed to Octavius Rickaby, Esq., Holborn Viaduct.

"Go there," she said, shortly.

"Who is Octavius Rickaby?" I asked feebly.

My mother smiled contemptuously. "Of course you wouldn't know," she said. "Mr. Rickaby is a very clever private detective — or rather the head of an admirably conducted private detective office. He conducts a great many society cases" — sinking her voice to a whisper — "in fact I could name several of my friends whom he has helped. Of course, Elsie, if you make a fool of yourself, and fail to put him in possession of every detail of your case — every detail, mind — you must not be surprised if he fails. If you make a confidant of him, he will be of very material assistance, in fact your husband will not be able to wink unless you know it. He is reasonable, and, my dear, he is perfectly upright. He will never trouble you after you have settled his bill."

My heart sank within me. The word detective had an awful significance in my mind. In fact, I think I would as soon have invoked the aid of Mephistopheles. Detectives always suggested murders and abductions and burglaries to me. A great many people will doubtless sympathize with this feeling.

My mother was "eyeing" me. "You do not intend to consult Mr. Rickaby, I see plainly," she said. "You will be sorry for it one of these days."

She might be right. After all, a detective might be of great service, and something must be done. "I will see Mr. Rickaby, and at once," I declared, rising with determination. "I am much obliged to you, mother. I am sorry to have disturbed you," I said, really becoming cheerful as I resolved upon immediate action; "I know I am an awful nuisance. Now go on with your dressing." I meant painting, but accuracy at times is detestable.

I drove at once to Mr. Rickaby's office in Holborn Viaduct, and was soon in front of a large glass door with the words "Octavius Rickaby" in gleaming black letters staring me in the face. I did not dare to stop and think for one moment. I walked straight in, just as my excitement, born of my eagerness to act, was wearing away like the effect of a much abused drug. I found myself in a neat little office, comfortably furnished, and not at all murderous or penny-dreadful looking. A polite young clerk, in a blue tie and a jovial face, which he seemed perpetually endeavoring to harmonize with the solemnity of his position, received me.

"Please take my card and this letter to Mr. Rickaby," I said, trying to appear as indifferent as though it were part of the daily routine of my life to consult with private detectives.

Of course I expected to be kept waiting. I ignorantly classed detectives with doctors and lawyers and editors, who are always "very busy just now," or if they are not, they pretend to be for the sake of appearances. I was agreeably surprised when Mr. Rickaby said he would see me at once. No, there could be no humbug about that man.

The great Octavius was stout and rubicund — another favorable point with me. No one could have looked less mysterious, and more matter of fact. I believe I half expected to enter his presence with an "open sesame," and to behold two or three imps of darkness skipping about with a caldron between them. He rose as I entered, placed a chair for me, and leaned back in his own cosy, cushioned seat.

"Tell me everything, Mrs. Ravener," said Mr. Rickaby suavely, "no one comes to see me unless he has something to tell. Consider me your doctor or your lawyer. Explain your case, and I will diagnose it."

He said all this in rather a fragmentary manner, expecting me to begin, and uttering each new sentence as he noticed that I remained silent.

He encouraged me by his patience and well-bred demeanor. I told him my story, — at least as much as I could of it. I omitted the fact that Arthur left me a few hours after our wedding. Mr. Rickaby remained silent for some moments after I had finished. Then he asked me if I had taxed Arthur with neglect. I told him I had done so in a very vigorous manner.

"You suspect that you have a rival?" he asked, looking at me keenly.

"What am I to think?"

"Have you ever discovered any letters or papers in your husband's possession that would lead you to such a belief?"

"I have not tried to discover any," I said.

"Will you do so?"

I promised that I would, but begged him not to wait for any possible discoveries on my part before he began proceedings in the matter.

"You have not told me everything, Mrs. Ravener." Mr. Rickaby said this with such an air of certainty that I was dumfounded. He had not removed his eyes from my face during the progress of my story, or during the time he had interrogated me.

"I have told you all — all I — I can tell you," I said in a low tone, averting my head. Still those eagle eyes were rivetted upon me. They seemed to burn into my soul. I was disconcerted and rose hastily.

"Do not stare at me so," I said angrily, walking to the window.

"I beg your pardon, Mrs. Ravener," he remarked quietly, "I am sorry to annoy you. Sit down." I sat down. "You know," playing musingly with a paper-knife, "I often have customers who tell me all they can — like you," he said, "so I have to adopt other means to learn the information withheld. I read it in their faces."

"Then — ?" I began furiously.

"You need not trouble to tell me any more," he said quietly. "It is not necessary."

I cannot describe my sensations. They were too painful to be recognizable in pen and ink. My face burned and my lips were parched. I was almost sorry I had come. But the worst was over, and I must bring this loathsome interview to an end.

"Do you think that — that," I hated to use the horrible expression that I had heard from my mother's lips — "there is a woman in — in the case?"

"It is possible," he said indefinitely.

"Possible!" I echoed in surprise. "What do you mean?"

"Mrs. Ravener," said Mr. Rickaby, "I will not express an opinion; I have no right to do so. I will possess myself of all the information I can. I will find out where your husband goes."

"You will?" I exclaimed joyfully. "Then, Mr. Rickaby, if you will do that you can leave the rest to me. Just find out for me where he goes, and I will then see what it will be best for me to do. Leave me to discover who the woman is. I — I should like to know — exclusively."

I told the truth. I did not want even a detective to possess himself of all my husband's secrets. To my surprise Mr. Rickaby seemed relieved.

"You will do this," I asked, "without going any farther?"

"Most willingly," he replied, "I will obey your instructions to the letter. It is to my interest to do so." That satisfied me.

CHAPTER 16

I returned quietly home — that is to say, I was quiet when I reached Tavistock Villa. The interval between my departure from the office of Mr. Octavius Rickaby and my arrival in Kew was spent in the tedious process of schooling myself to be what I was not, and never could be — cold and stony. I felt that everything depended upon the systematic manner in which I conducted my investigation. If I gave the reins to my impulsiveness, I knew I should ruin my case.

My case! How I hated the sound of the words. The love I had brought to my wedded life had resolved itself into a subject for detectives; the husband, whom a few months back I had sworn at the altar to love and honor and obey, had become a suspect, whose conduct must be investigated; the promise of wedded felicity had degenerated into the certainty of — a case.

I might desist even now in my attempt to understand my situation. If I did so I could live comfortably, even luxuriously to the end of my days. I was rich, and could consequently make as many friends as I chose; I was intelligent — passably so — and could interest myself in the current events of the day. I was young — ah! that was it. Why was I young? Alas! I needed love, sympathy and respect. I was womanly in spite of my eccentricities, which were those of an ignorant, obstinate girl. What woman, young and impulsive, would consent to accept a situation such as that which had been thrust upon me — or into which I had voluntarily stepped, if you will, — for I do not attempt to defend myself?

No, I would not suffer such humiliation. "Let this be the last of my scruples," I said to myself as I dressed for dinner. "Let me know exactly what stands between me and my husband's love. It may possibly be removed, and then —." I loved Arthur desperately. If I could only have hated him, how much better would it have been for me — and for him.

"Madame is feverish," said Marie, suddenly, as she watched me in my efforts to beautify myself with those fine feathers which are correctly supposed to make fine birds.

Her words gave me a shock. I looked in the glass. Yes, I was feverish. My cheeks were burning. There was a hectic red upon each. Evidently I had not succeeded in schooling myself into composure.

"What can I do, Marie?" I asked helplessly. "I do not want to have red cheeks."

Marie looked rather surprised, but her French experience thus appealed to, did me excellent service. At the end of ten minutes the color of my countenance was beautifully normal. The hectic spots had disappeared, at least from sight.

I went down to the dining room to eat my hateful dinner with Arthur. He was in a hopelessly conventional good humor. I succeeded — admirably, I thought — in emulating his complacence. To show the effect of my determination to keep from my husband any suspicion of my thoughts and actions, I chatted pleasantly upon a variety of subjects — the hackneyed aggressiveness of Lord Randolph Churchill; the new comic opera at the Savoy; the coming concert at St. James' Hall; Lady Toadyby's costume at the Queen's drawing-room; the accounts of Sardou's new play in Paris, with Bernhardt in the title role and — yes! I did it — the latest divorce case, minus the details, of course.

I read everything, understood nearly all that I read, focussed it in my mind, and you see was prepared to present it in good evening dress as an accessory to the dinner of my lord and master. I consider I did bravely. I had never done better. Arthur looked up thoroughly pleased. He little knew that beneath my coat — the coat that Marie put upon my cheeks — two scarlet spots were burning, and that my soul sickened of Lord Randolph Churchill, the Savoy Theatre, St. James' Hall, Lady Toadyby and all the rest of it.

Dinner was over — thank goodness!

"Are you going out to-night, Arthur?" I asked carelessly.

"Yes, Elsie, I — I — think so. Why?"

I had long ceased to interest myself in his actions as far as he could see. He had, therefore, a right to feel rather surprised when I questioned him on the subject now.

"Nothing," I answered vaguely.

"Can I do anything for you?"

"Oh, no, thank you." I was so amiable that he was more taken aback. "I must be careful," I said to myself.

As I vouchsafed no further remark, he left me, and half an hour afterwards I heard the front door close behind him.

Now, then, if I could only aid Detective Rickaby in any way. I had several long hours before me, with nothing more inviting than a novel which had been recommended to me by dear Miss Euphemia Dasy, and which I knew I should hate, with which to distract myself.

I went at once to Arthur's study, at least as far as the door, which I found locked. I shook it rather severely, in the silly hope that it would yield to such inducements. The chivalrous and interesting James happened to pass me at the time. He cast a look of intense surprise in my direction.

"You can't get in," he said with a grin.

"So I perceive," I remarked with affected resignation, walking slowly away as James departed for the lower regions. I slipped on a big straw hat, ran into the garden, and surveyed the prospect of effecting an entrance into my husband's sanctum from that point. It was not so hopeless. The room had a large window, not more than three feet from the ground, opening into the garden. The window was shrouded with thick curtains, so that it was impossible to see from the garden into the room.

With supreme satisfaction I noticed that the window was unlocked. My course was not left long undecided. It may not have been a particularly ladylike, but it was a vigorous one. I sprang upon the window sill, stood up, and very soon saw the glass obstacle raised sufficiently to permit my entrance into the apartment.

Arthur's sanctum was a rather large room, divided by heavy plush portières into two. That in which I now stood was fitted up comfortably as a writing room. There was an oak desk; one of those delightful leather-cushioned reading chairs which adjust themselves so amiably to the various positions of the most exacting body; a teeming book-case, a music canterbury filled with music, and other useful articles of furniture. There were some charming pictures upon the wall and, in a word, the apartment was evidently that of a man of refinement. Bitterly, I acknowledged that fact to myself, and thus began a little logical process of reasoning which rendered me all the more miserable. Arthur was a man of refinement — he must be; there could be no use denying it; he appreciated what was refined, and despised the vulgar and the common — his room showed that. He did not appreciate me — therefore I could not be refined; he despised me — therefore I was vulgar and common. The fallacy of this reasoning is of course very evident, but it was not evident to me at that time. Can you wonder at it?

I had sunk into this reading chair, and was evidently forgetting the real object of my intrusion. I had not come here to meditate. Heaven knows, I had ample time and opportunities for that pastime elsewhere.

I pushed back the plush portières, and stood in the back portion of Arthur's sanctum. It was fitted up as a bedroom. There was a large brass bedstead, a wash-stand, closets for clothes. So, when my husband did not spend the night out — and I had imagined he always did so — this was where he slept. It was rather a curious notion — but I had come to the conclusion that Arthur was rather a curious man. I wondered why he had objected to my visiting his sanctum. Surely he must have been aware that I would have preferred knowing he was in the house than supposing him out of it. Then a number of odious ideas came rushing into my head to bewilder me with the hideous probability that they were facts.

Could I discover no evidence against him without the aid of detectives? I went into the first half of the room, and tried the oak desk. The keys were in it — thank goodness! My lord had evidently grown careless, in the belief that he had an obedient little fool of a wife who would never dare to disobey his slightest behest. Ah! he made a mistake. I remembered my wedding day, and my mild, dutiful pleading to be allowed to inspect my husband's rooms. "They are in great disorder, Elsie," he had said. "You had better not venture into them." And my laughing rejoinder had been, "I believe you're a Bluebeard, Arthur, and that the bodies of a dozen preceding Mrs. Ravener's lie festering in that room." I opened the oak desk. It was filled with neatly arranged papers. I examined them all carefully. Alas; they were fearfully uninteresting. Old letters from his parents — I did not read them; literary efforts with the "returned with thanks," marked in tell-tale prominence; bills paid and unpaid, and similar documents of an equally useless description, as far as I was concerned. I went through them all with trembling fingers, dreading and hoping to find some incriminating papers. I was just about to leave the desk, when it suddenly occurred to me that I had missed opening one of the little drawers. I returned to my task, opened the drawer, and came across a little file of receipted bills. I had discovered so many already that I saw no use in examining them. Something prompted me however to glance at them.

They were monthly rent receipts. I read: "Received from Mr. Arthur Ravener the sum of twelve pounds for one month's rent in advance, for the furnished house, No. 121 Lancaster Road, Notting Hill, London, W., due 1st inst. Received payment, B. J. Smith."

How could that interest me? Arthur had probably lived in Lancaster Road, Notting Hill, at one period of his existence. I saw no reason why he should not have done so.

My eyes fell upon the date of the uppermost receipt. The papers dropped from my hands. I started back in terror.

The last twelve pounds acknowledged by Mr. B. J. Smith had been paid for the use of No. 121 Lancaster Road, during this month — this very month of May. Arthur had a perfect right to those premises at the present moment. He might be there now.

Oh! I saw it all now clearly before me. Tavistock Villa was the home of Arthur's neglected, despised wife; No. 121 Lancaster Road, Notting Hill, was the abode of his mistress. He loved her so well, that he could sacrifice his reputation for her. Perhaps he brought her occasionally to the room in which I now stood. To no other part of the house did he dare to take her. Over Tavistock Villa his hated wife reigned; her supremacy must not be called into question. Even then I felt a spasm of pity for Arthur. He was kind to me after all. He consulted my wishes, he gratified them, he was good and brotherly. And how difficult such a course of action must have been to him, when he daily and hourly had the image of a dearly beloved one in his mind. I loved Arthur dearly; I could not have shown the amount of endurance to another man that Arthur manifested to me. As I said, I felt a spasm of pity for Arthur. The spasm was soon over, and in its place a fury of bitterness swept over me. Who was the wretch who could take a husband so shamelessly from his wife? How did she dare to do such a thing? Had she so little knowledge of her own sex as to suppose that she would remain undiscovered very long? Did she not dread that discovery, or tremble at the inevitable meeting with an insulted and indignant wife?

I suddenly remembered where I was — in his room, and possibly in hers. I made haste to leave it. I was anxious to start for Notting Hill that moment, while the fever of animosity was burning so fiercely within me.

The cool night air calmed me somewhat. I reflected upon the inadvisability of such a hasty course. I had put my case in the hands of an able detective. I had better wait at least until I heard from him. He had asked me to try and discover any letters or papers in my husband's possession, that would lead me to the belief that I had a rival. I had been successful, I thought. Mr. Rickaby had promised to let me know where my husband went each night. I would wait until I heard from him.

I did not have to wait long. Two days later a gentleman called to see me. He would not disclose his business to James. He must see Mrs. Ravener. It was a special agent of Mr. Rickaby's private detective bureau. He had come to inform me that he had tracked my husband for two nights to — I almost laughed as he gave the address — No. 121 Lancaster Road, Notting Hill, W.

"I will go there myself," I said mentally, "I will see him in the house. I will see her — and then —" well, subsequent events should take care of themselves.

CHAPTER 17

It was a dark, dismal sort of an evening. A small provoking rain was falling, the trees dripped incessantly, and the mud in the Kew thoroughfares was horribly and consistently thick. I sat at the window of Tavistock Villa, watching the men returning from the city to their quiet, suburban homes. I wondered if they were glad to free themselves from the much maligned atmosphere of London for this invigorating air, or if they would have preferred the metropolis, with all its unhealthy faults, to the sedate and monotonous wholesomeness of Kew.

I would sooner live ten years in the city than fifty years in the country. I hate the balmy atmosphere of rurality; I loathe the suburban surroundings. Give me the city with its life, its motion, its meaning, its excitement. I could not sympathize with rural man.

> "Fixed like a plant on his peculiar spot,
> To draw nutrition, propagate — and rot."

We had just dined. In a few moments I should doubtless see my husband set out for the city, and I had made up my mind that after having given him a good hour's start, I would follow him. I had matured no plans. The only thing I had decided upon doing was gaining admittance to No. 121 Lancaster Road, and then suddenly confronting the guilty couple. I would not permit any one to announce me. If Arthur in his unhallowed household kept servants, I would dispense with their aid. I would confound my husband and his paramour; I would glory in his trembling confusion, and gloat over the irremediable, hopeless guilt in which I had surprised him.

I was a jealous woman, goaded to action. There is nothing more dangerous in the animal kingdom.

I did not have to wait long for my husband's departure. I saw him hurry out into the wet, uncomfortable night, with a protecting umbrella above his head. He had merely uttered a conventional "good-night" to me, when he left the dining room. I believe he now imagined that I had settled down into the placid daily enactment of the role of an injured wife. I had fretted at first, protested, even rebelled, but now it was all over; the uselessness of such revolt had become apparent. I am convinced that those were his ideas.

I rang the bell for Marie. "Bring me my long cloak, hat and veil," I ordered; "I am going up to London at once."

"At once!" echoed Marie in surprise, "this wet night?"

"Yes," I replied impatiently, "if any one should call, you can say I have gone — Oh, anywhere."

"To Madame, your mother — to Grosvenor Square?"

"Exactly," I replied, happily untruthful. No one would call, but it was best to be on the safe side.

I covered my face with a dark veil, the hackneyed device of the mysterious woman. I did this because I was afraid I might be recognized on my way to London. I did not want tongues to wag, at least until I gave them an unqualified right to do so. I was dressed long before it was advisable to start, and threw myself into an arm-chair in the drawing-room, waiting for the minutes to pass. I was wonderfully calm, and rejoiced at that fact. Angry people generally get the worst of it in this world. Quiet wrath does more effective work than an ebullition of fury.

Half an hour later I was in the damp night air, ploughing my way through the mud. I had decided that I would go to Notting Hill by the democratic Underground Railway. So I walked as quickly as I could to the Kew station, which was not far from Tavistock Villa. I had not very long to wait for the arrival of the train. It soon came roaring into the station. I ensconced myself comfortably in a first-class carriage, and threw myself lazily back in its blue cushioned seat.

I was not alone. Two young men sat opposite to me, and to my dismay I recognized Archie Lucknow and Melville Potterby, two detestable society whipper-snappers, whose hideous mission on earth, it seemed to me, was to persecute the gentler sex with attention. Thank goodness they did not recognize me through my veil. I had no particular anxiety to be seen on the road to London at eight o'clock at night, and alone.

"I can't help thinking, dear boy," Mr. Lucknow was saying in a low tone, "how deucedly uncharitable you are. Now you brand young Honeyworth with a mark of Cain, in sheer wilfulness. You have no evidence to substantiate what you say. It is cruel, positively it is, my dear boy. I am not a very straight-laced fellow, as you know, Potterby, but hang it all, if I care to hear this kind of thing."

"It is true, nevertheless," said Mr. Potterby, imperturbably. "No evidence is necessary. Eyes are evidence in this case."

"Well, we will drop the subject. You see how mistaken you were in the case of Arthur Ravener. You had branded him — everybody had, in fact. His name was on the lips of all fellows. He was shunned. What happened? He married; tongues ceased wagging, and now there is not a fellow in the crowd that maligned him, who would not be glad to apologize for his brutality."

Mr. Lucknow came to a pause. Oh! if they would continue talking! If they could only imagine how vitally interesting to me their conversation was! Perhaps it was just as well they could not imagine this, however.

"I would not apologize to Arthur Ravener," said Mr. Potterby in the same low tones, which, however, were distinctly audible to me.

"Then you are not the fellow I thought you" — very severely.

"Sorry, my dear boy, but can't help it. Before I apologize to Ravener, I'd like to know Mrs. Ravener's side of the story. People may have ceased talking. Ravener's marriage was always, in my opinion, brought about solely with that object in view. And he married a very young girl, as ignorant as a new-born babe."

"She was a silly little fool," said Mr. Lucknow, rather savagely.

I had snubbed him with great persistency, so I could not complain at his vehemence.

"Yes, and you know —" What Mr. Lucknow knew I could not learn, as Mr. Potterby's voice sank into a whisper which was hopelessly beyond my scope. They said no more. What I had heard simply whetted the edge of my curiosity. I wondered what Arthur had done, before I knew him, to cause gossip. It seemed to me that a quiet, refined young man, such as I previously supposed him to be, could not have given any very serious offence.

Perhaps, however, it was this very *liaison*, which I was now bent upon breaking, that had set his friends talking. That must be it. This horrible woman had been his bane. People had discovered her existence, and of course no young man in this enlightened century would recognize Arthur's unsavory life. I supposed that although the youths of to-day were silly and tedious they were at least strictly moral.

"Notting Hill."

Here I was at my destination. I alighted hurriedly, not daring to look at my fellow travelers, and was soon in the street. Now for No. 121 Lancaster Road.

I had no idea where it was, but a kindly policeman informed me that it was not more than seven minutes' walk from the station. He spoke the truth. Lancaster Road was so easy to find that even I could make no mistake about it.

When I had reached the thoroughfare, and commenced my search for No. 121, all the semi-jauntiness which I had called to my assistance, left me. The thought of my mission, and indignation at the causes of it, filled my mind. I began to dread my task.

Lancaster Road seemed to be deserted at this early hour. It was only nine o'clock. Not a solitary person had I passed yet. The big grey houses towered gloomily on each side of me. Bright lights shone from the windows, probably illuminating those happy homes which are in no city more plentiful than in London.

I was counting the numbers, my heart palpitating as I slowly approached that at which I should stop. I felt half inclined to go back at this eleventh hour, and live as I had been living these past few months, contentedly. No! content was no longer possible for me. I could not meet my husband again until I had seen my rival; and until he knew that I had seen her.

I stopped in front of a small gray house involuntarily. I seemed to feel instinctively, even before I had looked, that it was No. 121, and I was right. There were the three figures that to me made so sinister a combination, engraved on a little brass plate on the door. Then I took a leisurely view of the house in which Arthur chose to live, apart from his wife. It was a little, two story, gray-stone house, old fashioned, and rather unusual in its appearance. There was a tiny green grass plot in front, separated from the road by an iron railing, in which was a small, unlatched gate. It would have been a very ordinary looking house in a provincial city, but it was not at all suggestive of London. I looked at it with genuine curiosity, which for a moment swallowed up my anger. It was a very inexpensive place, but, love — guilty and illegitimate, but still love — dwelt there. Arthur preferred that simple little house, with one to whom he could give his heart, than the costly beauty of Tavistock Villa, with the wife whom he despised.

I brushed away the tears that rose unbidden to my eyes, with angry hands. This was no place for sentimental regret. I was here to act, and act I would.

There seemed to be only one room in the house which was lighted, and that was situated to the left of the front door. A light, reddened by warm, thick curtains, shone from its windows. Darkness reigned everywhere else. There was no light even in the hall. The glass above the front door looked black.

How was I to gain admittance? If I rang the rusty looking front door bell it would probably alarm them both. They were doubtless prepared in case of surprise of that kind, and such a course would certainly place me at a disadvantage. It was not likely that they kept servants, who might in the future prove unfortunate witnesses against them.

What could I do? I pushed open the gate and walked towards the stone steps leading to the front door. A thin iron grating separated me from the basement entrance. I touched it, and I could feel the gritty rust on my fingers. This basement entrance was in all likelihood never used now. I shook the grating slightly. Imagine my surprise, my joy, when it yielded without any difficulty to my gentle persuasion, and stood open. I entered immediately, only too pleased to be shut out from the sight of any passer-by, or of any policeman, to whom my position would have appeared rather strange.

I shut the iron gate behind me, descended two steps, and walked into the kitchen. It was in utter darkness. Not an object in front of me could I see. I groped my way about, feeling distinctly uneasy. Whether this kitchen were ever used, or whether it were in ruins I could not tell. I would have given a sovereign for a match — for one moment's light.

I presumed that this house was built like most houses, so I did not despair of finding my way upstairs. I could not discover the door leading to the basement hall, nor that by which I had entered. I grew frightened. The awful idea dawned upon me that I might have to stay where I was until daylight. I almost shrieked as I stumbled against some resisting object. It was nothing more alarming than a chair. I sat down and tried to quiet myself. My heart was throbbing wildly, and I could feel violent pulsations in my temples. They might hear me upstairs. The noise I made might alarm them. They would leave the house. I should be its sole tenant, and —

I started up. I would not terrify myself by such thoughts. By a mighty effort I collected myself as it were, and began my ridiculous hunt for the door with more deliberation. I was rewarded by success.

I had gained the stairs. I walked slowly upwards, found the door at the top of the stairs open — what should I have done had it been locked? — and stood in the hall. Now I could see the door of the room for which I was bound. The hall was in absolute darkness, but faint streaks of light, which would have been unnoticed under less obscure circumstances, revealed to me the whereabouts of the guilty couple. It was impossible now that they could escape me. I must see them. As this certainty forced itself upon me, my excitement became all the more intense.

I did not dare to move. From behind the hall door where I had retreated, I surveyed the situation. Six or eight steps would take me to the room where I could discover all. The door would in all probability be unlocked. From whom had they to fear intrusion? They were safely secluded — or they fancied they were — in their own castle. I had only to suddenly open the door and face them.

My courage began to fail me. My position was an unenviable one. I wondered how matters would be three hours from now — if everything would be settled; if I should have discovered all. Then I carefully lacerated my feelings by reviewing events connected with my unhappy marriage. I pictured my absurd scruples. I had heard that evening that I was a silly little fool. That was the truth. I was silly, I was unworthy —

Without concluding my self-condemnation, I rushed from my hiding-place to the door of the room whence came the light. Without hesitating one moment I turned the handle, and giving a mighty push, which was absolutely unnecessary, I entered.

The sudden light coming upon my eyes, accustomed for the last half hour to utter darkness, blinded me. I could see nothing. Then two figures abruptly moving stood out before me in the glare. My dazzled inability lasted but a few seconds. Then before me I saw my husband, pale as death, trembling, his eyes wide with amazement, advancing towards me. I waved him off, standing with my back to the door. The room was a small one. At the other end of it was his companion.

The amazement of Arthur was not as great as that which must have been visible on my own face, as I beheld, ghastly in his pallor, but still boldly defiant — Captain Jack Dillington.

I burst into hysterical laughter.

CHAPTER 18

Captain Dillington and my husband seemed unable to utter a word. My laughter did not last long. Quick as a flash of lightning came the thought to me that I was in a very ridiculous situation. After having shown my hand in a most hopeless manner, I had discovered my husband *tête-à-tête* with — the abandoned woman I had pictured, the wanton destroyer of my domestic happiness I had imagined? No, with his bosom friend — the friend who long before I had come upon the scene had played the role of Damon to Arthur's Pythias.

Of course, as I stood before them, my hysterical laughter silenced, my breast heaving with emotion, and the fever spot burning on each cheek, they knew why I was there, what I suspected. But was it merely my sudden arrival that was responsible for the death-like pallor of my husband's face? Why did Captain Dillington assume such a palpably defiant air, if there were no reason why he should defy me?

Such thoughts coursed through my mind much quicker than they can flow from my pen. After all had I shown my hand? Yes and no. I remembered that my mother had suggested Captain Dillington as the medium by which my husband communicated with his paramour. Why not assume that, in default of anything more substantial? That Captain Dillington was in some way responsible for my husband's despicable conduct, I was now as convinced as that I saw him before me. He had some influence over Arthur Ravener, the weaker vessel. This idea gained complete supremacy over me. It was then with Captain Dillington that I would deal — this deadly friend whom I would hold responsible.

I stood before the door, as I said, and simply stared at the two men, after my laughter had been subdued. Arthur grasped the back of a chair, and stood looking at me, as though he were obliged to look. Captain Dillington took a seat with a mighty show of composure, and awaited developments.

Arthur was the first to speak, and he did so gaspingly, "Why — why — d-did you c-come here, Elsie?" he asked.

"Why — why — did I come here?" I repeated mockingly.

"It is quite natural that your wife should be here, Arthur," said the Captain in his most elaborate manner. "She had suspicions — most natural, my dear fellow. She was jealous. You have no right to complain. Jealousy, as I look upon it, is merely an outcome of love. Is that not so, Mrs. Ravener?" (turning to me) "You — pardon my curiosity — thought that you would find a — a — well — a lady with your husband?"

The leer with which he accompanied these remarks was too indescribably repulsive to analyze. I determined to contain myself as much as possible.

"It is with no lady that I have business here," I said, with a miserable attempt at loftiness. "It is with you, Captain Dillington, and with no other."

I watched the effect of these words, shot at random. It was undeniable. Captain Dillington gasped. The blood left his cheeks and his lips. He was taken utterly aback. I had evidently started in the right direction. He must be the go between, but as I had seen no woman, it was not necessary that I should mention one.

"You are surprised, Captain Dillington?" I demanded quietly, though I was trembling with agitation.

"I — I simply do not understand you."

"Do you understand me, Arthur?" I asked, turning to my husband.

"I — I will not listen to your suspicions," began my husband, with such a weak attempt at resistance that it sounded more like an entreaty. "Elsie, you have no right here. You — you betray w-want of confidence in — in me. I will not stay —"

"You will!" I cried, placing my back to the door. "You shall not leave this room. Don't dare to try it," I continued, losing all my calmness, as a tide of anger swept over me, overwhelming caution. "Captain Dillington, if you attempt to stir from the room" (he had made a step forward) "I will open the window and rouse the neighbors. I don't mind scandal, perhaps, as much as you and he do. I can explain my presence here. You cannot."

"This is your husband's house," said Captain Dillington, angrily. "He has invited me here. I have nothing to explain. While I was a guest at your house, it was easy to see that I was not welcome. Your husband saw it. I saw it. So as we have always been great friends, he chose to invite me where there was no danger of my being insulted. That explains my presence here, I think."

"No, it does not. That does not explain your presence here, and you know it. You know it too, Arthur Ravener," I cried, turning to the helplessly distressed object all in a heap on the back of a chair. "Do you think, Captain Dillington, that I will continue to tolerate the conduct of this man, who left me on my wedding day, and who kept you, a hated guest — yes, you are right, a hated, detested, loathed guest — in our house, when it should have been sacred to ourselves? Do you think that because I am young and igno-rant — no, I am no longer ignorant — that I will bear with this? You know very little of women if you can suppose it. You probably thought you were dealing with a helpless fool. Let me tell you that you have been watched by detectives for the past week, at my instigation, and that I know all."

It was a desperate game of bluff, but it met with triumphant success. As I paused for want of breath, I saw that Captain Dillington was literally unable to speak.

He had warmed himself into anger a few moments before, but in the shock of this great surprise, it had died away. My husband had averted his face, and was looking at the wall with very great persistence. So far the field was my own. I had worked myself into a great passion, and these hits had not been premeditated.

"I will live no longer as I have been doing," I went on, "I have discov-ered enough. I have hoped against hope. I have dreaded this hour. But it has come, and I will not fear it. I have told you that I do not mind scandal, and I shall not hesitate to apply to the Divorce Court."

Captain Dillington pressed his hand to his heart. My husband came towards me, and took my hand.

"Elsie," he said, "do not — do not, for the love of Heaven speak like this. You cannot mean what you say. You cannot, you would not do it?"

"I would," I exclaimed, furiously, "I would do it. You have tried my patience. I have no interest in you any more. I gave you all, and you have treated me with contempt. I will not live with you any longer. I will not — I could not. The thought of your infamy would rise up before me at all times. I will be free, and you shall, you must be free, too."

I burst into tears, I could not help it. After all, I had done bravely, and I was not made of stone. I had ceased to wonder who was the woman in the case. I had succeeded in confounding the two men so well without her aid, that I felt comparatively satisfied. In fact I did not want to know who she was.

Captain Dillington recovered himself some what when he saw my tears. "Mrs. Ravener forgets that in a divorce suit a great many things must be proved. You say you have had us watched by detectives. May I ask if they have discovered the identity of the co-respondent?"

The coolness with which he spoke almost amused me. I laughed amidst my sobs. "I — I have all the evidence I need," I managed to say. "Suppose," with an attempt at mirth, "I — I should make you co-respondent, Captain Dillington?"

He smiled, but it was with a great effort, I could see.

"Very good, very good," he said, with manifest uneasiness.

"Do not — do not talk like that, Elsie," said Arthur, imploringly. "You will not bring this — this scandal upon us all. You — you did love me, Elsie. I do not believe that I have quite killed your love. You would not ruin me like this. You would not bring disgrace upon your family." He broke down, sobbing.

"The disgrace," I said sternly, feeling contempt for these pitiful arguments, "is brought by you, sir. My character is spotless, as you well know. I have given you every opportunity to avoid scandal, but you failed to suppose that I could do anything but submit to your heartless neglect. You have aroused me. It has taken you twelve months to do it. If you had married a girl who had mixed more with the world, she would not have lived with you one week. I had peculiarities, however, and you thought they would give you an opportunity to carry out your wretched plans without interruption; that is why you married me. I was warned against you — you need not start — but I disregarded the warning, and I have dearly paid for my folly. My punishment has been great, but it shall end from to-day. To-morrow I will leave Tavistock Villa, and I never want to see it again."

I began to button my cloak and gloves. I had said enough. I would now leave them to do exactly what they chose. I had no more interest in my husband, I told myself.

"You are going, Mrs. Ravener?" queried Captain Dillington in a mocking tone, his jeering exuberance once more asserting itself.

"I am going," I said.

Arthur seized his hat, and sprang towards the door. "I will go with you, Elsie," he said in a pleading tone.

"You will not," I exclaimed. "You shall not enter the house — with me, at any rate."

"He has a perfect right to do so," remarked Captain Dillington. "It is his home; you are his wife."

"And you —?" I asked pointedly. My jest about the co-respondent in the case had annoyed him so much before, that I thought I would administer another stab with the same weapon.

He turned away hastily for a moment. "I am his friend," he then said, "and" — boldly — "I am not ashamed of it. We were at college together, and our intimacy has been continued since those days. I will aid Arthur Ravener whenever I can; I will do anything for him. He is my bosom friend, and I am ready to say so before anybody. Now, are you satisfied?"

He snapped his fingers defiantly, but I was not going to allow myself to be beaten. My game of bluff had been successful. Perhaps he was trying the same tactics. He should not succeed.

"As far as you are concerned — perfectly," I said.

I opened the door. Arthur followed me.

"If you persist in coming," I said, "of course you must do so. After all, it does not make much difference; your apartments do not clash with mine."

He winced, but said nothing. He cast a glance, uneasy, suspicious, wretched, at Captain Dillington, and then left the room with me. He opened the front door, and we stepped out into the night air. Captain Dillington remained where we left him. Not another word did he utter.

"Shall I call a cab?" asked Arthur, nervously.

"If you choose," I said carelessly. "You insist upon accompanying me, so that I cannot help myself. Oblige me, however, by not troubling to talk. I have nothing to say. I don't want any explanation. That house," pointing to No. 121 Lancaster Road, "speaks for itself."

He hailed a passing four-wheeler, and we were soon rolling homewards. I buried my face in the cushions, and resolutely declined to think of my grievance during the long, weary ride home. Arthur made no attempt to speak. He stared, in a dazed way, out of the side windows, though he could not have seen much; and so we reached Tavistock Villa.

CHAPTER 19

There is one malady dear to the heart of modern novel-writers. It is helpful, pleasantly dangerous, and yet to be vanquished. Of course I allude to brain fever. Once get your hero into some scrape from which there is no outlet, and you are forced to call upon brain fever for help. He lies dangerously ill for weeks, months; makes several delirious confessions; arises once more the ghost of his former self, and in the meantime, what? All difficulties have been smoothed away, and the eager interest of the unsuspecting reader has been relieved of its keen edge. Brain fever is a boon to the novel-writer, and like all cheap boons it has been woefully abused.

Brain fever, however, is not nearly as frequent in real life as it is in novels. It is fiction's way out of a climax.

I have jotted down these thoughts because I remember they occurred to me during the days which followed the events described in the preceding chapter, when time hung heavily on my hands, and I could settle to nothing.

When we reached Tavistock Villa on that important night, Arthur retired to the rooms he had fitted up for himself, and I went silently to my own apartments. We attempted no explanations. We had no word to say. There was not even an uttered "good-night."

Next morning my husband sent for me, and I went at once to his room. He told me he had not slept all night, except for a few minutes at a time, when he had been awakened by alarming dreams. His face was flushed and his eyes moved constantly. It was easy to see that he was ill.

"Elsie," he said, "if people should call to-day, t-tell them that I — I am indisposed — th-that I cannot see them. You will do this?"

"No one shall disturb you," I promised. "We will have a doctor, presently, for I am afraid you are indeed indisposed."

"Do not send for a doctor," he said, excitedly, "I do not need one. I do not, indeed, Elsie, I assure you."

"You are mistaken," I said, coldly. "I insist upon sending for Dr. White. Perhaps you will allow me to have my own way for once."

He looked at me reproachfully. I felt guilty — as though I were hitting a man when he was down. Dr. White came. He said that Arthur must have been subjected to some long-continued mental anxiety, and that he needed careful nursing. I was not to be unnecessarily alarmed if at times he had hallucinations, such as imagining himself surrounded by enemies, or suspecting that people were plotting to do him harm. His nervous system was run down.

"Your husband has not been living as quietly as he might have done, I infer, Mrs. Ravener?" Dr. White asked rather hesitatingly.

I crimsoned. How could I tell this man that my husband's pursuits were unknown to me? He noticed my confusion.

"Dr. White," I said at last, deliberately, resolved to tell as much as I could, "I see no use in concealment. A medical man must receive strange confidences. The truth is that I know little more about my husband's life than you do. All I can tell you is that during the last year he has spent most of his time out of the house."

"Exactly," with significance. "I thought as much," with sapient consideration; then, "Well, Mrs. Ravener, if you will take my advice, you will forgive everything, and make no allusion whatever to the past. What your husband needs is complete rest and change, and a few months' devotion to him on your part will restore him to you. My dear young lady, this is not an unusual case —"

I started up. "Not unusual?" I interrupted. Then I reflected that all he knew of the case, and all that I intended he should know, might not be unusual.

"Not unusual," he said. "Young men of fortune like your husband, marrying at an early age, cannot break suddenly from old associations, from bachelor friends, from — ah! how do I know? That is why I always say to friends who I hear are about to wed: 'Reflect well, my boy. A wife is exacting. She will call you to account for yourself. All your gay doings must be renounced. A woman gives herself up to you. You must reciprocate.' You love your husband?" he asked, suddenly jerking his voice from an anecdotal crooning to a professional tone.

"Yes," I said in a low voice.

"Then, Mrs. Ravener, it is a case of plain sailing. Try to forget your injuries. Leave this country as soon as you conveniently can, and take your husband with you. What would you think of a trip across the Atlantic to America? It would be the making of you both. If," stammering, "as y-you suspect, and — as — I — suspect, Mr. Ravener — er — has — er — ties — er — here, which he should not have — er — what better means of breaking them could you possibly discover?"

He was right, the scheme was an excellent one. All this time I had been giving way to my indignant anger at my husband's cruel treatment, but I had never thought of attempting to remove him from temptation. Here was I planning separation, divorce and other scandalously revengeful proceedings, when, in reality, perhaps all my husband wanted was a change. He was weak, and he was under the influence of a man with an iron will, I felt sure. Perhaps I might be a little too submissive, but Arthur was my husband and I loved him.

"Dr. White," I said, rising and taking the old man's hand, "I — I thank you, your suggestion is a kind one — so kind and good that — that — it would not have occurred to me."

I buried my face in my hands. Yes, I was too vindictive. Even this morning, when I had seen Arthur feverish and oppressed, I could not forget the past few months. I thought only of my own wrongs. Who knew but that Arthur was as much sinned against as sinning? In this world too much charity is impossible.

"Mrs. Ravener," said Dr. White, pretending not to see my tears, "I have left a prescription on the little table in your husband's room. See that it is made up. I will look in again. You have nothing to be alarmed about. Your husband will recover, and — my dear — I hope that·you will both, like the good people in the fairy tales, live happily ever after. Now, now — no tears," he said, placing his hand on my bowed head. "Be as cheerful as you possibly can. I always say that my prescriptions should be diluted with cheerfulness. Ah! it is a wonderful thing."

While he was talking, I rose and dried my eyes. By the time he had finished, I could smile at him. He was satisfied and left me. As he went from the room, James entered with a card. "The gentleman is waiting," he said, with a quick look in my face.

The card was that of Captain Dillington. I tore it up savagely, forgetful of the servant's presence, and flung the pieces into the empty fireplace.

"Tell Captain Dillington," I said, "that Mr. Ravener is ill this morning and cannot be seen. If he calls again, tell him the same thing. James," approaching him, "do me a favor — it will indeed be a great one. Never permit Captain Dillington to set his foot within this house again. You will do this?"

"Yes, ma'am," he said, pleased at being asked to confer a favor, "I will. The Captain tried to brush past me this morning, but I heard the master tell you not to let people see him. I was in the room at the time, you know. So I just pushed the Captain back. He gives me a terrible look, but looks don't hurt any one. 'I'll take your card,' says I, and when he sees that I mean it he hands me one."

"You have done well," I said.

I was determined that Captain Dillington should see Arthur no more. Exactly what was the understanding between them, I did not know, but that the elder man was partly accountable for the delinquencies of the younger, I was perfectly persuaded. At any rate I would be on the safe side. I would refuse Captain Dillington admittance every time he applied for it, without consulting Arthur.

During the next few days I was constantly in my husband's room. As Dr. White led me to expect, he had hallucinations. He seemed to fancy that some one was pursuing him, but it was impossible to shape his incoherent utterances into any intelligible form. They lasted but for a short time, and left him weak, but entirely rational.

"Arthur," I said on one of these occasions, "I have a proposition to make to you. We have never taken any journey together" — I was going to refer to the lacking honeymoon, but determined to avoid any allusion to the past — "and I should like to go away very much. Suppose we were to take a trip to America?" I watched his face. His eyes fell. He turned away his head.

"It is very far," he said vaguely.

"Yes," I assented cheerfully, "that is why I am so anxious to take the trip. I think a little sail on the herring-pond would do us good," I continued, with an abortive attempt to be funny. "Dr. White said you needed a change."

"When would you want to go?" he asked uneasily.

"Any time, dear" I said. Then, as if the idea had come to me suddenly, "I think it would be best to start at once. Suppose that as soon as you are able to go out, your first ride be to Liverpool?"

He was embarrassed. "I will think it over," he said weakly. He never alluded to my threats of divorce. He seemed to have forgotten all about them. Since he had been ill, I had been kind, and as much like my former self as I possibly could.

Two days passed. Arthur's health was improving rapidly. We could start now at any time he chose to name, but he seemed in no hurry to refer to our American trip.

On the third day, when I tried to enter Arthur's room, I found the door locked. I was alarmed and knocked until my knuckles complained very painfully. I stopped suddenly, arrested by a noise I heard in the room. It could only have been the opening or shutting of the window, but it sounded strangely to me. I knocked again. Arthur hastened to the door and opened it. His face was red, and he seemed agitated. I looked at him in surprise.

"Why did you lock the door?" I asked, not sharply but curiously.

"Why not?" he said with a nervous laugh, "is there any law against it, Elsie?"

"None that I know of," I said, still rather uneasy in my mind. "Were you out in the garden, Arthur?"

"I? No."

"I thought I heard the window open?"

"My dear Elsie," he said, "why should I go into the garden by the window? You forget I am not strong enough yet to jump. If I wanted a walk, I should suggest an airing in a proper way." Arthur's manner was by no means reassuring.

"Then the window was not open?" I asked carelessly.

He hesitated a moment. "No," he replied, "it was not."

The matter was certainly not worth pursuing any further. I could have sworn that I had heard the window shut, but then perhaps my imagination, stimulated by a locked door, may have led me into error.

That night Arthur informed me he would accompany me to America any time I chose. I was delighted, and thought of nothing but the probable success of our journey away from scenes fraught with so many painful associations.

CHAPTER 20

Once away from Kew, and my old spirits reasserted themselves. As we rolled away from Euston to Liverpool's only and original Lime Street, I was as happy as — I was going to say — a newly made bride, but, alas, that hackneyed simile has no meaning for me. Every old corn field we passed delighted me; I made Arthur buy me illustrated papers and fruit at every station, and nearly caused him to miss the train at one halting place because in my insatiable desire for chocolate I sent him forth to the refreshment room.

Arthur was at first inclined to be subdued, as I suppose it was proper he should be, but I soon thwarted his intentions. I was determined that we would both of us forget the past, and start out afresh. I would be as engaging as a maiden yet to be wooed, and he, — well, he should woo me. I was resolved that I would not be wifely. I would consider that we were simply on good terms, and I was going to try hard to make him love me. Pshaw! A fig for the fact that I was really his wife. He would be glad to remember that by and by, I told myself.

So I broke every bit of ice I saw, and long before we had reached Lime Street, he was laughing at my idiotic behavior. We made a couple of fools of ourselves.

I wonder why English people who take railway journeys feel that they must eat as soon as the train starts. It has always caused me a great deal of amusement. On this particular occasion, a phlethoric old matron waited until she had waved her chubby hand at about fifty fond relations on the platform, allowed a tear or two to course portentously down her cheeks, and then sought consolation in her hamper. For the next thirty minutes she was busily engaged in dissecting a chicken. Ugh! how greasy she was at the end of that time. I was rude enough to stare at her, and I presume the poor old soul thought I coveted her chicken. She offered me some. At first I thought of accepting it and going halves with Arthur, but I caught his imploring glance and decided to be abstemious.

Of course we traveled with the usual ruddy-faced Briton, who before he was fifteen minutes out was caught peeping into a little spirit flask. They always amuse me — those exploring tipplers who seem anxious to impress you with the idea that they are merely making a scientific test. I have a detestation for red noses, both male and female, which of course means that I very frequently have one in cold weather — or at least used to do so, until I discovered that perfect French jewel, Marie, my maid. Dear readers, you will never know what comfort is until you have a Gallic "assistant." Of course they are expensive luxuries, but you can economize elsewhere.

My pen runs on. As I think of that delightful trip, coming as it did when life seemed darkest, all my happiness comes back to me, and I write now as I felt then.

As I was not desirous of parading myself, limp and seasick, before a select and fashionable audience, we decided not to patronize a Cunarder, even though it be so rapid. I was not so burningly anxious to be in America. I did not care where I was, so rejoiced was I to be away from London. So we ensconced ourselves meekly on one of the Inman steamers, which was quite good enough for me.

It seemed unnatural, going away without anyone to see us off, especially as nearly every one on board cried farewell to somebody on the tender. I felt hard-hearted because I "sailed away from my native land," without a tear. I tried to be affected, but I couldn't. I wished that I had given the polite little fellow, who had carried my valise for me, half-a-crown extra to cry when the steamer started, and wave his hand to me.

"You are as bad as I am, Arthur," I said, as we stood at the rail and watched the tender taking its farewell-sayers back to the dock. "There's not a solitary tear trickling down your countenance. I'm really vexed with myself, but they won't trickle. I can't help it."

"I am glad of it, Elsie," said Arthur, fervently. I knew he was thinking that they had trickled sufficiently during the past few sad weeks.

"I am not," I persisted in declaring. "It is unseemly to go about with all one's unshed tears while everybody else is lavishly distributing them in all directions."

No sooner had the tender disappeared from sight, and our own anchor had been lifted (isn't that deliciously nautical? I flatter myself it is extremely creditable), than I saw sixteen people — I counted them — rush up to the Captain and ask him if it were going to be "rough." Poor man! I suppose he is overwhelmed in this manner at every trip.

He thought it was going to be one of the finest voyages he had ever made, he said, and the sixteen timid ones went their way rejoicing.

It is the correct thing, nowadays, to be eternally and consistently *blasé*, as my dear mother would say, especially on one's travels. To speak of my transatlantic trip of course makes it at once apparent that I have never been to America before. I admit it, and must also confess that my voyage interested me immensely, and all the more because my expected seasickness was never realized.

To have seen us all in the saloon on the first night was in itself an entertainment. We were all very stiff, and suspicious, and unfriendly, being mostly English, and took our places at the table under protest as it were. We were soon supplied with passenger lists, and before attempting to nourish our bodies we fed our curiosity by wondering "who was who," and trying to "locate" the different passengers.

There were at least a score whose identity we soon discovered. They belonged to that class which an American on board declared to be composed of "chronic kickers — gentlemen who, if they went to Heaven, would vow their halo's didn't fit." They found that their names had been spelled wrong, and complained loudly:

"I made a point of spelling S-m-y-t-h-e and here they have me down as Smith."

"I call it disgusting. They've made me John P. Bodley, when I distinctly remember telling them my name was J. Porterhouse Bodley."

"Oh, Mamma, they've never mentioned Jane. I wanted them to put 'and maid.' How annoying!"

"Why, Eliza! They've actually got us 'J. Rogers, wife and family,' in one line, instead of mentioning each of our names, as I asked them to do."

And so they made themselves known.

The first meal was the only one of which many of the passengers approved. They had made up their minds to be seasick, and seasick they were. One young woman announced that she had been under medical treatment for three days before starting, and that her doctor had advised her after the first meal to go to bed during the rest of the voyage. That such a man should be allowed to practice!

Arthur and I sat at the Captain's table, close by the Captain, which I am told was a great honor. That dignitary seemed to wish us to think so, at any rate. He was full of graceful condescension at first, and three courses had sped quickly away before he favored us with our first nautical story. Of course everyone at the table was convulsed with laughter. It put us all in a good temper, and led us to look upon one another with less suspicion.

After dinner Arthur and I walked up and down deck, talking gaily of our plans. Not a sentimental word passed from my lips; no one could have been more affectionate and sisterly than I was. I firmly believe that he understood and appreciated my efforts. He looked at me gratefully from time to time. That friendliness which had been so oppressive in his manner to me formerly, was not so apparent.

I pictured our return to England, the past forgotten like an ugly dream; the future full of promise; the present given up utterly to the love which though late might overwhelm us with its long delayed delight. As I painted the glowing probabilities on my susceptible mind-canvas, I could not school my voice to the mild, platonic utterances which I felt I must affect. Words of love rose to my lips; I trembled at my own emotion.

"Are you not glad to be — to be here?" I asked him as quietly as I could.

He paused for one moment. Then in a low tone — "Yes," he said.

He was sincere. But there was none of the passion in his voice that I — unhappy girl! — could not keep from mine. He gave me affection in return for love. Well, at any rate, he seemed to be thawing. I had every reason to rejoice.

As I said before, I was not seasick. When we arrived at Queenstown, I recognized the fact that I had slept soundly, and arose in the best of spirits. I found my husband on deck, watching the men carrying the mail-bags on board. He also had slept well, he informed me.

It was a superb day, a bright sky overhead, a lovely green opaque sea around us, while the pretty coast of Ireland, as seen from Queenstown's snug little harbor, completed a most fascinating picture. We were both of us in excellent spirits, and chatted lightly on every subject but that of ourselves. We laughed at the queer old creatures who clambered up the sides of the big ship and cajoled us into purchasing murderous looking blackthorns, bog-oak ornaments of the most funereal type, and other quaintly Hibernian wares. How charming Ireland is — from a distance!

As we left Queenstown, people seemed to have made themselves at home on board, and to have resigned themselves to something more than a week of irrevocable sea. Men who had made their first appearance clad in the height of fashion, were hardly to be known in their hideous-comfortable sea-garments. Traveling caps replaced the shining *chapeau-de-soie;* loose warm ulsters, the daintily fitting overcoats; while time-honored trousers were called into a brief resurrection. The ladies donned their plainest, most unbecoming attire. Any one who had a grudge against any particular dress, wore it. There is little coquetry in attire on shipboard. Woman, from a pictorial point of view at any rate, is at her worst. Perhaps for the first time in her life, she is caught napping, so far as her attire is concerned.

A great number of the feminine passengers installed themselves with graceful invalidism on steamer chairs rug-enveloped. They were so determined to be ill that I should really have sympathized with their disappointment had Neptune declined to affect them as they expected to be affected.

We were soon one big family, united in the common desire of reaching port speedily and safely. I had so many acquaintances before a week was ended, that my days were entirely taken up with them. We had our little scandal society on board, and discussed at afternoon tea those who were not at the table. Womanhood always finds its level, and womanhood is not womanhood without gossip.

The queer things I was told about America on that ship! One portly damsel took me to one side and informed me in a mysterious whisper that clothes were terribly expensive in America, but that I could purchase undergarments for next to nothing. Another American told me that New York houses were so much more civilized than London dwellings, because they all had stoops. What a stoop was, I had no idea. After a time it occurred to me that the houses must be trying to follow the example of the leaning tower of Pisa. That stooped. I received information on all sides, and as my mind was pleasantly blank in regard to the country discovered by Christopher Columbus, I was pounced upon by everybody who wanted to talk.

My husband rarely left my side. He never entered the smoking-room, and kept distinctly aloof from the other men. We were hardly ever alone. With the exception of a half-hour's stroll on deck each evening after dinner, my husband and I never enjoyed a *solitude à deux*. Those brief half hours were devoted to general conversation. We never referred to the troublous period that had preceded our voyage.

I was rather glad that my time was so much occupied by my friend-passengers. I was able to acknowledge very soon the fact that my husband found increasing pleasure in my society. Our after dinner walks, I could see, were very pleasant to him, and at the end of a week conversation grew less general.

One evening he was unusually silent, and I made no effort to talk. We sat looking at the foamy milk-path that marked the course of the ship. I soon felt that his eyes were fastened on my face. I did not speak. My policy was not to attempt to force results in any way.

"Elsie," he said, presently, "some time ago I remember saying to you that perhaps our marriage was a mistake." I started. He went on: "I now believe that it was not. Elsie, no other woman would have been as patient as you have been, or made the sacrifice you have made in — in — really expatriating yourself for my sake. I — I — am very grateful, dear."

"You have nothing to be grateful for," I said, gravely. Then lightly throwing off the sentimental mood to which I would have loved to give sway, "I don't consider this expatriation, this is merely a pleasant voyage, and it is even more delightful than I anticipated."

"It is delightful," he said, seriously.

I imagine our fellow-passengers considered that we were rather eccentric. The men seemed to look down upon Arthur — or at least I thought so. What looked to me like contemptuous glances were cast by them at my husband when he was sitting in the midst of the medley of feminine passengers, who had evidently "taken a fancy" to me. Arthur seemed indifferent to these manifestations, if he noticed them at all. But they aroused in me a feeling of violent indignation. I could have gone up to these whippersnappers and told them that I believed my husband to be better than they were; but perhaps it was lucky I did not adopt this course.

I was quite ready and eager to forgive Arthur everything. I had resolved that not a single allusion to my unknown rival should ever cross my lips, unless, of course, my husband showed himself to be subsequently unworthy of my love, which I did not believe he would do. I had not the faintest curiosity to know who the woman was. In fact I was glad I was absolutely ignorant on the subject. As soon as I felt convinced that our happiness was assured, I had promised myself that I would try to understand the influence which Captain Dillington possessed over my husband, and then gently to withdraw him from it. It was bad. I was quite certain of that.

And so, more happily than I had imagined even in my most sanguine moments, our voyage across the Atlantic was accomplished. We said goodbye to the friends we had made on board as sorrowfully as though we had known them for a lifetime, and prepared to join the busy throng in the American metropolis.

CHAPTER 21

We went to a quiet hotel, "on" Broadway, but far from the noise and bewildering traffic of that turbulent thoroughfare. It was a comfortable, unostentatious little house, not startlingly impressive, like some of the caravansaries miles above us, nor gloomily monotonous like the so-called family hotels where women who are too disgracefully lazy to attend to household duties, and men who are too idiotically weak-willed to protest against this, abide in stupid sloth.

We had a dainty little suite of three rooms. There was a small, prettily furnished parlor, from one side of which Arthur's room opened, while from the other side my own chamber could be entered. It was a tiny, kitchenless flat, and — as the colored handmaiden who attended to our wants, expressed it — it was "just as cute as could be."

No more complete diversion from the painful events of the past could have been desired than this visit to New York, where everything was new to us; where suggestion from associations was out of the question; where we were unlikely to meet a soul whom we knew; where even the English newspapers, when they reached us, were ten days old, and consequently uninteresting, and where no social claims could form an excuse for separation.

The programme of our first few days in America was as follows: Breakfast at ten o'clock in that dear little parlor, which, I reflected, was gradually becoming all that separated us the one from the other; a glance through the American newspapers, so that no one could accuse us of living entirely out of the world; a drive, either through that magnificent park, which does not boast what I have always wilfully considered an intolerable nuisance, a "Rotten Row," upon what New Yorkers call "the road;" then dinner in the big dining-room. After dinner we retired to our own little parlor and I read from some popular novel to my husband. I did not weary him with instructive books, because I thought he needed recreation, and because I hate instructive books myself. I recollect how I used to have Smiles' "Self-Help," thrust upon me by an enterprising governess, because she said it was "the most instructive, and at the same time the most amusing book," she could find.

I read to Arthur some good modern novels. When I saw that the dose was sufficient, I desisted, quickly closed my book, kissed him, and departed into my room.

And this treatment, I flattered myself, was most efficacious. I do not believe I gave a thought to my unknown rival during all those pleasant, happy days. I am sure I should have known it if I had. I loved my husband so dearly in this voluntary exile, that I was quick to notice his every look and expression, to account for them, to understand them.

He was gratified. Slowly but surely I was able to recognize in his manner a change from the wooed to the wooer. Alas! that a woman should ever be forced to woo a man. Still, when that man is her own husband, there are extenuating circumstances to be placed to her credit, as I think you will readily agree. My attentions did not weary him. Once or twice I grew tired of reading aloud, and he noticed it before I did. Then quietly but firmly he took the book from my unwilling hands, closed it, and laid it gently on the sofa. The slight but embarrassing pause which followed that action was broken by comments he made upon the story in question, that led to an amiable discussion of its merits, its probabilities, its characters. I gave my views with my usual flippant recklessness, and at last had the delight of knowing that I entertained him.

I believe I have called my married life unhappy. Ah! why should I say that, with the memory of those few sunny days vividly before me? Nothing can take that memory away from me. Those days were mine; I had worked for them laboriously, and they came simply as the reward of labor.

I earned them. They were not the fullest joy that could have been given me, but they were inexpressibly dear, and as I think of them my eyes moisten and my lips tremble.

At the dinner-table, one night, we heard a very spirited discussion upon the merits of a sensational preacher, who was attracting large audiences — yes, "audiences" is the correct word — to his church, and exciting a good deal of newspaper comment at the same time. The majority of those who took part in the discussion were inclined to the opinion that the reverend gentleman was far too secular in his pulpit addresses; while the minority contended that he struck bravely at the root of crying evils from the very best place where it was possible for a man to strike at them. What was a pulpit for, said they, if not to redress evils by ventilating them? They, for their part, did not care to listen to the old-fashioned sermons that pleased generations past. The sermons might not be orthodox in the accepted meaning of the word, but they were interesting, clever and virile.

"Let us go to-morrow and hear this much-talked-about gentleman, Arthur," I said to my husband as we returned to our parlor after dinner. "We can then pass upon his merits or demerits in our own particularly learned way. What say you?"

He laughed.

"We will go, Elsie," he said. "You shall pass upon his merits or demerits as usual, and I will simply curb your impetuosity in whatever direction you may argue — also, as usual."

So the following morning, which happened to be Sunday, instead of casting our eyes through the voluminous newspapers, we disposed ourselves to thoughts of church, a novelty to both of us, I am sorry, though obliged, to confess.

This home of sensationalism was a very modern-looking building — as, of course, was appropriate. I was surprised when I found that it was a church, so extremely secular was its appearance.

It was situated a long way from our hotel, but in what street I cannot remember, though I am quite sure it was above Fortieth Street and below Fiftieth.

Crowds of people were entering the building as we reached it — exquisitely dressed women, black clad respectable looking men, and comely children in all their Sunday finery. I was told that this was a distinctly American congregation. It was certainly a most refined and intelligent looking gathering of men and women.

We took our seats in a pew, from which we had an excellent view of the presiding minister. He was a tall, thin, dignified, quiet looking man. At the first glance one might have expected an orthodox, prosy, soporific sermon, but a more careful inspection of the man revealed a pair of keen, bead like eyes, which seemed to "take in" every man or woman present in a most unusual manner; tightly compressed lips, and fingers that spasmodically clutched the book they held.

"He doesn't look sensational," I whispered conclusively to my husband.

"He looks very sensational," was the reply.

The preliminary service was a short one, and at the close of a hymn, exquisitely sung, suddenly looking up I saw the minister in the pulpit ready to begin. He made none of those prefatory announcements which are death to the artistic impressiveness of a sermon. Standing in his pulpit, he waited till the last deliciously tuneful strain of the choir had died away, and then gave out his text, clearly and deliberately. Before he had reached the end of the text, he had rivetted my attention, and during the entire sermon I listened to him spell-bound, unconscious of my surroundings.

This was the text:

> "Then the Lord rained upon Sodom and upon Gomorrah brimstone and fire from the Lord out of Heaven;
> "And he overthrew those cities, and all the plain, and all the inhabitants of the cities, and that which grew upon the ground.
> "And he (Abraham) looked towards Sodom and Gomorrah, and toward all the land of the plain, and beheld, and lo, the smoke of the country went up as the smoke of a furnace."

He spoke of the optimists who flatter themselves that the sins of the earlier ages are unknown to-day; who believe that civilization has dealt out death to the evils that corrupted a younger world. He tried to show that optimism was the natural sequence of ignorance; that all sin was the result of human weakness, inherited, or by some physiological freak, innate; that there was not a solitary vice recorded in the times gone by that did not exist to-day, magnified and multiplied. Sin could take no new shape, and no one could assert after a careful study of humanity, that it had forgotten any of its old forms. Men were the same now as they were when we first heard of them. Their lives, shortened slightly perhaps by civilization, were identical; their death as inevitable; their physical sufferings synonymous; their joys similar.

He alluded to those who knew of the existence of hateful sins, and who from misplaced scruple, failed to mention them.

"Do not call me illogical," he said, "I do not believe that sin could be abolished by all the sermons in the world. But at least it should be diligently pointed out that it may not gather increased victims. Its spread can be avoided; its contagion diminished. Men will sin as long as the world exists; but many sin voluntarily, won over by those with whom vice is natural."

The pessimism of the sermon frightened me. With him there was no hope of eradicating evil; merely of lessening its influence upon those with whom it was forced to come in contact. It was a very deep, obtuse lecture — too deep for me, I am afraid. I did not understand it thoroughly, though its gist was perfectly clear to me. The methods of the man would have attracted attention anywhere, but I never want to hear another such sermon. I do not believe it could do good. People do not want to be thrilled on Sunday. They need to be comforted and taught to hope for the best. As his last words were uttered, and the congregation, which had listened breathlessly, eagerly, to every word, watched the speaker descend from his pulpit, I looked for the first time since the beginning of the discourse at my husband.

His face was as white as death. His eyes, widely open, were staring fixedly at the pulpit, which was now empty, as though he expected further utterances. His hands hung limp and nerveless at his side.

I touched his arm. He started violently, and turned a face from which every expression of good-fellowship, trust and hope seemed to have fled.

"Arthur," I said, seriously alarmed, "what is the matter? Are you ill? Don't — don't look at me like that."

He tried to smile.

"I wonder if he has delivered that lecture before," he said huskily.

His strange tone surprised me — accustomed as I was, by this time, to surprise.

"Probably not," I said. "Popular preachers, as a rule, do not deliver old sermons, I should think, — for their own sakes."

"Let us go home," he said. "I can't sit through the rest of the service."

As we were going out Arthur asked one of the ushers anxiously if the Doctor were going to speak again that night. The usher smiled.

"No," he said. "One lecture is all he can manage. He exhausts himself. He's as weak as a rat after one of his talks."

My ideas upon the weakness of rats being decidedly limited, I could only infer from the context that it was extreme. We passed out into the street.

"I did not want to hear him again," said Arthur presently, as we walked homewards, "but if he had spoken to-night I feel I must have gone. What an awful sermon!"

"It was indeed," I assented, "we are surely not such hopeless cases as that man wants to make out."

"Do you think so?" he asked.

I looked at him, wondering.

"I am sure of it," I said, with the beautiful certainty of one who never studies any question except upon the surface.

"You are a dear little girl," he said suddenly, with what I considered absolute irrelevance, "and I would believe you rather than — than him. Let us go home and talk. Do you know, dear, I am beginning to feel so happy in your society — No, no" (hastily), "not as I used to be, Elsie. You are doing so much good. I bless the day when we left London."

I looked up at him gladly; could any words have been sweeter than these to me? I doubt it.

CHAPTER 22

We dined with the multitude that afternoon, and I was glad of it. Arthur was feverishly uneasy. He seemed unable to forget the sermon he had heard in the morning, though why it should have affected him so painfully, I could not exactly understand. Of course I supposed he felt remorse for that part of his life — of our lives — which had brought us to this far off country, and exiled us on its hospitable shores.

Women are not uncharitable, say what you will. I was anxious that my husband should suffer no more for those misdeeds which, it seemed to me, had been so thoroughly left to the past. I wanted him to forget them. I was trying to forget them myself. I flattered myself that my most sanguine hopes would be realized, and that we should return to England as warmly devoted a couple as readers could ever hope to consign to "living happily" ever after.

I was on "pins and needles" lest the subject of the popular preacher should be broached at the dinner-table. There was one old bore present, whom I had seen at the church, and as I knew he was a person with a distinct desire to talk upon the least provocation, I dreaded any opportunity occurring for an outbreak on his part. No one else appeared to have attended divine service that morning, thank goodness! The conversation was beautifully secular, referring to the stage, for the most part.

I had hard work to keep the guests to that subject, but I succeeded. I asked fifty idiotic questions, in the answers to which I had not the faintest interest, beyond the fact that they took up considerable time. I caught the eye of the bore, as I mentally christened him, angrily fixed upon me. He was waiting his opportunity to talk preacher. I knew that. I was determined to prevent his attacking the subject, and I was successful. When I felt a pause coming, I had another question ready to fling broadcast at any one who chose to answer it. I was unfailing in my efforts.

When we finally rose from the table, I cast a look of triumph at the poor old fellow opposite to me. He was biting his stubbly moustache to hide his mortification. He had not been allowed to put in a word edgeways, and he was keenly miserable.

"Was I not thirsty for information, Arthur?" I asked my husband, as he settled himself in our mutual parlor to read the paper, a task with which our church-going had interfered.

"Horribly so," he said, laughing. He seemed to have somewhat recovered himself, though his face was still flushed, and I could see that his hands shook slightly as he held the paper. "What induced you to talk so much, Elsie?"

Oh, men are obtuse beings! He had no idea that my conversational efforts were merely made to spare him pain.

"I had nothing else to do," I answered flippantly. "And I thought my voice sounded well to-day; then, you know, it was Sunday, and I wanted to give them all a treat. Do you see?"

He laughed again. "Elsie," he said, "sometimes I wonder, after listening to your speeches, how it is that you really have depth after all. People who never heard anything but your small talk would think you were good for nothing else."

"Do you think that?" I asked, trying not to appear anxious.

"No, Elsie. Indeed I do not." He glanced at me lovingly. There was a look in his eyes that I had never seen there before. I dropped mine in embarrassment. "I am only thankful — yes, thankful from the bottom of my heart — that you can still be the same little girl as before, after — after what you have endured, since our — our marriage. No, Elsie —" as I made a gesture of disapproval — "there is no reason why we should not discuss the past now, because — because —"

"Because?" I asked breathlessly.

"Because it is losing its interest for me, I am sure," he said in a low tone.

I felt convinced that he spoke the truth. I was confident that no rival supplanted me now, and I saw no harm in congratulating myself already upon the success of my plan. That evening I was in an unusually hilarious mood. I saw success before me in large shining letters. Imperceptibly my manner changed, from that of the love-sick girl, yearning for one kind word from the man upon whom she has lavished all her affection, to the half arrogant self-consciousness of the woman who knows her power. The fool that I was! Great heavens! That such a thing as feminine coquetry should ever be spoken of as charming!

I talked so much nonsense, chatted away so incessantly, and put such a decided veto upon any serious conversation, that Arthur looked at me reproachfully. Surely I had won the right to be gay, I told myself. It had not been often that I had been able to indulge in any frivolity.

"One would think you were on wires to-night, Elsie," said Arthur, in a tone of gentle protest, as after having fluttered all around the room, I sat down beside him.

He took my hand. It was the first time he had ever voluntarily done so. Months ago I would have given years of my life for that little endearment. My heart beat violently as his burning fingers closed over mine; but the devilish spirit of feminine coquetry possessed me; I withdrew my hand abruptly.

"Don't!" I said, rather pettishly.

There was an embarrassing pause; at least it must have been embarrassing for him. I can only think that I was out of my mind that night.

"I suppose when I get back to England," I went on quickly, "that I shall have to set to work and write my impressions of America. Dear me! how extensive they are. Their range is so wide, reaching from this hotel to Central Park, and from Central Park to this hotel. You shall do the editing for me, if you will, and I shall begin as soon as we reach London. Do you consent, Arthur?"

"I cannot think yet of returning to London," he said, almost inaudibly. "I — I — do not want to think of it."

"But you must," I remarked, fanning myself with the newspaper which I had taken from him and folded into a convenient shape. "I am sure neither of us intend to become naturalized Americans, so I don't see why we should remain much longer. I like New York — that is impression No. 1 — don't you?"

"I love New York," he said fervently.

"Like the actors and actresses who are interviewed in the newspapers. They all of them seem to love America before they have seen it. I suppose they hope to go home with lots of dollars in their pockets, and want to impress the Americans favorably by liking their country. Don't you think that is a fact, dear?"

I waited for a reply as anxiously as if the question had been one of vital importance.

"Very probably," was the absent rejoinder.

I took up a book and tried to settle down to reading. The letters danced before my eyes, and I flung the book aside with a laugh. I unfolded Arthur's newspaper and gazed stupidly at the advertisements. A dentist offered to extract teeth free of charge, if only the extractee would consent to wear the false article. He had for sale "elegant full gum sets," "gold combination sets," and "platina lined, porcelain enamelled sets." Of course they were all fearfully cheap. I noted that Mr. John Smith had a two-year-old colt to offer the public for a consideration. It was brown, and had no spots, though it possessed the luxury of a half brother with a record of 2.23; warranted sound. I smiled at the tailor who declared he would make any man a "nobby" suit of clothes for a mere song, and pitied the poor lady who wanted a loan to finish a new house. Poor thing! Why did she begin it, without sufficient money to see the building to its bitter end? I was genuinely interested.

The little clock upon the mantelpiece struck eleven o'clock. How late it was getting! I folded up the newspaper, and sat bolt upright in my chair. I looked at Arthur. His eyes, which seemed to shine like live coals, were fixed upon mine. I crimsoned, for no reason that I can think of.

"It is getting late," I said in a low tone, looking helplessly at the clock.

"Yes."

"We have cooped ourselves up too much to-day," I said, at random. "I wonder why we did not go out this afternoon; the weather was beautiful, and we — we —"

I could not finish the sentence, simply because I did not know what I was going to say when I began it. I sat uneasily listening to the ticking of the clock. It irritated me, and sounded loud as the tramp of soldiers, in the uncomfortable silence that prevailed.

"To-morrow, Arthur," I said, with an effort at levity, as I rose to go, "I shall make you take me for a long walk, as I think it will do us both good. Exercise, you know, is always desirable, and — and — good-night."

I gave him my hand. He took it and, rising, drew me towards him, holding me fondly, firmly in his arms. Bending forward he murmured hoarsely, "Why need we say good-night?"

For one moment I lay quiescent upon his bosom. The next, though my pulses throbbed painfully, and I could feel the hot, feverish blood burning through my veins, I withdrew myself from his clasp, and ran precipitately into my room.

I remained breathless behind the closed door, waiting for him to speak, or at least to let me know that I had not offended him by my abruptness. I waited in vain for five minutes; then I opened my door. He had retired to his room. Looking up at the glass ventilator, I saw that he had put his light out.

In an agony of mortification I retired to my chamber, and throwing myself upon the bed, I cried out against the coquetry inherent in the best of my sex. I had reason to cry out against it.

CHAPTER 23

My sleep that night was fitful and troubled, and I arose the next morning with a sense of oppression quite unusual with me. Hitherto, when I had retired at night a pessimist, the morning sun invariably brought with it relief, which I believe it is its pleasant mission to do, and I awoke an optimist. But as I dressed on this particular day, I felt uneasy, and anxious without any apparent cause, I told myself.

What had happened to justify this state of mind, I asked? Certainly my wedded life had never looked so promising as it did now. I had won my husband's love, most surely. Could a caprice or two on my part extinguish the flame which I had fanned so long and so diligently? Pshaw! The idea was ridiculous. I was out of sorts. I would not give way to my gloomy thoughts. I would exercise my will, and be happy in spite of myself.

That night Arthur and I were to accompany a charming English couple, whose acquaintance we had made at the hotel, to the opera. It was an appointment dating from a week ago, and I remembered it with regret. I would have preferred passing the evening alone with my husband. However, I reflected that I could not offend these people, who were of that genial, whole-souled class, whose acquaintance is a privilege, and whose friendship is nothing less than a boon. After all, a future of unoccupied evenings was before me. Arthur and I undoubtedly had time even to grow tired of one another, I thought, and I smiled at the idea.

At that moment an ebony head-waiter knocked at the door and brought in our breakfast, and two minutes later my husband emerged from his chamber, looking bright and pleasant. At all events, I said to myself, if there were any presentiments in the atmosphere, they had all fallen to my share.

"What a lovely day," remarked Arthur, with daring originality as we took our seats at the cosy little round table, and I began to pour out the coffee.

"Yes," I assented, handing him his cup. "After breakfast we are to go for a nice long walk on Broadway to look at the people, and after dinner we are engaged to Mr. and Mrs. Donaldson for the opera."

"You have the programme carefully mapped out," he said, laughing. "Have you been thinking about it long?"

"All night," I said, thoughtlessly.

He looked at me for a moment. My words had no significance, however, other than their literal meaning.

"What do they sing at the opera to-night?" he asked, carelessly.

"Lohengrin."

"I hate Wagner."

"Then you have no right to say so," I assented vigorously, as I dropped an extra piece of sugar into my cup. "If you dare to tell Mr. and Mrs. Donaldson such a thing, the same hotel will never hold us."

He laughed. He was evidently happy this morning. We chatted pleasantly until breakfast was a thing of the past. Then, after having dismissed the morning papers, as was our custom, we started out from the hotel for our walk.

I felt better. My husband's good humor was contagious. It affected me, and I can assure you I was not unwilling to be affected. It was a lovely sunshiny spring day, and Broadway was at its best. It was thronged. Dainty women tripped in and out of the big, well-stocked shops; the beautifully dressed children attracted my attention, and filled me with admiration of juvenile Americans; dapper little men walked quickly by, always in a hurry on general principles. There was a blue sky overhead. Winter had been successfully vanquished and humanity seemed anxious to celebrate its defeat.

I hummed the one song my mother used to make me sing "before company," when I was at home, and its refrain:

"The merry, merry sun, the mer-ry sun,
The merry, merry sun for me-e-e-e."

Then there was a high note at which I had always quaked, and occasionally lowered, much to the anguish of my maternal parent, who liked a good, tuneful shriek, laboring under the impression that it indicated a cultivated voice.

Arthur and I did not talk much, as we were both too intent looking about us to enjoy conversation. The most delightful thing about this walk was that we were not perpetually stopped by a friendly "How d'ye do?" "Fine day," or similar every day greetings. In London we should have been thus annoyed every five minutes if we had selected Regent Street or Oxford Street, the Broadways of the English metropolis. We were absolutely unnoticed, and it was unspeakably pleasant. I began to think that after all there were worse places than New York in which to make a home.

We were now approaching Madison Square, and I looked around with interest at the lively scene; at the big buildings; the people hurrying about in every direction; the tinkling tram-cars on all sides; the large, lumbering "four-wheelers" jolting over the uneven pavements; the nurses and perambulators just visible on the square; Fifth Avenue stretching far away; the curious, uncomfortable looking omnibusses; and the quaint, Swiss-chalet-like structure marking a station on the elevated railway, to be seen traversing the wide thoroughfare on the left. I was fascinated. We crossed the street and found ourselves in front of an enormous, ponderous, gray hotel. A large portico stretched from the entrance to this building, and afforded a standing place for a score or so of men, apparently bent upon ogling passers-by, who unfortunately could not avoid passing them.

I hate a congregation of men, anywhere, so I walked quickly past this group and stopped before I reached the corner to allow Arthur to come up with me. I turned. He was not by my side. He was standing in front of the portico gazing into the lobby. As I waited, he approached me, and I was startled as I looked at his face.

It was livid, and he was trembling violently.

"I am ill, Elsie," he said, quickly. "I must be ill. Perhaps it is my heart. I — I think so. Let us go home."

He looked ill indeed. I told myself that it must be heart trouble, as a few moments before he had been perfectly well, and there was nothing else I could think of to affect him in that manner. We returned to the hotel, and I insisted upon sending for a doctor. Arthur rebelled, but I would not give way. The Doctor declared that there was nothing at all the matter with Arthur's heart. It was sound. He thought his system was out of order generally, and wrote out a prescription. In fact he did what most doctors do, in the usual pompous, would-be impressive way.

"I am going to send down word to Mrs. Donaldson," I said, half an hour later, "that we cannot accompany her to the Opera to-night. I can't say I'm particularly sorry," I added, carelessly.

Arthur started up quickly from the sofa upon which he had been reclining. "You must go," he declared, "there is no reason why you should not do so. Do not offend these people, Elsie. We have found them very pleasant acquaintances, and I believe they are only going to accommodate us."

I looked at him in amazement. His eagerness was almost painful to see; there was a bright red spot upon each cheek, and his eyes shone fiercely. His gentle, sympathetic manner of the past few days seemed to have disappeared.

"If you insist upon my going," I said, to humor him, "I will go; but I would sooner stay at home with you."

"Nonsense." He spoke so roughly that the tears started to my eyes. He saw this and looked remorseful.

"I will follow you, Elsie, if I can," he said. "Perhaps I m-may join you during the evening, though —"

He got no farther. He was ill, I thought, and possibly an evening alone would do him good. I had given him no opportunities to miss me since we had been in America. I had found so much pleasure in his society, that I was determined to enjoy it. Did I not know, clearly enough, that he loved me, at last? Had I not been able to recognize that fact with sufficient distinctness? Of course I had. He wanted me to go to the opera, and I would go and amuse myself. I should be able to think of him waiting for me at home, and growing perhaps miserably lonely in my absence. He would possibly tell me when I returned that he could not spare me again, and then how thoroughly happy I should feel! Perhaps, after all, Arthur's indisposition was for the best. I felt that it might be, and my spirits, which had been rapidly sinking since my return from our walk, rose with considerable energy.

We dined in the big dining-room, Arthur declaring that he was not ill enough to be treated as an invalid, and after that meal I robed myself in gorgeous apparel. Arthur walked up and down the parlor, and through my closed door I could hear his quick uneven footsteps. I was soon ready, and my husband wrapped me up in my *sortie de bal.*

"Good-night, dear," I said briskly.

"Good-night."

"Are you not going to kiss me?" I asked, reproachfully, as he took my hand, and let it drop rather coldly, evidently inclined to make this do duty as a farewell salutation.

He bent over me in silence, and pressed his lips to my upturned face. The kiss chilled me. It reminded me of the first he had ever given me, and I shuddered slightly. For one moment a great feeling of disappointment came over me; the next brought with it the remembrance of last night, and my anxiety was swept away as by a consuming flame.

I ran lightly down stairs and joined the genial Donaldsons. They were waiting for me in the parlors. When I saw Mrs. Donaldson, I really felt pleased that my husband was absent. She was *décolletée* in a way that made my cheeks burn. The strip of satin that, for politeness' sake she called a bodice, was so bewilderingly narrow, that one had to look for it carefully, in order to find it. She was a nice little woman, this Mrs. Donaldson. I liked what I knew of her, but I had no desire to know quite as much as her attire revealed.

"How charming you look," she said as I entered the room, and turned my eyes away from her chubby beauty, "and what a bright color you have in your cheeks. One might almost suspect rouge," she added, laughing.

The bright color was all on her account. I have no doubt it looked very pleasing, but I knew it would not remain. I was one of those unfortunate girls who rarely look rosy unless they are blushing or suffering from indigestion.

Mr. Donaldson was delighted with his wife. To him she was a perpetual source of pleasing astonishment. He saw nothing improper in her costume — or rather want of costume — and I am quite convinced that if she had set forth for the Opera, attired in a sweet smile and a tunic, he would have been satisfied. I reflected that there would probably be other women as outrageously clad as my friend, and reconciled myself in this manner to being seen with her.

I was right. In the vast Opera House the display of feminine undress was so startling, that it took my breath away. It was ten times worse than anything I had ever seen in London. I had been told that New York was, in many respects, an exaggeration of London, and I felt I could believe it.

"Lohengrin," as I had already said, was the opera; not that it mattered much. The occupants of the boxes paid very little attention to what was going on upon the stage. They talked and laughed and recognized one another; opera-glassed the other side of the house, and commented upon each new arrival within range of their vision. It was a lively scene, at any rate.

Mr. and Mrs. Donaldson pretended to be very fond of Wagner, and I believe they imagined that they were. Being strangers in the city they had few friends to recognize, and were tolerably interested in the opera. Mrs. Donaldson's costume proved to be positively prudish. There were others that were so much more astonishing, that I felt quite sorry for her. She had started out prepared to astonish the natives, and lo! it was the natives who were astonishing her.

I treasured up a few descriptions with which to regale Arthur when I went home. I imagined I heard his hearty laugh, and that phrase of his, "Your speeches always amuse me so, Elsie."

Dear old man! How pleasant the future looked, stretched out before us! What happiness there seemed to be held in store for us by coming years.

I looked at Mrs. Donaldson. She was yawning desperately, and seemed vexed to be caught in the act.

"It is not a good performance, by any means," she said to justify herself. I agreed with her. I was anxious to go home. Arthur had not joined us, and I had heard all the Wagner I wanted for this evening. I tried to delicately insinuate to Mrs. Donaldson that it would be advisable to leave early and avoid the crush. She would not hear of this, however, and favored me with such a Medusa-like stare, that I was silenced most effectually.

The opera was over at last, and slowly and solemnly we wound our way down the broad, red carpeted staircase. A carriage was awaiting us and we were soon rolling hotelward. On the whole I was rather glad I had accompanied the Donaldsons. The scene at the Opera House had amused me somewhat, and I had plenty to say to Arthur, which was in itself a boon. As my husband was not sentimental, and I was determined to be as prosaic as possible, a few novelties to be added to our conversational stock would not be amiss. I wondered if the evening had seemed very long to him. I felt he would not like to admit that it had, but I was resolved that my object should be to force him to make that confession. I pictured him seated in the arm-chair reading and waiting for me — especially waiting.

I said good-night to the Donaldsons as soon as we arrived at the hotel, and resisted their invitation to supper. Supper indeed! Going quietly upstairs I coyly knocked at the parlor door, and then drawing back into the shadow, waited for it to be opened. There was no answer. In my coyness, I supposed I had not made myself heard, so with decidedly more energy, I knocked again.

It was long past midnight. Arthur must have fallen asleep, I reflected. He was tired, and such a vigil was by no means encouraging. So I turned the knob of the door and walked in.

The gas was burning brightly; there was an untidy gathering of newspapers upon the sofa, and the room had all the appearance of an extremely occupied apartment. Arthur was not there, however. With a little sob of utter disappointment, I told myself that he had not waited up for me. Oh! how unkind of him, when he knew how much I should have appreciated that little act of attention! In his place, I would have remained awake all night. Pshaw! What peculiar creatures men were, I thought. Their ideas were so absolutely opposed to ours that it was wonderful such a thing as a matrimonial partnership could ever exist for any length of time. Then I stopped in my mental deliberations to remember that I had left Arthur avowedly indisposed. How could I tell that he had not been taken worse during the evening? Surely it was my duty to ascertain the facts of the case. I felt a qualm of remorse as I saw how ready I was to place my husband in the wrong.

I went to the door of his bed-room and knocked. There was no answer.

Becoming seriously alarmed, I knocked again; this time loudly, with the same result. Then, resolved to stand upon no ceremony, I opened the door and walked into his room. It was in complete darkness. A cold apprehension of trouble seized me, and I shivered violently. I went to the table where I knew he kept his matches, and with trembling fingers drew one from the box. I dreaded to light it. I struck the match, however, and closed my eyes for a second. When I had summoned up courage to look around me, I saw that the room was empty. The bed had not been occupied, and my husband's coats had disappeared from their hooks in the closet, as I could see through its open door. My knees shook, and I almost fell, as I saw that his trunk and valise had also gone.

For a moment I was too dazed to realize what all this meant. I sat down upon the bed, and held my hands to my forehead, which was throbbing so vigorously that it almost deadened the recognition of any other fact. Arthur had gone and taken his trunk with him. He had left me without a word of explanation. I sprang up, rushed from the room, and started down stairs to see the hotel clerk and ask him if my husband had left any message with him. I dreaded to face the man at such an hour, and then I suddenly remembered that the clerk who had been on duty before midnight had undoubtedly been succeeded by this time.

I ran back to my rooms. The perspiration was dripping from my forehead and the glimpse I caught of my ghastly face in the looking-glass, which hung above the mantelpiece, frightened me. Ah! there was an envelope in the frame of this looking-glass, which was evidently meant to attract my attention. I made a bound forward and seized it. It was addressed simply to "Elsie."

A cry escaped my lips as I saw this. He had left me, and this was his explanation. The letters on the envelope became enveloped in a blurred mist, and I could see nothing. I steadied myself by grasping the mantelpiece with one hand, while I pressed the other, holding the letter, against my heart. I must have stood thus for a minute; then, with a feeling of astonishment at my own helplessness, I broke open the envelope and read this, written in a trembling, hurried hand, mis-spelt and blotted:

> "ELSIE:
>
> "No one will ever know how I have tried to obliterate the memory of a sinful past, and make you the husband, which — noble girl that you are — you deserve. I have long recognized the fact that the old miserable ideas which we have discussed so often, and which led to our marriage, were impossible. I say I have tried to become a good, manly husband to you. I thought I had succeeded until this morning, and so did you, poor girl, but it seems we were both mistaken. I am a wretch. Forget me. Return to England with the Donaldsons next week. I shall come to you no more. After this final step, it would of course be impossible. I make no excuses for myself. I am not worth any, and no one recognizes that fact more than,
>
> "ARTHUR RAVENER"

The room seemed to be revolving. An awful giddiness overwhelmed me, and I fell heavily to the floor.

CHAPTER 24

I do not know how I passed that awful night. I have a dim recollection of sitting up in hopeless dejection, on the sofa, conscious only of my intense longing for daylight. I could do nothing while darkness reigned; in fact I was absolutely helpless. I could only hope that the darkness which rendered me powerless to act, would have the same effect upon my husband. I could understand nothing. I seemed to be dazed. Not an idea of the truth dawned upon me. Our relations had been so pleasant; I was just about to attain the object of my visit to America, when, in the most inexplicable manner, my husband had left me. As I look back now I wonder how I could have been so dense. It appears to me now that the veriest blockhead could have grasped the situation.

At seven o'clock I sent for the hotel clerk, and asked him if he could tell me anything about my husband's departure from the hotel. In his suave, horribly superior manner, he informed me that he had not been on duty, and the "gentleman" who had been in charge of the desk before midnight, would not be "around" again until noon. I was in despair. I told this fat, oily official that it was really a matter of life and death with me. If he would only send for the clerk who had last seen my husband, I would pay liberally for the trouble I gave. This, and this alone, seemed to invest the case with interest for him. He promised to send for the day clerk, and in a short time I found him in my room. He could tell me very little. At about nine o'clock Mr. Ravener had ordered a carriage, and had taken a small trunk and a valise with him. He had not said where he was going, or anything concerning his return.

I begged the clerk to send for the man who had driven Mr. Ravener from the hotel. He looked with gentle surprise at my distress, as though it were extremely incomprehensible to him. Arthur had left with the few lines he had written me, money to the amount of five hundred pounds, and I tipped the clerk recklessly. He was thereupon much impressed with my case, and promised to do all he could to help me.

The driver was a big, burly fellow, with a red nose, and a florid, bull-dog face. My heart sank when I saw him. Heaven help all who have to depend upon so sottish a class of people for important information. He had great trouble in remembering the fact that he had taken anybody from the hotel at nine o'clock the evening before.

"Think! think! man," I cried frantically. "If you will remember everything, and tell me what I want to know, I'll give you this."

I held up a ten-dollar bill before him, and his eyes flashed with eager desire through the heavy, drunken film that covered them, as he saw the money. He sat down, stopped chewing the tobacco which he had been masticating vigorously and attempted to think, with a brutish effort. Then he referred to a little book that he carried in his pocket, and in a few minutes a ray of something distantly related to intelligence lighted up his features.

"The gen'lman told me ter take him to the big marble building on the corner o' Twen'y-third Street and Broadway," said he stolidly. "He said he guessed it was an hotel, and I said I guessed he meant the Fifth Avenue. When we got there, a man come to the carriage and helped him out. I guess the man was expectin' him. No, I didn't hear what they says. A porter come up and took the gen'lman's baggage. He give me a five dollar bill, and told me not to wait. That's all I know, mum."

"What kind of a man met Mr. Ravener at the hotel?" I exclaimed, gasping, with a terrible fear upon me.

"I dunno, mum," was the answer. "A ordinary, every-day gen'lman, he seemed to me. He was rather stout, I think, but I didn't pay no partickler attention to him, mum. I ain't in the habit of lookin' at every man I meet so as I can give a description of him afterwards, mum."

"Was Mr. Ravener's baggage taken upstairs?" I asked, trying to speak calmly.

"I dunno, mum. Ye see when I got my fare I just skipped. T'wasn't no good my waitin' around."

"All right — now go," I said hurriedly. "Here's the money."

I wanted to be alone. I dismissed the hotel clerk, and began to dress quickly. I would go to the Fifth Avenue Hotel at once. I should doubtless find Arthur there. I absolutely declined to think at all until I could solve the case. I would not torture my mind by imagining this, and suspecting that. I would, if possible, deal with facts only. I had no difficulty in keeping my mind a blank. I was bewildered by the magnitude of the misfortune that had fallen upon me in a strange country. I was soon ready to start, and ordering a carriage, I told the driver to take me to the Fifth Avenue Hotel, and wait for me there.

No sooner had I arrived at the hotel, than quick as a flash of lightning, a great deal of what had been inexplicable lay solved before me. This was the big building that Arthur and I had passed the preceding day. I remembered the crowd of men standing under the porch, and the annoyance I felt at being ogled. I had walked alone to the corner of the street, and, turning, had beheld Arthur gazing in at the lobby. His livid face had filled me with alarm, and he had declared that he was ill. That night he had been driven to this hotel. The reason was too clear for even a blind fool like myself to fail to understand. He had seen some one in the lobby — some one whom he had not expected to see. I could not doubt who it was — no, I could not doubt it, though I would have given all I possessed to be able to do so.

I walked into the hotel, elbowing my way through a crowd of wide-staring men, and went at once to the clerk. I asked him if a young man named Arthur Ravener had arrived at the hotel the previous night. He referred to his register, but could find no such name. I told him he must be mistaken, but this had the effect of rendering him mute. I forgot that an American hotel clerk could not possibly, under any circumstances, be mistaken. I then informed him that I had just spoken with the driver who had conducted Mr. Ravener, with his baggage, to the hotel, and left him there. He was surprised, but he had not been "on duty" at that time. He suggested that I speak to Mr. Price, the detective of the hotel, who was always in the lobby, and whose keen eyes saw everybody who came in and who went out.

I found this detective courteous, well-informed, and remarkably intelligent. I explained my case to him.

"Last night," he said, "shortly after nine o'clock, a carriage drove up to the hotel. It contained a young man, and I noticed that his face was deathly white. In fact, it was this circumstance that interested me at first. This ghastly hue could not have been normal with any living being. Before he had time to leave the carriage, a fellow, of whom I will speak presently, rushed out and opened the door. He called to a porter, and after having dismissed the carriage, ordered that the trunk and valise which the gentleman with the white face brought, be sent to the dock of the Guion line of steamers, with his own."

I uttered an exclamation of horror, and the detective stopped in alarm. "Go on," I cried.

"The two then went upstairs. The young man seemed to be much excited. He could hardly reply to the glib remarks of his companion. He appeared to be in a dream. I suspected that there was something strange about this, Madame," said Mr. Price, safely, "but I did not see on what ground I could interfere. The gentleman who met your — your — husband? — arrived from England about three days ago. He brought a big black trunk, labelled conspicuously "J.D.," while he registered under the name of Frank Clarke. A leather pocket-book was found in the hotel the other day. It contained a large sum of money. Mr. Clarke claimed it, and declared that it belonged to him, although the name on the cards which were in it was —"

"What?" I asked breathlessly, although I knew full well.

Mr. Price drew a slip of paper from his pocket. "The name was Jack Dillington," he said. "Captain Jack Dillington. I was very suspicious when he claimed this pocket-book. He was able to tell me exactly its contents. He explained that the cards belonged to a friend, and I had to believe him."

"Although you saw his trunk marked 'J.D.'?" I asked impatiently.

"Yes," replied the detective. "I had my suspicions, but what could I do? A man can travel under any name he likes; we may suspect that he is doing so for some improper purpose, but unless he does something which justifies our suspicions, I am afraid we could not make out a case. Mr. Clarke, or Dillington, behaved himself properly. I was not asked to watch him. I could not suppose that he — he —"

"Was running away with a woman's husband," I said, wearily. Fate seemed to be against me. I felt it was useless to struggle.

"Exactly," he assented, looking at me keenly.

"I am much obliged to you for having told me all that you know," I said, in the same tired way. He bowed, and I went out to my carriage. I told the driver to take me to the Guion line dock.

It was not much use, though I thought I might as well drain my cup of misery to the dregs. I saw it all. Arthur had told Captain Dillington of our proposed trip to America. I remembered the day when I had gone to his room and found the door locked. I called to mind the sudden shutting of the window which I had unmistakably heard. Captain Dillington had probably consented to this departure, and the fool whom I had married had not suspected that he would be followed. Consequently, when by mere chance Arthur had seen Dillington in the lobby of the Fifth Avenue Hotel, he had been astounded. The horrible influence which this man exerted over the weaker vessel must have been all-powerful. It had in one moment knocked away the barriers which in weeks of perseverance I had raised. I had been right in one respect. It was only by removing him from this man, whom I felt to be his evil genius, that I could have hoped to win my husband.

For the first time I began to doubt if there were a "woman in the case," after all. But the doubt brought no relief to my mind. I almost wished that I could have known that my husband was on his way to some woman who loved him well, even if unwisely. As it was, I could only suppose that the Captain's evil influence was exerted over Arthur for some object that I could not guess at, though I felt sure it must be wicked, and to be feared.

At the Guion dock, I learned that the Alaska had sailed for Liverpool at six o'clock that morning. I had no difficulty in ascertaining that two gentlemen had driven up about ten minutes before the vessel sailed. One of them was stout; the other slight and with a pale face.

I almost laughed at the completeness with which one piece of evidence fitted into the other.

I drove back to my hotel. I was alone in a strange country, but it was not that fact which annoyed me. No one would run away with me, I was sorry to say. I thought of the future, and it seemed so black that I could not look into it.

I resolved to make one more effort to save my husband from a fate which I did not understand. I saw that a Cunard steamer was sailing the next day — the fast Etruria. I could reach Liverpool before the Alaska.

I had no sooner seen this than one last ray of hope roused me to energy. I packed up my few goods, and the next day I was speeding across the ocean.

I have little more to say. I arrived in Liverpool, as I thought I should do, a day before the Alaska. I put up at the Adelphi Hotel, and gave orders that as soon as the Alaska was sighted I should be notified. I went down to the dock in due course. I watched the crowd of cabin passengers alight from the tender, but my husband and his accomplice were not to be found. Later, I learned that several passengers had landed at Queenstown, and I could not doubt but that they had been among them. They had probably suspected that I might follow on a fast Cunarder, and had rightly thought that I should not stop at Queenstown.

Well, they had won the battle, and if two men could find any glory in having vanquished one weak woman, let them find and keep it, I said to myself bitterly.

I was defeated and heart-broken. I returned to the house in Kew, "wound up" my affairs there — as they say in the mercantile world — and went abroad, in seclusion.

CHAPTER 25

A grave scandal was agitating the never very placid surface of Parisian society, and causing an immense sensation in the French metropolis. Men of high standing were involved, and names that had hitherto stood in lofty superiority, were mentioned in connection with one of the most disgraceful revelations that Paris had known in many years. The newspapers might possibly have ignored the affair as much as possible on account of the nauseating nature of the details, but this course could not be pursued. The names of the malefactors were too well known and too prominent. The people demanded that the details be made public, and when the reputable journals maintained a silence upon the matter, they transferred their allegiance to one or two disreputable papers that dealt with scandal without gloves. It was evident that the case must be ventilated, and bowing to the inevitable, each journal took it up. Everybody knows that the French papers are none too nice, so it will be readily understood that happenings bad enough for them to endeavor to suppress must indeed have been bad.

The London papers devoted a great deal of space to the scandal; in fact they seemed to gloat over it, and when it was subsequently hinted that the contagion had spread to the English metropolis, Londoners grew more and more interested each day.

"We know of no spectacle so ridiculous as the British public in one of its periodical fits of morality," says Macaulay. "In general, elopements, divorces, and family quarrels pass with little notice. We read the scandal, talk about it for a day, and forget it. But once in six or seven years, our virtue becomes outrageous."

It seemed as though this "once in six or seven years" had come.

I was in London at the time of which I write, brought from the seclusion into which I had withdrawn, by business connected prosaically with my financial affairs, and requiring my presence. For two years I had been trying to live down the memory of the events that had wrecked my life. I had not seen my husband since the night I had left him to go to the opera. We were still bound by the ties of matrimony. My friends had suggested divorce, but I dreaded the publicity of the courts, and, after all, why should I suffer it? The tie that bound me was not irksome, since he, to whom I was bound, left me to my own resources.

One afternoon, shortly after my arrival in London, I picked up the *Daily Telegraph*, more in idleness than in curiosity. Of course I had heard about the scandal which seemed to be dragging London and Paris into a cesspool of vice. The journal in question was particularly sensational on the day in question. In spite of myself, I was compelled to read. I had not gone far, before I was startled into painful interest. One of the ringleaders of the evil-doers had been arrested at Newhaven, where he had just landed from Dieppe and Paris. He had made a full confession, and the London police had seized upon it with avidity. He declared that there were many Londoners in Paris at the present time, who were deeply involved in the matter. The principal of these, he said, was a man who was passing under the assumed name of Delácroix. He was an Englishman whose real name was Dillington.

I uttered a cry as this name, fraught with such bitter recollections for me, was thus brought to my attention. For two years, I had neither heard nor seen it, and now, in cold type, it stood before me. I could not doubt that the Dillington mentioned, was the one who had been instrumental in destroying my happiness. The article went on to say that he was staying at present at a little hostelry known as the Hotel Vaupin, in the Rue Geoffroy-Marie.

I rose with an impulse of overwhelming force upon me. Dillington at the Hotel Vaupin; my husband must be there too. Yes, he was still my husband in the eyes of God and man, and he must be saved while there was yet time. The thought of his danger swept away for the moment all memories of the bitter wrongs I had suffered at his hands. They faded from my mind as though they had not existed. I saw him only as he was that night when he had asked me why I need leave him, and I, impelled by a fatal feminine coquetry, had rushed away, leaving his passionate question unanswered. Perhaps I might have saved him then if — no, it would not bear thinking about. I would go to his assistance at once, flinging all conventionalities to the winds.

I hastily packed a small valise, ordered a hansom, and one hour after I had become acquainted with the *Telegraph* article, I was on my way to the Charing Cross Station. I was not afraid of meeting anybody, as I had been on a former journey, also taken in the interests of my miserable marriage. I did not care who saw me, and yet, as though to contradict this mental avowal, I gave a sigh of relief as I found the railway carriage, which took me to Folkestone, unoccupied.

I arrived in Paris early the following morning, before the sleepy officials at the Gare du Nord, seemed to have shaken off their slumbers. I had no time to think of putting up at any hotel; speed was a question of life and death with me; so summoning a *fiacre*, I had my valise put inside, and told the driver to take me to the Hotel Vaupin. He had never heard of it, he said. I started, surprised that a man like Captain Dillington, whose ideas I had always thought were of the most extravagant, could be found at an hotel unknown to a station cab driver. I told the man that the Vaupin was in the Rue Geoffroy-Marie, and then it was his turn to stare. I urged him to hurry, and he did so, seemingly under protest. Down the interminable Rue de Lafayette we went. It had just begun its day's life, and the last of the *chiffoniers* was seen vanishing as though he could not stand the glare of the morning. Soon we turned into the Rue de Trevise; then, crossing the Rue Richer, we entered the Rue Geoffroy-Marie.

It is a narrow, dirty little street, in the centre of the commerce of Paris. The Hotel Vaupin had a conspicuous gilt sign in front of it; the driver drew up, and opening the door of the carriage, assisted me to alight. I told him to wait for me, as I had no idea of remaining in the semi-squalor of this locality very long. He eyed me suspiciously, and said he would wait, but he would like to be paid for the trip we had already made. Angry, even at this delay, I paid him, and passed at once into the hotel.

The proprietor was a big, burly, flaxen-haired fellow, phlegmatic, yet still a Frenchman. He came to the door to meet me. I hesitated for a moment, and then asked:

"Is M. Delacroix in?"

He looked at me keenly, and did not answer at once. "Does Madame not know?" he asked, haltingly.

"Know what?" I demanded, with a sinking heart.

"M. Delacroix was arrested this morning," said the proprietor, "at my hotel, too — alas! that I should tell it. He is charged with being involved in these — in these scandals, and —"

He went on in an affably recitative manner, but I heard no more. What a fool I had been to imagine that the French authorities would ignore the confession that I had read in the *Telegraph*. They had acted upon it at once. It had probably been known to them before the *Telegraph* had gone to press.

"Was M. Delacroix alone at this hotel?" I asked breathlessly. The proprietor seemed to be taken aback at my excitement — for a moment only, however.

"M. Delacroix came to this house some weeks ago," he said. "He was accompanied by a young gentleman, *un charmant garcon,* who occupied a room adjoining his, and —"

"Go on," I cried, frantically.

"He is still here."

"Ah!" This exclamation escaped me; I could not help giving it utterance. "I will go up to his room," I said, trying to quiet my throbbing pulses. I felt that I could not move. Now that I knew Arthur was here, I hated to see him; to confess, by this interview, that I understood his unhappy life. I made a mighty effort, however, and was ready, when the proprietor told me that the apartment was the first room to the right, on the second floor, to seek it.

I slowly ascended the uneven, miserably carpeted staircase. Not a soul did I meet. If there were any other occupants than Arthur in the hotel, they kept themselves out of sight. I stopped in front of room No. 18. It was the first to the right on the second floor. I knocked at the door, but received no answer. I listened, but nobody seemed to be behind the thin, cracked door to which a lock and key offered but slight security. I repeated my knocks without the least success, and, at last, I retraced my steps, found the proprietor, and told him that he must be mistaken; that the young Englishman must be out.

"No, he is not out," said the man vigorously. "I have stood here all day. I wished to warn him," hesitatingly, "for — for I liked him. He has not left his room. I can swear to that. Come with me; I think I can make him hear."

Oppressed by the awful character of the events in which I seemed myself to be involved, I followed him, and again ascended the creaking staircase. The proprietor's emphatic knock was as unsuccessful as mine. He waited for a minute or two, and then opening the door of the room next to No. 18, which he told me had been occupied by M. Delacroix, he entered that apartment. He tried a door inside, connecting the two rooms. It was locked.

There was a strange look upon his face as he came out. "I will break open the door," he said.

The task was not a hard one. An application of his big shoulder to the frail portal; a not very powerful push, and the lock gave way. We stood inside the room. It was darkened. The proprietor went to the window and drew up the shabby blinds. As much light as the close proximity of another house would allow struggled into the room. It was in complete disorder. The bed had not been slept in. The floor was littered with books, newspapers and clothes.

I turned, and in an old chintz-covered arm-chair by the fire-place, saw my husband. His face was white, his head was bent slightly forward. He looked as though he had fallen asleep in an uncomfortable position.

"Arthur," I cried, springing forward with a loud cry; but the proprietor, who had been standing by the chair for a minute, came forward and pulled me towards the door.

"He is dead," he said simply.

Dead!

In a dazed way I walked up to the chair and coldly glanced at the face, which, white and expressionless, looked to me unlike that which I had known as my husband's. The proprietor quietly went from the room and left me alone with Arthur. On the mantel-piece my staring eyes saw a small bottle, on which a label marked "laudanum" stood out with fearful clearness. Then I realized it all. With an agonized cry I flung myself into the unresisting arms of my husband. I kissed his cold, dead lips, his face, and the open, unseeing eyes, as I would have kissed him in life, had he willed it so. Ah! he could not ward me off now. He was mine, and I would cherish him forever.

Suddenly I sprang back, a horrible feeling of repulsion creeping over me. Just above Arthur's head, on the wall, I saw two portraits, placed together in a single frame. One represented my husband, happy and smiling; the other showed the hateful features of Captain Dillington. My grief gave place to a violent, overpowering sense of anger. Tearing the frame from the wall, I threw it roughly to the floor. The glass broke with a crisp, short noise; but with my feet I crushed it into atoms. Then stooping down, I picked up the photographs, and tore them into smallest pieces. In the same frenzied manner, I went to the window, opened it, and gathering up the bits of glass — regardless of the fact that they cut my hands until the blood flowed freely — I flung them with the torn photographs from the window and looked from it until I saw them scatter in all directions. Then turning away, and without another look at the dead form in the chair, I left the room and the hotel.

{1889}

HOWARD OVERING STURGIS
{1855–1920}

Howard Overing Sturgis is one of those novelists destined to be remembered less for his own contributions to literature than for his close friendship with a writer of greater fame: in his case, Henry James. The son of wealthy American expatriates, he lived most of his life in England, retiring eventually to an estate called Queen's Acre (or Qu'Acre), which he shared until his death with the much younger William Haynes-Smith, a distant relation. Apparently he was quite queeny; George Santayana, to whom he was also related, described him as, "save for the accident of sex, which was not yet a serious encumbrance, a perfect young lady of the Victorian type." Forster, in a 1935 essay on Sturgis collected in *Abinger Harvest*, recalled that "he was neat in everything. He has been compared to a clean, plump, extremely kind yet distinctly formidable old lady, the sort of old lady who seems all benignity and knitting but who follows everything that is said and much that isn't, and pounces and scratches before you know where you are — pounces on the present company and scratches the absent."

Sturgis published three novels, *Tim* (1891), *All That Was Possible* (1895), and *Belchamber* (1904); the first of them, the title page of which bears the epigraph "Thy love to me was wonderful, passing the love of women," appeared anonymously. Forster called *Tim* "an Etonian meditation rather than a novel . . . a wistful, 'pretty' book, unlikely to find favour in this hard-boiled age." Yet *Tim*'s evocation of one-sided schoolboy love also epitomized what James referred to as "the age of trash triumphant." Indeed, some few years later, James criticized *Belchamber* so heavily (calling it a "mere ante-chamber") that Sturgis stopped writing altogether. In light of James's homophobia, the possibility that he might have had an extra-literary motive in encouraging such a violent act of repudiation is difficult to dismiss. 🙚

FROM *Tim: A Story of Eton*

CHAPTER 13

> . . . Even the weariest river
> Winds, somewhere, safe to sea.
> —SWINBURNE's *Garden of Proserpine*

As the weeks succeeded each other, one thought was ever present in the mind of Tim. "Shall I see him again before I die? It can do him no harm now. I shall so soon be out of the way; I cannot come between him and his love any more."

As his poor hands, whose hold on this world was loosening day by day, grew thinner and more transparent, his face paler, his step slower upon the gravel, his heart yearned ever with a patient longing for just one more sight of the friend to whom his whole life had been true. But he had given the crowning proof of his devotion — renunciation. The arms that should have been upholding him in his last sore struggle, he had himself unclasped; the dear lips and eyes that should even now be smiling on his sickbed, his own free act had sent far away from him.

"He will never know that I was true to him. I shall never see him again." Through all the long empty hours this one cry repeats itself in his soul. All the little life that is left to him seems concentrated in this one intense longing for Carol. To see his face, to hear his loved voice again, if only for a moment; to tell him the truth at last; only once, just once, before he died. And yet even now he could not put his thought into words, — could not bring himself to make this last request to his father.

As for Mr. Ebbesley, he too was troubled by one thought which he could not find the courage to speak. He was always with Tim now. It was his arm which supported the boy into the garden where he loved to sit, and back to the house; no tending could have been more loving, more sympathetic. But, as I have said, no one changes his whole nature at a leap, even in the great crises of life; and there was yet one struggle to be made with his pride before perfect ease and confidence could exist between them.

Hour after hour would Tim lie silent and uncomplaining, yearning for Carol, but dreading to endanger the new-found treasure of his father's love; dreading to see the old cloud settle on the face that he was watching, the hard look grow round the mouth, as it was wont to do when in the old days he had been obliged to mention his friend's name. And William

Ebbesley would sit beside him all the while, divining his thoughts, knowing there was one supreme proof of his affection to be given to his son, one sacrifice that he could make for him, one happiness that he could give him, and longing to make the effort, yet ever just kept from it by some strange inexplicable shyness and reserve. For a long time he hoped that Tim would break the silence, would be the first to approach the subject; but at last he saw that that was not to be hoped, and he was half angry with himself for the cowardice that made him wish to shift this burthen to those poor weak shoulders. No. It was clearly for him to take the first step; had he not ardently desired some way of showing his devotion to his son, and when he had it, was it possible that he should hesitate?

So one evening when they had been watching the sunset, which had left a sham glow on Tim's white cheeks, William Ebbesley, holding his son's hand, and with face half-turned away, said suddenly, "Tim, dear, you have not everything you want; there is one thing I have not done for you."

There was a real glow in Tim's cheeks now; the sunset light had faded, but in its place an inward radiance, brighter but almost as transient, had spread over the delicate face. Feeling his grasp tighten, his father stole a look at him, and even then a pang shot through him at the thought of the love that had called forth this happy flush at the bare chance of a meeting, the love that was not for him, that might perhaps have been his.

"Oh, father! you mean —" Tim began tremulously, and paused; he dared hardly complete the sentence even in his own mind.

William Ebbesley choked down the last touch of the old jealousy. "I will write to-night," he said quietly, answering the other's unspoken thought.

But a new trouble had fallen on Tim. "Will he come?" he said half to himself; and then, "Oh yes. If I know him for the kind, generous Carol I think him, he will surely come."

Then he asked, "Father, may *I* write?"

"You know, dear boy, the doctor has forbidden you to write a word."

"Yes, I know; but this will do me good. I shall not be easy unless I may."

"Won't it do if you dictate to me?"

"No. I must write myself; nothing else will do."

"Well, if you are sure it will not tire you." And he went and brought the writing things.

Tim took them eagerly, and was beginning to write, when he stopped suddenly and looked up. "Father, forgive me; I am selfish. You are sorry at this."

It was so unexpected, the little impulse of unselfish consideration, that at its contact the last drop of bitterness fell from the father's heart, and in his eyes for the first time for more years than he could remember shone the blessed healing tears to which he had so long been a stranger.

"No, no, my darling," he faltered hastily; "whatever makes you happy — I —" then his voice broke, and he could not finish.

"God bless you, dear dear father. I am quite happy now."

And this was Tim's letter: "I am very ill, Carol — dying, I think. Dear Carol, if I have seemed ungrateful, can you and will you forgive me? I could explain to you if I had you here, but I can't write. Come to me, Carol dear. — Your loving Tim."

"Father."

"Yes, dear."

"Do you want to see what I have written?"

"No, my boy, no."

Mr. Ebbesley took the letter and sealed it; then he sent it to the address that he had already got from the servants at the Court.

Whether it was the reaction from the tense longing in which he had been living, or merely that as his strength decreased the change in him grew more apparent, Tim seemed to get worse much more quickly after his letter had gone.

The doctor came and went, shaking his head sadly, and saying, "It is quicker than I thought," and despair settled down upon the two watchers by the sick boy.

But still Tim waited day by day for the answer that was to bring peace to his soul. Life was slipping away too fast. "Oh! come, Carol," he would whisper, "or it may be too late; she will surely spare you just for a little."

Tim had been at home nearly a month now; the blazing July weather had ended in a rather wet August. All around, the harvest lay beaten down by the rain; not the only grain stricken ere it had come to maturity. One evening, after a more than usually dreary day, the clouds had broken, giving place to a gorgeous sunset. Tim had been placed on a sofa in the open window, from which he could watch the purple and crimson and gold, and the delicate green and lilac tints of the western sky; the same sofa on which he had lain eight years before, pondering on his "angel," and had seen Carol come in with his offering of grapes.

"Father."

"Yes, my boy." He knew too well what question was coming.

"Has the postman been?"

"Yes, dear."

Alas! no letter. Tim did not even ask, knowing that if there were one, it would be given to him at once. He closed his eyes and lay quite still. His father looked wearily out of the window; he knew what was passing in the lad's mind, and had come to desire the letter almost as much as the sick boy himself.

The air was cool and fresh. The garden was yielding a thousand scents to the soft touch of the summer rain. The setting sun lit little coloured lamps in the large drops that hung from every leaf of the grateful trees and shrubs; the birds kept up a drowsy twittering. A few knowing old blackbirds and thrushes, well aware that the moisture brings out the fine fat worms, were hopping about on the grass-plot in search of their supper. All sounds were strangely distinct that evening.

Hark! what was that? surely a step on the wet gravel; not old Richard the gardener's step. No, it was a young foot that struck the ground lightly, and scrunched stoutly along the little approach to the house. Tim's ears had caught the sound, and he started up from his pillows, his cheeks aflame, his eyes bright and eager, while his heart beat loud and fast. He would know that dear step among a thousand.

He had come — at last, at last!

Mr. Ebbesley stole noiselessly away, with a heavy dull ache in his heart, and I am afraid neither of the friends noticed his absence. In the same room, in the same place, in the same attitudes in which they had met as children, they had come together again.

"Oh, Carol! are you come to me?"

"Oh, my poor dear Tim!"

Carol could say no more. He was shocked at the havoc these few short weeks had wrought. A sacred silence rested between them for a few minutes. Enough for Tim that he was there; no need of words. Carol was the first to speak; his voice was hushed and full of awe.

"I was not with my family when your letter came, dear Tim, and they did not know where to forward it to me, as I was moving about; so I never got it for nearly ten days, or I should have been here long ago."

"Oh, Carol! how good of you to come. I half thought sometimes — forgive me for doubting you — but I thought you might not come at all — after — after the way I treated you."

"Don't let's talk of that now, Tim; it's past and gone. I don't want you to explain; I am content not to understand. I remember only the dear good friend of the old days, who is come back to me."

"But I *must* talk of it, please, Carol; I must tell you how it was. It can do no harm now, and I can't leave you thinking hardly of me, for you know I have not very long to live; something tells me you are come only just in time."

"Oh! dear dear boy, for God's sake, don't talk like that," said Carol, with a great lump rising in his throat. "You are not going to — to —" He felt all the repugnance of the young and strong to face the thought, or say the word.

"To die." Tim finished the sentence for him quite simply. "Yes, I think so."

"No, no; you will get well and strong. You must, for all our sakes."

Tim smiled and shook his head; it did not seem to him worth while to argue the point; that was not what he wanted to say.

"Never mind," he said gently, in a way that put the subject aside as unimportant. "If I had lived I could not have had you with me now. I could never have told you what I am going to tell you. Carol, will you believe me when I say that I never wavered for an instant in my love for you; never loved you better than when I seemed to give you up?" Tim was getting excited, and Carol, fearing it would be bad for him, tried in vain to stop him. "Oh, Carol! it was for your sake I did it; will you believe me when I tell you all this?"

"For my sake, dear old boy? I don't understand you." He thought his friend's mind was wandering, but he was very patient and tender with him, humouring him, as one would a sick child.

"She said — I heard her say — that I came between you. You know, Carol, it was when you were so unhappy; and then I saw that I was the cause of it all; and so I determined not to come between you any more; and, indeed, indeed, dear Carol, I would have held my tongue for ever, only there is no more need now. I could not die and leave you thinking ill of me. I suppose I ought to have, but I couldn't do it."

A new light was breaking in upon Carol. "And did you do all this for me?" he asked wonderingly. "Why, Tim, I knew you liked me absurdly, much more than I deserved, but I never dreamt you cared as much for me as that."

"And you understand now, Carol, don't you, why I didn't answer your dear letter? See, I have it here; it never leaves me."

"I was a beast and a fool to doubt you, Tim. How could I ever have done it? but it *did* seem as though you must be bored with me and my affairs. And all the time you were doing this for me!"

"Carol, did she mind your coming to me? Tell me I have not made fresh mischief between you?"

"She was very unhappy when I told her how ill you were, and she said, 'Oh! go at once to him; I can guess what it would be to be ill and wanting you; and he has been waiting so long already.' And then she cried, and said a great deal I did not understand at the time about having been jealous of my friendship for you, and having had hard thoughts of you some-times, and that she was so ashamed of herself now that you were so ill. I was to be sure and tell you, and to ask if you would ever forgive her."

"There is nothing to forgive," Tim answered indifferently.

"But how did you guess," Carol continued, "how could you imagine that she felt anything of the sort?"

Then Tim told him all that he had overheard Violet say, only soften-ing it off, and generalising a little with fine tact. And then, the floodgates once open, he went on with sudden eloquence, the more touching from its sheer simplicity, and told all the long story of his constant love, but with as little mention as possible of his father throughout, and of the part he had played in it. And this short hour, which some may think was a sad one, was just the happiest of Tim's whole life.

Carol listened in wonder and awe, not unmingled with compunction, as the description of the feeling he had so unconsciously excited unrolled itself before him. He forgot himself, Violet, his love for her, everything for the moment in contemplation of this devotion, so single-hearted, so lofty, so pure and so unselfish, which had been his, all his, and at which he had been so far from guessing.

"I had no idea of anything of the kind," he said, more to himself than to Tim. "I knew the old people were awfully fond of me, God bless them; and I understand what I feel for Violet. But this beats me; I've always been what's called popular, I suppose. I never thought much about it, but fel-lows have always been jolly to me, and seemed to like me. Oh! my dear friend, what have I ever done that you should care about me like this?"

Tim's face lit up exultingly. " 'Passing the love of women,' " he said; "that was it, Carol, wasn't it? 'Thy love to me was wonderful, passing the love of women.' Do you remember the day when they read it in the lesson in chapel at Eton?"

Carol had forgotten, but Tim's words brought back the scene with strange distinctness: the big chapel in its stillness, the silence of a great crowd, and of a crowd unused to be still, the little flecks of light from the air-holes in the roof, the ugly picture of the finding of Moses in the window op-posite his seat, the droning voice of the reader, and the flash of the little face that turned up to his, with the expression that had puzzled him at the time.

"Yes, I remember," he answered.

"I have thought of it so often since. It would be grand for one's friend to be able to say that of one, after one was dead. Put your strong arms round me, Carol, and raise me a little; I can talk better so."

Carol lifted the poor thin body as easily as a baby, and propped it up on the cushions.

"Thank you, that is better. Ah! don't take your arms away; let me feel them round me for a little. Carol, when I am buried, I want those words to be put on the stone. My father will let it be so, I know, if I wish it; I shall ask him the last thing. But you must remind him."

"Oh! Tim, I can't bear to hear you talk so. You mustn't die; we all want you so much."

"Don't cry, Carol; you will do as I wish, won't you? And, Carol, tell her how I tried to make things happy for her and you; I want her to think kindly of me too."

He laid his head on his friend's breast and closed his eyes; the effort of talking so much had tired him. Carol thought he was asleep, and dared not move for fear of waking him; but by and by he said, "Do you remember, Carol? I lay on this sofa when you first came to see me after the accident. I had been dreaming of you without knowing it; I thought you were an angel. And then I turned and saw you standing there in the doorway. You kissed me that day, Carol. Will you kiss me now?"

Carol bowed his head without a word and kissed him. And thus their friendship was sealed at either end.

"Father," said Tim, after a little, "are you there?"

"Yes, my boy." He had come in, and was standing a little apart in the deepening twilight, humbly watching the friends. How unlike the proud man who had so bitterly resented his little son's preferring another to himself!

"Will you come here, father? I cannot see you there." He came round the sofa, and Tim held out his hand to him. "You and Carol must love one another," he said, looking from one to the other, "for my sake." Silently the two men clasped hands over the couch.

"You must leave us now, Carol dear," Tim went on; "I must be alone with my father."

Carol longed to say something, but could not; he went out without a word. Tim watched him walk away with eyes that knew they were taking their last look. Then a satisfied smile lit up his face as he turned it to his father.

{1891}

AMBROSE BIERCE
{1842–1913?}

Ambrose Bierce's best-known works are surely *The Devil's Dictionary* (1911) and the *Tales of Soldiers and Civilians* (1891; the most famous being "An Occurrence at Owl Creek Bridge"). "The Mocking-Bird" is very different from the rest of Bierce's work, for though the story describes an episode of the Civil War, and was published at the beginning of the 1890s, it reads as a pastiche of fiction from the end of that decade. Death is poeticized to an extraordinary degree, as it is in some of Stenbock, or Wilde. And yet, there is a fairy-tale quality to the story: when the soldier fighting for the Union troops discovers the body of his twin brother who fought for the Confederacy ("to whom he gave his heart and soul in love"), one is forcibly reminded of the Prince's discovery of Sleeping Beauty, or of Narcissus (whose story Wilde reinvents to make the pool love Narcissus back because "in the mirror of his eyes I saw ever my own beauty mirrored"). Bierce further participates in the tradition of naming a homosexual utopia; in his case a place that is not merely homosexual, but incestuous. In the end, the soldier who has slain his brother cannot bear the song of the mockingbird that sings over the youth whose body is warm and whose gray uniform is stained only by a spot of blood on the breast — the song that was to him "the meaning and interpretation to sense of the mysteries of life and love." Like Isolde, life without his Tristan is impossible.

Bierce disappeared, in Mexico, in 1913. ✷

FROM *Tales of Soldiers and Civilians*

The Mocking-Bird

THE TIME, a pleasant Sunday afternoon in the early autumn of 1861. The place, a forest's heart in the mountain region of southwestern Virginia. Private Grayrock of the Federal Army is discovered seated comfortably at the root of a great pine tree, against which he leans, his legs extended straight along the ground, his rifle lying across his thighs, his hands (clasped in order that they may not fall away to his sides) resting upon the barrel of the weapon. The contact of the back of his head with the tree has pushed his cap downward over his eyes, almost concealing them; one seeing him would say that he slept.

Private Grayrock did not sleep; to have done so would have imperiled the interests of the United States, for he was a long way outside the lines and subject to capture or death at the hands of the enemy. Moreover, he was in a frame of mind unfavorable to repose. The cause of his perturbation of spirit was this: during the previous night he had served on the picket-guard, and had been posted as a sentinel in this very forest. The night was clear, though moonless, but in the gloom of the wood the darkness was deep. Grayrock's post was at a considerable distance from those to right and left, for the pickets had been thrown out a needless distance from the camp, making the line too long for the force detailed to occupy it. The war was young, and military camps entertained the error that while sleeping they were better protected by thin lines a long way out toward the enemy than by thicker ones close in. And surely they needed as long notice as possible of an enemy's approach, for they were at that time addicted to the practice of undressing — than which nothing could be more unsoldierly. On the morning of the memorable 6th of April, at Shiloh, many of Grant's men when spitted on Confederate bayonets were as naked as civilians; but it should be allowed that this was not because of any defect in their picket line. Their error was of another sort: they had no pickets. This is perhaps a vain digression. I should not care to undertake to interest the reader in the fate of an army; what we have here to consider is that of Private Grayrock.

For two hours after he had been left at his lonely post that Saturday night he stood stock-still, leaning against the trunk of a large tree, staring into the darkness in his front and trying to recognize known objects; for he had been posted at the same spot during the day. But all was now different; he saw nothing in detail, but only groups of things, whose shapes, not observed when there was something more of them to observe, were now unfamiliar. They seemed not to have been there before. A landscape that is all trees and undergrowth, moreover, lacks definition, is confused and without accentuated points upon which attention can gain a foothold. Add the gloom of a moonless night, and something more than great natural intelligence and a city education is required to preserve one's knowledge of direction. And that is how it occurred that Private Grayrock, after vigilantly watching the spaces in his front and then imprudently executing a circumspection of his whole dimly visible environment (silently walking around his tree to accomplish it) lost his bearings and seriously impaired his usefulness as a sentinel. Lost at his post — unable to say in which direction to look for an enemy's approach, and in which lay the sleeping camp for whose security he was accountable with his life — conscious, too, of many another awkward feature of the situation and of considerations affecting his own safety, Private Grayrock was profoundly disquieted. Nor was he given time to recover his tranquillity, for almost at the moment that he realized his awkward predicament he heard a stir of leaves and a snap of fallen twigs, and turning with a stilled heart in the direction whence it came, saw in the gloom the indistinct outlines of a human figure.

"Halt!" shouted Private Grayrock, peremptorily as in duty bound, backing up the command with the sharp metallic snap of his cocking rifle — "who goes there?"

There was no answer; at least there was an instant's hesitation, and the answer, if it came, was lost in the report of the sentinel's rifle. In the silence of the night and the forest the sound was deafening, and hardly had it died away when it was repeated by the pieces of the pickets to right and left, a sympathetic fusillade. For two hours every unconverted civilian of them had been evolving enemies from his imagination, and peopling the woods in his front with them, and Grayrock's shot had started the whole encroaching host into visible existence. Having fired, all retreated, breathless, to the reserves — all but Grayrock, who did not know in what direction to retreat. When, no enemy appearing, the roused camp two miles away had undressed and got itself into bed again, and the picket line was cautiously reestablished, he was discovered bravely holding his ground, and was complimented by the officer of the guard as the one soldier of that devoted band who could rightly be considered the moral equivalent of that uncommon unit of value, "a whoop in hell."

In the mean time, however, Grayrock had made a close but unavailing search for the mortal part of the intruder at whom he had fired, and whom he had a marksman's intuitive sense of having hit; for he was one of those born experts who shoot without aim by an instinctive sense of direction, and are nearly as dangerous by night as by day. During a full half of his twenty-four years he had been a terror to the targets of all the shooting-galleries in three cities. Unable now to produce his dead game he had the discretion to hold his tongue, and was glad to observe in his officer and comrades the natural assumption that not having run away he had seen nothing hostile. His "honorable mention" had been earned by not running away anyhow.

Nevertheless, Private Grayrock was far from satisfied with the night's adventure, and when the next day he made some fair enough pretext to apply for a pass to go outside the lines, and the general commanding promptly granted it in recognition of his bravery the night before, he passed out at the point where that had been displayed. Telling the sentinel then on duty there that he had lost something, — which was true enough — he renewed the search for the person whom he supposed himself to have shot, and whom if only wounded he hoped to trail by the blood. He was no more successful by daylight than he had been in the darkness, and after covering a wide area and boldly penetrating a long distance into "the Confederacy" he gave up the search, somewhat fatigued, seated himself at the root of the great pine tree, where we have seen him, and indulged his disappointment.

It is not to be inferred that Grayrock's was the chagrin of a cruel nature balked of its bloody deed. In the clear large eyes, finely wrought lips, and broad forehead of that young man one could read quite another story, and in point of fact his character was a singularly felicitous compound of boldness and sensibility, courage and conscience.

"I find myself disappointed," he said to himself, sitting there at the bottom of the golden haze submerging the forest like a subtler sea — "disappointed in failing to discover a fellow-man dead by my hand! Do I then really wish that I had taken life in the performance of a duty as well performed without? What more could I wish? If any danger threatened, my shot averted it; that is what I was there to do. No, I am glad indeed if no human life was needlessly extinguished by me. But I am in a false position. I have suffered myself to be complimented by my officers and envied by my comrades. The camp is ringing with praise of my courage. That is not just; I know myself courageous, but this praise is for specific acts which I did not perform, or performed — otherwise. It is believed that I remained at my post bravely, without firing, whereas it was I who began the fusillade, and I did not retreat in the general alarm because bewildered. What, then, shall I do? Explain that I saw an enemy and fired? They have all said that of themselves, yet none believes it. Shall I tell a truth which, discrediting my courage, will have the effect of a lie? Ugh! it is an ugly business altogether. I wish to God I could find my man!"

And so wishing, Private Grayrock, overcome at last by the languor of the afternoon and lulled by the stilly sounds of insects droning and prosing in certain fragrant shrubs, so far forgot the interests of the United States as to fall asleep and expose himself to capture. And sleeping he dreamed.

He thought himself a boy, living in a far, fair land by the border of a great river upon which the tall steamboats moved grandly up and down beneath their towering evolutions of black smoke, which announced them long before they had rounded the bends and marked their movements when miles out of sight. With him always, at his side as he watched them, was one to whom he gave his heart and soul in love — a twin brother. Together they strolled along the banks of the stream; together explored the fields lying farther away from it, and gathered pungent mints and sticks of fragrant sassafras in the hills overlooking all — beyond which lay the Realm of Conjecture, and from which, looking southward across the great river, they caught glimpses of the Enchanted Land. Hand in hand and heart in heart they two, the only children of a widowed mother, walked in paths of light through valleys of peace, seeing new things under a new sun. And through all the golden days floated one unceasing sound — the rich, thrilling melody of a mocking-bird in a cage by the cottage door. It pervaded and possessed all the spiritual intervals of the dream, like a musical benediction. The joyous bird was always in song; its infinitely various notes seemed to flow from its throat, effortless, in bubbles and rills at each heartbeat, like the waters of a pulsing spring. That fresh, clear melody seemed, indeed, the spirit of the scene, the meaning and interpretation to sense of the mysteries of life and love.

But there came a time when the days of the dream grew dark with sorrow in a rain of tears. The good mother was dead, the meadowside home by the great river was broken up, and the brothers were parted between two of their kinsmen. William (the dreamer) went to live in a populous city in the Realm of Conjecture, and John, crossing the river into the Enchanted Land, was taken to a distant region whose people in their lives and ways were said to be strange and wicked. To him, in the distribution of the dead mother's estate, had fallen all that they deemed of value — the mocking-bird. They could be divided, but it could not, so it was carried away into the strange country, and the world of William knew it no more forever. Yet still through the aftertime of his loneliness its song filled all the dream, and seemed always sounding in his ear and in his heart.

The kinsmen who had adopted the boys were enemies, holding no

communication. For a time letters full of boyish bravado and boastful nar-
ratives of the new and larger experience — grotesque descriptions of their
widening lives and the new worlds they had conquered — passed between
them; but these gradually became less frequent, and with William's re-
moval to another and greater city ceased altogether. But ever through it all
ran the song of the mocking-bird, and when the dreamer opened his eyes
and stared through the vistas of the pine forest the cessation of its music
first apprised him that he was awake.

The sun was low and red in the west; the level rays projected from the
trunk of each giant pine a wall of shadow traversing the golden haze to
eastward until light and shade were blended in undistinguishable blue.

Private Grayrock rose to his feet, looked cautiously about him, shoul-
dered his rifle and set off toward camp. He had gone perhaps a half-mile,
and was passing a thicket of laurel, when a bird rose from the midst of it
and perching on the branch of a tree above, poured from its joyous breast
so inexhaustible floods of song as but one of all God's creatures can utter in
His praise. There was little in that — it was only to open the bill and
breathe; yet the man stopped as if struck — stopped and let fall his rifle,
looked upward at the bird, covered his eyes with his hands and wept like a
child! For the moment he was, indeed, a child, in spirit and in memory,
welling again by the great river, over-against the Enchanted Land! Then
with an effort of the will he pulled himself together, picked up his weapon
and audibly damning himself for an idiot strode on. Passing an opening
that reached into the heart of the little thicket he looked in, and there,
supine upon the earth, its arms all abroad, its gray uniform stained with a
single spot of blood upon the breast, its white face turned sharply upward
and backward, lay the image of himself! — the body of John Grayrock,
dead of a gunshot wound, and still warm! He had found his man.

As the unfortunate soldier knelt beside that masterwork of civil war the
shrilling bird upon the bough overhead stilled her song and, flushed with
sunset's crimson glory, glided silently away through the solemn spaces of
the wood. At roll-call that evening in the Federal camp the name William
Grayrock brought no response, nor ever again thereafter.

{1891}

HENRY JAMES
{1843–1916}

Millicent Bell, in a review of Sheldon M. Novick's *Henry James: The Young Master* (1995), takes issue with Novick's "novelistic" approach to biography, particularly to the thorny question of James's homosexuality. As it happens, Novick gives his hero an active sex life (one, he writes, that began with Oliver Wendell Holmes, whose biography Novick also wrote), while the more scrupulous Fred Kaplan (*Henry James: The Imagination of Genius*, 1992) found no evidence to support claims that James's homosexuality was actual rather than theoretical, and Leon Edel, in his five-volume biography of the master (published between 1953 and 1972), held that James began to have sex with men only in his last years. Failing the discovery of love letters from James to a young man — a version of his own novella, *The Aspern Papers* — his homosexuality must remain theoretical.

That said, one fact is certain: James shunned any association with obvious homosexual situations, whether literary or personal. In 1895, when Stuart Merrill asked James to sign a petition requesting that Oscar Wilde's prison sentence be mitigated, James refused. He felt little sympathy toward the writer he had once called an "unclean beast" — and whose plays had bested his own disastrous *Guy Domville* (1895), after the premiere of which James, when he came forward to take his bow, was booed off the stage. Later, he remarked in a letter that in his view Wilde's sentence of hard labor was overly severe; isolation, he thought, would have been more just. Likewise, when the young novelist Forrest Reid dedicated *The Garden God: A Tale of Two Boys* (1905) to him, James responded by severing the friendship.

Not surprisingly, the homosexual content in James's *oeuvre* is rarely explicit. Aside from the much anthologized (and analyzed) "The Pupil" and "The Turn of the Screw," notable examples include "The Author of Beltraffio," with its Symonds-like "aesthetic" hero; "The Great Good Place," of which both James Gifford and Brad Leithauser offer superb analyses; and *The Ambassadors* (1903), in which Strether's first Parisian encounter with the American runaway Chad evokes an intense, if subconscious, desire for the boy, a "rush . . . both vague and multitudinous" that "lasted a long time, protected, as it were, yet at the same aggravated, by the circumstance of its coinciding with a decorous silence." Sitting next to Chad at the theater, it is "truly the life of high pressure that Strether had seemed to feel himself lead . . . close to Chad, during the long tension of the act."

> He was in presence of a fact that had occupied his whole mind, that occupied for the half-hour his senses themselves all together; but he couldn't without inconvenience show anything — which moreover might count really as luck . . . The phenomenon that had suddenly sat down there with him was a phenomenon of change so complete that his imagination, which had worked so beforehand, felt itself, in the connexion, without margin or allowance. It had faced every contingency but that Chad should not *be* Chad, and this was what it now had to face with a mere strained smile and an uncomfortable flush.

James's typically tormented "late style" prose here chokes an erotic response that the use of words such as "rush," "flush," "strained" and "pressure" only serves to underscore — so much so that the carnal implications of the phrase "the long tension of the act" ring out loud and clear, despite (or perhaps because of) James's efforts to suppress them. ❧

Collaboration

I DON'T KNOW HOW MUCH people care for my work, but they like my studio (of which indeed I am exceedingly fond myself), as they show by their inclination to congregate there at dusky hours on winter afternoons, or on long dim evenings when the place looks well with its rich combinations and low-burning lamps and the bad pictures (my own) are not particularly visible. I won't go into the question of how many of these are purchased, but I rejoice in the distinction that my invitations are never declined. Some of my visitors have been good enough to say that on Sunday evenings in particular there is no pleasanter place in Paris — where so many places are pleasant — none friendlier to easy talk and repeated cigarettes, to the exchange of points of view and the comparison of accents. The air is as international as only Parisian air can be; women, I surmise, think they look well in it; they come also because they fancy they are doing something Bohemian, just as many of the men come because they suppose they are doing something correct. The old heraldic cushions on the divans, embossed with rusty gold, are favourable both to expansion and to contraction — that of course of contracting parties — and the Italian brocade on the walls appeals to one's highest feelings. Music makes its home there — though I confess I am not quite the master of *that* house, and when it is going on in a truly receptive hush I enjoy the way my company leans back and gazes through the thin smoke of cigarettes up at the distant Tiepolo in the almost palatial ceiling. I make sure the piano, the tobacco and the tea are all of the best.

For the conversation, I leave that mostly to take care of itself. There are discussions of course and differences — sometimes even a violent circulation of sense and sound; but I have a consciousness that beauty flourishes and that harmonies prevail in the end. I have occasionally known a visitor to be rude to me because he disliked another visitor's opinions — I had seen an old habitué slip away without bidding me good night on the arrival of some confident specimen of *les jeunes;* but as a general thing we have it out together on the spot — the place is really a chamber of justice, a temple of reconciliation: we understand each other if we only sit up late enough. Art protects her children in the long run — she only asks them to trust her. She is like the Catholic Church — she guarantees paradise to the faithful. Music moreover is a universal solvent; though I've not an infallible ear I've a sufficient sense of the matter for that. Ah, the wounds I've known it to heal — the bridges I've known it to build — the ghosts I've known it to lay! Though I've seen people stalk out I've never observed them not to steal back. My studio in short is the theatre of a cosmopolite drama, a comedy essentially "of character."

One of the liveliest scenes of the performance was the evening, last winter, on which I became aware that one of my compatriots — an American, my good friend Alfred Bonus — was engaged in a controversy somewhat acrimonious, on a literary subject, with Herman Heidenmauer, the young composer who had been playing to us divinely a short time before and whom I thought of neither as a disputant nor as an Englishman. I perceived in a moment that something had happened to present him in this combined character to poor Bonus, who was so ardent a patriot that he lived in Paris rather than in London, who had met his interlocutor for the first time on this occasion, and who apparently had been misled by the perfection with which Heidenmauer spoke English — he spoke it really better than Alfred Bonus. The young musician, a born Bavarian, had spent a few years in England, where he had a commercial step-brother planted and more or less prosperous — a helpful man who had watched over his difficult first steps, given him a temporary home, found him publishers and pupils, smoothed the way to a stupefied hearing for his first productions. He knew his London and might at a first glance have been taken for one of its products; but he had, in addition to a genius of the sort that London fosters but doesn't beget, a very German soul. He brought me a note from an old friend on the other side of the Channel, and I liked him as soon as I looked at him; so much indeed that I could forgive him for making me feel thin and empirical, conscious that *he* was one of the higher kind whom the future has looked in the face. He had met through his gold spectacles her deep eyes, and some mutual communication had occurred. This had given him a confidence which passed for conceit only with those who didn't know the reason.

I guessed the reason early, and, as may be imagined, he didn't grudge me the knowledge. He was happy and various — as little as possible the mere long-haired musicmonger. His hair was short — it was only his legs and his laughter that were long. He was fair and rosy, and his gold spectacles glittered as if in response to the example set them by his beautiful young golden beard. You would have been sure he was an artist without going so far as to decide upon his particular passion; for you would have been conscious that whatever this passion might be it was acquainted with many of the others and mixed with them to its profit. Yet these discoveries had not been fully made by Alfred Bonus, whose occupation was to write letters to the American journals about the way the "boys" were coming on in Paris; for in such a case he probably would not have expected such nebulous greatness to condense at a moment's notice. Bonus is clever and critical, and a sort of self-appointed emissary or agent of the great republic. He has it at heart to prove that the Americans in Europe *do* get on — taking for granted on the part of the Americans at home an interest in this subject greater, as I often assure him, than any really felt. "Come, now, do *I* get on?" I often ask him; and I sometimes push the inquiry so far as to stammer: "And you, my dear Bonus, do *you* get on?" He is apt to look a little injured on such occasions, as if he would like to say in reply: "Don't you call it success to have Sunday evenings at which I'm a regular attendant? And can you question for a moment the figure I make at them?" It has even occurred to me that he suspects me of painting badly on purpose to spite him — that is to interfere with his favourite dogma. Therefore to spite me in return he's in the heroic predicament of refusing to admit that I'm a failure. He takes a great interest in the plastic arts, but his intensest sympathy is for literature. This sentiment is somewhat starved, as in that school the boys languish as yet on a back seat. To show what they are doing Bonus has to retreat upon the studios, but there is nothing he enjoys so much as having, when the rare chance offers, a good literary talk. He follows the French movement closely and explains it profusely to our compatriots, whom he mystifies, but who guess he's rather loose.

I forget how his conversation with Heidenmauer began — it was, I think, some difference of opinion about one of the English poets that set them afloat. Heidenmauer knows the English poets, and the French, and the Italian, and the Spanish, and the Russian — he is a wonderful representative of that Germanism which consists in the negation of intellectual frontiers. It is the English poets that, if I'm not mistaken, he loves best, and probably the harm was done by his having happened to say so. At any rate Alfred Bonus let him have it, without due notice perhaps, which is rather Alfred's way, on the question (a favourite one with my compatriot) of the backward state of literature in England, for which after all Heidenmauer was not responsible. Bonus believes in responsibility — the responsibility of others, an attitude which tends to make some of his friends extremely secretive, though perhaps it would have been justified — as to this I'm not sure — had Heidenmauer been, under the circumstances, technically British. Before he had had time to explain that he was not, the other persons present had become aware that a kind of challenge had passed — that nation, in a sudden startled flurry, somehow found itself pitted against nation. There was much vagueness at first as to which of the nations were engaged and as to what their quarrel was about, the question coming presently to appear less simple than the spectacle (so easily conceivable) of a German's finding it hot for him in a French house, a house French enough at any rate to give countenance to the idea of his quick defeat.

How could the right cause fail of protection in any house of which Madame de Brindes and her charming daughter were so good as to be assiduous frequenters? I recollect perfectly the pale gleam of joy in the mother's handsome face when she gathered that what had happened was that a detested German was on his defence. She wears her eternal mourning (I admit it's immensely becoming) for a triple woe, for multiplied griefs and wrongs, all springing from the crash of the Empire, from the battle-fields of 1870. Her husband fell at Sedan, her father and her brother on still darker days; both her own family and that of M. de Brindes, their general situation in life, were, as may be said, creations of the Empire, so that from one hour to the other she found herself sinking with the wreck. You won't recognise her under the name I give her, but you may none the less have admired, between their pretty lemon-coloured covers, the touching tales of Claude Lorrain. She plies an ingenious, pathetic pen and has reconciled herself to effort and privation for the sake of her daughter. I say privation, because these distinguished women are poor, receive with great modesty and have broken with a hundred of those social sanctities that are dearer to French souls than to any others. They have gone down into the market-place, and Paule de Brindes, who is three-and-twenty to-day and has a happy turn for keeping a water-colour liquid, earns a hundred francs here and there. She is not so handsome as her mother, but she has magnificent hair and what the French call a look of race, and is, or at least was till the other day, a frank and charming young woman. There is something exquisite in the way these ladies are earnestly, conscientiously modern. From the moment they accept necessities they accept them all, and poor Madame de Brindes flatters herself that she has made her dowerless daughter one of us others. The girl goes out alone, talks with young men and, although she only paints landscape, takes a free view of the *convenances*. Nothing can please either of them more than to tell them they have thrown over their superstitions. They haven't, thank heaven; and when I want to be reminded of some of the prettiest in the world — of a thousand fine scruples and pleasant forms, and of what grace can do for the sake of grace — I know where to go for it.

It was a part of this pious heresy — much more august in the way they presented it than some of the aspects of the old faith — that Paule should have become "engaged," quite like a *jeune mees*, to my brilliant friend Félix Vendemer. He is such a votary of the modern that he was inevitably interested in the girl of the future and had matched one reform with another, being ready to marry without a penny, as the clearest way of expressing his appreciation, this favourable specimen of the type. He simply fell in love with Mademoiselle de Brindes and behaved, on his side, equally like one of us others, except that he begged me to ask her mother for her hand. I was inspired to do so with eloquence, and my friends were not insensible of such an opportunity to show that they now lived in the world of realities. Vendemer's sole fortune is his genius, and he and Paule, who confessed to an answering flame, plighted their troth like a pair of young rustics or (what comes for French people to the same thing) young Anglo-Saxons. Madame de Brindes thinks such doings at bottom very vulgar; but vulgar is what she tries hard to be, she is so convinced it is the only way to make a living. Vendemer had had at that time only the first of his successes, which was not, as you will remember — and unfortunately for Madame de Brindes — of this remunerative kind. Only a few people recognised the perfection of his little volume of verse: my acquaintance with him originated in my having been one of the few. A volume of verse was a scanty provision to marry on, so that, still like a pair of us others, the luckless lovers had to bide their time. Presently however came the success (again a success only with those who care for quality, not with the rough and ready public) of his comedy in verse at the Français. This charming work had just been taken off (it had been found not to make money), when the various parties to my little drama met Heidenmauer at my studio.

Vendemer, who has, as indeed the others have, a passion for music, was tremendously affected by hearing him play two or three of his compositions, and I immediately saw that the immitigable German quality was a morsel much less bitter for him than for the two uncompromising ladies. He went so far as to speak to Heidenmauer frankly, to thank him with effusion, an effort of which neither of the quivering women would have been capable. Vendemer was in the room the night Alfred Bonus raised his little breeze; I saw him lean on the piano and listen with a queer face looking however rather wonderingly at Heidenmauer. Before this I had noticed the instant paleness (her face was admirably expressive) with which Madame de Brindes saw her prospective son-in-law make up, as it were, to the original Teuton, whose national character was intensified to her aching mind, as it would have been to that of most Frenchwomen in her place, by his wash of English colour. A German was bad enough — but a German with English aggravations! Her senses were too fine to give her the excuse of not feeling that his compositions were interesting, and she was capable, magnanimously, of listening to them with dropped eyes; but (much as it ever cost her not to be perfectly courteous), she couldn't have made even the most superficial speech to him about them. Marie de

Brindes could never have spoken to Herman Heidenmauer. It was a narrowness if you will, but a narrowness that to my vision was enveloped in a
dense atmosphere — a kind of sunset bloom — of enriching and fortifying
things. Herman Heidenmauer himself, like the man of imagination and
the lover of life that he was, would have entered into it delightedly, been
charmed with it as a fine case of bigotry. This was conspicuous in Marie de
Brindes: her loyalty to the national idea was that of a *dévote* to a form of
worship. She never spoke of France, but she always made me think of it,
and with an authority which the women of her race seem to me to have in
the question much more than the men. I dare say I'm rather in love with
her, though, being considerably younger, I've never told her so — as if
she would in the least mind that! I have indeed been a little checked by a
spirit of allegiance to Vendemer; suspecting always (excuse my sophistica-
tion) that in the last analysis it is the mother's charm that he feels — or
originally felt — in the daughter's. He spoke of the elder lady to me in
those days with the insistence with which only a Frenchman can speak of
the objects of his affection. At any rate there was always something symbolic and slightly ceremonial to me in her delicate cameo-face and her
general black-robed presence; she made me think of a priestess or a
mourner, of revolutions and sieges, detested treaties and ugly public
things. I pitied her, too, for the strife of the elements in her — for the way
she must have felt a noble enjoyment mutilated. She was too good for that,
and yet she was too rigid for anything else; and the sight of such dismal
perversions made me hate more than ever the stupid terms on which nations have organised their intercourse.

When she gathered that one of my guests was simply cramming it
down the throat of another that the English literary mind was not even literary, she turned away with a vague shrug and a pitiful look at her daughter for the taste of people who took their pleasure so poorly: the truth in
question would be so obvious that it was not worth making a scene about.
Madame de Brindes evidently looked at any scene between the English
and the Americans as a quarrel proceeding vaguely from below stairs — a
squabble sordidly domestic. Her almost immediate departure with her
daughter operated as a lucky interruption, and I caught for the first time in
the straight, spare girl, as she followed her mother, a little of the air that
Vendemer had told me he found in her, the still exaltation, the brown uplifted head that we attribute, or that at any rate he made it visible to me
that he attributed, to the dedicated Maid. He considered that his intended
bore a striking resemblance to Jeanne d'Arc, and he marched after her on
this occasion like a square-shouldered armour-bearer. He reappeared,
however, after he had put the ladies into a cab, and half an hour later the

rest of my friends, with the sole exception of Bonus, having dispersed, he was sitting up with me in the empty studio for another *bout de causerie*. At first perhaps I was too occupied with reprimanding my compatriot to give much attention to what Vendemer might have to say; I remember at any rate that I had asked Bonus what had induced him to make so grave a blunder. He was not even yet, it appeared, aware of his blunder, so that I had to inquire by what odd chance he had taken Heidenmauer for a bigoted Briton.

"If I spoke to him as one he answered as one; that's bigoted enough," said Alfred Bonus.

"He was confused and amused at your onslaught: he wondered what fly had stung you."

"The fly of patriotism," Vendemer suggested.

"Do *you* like him — a beast of a German?" Bonus demanded.

"If he's an Englishman he isn't a German — *il faut opter*. We can hang him for the one or for the other, we can't hang him for both. I was immensely struck with those things he played."

"They had no charm for me, or doubtless I too should have been demoralised," Alfred said. "He seemed to know nothing about Miss Brownrigg. Now Miss Brownrigg's great."

"I like the things and even the people you quarrel about, you big babies of the same breast. *C'est à se tordre!*" Vendemer declared.

"I may be very abject, but I *do* take an interest in the American novel," Alfred rejoined.

"I hate such expressions: there's no such thing as the American novel."

"Is there by chance any such thing as the French?"

"*Pas davantage* — for the artist himself: how can you ask? I don't know what is meant by French art and English art and American art: those seem to me mere cataloguers' and reviewers' and tradesmen's names, representing preoccupations utterly foreign to the artist. Art is art in every country, and the novel (since Bonus mentions that) is the novel in every tongue, and hard enough work they have to live up to that privilege, without our adding another muddle to the problem. The reader, the consumer may call things as he likes, but we leave him to his little amusements." I suggested that we were all readers and consumers; which only made Vendemer continue: "Yes, and only a small handful of us have the ghost of a palate. But you and I and Bonus are of the handful."

"What do you mean by the handful?" Bonus inquired.

Vendemer hesitated a moment. "I mean the few intelligent people, and even the few people who are not —" He paused again an instant, long enough for me to request him not to say what they were "not," and then went on: "People in a word who have the honour to live in the only country worth living in."

"And pray what country is that?"

"The land of dreams — the country of art."

"Oh, the land of dreams! I live in the land of realities!" Bonus exclaimed. "What do you all mean then by chattering so about *le roman russe?*"

"It's a convenience — to identify the work of three or four, *là-bas*, because we're so far from it. But do you see them *writing* 'le roman russe'?"

"I happen to know that that's exactly what they want to do, some of them," said Bonus.

"Some of the idiots, then! There are plenty of those everywhere. Anything born under that silly star is sure not to count."

"Thank God I'm not an artist!" said Bonus.

"Dear Alfred's a critic," I explained.

"And I'm not ashamed of my country," he subjoined.

"Even a critic perhaps may be an artist," Vendemer mused.

"Then as the great American critic Bonus may be the great American artist," I went on.

"Is that what you're supposed to give us — 'American' criticism?" Vendemer asked, with dismay in his expressive, ironic face. "Take care, take care, or it will be more American than critical, and then where will *you* be? However," he continued, laughing and with a change of tone, "I may see the matter in too lurid a light, for I've just been favoured with a judgment conceived in the purest spirit of our own national genius." He looked at me a moment and then he remarked: "That dear Madame de Brindes doesn't approve of my attitude."

"Your attitude?"

"Toward your German friend. She let me know it when I went down stairs with her — told me I was much too cordial, that I must observe myself."

"And what did you reply to that?"

"I answered that the things he had played were extraordinarily beautiful."

"And how did she meet that?"

"By saying that he's an enemy of our country."

"She had you there," I rejoined.

"Yes, I could only reply '*Chère madame, voyons!*' "

"That was meagre."

"Evidently, for it did no more for me than to give her a chance to declare that he can't possibly be here for any good and that he belongs to a race it's my sacred duty to loathe."

"I see what she means."

"I don't then — where artists are concerned. I said to her: '*Ah, madame, vous savez que pour moi il n'y a que l'art!*' "

"It's very exciting!" I laughed. "How could she parry that?"

" 'I know it, my dear child — but for *him*?' That's the way she parried it. 'Very well, for him?' I asked. 'For him there's the insolence of the victor and a secret scorn for our incurable illusions!' "

"Heidenmauer has no insolence and no secret scorn."

Vendemer was silent a moment. "Are you very sure of that?"

"Oh, I like him! He's out of all that, and far above it. But what did Mademoiselle Paule say?" I inquired.

"She said nothing — she only looked at me."

"Happy man!"

"Not a bit. She looked at me with strange eyes, in which I could read 'Go straight, my friend — go straight!' Oh, *les femmes, les femmes!*"

"What's the matter with them now?"

"They've a mortal hatred of art!"

"It's a true, deep instinct," said Alfred Bonus.

"But what passed further with Madame de Brindes?" I went on.

"She only got into her cab, pushing her daughter first; on which I slammed the door rather hard and came up here. *Cela m'a porté sur les nerfs.*"

"I'm afraid I haven't soothed them," Bonus said, looking for his hat. When he had found it he added: "When the English have beaten us and pocketed our *milliards* I'll forgive them; but not till then!" And with this he went off, made a little uncomfortable, I think, by Vendemer's sharper alternatives, while the young Frenchman called after him: "My dear fellow, at night all cats are grey!"

Vendemer, when we were left alone together, mooned about the empty studio awhile and asked me three or four questions about Heidenmauer. I satisfied his curiosity as well as I could, but I demanded the reason of it. The reason he gave was that one of the young German's compositions had already begun to haunt his memory; but that was a reason which, to my sense, still left something unexplained. I didn't however challenge him, before he quitted me, further than to warn him against being deliberately perverse.

"What do you mean by being deliberately perverse?" He fixed me so with his intensely living French eye that I became almost blushingly conscious of a certain insincerity and, instead of telling him what I meant, tried to get off with the deplorable remark that the prejudices of Mesdames de Brindes were after all respectable. "That's exactly what makes them so odious!" cried Vendemer.

A few days after this, late in the afternoon, Herman Heidenmauer came in to see me and found the young Frenchman seated at my piano — trying to win back from the keys some echo of a passage in the *Abendlied* we had listened to on the Sunday evening. They met, naturally, as good friends, and Heidenmauer sat down with instant readiness and gave him again the page he was trying to recover. He asked him for his address, that he might send him the composition, and at Vendemer's request, as we sat in the firelight, played half-a-dozen other things. Vendemer listened in silence but to my surprise took leave of me before the lamp was brought in. I asked him to stay to dinner (I had already appealed to Heidenmauer to stay), but he explained that he was engaged to dine with Madame de Brindes — *à la maison* as he always called it. When he had gone Heidenmauer, with whom on departing he had shaken hands without a word, put to me the same questions about him that Vendemer had asked on the Sunday evening about the young German, and I replied that my visitor would find in a small volume of remarkable verse published by Lemerre, which I placed in his hands, much of the information he desired. This volume, which had just appeared, contained, beside a reprint of Vendemer's earlier productions, many of them admirable lyrics, the drama that had lately been played at the Français, and Heidenmauer took it with him when he left me. But he left me late, and before this occurred, all the evening, we had much talk about the French nation. In the foreign colony of Paris the exchange of opinions on this subject is one of the most inevitable and by no means the least interesting of distractions; it furnishes occupation to people rather conscious of the burden of leisure. Heidenmauer had been little in Paris, but he was all the more open to impressions; they evidently poured in upon him and he gave them a generous hospitality. In the diffused white light of his fine German intelligence old colours took on new tints to me, and while we spun fancies about the wonderful race around us I added to my little stock of notions about his own. I saw that his admiration for our neighbours was a very high tide, and I was struck with something bland and unconscious (noble and serene in its absence of precautions) in the way he let his doors stand open to it. It would have been exasperating to many Frenchmen; he looked at them through his clear spectacles with such an absence of suspicion that they might have anything to forgive him, such a thin metaphysical view of instincts and passions. He had the air of not allowing for recollections and nerves, and would doubtless give them occasion to make afresh some of their reflections on the tact of *ces gens-là.*

A couple of days after I had given him Vendemer's book he came back to tell me that he found great beauty in it. "It speaks to me — it speaks to me," he said with his air of happy proof. "I liked the songs — I liked the songs. Besides," he added, "I like the little romantic play — it has given me wonderful ideas; more ideas than anything has done for a long time. Yes — yes."

"What kind of ideas?"

"Well, this kind." And he sat down to the piano and struck the keys. I listened without more questions, and after a while I began to understand. Suddenly he said: "Do you know the words of *that?*" and before I could answer he was rolling out one of the lyrics of the little volume. The poem was strange and obscure, yet irresistibly beautiful, and he had translated it into music still more tantalizing than itself. He sounded the words with his German accent, barely perceptible in English but strongly marked in French. He dropped them and took them up again; he was playing with them, feeling his way. "*This* is my idea!" he broke out; he had caught it, in one of its mystic mazes, and he rendered it with a kind of solemn freshness. There was a phrase he repeated, trying it again and again, and while he did so he chanted the words of the song as if they were an illuminating flame, an inspiration. I was rather glad on the whole that Vendemer didn't hear what his pronunciation made of them, but as I was in the very act of rejoicing I became aware that the author of the verses had opened the door. He had pushed it gently, hearing the music; then hearing also his own poetry he had paused and stood looking at Heidenmauer. The young German nodded and laughed and, irreflectively, spontaneously, greeted him with a friendly "*Was sagen Sie dazu?*" I saw Vendemer change colour; he blushed red and, for an instant, as he stood wavering, I thought he was going to retreat. But I beckoned him in and, on the divan beside me, patted a place for him to sit.

He came in but didn't take this place; he went and stood before the fire to warm his feet, turning his back to us. Heidenmauer played and played, and after a little Vendemer turned round; he looked about him for a seat, dropped into it and sat with his elbows on his knees and his head in his hands. Presently Heidenmauer called out, in French, above the music: "I like your songs — I like them immensely!" but the young Frenchman neither spoke nor moved. When however five minutes later Heidenmauer stopped he sprang up with an entreaty to him to go on, to go on for the love of God. "*Foilà — foilà!*" cried the musician, and with hands for an instant suspended he wandered off into mysterious worlds. He played Wagner and then Wagner again — a great deal of Wagner; in the midst of which, abruptly, he addressed himself again to Vendemer, who had gone still fur-

ther from the piano, launching to me, however from his corner a *"Dieu, que
c'est beau!"* which I saw that Heidenmauer caught. "I've a conception for an
opera, you know — I'd give anything if you'd do the libretto!" Our German friend laughed out, after this, with clear good nature, and the rich appeal brought Vendemer slowly to his feet again, staring at the musician
across the room and turning this time perceptibly pale.

I felt there was a drama in the air, and it made me a little nervous; to
conceal which I said to Heidenmauer: "What's your conception? What's
your subject?"

"My conception would be realized in the subject of M. Vendemer's
play — if he'll do that for me in a great lyric manner!" And with this the
young German, who had stopped playing to answer me, quitted the piano
and Vendemer got up to meet him. "The subject is splendid — it has
taken possession of me. Will you do it with me? Will you work with me?
We shall make something great!"

"Ah, you don't know what you ask!" Vendemer answered, with his
pale smile.

"I do — I do: I've thought of it. It will be bad for me in my country; I
shall suffer for it. They won't like it — they'll abuse me for it — they'll say
of me *pis que pendre.*" Heidenmauer pronounced it *bis que bendre.*

"They'll hate my libretto so?" Vendemer asked.

"Yes, your libretto — they'll say it's immoral and horrible. And
they'll say *I'm* immoral and horrible for having worked with you," the
young composer went on, with his pleasant healthy lucidity. "You'll injure
my career. Oh yes, I shall suffer!" he joyously, exultingly cried.

"Et moi donc!" Vendemer exclaimed.

"Public opinion, yes. I shall also make *you* suffer — I shall nip your
prosperity in the bud. All that's *des bêtises — tes pètisses,*" said poor Heidenmauer. "In art there are no countries."

"Yes, art is terrible, art is monstrous," Vendemer replied, looking at
the fire.

"I love your songs — they have extraordinary beauty."

"And Vendemer has an equal taste for *your* compositions," I said to
Heidenmauer.

"Tempter!" Vendemer murmured to me, with a strange look.

"C'est juste! I mustn't meddle — which will be all the easier as I'm dining out and must go and dress. You two make yourselves at home and fight
it out here."

"Do you *leave* me?" asked Vendemer, still with his strange look.

"My dear fellow, I've only just time."

"We will dine together — he and I — at one of those characteristic places, and we will look at the matter in its different relations," said Heidenmauer. "Then we will come back here to finish — your studio is so good for music."

"There are some things it *isn't* good for," Vendemer remarked, looking at our companion.

"It's good for poetry — it's good for truth," smiled the composer.

"You'll stay *here* and dine together," I said; "my servant can manage that."

"No, no — we'll go out and we'll walk together. We'll talk a great deal," Heidenmauer went on. "The subject is so comprehensive," he said to Vendemer, as he lighted another cigar.

"The subject?"

"Of your drama. It's so universal."

"Ah, the universe — *il n'y a que ça!*" I laughed, to Vendemer, partly with a really amused sense of the exaggerated woe that looked out of his poetic eyes and that seemed an appeal to me not to forsake him, to throw myself into the scale of the associations he would have to stifle, and partly to encourage him, to express my conviction that two such fine minds couldn't in the long run be the worse for coming to an agreement. I might have been a more mocking Mephistopheles handing over his pure spirit to my literally German Faust.

When I came home at eleven o'clock I found him alone in my studio, where, evidently, for some time, he had been moving up and down in agitated thought. The air was thick with Bavarian fumes, with the reverberation of mighty music and great ideas, with the echoes of that "universe" to which I had so mercilessly consigned him. But I judged in a moment that Vendemer was in a very different phase of his evolution from the one in which I had left him. I had never seen his handsome, sensitive face so intensely illumined.

"*Ça y est — ça y est!*" he exclaimed, standing there with his hands in his pockets and looking at me.

"You've really agreed to do something together?"

"We've sworn a tremendous oath — we've taken a sacred engagement."

"My dear fellow, you're a hero."

"Wait and see! *C'est un très-grand esprit.*"

"So much the better!"

"*C'est un bien beau génie.* Ah, we've risen — we soar; *nous sommes dans les grandes espaces!*" my friend continued with his dilated eyes.

"It's very interesting — because it will cost you something."

"It will cost me everything!" said Félix Vendemer in a tone I seem to hear at this hour. "That's just the beauty of it. It's the chance of chances to testify for art — to affirm an indispensable truth."

"An indispensable truth?" I repeated, feeling myself soar too, but into the splendid vague.

"Do you know the greatest crime that can be perpetrated against it?"

"Against it?" I asked, still soaring.

"Against the religion of art — against the love for beauty — against the search for the Holy Grail?" The transfigured look with which he named these things, the way his warm voice filled the rich room, was a revelation of the wonderful talk that had taken place.

"Do you know — for one of *us* — the really damnable, the only unpardonable, sin?"

"Tell me, so that I may keep clear of it!"

"To profane *our* golden air with the hideous invention of patriotism."

"It was a clever invention in its time!" I laughed.

"I'm not talking about its time — I'm talking about its place. It was never anything but a fifth-rate impertinence here. In art there are no countries — no idiotic nationalities, no frontiers, nor *douanes*, nor still more idiotic fortresses and bayonets. It has the unspeakable beauty of being the region in which those abominations cease, the medium in which such vulgarities simply can't live. What therefore are we to say of the brutes who wish to drag them all in — to crush to death with them all the flowers of such a garden, to shut out all the light of such a sky?" I was far from desiring to defend the "brutes" in question, though there rose before me even at that moment a sufficiently vivid picture of the way, later on, poor Vendemer would have to face them. I quickly perceived indeed that the picture was, to his own eyes, a still more crowded canvas. Félix Vendemer, in the centre of it, was an admirable, a really sublime figure. If there had been wonderful talk after I quitted the two poets the wonder was not over yet — it went on far into the night for my benefit. We looked at the prospect in many lights, turned the subject about almost every way it would go; but I am bound to say there was one relation in which we tacitly agreed to forbear to consider it. We neither of us uttered the name of Paule de Brindes — the outlook in that direction would be too serious. And yet if Félix Vendemer, exquisite and incorruptible artist that he was, had fallen in love with the idea of "testifying," it was from that direction that the finest part of his opportunity to do so would proceed.

I was only too conscious of this when, within the week, I received a hurried note from Madame de Brindes, begging me as a particular favour to come and see her without delay. I had not seen Vendemer again, but I had had a characteristic call from Heidenmauer, who, though I could imagine him perfectly in a Prussian helmet, with a needle-gun, perfectly, on definite occasion, a sturdy, formidable soldier, gave me a renewed impression of inhabiting, in the expansion of his genius and the exercise of his intelligence, no land of red tape, no province smaller nor more pedantically administered than the totality of things. I was reminded afresh too that *he* foresaw no striking salon-picture, no *chic* of execution nor romance of martyrdom, or at any rate devoted very little time to the consideration of such objects. He doubtless did scant justice to poor Vendemer's attitude, though he said to me of him by the way, with his rosy deliberation: "He has good ideas — he has good ideas. The French mind has — for me — the taste of a very delightful *bonbon!*" He only measured the angle of convergence, as he called it, of their two projections. He was in short not preoccupied with the personal gallantry of their experiment; he was preoccupied with its "aesthetic and harmonic basis."

It was without her daughter that Madame de Brindes received me, when I obeyed her summons, in her scrap of a *quatrième* in the Rue de Miromesnil.

"Ah, *cher monsieur,* how could you have permitted such a horror — how could you have given it the countenance of your roof, of your influence?" There were tears in her eyes, and I don't think that for the moment I have ever been more touched by a reproach. But I pulled myself together sufficiently to affirm my faith as well as to disengage my responsibility. I explained that there was no horror to me in the matter, that if I was not a German neither was I a Frenchman, and that all I had before me was two young men inflamed by a great idea and nobly determined to work together to give it a great form.

"A great idea — to go over to *ces gens-là?*"

"To go over to them?"

"To put yourself on their side — to throw yourself into the arms of those who hate us — to fall into their abominable trap!"

"What do you call their abominable trap?"

"Their false *bonhomie,* the very impudence of their intrigues, their profound, scientific deceit and their determination to get the advantage of us by exploiting our generosity."

"You attribute to such a man as Heidenmauer too many motives and too many calculations. He's quite ideally superior!"

"Oh, German idealism — we know what that means! We've no use for their superiority; let them carry it elsewhere — let them leave us alone. Why do they thrust themselves in upon us and set old wounds throbbing by their detested presence? We don't go near *them,* or ever wish to hear their ugly names or behold their *visages de bois;* therefore the most rudimentary good taste, the tact one would expect even from naked savages, might suggest to them to seek their amusements elsewhere. But *their* taste, *their* tact — I can scarcely trust myself to speak!"

Madame de Brindes did speak however at considerable further length and with a sincerity of passion which left one quite without arguments. There was no argument to meet the fact that Vendemer's attitude wounded her, wounded her daughter, *jusqu'au fond de l'âme,* that it represented for them abysses of shame and suffering and that for himself it meant a whole future compromised, a whole public alienated. It was vain doubtless to talk of such things; if people didn't *feel* them, if they hadn't the fibre of loyalty, the high imagination of honour, all explanations, all supplications were but a waste of noble emotion. M. Vendemer's perversity was monstrous — she had had a sickening discussion with him. What she desired of me was to make one last appeal to him, to put the solemn truth before him, to try to bring him back to sanity. It was as if he had temporarily lost his reason. It was to be made clear to him, *par exemple,* that unless he should recover it Mademoiselle de Brindes would unhesitatingly withdraw from her engagement.

"Does she *really* feel as you do?" I asked.

"Do you think I put words into her mouth? She feels as a *fille de France* is obliged to feel!"

"Doesn't she love him then?"

"She adores him. But she won't take him without his honour."

"I don't understand such refinements!" I said.

"Oh, *vous autres!*" cried Madame de Brindes. Then with eyes glowing through her tears she demanded: "Don't you know she knows how her father died?" I was on the point of saying "What has that to do with it?" but I withheld the question, for after all I could conceive that it might have something. There was no disputing about tastes, and I could only express my sincere conviction that Vendemer was profoundly attached to Mademoiselle Paule. "Then let him prove it by making her a sacrifice!" my strenuous hostess replied; to which I rejoined that I would repeat our conversation to him and put the matter before him as strongly as I could. I delayed a little to take leave, wondering if the girl would not come in — I should have been so much more content to receive her strange recantation from her own lips. I couldn't say this to Madame de Brindes; but she guessed I meant it, and before we separated we exchanged a look in which our mutual mistrust was written — the suspicion on her side that I should not be a very passionate intercessor and the conjecture on mine that she might be misrepresenting her daughter. This slight tension, I must add, was only momentary, for I have had a chance of observing Paule de Brindes since then, and the two ladies were soon satisfied that I pitied them enough to have been eloquent.

My eloquence has been of no avail, and I have learned (it has been one of the most interesting lessons of my life) of what transcendent stuff the artist may sometimes be made. Herman Heidenmauer and Félix Vendemer are, at the hour I write, immersed in their monstrous collaboration. There were postponements and difficulties at first, and there will be more serious ones in the future, when it is a question of giving the finished work to the world. The world of Paris will stop its ears in horror, the German Empire will turn its mighty back, and the authors of what I foresee (oh, I've been treated to specimens!) as a perhaps really epoch-making musical revelation (is Heidenmauer's style rubbing off on me?) will perhaps have to beg for a hearing in communities fatally unintelligent. It may very well be that they will not obtain any hearing at all for years. I like at any rate to think that time works for them. At present they work for themselves and for each other, amid drawbacks of several kinds. Separating after the episode in Paris, they have met again on alien soil, at a little place on the Genoese Riviera where sunshine is cheap and tobacco bad, and they live (the two together) for five francs a day, which is all they can muster between them. It appears that when Heidenmauer's London step-brother was informed of the young composer's unnatural alliance he instantly withdrew his subsidy. The return of it is contingent on the rupture of the unholy union and the destruction by flame of all the manuscript. The pair are very poor and the whole thing depends on their staying power. They are so preoccupied with their opera that they have no time for potboilers. Vendemer is in a feverish hurry, lest perhaps he should find himself chilled. There are still other details which contribute to the interest of the episode and which, for me, help to render it a most refreshing, a really great little case. It rests me, it delights me, there is something in it that makes for civilization. In their way they are working for human happiness. The strange course taken by Vendemer (I mean his renunciation of his engagement) must moreover be judged in the light of the fact that he was really in love. Something had to be sacrificed, and what he clung to most (he's extraordinary, I admit) was the truth he had the opportunity of proclaiming. Men give up their love for advantages every day, but they rarely give it up for such discomforts.

Paule de Brindes was the less in love of the two; I see her often enough to have made up my mind about that. But she's mysterious, she's odd; there was at any rate a sufficient wrench in her life to make her often absent-minded. Does her imagination hover about Félix Vendemer? A month

ago, going into their rooms one day when her mother was not at home (the
bonne had admitted me under a wrong impression) I found her at the piano,
playing one of Heidenmauer's compositions — playing it without notes
and with infinite expression. How had she got hold of it? How had she
learned it? This was her secret — she blushed so that I didn't pry into it.
But what is she doing, under the singular circumstances, with a composition of Herman Heidenmauer's? She never met him, she never heard him
play but that once. It will be a pretty complication if it shall appear that the
young German genius made on that occasion more than one intense impression. This needn't appear, however, inasmuch as, being naturally in
terror of the discovery by her mother of such an anomaly, she may count
on me absolutely not to betray her. I hadn't fully perceived how deeply
susceptible she is to music. She must have a strange confusion of feelings
— a dim, haunting trouble, with a kind of ache of impatience for the wonderful opera somewhere in the depths of it. Don't we live fast after all, and
doesn't the old order change? Don't say art isn't mighty! I shall give you
some more illustrations of it yet.

{1891–1892}

ANONYMOUS

Teleny — a high watermark of Victorian pornography first published by Leonard Smithers in an edition of two hundred copies — tells the story of a young Hungarian virtuoso pianist (an *hommage* to the Liszt legend) and his lover, Des Grieux (the surname of Manon Lescaut's lover). Although highly compelling in its own right, the novel has gained in literary importance as a consequence of its historical link to Oscar Wilde, who has been put forward as a candidate for its authorship. Whether Wilde ultimately penned *Teleny* (or part of it) is of little consequence (the novel would be neither better nor worse for this knowledge), but playing detective is irresistible.

Two points are worth noting in particular. First, Wilde was the only important English writer of the time in whose works men commonly play the piano. Both Algernon Moncrieff, in *The Importance of Being Earnest*, and Dorian Gray do so. They, of course, are avowed amateurs, whereas Teleny is a concert pianist. Here is the scene from chapter 1 in which Des Grieux first hears Teleny — an extravagant, but fairly archetypal response to the virtuoso:

> That thrilling longing I had felt grew more and more intense, the craving so insatiable that it was changed to pain; the burning fire had now been fanned into a mighty flame, and my whole body was convulsed and writhed with mad desire. My lips were parched, I gasped for breath; my joints were stiff, my veins were swollen, yet I sat still, like all the crowd around me. But suddenly a heavy hand seemed to be laid upon my lap, something was hent and clasped and grasped, which made me faint with lust. The hand was moved up and down, slowly at first, then faster and faster it went in rhythm with the song. My brain began to reel as throughout every vein a burning lava coursed, and then, some drops even gushed out — I panted —

Second, the suite of Teleny's rooms described in the passage excerpted here gives more than a passing nod to rooms in Wilde's own house on London's Tite Street, number 16. There was a white room there, but it was the dining room rather than the bedroom. The bathroom, however, was also lit by a skylight, and the decor of Wilde's smoking room (as Vyvyan Holland recollects in his memoir, *Son of Oscar Wilde*) was also North African: "Divans, ottomans, Moorish hangings and lanterns filled the room." Moreover, the wallpaper in that room, known as Lincrusta-Walton, had "a William Morris pattern of dark red and dull gold."

Teleny is enormously superior to two notable pornographic works from the same period: Jack Saul's *Sins of the Cities of the Plain, or The Recollections of a Mary-Ann* (published in a private edition of 250 copies) and Aubrey Beardsley's *Under the Hill*. Saul was a "professional sodomite" in Victorian London, and his 1881 "memoirs" recount a lively career in the English capital's sexual underworld. In the following example, all of the "women" are, in fact, men in drag:

> He rose from the breakfast-table, and opening the piano, ran his fingers over the keys; then motioning me to come to him, gave me a luscious kiss. "You darling Eveline, I'm sure your prick stands," he said, groping under my dress and finding it was as he said. "Now I will play you a nice piece, only I have a fancy to have you in me, and you must both fuck and frig me as I play to you," he said, as he made me sit on the music-stool, then raised my dress, and turning his bottom to me, lifted his own clothes and gradually sat down in my lap; as my stiff prick went up his bottom, my hands went 'round his waist, and I clasped the glorious cock of his, and he began to play and sing "Don't you remember sweet Alice, Ben Bolt?" from a parody in the *Pearl Magazine*, which he had set to music.

Sins of the Cities of the Plain has met with the dubious honor of being recently reprinted — with liberties — by Badboy Books.

Under the Hill (1904) is one of those works that, while being the fruit of a highly cultivated homosexual aesthetic, contains but one homosexual sequence. From chapter 7 ("How Tannhäuser Awakened and Took His Morning Ablutions in the Venusberg"):

> "Splash me a little," he cried and the boys teased him with water and quite excited him. He chased the prettiest of them and bit his fesses, and kissed him upon the perineum till the dear fellow banded like a carmelite, and its little bald top-knot looked like a great pink pearl under the water. As the boy seemed anxious to take up the active attitude, Tannhäuser graciously descended to the passive — a generous trait that won him the complete affections of his valets de bain, or pretty fish, as he liked to call them, because they loved to swim between his legs.

"Pretty fish," which will be familiar to those who have read Suetonius's *The Twelve Caesars*, recalls an episode in the history of the vicious Tiberius on Capri. From the translation by Robert Graves: "Imagine training little boys, whom he called his 'minnows,' to chase him while he went swimming and get between his legs to lick and nibble him."

Beardsley died before finishing the manuscript of *Under the Hill.* John Glassco completed it, and Maurice Girodias published it in the Traveller's Companion Series of the Olympia Press (1959). ✸

FROM *Teleny; or The Reverse of the Medal*

" 'COME HOME WITH ME,' said Teleny, in a low, nervous, and trembling voice; 'come and sleep with me,' added he, in the soft, hushed, and pleading tone of the lover who would fain be understood without words.

"I pressed his hands for all answer.

" 'Will you come?'

" 'Yes,' I whispered, almost inaudibly.

"This low, hardly-articulate sound was the hot breath of vehement desire; this lisped monosyllable was the willing consent to his eagerest wish.

"Then he hailed the passing cab, but it was some moments before the driver could be awakened and made to understand what we wanted of him.

"As I stepped into the vehicle, my first thought was that in a few minutes Teleny would belong to me. This thought acted upon my nerves as an electric current, making me shiver from head to foot.

"My lips had to articulate the words, 'Teleny will be mine,' for me to believe it. He seemed to hear the noiseless movement of my lips, for he clasped my head between his hands, and kissed me again and again.

"Then, as if feeling a pang of remorse — 'You do not repent, do you?' he asked.

" 'How can I?'

" 'And you will be mine — mine alone?'

" 'I never was any other man's, nor ever shall be.'

" 'You will love me for ever?'

" 'And ever.'

" 'This will be our oath and our act of possession,' added he.

"Thereupon he put his arms around me and clasped me to his breast. I entwined my arms round him. By the glimmering, dim light of the cab-lamps I saw his eyes kindle with the fire of madness. His lips — parched with the thirst of his long-suppressed desire, with the pent-up craving of possession — pouted towards mine with a painful expression of dull suffering. We were again sucking up each other's being in a kiss — a kiss more intense, if possible, than the former one. What a kiss that was!

"The flesh, the blood, the brain, and that undefined subtler part of our being seemed all to melt together in an ineffable embrace.

"A kiss is something more than the first sensual contact of two bodies; it is the breathing forth of two enamoured souls.

"But a criminal kiss long withstood and fought against, and therefore long yearned after, is beyond this; it is as luscious as forbidden fruit; it is a glowing coal set upon the lips; a fiery brand that burns deep, and changes the blood into molten lead or scalding quicksilver.

"Teleny's kiss was really galvanic, for I could taste its sapidity upon my palate. Was an oath needed, when we had given ourselves to one another with such a kiss? An oath is a lip-promise which can be, and is, often forgotten. Such a kiss follows you to the grave.

"Whilst our lips clung together, his hand slowly, imperceptibly, unbuttoned my trousers, and stealthily slipped within the aperture, turning every obstacle in its way instinctively aside, then it lay hold of my hard, stiff, and aching phallus which was glowing like a burning coal.

"This grasp was as soft as a child's, as expert as a whore's, as strong as a fencer's. He had hardly touched me than I remembered the Countess's words.

"Some people, as we all know, are more magnetic than others. Moreover, whilst some attract, others repel us. Teleny had — for me, at least — a supple, mesmeric, pleasure-giving fluid in his fingers. Nay, the simple contact of his skin thrilled me with delight.

"My own hand hesitatingly followed the lead his had given, and I must confess the pleasure I felt in paddling him was really delightful.

"Our fingers hardly moved the skin of the penis; but our nerves were so strained, our excitement had reached such a pitch, and the seminal ducts were so full, that we felt them overflowing. There was, for a moment, an intense pain, somewhere about the root of the penis — or rather, within the very core and centre of the reins, after which the sap of life began to move slowly, slowly, from within the seminal glands; it mounted up the bulb of the urethra, and up the narrow column, somewhat like mercury within the tube of a thermometer — or rather, like the scalding and scathing lava within the crater of a volcano.

"It finally reached the apex; then the slit gaped, the tiny lips parted, and the pearly, creamy, viscous fluid oozed out — not all at once in a gushing jet, but at intervals, and in huge, burning tears.

"At every drop that escaped out of the body, a creepy almost unbearable feeling started from the tips of the fingers, from the ends of the toes, especially from the innermost cells of the brain; the marrow in the spine and within all the bones seemed to melt; and when the different currents — either coursing with the blood or running rapidly up the nervous fibres — met within the phallus (that small instrument made out of muscles and blood-vessels) a tremendous shock took place; a convulsion which annihilated both mind and matter, a quivering delight which everyone has felt, to a greater or lesser degree — often a thrill almost too intense to be pleasurable.

"Pressed against each other, all we could do was to try and smother our groans as the fiery drops slowly followed one another.

"The prostration which followed the excessive strain of the nerves had set in, when the carriage stopped before the door of Teleny's house — that door at which I had madly struck with my fist a short time before.

"We dragged ourselves wearily out of the carriage, but hardly had the portal shut itself upon us than we were again kissing and fondling each other with renewed energy.

"After some moments, feeling that our desire was too powerful to be withstood any longer — 'Come,' said he, 'why should we linger any longer, and waste precious time here in the darkness and in the cold?'

" 'Is it dark and is it cold?' was my reply.

"He kissed me fondly.

" 'In the gloom you are my light; in the cold you are my fire; the frozen wastes of the Pole would be a Garden of Eden for me, if you were there,' I continued.

"We then groped our way upstairs in the dark, for I would not allow him to light a wax match. I therefore went along, stumbling against him; not that I could not see, but because I was intoxicated with mad desire as a drunken man is with wine.

"Soon we were in his apartment. When we found ourselves in the small, dimly-lighted antechamber, he opened his arms and stretched them out towards me.

" 'Welcome!' said he. 'May this home be ever thine.' Then he added, in a low tone, in that unknown, musical tongue, 'My body hungereth for thee, soul of my soul, life of my life!'

"He had barely finished these words before we were lovingly caressing each other.

"After thus fondling each other for a few moments — 'Do you know,' said he, 'that I have been expecting you today?'

" 'Expecting me?'

" 'Yes, I knew that sooner or later you would be mine. Moreover, I felt that you would be coming today.'

" 'How so?'

" 'I had a presentiment.'

" 'And had I not come?'

" 'I should have done what you were going to do when I met you, for life without you would have been unbearable.'

" 'What! drowned yourself?'

" 'No, not exactly: the river is too cold and bleak, I am too much of a Sybarite for that. No, I should simply have put myself to sleep — the eternal slumber of death, dreaming of you, in this room prepared to receive you, and where no man has ever set his foot.'

"Saying these words he opened the door of a small chamber, and ushered me into it. A strong, overpowering smell of white heliotrope first greeted my nostrils.

"It was a most peculiar room, the walls of which were covered over with some warm, white, soft, quilted stuff, studded all over with frosted silver buttons; the floor was covered with the curly white fleece of young lambs; in the middle of the apartment stood a capacious couch, on which was thrown the skin of a huge polar bear. Over this single piece of furniture, an old silver lamp — evidently from some Byzantine church or some Eastern synagogue — shed a pale glimmering light, sufficient, however, to light up the dazzling whiteness of this temple of Priapus whose votaries we were.

" 'I know,' said he, as he dragged me in, 'I know that white is your favourite colour, that it suits your dark complexion, so it has been fitted up for you and you alone. No other mortal shall ever set his foot in it.'

"Uttering these words, he in a trice stripped me deftly of all my clothes — for I was in his hands like a slumbering child, or a man in a trance.

"In an instant I was not only stark naked, but stretched on the bearskin, whilst he, standing in front of me, was gloating upon me with famished eyes.

"I felt his glances greedily fall everywhere; they sank in my brain, and my head began to swim; they pierced through my heart, whipping my blood up, making it flow quicker and hotter through all the arteries; they darted within my veins, and Priapus unhooded itself and lifted up its head violently so that all the tangled web of veins in its body seemed ready to burst.

"Then he felt me with his hands everywhere, after which he began to press his lips on every part of my body, showering kisses on my breast, my arms, my legs, my thighs, and then, when he had reached my middle parts, he pressed his face rapturously on the thick and curly hair that grows there so plentifully.

"He shivered with delight as he felt the crisp locks upon his cheek and neck; then, taking hold of my phallus, he pressed his lips upon it. That seemed to electrify him; and then the tip and afterwards the whole glans disappeared within his mouth.

"As it did so, I could hardly keep quiet. I clasped within my hands his curly and scented head; a shiver ran through my whole body; all my nerves were on edge; the sensation was so keen that it almost maddened me.

"Then the whole column was in his mouth, the tip was touching his palate; his tongue, flattened or thickened, tickling me everywhere. Now I was sucked greedily, then nibbled or bitten. I screamed, I called on him to stop. I could not bear such intensity any longer; it was killing me. If it had lasted but a trice longer I should have lost my senses. He was deaf and ruthless to my entreaties. Flashes of lightning seemed to be passing before my eyes; a torrent of fire was coursing through my body.

" 'Enough — stop, enough!' I groaned.

"My nerves were extended; a thrill came over me; the soles of my feet seemed to have been drilled through. I writhed; I was convulsed.

"One of his hands which had been caressing my testicles slipped under my bum — a finger was slipped in the hole. I seemed to be a man in front, a woman behind, for the pleasure I felt either way.

"My trepidation had reached its climax. My brain reeled; my body melted; the burning milk of life was again mounting up, like a sap of fire; my bubbling blood mounted up to my brain, maddening me. I was exhausted; I fainted with pleasure: I fell upon him — a lifeless mass!

"In a few minutes I was myself again — eager to take his place, and to return the caresses I had just received.

"I tore the clothes from his body, so that he was speedily as naked as I was. What a pleasure it was to feel his skin against mine from head to foot! Moreover, the delight I had just felt had only increased my eagerness, so that, after clasping each other and wrestling together for a few moments, we both rolled on the floor, twisting, and rubbing, and crawling, and writhing, like two heated cats exciting each other into a paroxysm of rage.

"But my lips were eager to taste his phallus — an organ which might have served as a model for the huge idol in the temple of Priapus, or over the doors of the Pompeian brothels, only that at the sight of this wingless god most men would' have — as many did — discarded women for the love of their fellow-men. It was big without having the proportion of an ass's; it was thick and rounded, though slightly tapering; the glans — a fruit of flesh and blood, like a small apricot — looked pulpy, round and appetizing.

"I feasted my hungry eyes upon it; I handled it; I kissed it; I felt its soft glossy skin upon my lip; it moved with an inward motion of its own, as I did so. My tongue then deftly tickled the tip, trying to dart itself between those tiny rosy lips that, bulged out with love, opened and spattered a tiny drop of sparkling dew. I licked the foreskin, then sucked the whole of it, pumping it greedily. He moved it vertically whilst I tried to clasp it tightly with my lips; he thrust it further every time, and touched my palate; it almost reached my throat, and I felt it quivering with a life of its own; I moved quicker, quicker, quicker. He clasped my head furiously; all his nerves were throbbing.

" 'Your mouth is burning — you are sucking out my very brain! Stop, stop! my whole body is aglow! I can't — any more! I can't — it is too much!'

"He grasped my head tightly to make me stop, but I pressed his phallus tightly with my lips, my cheeks, my tongue; my movements were more and more rapid, so that after a few strokes I felt him shudder from head to foot, as if seized by a fit of giddiness. He sighed, he groaned, he screamed. A jet of warm, soapy, acrid liquid filled my mouth. His head reeled; the pleasure he felt was so sharp that it verged upon pain.

" 'Stop, stop!' he moaned faintly, shutting his eyes and panting.

"I, however, was maddened by the idea that he was now truly mine; that I was drinking down the fiery foaming sap of his body, the real elixir of life.

"His arms for a moment clasped me convulsively. A rigidity then came over him; he was shattered by such an excess of wantonness.

"I myself felt almost as much as he did, for in my fury I sucked him eagerly, greedily, and thus provoked an abundant ejaculation; and at the same time small drops of the same fluid which I was receiving in me, coursed slowly, painfully, out of my body. As this happened, our nerves relaxed and we fell exhausted upon one another.

"A short space of rest — I cannot tell how long, intensity not being measured by Time's sedate pace — and then I felt his nerveless penis reawaken from its sleep, and press against my face; it was evidently trying to find my mouth, just like a greedy but glutted baby even in its sleep holds firm the nipple of its mother's breast simply for the pleasure of having it in its mouth.

"I pressed my mouth upon it, and, like a young cock awakened at early dawn stretches forth its neck and crows lustily, it thrust its head towards my warm, pouted lips.

"As soon as I had it in my mouth, Teleny wheeled himself around, and placed himself in the same position that I was to him; that is, his mouth was at the height of my middle part, only with the difference that I was on my back and he was over me.

"He began to kiss my rod; he played with the bushy hair that grew around it; he patted my buttocks, and, especially, he caressed my testicles with a knack all his own that filled me with unutterable delight.

"His hands so increased the pleasure his mouth and his own phallus were giving me that I was soon beyond myself with excitement.

"Our two bodies were one mass of quivering sensuality; and although we were both increasing the rapidity of our movements, still we were so maddened with lust that in that tension of the nerves the seminal glands refused to do their work.

"We laboured on in vain. My reason all at once left me; the parched blood within me vainly tried to ooze out, and it seemed to swirl in my injected eyes; it tingled in my ears. I was in a paroxysm of erotic rage — in a paroxysm of mad delirium.

"My brain seemed trepanned, my spine sawn in two. Nevertheless I sucked his phallus quicker and quicker; I drew it like a teat; I tried to drain it; and I felt him palpitate, quiver, shudder. All at once the gates of the sperm were opened, and from hellish fires we were uplifted, amidst a shower of burning sparks, into a delightfully calm and ambrosial Olympus.

"After a few moments' rest I uplifted myself on my elbow, and delighted my eyes with my lover's fascinating beauty. He was a very model of carnal comeliness; his chest was broad and strong, his arms rounded; in fact, I have never seen such a vigorous and at the same time agile frame; for not only was there not the slightest fat but not even the least superfluous flesh about him. He was all nerve, muscle, and sinew. It was his wellknit and supple joints that gave him the free, easy, and graceful motion so characteristic of the Felidæ, of which he had also the flexibility, for when he clasped himself to you he seemed to entwine himself around you like a snake. Moreover, his skin was of a pearly almost iridescent whiteness, whilst the hair on the different parts of his body except the head was quite black.

"Teleny opened his eyes, stretched his arms towards me, took hold of my hand, kissed, and then bit me on the nape of my neck; then he showered a number of kisses all along my back, which, following one another in quick succession, seemed like a rain of rose-leaves falling from some fullblown flower.

"Then he reached the two fleshy lobes which he pressed open with his hands, and darted his tongue in that hole where a little while before he had thrust his finger. This likewise was for me a new and thrilling sensation.

"This done, he rose and stretched forth his hand to lift me up.

"'Now,' said he, 'let us go in the next room, and see if we can find something to eat; for I think we really require some food, though, perhaps, a bath would not be amiss before we sit down to supper. Should you like to have one?'

"'It might put you to inconvenience.'

"For all answer he ushered me into a kind of cell, all filled with ferns and feathery palms, that — as he shewed me — received during the day the rays of the sun from a skylight overhead.

" 'This is a kind of make-shift for a hot-house and a bath-room, which every habitable dwelling ought to have. I am too poor to have either, still this hole is big enough for my ablutions, and my plants seem to thrive pretty well in this warm and damp atmosphere.'

" 'But it's a princely bath-room!'

" 'No, no!' said he, smiling; 'it's an artist's bath-room.'

"We at once plunged into the warm water, scented with essence of heliotrope; and it was so pleasant to rest there locked in each other's arms after our last excesses.

" 'I could stay here all night,' he mused, 'it is so delightful to handle you in this warm water. But you must be famished, so we had better go and get something to satisfy the inward cravings.'

"We got out, and wrapped ourselves up for a moment with hot *peignoirs* of Turkish towelling.

" 'Come,' said he, 'let me lead you to the dining-room.'

"I stood hesitating, looking first at my nakedness, then upon his. He smiled, and kissed me.

" 'You don't feel cold, do you?'

" 'No, but —'

" 'Well, then, don't be afraid; there is no one in the house. Everyone is asleep on the other flats, and besides, every window is tightly shut, and all the curtains are down.'

"He dragged me with him into a neighbouring room all covered with thick, soft, and silky carpets, the prevailing tone of which was dull Turkish red.

"In the centre of this apartment hung a curiously-wrought, starshaped lamp, which the faithful — even now-a-days — light on Friday eve.

"We sat down on a soft-cushioned divan, in front of one of those ebony Arab tables all inlaid with coloured ivory and iridescent mother-of-pearl.

" 'I cannot give you a banquet, although I expected you; still, there is enough to satisfy your hunger, I hope.'

"There were some luscious Cancale oysters — few, but of an immense size; a dusty bottle of Sauternes, then a *pâté de foie gras* highly scented with Perigord truffles; a partridge, with *paprika* or Hungarian curry, and a salad made out of a huge Piedmont truffle, as thinly sliced as shavings, and a bottle of exquisite dry sherry.

"All these delicacies were served in dainty blue old Delft and Savona ware, for he had already heard of my hobby for old majolica.

"Then came a dish of Seville oranges, bananas, and pineapples, flavoured with Maraschino and covered with sifted sugar. It was a savoury, tasty, tart and sweet medley, combining together the flavour and perfume of all these delicious fruits.

"After having washed it down with a bottle of sparkling champagne, we then sipped some tiny cups of fragrant and scalding Mocha coffee; then he lighted a narghilè, or Turkish water pipe, and we puffed at intervals the odorous Latakiah, inhaling it with our ever-hungry kisses from each other's mouths.

"The fumes of the smoke and those of the wine rose up to our heads, and in our re-awakened sensuality we soon had between our lips a far more fleshy mouth-piece than the amber one of the Turkish pipe.

"Our heads were again soon lost between each other's thighs. We had once more but one body between us, juggling with one another, ever seeking new caresses, new sensations, a sharper and more inebriating kind of lewdness, in our anxiety not only to enjoy ourselves but to make the other one feel. We were, therefore, very soon the prey of a blasting lust, and only some inarticulate sounds expressed the climax of our voluptuous state, until, more dead than alive, we fell upon each other — a mingled mass of shivering flesh.

"After half an hour's rest and a bowl of arrak, curaçao and whisky punch, flavoured with many hot, invigorating spices, our mouths were again pressed together.

"His moist lips grazed mine so very slightly that I hardly felt their touch; they thus only awakened in me the eager desire to feel their contact more closely, whilst the tip of his tongue kept tantalizing mine, darting in my mouth for a second and rapidly slipping out again. His hands in the meanwhile passed over the most delicate parts of my body as lightly as a soft summer breeze passes over the smooth surface of the waters, and I felt my skin shiver with delight.

"I happened to be lying on some cushions on the couch, which thus elevated me to Teleny's height; he swiftly put my legs on his shoulders, then, bending down his head, he began first to kiss, and then to dart his pointed tongue in the hole of my bum, thrilling me with an ineffable pleasure. Then rising when he had deftly prepared the hole by lubricating it well all round, he tried to press the tip of his phallus into it, but though he pressed hard, still he could not succeed in getting it in.

" 'Let me moisten it a little, and then it will slip in more easily.'

"I took it again in my mouth. My tongue rolled deftly all around it. I sucked it down almost to its very root, feeling it up to any little trick, for it was stiff, hard, and frisky.

" 'Now,' said I, 'let us enjoy together that pleasure which the gods themselves did not disdain to teach us.'

"Thereupon the tips of my fingers stretched the edges of my unexplored little pit to their very utmost. It was gaping to receive the huge instrument that presented itself at the orifice.

"He once more pressed the glans upon it; the tiny little lips protruded themselves within the gap; the tip worked its way inside, but the pulpy flesh bulged out all around, and the rod was thus arrested in its career.

" 'I am afraid I am hurting you?' he asked, 'had we not better leave it for some other time?'

" 'Oh, no! It is such a happiness to feel your body entering into mine.'

"He thrust gently but firmly; the strong muscles of the anus relaxed; the glans was fairly lodged; the skin extended to such a degree that tiny, ruby beads of blood trickled from all around the splitting orifice; still, notwithstanding the way I was torn, the pleasure I felt was much greater than the pain.

"He himself was so tightly clasped that he could neither pull his instrument out nor push it in, for when he tried to press it down he felt as if he was being circumcised. He stopped for a moment, and then, after having asked whether he was not hurting me too much, and having received a negative reply, he thrust it in with all his might.

"The Rubicon was crossed; the column began to slide softly in; he could begin his pleasurable work. Soon the whole penis slipped in; the pain that tortured me was deadened; the delight was ever so much increased. I felt the little god moving within me; it seemed to be tickling the very core of my being; he had shoved the whole of it into me, down to its very root; I felt his hair crushed against mine, his testicles gently rubbing against me.

"I then saw his beautiful eyes gazing deep into mine. What unfathomable eyes they were! Like the sky or the main, they seemed to reflect the infinite. Never again shall I see eyes so full of burning love, of such smouldering languor. His glances had a mesmeric spell over me; they bereft me of my reason; they did even more — they changed sharp pain into delight.

"I was in a state of ecstatic joy; all my nerves contracted and twitched. As he felt himself thus clasped and gripped, he shivered, he ground his teeth; he was unable to bear such a strong shock; his outstretched arms held fast on my shoulders; he dug his nails into my flesh; he tried to move, but he was so tightly wedged and grasped that it was impossible to push himself any further in. Moreover, his strength was beginning to fail him, and he could then hardly stand upon his feet.

"As he tried to give another jerk, I myself, that very moment squeezed the whole rod with all the strength of my muscles, and a most violent jet, like a hot geyser, escaped from him, and coursed within me like some scorching, corroding poison; it seemed to set my blood on fire, and transmuted it into some kind of hot, intoxicating alcohol. His breath was thick and convulsive; his sobs choked him; he was utterly done up.

" 'I am dying!' he gasped out, his chest heaving with emotion; 'it is too much.' And he fell senseless in my arms.

"After half an hour's rest he woke up, and began at once to kiss me with rapture, whilst his loving eyes beamed with thankfulness.

" 'You have made me feel what I never felt before.'

" 'Nor I either,' quoth I, smiling.

"I really did not know whether I was in heaven or in hell. I had quite lost my senses.

"He stopped for a moment to look at me, and then — 'How I love you, my Camille!' he went on, showering kisses on me; 'I have loved you to distraction from the very moment I saw you.'

"Then I began to tell him how I had suffered in trying to overcome my love for him; how I was haunted by his presence day and night; how happy I was at last.

" 'And now you must take my place. You must make me feel what you felt. You will now be active and I passive; but we must try another position, for it is really tiresome to stand after all the fatigue we have undergone.'

" 'And what am I to do, for you know I am quite a novice?'

" 'Sit down there,' he replied, pointing to a stool constructed for the purpose, 'I'll ride on you whilst you impale me as if I were a woman. It is a mode of locomotion of which the ladies are so fond tha. they put it into practice whenever they get the slightest chance. My moth r actually rode a gentleman under my very eyes. I was in the parlour when a friend happened to call, and had I been sent out suspicions might have been aroused, so I was made to believe that I was a very naughty little boy, and I was put in a corner with my face to the wall. Moreover, she told me that if I cried or turned round she'd put me to bed; but if I wer good she'd give me a cake. I obeyed for one or two minutes, but after th t, he ring an unusual rustle, and a loud breathing and panting, I saw what I could not understand at the time, but what was clear to me many years afterwards.'

"He sighed, shrugged his shoulders, then smiled ... d added — 'Well, sit down there.'

"I did as I was bidden. He first knelt down to say ... prayers to Priapus — which was, after all, a more dainty bit to kiss than the old Pope's gouty toe — and having bathed and tickled the little god with his tongue, he got a straddle over me. As he had already lost his maidenhood long ago, my rod entered far more easily in him than his had done in me, nor did I give him the pain that I had felt, although my tool is of no mean size.

"He stretched his hole open, the tip entered, he moved a little, half the phallus was plunged in; he pressed down, lifted himself up, then came down again; after one or two strokes the whole turgid column was lodged within his body. When he was well impaled he put his arms round my neck, and hugged and kissed me.

" 'Do you regret having given yourself to me?' he asked, pressing me convulsively as if afraid to lose me.

"My penis, which seemed to wish to give its own answer, wriggled within his body. I looked deep into his eyes.

" 'Do you think it would have been pleasanter to be now lying in the slush of the river?'

"He shuddered and kissed me, then eagerly — 'How can you think of such horrible things just now; it is real blasphemy to the Mysian god.'

"Thereupon he began to ride a Priapean race with masterly skill; from an amble he went on to a trot, then to a gallop, lifting himself on the tips of his toes, and coming down again quicker and ever quicker. At every movement he writhed and wriggled, so that I felt myself pulled, gripped, pumped, and sucked at the same time.

"A rigid tension of the nerves took place. My heart was beating in such a way that I could hardly breathe. All the arteries seemed ready to burst. My skin was parched with a glowing heat; a subtle fire coursed through my veins instead of blood.

"Still he went on quicker and quicker. I writhed in a delightful torture. I was melting away, but he never stopped till he had quite drained me of the last drop of life-giving fluid there was in me. My eyes were swimming in their sockets. I felt my heavy lids half close themselves; an unbearable voluptuousness of mingled pain and pleasure, shattered my body and blasted my very soul; then everything waned in me. He clasped me in his arms, and I swooned away whilst he was kissing my cold and languid lips."

{1893}

The REVEREND EDWIN EMANUEL BRADFORD
{1860–1944}

The most prolific of the Uranian poets, the Reverend Edwin Emanuel Bradford studied at Exeter College, Oxford, where his friends included John Francis Bloxam (the author of the next selection). In 1887, after serving as a curate in High Ongar (formerly the terminus of the Central Line) and St. Swithin's, Walthamstow (now the terminus of the Victoria Line), he was appointed chaplain at St. Petersburg and so moved to Russia. "Boris Orloff," set in St. Petersburg, appeared in two issues of the *Boy's Own Paper* in September 1893. To the innocent reader, "Boris Orloff" was a sentimental tale of youthful jealousy and friendship; to the knowing Uranian, a harrowing romantic melodrama in which the conventions of fable — the big bad wolf, for example — are married to those of the sexual triangle.

Bradford's pederastic interests are more explicitly revealed in his poems, one of which depicts a boy swimming in the Blue Grotto at Capri:

> Prepared to dive, he flings aside his vest,
> And waits the signal. Brown's his curly hair,
> Deep brown his eyes, and now we see it bare,
> Though face and hands are browner than the rest,
> Save two brown nipples on the boyish breast,
> His sun-burnt body's nut brown everywhere.

Boris Orloff

WHEN I WAS A BOY OF FOURTEEN, my father, who till then had been attached to the British Embassy in Paris, was appointed first secretary to the embassy at St. Petersburg; and my poor mother, who had always been delicate, insisted, in spite of medical warnings that she was not strong enough to endure the rigour of a Russian winter, upon accompanying him. As for me, I was sent to England, to be educated in the family of a Yorkshire clergyman, a Mr. Courtenay, Vicar of Anstey, a small village in the East Riding.

I cannot honestly say that I felt the parting from my parents very keenly. My mother had been under the influence of an eloquent French preacher, some four years ago, soon after she first came to reside in Paris, and since that time she had been strangely imbued with a sense of the danger, if not the absolute sinfulness, of all human affection. Her influence over my father was unbounded, and they both felt themselves constrained to treat me with a coldness and severity that made it impossible for me to love them as warmly as I felt I ought.

Accordingly, though I was half ashamed of it, and would scarcely acknowledge it to myself, I am afraid that I experienced a sensation of relief rather than sorrow, when I heard that I was to be sent away; and I think that the two years which I spent in my new home were the very brightest and happiest in my whole life.

Mr. Courtenay's family was a large one, consisting of himself, one of the kindest and most genial men I have ever met; his wife, a gentle, aristocratic, south-countrywoman; and seven children, all boys, who mostly took after their father. My especial favourite was the second boy, Arthur, and though he was some three or four years my junior, it was he who became my chosen companion and confidant. He was the only one of the young Courtenays who took after his mother, being of a more romantic and imaginative temperament than his brothers, who often used to tease him and laugh at his strange fancies. Probably it was partly this that first attracted me to him.

There were times when, in spite of all the kindness and affection lavished upon me, I could not help being a little homesick, and then Artie's delicate childish sympathy was just what I needed to keep me from feeling lonely and low-spirited. Looking back, I sometimes think that our life was then so bright and unclouded that we used to rather enjoy *playing at being unhappy*; he misunderstood by his brothers, and I parted from my parents;

it gave a touch of romance to our affection which made it all the sweeter. Ah! me, if sorrow gives romance to life, I was to have plenty of it soon.

The first blow fell toward the close of the second year of my stay at Anstey.

I was now a big boy of sixteen, and, as such, admitted to the dignity of late dinners. But on Sundays we all dined early, and had a meat tea together at five o'clock, in order to be able to attend evening service at church. Mrs. Courtenay used to take such pains to provide delightful delicacies for this Sunday tea, so that we might not miss the more substantial dinner, that we young people grew to look upon it as the great feast of the week. How well I remember the last at which I was ever present!

It was late in November, the cosy red curtains were drawn across the windows to shut out the cold raw air outside, and a huge coal fire was blazing brightly in the great old fashioned chimney. The long dining-room table, gay with a profusion of cut flowers, and lit by numerous wax-candles, in quaint old silver candelabra which had been in the Courtenay family for centuries, had something of the stately air which it assumed when decked for a grand dinner-party; while the great silver kettle and tea-pot, the pretty china cups and saucers painted with wildflowers, ranged before Mrs. Courtenay, and the smiling childish faces all around, gave it the more homely and familiar look which befitted a meal which Artie once described as "a kind of cross between a swell dinner and a glorified school-room tea."

As we were busily engaged in doing full justice to the good cheer before us, all talking at once, contradicting each other at every turn, making fun of each other's personal peculiarities, and laughing boisterously at everything and nothing, after the usual fashion of family parties where boys are in the majority, a servant entered with two letters, one for Mr. Courtenay and one for me, both bearing the familiar Russian post-mark.

This caused a momentary lull in the hum of conversation, for letters were regarded at Anstey more or less in the light of public property, and the happy recipient of one was expected either to read it aloud, or at least to give a *résumé* of its contents. I saw at once from the handwriting that mine was from my father, and a strange presentiment of evil made my fingers tremble as I tore open the envelope.

I had scarcely glanced at the letter inside before I saw that my worst fears were realised. My eyes filled with tears, and as I raised them for a moment and looked round on the familiar home-circle before me, all appeared to be changed and glorified with the strange pathetic beauty which invests faces and scenes upon which one looks for the last time; and as the solemn-toned clock on the mantelpiece slowly chimed the quarter after five, I felt as if it were some supernatural bell tolling the knell of my earthly happiness!

My mother, I had read, had died quite suddenly from a chill caught in driving home from a dinner-party in an open sleigh; I was to come home at once; all the necessary arrangements were contained in the letter which my father was sending by the same post to Mr. Courtenay.

I was, of course, very sad at hearing of my mother's death, and yet I must confess that what I felt most of all was the parting from the Courtenays — and especially my little friend Artie. As for him, poor child, if it were possible, I think he was even more wretched than I. As we walked home from church together that evening he was inconsolable, and kept protesting sadly that at St. Petersburg I should soon make new friends and forget him. All I could do in any way to comfort him was to accede to one of his strange, fanciful requests — that I would promise faithfully to write to him every Sunday at St. Petersburg, if it were only a few words, exactly at quarter-past seven — the hour corresponding with quarter-past five in England — and he would write to me at the same time; so that we might always be sure that we were thinking of each other when every Sunday brought round the weekly anniversary of the fatal moment when we first learnt that we were to part.

They were dreary days that followed. Next morning I set off sadly — it seemed almost a mockery to say "homewards" — and when after my weary three days' journey I arrived at St. Petersburg, I found my father sterner and colder in manner than ever. I dimly wondered why he cared to have me with him, so little notice did he seem to take of my presence; and I was almost relieved when he announced to me that he had decided to send me for a term, as a day-boarder, to one of the great German schools, of which there are two or three in St. Petersburg, in order, as he said, that I might improve my knowledge of that language, in which he found me disgracefully backward.

How I hated that great gloomy, prison-like school, and those grave, studious, German boys, who never seemed to play any games, but went straight home as soon as they had finished their work for the day.

The only friend I made there was a strange, wild little Russian boy, called Boris Orloff, who came from the country near Kiev, and had never been to school before this term; and who, when I first saw him, had absolutely startled me by his wonderful likeness to Artie Courtenay. He interested me in many ways. First and foremost, naturally, because he was so remarkably like my little friend at Anstey; secondly, because he spoke English quite fluently, if not always grammatically; and lastly, because he was such a complete little Russian, so utterly untouched by western civilisation, he was almost like a little savage. How well I remember the first afternoon that the Lutheran clergyman came to give religious instruction to the German boys! As the worthy pastor entered the class-room where we were sitting, Boris, struck by his dress, asked his neighbour who he might be, and on hearing that it was the minister, he exclaimed in his stage whisper, which could be heard all over the school, "He doesn't look a bit like a *batoushka*!" Then after eyeing him doubtfully for a minute, and apparently coming to the conclusion that after all "it isn't the cowl that makes the friar," and possibly the "popes" of St. Petersburg dressed differently from those at Kiev, he made a sudden dive at him, caught hold of his hand, impressed upon it a sounding kiss that might have been heard in the street outside, and was back at his desk again before the reverend gentleman well knew what had taken place.

Boris was now the one interest in my dull, monotonous life, and a description of his funny sayings and doings filled up a good deal of my first letters to Artie. But I soon found, from sundry little hints, that my old friend was decidedly jealous of the new, and that henceforth I must be more careful of what I wrote.

Boris, on the contrary, took the warmest interest in Artie, and was never tired of hearing me speak of him. When I told him of Artie's fanciful proposal that he and I should always write to each other on the same day and at the same hour, the romantic little Slav was quite touched, and wanted me to enclose a few words from him in each of my letters to Artie. I didn't like to deceive him by pretending to send his messages and not doing so, and yet I well knew that Artie would be terribly grieved if all my letters to him were coupled with notes from the little Russian boy whom he foolishly regarded as his rival. Accordingly I had to confess to Boris that Artie was a little jealous of him, which filled him with great sorrow.

"Well," he said, with a sigh, "if you think it would vex him, never mind. But I shall at least always think of him at that hour, and perhaps, by-and-by, he'll let me write to him."

So we left it thus for the present, I promising, for my part, to do my best to bring Artie to a better mind.

Boris was never tired of hearing me describe our life at Anstey, and especially the famous Sunday teas. Sometimes he would think quietly for a minute, and then give me his version of what I had just said; which was often exceedingly droll, from its careful reproduction of the facts I had told him unconsciously varied by foreign additions.

"I think I see it all with my mind's eye," he would say. "It is evening. The wax tapers are lit before the icon in the corner of the room. Madame Courtenay presides at the tea-table; before her is the great steaming brass *samovar*, surrounded by tea-glasses and lemons. The *pope* (this was Mr. Courtenay) stands in his flowing cassock to ask a blessing, while the children are grouped smiling around. It is so with us too; England is far away, but your customs and ours are the same." I wondered if he would find it so if he ever went to England.

One day Boris brought me an invitation. One of his uncles was governor of the fortress of Schlüsselburg, on Lake Ladoga, about forty miles from St. Petersburg, and whenever two or three holidays happened to succeed each other, he used to invite Boris to spend them with him. One week when Monday was some church festival — I forget which — and Tuesday was the Emperor's birthday, Boris brought me an invitation from his uncle to spend Sunday and the two following days at Schlüsselburg.

Punctually at half-past four a tremendous jingling of bells announced the arrival of Boris's *troïka*. I was on the look-out, and as soon as I had sighted it hastily muffled myself up in my great driving *shooba* and fur cap, and hurried down the stairs as fast as my heavy clothing permitted, where, with the help of the coachman on the one side and one of our *dvorniks* on the other, I was heaved into the sledge, and, tumbling down into the straw with which it was filled, was soon covered with great fur rugs, which were tucked round me as if I were in bed.

"What is this?" I asked, knocking against something by my side.

"Take care," cried Boris, "that is my uncle's gun; he sent it to St. Petersburg to be repaired, and I am bringing it back for him; and I've loaded it, because, one never knows, we might see some wolves on the way. Wouldn't it be fun if we could shoot one and bring it to uncle!"

Before I had time to reply, our coachman, uttering a series of strange guttural sounds which conveyed nothing to me, but which seemed to be perfectly intelligible to the horses, had shaken his rough-looking animals into a gallop, and I was now enjoying for the first time one of the most delightful sensations that can be imagined — a drive in a troïka sledge on a clear fine night. Without the slightest jolt or jerk we glided swiftly over the smooth, feathery snow; not a sound was heard but the soothing jingle of the sledge bells, the muffled galloping of the horses' hoofs, and a soft rushing noise like that of the wind in the trees of a forest, made by the bottom of our sledge passing over the snowy ground.

In spite of the keenness of the air, a delicious warmth gradually pervaded me through and through, and as the deepening darkness and the rapid pace at which we were flying along prevented me from seeing anything very distinctly, I was soon lost in a gentle dreamy reverie on the borderland between sleeping and waking, half thinking my own thoughts, and half listening to Boris's stories of adventures with wolves. I think I must have just crossed the border when I was roused by Boris exclaiming in a loud, joyous voice, "Look! look! this is the beginning of the forest. See! Isn't it beautiful?"

I opened my eyes and looked round. The moon had risen, and was now shining almost as brightly as the sun by day, only flinging darker shadows, and thus giving a strangely fantastic appearance to the quaint little wooden houses which abound in the suburbs of St. Petersburg, bringing out and accentuating all the oddities and eccentricities of their architecture. Straight before us, looking all the darker from the contrast with the dazzling whiteness of the moonlit snow, were some great clumps of fir trees.

By degrees the houses grew rarer, and the clumps of trees larger and closer together, till at last they were no longer divided at all, but swept away continuously on either side, forming one vast shadowy mantle of green which covered everything but the snowy road, glistening with innumerable diamonds in the clear light of the moon. But I was so struck by the change in Boris himself, that I could hardly look at anything else. I felt as if for the first time I saw him as he really was. At school he had always seemed out of his element, uncomfortable and awkward. But now he was like the Highlander "whose foot is on his native heath."

While I had the collar of my *shooba* turned up over my ears, and my fur cap pulled down over my eyes, Boris's cap, jauntily pushed back from his forehead, left a great fringe of golden hair to blow about carelessly in the wind, and his bare throat was exposed to the icy air as unconcernedly as if it were a balmy morning in June instead of a bitter night in December.

"I am nearly sure I saw a wolf just now," all at once he cried, peering eagerly into the darkness of the forest. I was almost as excited as he himself, for I had heard a gentleman tell my father only a few days before, that wolves, though rare, were still occasionally to be met with in the forest near Schlüsselburg; and if by some lucky chance we *should* happen to meet with one and shoot it, what a glorious item of news it would make for my next letter to Anstey, and what a hero I should become in Artie's eyes!

"Quick! quick!" Boris cried suddenly, half beside himself with excitement, "give me the gun — it is in the straw by your side." With trembling hands I fumbled in the straw; I knew where it was, for I had knocked against it in getting into the sledge, but the stock had got entangled in something, probably one of the rugs, and as I was trying to disengage it, all at once there was a bang, a flash, a cloud of blinding smoke — the sledge stopped and the driver sprang to the ground, while Boris sunk back upon the cushions of the sledge, and remained speechless and motionless.

"Boris dear, are you hurt?" I cried wildly, looking at the strange, expressionless face and fixed eyes of my little friend. As I turned back the rug which covered him, a thrill of horror ran through my whole frame — it was wet with blood!

Our driver had already left the sledge, and was running for the nearest cottage, shouting for assistance as he went.

"Boris, dear, speak to me! Say just one word!" Thank Heaven! my first horrible fear was not realised — he still lived. He slowly opened his eyes and looked at me with a faint smile, making an almost imperceptible attempt to shake his head, as I tore out my handkerchief and pressed it against his chest; in a moment it was soaked with the blood that was now welling up as from a fountain.

"What time is it, dear?" he breathed faintly. Mechanically I looked at my watch: it was fourteen minutes past seven. Boris's face lit up with a bright expression when I told him. "Do you think I may send a message to the little English boy now?" he whispered, with a little smile. And then, scarcely waiting for an answer, he continued, "Quick! write what I say."

I felt hypnotised: all personal thought and will were gone from me; I obeyed blindly like a machine, taking my note-book and pencil from my pocket, and writing what Boris slowly and painfully dictated.

"Dear little English boy . . . you need not be jealous . . . any more . . . of poor Boris . . . he is —" he broke off, paused for a moment, gave one last little faint, flickering smile, and whispered "dead!"

As the word left his lips I heard the bells from Schlüsselburg chime the quarter-past seven; as by a lightning-flash I seemed to see the bright, happy party gathered round the tea-table at dear old Anstey, I heard their careless chat and light laughter as in the days of old that now seemed so long, long ago, when I was one of them; and when I looked down again on the pale, placid face of the child before me, I saw that his message was true — my little friend Boris was dead!

{1893}

JOHN FRANCIS BLOXAM
{1873–1928}

John Francis Bloxam was a student at Exeter College, Oxford, when in December 1894 he edited and published the single issue of *The Chameleon: A Bazaar of Dangerous and Smiling Chances.* (The title was borrowed from Robert Louis Stevenson.) The contents of this magazine included Oscar Wilde's "Phrases and Philosophies for the Use of the Young" (offered as a favor to Bloxam's friend Lord Alfred Douglas), Douglas's poems "In Praise of Shame" and "Two Loves" (one of which dared not speak its name), and an anonymous short story entitled "The Priest and the Acolyte." While many readers assumed Wilde to be the author of this story, his friend Ada Leverson ("the Sphinx") suspected the poet John Gray, whom Wilde called Dorian. But: " 'The Priest and the Acolyte' is not by Dorian," Wilde replied in a letter, "though you were right in discerning by internal evidence that the author has a profile. He is an undergraduate of strange beauty." Although Bloxam himself had written the story, the mere association of "The Priest and the Acolyte" with Wilde's name would harm him during his trials.

From the beginning, *The Chameleon* offended Mrs. Grundy. Jerome K. Jerome, in an editorial in his paper *To-Day* (December 29, 1894), accused the publication of being "nothing more nor less than an advocacy for indulgence in the cravings of an unnatural disease."

> That young men are here and there cursed with these unnatural cravings, no one acquainted with our public school life can deny. It is for such to wrestle with the devil within them; and many a long and agonized struggle is fought, unseen and unknown, within the heart of a young man. A publication of this kind, falling into his hands before the victory is complete, would, unless the poor fellow were of an exceptionally strong nature, utterly ruin him for all eternity.

Aside from a few verse contributions to Charles Kains Jackson's Uranian magazine *The Artist* (submitted under the pseudonym Bertram Lawrence), Bloxam never published anything else in his lifetime. Later, he was ordained a minister in the Church of England. Having served as chaplain to the forces in the First World War, he was awarded the Military Cross and Bar, and went on to hold various livings in the East End of London. When he died, he was vicar of St. Saviour, Hoxton.

The Priest and the Acolyte

Honi soit qui mal y pense

PART ONE

"Pray, father, give me thy blessing, for I have sinned."

The priest started; he was tired in mind and body; his soul was sad and his heart heavy as he sat in the terrible solitude of the confessional ever listening to the same dull round of oft-repeated sins. He was weary of the conventional tones and matter-of-fact expressions. Would the world always be the same? For nearly twenty centuries the Christian priests had sat in the confessional and listened to the same old tale. The world seemed to him no better; always the same, the same. The young priest sighed to himself, and for a moment almost wished people would be worse. Why could they not escape from these old wearily-made paths and be a little original in their vices, if sin they must? But the voice he now listened to aroused him from his reverie. It was so soft and gentle, so diffident and shy.

He gave the blessing, and listened. Ah, yes! he recognized the voice now. It was the voice he had heard for the first time only that very morning: the voice of the little acolyte that had served his Mass.

He turned his head and peered through the grating at the little bowed head beyond. There was no mistaking those long soft curls. Suddenly, for one moment, the face was raised, and the large moist blue eyes met his; he saw the little oval face flushed with shame at the simple boyish sins he was confessing, and a thrill shot through him, for he felt that here at least was something in the world that was beautiful, something that was really true. Would the day come when those soft scarlet lips would have grown hard and false? when the soft shy treble would have become careless and conventional? His eyes filled with tears, and in a voice that had lost its firmness he gave the absolution.

After a pause, he heard the boy rise to his feet, and watched him wend his way across the little chapel and kneel before the altar while he said his penance. The priest hid his thin tired face in his hands and sighed wearily. The next morning, as he knelt before the altar and turned to say the words of confession to the little acolyte whose head was bent so reverently towards him, he bowed low till his hair just touched the golden halo that surrounded the little face, and he felt his veins burn and tingle with a strange new fascination.

When that most wonderful thing in the whole world, complete soul-absorbing love for another, suddenly strikes a man, that man knows what heaven means, and he understands hell: but if the man be an ascetic, a priest whose whole heart is given to ecstatic devotion, it were better for that man if he had never been born.

When they reached the vestry and the boy stood before him reverently receiving the sacred vestments, he knew that henceforth the entire devotion of his religion, the whole ecstatic fervour of his prayers, would be connected with, nay, inspired by, one object alone. With the same reverence and humility as he would have felt in touching the consecrated elements he laid his hands on the curl-crowned head, he touched the small pale face, and, raising it slightly, he bent forward and gently touched the smooth white brow with his lips.

When the child felt the caress of his fingers, for one moment everything swam before his eyes; but when he felt the light touch of the tall priest's lips, a wonderful assurance took possession of him: he understood. He raised his little arms, and, clasping his slim white fingers around the priest's neck kissed him on the lips. With a sharp cry the priest fell upon his knees, and, clasping the little figure clad in scarlet and lace to his heart, he covered the tender flushing face with burning kisses. Then suddenly there came upon them both a quick sense of fear; they parted hastily, with hot trembling fingers folded the sacred vestments, and separated in silent shyness.

The priest returned to his poor rooms and tried to sit down and think, but all in vain: he tried to eat, but could only thrust away his plate in disgust: he tried to pray, but instead of the calm figure on the cross, the calm, cold figure with the weary, weary face, he saw continually before him the flushed face of a lovely boy, the wide star-like eyes of his new-found love.

All that day the young priest went through the round of his various duties mechanically, but he could not eat nor sit quiet, for when alone, strange shrill bursts of song kept thrilling through his brain, and he felt that he must flee out into the open air or go mad.

At length, when night came, and the long, hot day had left him exhausted and worn out, he threw himself on his knees before his crucifix and compelled himself to think.

He called to mind his boyhood and his early youth; there returned to him the thought of the terrible struggles of the last five years. Here he knelt, Ronald Heatherington, priest of Holy Church, aged twenty-eight: what he had endured during these five years of fierce battling with those terrible passions he had fostered in his boyhood, was it all to be in vain? For the last year he had really felt that all passion was subdued, all those

terrible outbursts of passionate love he had really believed to be stamped
out for ever. He had worked so hard, so unceasingly, through all these five
years since his ordination — he had given himself up solely and entirely to
his sacred office; all the intensity of his nature had been concentrated,
completely absorbed, in the beautiful mysteries of his religion. He had
avoided all that could affect him, all that might call up any recollection of
his early life. Then he had accepted this curacy, with sole charge of the little chapel that stood close beside the cottage where he was now living, the
little mission-chapel that was the most distant of the several grouped round
the old Parish Church of St. Anselm. He had arrived only two or three
days before, and, going to call on the old couple who lived in the cottage,
the back of which formed the boundary of his own little garden, had been
offered the services of their grandson as acolyte.

"My son was an artist fellow, sir," the old man had said: "he never was
satisfied here, so we sent him off to London; he was made a lot of there, sir,
and married a lady, but the cold weather carried him off one winter, and
his poor young wife was left with the baby. She brought him up and taught
him herself, sir, but last winter she was taken too, so the poor lad came to
live with us — so delicate he is, sir, and not one of the likes of us; he's a
gentleman born and bred, is Wilfred. His poor mother used to like him to
go and serve at the church near them in London, and the boy was so fond
of it himself that we thought, supposing you did not mind, sir, that it would
be a treat for him to do the same here."

"How old is the boy?" asked the young priest.

"Fourteen, sir," replied the grandmother.

"Very well, let him come to the chapel tomorrow morning," Ronald
had agreed.

Entirely absorbed in his devotions, the young man had scarcely noticed
the little acolyte who was serving for him, and it was not till he was hearing
his confession later in the day that he had realized his wonderful loveliness.

"Ah God! help me! pity me! After all this weary labour and toil, just
when I am beginning to hope, is everything to be undone? am I to lose
everything? Help me, help me, O God!"

Even while he prayed; even while his hands were stretched out in agonized supplication towards the feet of that crucifix before which his hardest
battles had been fought and won; even while the tears of bitter contrition
and miserable self-mistrust were dimming his eyes — there came a soft tap
on the glass of the window beside him. He rose to his feet, and wonderingly drew back the dingy curtain. There in the moonlight, before the
open window, stood a small white figure — there, with his bare feet on the

moon-blanched turf, dressed only in his long white night-shirt, stood his little acolyte, the boy who held his whole future in his small childish hands.

"Wilfred, what are you doing here?" he asked in a trembling voice.

"I could not sleep, father, for thinking of you, and I saw a light in your room, so I got out through the window and came to see you. Are you angry with me, father?" he asked, his voice faltering as he saw the almost fierce expression in the thin ascetic face.

"Why did you come to see me?" The priest hardly dared recognize the situation, and scarcely heard what the boy said.

"Because I love you, I love you — oh, so much! but you — you are angry with me — oh, why did I ever come! why did I ever come! — I never thought you would be angry!" and the little fellow sank on the grass and burst into tears.

The priest sprang through the open window, and seizing the slim little figure in his arms, he carried him into the room. He drew the curtain, and, sinking into the deep arm-chair, laid the little fair head upon his breast, kissing his curls again and again.

"O my darling! my own beautiful darling!" he whispered, "how could I ever be angry with you? You are more to me than all the world. Ah, God! how I love you, my darling! my own sweet darling!"

For nearly an hour the boy nestled there in his arms, pressing his soft cheek against his; then the priest told him he must go. For one long last kiss their lips met, and then the small white-clad figure slipped through the window, sped across the little moonlit garden, and vanished through the opposite window.

When they met in the vestry next morning, the lad raised his beautiful flower-like face, and the priest, gently putting his arms round him, kissed him tenderly on the lips.

"My darling! my darling!" was all he said; but the lad returned his kiss with a smile of wonderful almost heavenly love, in a silence that seemed to whisper something more than words.

"I wonder what was the matter with the father this morning?" said one old woman to another, as they were returning from the chapel; "he didn't seem himself at all; he made more mistakes this morning than Father Thomas made in all the years he was here."

"Seemed as if he had never said a Mass before!" replied her friend, with something of contempt.

And that night, and for many nights after, the priest, with the pale tired-looking face, drew the curtain over his crucifix and waited at the window for the glimmer of the pale summer moonlight on a crown of golden curls, for the sight of slim boyish limbs clad in the long white night-shirt, that only emphasized the grace of every movement, and the beautiful pallor of the little feet speeding across the grass. There at the window, night after night, he waited to feel tender loving arms thrown round his neck, and to feel the intoxicating delight of beautiful boyish lips raining kisses on his own.

Ronald Heatherington made no mistakes in the Mass now. He said the solemn words with a reverence and devotion that made the few poor people who happened to be there speak of him afterwards almost with awe; while the face of the little acolyte at his side shone with a fervour which made them ask each other what this strange light could mean. Surely the young priest must be a saint indeed, while the boy beside him looked more like an angel from heaven than any child of human birth.

PART TWO

The world is very stern with those that thwart her. She lays down her precepts, and woe to those who dare to think for themselves, who venture to exercise their own discretion as to whether they shall allow their individuality and natural characteristics to be stamped out, to be obliterated under the leaden fingers of convention.

Truly, convention is the stone that has become head of the corner in the jerry-built temple of our superficial, self-assertive civilization.

"And whosoever shall fall on this stone shall be broken: but on whomsoever it shall fall, it will grind him to powder."

If the world sees anything she cannot understand, she assigns the basest motives to all concerned, supposing the presence of some secret shame, the idea of which, at least, her narrow-minded intelligence is able to grasp.

The people no longer regarded their priest as a saint, and his acolyte as an angel. They still spoke of them with bated breath and with their fingers on their lips; they still drew back out of the way when they met either of them; but now they gathered together in groups of twos and threes and shook their heads.

The priest and his acolyte heeded not; they never even noticed the suspicious glances and half-suppressed murmurs. Each had found in the other perfect sympathy and perfect love: what could the outside world matter to them now? Each was to the other the perfect fulfilment of a scarcely preconceived ideal; neither heaven nor hell could offer more. But the stone of convention had been undermined; the time could not be far distant when it must fall.

The moonlight was very clear and very beautiful; the cool night air was heavy with the perfume of the old-fashioned flowers that bloomed so profusely in the little garden. But in the priest's little room the closely drawn curtains shut out all the beauty of the night. Entirely forgetful of all the world, absolutely oblivious of everything but one another, wrapped in the beautiful visions of a love that far outshone all the splendour of the summer night, the priest and the little acolyte were together.

The little lad sat on his knees with his arms closely pressed round his neck and his golden curls laid against the priest's close-cut hair; his white night-shirt contrasting strangely and beautifully with the dull black of the other's long cassock.

There was a step on the road outside — a step drawing nearer and nearer; a knock at the door. They heard it not; completely absorbed in each other, intoxicated with the sweetly poisonous draught that is the gift of love, they sat in silence. But the end had come: the blow had fallen at last. The door opened, and there before them in the doorway stood the tall figure of the rector.

Neither said anything; only the little boy clung closer to his beloved, and his eyes grew large with fear. Then the young priest rose slowly to his feet and put the lad from him.

"You had better go, Wilfred," was all he said.

The two priests stood in silence watching the child as he slipped through the window, stole across the grass, and vanished into the opposite cottage.

Then the two turned and faced each other.

The young priest sank into his chair and clasped his hands, waiting for the other to speak.

"So it has come to this!" he said: "the people were only too right in what they told me! Ah, God! that such a thing should have happened here! that it has fallen on me to expose your shame — our shame! that it is I who must give you up to justice, and see that you suffer the full penalty of your sin! Have you nothing to say?"

"Nothing — nothing," he replied softly. "I cannot ask for pity: I cannot explain: you would never understand. I do not ask you anything for myself, I do not ask you to spare me; but think of the terrible scandal to our dear Church."

"It is better to expose these terrible scandals and see that they are cured. It is folly to conceal a sore: better show all our shame than let it fester."

"Think of the child."

"That was for you to do: you should have thought of him before. What has his shame to do with me? it was your business. Besides, I would not spare him if I could: what pity can I feel for such as he —?"

But the young man had risen, pale to the lips.

"Hush!" he said in a low voice; "I forbid you to speak of him before me with anything but respect"; then softly to himself, "with anything but reverence; with anything but devotion."

The other was silent, awed for the moment. Then his anger rose.

"Dare you speak openly like that? Where is your penitence, your shame? have you no sense of the horror of your sin?"

"There is no sin for which I should feel shame," he answered very quietly. "God gave me my love for him, and He gave him also his love for me. Who is there that shall withstand God and the love that is His gift?"

"Dare you profane the name by calling such a passion as this 'love'?"

"It was love, perfect love: it *is* perfect love."

"I can say no more now; tomorrow all shall be known. Thank God, you shall pay dearly for all this disgrace," he added, in a sudden outburst of wrath.

"I am sorry you have no mercy; — not that I fear exposure and punishment for myself. But mercy can seldom be found from a Christian," he added, as one that speaks from without.

The rector turned towards him suddenly, and stretched out his hands.

"Heaven forgive me my hardness of heart," he said. "I have been cruel; I have spoken cruelly in my distress. Ah, can you say nothing to defend your crime?"

"No: I do not think I can do any good by that. If I attempted to deny all guilt, you would only think I lied: though I should prove my innocence, yet my reputation, my career, my whole future, are ruined for ever. But will you listen to me for a little? I will tell you a little about myself."

The rector sat down while his curate told him the story of his life, sitting by the empty grate with his chin resting on his clasped hands.

"I was at a big public school, as you know. I was always different from other boys. I never cared much for games. I took little interest in those things for which boys usually care so much. I was not very happy in my boyhood, I think. My one ambition was to find the ideal for which I longed. It has always been thus: I have always had an indefinite longing for something, a vague something that never quite took shape, that I could never quite understand. My great desire has always been to find something that would satisfy me. I was attracted at once by sin: my whole early life is stained and polluted with the taint of sin. Sometimes even now I think that there are sins more beautiful than anything else in the world. There are vices that are bound to attract almost irresistibly anyone who loves beauty above everything. I have always sought for love: again and again I have been the victim of fits of passionate affection: time after time I have seemed to have found my ideal at last: the whole object of my life has been, times without number, to gain the love of some particular person. Several times my efforts were successful; each time I woke to find that the success I had obtained was worthless after all. As I grasped the prize, it lost all its attraction — I no longer cared for what I had once desired with my whole heart. In vain I endeavoured to drown the yearnings of my heart with the ordinary pleasures and vices that usually attract the young. I had to choose a profession. I became a priest. The whole aesthetic tendency of my soul was intensely attracted by the wonderful mysteries of Christianity, the artistic beauty of our services. Ever since my ordination I have been striving to cheat myself into the belief that peace had come at last — at last my yearning was satisfied: but all in vain. Unceasingly I have struggled with the old cravings for excitement, and, above all, the weary, incessant thirst for a perfect love. I have found, and still find, an exquisite delight in religion: not in the regular duties of a religious life, not in the ordinary round of parish organizations; — against these I chafe incessantly; — no, my delight is in the aesthetic beauty of the services, the ecstasy of devotion, the passionate fervour that comes with long fasting and meditation."

"Have you found no comfort in prayer?" asked the rector.

"Comfort? — no. But I have found in prayer pleasure, excitement, almost a fierce delight of sin." .

"You should have married. I think that would have saved you."

Ronald Heatherington rose to his feet and laid his hand on the rector's arm.

"You do not understand me. I have never been attracted by a woman in my life. Can you not see that people are different, totally different, from one another? To think that we are all the same is impossible; our natures, our temperaments, are utterly unlike. But this is what people will never see; they found all their opinions on a wrong basis. How can their deductions be just if their premisses are wrong? One law laid down by the majority, who happen to be of one disposition, is only binding on the minority *legally*, not *morally*. What right have you, or anyone, to tell me that such and such a thing is sinful for me? Oh, why can I not explain to you and force you to see?" and his grasp tightened on the other's arm. Then he continued, speaking fast and earnestly:

"For me, with my nature, to have married would have been sinful: it would have been a crime, a gross immorality, and my conscience would have revolted." Then he added bitterly: "Conscience should be that divine instinct which bids us seek after that our natural disposition needs — we have forgotten that; to most of us, to the world, nay, even to Christians in general, conscience is merely another name for the cowardice that dreads to offend against convention. Ah, what a cursed thing convention is! I have committed no moral offence in this matter; in the sight of God my soul is blameless; but to you and to the world I am guilty of an abominable crime — abominable, because it is a sin against convention, forsooth! I met this boy: I loved him as I had never loved anyone or anything before: I had no need to labour to win his affection — he was mine by right: he loved me, even as I loved him, from the first: he was the necessary complement to my soul. How dare the world presume to judge us? What is convention to us? Nevertheless, although I really knew that such a love was beautiful and blameless, although from the bottom of my heart I despised the narrow judgement of the world, yet for his sake and for the sake of our Church, I tried at first to resist. I struggled against the fascination he possessed for me. I would never have gone to him and asked his love; I would have struggled on till the end: but what could I do? It was he that came to me, and offered me the wealth of love his beautiful soul possessed. How could I tell to such a nature as his the hideous picture the world would paint? Even as you saw him this evening, he has come to me night by night, — how dare I disturb the sweet purity of his soul by hinting at the horrible suspicions his presence might arouse? I knew what I was doing. I have faced the world and set myself up against it. I have openly scoffed at its dictates. I do not ask you to sympathize with me, nor do I pray you to stay your hand. Your eyes are blinded with a mental cataract. You are bound, bound with those miserable ties that have held you body and soul from the cradle. You must do what you believe to be your duty. In God's eyes we are martyrs, and we shall not shrink even from death in this struggle against the idolatrous worship of convention."

Ronald Heatherington sank into a chair, hiding his face in his hands, and the rector left the room in silence.

For some minutes the young priest sat with his face buried in his hands. Then with a sigh he rose and crept across the garden till he stood beneath the open window of his darling.

"Wilfred," he called very softly.

The beautiful face, pale and wet with tears, appeared at the window.

"I want you, my darling; will you come?" he whispered.

"Yes, father," the boy softly answered.

The priest led him back to his room; then, taking him very gently in his arms, he tried to warm the cold little feet with his hands.

"My darling, it is all over." And he told him as gently as he could all that lay before them.

The boy hid his face on his shoulder, crying softly.

"Can I do nothing for you, dear father?"

He was silent for a moment. "Yes, you can die for me; you can die with me."

The loving arms were about his neck once more, and the warm, loving lips were kissing his own. "I will do anything for you. O father, let us die together!"

"Yes, my darling, it is best: we will."

Then very quietly and very tenderly he prepared the little fellow for his death; he heard his last confession and gave him his last absolution. Then they knelt together, hand in hand, before the crucifix.

"Pray for me, my darling."

Then together their prayers silently ascended that the dear Lord would have pity on the priest who had fallen in the terrible battle of life. There they knelt till midnight, when Ronald took the lad in his arms and carried him to the little chapel.

"I will say Mass for the repose of our souls," he said.

Over his night-shirt the child arrayed himself in his little scarlet cassock and tiny lace cotta. He covered his naked feet with the scarlet sanctuary shoes; he lighted the tapers and reverently helped the priest to vest. Then before they left the vestry the priest took him in his arms and held him pressed closely to his breast; he stroked the soft hair and whispered cheeringly to him. The child was weeping quietly, his slender frame trembling with the sobs he could scarcely suppress. After a moment the tender embrace soothed him, and he raised his beautiful mouth to the priest's. Their lips were pressed together, and their arms wrapped one another closely.

"Oh, my darling, my own sweet darling!" the priest whispered tenderly.

"We shall be together for ever soon; nothing shall separate us now," the child said.

"Yes, it is far better so; far better to be together in death than apart in life."

They knelt before the altar in the silent night, the glimmer of the tapers lighting up the features of the crucifix with strange distinctness. Never had the priest's voice trembled with such wonderful earnestness, never had the acolyte responded with such devotion, as at this midnight Mass for the peace of their own departing souls.

Just before the consecration the priest took a tiny phial from the pocket of his cassock, blessed it, and poured the contents into the chalice.

When the time came for him to receive from the chalice, he raised it to his lips, but did not taste of it.

He administered the sacred wafer to the child, and then he took the beautiful gold chalice, set with precious stones, in his hand; he turned towards him; but when he saw the light in the beautiful face he turned again to the crucifix with a low moan. For one instant his courage failed him; then he turned to the little fellow again, and held the chalice to his lips:

"The Blood of our Lord Jesus Christ, which was shed for thee, preserve thy body and soul unto everlasting life."

Never had the priest beheld such perfect love, such perfect trust, in those dear eyes as shone from them now; now, as with face raised upwards he received his death from the loving hands of him that he loved best in the whole world.

The instant he had received, Ronald fell on his knees beside him and drained the chalice to the last drop. He set it down and threw his arms round the beautiful figure of his dearly loved acolyte. Their lips met in one last kiss of perfect love, and all was over.

When the sun was rising in the heavens it cast one broad ray upon the altar of the little chapel. The tapers were burning still, scarcely half-burnt through. The sad-faced figure of the crucifix hung there in its majestic calm. On the steps of the altar was stretched the long, ascetic frame of the young priest, robed in the sacred vestments; close beside him, with his curly head pillowed on the gorgeous embroideries that covered his breast, lay the beautiful boy in scarlet and lace. Their arms were round each other; a strange hush lay like a shroud over all.

"And whosoever shall fall on this stone shall be broken: but on whomsoever it shall fall, it will grind him to powder."

{1894}

STANISLAUS ERIC, COUNT STENBOCK
{1860–1895}

Stanislaus Eric, Count Stenbock, was conspicuous even among the decadents of the 1890s. His original published works include three volumes of poetry — *Love, Sleep and Dreams: A Volume of Verse* (circa 1881, of which but two copies are extant); *Myrtle, Rue and Cypress: A Book of Poems, Songs, and Sonnets* (1883); and *The Shadow of Death: A Collection of Poems, Songs, and Sonnets* (1893) — as well as fiction (apart from the seven stories in *Studies of Death*, which appeared the year before his own death, the story " 'The Other Side': A Breton Legend," about lycanthropy, written for Lord Alfred Douglas's *Spirit Lamp*). With William Wilson, he also translated "shorter stories" of Balzac into English (1890). His masterwork, however, was undoubtedly himself.

Unlike Baron Corvo, Stenbock came by his title honestly: his father was an Estonian nobleman. Indeed, he returned to Estonia in 1885 and remained there two years before returning to London. This Estonian period may be seen as a rehearsal for the image he cultivated in London. From Matthew Sturgis's description of Stenbock's Estonian household in *Passionate Attitudes: The English Decadence of the 1890s* (1995):

> The upper storey he transformed into an artificial paradise, heavy with the perfumes of incense and opium; tortoises trundled across the thick Smyrna carpets; hot-house flowers and caged song-birds proclaimed the subjugation of nature to artifice; the snake that protruded from the cuff of his dressing-gown and the toads that littered his table made their separate claims for the beauties of ugliness; and the presence of a beloved dachshund called Trixie added a note of unmistakable camp.

As for Stenbock's physical aspect, we have this verbal sketch by the artist Simeon Solomon (from a letter to the photographer Frederick Hollyer, for whom Stenbock sat, quoted in Brian Reade's 1970 anthology *Sexual Heretics: Male Homosexuality in English Literature from 1850–1900*): "His appearance was that of a tall, graceful intellectual looking girl and although he is not exactly good-looking, his eyes and expression are very beautiful."

A key work for any study of Stenbock is John Adlard's *Stenbock, Yeats and the Nineties* (1969), which includes both an essay on Stenbock by Arthur Symons titled "A Study in the Fantastic" and a bibliography of his works by Timothy d'Arch Smith. A number of Stenbock's manuscripts and typescripts, as well as some of his correspondence, can be found in the Villa I Tatti in Florence because the author's lawyer was the first husband of Bernard Berenson's wife, Mary. Durtro Press has republished *Studies of Death* as well as an edition of four further stories by Stenbock: "La Girandola," "The Child of the Soul — a Story in Thirteen Chapters," "A Modern Saint," and "Story of a Scapular." ⚘

FROM *Studies of Death: Romantic Tales*

Hylas

I WAS INTENDING to paint a picture of David as the Shepherd, but nowhere could I find a suitable model for the face; there were several "white and ruddy," but none which had on them the impress of the born King, or the inspiration of the Psalmist. One day I was rowing up the river, and came across the very face I had been seeking for so long. He was a boy of about fifteen, clad in flannels, alone in a boat which he had moored to the shore of a little island in the middle of the river; he was occupied in sketching. "This is lucky," I thought, "it will be a good excuse to begin a conversation," so I rowed up to him, and saying that I was an artist, asked to see what he was drawing; he blushed, and showed me. Of course I had expected the usual smudged landscape; but imagine my surprise to find a certainly beautifully conceived drawing of Hylas by the river's brink, with the Nymph stretching out her arms towards him. He was merely copying the rushes and trees of the island as a background. The Hylas was not at all a bad portrait of himself, but my surprise was still greater to find that the face of the Nymph was an evident copy of my own last picture called "The Siren," which I had recently sold to a certain Professor Langton (at a very low price, as I knew the Professor was not well off, and his genuine enthusiasm for my work was so refreshing after the inane compliments of those who thought it the "thing" to admire me because I happened to be the "fashion" just then). I praised the drawing, and pointed out one or two faults, then asked for paper and pencil, and reproduced the drawing as it should have been. The boy watched with ever-increasing eagerness; at last he said with a deep blush, "May I ask you what your name is?"

"My name is Gabriel Glynde," I replied.

"Ah, I thought so all the time you were drawing. Do you know, your pictures have always had a peculiar fascination for me; father has lots of them, at least *drawings*, only one *painting*, that one called 'The Siren,' from which I copied *that*; you must know father, he went to see your studio the other day"; then, blushing still deeper, "May I come and see your studio too?"

"Certainly you may; but I ask something in return: that is, that you will sit as model for the 'shepherd David.' I guess from what you say that you are the son of Professor Langton; am I not right? May I ask what is your Christian name?"

"Oh, Lionel," he said simply; "there's only father and me; I don't mind being a model if you like, and will let me see your studio, though why you should think I should make a suitable David I am at a loss to understand."

There was a mixture of simple boyishness, and at the same time education, about his way of talking which puzzled me, but the explanation was not difficult to unravel. We rowed down together: I took him to tea at an old wayside inn covered with honeysuckle, then went straight with him to his father's. He had told me all about himself on the way. He was his father's only son, he had never been to school, his father had taught him everything himself, he had no companions of his own age, and amused himself alone. He liked riding and rowing and swimming, but hated shooting and fishing (curious this, that he should share my own ingrained dislikes), but what he loved above all was drawing and painting; he had never learnt to draw, but he had always drawn ever since he could remember. His father knew everything, but could not draw, but was very fond of pictures, but nevertheless would not let him go to an art school, etc. So he prattled on. I could not help remarking that he seemed *very* much more educated than boys of his age usually are, though wholly unconscious of the fact, and yet, at the same time, showed a singular artlessness and innocence about the most commonplace things.

Professor Langton received me with the utmost amiability, and the end of it was that I stayed there the evening. After he had sent his son to bed, he expounded to me his ideas on education. He did not approve of schools of any kind, he said; boarding schools were an abomination, but day schools, perhaps, were a necessity. "But in my case," he said, "happily *not*; indeed, what is the use of being a Professor if I cannot instruct my own boy?"

Well, the end of all this was, that having Lionel as a model, I took a great fancy to him, and the more I saw of him the less I liked the idea of his going to an Academy school. Perhaps to a boy ordinarily brought up the usual conversation of art students would not do much harm, but to Lionel — this exotic flower — I shuddered to think of it. I never before had had any pupils, wishing to be individual, and *not* to create a school, but then Lionel was of my school already. So the end of it was that I offered to take him as a gratuitous and exclusive pupil, for which his father was intensely grateful.

Years passed by, and I taught him to draw and to paint very well; perhaps I impregnated him a little too much with my own individuality. I used to chuckle to myself, "This is just like Leonardo da Vinci and Salaino. Critics in the future will be disputing which is a genuine 'Glindio.' " I do not mean by this that Lionel had no imagination or inventive power — on the contrary, he was, as I have said before, a "genius," an artist, born, not made — but merely that his style of execution was based on mine; indeed, I even hoped that he might surpass in my own line.

One does not realise what a frightful responsibility one incurs in introducing one person to another. In nine cases out of ten nothing particular may ensue, but the tenth case may be the turning-point in a life for good or for evil. Thus it was when I introduced Lionel to Lady Julia Gore Vere. When I say I introduced him, I did nothing of the kind; she was having tea with me in my studio, and Lionel, who I thought was going up the river that day (that was one of the reasons I had selected that day to ask her), suddenly walked in. Well! what could I do but introduce them.

Lady Julia bore the name Gore Vere because she had two husbands, both alive and kicking, and through some anomaly of the Divorce Court, she could not legally ascertain whether she ought to bear the name of Mr. Gore or Mr. Vere, so she split the difference by giving herself both appellations. What her past was I did not know, and did not care to inquire — it was no concern of mine; what did concern me was that she bought my pictures. She was certainly the last person I should have liked Lionel to meet. She was a very lovely woman and very clever (when I say clever I do not merely mean sharp and witty, but really cultured), and when she talked about Art she really knew what she was talking about. Except for a moment of irritation, I did not see any particular harm. Lionel knew nothing about her; there was nothing remarkable in the fact that she took an interest in him; and he took a childish pleasure in showing her his sketches, which she criticised and admired, justly, for, as I have said before, they were remarkably good.

I had always thought of Lionel as a child, and never realised that he was now grown up. Happening to know Lady Julia's age, it did not occur to me that to people in general she looked a very great deal younger than she really was. Well, they met several times. One day Lionel said, "How like Lady Julia is to your picture 'The Siren.'" I have always maintained that artists give models for faces, as much as faces give models for artists. I had done so many pictures since, I had quite forgotten about "The Siren." Now "The Siren" was entirely an imaginative face, taken from no model at all, but when Lionel said so, it struck me she *was* like "The Siren." Then I thought of his drawing the first day I had met him. A disagreeable sensation and vague fear haunted me; I took to watch him more closely. Then the truth flashed upon me — he was hopelessly in love with her. She was doing her best to egg him on; what an idiot I was not to have seen that before, I who pretend to be observant of all things.

No, this would not do at all, it would be the ruin of his life. I must save him at any cost. Perhaps I had been wrong all the time, I had kept him too much under a glass case; perhaps if he had had more experience he would not have become so suddenly and completely infatuated. Oh, how wicked of her! I raged and gnashed my teeth. Had she not the whole world for prey that she could not spare this poor boy? What could he be to her? But then, perhaps, she did not realise what harm she was doing. I would go and expostulate with her myself; from what I knew of her she was by no means heartless.

So next day I called on her, and somewhat rudely came to the point at once. "Why," I said, "do you seek to ruin that poor boy's life? You know whom I mean — Lionel. Surely such a conquest must be nothing to you?"

I spoke very bitterly, she answered calmly, "You ask me why? I will tell you the reason quite simply: first, because I am jealous of him; secondly, because I thought you cared for me a little, and I thought I might make you jealous of me, and finally, because *I love you*."

I was utterly dumfounded; for some time I could not speak at all. Then I said, "If it is true, as you say, that you love me, do at least this one thing for me — spare *him*." She answered in the same calm voice. "There is one way to overcome the difficulty." I went out without a word.

All that night I remained without sleep, thinking. "There was one way to overcome the difficulty." I had said I would save him at any cost, and the cost was to sacrifice myself. However unselfish one's motive may be, selfish considerations are inevitably intermingled. I thought, After all, the sacrifice is not so very terrible, the way out of the difficulty comparatively easy — I certainly liked her well enough, and now that my studio parties were on a much larger scale than heretofore, it would really be a great convenience to have a lady in the house. And then I thought, trying to be unselfish again, I shall be doing a good turn to her; by giving her my name I shall re-establish her reputation, and people will soon forget that her name has ever been Gore or Vere. . . . Lionel would soon realise the absurdity of his own position, and of course would not think of making love to my wife.

So next morning I wrote to Lady Julia, asking her if she would be willing to exchange the ambiguous name of Gore-Vere for that of Glynde. She wrote back to say she would be very pleased to accept my offer, but she thought I might have phrased it more kindly.

Fortunately Lionel was going away the next day on a walking tour by himself (a thing which he was very fond of doing), for I could not bring myself to tell Lionel about it just yet, or indeed till the whole thing was over. There was no reason whatever for delay, so we arranged to be married quietly in Paris before a Maire, as, for obvious reasons, it would be better not to be married in London. When the marriage was over I made up my mind to write to Lionel. I tore up several letters in various styles; at last I resolved to adopt the flippantly facetious. I said, "I am now in Paris, and *who* do you think is my companion? You will never guess — Lady Julia Gore-Vere, only her name isn't Gore-Vere now, but Glynde, because I have married her; but it won't make any difference, you must call her Lady Julia all the same."

To this letter there was no response; to this I attached but little importance. "Of course," I thought, "he will be a little sulky at first, but he will soon get over it; his innate sense of humour will show him how foolish he has been."

In spite of all people might say against my wife, there could be no more charming travelling companion, always amusing and amused, and intelligently critical; indeed, if I had not always had the haunting thought of Lionel, I think we should have enjoyed ourselves very much.

Will you understand me if I say that I was sorry to find out my wife's past was by no means as black as it was painted; indeed, she was much more the wronged than the wrongdoer. This, I suppose, is inverted selfishness; it is a luxury to pose as a hero. What was my heroic self-sacrifice? Simply getting a charming wife, who really loved me, and who had never loved any one else before. I wrote to Lionel once more — a long, lively letter describing the places we had been to, interspersed with graphic sketches of persons and places. To this again I received no answer. But then as I had addressed it to the last country place where I knew Lionel had been staying, I came to the conclusion he could not have received it, possibly having left no address behind him.

At last we came home; I learned that Lionel was staying with his father. I sent a note, saying: "I insist on seeing you. Come this evening. Waiting for an answer."

There was *no* answer; but in the evening Lionel came in person.

Lionel, I say? Could *this* be Lionel? He was utterly changed. All youth and buoyancy had gone from him; he rather dragged himself along than walked; he was quite pale, and wore a look of utter, absolute dejection. I tried to pretend to take no notice.

"Well, Lionel," I said, with sham cheerfulness, "what have *you* been doing all this time?" He answered in a dull, apathetic voice, "Painting a picture."

"A picture? What about?"

"You will get it the day after to-morrow," he said in the same dull monotone.

"Child, what has come over you? Why do you keep aloof from me? Why did you not answer my letters?"

"I think it is somewhat needless for you to ask that question," he said.

"No, but tell me — explain," I cried, stretching out my hands to him. He went backwards to the other end of the room, and then said in a voice filled with tears, "You have taken from me all that I loved; I should not have thought that of *you*. Of course you had a perfect right to do so, but still, at least, you might have told me first."

"*All* that you loved?" I said.

"Yes! *All* except yourself, and you have killed my love for you," he said, almost with a wail.

"But, Lionel, listen; I do not love her."

"Do you consider that an excuse?" he said fiercely; "if you *did* I might forgive you; but as it is I cannot."

"But listen, child," I cried; "hear me out; it is not *her* that I love but *you*; it was to save you from what I thought would be your utter ruin that I married her."

"A strange way of showing love to break my heart," he said in the same spiritless voice as before; "Good-bye," and then he turned his back on me, and held out his left hand — it was quite cold, and fell limp to his side; he turned once round as he opened the door with a look of mute reproach which will haunt me for ever.

The day after the morrow I took up the morning paper, and saw this: —

SHOCKING ACCIDENT WHILE BATHING.

Near ——— Island (the island where I first met Lionel), the body of a young man was found yesterday. There was little difficulty in identifying the body as that of Mr. Lionel Langton, a young artist of much promise, as his clothes were on the shore, and a pocket-book containing cards and letters was found in the coat pocket, and also as Mr. Langton was well known in this neighbourhood, being particularly fond of bathing at this spot. The fact of his being drowned has caused much astonishment, as he was known to be a remarkably good swimmer. Death was attributed to sudden cramp. His father, Professor Langton, was immediately telegraphed for, and seemed quite overcome with grief. He deposed that lately he had been much distressed about his son; he had been unwell and very depressed, also strange in his manner, for which he, his father, could assign no cause.

Hardly had I read this, when there was a violent knock at the door, and two men came in bringing a picture. Never had I seen anything so good from Lionel's hand; it was simply wonderful. It represented Hylas lying at the bottom of a river, seen through water. The figure of Hylas was a portrait of himself as he was when I first saw him, but somehow into the closed eyes he had infused the expression which I had last seen in his face. Looking down, reflected in the water, was my own face. Starting up, I caught a sight of my face in a mirror; by what prescience did he know that I should look thus on hearing the tidings of his death?

Narcissus

MY FATHER DIED before I was born, and my mother in giving birth to me, so I was born at once to a title and a fortune. I merely mention this to show that Fortune, in a way, seemed from the first to smile upon me. The one passion of my life was beauty, and I thought myself specially *fortunate* that I realised my own ideal in myself. Even now that I am writing I look round the room, and see portraits of myself at various stages of my life: as a child, a boy, and a young man. Never have I seen a face as lovely as my own was. That glorious classic outline, those large, lustrous, dark blue eyes, that curled gold hair, like woven sunshine, that divinely curved mouth and exquisite grace of lips, that splendid poise of neck and throat! I was not vain in the proper sense of the word, for vanity means desire for the approbation of others, and getting up oneself to please others. But I, on the contrary, did not care what others thought; I would remain for hours before the mirror in a kind of ecstasy. No! no single picture I had ever seen could come up to me!

I was spoilt as a child. At school my life was made easy for me. Others did my impositions, and masters overlooked my peccadilloes; and if the boys of my own form hated and envied me, they knew that if they dared lift a finger against me, they would have their lives thrashed out of them by my champions in the upper forms. I do not mean to say by this that my school career was not a success in the ordinary sense of the word; because, besides being beautiful, I was brilliantly clever, and learnt in a day what it would take others months to learn. And if I say I was spoilt, I at least was not pettish and fretful as spoilt children usually are; on the contrary, I was invariably amiable, perhaps because my will was never gainsaid. Unlike most in whom the æsthetic sense is abnormally developed, I had absolutely no passions. I did not love any one — but then, I allowed myself very gracefully to be loved, and always sought to please those who loved me, so that I actually got the reputation of being unselfish.

This was all very well as a boy. When I became of age I was launched into society. Women, one and all, appeared to fall in love with me. I don't mean fortune-seekers and tuft-hunters, but such as had the same wealth and social position as myself. I was congratulated on my conquests, and told that my admirers were celebrated beauties. Beauties, indeed! What was their beauty to mine? I did not understand women or their sentiments at all; but I had read several novels, and tried to be amiable to one and all, and make love to them in the conventional way, as I had read. One time there appeared on the scene a girl who was considered dazzlingly beautiful. She really was rather handsome. She was the daughter of a Mexican millionaire, and, of course, was sought after by every one. Indeed, I was reminded at the time of the Bab Ballad, "Dukes with the humble maiden dealt," and, unlike Duke Baily and Duke Humphey, they were willing to cast their coronets and their lands at her feet. But she, unlike the heroine of the Bab Ballad, preferred my "miserable and grovelling" self. I must say here that my *vanity* was this time rather flattered; it rather pleased me to think that they should be put in the background for my sake, and I was as amiable to her as possible, and used to take her out everywhere. She was certainly clever, but there was a certain savage passionateness about her nature that jarred upon me.

One day her father said to me, "You can't think how glad I am to hear that you are engaged to my daughter. As we happen to be alone together, perhaps you wouldn't mind if we settle all the particulars of this business. I intend to behave very handsomely to her, and will give her a dowry of ————." (Good heavens! This parvenu!)

"Engaged to your daughter!" I cried, "there has been no such understanding between us. I am extremely sorry, but I cannot imagine who could have been your informant. The information is wholly and entirely false."

"What?" he said, "not engaged to Enriqueta? What on earth do you mean? Do you suppose I should have allowed you to go about with my girl as you have been doing? Again, I ask, what do you mean?"

"I am sorry," I replied, "that you should have been labouring under such a misapprehension. In proof that I mean what I say, I will avoid all intercourse with your daughter for the future. And I can scarcely believe she is under the same misapprehension as yourself." With that remark I left the house abruptly.

A short time afterwards, when I was seated by the fire in my drawing-room reading, who should walk in suddenly but Enriqueta herself, with furiously flashing eyes. She looked like a fiend incarnate. The emblem of anger in the abstract. I remember at that moment the words of the proverb flashing across me, "Non est ira sicut ira mulieris."

"So," she said, "this is how you behave! Well, then, take that!" and saying this, she threw a fluid from a glass phial into my face. It was not vitriol; that would have blinded me: this, unfortunately, did not!

A sudden smart on one side of the face, then gradually the whole face corroded. The cheeks fell in, the flesh part of the nose dropped off, the hair came out in handfuls, several of the teeth dropped out, the mouth contorted into a ghastly grin, the eyes became cavernous and horrible, denuded of eyebrows and lashes. I saw myself in a mirror *once;* anything more loathsome it would be impossible to imagine.

Some friends called to sympathise with me, but on no consideration would I admit any one. I had every mirror in the house broken and thrown away, and could scarcely bear to look into a washing-basin. I spoke to my servants from behind a screen, and lived utterly alone, and by night. I had only one opportunity of air and exercise, so I managed to bribe the policeman to let me into Hyde Park just before the gates closed at night, and there I would wander about all night through, till at dawn the gates opened again, when I would hurry home.

One night, when I was going on my usual lonely walk, the wailing voice of a child came out of the darkness.

"Do please help me," it cried, "mother left me here, and said she would come back directly, and now I have heard the clock strike the hour four times, and mother hasn't come back, and I am blind, quite blind."

I lit my lantern; it was a child of about nine or ten years old. It was clad in rags — yet the voice had the accent of a gentleman.

I said, "It's impossible to get out now; you must wait till the gates open in the morning. Come and sit here? Are you hungry?"

"Yes," said the child simply.

"Well, then, let's have something to eat." Then I undid my knapsack, wherein I always took with me provisions of various dainties, and wine, for my nocturnal meal, and spreading a napkin, prepared a repast.

Then the child told me his story. I cannot repeat it in the artless way he told it; I can only give the gist of it. He was very delicate-looking, with a very sweet face, and an infinite pathos in the expression of the closed eyes. It appeared he lived alone with his mother. His name, he said, was Tobit: that he had been born blind, and did not know what seeing anything meant. He did not think he had any surname; his mother was always called "Bonny Bess," because people said she was so *handsome.*

"What does handsome mean?" he asked. I shuddered.

"Oh!" I said, "it means good-looking; but it's no use being handsome. It's better to be good."

He said his mother was very unkind to him, and was always beating him; but there was a gentleman, who used to come about every three months, who was very kind to him, and used to bring him presents, and give his mother money. The gentleman was an officer, he said. He always knew when the gentleman was coming, because his mother did not beat him for three weeks beforehand, because one time the gentleman had seen some bruises on him, and had been very angry, and had beaten his mother. And when the gentleman had gone, his mother had said: "If you dare to tell the gentleman anything about me again, I'll thrash you within an inch of your life."

The gentleman used to talk to him, and take him out for walks. But all toys the gentleman brought him his mother would take away from him, and sell them in order to get drink. Twice he had taken him to a place called "the country" for a whole week. There were flowers and birds singing; then he was really happy.

"The only thing she didn't take away from me," he said, "is this," and from his pocket he produced a penny whistle, "because she said she could not get anything for it, and I might go and play it in the street. Then, perhaps, people would give me pennies." Then he proceeded to perform on the penny whistle. Good heavens! I had no idea that out of a thing like that so much tone could be elicited! He began with a well-known organ-grinder tune, then came variations filled with roulades. I was simply astounded.

"A great many people give me pennies," he said, naïvely, "but mother takes them all away from me."

One day he had overheard the gentleman quarrelling with his mother. "Then why don't you make me an honest woman?" she had said.

"It would be quite impossible to make *you* an honest woman. Shut up your cant. You know perfectly well I can't marry you. Even if I could, I wouldn't. I only wish to God I could take poor little Tobit away with me."

"Rob a mother of her only child," said the mother, whimpering, "fortunately the law of England does not allow that."

"Blast your infernal humbug!" said the gentleman, "I know you don't care a hang about the child. You only want the money. I feel quite certain that you ill-treat him, though he has never said a word to me about it. Bah! you talk of being an *honest* woman. Look how the child is dressed — look how you are!"

As soon as the gentleman had gone his mother seized upon him, and beat him so severely that he screamed for help. A man came in, and seized her arms and pinned her to the ground.

"Look here," the man had said, "that's enough of that, you she-devil! If you try that sort of game again you'll get the worst of it!"

The last time he saw the gentleman he had been more tender than ever before. He had felt hot tears falling on his face.

"Poor little Tobit!" he had said. "I am going away to a far country, and perhaps may never see you again."

Then he had heard the gentleman talking to his mother. "Look here, Bess," he said, "this is all the money I can scrape together, and this must last you out while I am away. But I hope to be back soon, and then I shall have higher pay."

He had cried for many days afterwards, which made his mother very angry. One day, after waiting some time, he had asked when the gentleman would be coming back again from the far country. "He won't be coming back again at all," answered his mother snappishly. "He's dead — got shot in Africa, blast him! Get out and play the whistle."

He had gone out in the streets, and cried very much at first, and then it seems he put his grief into music: "Because," he said, "he had got more pennies than he had ever got before." A little while after he had heard his mother whispering to a man. "Damn it!" said the man, "we can't take that bloody brat with us."

"Oh, I'll manage that," the mother had said. And that evening his mother had taken him out into the park, and had told him she wanted to speak with somebody, and was coming back directly, and told him to stay there. He had heard a man's voice, but his mother had never come back again.

Fortunately, as soon as the child had finished his story he went fast asleep. I do not know what I should have said. Its utter loathsomeness reminded me of the one sight I had had of my own face. At dawn I woke the child up. Putting down my thick black veil I turned home, taking the child with me. I sent a servant to make inquiries, and the result was as I had expected — the mother had decamped with all her possessions, and not paid the rent.

So at last one consolation was sent me. After having been so long alone, at last I had a companion — one who would not recoil from the sight of me. I determined to give up my nocturnal life, and managed to secure a cottage in a remote and desolate part of the country, where one could walk for miles without seeing any one, and in mercy to my servants, stationed them in the nearest town, requiring them only to bring me provisions and do the house once a day.

The child was delighted with the country. His placid, absolute happiness, in all his blindness, was much more than I ever experienced in the delight in beauty by the sense of sight. He was very intelligent and phenomenally good, and I managed to teach him music, in which he took the keenest pleasure. The piano, of course, was a thing unknown to him before. His only instrument had been a penny whistle!

One day I read in the paper that an operation had been successfully performed by a certain eminent oculist on a person born blind. An awful struggle rose in my mind; supposing the child could be made to see! I thought of the frightful blank all things which to me had seemed of the greatest value must be to him, and was I to deprive him of that? Then, if he could see, and saw me, he would recoil from me in horror. But then I knew that my health was failing — that I should not live long, and was I, just to gratify my own selfishness for a short time, to condemn him to perpetual darkness, when it lay within my reach to save him? It was, as I said before, a frightful struggle. At last I decided I would consult the oculist. I took the child to London.

The oculist came, and said in his case the operation would be quite simple — not nearly so difficult as the case mentioned in the papers. It would merely require — well, I don't know what. I know nothing of medical terms, so I consented to have the operation performed. The child was given chloroform, and, the operation completed, his eyes were bound with bandages, which I was told to take off on the third day.

On the third day I did so. I had always thought that the blind, even though born blind, made visual images of things. In his case it was not so. The operation had been successful, and he could see. He knew well enough, by the touch, what a chair or a table was, but I had the greatest difficulty in explaining this or that was a chair or table as he saw it. He seemed quite dazed. Then he said ultimately: —

"And you are the most beautiful person in all the world!"

The True Story of a Vampire

VAMPIRE STORIES ARE generally located in Styria; mine is also. Styria is by no means the romantic kind of place described by those who have certainly never been there. It is a flat, uninteresting country, only celebrated by its turkeys, its capons, and the stupidity of its inhabitants. Vampires generally arrive at night, in carriages drawn by two black horses.

Our Vampire arrived by the commonplace means of the railway train, and in the afternoon. You must think I am joking, or perhaps that by the word "Vampire" I mean a financial vampire. No, I am quite serious. The Vampire of whom I am speaking, who laid waste our hearth and home, was a *real* vampire.

Vampires are generally described as dark, sinister-looking, and singularly handsome. Our Vampire was, on the contrary, rather fair, and certainly was not at first sight sinister-looking, and though decidedly attractive in appearance, not what one would call singularly handsome.

Yes, he desolated our home, killed my brother — the one object of my adoration — also my dear father. Yet, at the same time, I must say that I myself came under the spell of his fascination, and, in spite of all, have no ill-will towards him now.

Doubtless you have read in the papers *passim* of "the Baroness and her beasts." It is to tell how I came to spend most of my useless wealth on an asylum for stray animals that I am writing this.

I am old now; what happened then was when I was a little girl of about thirteen. I will begin by describing our household. We were Poles; our name was Wronski: we lived in Styria, where we had a castle. Our household was very limited. It consisted, with the exclusion of domestics, of only my father, our governess — a worthy Belgian named Mademoiselle Vonnaert — my brother, and myself. Let me begin with my father: he was old, and both my brother and I were children of his old age. Of my mother I remember nothing: she died in giving birth to my brother, who is only one year, or not as much, younger than myself. Our father was studious, continually occupied in reading books, chiefly on recondite subjects and in all kinds of unknown languages. He had a long white beard, and wore habitually a black velvet skull-cap.

How kind he was to us! It was more than I could tell. Still it was not I who was the favourite. His whole heart went out to Gabriel — Gabryel as we spelt it in Polish. He was always called by the Russian abbreviation Gavril — I mean, of course, my brother, who had a resemblance to the only portrait of my mother, a slight chalk sketch which hung in my father's study. But I was by no means jealous: my brother was and has been the only love of my life. It is for his sake that I am now keeping in Westbourne Park a home for stray cats and dogs.

I was at that time, as I said before, a little girl; my name was Carmela. My long tangled hair was always all over the place, and never would be combed straight. I was not pretty — at least, looking at a photograph of me at that time, I do not think I could describe myself as such. Yet at the same time, when I look at the photograph, I think my expression may have been pleasing to some people: irregular features, large mouth, and large wild eyes.

I was by way of being naughty — not so naughty as Gabriel in the opinion of Mlle. Vonnaert. Mlle. Vonnaert, I may intercalate, was a wholly excellent person, middle-aged, who really *did* speak good French, although she was a Belgian, and could also make herself understood in German, which, as you may or may not know, is the current language of Styria.

I find it difficult to describe my brother Gabriel; there was something about him strange and superhuman, or perhaps I should rather say præter-human, something between the animal and the divine. Perhaps the Greek idea of the Faun might illustrate what I mean; but that will not do either. He had large, wild, gazelle-like eyes: his hair, like mine, was in a perpetual tangle — that point he had in common with me, and indeed, as I afterwards heard, our mother having been of gipsy race, it will account for much of the innate wildness there was in our natures. I was wild enough, but Gabriel was much wilder. Nothing would induce him to put on shoes and stockings, except on Sundays — when he also allowed his hair to be combed, but only by me. How shall I describe the grace of that lovely mouth, shaped verily "en arc d'amour." I always think of the text in the Psalm, "Grace is shed forth on thy lips, therefore has God blessed thee eternally" — lips that seemed to exhale the very breath of life. Then that beautiful, lithe, living, elastic form!

He could run faster than any deer: spring like a squirrel to the topmost branch of a tree: he might have stood for the sign and symbol of vitality itself. But seldom could he be induced by Mlle. Vonnaert to learn lessons; but when he did so, he learnt with extraordinary quickness. He would play upon every conceivable instrument, holding a violin here, there, and everywhere except the right place: manufacturing instruments for himself out of reeds — even sticks. Mlle. Vonnaert made futile efforts to induce him to learn to play the piano. I suppose he was what was called spoilt, though merely in the superficial sense of the word. Our father allowed him to indulge in every caprice.

One of his peculiarities, when quite a little child, was horror at the sight of meat. Nothing on earth would induce him to taste it. Another thing which was particularly remarkable about him was his extraordinary power over animals. Everything seemed to come tame to his hand. Birds would sit on his shoulder. Then sometimes Mlle. Vonnaert and I would lose him in the woods — he would suddenly dart away. Then we would find him singing softly or whistling to himself, with all manner of woodland creatures around him, — hedgehogs, little foxes, wild rabbits, marmots, squirrels, and such like. He would frequently bring these things home with him and insist on keeping them. This strange menagerie was the terror of poor Mlle. Vonnaert's heart. He chose to live in a little room at the top of a turret; but which, instead of going upstairs, he chose to reach by means of a very tall chestnut-tree, through the window. But in contradiction to all this, it was his custom to serve every Sunday Mass in the parish church, with hair nicely combed and with white surplice and red cassock. He looked as demure and tamed as possible. Then came the element of the divine. What an expression of ecstasy there was in those glorious eyes!

Thus far I have not been speaking about the Vampire. However, let me begin with my narrative at last. One day my father had to go to the neighbouring town — as he frequently had. This time he returned accompanied by a guest. The gentleman, he said, had missed his train, through the late arrival of another at our station, which was a junction, and he would therefore, as trains were not frequent in our parts, have had to wait there all night. He had joined in conversation with my father in the too-late-arriving train from the town: and had consequently accepted my father's invitation to stay the night at our house. But of course, you know, in those out-of-the-way parts we are almost patriarchal in our hospitality.

He was announced under the name of Count Vardalek — the name being Hungarian. But he spoke German well enough: not with the monotonous accentuation of Hungarians, but rather, if anything, with a slight Slavonic intonation. His voice was peculiarly soft and insinuating. We soon afterwards found out he could talk Polish, and Mlle. Vonnaert vouched for his good French. Indeed he seemed to know all languages. But let me give my first impressions. He was rather tall, with fair wavy hair, rather long, which accentuated a certain effeminacy about his smooth face. His figure had something — I cannot say what — serpentine about it. The features were refined; and he had long, slender, subtle, magnetic-looking hands, a somewhat long sinuous nose, a graceful mouth, and an attractive smile, which belied the intense sadness of the expression of the eyes. When he arrived his eyes were half closed — indeed they were habitually so — so that I could not decide their colour. He looked worn and wearied. I could not possibly guess his age.

Suddenly Gabriel burst into the room: a yellow butterfly was clinging to his hair. He was carrying in his arms a little squirrel. Of course he was bare-legged as usual. The stranger looked up at his approach; then I noticed his eyes. They were green: they seemed to dilate and grow larger. Gabriel stood stock-still, with a startled look, like that of a bird fascinated by a serpent. But nevertheless he held out his hand to the newcomer. Vardalek, taking his hand — I don't know why I noticed this trivial thing,

— pressed the pulse with his forefinger. Suddenly Gabriel darted from the room and rushed upstairs, going to his turret-room this time by the staircase instead of the tree. I was in terror what the Count might think of him. Great was my relief when he came down in his velvet Sunday suit, and shoes and stockings. I combed his hair, and set him generally right.

When the stranger came down to dinner his appearance had somewhat altered; he looked much younger. There was an elasticity of the skin, combined with a delicate complexion, rarely to be found in a man. Before, he had struck me as being very pale.

Well, at dinner we were all charmed with him, especially my father. He seemed to be thoroughly acquainted with all my father's particular hobbies. Once, when my father was relating some of his military experiences, he said something about a drummer-boy who was wounded in battle. His eyes opened completely again and dilated: this time with a particularly disagreeable expression, dull and dead, yet at the same time animated by some horrible excitement. But this was only momentary.

The chief subject of his conversation with my father was about certain curious mystical books which my father had just lately picked up, and which he could not make out, but Vardalek seemed completely to understand. At dessert-time my father asked him if he were in a great hurry to reach his destination: if not, would he not stay with us a little while: though our place was out of the way, he would find much that would interest him in his library.

He answered, "I am in no hurry. I have no particular reason for going to that place at all, and if I can be of service to you in deciphering these books, I shall be only too glad." He added with a smile which was bitter, very very bitter: "You see I am a cosmopolitan, a wanderer on the face of the earth."

After dinner my father asked him if he played the piano. He said, "Yes, I can a little," and he sat down at the piano. Then he played a Hungarian csardas — wild, rhapsodic, wonderful.

That is the music which makes men mad. He went on in the same strain.

Gabriel stood stock-still by the piano, his eyes dilated and fixed, his form quivering. At last he said very slowly, at one particular motive — for want of a better word you may call it the *relâche* of a csardas, by which I mean that point where the original quasi-slow movement begins again — "Yes, I think I could play that."

Then he quickly fetched his fiddle and self-made xylophone, and did actually, alternating the instruments, render the same very well indeed.

Vardalek looked at him, and said in a very sad voice, "Poor child! you have the soul of music within you."

I could not understand why he should seem to commiserate instead of congratulate Gabriel on what certainly showed an extraordinary talent.

Gabriel was shy even as the wild animals who were tame to him. Never before had he taken to a stranger. Indeed, as a rule, if any stranger came to the house by any chance, he would hide himself, and I had to bring him up his food to the turret chamber. You may imagine what was my surprise when I saw him walking about hand in hand with Vardalek the next morning, in the garden, talking livelily with him, and showing his collection of pet animals, which he had gathered from the woods, and for which we had had to fit up a regular zoological gardens. He seemed utterly under the domination of Vardalek. What surprised us was (for otherwise we liked the stranger, especially for being kind to him) that he seemed, though not noticeably at first — except perhaps to me, who noticed everything with regard to him — to be gradually losing his general health and vitality. He did not become pale as yet; but there was a certain languor about his movements which certainly there was by no means before.

My father got more and more devoted to Count Vardalek. He helped him in his studies: and my father would hardly allow him to go away, which he did sometimes — to Trieste, he said: he always came back, bringing us presents of strange Oriental jewellery or textures.

I knew all kinds of people came to Trieste, Orientals included. Still, there was a strangeness and magnificence about these things which I was sure even then could not possibly have come from such a place as Trieste, memorable to me chiefly for its necktie shops.

When Vardalek was away, Gabriel was continually asking for him and talking about him. Then at the same time he seemed to regain his old vitality and spirits. Vardalek always returned looking much older, wan, and weary. Gabriel would rush to meet him, and kiss him on the mouth. Then he gave a slight shiver: and after a little while began to look quite young again.

Things continued like this for some time. My father would not hear of Vardalek's going away permanently. He came to be an inmate of our house. I indeed, and Mlle. Vonnaert also, could not help noticing what a difference there was altogether about Gabriel. But my father seemed totally blind to it.

One night I had gone downstairs to fetch something which I had left in the drawing-room. As I was going up again I passed Vardalek's room. He was playing on a piano, which had been specially put there for him, one of Chopin's nocturnes, very beautifully: I stopped, leaning on the banisters to listen.

Something white appeared on the dark staircase. We believed in ghosts in our part. I was transfixed with terror, and clung to the banisters. What was my astonishment to see Gabriel walking slowly down the staircase, his eyes fixed as though in a trance! This terrified me even more than a ghost would. Could I believe my senses? Could that be Gabriel?

I simply could not move. Gabriel, clad in his long white night-shirt, came downstairs and opened the door. He left it open. Vardalek still continued playing, but talked as he played.

He said — this time speaking in Polish — *Nie umiem wyrazic jak ciehie kocham*, — "My darling, I fain would spare thee; but thy life is my life, and I must live, I who would rather die. Will God not have *any* mercy on me? Oh! oh! life; oh, the torture of life!" Here he struck one agonised and strange chord, then continued playing softly, "O Gabriel, my beloved! my life, yes *life* — oh, why life? I am sure this is but a little that I demand of thee. Surely thy superabundance of life can spare a little to one who is already dead. No, stay," he said now almost harshly, "what must be, must be!"

Gabriel stood there quite still, with the same fixed vacant expression, in the room. He was evidently walking in his sleep. Vardalek played on: then said, "Ah!" with a sigh of terrible agony. Then very gently, "Go now, Gabriel; it is enough." And Gabriel went out of the room and ascended the staircase at the same slow pace, with the same unconscious stare. Vardalek struck the piano, and although he did not play loudly, it seemed as though the strings would break. You never heard music so strange and so heart-rending!

I only know I was found by Mlle. Vonnaert in the morning, in an unconscious state, at the foot of the stairs. Was it a dream after all? I am sure now that it was not. I thought then it might be, and said nothing to any one about it. Indeed, what could I say?

Well, to let me cut a long story short, Gabriel, who had never known a moment's sickness in his life, grew ill: and we had to send to Gratz for a doctor, who could give no explanation of Gabriel's strange illness. Gradual wasting away, he said: absolutely no organic complaint. What could this mean?

My father at last became conscious of the fact that Gabriel was ill. His anxiety was fearful. The last trace of grey faded from his hair, and it became quite white. We sent to Vienna for doctors. But all with the same result.

Gabriel was generally unconscious, and when conscious, only seemed to recognise Vardalek, who sat continually by his bedside, nursing him with the utmost tenderness.

One day I was alone in the room: and Vardalek cried suddenly, almost fiercely, "Send for a priest at once, at once," he repeated. "It is now almost too late!"

Gabriel stretched out his arms spasmodically, and put them round Vardalek's neck. This was the only movement he had made for some time. Vardalek bent down and kissed him on the lips. I rushed downstairs: and the priest was sent for. When I came back Vardalek was not there. The priest administered extreme unction. I think Gabriel was already dead, although we did not think so at the time.

Vardalek had utterly disappeared; and when we looked for him he was nowhere to be found; nor have I seen or heard of him since.

My father died very soon afterwards: suddenly aged, and bent down with grief. And so the whole of the Wronski property came into my sole possession. And here I am, an old woman, generally laughed at for keeping, in memory of Gabriel, an asylum for stray animals — and — people do not, as a rule, believe in Vampires!

{1894}

KENNETH GRAHAME

{1859–1932}

Mostly remembered now for his masterpiece *The Wind in the Willows* (1908), Kenneth Grahame began his professional life as a gentleman-clerk in the Bank of England after financial problems prohibited him from attending Oxford. Although unhappy in his work, he nonetheless became an officer of the bank at thirty-nine, while simultaneously pursuing a literary career that placed him squarely in the *fin de siècle* tradition: among the periodicals to which he contributed essays were the *National Observer* and *The Yellow Book* (where "The Roman Road" was first published). In 1899 he married Elspeth Thomson, and the following year their only child, Alastair, was born. (Alastair Grahame would die in a train accident, a probable suicide, in 1920.) As Oscar Wilde's fairy tales began as tales told to his two sons, so the early chapters of *The Wind in the Willows* had their origins in bedtime stories and letters written to Alastair, an unhappy and sickly boy.

That Grahame was never very comfortable being a grown-up is evident from two of his earlier books, *The Golden Age* (1895) and *Dream Days* (1898), both of which take place in a realm of idealized and perpetual childhood, an adultless world that in *The Wind in the Willows* becomes a humanless world — one that Grahame, for what his biographer Peter Green calls "surmisable reasons," keeps strictly "clean of the clash of sex." Instead, in his riverbank society of bachelor animals living in pairs (as in Carpenter's *Ioläus*) brotherhood, not marriage, is the defining social term. A wistful longing for such an arcadia resonates as well in *The Golden Age*, where Edward consoles his sister Charlotte with "a jolly story" about a pair of storks:

> And one stork died — it was the she stork . . . And the other stork was quite sorry, and moped, and went on, and got very miserable. So [the stork's owners] looked about and found a duck, and introduced it to the stork. The duck was a drake, but the stork didn't mind, and they loved each other and were as jolly as could be. By and by another duck came along — a real she-duck this time — and when the drake saw her he fell in love, and left the stork, and went and proposed to the duck: for she was very beautiful. But the poor stork who was left, he said nothing at all to anybody, but just pined and pined and pined away, till one morning he was found quite dead: But the ducks lived happily ever afterwards!

It is significant that the source of this story, the children's aunt Eliza, has carried it over from "that beastly abroad," the non-English (and literally beastly) world where such love as that of the stork for the drake becomes possible. 🐾

FROM *The Golden Age*

The Roman Road

ALL THE ROADS of our neighbourhood were cheerful and friendly, having each of them pleasant qualities of their own; but this one seemed different from the others in its masterful suggestion of a serious purpose, speeding you along with a strange uplifting of the heart. The others tempted chiefly with their treasures of hedge and ditch; the rapt surprise of the first lords-and-ladies, the rustle of a field-mouse, the splash of a frog; while cool noses of brother beasts were pushed at you through gate or gap. A loiterer you had need to be, did you choose one of them, so many were the tiny hands thrust out to detain you, from this side and that. But this one was of a sterner sort, and even in its shedding off of bank and hedgerow, as it marched straight and full for the open downs, it seemed to declare its contempt for adventitious trappings to catch the shallow-pated. When the sense of injustice or disappointment was heavy on me, and things were very black within, as on this particular day, the road of character was my choice for that solitary ramble when I turned my back for an afternoon on a world that had unaccountably declared itself against me.

"The Knights' Road" we children had named it, from a sort of feeling that, if from any quarter at all, it would be down this track we might some day see Lancelot and his peers come pacing on their great war-horses — supposing that any of the stout band still survived in nooks and unexplored places. Grown-up people sometimes spoke of it as the "Pilgrims' Way;" but I didn't know much about pilgrims — except Walter in the Horselberg story. Him I sometimes saw, breaking with haggard eyes out of yonder copse, and calling to the pilgrims as they hurried along on their desperate march to the Holy City, where peace and pardon were awaiting them. "All roads lead to Rome," I had once heard somebody say; and I had taken the remark very seriously, of course, and puzzled over it many days. There must have been some mistake, I concluded at last; but of one road at least I intuitively felt it to be true. And my belief was clinched by something that fell from Miss Smedley during a history lesson, about a strange road that ran right down the middle of England till it reached the coast, and then began again in France, just opposite, and so on undeviating, through city and vineyard, right from the misty Highlands to the Eternal City. Uncorroborated, any statement of Miss Smedley's usually fell on incredulous ears; but here, with the road itself in evidence, she seemed, once in a way, to have strayed into truth.

Rome! It was fascinating to think that it lay at the other end of this white ribbon that rolled itself off from my feet over the distant downs. I was not quite so uninstructed as to imagine I could reach it that afternoon; but some day, I thought, if things went on being as unpleasant as they were now — some day, when Aunt Eliza had gone on a visit — some day, we would see.

I tried to imagine what it would be like when I got there. The Coliseum, I knew, of course, from a woodcut in the history-book; so to begin with I plumped that down in the middle. The rest had to be patched up from the little gray market-town where twice a year we went to have our hair cut; hence, in the result, Vespasian's amphitheatre was approached by muddy little streets, wherein the Red Lion and the Blue Boar, with Somebody's Entire along their front, and "Commercial Room" on their windows; the doctor's house, of substantial red brick; and the façade of the New Wesleyan chapel, which we thought very fine, were the chief architectural ornaments: while the Roman populace pottered about in smocks and corduroys, twisting the tails of Roman calves and inviting each other to beer in musical Wessex. From Rome I drifted on to other cities, faintly heard of — Damascus, Brighton (Aunt Eliza's ideal), Athens, and Glasgow, whose glories the gardener sang; but there was a certain sameness in my conception of all of them — that Wesleyan chapel would keep cropping up everywhere. It was easier to go a-building among those dream-cities where no limitations were imposed, and one was sole architect, with a free hand. Down a delectable street of cloud-built palaces I was mentally pacing, when I happened upon the Artist.

He was seated at work by the roadside, at a point whence the cool large spaces of the downs, juniper-studded, swept grandly westwards. His attributes proclaimed him of the artist tribe: besides, he wore knickerbockers like myself — a garb confined, I was aware, to boys and artists. I knew I was not to bother him with questions, nor look over his shoulder and breathe in his ear — they didn't like it, this *genus irritabile*. But there was nothing about staring in my code of instructions, the point having somehow been overlooked; so, squatting down on the grass, I devoted myself to the passionate absorbing of every detail. At the end of five minutes there was not a button on him that I could not have passed an examination in; and the wearer himself of that homespun suit was probably less familiar with its pattern and texture than I was. Once he looked up, nodded, half held out his tobacco pouch, mechanically as it were, then returning it to his pocket, resumed his work, and I my mental photography.

After another five minutes or so had passed, he remarked, without looking my way: "Fine afternoon we're having; going far to-day?"

"No, I'm not going any farther than this," I replied. "I *was* thinking of going on to Rome, but I've put it off."

"Pleasant place, Rome," he murmured; "you'll like it." It was some minutes later that he added, "But I wouldn't go just now, if I were you: too jolly hot."

"*You* haven't been to Rome, have you?" I inquired.

"Rather," he replied briefly: "I live there."

This was too much, and my jaw dropped as I struggled to grasp the fact that I was sitting there talking to a fellow who lived in Rome. Speech was out of the question: besides, I had other things to do. Ten solid minutes had I already spent in an examination of him as a mere stranger and artist; and now the whole thing had to be done over again, from the changed point of view. So I began afresh, at the crown of his soft hat, and worked down to his solid British shoes, this time investing everything with the new Roman halo; and at last I managed to get out, "But you don't really live there, do you?" never doubting the fact, but wanting to hear it repeated.

"Well," he said, good-naturedly overlooking the slight rudeness of my query, "I live there as much as I live anywhere; about half the year sometimes. I've got a sort of a shanty there. You must come and see it some day."

"But do you live anywhere else as well?" I went on, feeling the forbidden tide of questions surging up within me.

"Oh yes — all over the place," was his vague reply. "And I've got a diggings somewhere off Piccadilly."

"Where's that?" I inquired.

"Where's what?" said he. "Oh, Piccadilly! It's in London."

"Have you a large garden?" I asked; "and how many pigs have you got?"

"I've no garden at all," he replied sadly, "and they don't allow me to keep pigs, though I'd like to, awfully. It's very hard."

"But what do you do all day, then?" I cried; "and where do you go and play, without any garden, or pigs, or things?"

"When I want to play," he said gravely, "I have to go and play in the street; but it's poor fun, I grant you. There's a goat, though, not far off, and sometimes I talk to him when I'm feeling lonely; but he's very proud."

"Goats *are* proud," I admitted. "There's one lives near here, and if you say anything to him at all, he hits you in the wind with his head. You know what it feels like when a fellow hits you in the wind?"

"I do, well," he replied, in a tone of proper melancholy, and painted on.

"And have you been to any other places," I began again presently, "besides Rome and Piccy-what's-his-name?"

"Heaps," he said. "I'm a sort of Ulysses — seen men and cities, you know. In fact, about the only place I never got to was the Fortunate Island."

I began to like this man. He answered your questions briefly and to the point, and never tried to be funny. I felt I could be confidential with him.

"Wouldn't you like," I inquired, "to find a city without any people in it at all?"

He looked puzzled. "I'm afraid I don't quite understand," said he.

"I mean," I went on eagerly, "a city where you walk in at the gates, and the shops are all full of beautiful things, and the houses furnished as grand as can be, and there isn't anybody there whatever! And you go into the shops, and take anything you want — chocolates and magic-lanterns and injirubber balls — and there's nothing to pay; and you choose your own house and live there and do just as you like, and never go to bed unless you want to!"

The artist laid down his brush. "That *would* be a nice city," he said — "better than Rome. You can't do that sort of thing in Rome — or in Piccadilly either. But I fear it's one of the places I've never been to."

"And you'd ask your friends," I went on, warming to my subject — "only those you really like, of course; and they'd each have a house to themselves — there'd be lots of houses: and there wouldn't be any relations at all, unless they promised they'd be pleasant; and if they weren't they'd have to go."

"So you wouldn't have any relations?" said the artist. "Well, perhaps you're right. We have tastes in common, I see."

"I'd have Harold," I said reflectively, "and Charlotte. They'd like it awfully. The others are getting too old. Oh, and Martha — I'd have Martha to cook and wash up and do things. You'd like Martha. She's ever so much nicer than Aunt Eliza. She's my idea of a real lady."

"Then I'm sure I should like her," he replied heartily, "and when I come to — what do you call this city of yours? Nephelo — something, did you say?"

"I — I don't know," I replied timidly. "I'm afraid it hasn't got a name — yet."

The artist gazed out over the downs. " 'The poet says, dear city of Cecrops,' " he said softly to himself; " 'and wilt not thou say, dear city of Zeus?' That's from Marcus Aurelius," he went on, turning again to his work. "You don't know him, I suppose; you will some day."

"Who's he?" I inquired.

"Oh, just another fellow who lived in Rome," he replied, dabbing away.

"Oh dear!" I cried disconsolately. "What a lot of people seem to live at Rome, and I've never even been there! But I think I'd like *my* city best."

"And so would I," he replied, with unction. "But Marcus Aurelius wouldn't, you know."

"Then we won't invite him," I said; "will we?"

"*I* won't if you won't," said he. And that point being settled, we were silent for a while.

"Do you know," he said presently, "I've met one or two fellows from time to time who have been to a city like yours — perhaps it was the same one. They won't talk much about it — only broken hints, now and then; but they've been there sure enough. They don't seem to care about anything in particular — and everything's the same to them, rough or smooth; and sooner or later they slip off and disappear, and you never see them again. Gone back, I suppose."

"Of course," said I. "Don't see what they ever came away for; *I* wouldn't. To be told you've broken things when you haven't, and stopped having tea with the servants in the kitchen, and not allowed to have a dog to sleep with you. But *I've* known people, too, who've gone there."

The artist stared, but without incivility.

"Well, there's Lancelot," I went on. "The book says he died, but it never seemed to read right, somehow. He just went away, like Arthur. And Crusoe, when he got tired of wearing clothes and being respectable. And all the nice men in the stories who don't marry the Princess, 'cos only one man ever gets married in a book, you know. They'll be there!"

"And the men who never come off," he said, "who try like the rest, but get knocked out, or somehow miss — or break down or get bowled over in the *mêlée* — and get no Princess, nor even a second-class kingdom — some of them'll be there, I hope?"

"Yes, if you like," I replied, not quite understanding him; "if they're friends of yours, we'll ask 'em, of course."

"What a time we shall have!" said the artist reflectively; "and how shocked old Marcus Aurelius will be!"

The shadows had lengthened uncannily, a tide of golden haze was flooding the gray-green surface of the downs, and the artist began to put his traps together, preparatory to a move. I felt very low: we would have to part, it seemed, just as we were getting on so well together. Then he stood up, and he was very straight and tall, and the sunset was in his hair and beard as he stood there, high over me. He took my hand like an equal. "I've enjoyed our conversation very much," he said. "That was an interesting subject you started, and we haven't half exhausted it. We shall meet again, I hope?"

"Of course we shall," I replied, surprised that there should be any doubt about it.

"In Rome perhaps?" said he.

"Yes, in Rome," I answered; "or Piccy-the-other-place, or somewhere."

"Or else," said he, "in that other city — when we've found the way there. And I'll look out for you, and you'll sing out as soon as you see me. And we'll go down the street arm in arm, and into all the shops, and then I'll choose my house, and you'll choose your house, and we'll live there like princes and good fellows."

"Oh, but you'll stay in my house, won't you?" I cried. "I wouldn't ask everybody, but I'll ask *you*."

He affected to consider a moment; then "Right!" he said: "I believe you mean it, and I *will* come and stay with you. I won't go to anybody else, if they ask me ever so much. And I'll stay quite a long time too, and I won't be any trouble."

Upon this compact we parted, and I went down-heartedly from the man who understood me, back to the house where I never could do anything right. How was it that everything seemed natural and sensible to him, which these uncles, vicars, and other grown-up men took for the merest tomfoolery? Well, he would explain this, and many another thing, when we met again. The Knights' Road! How it always brought consolation! Was he possibly one of those vanished knights I had been looking for so long? Perhaps he would be in armour next time; why not? He would look well in armour, I thought. And I would take care to get there first, and see the sunlight flash and play on his helmet and shield, as he rode up the High Street of the Golden City.

Meantime, there only remained the finding it. An easy matter.

{1895}

FREDERICK ROLFE, BARON CORVO
{1860–1913}

Frederick William Serafino Austin Lewis Mary Rolfe remains one of the most curious and pathetic figures in English letters. His most celebrated work is *The Desire and Pursuit of the Whole: A Romance of Modern Venice* (written in 1909 but not published until 1934), and yet the majority of readers, in a moment of honesty, would admit to calling the book unreadable. For, though Rolfe produced much remarkable prose, its merits were not thoroughgoing. His was, in the end, an abstruse species of genius. "In Praise of Billy B." is included here because its content is characteristic of Rolfe even if its concision is not.

Rolfe passed much of his life in Venice — he worked as a gondolier and is buried on the island cemetery of San Michele. The student of Corvo would do well to look up *Baron Corvo's Venice Letters* (1987). These two dozen or so missives were addressed to Charles Masson Fox, whose intimates included John Gambril Nicholson (he plagiarized one of Rolfe's poems in his collection *Love in Earnest*), the painter Henry Tuke, and Louis Wilkinson, and date from 1909 and 1910. They are valuable above all for their frank sexuality: Rolfe's own experiences (with boys "16, 17, 18 and large . . . strong enough to struggle and to give as much joy as I take"), as well as his minor history of the homosexual *ambiente*. At the same time, the letters disclose that what even an extravagant, almost romantic, figure such as Rolfe wrote for public consumption was more reticent by far than what he was willing to write to a friend. From Letter XI (January 27, 1910):

> I never knew that I loved and was loved so passionately with so much of me by so much another. . . .
>
> I was waked by a gentle voice "Sior, Sior, Sior, with permission!" And his rod was rigid and ready. I took him on me. "Slowly, and as hard as you like" I said. Oh what a time we had. He took me at my word splendidly and laboured with the sumptuous abandon of a true artist, straining his young body to his very utmost but holding himself in control prolonging the pleasure for the pure joy of it.

Rolfe is fortunate to be the subject of one of the most interesting of all literary biographies, A.J.A. Symons's *The Quest for Corvo: An Experiment in Biography* (1934). ❧

In Praise of Billy B.

THIS IS NEARLY the true story of the Row at Magdalen.

There was a Magdalen man who decided to pose as an aesthete. He was a nasty little skunk with depraved tastes, disgusting habits and a vitriolic tongue. The naked legs and muscular *torsi* of the boating men filled him with envious longing for what could never be his. Like the fox who said he didn't want the grapes, he never spoke without some cut or gibe at those whose healthy physique and wholesome virility should have made him blush for his own puny insignificance.

His sarcasms when Magdalen got to the head of the river, passed all bounds of decency; and at the bump-supper the boating men, who were certainly a little intoxicated with their athletic successes and other things, resolved for once to take the law into their own hands and make the little beast rue his insulting words. The idea was a charming one, and a rush was made for the New Buildings where the miscreant had his lair. His rooms were lighted, but there was no response to the invitation for him to come out and meet the athletes he had vilified. A search was made, but the aesthete was nowhere to be found.

Now you must clearly understand that had the DISGRACE TO HIS SEX been forthcoming the athletes would probably have had their halfpenny worth out of him: either by cutting his long, greasy, and perfumed hair, or by dangling him at the end of a string from the little bridge in the Water Walk close at hand, or by making him run round and round the quad attired in a sage-green billycock, a pair of Oriental slippers, a peacock's feather, and nothing else, the night being warm for the time of the year.

The idea was simply to give the animal an unhappy quarter of an hour.

Disappointed in this laudable desire, there was only one course open to the athletes. They proceeded to make hay of his furniture.

A haycock was formed of the chairs and tables and heavier furniture in the middle of the room, and the interstices were stuffed with books and pictures. A china pot crowned the summit wreathed with a garland of sham sunflowers. Sheets, counterpanes, curtains and rugs draped the ceiling-reaching pile, and at its base there was a cycle of pots and pans filled with water and with a choir-boy's photograph floating on each surface.

Around this haycock the athletics danced hand in hand with artless glee, singing boating songs.

In the midst of it all the aesthete came home. Hearing the noise as he went up the stair, he began to suspect something. On arriving at his own half-open door he took a cautious peep before declaring his presence.

What he saw frightened him so dreadfully that he ran away.

All the rooms on his own stair were dark, and there seemed no refuge for the fugitive. Mad with fear he tore along the portico and up a neighbouring staircase. Seeing a light under a door he dashed into the room of he knew not whom and with gasping sobs besought the occupant to save his life.

Now the man whose premises were thus unceremoniously invaded was neither an athlete nor an aesthete. He was a reading man who took pains with his personal appearance and was faultless in his attire. Athletic exercise he enjoyed in reason, and he was an accomplished musician. He was a well-bred good-natured man of the world, and later on he distinguished himself by taking a Triple First and a college fellowship. He made the palpitating aesthete comfortable in an easy chair, gave him some benedictine and cigarettes and set to work to console him and make him a cup of tea.

The aesthete said he was his saviour, described in lurid lights the danger he was in, and wept with terror and gratitude all over the fireplace. The said saviour whom we will call Billy B. tried to cheer him up, and was giving him good advice for his soul's health, when lo and behold, the athletes who, having finished their haymaking, had perceived the light in Billy B.'s room, came thither to relate the deed which had been done. The aesthete grew livid again, and begged permission to retire behind the curtains which hung before the window. He disappeared, and the next instant Billy B. was calmly entertaining the athletes. He fed them with curious drinks and tobacco in various forms, and as each hero confessed his share in the haymaking the aesthete behind the curtain took down his name and words.

It was perhaps a couple of hours before this pleasant party broke up, and the conversation had drifted into other channels to such an extent, that when the last athlete took his departure Billy B. had completely forgotten the presence of the aesthete behind the window curtains.

He went into the bedroom to wash his hands, and then sat down for half an hour of Balzac before going to bed, but as he drew his chair nearer the lamp his memory came back again, and he went and looked for his aesthete. That person was nowhere to be seen, and Billy B. very naturally concluded that he had found an opportunity of slipping off while his foes had their attention otherwise engaged.

The next morning there were shocks.

The Warden sent for certain athletes, and charged them with having committed an outrage on the previous evening in the rooms of Mr Simone Memmi Simpkinson. He was appallingly definite in his details. "You, Mr A., did this, and you, Mr B., did that," and so on through the whole bag of tricks. Nothing was ever more complete.

The athletes were given the option of denying the charges, or of defending themselves; and of course there were no denials.

Some mention was made of a "lark," not by way of defence but of explanation.

"Sending down" was the natural sequence. No one was a bit surprised at that, but everybody did want to know who had sneaked to the Warden. The general feeling was in sympathy with the athletes, and it was argued that the only people who had the power to give such definite information to the Warden as had undoubtedly been given, were Billy B., the aesthete, and the athletes themselves. It was ridiculous to suppose that the athletes would give themselves away; the aesthete had not been seen by anybody during the function in his rooms; there remained only Billy B., and, as soon as an opinion had had time to be formulated, he fell under a good deal more than suspicion of being a filthy little sneak who had accepted the confidences of the athletes and then betrayed them to the Warden.

This suspicion soon betrayed itself in a very unpleasant way for poor Billy. Men gave him the cold shoulder, and in a very little while he began to realize that he had received the Order of the Cut. The reason of it never entered his head; and as he was a proud sort of beggar he made no attempt to enquire.

When the aesthete saw that Billy was cut, he cut him too. This did gall Billy and he asked him what the devil he meant by it. The aesthete meekly explained that he was only carrying out the advice Billy himself had given on the night of the haymaking, and he was endeavouring to copy the manners and customs of the majority in the college. He said further that he was much obliged to Billy for letting him stay behind his curtain and collect the evidence which he had given to the Warden, that he had remained in his hiding place until the last athlete had left and then slipped away during Billy B.'s temporary absence in the bedroom, and he asked for Billy's congratulations on the completeness of the revenge which he had been able to take.

Billy B. was horrified. He said several things; and he asked the aesthete if he intended to allow the college to cut him (Billy) for his own dirty tricks. The aesthete faltered out that he thought Billy wouldn't mind, that it wouldn't last long, and then he cried, and begged Billy not to ruin him.

Billy B. took him by the nose and shook him till he shrieked. Then he said that as the college had done him the injustice of suspecting him of sneaking, and had cut him without asking if he could defend himself, he should not deign to ask for a hearing now. If Simpkinson was so lost to all honourable feeling as to allow a perfectly innocent man to suffer for his misdeeds, he (Billy) disdained to suggest to such a vermin what his duty was.

And there the matter stood. Billy B. accepted the situation with a haughtiness which caused a good deal of surprise, and wrapped himself up in his books. As I said, he has since taken a Triple First. And he did not wear his heart upon his sleeve for daws to peck at.

He endured this martyrdom for a year. At the end of that time the aesthete left the place, and the real facts became known. Whether Billy B.'s heroism had been noticed by the Warden and he had, in common justice, compelled the aesthete to own up in writing (as he did), is not exactly known, but anyhow there was no one more affected and surprised than Billy B. at the dénouement and at the revulsion of feeling which took place in his favour.

{1897}

OWEN WISTER
{1860–1938}

*T*he Virginian (1902), dedicated to Wister's friend and Harvard class-
mate Theodore Roosevelt, is the wellspring of the American cowboy
myth. The novel is not, however, the first to introduce a handsome cow-
boy as an object of homosexual idealization: Theodore Winthrop's *John
Brent* (1862) possesses that distinction. When the narrator first sees John
Brent (an old schoolfellow), he does not recognize him because, as Brent
later says, "Ten years of experience have taken all the girl out of me."
Thus, in chapter 4, the narrator permits himself this over-the-top reverie:

> "The Adonis of the copper-skins!" I said to myself. "This is the
> 'Young Eagle,' or the 'Sucking Dove,' or the 'Maiden's Bane,' or
> some other great chief of the cleanest Indian tribe on the continent.
> A beautiful youth! O Fenimore, why are you dead! There are a
> dozen romances in one look of that young brave. One chapter
> might be written on his fringed buckskin shirt; one on his equally
> fringed leggings, with their stripe of porcupine-quills; and one short
> chapter on his moccasons [*sic*], with their scarlet cloth instep-piece,
> and his cap of otter fur decked with an eagle's feather. What a poem
> the fellow is! I wish I was an Indian myself for such a companion; or,
> better, a squaw, to be made love to by him."

Later in the same chapter:

> In all this time I learned to love the man John Brent, as I had
> loved the boy; but as mature man loves man. I have known no more
> perfect union than that one friendship. Nothing so tender in any of
> my transitory loves for women. We were two who though alike, but
> saw differently, and never quarrelled because the shield was to him
> gold and to me silver. Such a friendship justifies life. All bad faith is
> worth encountering for the sake of such good faith, — all cold
> shoulder for such warm heart.

(*John Brent*'s plot is nonetheless bound up with the eponymous hero's love
for a pure maiden ensnared by evil Mormons.)

Wister himself was not homosexual, but the Virginian, like John
Brent, is attractive to men and women alike. (He is rather like the actor
James Garner, whom everyone's mother loves and everyone's father ad-
mires.) The narrator of Wister's novel dusts off language startlingly simi-

lar to Winthrop's: "Had I been the bride, I should have taken the giant, dust and all"; "I have never seen a creature more irresistibly handsome"; and "the Virginian looked at her with such a smile that, had I been a woman, it would have made me his to do what he pleased with on the spot." Naturally enough, the narrator wants and hopes to be the Virginian's friend — as good and close a friend to him as Steve (eventually hanged for rustling cattle) — but he manages to achieve this only when together they care for a childless hen named Em'ly.

Of all the works included in this anthology, "Em'ly" is perhaps the most unlikely. And yet, childlessness is very much at the heart of homosexual experience: Bernard Cooper writes of it in "Childless," from *Maps to Anywhere;* Henry James in both "The Author of Beltraffio" and the unfinished "Hugh Merrow"; and, perhaps, the emptiness Forster discovered in the echoing walls of the Marabar Caves was the emptiness of childlessness.

The Virginian has engendered at least two films (the first, from 1929, starring Gary Cooper, who beautifully delivered the line "If you want to call me that, smile"; the second, from 1946, starring Joel McCrea), as well as a long-running television series in the 1960s. And, most appositely, a peak in the Tetons was named for Wister in 1939. ❧

FROM *The Virginian: A Horseman of the Plains*

EM'LY

My personage was a hen, and she lived at the Sunk Creek Ranch.

Judge Henry's ranch was notable for several luxuries. He had milk, for example. In those days his brother ranchmen had thousands of cattle very often, but not a drop of milk, save the condensed variety. Therefore they had no butter. The Judge had plenty. Next rarest to butter and milk in the cattle country were eggs. But my host had chickens. Whether this was because he had followed cock-fighting in his early days, or whether it was due to Mrs. Henry, I cannot say. I only know that when I took a meal elsewhere, I was likely to find nothing but the eternal "sowbelly," beans, and coffee; while at Sunk Creek the omelet and the custard were frequent. The passing traveller was glad to tie his horse to the fence here, and sit down to the Judge's table. For its fame was as wide as Wyoming. It was an oasis in the Territory's desolate bill-of-fare.

The long fences of Judge Henry's home ranch began upon Sunk Creek soon after that stream emerged from its cañon through the Bow Leg. It was a place always well cared for by the owner, even in the days of his bachelorhood. The placid regiments of cattle lay in the cool of the cottonwoods by the water, or slowly moved among the sage-brush, feeding upon the grass that in those forever departed years was plentiful and tall. The steers came fat off his unenclosed range and fattened still more in his large pasture; while his small pasture, a field some eight miles square, was for several seasons given to the Judge's horses, and over this ample space there played and prospered the good colts which he raised from Paladin, his imported stallion. After he married, I have been assured that his wife's influence became visible in and about the house at once. Shade trees were planted, flowers attempted, and to the chickens was added the much more troublesome turkey. I, the visitor, was pressed into service when I arrived, green from the East. I took hold of the farmyard and began building a better chicken house, while the Judge was off creating meadow land in his gray and yellow wilderness. When any cow-boy was unoccupied, he would lounge over to my neighborhood, and silently regard my carpentering.

Those cow-punchers bore names of various denominations. There was Honey Wiggin; there was Nebrasky, and Dollar Bill, and Chalkeye. And they came from farms and cities, from Maine and from California. But the romance of American adventure had drawn them all alike to this great playground of young men, and in their courage, their generosity, and their amusement at me they bore a close resemblance to each other. Each one would silently observe my achievements with the hammer and the chisel. Then he would retire to the bunk-house, and presently I would over-hear laughter. But this was only in the morning. In the afternoon on many days of the summer which I spent at the Sunk Creek Ranch I would go shooting, or ride up toward the entrance of the cañon and watch the men working on the irrigation ditches. Pleasant systems of water running in channels were being led through the soil, and there was a sound of rippling here and there among the yellow grain; the green thick alfalfa grass waved almost, it seemed, of its own accord, for the wind never blew; and when at evening the sun lay against the plain, the rift of the cañon was filled with a violet light, and the Bow Leg Mountains became transfigured with hues of floating and unimaginable color. The sun shone in a sky where never a cloud came, and noon was not too warm nor the dark too cool. And so for two months I went through these pleasant uneventful days, improving the chickens, an object of mirth, living in the open air, and basking in the perfection of content.

I was justly styled a tenderfoot. Mrs. Henry had in the beginning endeavored to shield me from this humiliation; but when she found that I was inveterate in laying my inexperience of Western matters bare to all the world, begging to be enlightened upon rattlesnakes, prairie-dogs, owls, blue and willow grouse, sage-hens, how to rope a horse or tighten the front cinch of my saddle, and that my spirit soared into enthusiasm at the mere sight of so ordinary an animal as a white-tailed deer, she let me rush about with my firearms, and made no further effort to stave off the ridicule that my blunders perpetually earned from the ranch hands, her own humorous husband, and any chance visitor who stopped for a meal or stayed the night.

I was not called by my name after the first feeble etiquette due to a stranger in his first few hours had died away. I was known simply as "the tenderfoot." I was introduced to the neighborhood (a circle of eighty miles) as "the tenderfoot." It was thus that Balaam, the maltreater of horses, learned to address me when he came a two days' journey to pay a visit. And it was this name and my notorious helplessness that bid fair to end what relations I had with the Virginian. For when Judge Henry ascertained that nothing could prevent me from losing myself, that it was not uncommon for me to saunter out after breakfast with a gun and in thirty minutes cease to know north from south, he arranged for my protection. He detailed an escort for me; and the escort was once more the trustworthy man! The poor Virginian was taken from his work and his comrades and set to playing nurse for me. And for a while this humiliation ate into his untamed soul. It was his lugubrious lot to accompany me in my rambles, preside over my blunders, and save me from calamitously passing into the next world. He bore it in courteous silence, except when speaking was necessary. He would show me the lower ford, which I could never find for myself, generally mistaking a quicksand for it. He would tie my horse properly. He would recommend me not to shoot my rifle at a white-tailed deer in the particular moment that the outfit wagon was passing behind the animal on the further side of the brush. There was seldom a day that he was not obliged to hasten and save me from sudden death or from ridicule, which is worse. Yet never once did he lose his patience; and his gentle, slow voice, and apparently lazy manner remained the same, whether we were sitting at lunch together, or up in the mountains during a hunt, or whether he was bringing me back my horse, which had run away because I had again forgotten to throw the reins over his head and let them trail.

"He'll always stand if yu' do that," the Virginian would say. "See how my hawss stays right quiet yondeh."

After such admonition he would say no more to me. But this tame nursery business was assuredly gall to him. For though utterly a man in countenance and in his self-possession and incapacity to be put at a loss, he was still boyishly proud of his wild calling, and wore his leathern shaps and jingled his spurs with obvious pleasure. His tiger limberness and his beauty were rich with unabated youth; and that force which lurked beneath his surface must often have curbed his intolerance of me. In spite of what I knew must be his opinion of me, the tenderfoot, my liking for him grew, and I found his silent company more and more agreeable. That he had spells of talking, I had already learned at Medicine Bow. But his present taciturnity might almost have effaced this impression, had I not happened to pass by the bunk-house one evening after dark, when Honey Wiggin and the rest of the cow-boys were gathered inside it.

That afternoon the Virginian and I had gone duck shooting. We had found several in a beaver dam, and I had killed two as they sat close together; but they floated against the breastwork of sticks out in the water some four feet deep, where the escaping current might carry them down the stream. The Judge's red setter had not accompanied us, because she was expecting a family.

"We don't want her along anyways," the cow-puncher had explained to me. "She runs around mighty irresponsible, and she'll stand a prairie-dog 'bout as often as she'll stand a bird. She's a triflin' animal."

My anxiety to own the ducks caused me to pitch into the water with all my clothes on, and subsequently crawl out a slippery, triumphant, weltering heap. The Virginian's serious eyes had rested upon this spectacle of mud; but he expressed nothing, as usual.

"They ain't overly good eatin'," he observed, tying the birds to his saddle. "They're divers."

"Divers!" I exclaimed. "Why didn't they dive?"

"I reckon they was young ones and hadn't experience."

"Well," I said, crestfallen, but attempting to be humorous, "I did the diving myself."

But the Virginian made no comment. He handed me my double-barrelled English gun, which I was about to leave deserted on the ground behind me, and we rode home in our usual silence, the mean little white-breasted, sharp-billed divers dangling from his saddle.

It was in the bunk-house that he took his revenge. As I passed I heard his gentle voice silently achieving some narrative to an attentive audience, and just as I came by the open window where he sat on his bed in shirt and drawers, his back to me, I heard his concluding words, "And the hat on his haid was the one mark showed yu' he weren't a snappin'-turtle."

The anecdote met with instantaneous success, and I hurried away into the dark.

The next morning I was occupied with the chickens. Two hens were fighting to sit on some eggs that a third was daily laying, and which I did not want hatched, and for the third time I had kicked Em'ly off seven potatoes she had rolled together and was determined to raise I know not what sort of family from. She was shrieking about the hen-house as the Virginian came in to observe (I suspect) what I might be doing now that could be useful for him to mention in the bunk-house.

He stood awhile, and at length said, "We lost our best rooster when Mrs. Henry came to live hyeh."

I paid no attention.

"He was a right elegant Dominicker," he continued.

I felt a little ruffled about the snapping-turtle, and showed no interest in what he was saying, but continued my functions among the hens. This unusual silence of mine seemed to elicit unusual speech from him.

"Yu' see, that rooster he'd always lived round hyeh when the Judge was a bachelor, and he never seen no ladies or any persons wearing female gyarments. You ain't got rheumatism, seh?"

"Me? No."

"I reckoned maybe them little old divers yu' got damp goin' afteh —" He paused.

"Oh, no, not in the least, thank you."

"Yu' seemed sort o' grave this mawnin', and I'm cert'nly glad it ain't them divers."

"Well, the rooster?" I inquired finally.

"Oh, him! He weren't raised where he could see petticoats. Mrs. Henry she come hyeh from the railroad with the Judge afteh dark. Next mawnin' early she walked out to view her new home, and the rooster was a-feedin' by the door, and he seen her. Well, seh, he screeched that awful I run out of the bunk-house; and he jus' went over the fence and took down Sunk Creek shoutin' fire, right along. He has never come back."

"There's a hen over there now that has no judgment," I said, indicating Em'ly. She had got herself outside the house, and was on the bars of a corral, her vociferations reduced to an occasional squawk. I told him about the potatoes.

"I never knowed her name before," said he. "That runaway rooster, he hated her. And she hated him same as she hates 'em all."

"I named her myself," said I, "after I came to notice her particularly. There's an old maid at home who's charitable, and belongs to the Cruelty to Animals, and she never knows whether she had better cross in front of a street car or wait. I named the hen after her. Does she ever lay eggs?"

The Virginian had not "troubled his haid" over the poultry.

"Well, I don't believe she knows how. I think she came near being a rooster."

"She's sure manly-lookin'," said the Virginian. We had walked toward the corral, and he was now scrutinizing Em'ly with interest.

She was an egregious fowl. She was huge and gaunt, with great yellow beak, and she stood straight and alert in the manner of responsible people. There was something wrong with her tail. It slanted far to one side, one feather in it twice as long as the rest. Feathers on her breast there were none. These had been worn entirely off by her habit of sitting upon potatoes and other rough abnormal objects. And this lent to her appearance an air of being décolleté, singularly at variance with her otherwise prudish ensemble. Her eye was remarkably bright, but somehow it had an outraged expression. It was as if she went about the world perpetually scandalized over the doings that fell beneath her notice. Her legs were blue, long, and remarkably stout.

"She'd ought to wear knickerbockers," murmured the Virginian. "She'd look a heap better'n some o' them college students. And she'll set on potatoes, yu' say?"

"She thinks she can hatch out anything. I've found her with onions, and last Tuesday I caught her on two balls of soap."

In the afternoon the tall cow-puncher and I rode out to get an antelope.

After an hour, during which he was completely taciturn, he said: "I reckon maybe this hyeh lonesome country ain't been healthy for Em'ly to live in. It ain't for some humans. Them old trappers in the mountains gets skewed in the haid mighty often, an' talks out loud when nobody's nigher 'n a hundred miles."

"Em'ly has not been solitary," I replied. "There are forty chickens here."

"That's so," said he. "It don't explain her."

He fell silent again, riding beside me, easy and indolent in the saddle. His long figure looked so loose and inert that the swift, light spring he made to the ground seemed an impossible feat. He had seen an antelope where I saw none.

"Take a shot yourself," I urged him, as he motioned me to be quick. "You never shoot when I'm with you."

"I ain't hyeh for that," he answered. "Now you've let him get away on yu'!"

The antelope had in truth departed.

"Why," he said to my protest, "I can hit them things any day. What's your notion as to Em'ly?"

"I can't account for her," I replied.

"Well," he said musingly, and then his mind took one of those particular turns that made me love him, "Taylor ought to see her. She'd be just the schoolmarm for Bear Creek!"

"She's not much like the eating-house lady at Medicine Bow," I said.

He gave a hilarious chuckle. "No, Em'ly knows nothing o' them joys. So yu' have no notion about her? Well, I've got one. I reckon maybe she was hatched after a big thunderstorm."

"A big thunderstorm!" I exclaimed.

"Yes. Don't yu' know about them, and what they'll do to aiggs? A big case o' lightnin' and thunder will addle aiggs and keep 'em from hatchin'. And I expect one came along, and all the other aiggs of Em'ly's set didn't hatch out, but got plumb addled, and she happened not to get addled that far, and so she just managed to make it through. But she cert'nly ain't got a strong haid."

"I fear she has not," said I.

"Mighty hon'ble intentions," he observed. "If she can't make out to lay anything, she wants to hatch somethin', and be a mother anyways."

"I wonder what relation the law considers that a hen is to the chicken she hatched but did not lay?" I inquired.

The Virginian made no reply to this frivolous suggestion. He was gazing over the wide landscape gravely and with apparent inattention. He invariably saw game before I did, and was off his horse and crouched among the sage while I was still getting my left foot clear of the stirrup. I succeeded in killing an antelope, and we rode home with the head and hind quarters.

"No," said he. "It's sure the thunder, and not the lonesomeness. How do yu' like the lonesomeness yourself?"

I told him that I liked it.

"I could not live without it now," he said. "This has got into my system." He swept his hand out at the vast space of world. "I went back home to see my folks onced. Mother was dyin' slow, and she wanted me. I stayed a year. But them Virginia mountains could please me no more. Afteh she was gone, I told my brothers and sisters good-by. We like each other well enough, but I reckon I'll not go back."

We found Em'ly seated upon a collection of green California peaches, which the Judge had brought from the railroad.

"I don't mind her any more," I said; "I'm sorry for her."

"I've been sorry for her right along," said the Virginian. "She does hate the roosters so." And he said that he was making a collection of every class of object which he found her treating as eggs.

But Em'ly's egg-industry was terminated abruptly one morning, and her unquestioned energies diverted to a new channel. A turkey which had been sitting in the root-house appeared with twelve children, and a family of bantams occurred almost simultaneously. Em'ly was importantly scratching the soil inside Paladin's corral when the bantam tribe of newly born came by down the lane, and she caught sight of them through the bars. She crossed the corral at a run, and intercepted two of the chicks that were trailing somewhat behind their real mamma. These she undertook to appropriate, and assumed a high tone with the bantam, who was the smaller, and hence obliged to retreat with her still numerous family. I interfered, and put matters straight; but the adjustment was only temporary. In an hour I saw Em'ly immensely busy with two more bantams, leading them about and taking a care of them which I must admit seemed perfectly efficient.

And now came the first incident that made me suspect her to be demented.

She had proceeded with her changelings behind the kitchen, where one of the irrigation ditches ran under the fence from the hay-field to supply the house with water. Some distance along this ditch inside the field were the twelve turkeys in the short, recently cut stubble. Again Em'ly set off instantly like a deer. She left the dismayed bantams behind her. She crossed the ditch with one jump of her stout blue legs, flew over the grass, and was at once among the turkeys, where, with an instinct of maternity as undiscriminating as it was reckless, she attempted to huddle some of them away. But this other mamma was not a bantam, and in a few moments Em'ly was entirely routed in her attempt to acquire a new variety of family.

This spectacle was witnessed by the Virginian and myself, and it overcame him. He went speechless across to the bunk-house, by himself, and sat on his bed, while I took the abandoned bantams back to their own circle.

I have often wondered what the other fowls thought of all this. Some impression it certainly did make upon them. The notion may seem out of reason to those who have never closely attended to other animals than man; but I am convinced that any community which shares some of our instincts will share some of the resulting feelings, and that birds and beasts have conventions, the breach of which startles them. If there be anything in evolution, this would seem inevitable. At all events, the chicken-house was upset during the following several days. Em'ly disturbed now the bantams and now the turkeys, and several of these latter had died, though I will not go so far as to say that this was the result of her misplaced attentions. Nevertheless, I was seriously thinking of locking her up till the broods should be a little older, when another event happened, and all was suddenly at peace.

The Judge's setter came in one morning, wagging her tail. She had had her puppies, and she now took us to where they were housed, in between the floor of a building and the hollow ground. Em'ly was seated on the whole litter.

"No," I said to the Judge, "I am not surprised. She is capable of anything."

In her new choice of offspring, this hen had at length encountered an unworthy parent. The setter was bored by her own puppies. She found the hole under the house an obscure and monotonous residence compared with the dining room, and our company more stimulating and sympathetic than that of her children. A much-petted contact with our superior race had developed her dog intelligence above its natural level, and turned her into an unnatural, neglectful mother, who was constantly forgetting her nursery for worldly pleasures.

At certain periods of the day she repaired to the puppies and fed them, but came away when this perfunctory ceremony was accomplished; and she was glad enough to have a governess bring them up. She made no quarrel with Em'ly, and the two understood each other perfectly. I have never seen among animals any arrangement so civilized and so perverted. It made Em'ly perfectly happy. To see her sitting all day jealously spreading her wings over some blind puppies was sufficiently curious; but when they became large enough to come out from under the house and toddle about in the proud hen's wake, I longed for some distinguished naturalist. I felt that our ignorance made us inappropriate spectators of such a phenomenon. Em'ly scratched and clucked, and the puppies ran to her, pawed her with their fat limp little legs, and retreated beneath her feathers in their games of hide and seek. Conceive, if you can, what confusion must have reigned in their infant minds as to who the setter was!

"I reckon they think she's the wet-nurse," said the Virginian.

When the puppies grew to be boisterous, I perceived that Em'ly's mission was approaching its end. They were too heavy for her, and their increasing scope of playfulness was not in her line. Once or twice they knocked her over, upon which she arose and pecked them severely, and they retired to a safe distance, and sitting in a circle, yapped at her. I think they began to suspect that she was only a hen after all. So Em'ly resigned with an indifference which surprised me, until I remembered that if it had been chickens, she would have ceased to look after them by this time.

But here she was again "out of a job," as the Virginian said.

"She's raised them puppies for that triflin' setter, and now she'll be huntin' around for something else useful to do that ain't in her business."

Now there were other broods of chickens to arrive in the hen-house, and I did not desire any more bantam and turkey performances. So, to avoid confusion, I played a trick upon Em'ly. I went down to Sunk Creek and fetched some smooth, oval stones. She was quite satisfied with these, and passed a quiet day with them in a box. This was not fair, the Virginian asserted.

"You ain't going to jus' leave her fooled that a-way?"

I did not see why not.

"Why, she raised them puppies all right. Ain't she showed she knows how to be a mother anyways? Em'ly ain't going to get her time took up for nothing while I'm round hyeh," said the cow-puncher.

He laid a gentle hold of Em'ly and tossed her to the ground. She, of course, rushed out among the corrals in a great state of nerves.

"I don't see what good you do meddling," I protested.

To this he deigned no reply, but removed the unresponsive stones from the straw.

"Why, if they ain't right warm!" he exclaimed plaintively. "The poor, deluded son-of-a-gun!" And with this unusual description of a lady, he sent the stones sailing like a line of birds. "I'm regular getting stuck on Em'ly," continued the Virginian. "Yu' needn't to laugh. Don't yu' see she's got sort o' human feelin's and desires? I always knowed hawsses was like people, and my collie, of course. It is kind of foolish, I expect, but that hen's goin' to have a real aigg di-rectly, right now, to set on." With this he removed one from beneath another hen. "We'll have Em'ly raise this hyeh," said he, "so she can put in her time profitable."

It was not accomplished at once; for Em'ly, singularly enough, would not consent to stay in the box whence she had been routed. At length we found another retreat for her, and in these new surroundings, with a new piece of work for her to do, Em'ly sat on the one egg which the Virginian had so carefully provided for her.

Thus, as in all genuine tragedies, was the stroke of Fate wrought by chance and the best intentions.

Em'ly began sitting on Friday afternoon near sundown. Early next morning my sleep was gradually dispersed by a sound unearthly and continuous. Now it dwindled, receding to a distance; again it came near, took a turn, drifted to the other side of the house; then, evidently, whatever it was, passed my door close, and I jumped upright in my bed. The high, tense strain of vibration, nearly, but not quite, a musical note, was like the threatening scream of machinery, though weaker, and I bounded out of the house in my pajamas.

There was Em'ly, dishevelled, walking wildly about, her one egg miraculously hatched within ten hours. The little lonely yellow ball of down went cheeping along behind, following its mother as best it could. What, then, had happened to the established period of incubation? For an instant the thing was like a portent, and I was near joining Em'ly in her horrid surprise, when I saw how it all was. The Virginian had taken an egg from a hen which had already been sitting for three weeks.

I dressed in haste, hearing Em'ly's distracted outcry. It steadily sounded, without perceptible pause for breath, and marked her erratic journey back and forth through stables, lanes, and corrals. The shrill disturbance brought all of us out to see her, and in the hen-house I discovered the new brood making its appearance punctually.

But this natural explanation could not be made to the crazed hen. She continued to scour the premises, her slant tail and its one preposterous feather waving as she aimlessly went, her stout legs stepping high with an unnatural motion, her head lifted nearly off her neck, and in her brilliant yellow eye an expression of more than outrage at this overturning of a natural law. Behind her, entirely ignored and neglected, trailed the little progeny. She never looked at it. We went about our various affairs, and all through the clear, sunny day that unending metallic scream pervaded the premises. The Virginian put out food and water for her, but she tasted nothing. I am glad to say that the little chicken did. I do not think that the hen's eyes could see, except in the way that sleep-walkers' do.

The heat went out of the air, and in the cañon the violet light began to show. Many hours had gone, but Em'ly never ceased. Now she suddenly flew up in a tree and sat there with her noise still going; but it had risen lately several notes into a slim, acute level of terror, and was not like machinery any more, nor like any sound I ever heard before or since. Below the tree stood the bewildered little chicken, cheeping, and making tiny jumps to reach its mother.

"Yes," said the Virginian, "it's comical. Even her aigg acted different from anybody else's." He paused, and looked across the wide, mellowing plain with the expression of easy-going gravity so common with him. Then he looked at Em'ly in the tree and the yellow chicken. "It ain't so damned funny," said he.

We went in to supper, and I came out to find the hen lying on the ground, dead. I took the chicken to the family in the hen-house.

No, it was not altogether funny any more. And I did not think less of the Virginian when I came upon him surreptitiously digging a little hole in the field for her.

"I have buried some citizens here and there," said he, "that I have respected less."

And when the time came for me to leave Sunk Creek, my last word to the Virginian was, "Don't forget Em'ly."

"I ain't likely to," responded the cow-puncher. "She is just one o' them parables."

Save when he fell into his native idioms (which, they told me, his wanderings had well-nigh obliterated until that year's visit to his home again revived them in his speech), he had now for a long while dropped the "seh," and all other barriers between us. We were thorough friends, and had exchanged many confidences both of the flesh and of the spirit. He even went the length of saying that he would write me the Sunk Creek news if I would send him a line now and then. I have many letters from him now. Their spelling came to be faultless, and in the beginning was little worse than George Washington's.

The Judge himself drove me to the railroad by another way — across the Bow Leg Mountains, and south through Balaam's Ranch and Drybone to Rock Creek.

"I'll be very homesick," I told him.

"Come and pull the latch-string whenever you please," he bade me.

I wished that I might! No lotus land ever cast its spell upon man's heart more than Wyoming had enchanted mine.

{1902}

EDWARD FREDERIC BENSON

{1867–1940}

The son of Edward White Benson, archbishop of Canterbury, "Fred" Benson was educated at Marlborough and King's College, Cambridge. From early on, he moved in both homosexual and literary circles; in addition to Margot Asquith and Marie Corelli, his close friends included Reginald Turner, Robert Hichens (author of *The Green Carnation*, an 1894 parody of Wilde), and Lord Alfred Douglas, in whose company he traveled to Egypt in 1894. Fred and Bosie "got on marvellously together," Hichens writes in *Yesterday* (1947), "the wit of one seeming to call out and polish the wit of the other." They also had similar fates, both growing from beautiful young men into unhappy old men.

Benson published ninety-three books in his lifetime (in 1903 alone he published six), among them story collections, biographies (of Sir Francis Drake, Charlotte Brontë, Alcibiades, and Ferdinand Magellan, among others), volumes on golf and "winter sports in Switzerland," and several dozen novels, of which the best remembered are surely the six Mapp and Lucia stories. Set in a thinly disguised version of Rye, where Benson lived in Lamb's House (the former residence of Henry James) and was mayor from 1934 to 1937, the sequence was made into a BBC television series with Prunella Scales and Geraldine McEwan in the late 1980s. That Tom Holt has written two further installments, *Lucia in Wartime* and *Lucia Triumphant*, testifies to their enduring popularity.

Benson was throughout his life highly circumspect about his own homosexuality, developing intense friendships with young men such as Wilfrid Coleridge, whom he trained in skating, and deriving what his biographer Brian Masters calls a "*frisson* from the knowledge that the friendship is bound to be sterile, that it must be denied and frustrated in order to be pure." Nonetheless, as Masters also observes, Benson once copied out the entirety of Wilde's *De Profundis* in a notebook marked PRIVATE, including those passages deleted from the 1905 edition. He did not always censor his own writing, however: indeed, when his brother Arthur read the novel *David Blaize* (1916), he was dismayed, and advised in tortured diction:

> this particular subject is *tacendum* . . . Personally, I should not wish to raise it as a problem because I don't think it is a thing which can be fought by talking. The more openly talked about the more likely to be experimented in. Why I think your book is risky is because you

speak in these pages very plainly . . . there is a chance of talk and criticism of an unpleasant kind . . . Of course I think it would be *most* unadvisable for you to open the whole subject — it could only be done by a fanatical medical man, with a knowledge of nervous pathology.

FROM *The Challoners*

CHAPTER 10

KARL RUSOFF got up rather wearily from the piano, where he had been practising for the last three hours, stretched himself, and for a few seconds held his fingers against his eyes, as if to rest them. The afternoon was a little chilly, and he walked over to the fireplace, where he stood warming himself. The cheerful flickering blaze shining through his thin long hands, made the fingers look transparent, as if they were luminous and lit with a red light from within.

From the windows the dun-coloured gloom of a cloudy Spring afternoon in London left the room vague and full of shadows that huddled into the corners, while the light of gas-lamps already lit in the street outside cast patches of yellow illumination high on the walls and on the mouldings of the ceiling. The room itself was large, lofty and well-proportioned, and furnished with a certain costly simplicity. A few Persian rugs lay on the parqueted floor, a French writing-table stood in the window, a tall bookcase glimmering with the gilt and morocco of fine bindings occupied nearly half of the wall in which the fireplace was set, two or three large chairs formed a group with a sofa in the corner, and the Steinway grand occupied more than the area taken up by all the rest of the furniture. There perhaps simplicity gained its highest triumph; the case was of rosewood designed by Morris, and the formal perfection of its lines was a thing only to be perceived by an artist. On the walls, finally, hung two or three prints, and on the mantelpiece were a couple of reproductions of Greek bronzes found at Herculaneum.

It was a room, in fact, that spoke very distinctly of an individual and flawless taste. Wherever the eye fell it lighted on something which, in its kind, was perfect: on the other hand there was nothing the least startling or arresting, and above all nothing fidgety. It was a room pre-eminently restful, where a tired mind might fall into reverie, or an active mind pursue its activities without challenge or annoyance from visible objects. Pre-eminently also it was a room instinct with form: nothing there should have been otherwise.

Karl stood in front of the fireplace for some minutes, opening and shutting his hands, which were a little cramped, a little tired, with the long practice they had just finished. His mind, too, was a little tired with the monotony of his work, for his three hours at the piano had been no glorious excursion into the sunlit lands of melody, but the repetition of about twelve bars all told from a couple of passages out of the "Waldstein Sonata" which he was to play next week at the last of his four concerts in St. James's Hall. And though perhaps not half-a-dozen people in that crowded hall would be able to tell the difference between the execution of those dozen bars as he played them yesterday and as he could play them now, he would not have been the pianist he was if it had been possible for him not to attempt to make them perfect, whether that took a week or a month. The need of perfection, which never says, "That will do" until the achievement cannot be bettered, was a ruling instinct to him.

Besides, to him just now the presence of one out of those possible six auditors who might be able to tell the difference, was more to him than all the rest of the ringing hall. Sometimes he almost wished he had never seen Martin, never at any rate consented to give him lessons, for in some strange way this pupil was becoming his master, and Rusoff was conscious that the lad's personality, never so vivid as when he was at his music, was beginning to cast a sort of spell over his own. Brilliant, incisive, full of fire as his own style was, he was conscious when Martin played certain things that his own rendering, far more correct, far more finished though it might be, was elderly, even frigid, compared to the other. The glorious quality of his exuberant youth, a thing which in most artists is beginning to pale a little before they have attained to that level of technical skill which is necessary to a pianist of any claim to high excellence, was in Martin at its height and its noonday; while it really seemed sometimes to his master that he had been, perhaps in his cradle, perhaps as he bent his unwilling head over the crabbed intricacies of Demosthenes, somehow mysteriously initiated into the secrets of technique. Anyhow that facility, that art of first mastering and then concealing difficulties which to most pianists only comes, as it had come to himself, through months and years of unremitting toil, seemed to be natural to his pupil. Martin had only got to be told what to do, and if he was in an obliging humour he did it. The difficulties of execution simply did not seem to exist for him. Immensely struck as Karl Rusoff had been with his performance last summer at Lord Yorkshire's, he felt now that he had not then half fathomed the depth of his power, which lay pellucid like a great ocean cave full of changing lights and shadows, suffused to its depths with sunlight, and by its very clearness and brightness baffling the eye that sought to estimate its depths.

And his temperament — that one thing that can never be taught — Karl Rusoff knew he had never come across a temperament that, artistically speaking, approached it. It was indeed not less than perfect from that point of view, sensitive, impressionable, divinely susceptible to beauty, hating — (here largely was the personal charm of it to his master) — hating the second-rate, especially the skilful second-rate, with glorious intensity. At the thought Karl's rather grim face relaxed into a smile as he remembered how Martin had sat down to the piano the other day in a sudden burst of Handel-hatred, and with his ten fingers which sounded like twenty, and a strangely unmelodious voice which sounded like a crow and ranged from high falsetto treble to the note of kettledrums, had given a rendering of the Hailstone Chorus, so ludicrous, yet catching so unerringly the cheap tumult of that toy-storm in a tea-cup, that he himself had sat and laughed till his eyes were dim.

"And why," asked Martin dramatically in conclusion, "did that German spend his long and abandoned life in England? Because he knew, sir, he knew that in any other country he would have been kindly but firmly put over the border. Now shall I sing you the 'Hallelujah Chorus'?"

Besides this facility in technique, the power of perception of beauty, which in many of the finest minds requires years of delicate cultivation before it becomes at all mature or certain, was already present in Martin in apparent fulness of growth; it was already an instinct exerting and asserting itself, not through habit, but through intuition. It was so much the dominating ingredient in the composition known as Martin Challoner, that almost everything else might be considered as a mere by-product. His whole will, his whole energy was at its service. When once it called to him as it had called to him in his adoption of the Roman faith, it seemed he had to obey, and could not question. It was to him a law that he could not transgress.

But all this, the charm of which Karl Rusoff felt almost too keenly for his peace of mind, he knew to be extremely dangerous; and to him this exultant, beautiful mind was entrusted with all the responsibility that it entailed, to fashion, to train, to prune. With a true and honest modesty, he recognised how menial, so to speak, his work in regard to Martin was; but this did not lessen the responsibility. He was, to rate himself at the highest, the gardener who had to bring this exquisite plant into fulness of flower, to feed, to water, to cut, and above all to let air and sun, the great natural influences, have their way with it. He did not believe in forced growth, or in sheltered cultivation; as he had told Martin in the summer, every emotion, every pain and joy, so long as it was not sensual, was his proper food. The richer his experience was, the richer would his music be. Karl had already seen a first clear endorsement of his view in the circumstances attending Martin's secession to the Roman Church. He himself did not know with any exactitude of detail what had passed between him and his father; but though the painfulness of that had knocked Martin completely up for a time, what he himself had foreseen had come true, and he could hardly help inwardly rejoicing at even the cruelty of Mr. Challoner's attitude to his son, so great had been the gain to Martin artistically. He had suffered horribly, and was the better for it. Afterwards — the thing had taken place now more than two months ago — the elastic fibre of his youth had re-asserted itself, and his exuberant health of body and mind had returned to their former vigour. The pain had passed, the gain remained.

Then to Karl's reverie there came the interruption he had been expecting: a quick step sounded outside, then a noise as of a large quantity of books being dropped in the passage, a loud and hollow groan, and after a short pause Martin, with half-a-dozen volumes of music, entered, flushed, vivid in face, muddy in boots.

"I am late," he said, "also I am sorry. But there was not a cab to be found. So I ran. I ran quicker than cabs. Oh, how hot I am!"

Karl's face lighted up as he saw him. He himself was unmarried and rather lonely in the world till this child of his old age had come to him, who should be, so he told himself, the crown of his life's work, and illuminate the dull world long after he himself was dead, with the melodious torch that he had helped to light.

"Are you late?" he said. "I have only just finished practising myself. My dear child, how hot you are! Let us have tea first. And are you dining out to-night? If not, have a chop with me here, and we can work a little afterwards as well. You have not been to me for a week."

"Yes, thanks, I should like that," said Martin. "I have been down at Chartries, as you know, for a couple of days."

He paused a moment, frowning at the fire.

"No, it was no good," he said. "My father would not see me. He even opposed Helen's coming to Uncle Rupert's while I was there. But she came."

"How is she?" asked Karl.

"Very well; and, what is so odd, extraordinarily happy: happy in some steadily-shining way. Deep, broad, bright happiness, like sunlight. Now, how do you account for that? Away from Frank — she doesn't even write to him or hear from him — continuing to do all that she found so intolerable under hugely aggravated conditions — he not there — and yet awfully happy. Not that father has changed to her at all — he is very silent, very sad, very — well, sometimes very cross. And she feels his sadness, too — feels it as if it was her own —"

"Ah, you have hit it," said Karl; "that is why she is happy. It is what I have always told you — the fact of sympathy, whether it is with joy or pain, is what enriches and perfects; the fact of sympathy is what makes her happy. You are as happy, with the broad sunshine of happiness, even though a bitter wind whistles, when Isolde sinks lifeless by the body of Tristan, as when Siegfried hears the singing of the bird."

He paused a moment, looking at the fire, then turned to Martin.

"Ah, my dear lad," he said, "pray that you drink to the dregs any cup of sorrow or of joy that may be given you. Never shrink from pain; you will not become your best self without it. But by it and through it, and in no selfish or egoistic manner, you will fulfil yourself."

He rose from his chair and turned on switch after switch of electric light.

"It is like this," he said, feeling in his sudden desire for light some instinctive connection with what he was saying. "Open the doors, open the windows of your soul; let the sun in and the wind. And this is a music-lesson," he added laughingly. "Well, I have given a good many in my life, and should be pleased to know I never gave a worse one. Now, what have you done since I saw you last?"

Martin walked quickly over to the piano with a laugh.

"Listen," he said.

He played a few bars of very intricate phrase after the manner of the opening of a fugue. Then in the bass half the phrase was repeated, but it finished with something perfectly different — a third and a fourth and a fifth joined in, and before the "whole kennel was a-yelp," the original subject had passed through rapid gradations until it had become something totally different to what it began with, though still an incessant jabber of cognate phrases, never quite coherent, were somehow strung together and worked against each other by a miracle of ingenuity. Then the original subject was repeated with emphatic insistence, as if to call renewed attention to itself, but it was answered this time by a phrase that had nothing whatever to do with it; a third short melody, totally different from anything that had gone before or was to come after, ran its brief and ridiculous course, and then a perfect hodge-podge of reminiscences of all that had previously occurred, handled with extraordinary dexterity, made the brain positively reel and swim. Finally, a huge bravura passage, as much decked out with ribands and lace as a fashionable woman at a party, brought this insane composition, which taxed even Martin's fingers, to a totally unexpected close.

Karl Rusoff had listened at first with sheer uncomprehending bewilderment, unable, since indeed there was neither head nor tail nor body to it, to make anything whatever out of it, and for a moment he wondered if Martin was merely playing the fool. But as he looked at his face bent over the piano, and saw even his fingers nearly in difficulties, a sudden light struck him, and he began to smile. And before the end was reached he sat shaking in his chair with hopeless laughter.

"Ah, you wicked boy!" he said. "Why, even our dear Lady Sunningdale would recognise herself."

Martin pushed his plume out of his left eye, and laughed.

"That's the joy of it," he said. "She did recognise it. About half-way through she said, 'Why, that's me!' You know you told me to do that, to take anything, the east wind, or a London fog, or a friend, and make music of it."

"Play it once more, if you will," said Karl, "and then to work. Not that that is not work. There is a great deal of work in that; also I perceive with secret satisfaction that you do not find it easy to play. But the bravura is rather unkind. She is never quite like that."

"Ah! the bravura is only her clothes," said Martin, preparing to begin again. "She even told me which hat she had on. It is the one she describes as a covey of birds of paradise which have been out all night in a thunderstorm, sitting on a tomato-salad."

Again Karl sat and listened to the torrent of fragments and currents of interrupted thoughts. Heard for the second time, it seemed to him even a more brilliantly constructed absence of construction than before, an anomalous farrago which could only have been attained by a really scholarly and studious disregard of all rules; no one who had not the rules at his finger-tips could have broken them so accurately. It was a gorgeous parody of musical grammar in exactly the mode in which Lady Sunningdale's conversation was a brilliant parody of speech, full of disconnected wit, and lit from end to end with humour, but as jerky as the antics of a monkey, as incapable of sustained flight in any one direction as a broken-winged bird, a glorious extravagance.

Karl had left his seat and stood near the piano as the bravura passage began. This time it seemed to present no difficulty to Martin, though his unerring hands were hardly more than a mist over the keys. And Karl felt a sudden spasm of jealousy of his pupil, as a huge cascade of tenths and octaves streamed out of Martin's fingers.

"Yes, indeed, the bravura is not easy," he remarked when Martin had finished, "and I think you played it without a mistake, did you not? Is it *quite* easy to play tenths like that?"

Martin laughed.

"I find I've got not to think of anything else," he said. "Will that do for my composition for the week?"

Karl laughed.

"Yes, very well indeed," he said. "It has lots of humour, and humour in music is rather rare. But don't cultivate it, or some day you will find yourself in the position of a man who can't help making puns. A dismal fate! Now let us leave it (it is admirable) and get to work. I think I told you to study the last of the 'Noveletten.' Play it, please."

This time, however, there was no laughter and no approbation. Karl looked rather formidable.

"It won't do; it won't do at all," he said. "You have the notes, but that is absolutely all. It is perfectly empty and dead; a pianola would do as well. What's the matter? Can't you read anything into it?"

Martin shrugged his shoulders.

"I know it's all wrong," he said. "But I can't make anything of it. It's stodgy."

Karl's eyes glared rather dangerously from behind his glasses.

"Oh, stodgy is it?" he said slowly. "Schumann is stodgy! That is news to me. I must try to remember that."

Martin looked sideways at his master, but Karl's face did not relax.

"Stodgy!" he repeated. "I know where the stodginess comes in. Ah! you are either idiotic or you have taken no trouble about it. Because you have found that the mere execution was not difficult to you, you have not troubled to get at the music. I gave you music to learn, and you have brought me back notes. Do not bring a piece to me like that again. If I give you a thing to learn, I do so for some reason. Get up, please."

Karl paused a moment, summoning to his aid all that he knew, all he had ever learned, to give cunning to his fingers and perception to his brain. Never perhaps in his life had he played with more fire, with more eagerness to put into the music all that was his to put there, and that in order to charm no crowded hall packed from floor to ceiling, but to show just one pupil the difference between playing the music and playing the notes.

Martin had left the music-stool in what may be called dignified silence, and was standing by the fire, but before long Karl saw him out of the corner of an eye (he could spare him neither thought nor look) steal back towards the piano, and though he could not look directly at his face he knew what was there: those wide-open black eyes, finely chiselled nostrils swelling and sinking with his quickened breath, mouth a little open, and the whole vivid brain that informed the face lost, absorbed.

He came to the end and sat silent.

"Is that there?" asked Martin in a half breathless whisper. "Is that really all there?"

Karl looked up. Martin's face was exactly as he had known it would be. But the first mood of the artist was of humility.

"I played wrong notes," he said. "Half-a-dozen at least."

"Oh, more than that," said Martin. "But what does that matter? You played it. My God, what a fool I have been! There I sat day after day, and never saw the music."

Karl Rusoff got up. It had been a very good music-lesson.

"It isn't 'stodgy,'" he said. "It isn't really. Do you now see one thing out of a hundred perhaps that it means? You have got to be the critic of the music you play; you have to interpret it. But out of all the ways of playing that, out of all that can be seen in it, you saw nothing; your rendering was absolutely without meaning or colour. To play needs all you are; you gave that fingers only. If I want you to practise fingers only, I will tell you so, and give you a finger exercise or Diabelli. Otherwise you may take it for granted that when your fingers are perfect your work begins. But to play — ah! — you have to burn before you play."

Martin still hung over the piano.

"And I thought it stodgy!" he repeated, looking shy and sideways at Karl's great grey head.

"Well, you won't again," said he. "Will you try it again now?"

"No, how can I?" said Martin. "I've got to begin it all over again."

"Then there was a piece of Bach. Play that. And now read nothing into it except the simplicity of a child. Just the notes, the more simply the better. Wait a moment, Martin. I want to enjoy it. Let me sit down."

Martin waited, and then began one of the "Suites Anglaises," and like a breath of fresh air in a stuffy room, or like a cloudless dawn with the singing of birds after a night of storm and thunder, the exquisite melody flowed from his fingers, precise, youthful and joyous. There was no introspection here, no moods of a troubled soul: no doubts or questioning: it sang as a thrush sings, changed and returned on itself, danced in a gavotte, moved slowly in a minuet, and romped through a Bourrée like a child.

At the end Martin laughed suddenly.

"Oh, how good!" he cried. "Did you know that Bach wrote that for me?" he asked, turning to Karl.

"Yes, I thought he must have," said Karl. "And with the command that you were to play it to me. You played that very well; all your fingers were of one weight. How did you learn that?"

Martin raised his eyebrows.

"Why, it would spoil it, would it not, to play it any other way?" he asked.

"Certainly it would."

Then he got up quickly.

"Oh, Martin, you child!" he said. "Did I speak too roughly about the Schumann?"

"You did rather," he said. "But I deserved to have my ears boxed."

The two dined alone, and held heated arguments, not like master and pupil but like two students who worked side by side, Karl as often as not deferring to the other, Martin as often as not blandly disagreeing with Karl.

"How can you pronounce, for instance," he asked, "that that 'Novelette' is to be played with those sweatings and groanings, the mere notes being of no use, whereas Bach is to be played with notes only?"

Karl gazed at him in silence.

"You impertinent infant!" he said. "What else do you propose? To play the Schumann as you played it? And the Bach as I played the Schumann?"

"That would sound extremely funny," remarked Martin. "No, I don't say you are not right, but how do you know you are right?"

"Because Bach wrote for the spinnet," said Karl. "Have you ever tried to play Schumann on a spinnet? It sounds exactly as you made it sound just now. A deplorable performance, my poor boy."

"You have told me that. Don't rub it in so. I shall play it very well to-morrow."

"Or next year," said Karl, still grim but inwardly full of laughter. "By the way, there was no 'dog' motive in the Lady Sunningdale composition."

"You can't have been attending," said Martin. "Suez Canal came in twice, and Sahara three times with shrill barks. Yes, please, another cutlet."

Karl watched him eat it: the process took about five seconds.

"You didn't taste that," he remarked.

"No, it was needed elsewhere," said Martin. "But I'm sure it was very good."

Karl lingered over the bouquet of his Burgundy.

"It is a strange thing," he said, "that mankind are so gross as to confuse the sense of taste with greediness. No, my dear boy, I am not at this moment attacking you. But there is no organ, even that of the ear, in this wonderful body of ours, so fine as that of taste. Yet to most people the sight of a man deeply appreciating his dinner conveys a feeling of greediness. But I always respect such a man. He has a sense more than most people."

"But isn't it greedy?" asked Martin.

Karl became deeply impressive.

"It is no more greedy," he said, "to catch the flavour of an olive or an oyster, than to catch the tone of a 'cello."

"But a hundred oysters?" said Martin.

"Ah, that would be like encoring a song in an opera — a most detestable habit — and hearing it over and over again. No artist desires that.

Fancy hearing Wotan's 'Abschied' twice. That would be greedy. The art of dining, like most arts, is frightfully neglected in England."

Martin laughed.

"I have been here, I suppose, a dozen times," he said, "and every time you give me some surprise. I had no idea you gave two thoughts as to what you ate."

"That was hasty of you. True, of all the senses I put the ear first. That is personal predilection. But all the senses really are equal; there is no shadow of reason for supposing that one is more elevated than another. True, some can be more easily misused than others, taste more particularly. But all are subtle gateways to the soul."

They had finished dinner and Karl pushed back his chair.

"Take an instance," he said. "Take incense. Does not that smell excite and inspire the devotional sense? Does not the smell of frangipanni — an unendurable odour — suggest a sort of hothouse sensualism? Does not the smell of a frosty November morning bring the sense of cleanness into the very marrow of your bones?"

Martin sniffed experimentally.

"Ah, I know that!" he said. "And the leaves on the beech-trees are red, and the grass underfoot a little crisp with frost. Oh, how good! But what then?"

Karl was watching him closely. It was his conscious object now and always to make Martin think, to excite anything in him that could touch his sense for beauty. He had found that this half-serious, half-flippant method was the easiest means of approach. For Martin was but a boy: discussions in an earnest, conscious German spirit both bored and alarmed him. This fact, had his father grasped it, might in years past have helped matters.

"Why, everything," he replied. "Each sense can be expressed in terms of another. Take magenta in colour: it is frangipanni in smell, in sound it is — what shall we say? — an Anglican chant of some sort, in taste it is the vague brown sauce in which a bad cook hides his horrors."

Martin laughed again, with the keen pleasure of youth in all things experimental.

"Yes, that is true," he said. "How do you go on? Take a fine colour, vermilion."

"The blind man said it must be like the sound of a trumpet," said Karl, "and the blind man, at that moment, saw. Brandy also for taste is red. So is ammonia: a pistol to your nostrils."

Martin dabbed his cigarette on to his dessert plate.

"Yes, yes," he cried, "and C major is red. And F sharp is blue, electric blue, like the grotto at Capri —"

He stopped suddenly.

"Am I talking nonsense?" he asked. "If so, it is your fault. You encouraged me. You meant to. And what do you mean me to get from it?"

Karl turned directly towards him.

"I mean you to think," he said. "To frame your life wholly for beauty, in whatever form you see it. It is everywhere, be assured of that; and if your eye sees it, store it up like a honey bee, and bring it home. If your mouth feels it, bring it home. If you smell the autumn morning, bring that home too. It all makes music."

He pushed his plate aside, and leaned forward towards Martin.

"All is food for you," he said. "It is only in that way, by harvesting every grain of corn you see, that you can be great. A lot of harvesting is done unconsciously. Supplement that by conscious harvesting. You may learn perfectly all the harmony and counterpoint that can be learned, you may learn to play things impossible, but all that is no good by itself. You can already play — I am not flattering you, but the reverse — if you practise a little, all the printed music ever written, as far as notes go. That is no good either. But — if I had not seen this when first I heard you play, I should never have wasted ten minutes of my time on you — you can do more than that. You can, if you are very alert, quite untiring, very critical, and always ready to catch beauty in whatever form it may present itself, you can do more than this. At least I believe so."

He got up from his seat, and leaned his hands on the boy's shoulders as he sat by the table.

"Ah, Martin, don't disappoint me," he said, "or, being old, I shall die of it. Drink from every spring but one, and drink deep."

Martin turned in his chair and faced him.

"Do I know what spring you mean?" he asked. "Love?"

Karl looked at him with a sort of wonder.

"No, I did not mean that," he said.

He drew a long breath.

"My God, if that had been granted to me," he said, "I too might have been great. But I never fell in love. Oh! I am successful; I know, I understand. I am the only person perhaps who does know what is missing in me. It is that. But missing that, I never, no not once, parodied what I did not know. Parody, parody!" he repeated.

Martin looked at him with that direct lucid gaze Karl knew so well, level beneath the straight line of his eyebrows. His smooth brown cheeks were a little flushed with some emotion he could not have put a name to. Slight injury was there, that Karl could possibly have supposed him bestial, the rest was clean modesty.

"I am not beastly," he said, "if you mean that."

"I did mean that," he said. "And I beg your pardon."

Martin stood up.

"I think you had no right to suppose that," he said.

"No, I had none. I did not suppose it. I warned you, though."

A tenderness such as he had never known rose like a blush into his old bones, tenderness for this supreme talent that had been placed in his hands.

"I only warned you," he said. "I looked for burglars under your bed, just because — because it is a boy like you that this stupid world tries to spoil. Aye, and it will try to spoil you. Women will make love to you. They will fall in love with you, too."

Again he paused.

"Things will be made poisonously pleasant for you," he said. "You can without effort capture brilliant success. But remember all that you get without effort is not, from the point of view of art, conceivably worth anything. Remember also that nothing fine ever grew out of what is horrible. More than that, what is horrible sterilises the soil — that soil is you, you will never get any more if you spoil it or let it get sour or rancid. Horror gets rooted there, it devours all that might have been good, all that might have been of the best."

There was a long silence. Then Karl stepped back and rang the bell. To Martin the silvery tinkle sounded remote. He certainly was thinking now.

"Well, I have done," said Karl. "Excuse the — the Nonconformist conscience."

Martin got up.

"I don't see how one can care — really care — for music and live grossly," he said. "Yet people appear to manage it. And mawkishness makes me feel sick," he added with apparent irrelevance.

But Karl understood.

"Somebody has been trying to pet him," he thought to himself.

They went upstairs to the music-room, and Martin stood before the fire a few moments smoking in silence.

"I like this room," he said. "It makes me feel clean like the November morning. I say, how is it that so many people, men and women alike, only think about one subject? Surely it is extraordinarily stupid of them, when there are so many jolly things in the world."

"Ah, if the world was not full of extraordinarily stupid people," remarked Karl, "it would be an enchanting place."

"Oh, it's enchanting as it is," cried Martin, throwing off his pre-occupation. "May I begin again at once? I want to get through a lot of work to-night. Heavens, there's a barrel-organ playing 'Cavalleria.' Frank is going to introduce a Bill next Session, he says, putting 'Cavalleria' in public on the same footing as obscene language in public. He says it comes to the same thing."

{1904}

JOHN GAMBRIL NICHOLSON
{1866–1931}

The fourteenth chapter of *The Romance of a Choir-Boy*, titled "A Catalogue," contains the first reference in literature to photographs of boys as erotic devices. The photographs of the Baron von Gloeden — Italian boys in stylized settings — were known in homosexual circles of the day, but the Baron's photographs were nonspecific idealizations of the eternal masculine. Similarly, in chapter 8 of Forrest Reid's *The Garden God*, Graham places his friend Harold in the attitudes of famous homoerotic sculptures such as the faun, the *Spinario* (the bronze statue of a boy pulling a thorn from his foot), the *Adorante* (presumably the bronze statue by Lysippus), and a youthful Dionysus with a face "like that of Leonardo's 'Bacchus.' " The gallery of photographs, or "harem," in Nicholson's novel, on the contrary, attests to a disturbingly pederastic, even pedophilic, preoccupation with quite particular boys, all aged between eleven and sixteen.

No figure of the period had so tortured and ambivalent a relationship to his own homosexuality as Nicholson. He once burned a ten-thousand-word erotic manuscript by the Baron Corvo because he feared that its mere existence would cause him to be false to his own exalted homosexual "ideal," and wrote the cautionary "A Story of Cliffe School," about the perils of masturbation, even as he fell chronically in love with boys: Victor Rushforth, the third love of his life, was but thirteen. Was it Rousseau who said, "Once a philosopher, twice a pederast"?

That photography, as both object and process, was the coming thing is further proved by this passage from André Gide's *Et Nunc Manet in Te* (1947; English translation, 1952) describing his wedding trip to Italy at the end of the nineteenth century:

> In Florence we visited together churches and museums; but in Rome, completely absorbed by the young models from Saracinesco who then used to come and offer themselves on the stairs of the Piazza di Spagna, I was willing (and here I cease to understand myself) to forsake [Madeleine] for long hours at a time, which she filled somehow or other, probably wandering bewildered through the city — while, on the pretext of photographing them, I would take the models to the little apartment we had rented in Piazza Barberini.

The Romance of a Choir-Boy was published privately in 1916, but written between 1896 and 1905. The title page bears this epigraph:

"All that life contains of torture, toil, and treason,
  Shame, dishonour, death, to him was but a name;
Here, a boy, he dwelt through all the singing season,
  And, ere the day of sorrow, departed as he came."

FROM *The Romance of a Choir-Boy*

A CATALOGUE

It was after eight when Philip got back to the clergy-house, and Gerrard soon came in, ready for supper.

"Hallo, old chap! What have you been up to?" was his greeting.

"Been exorcising Nebul?" responded Philip cheerfully.

"How do you spell that word, eh?"

"N-e-b-u-l!" said Philip, wilfully misunderstanding the question. Then he added, "Sometimes spelt P-h-i-l-i-p!"

And Gerrard replied,

"Or, more safely, S-e-l-f!"

Then they dropped their banter, and talked philosophy in Philip's room till nearly ten o'clock. Gerrard retired then, as it was his Early Celebration next day, leaving Philip to read the "Church Times." This failed to hold him for long, as his mind was still ruffled after the conflicts of the day. He wouldn't strum, for fear of disturbing his colleague, so he unlocked a drawer and took a packet of letters, and read a few here and there. They were all Teddy's letters, neatly and chronologically arranged in Philip's usual methodical fashion. Every scrap of the boy's correspondence was there, even to little pencilled notes on bits of exercise paper. Teddy had always written a neat, boyish hand, even from his early days; but now he was changing its character considerably, and Philip had noticed for the past few months how closely imitative it was of his own! In the form of the capitals Teddy, perhaps unconsciously, was copying his mentor; he also copied accurately Philip's heading of the paper; first the year in Roman numerals, under that the day of the month, written in words, and the address in the third line; and all these on the left-top corner of the paper. Most of these letters began with "*Dear Sir*"; some few had "*Dear Mr. Luard*"; some plunged at once *in medias res*. Nearly all ended with, "*Best love from Teddy*"; a few were signed "*E. T.*," and the first half-dozen concluded with "*Yours obediently, E. Faircloth*," but even some of those also contained, "*With best love.*" The affectionate little country lad of twelve had never questioned Philip's motives for the great interest in him and efforts in his behalf; had no more doubted that it was because of love than he doubted the love of his mother. And as Philip tied up once more his precious bundle, he felt that Teddy was content, even now, with no other explanation of it all. Had he but been able to take the love in the letters as literal, actual, and meaning just the same as he himself meant when he wrote, "*With best love,*" then (he told himself) all the doubts, perplexities, anxieties and grievances would vanish like smoke! But he had never yet been able to make himself believe that Teddy loved him; and, so foolish had he grown of late, that even if the boy had admitted it in just so many words, saying orally "*I love you!*" and look-ing into his face with those sweet, truthful, honest eyes, as he said it, — even then Philip knew he would be still sceptical!

Next he took out an envelope containing a few unmounted photo-graphs of Teddy. And he lingered long over the first snap-shot, which showed the little boy with nothing on but an old battered hat, dipping one foot into the cool summer stream. Teddy did not love this photo of himself. "Not because I'm naked," he had explained, more than once, "but be-cause I'm ugly and stupid-looking." Then Philip would kiss it, to Teddy's disgust, and would say, "It's sweet! It's beautiful! It is my own dear little sweetheart, and I love him!"

Putting the letters and photos back in the drawer of his writing-table, he wandered round the room gazing vacantly at the pictures on the walls. The writing-table stood under the window; on the right of it was "Beata Beatrix," — a twelve-by-ten Hollyer photograph. On the long wall be-tween window and door the place of honour was occupied by a wonderful nocturne, in blue, in a white frame; an oil-painting by a young Irish artist who had learned his methods in a French school; representing the Thames at night, looking from the Chelsea Embankment over to the Battersea side. The chimney-shafts and high factory buildings, scarcely outlined in the vague distance, were as light and aëry and picturesque as Venetian towers and cupolas; a splotch or two of yellow illumination among them was re-peated in the dark river in long reflections; in the left foreground a barge was moored, end-on to the spectator, with its sail loosely furled about its mainmast, its hull anchored in a patch of deepest shadowy night. It was a delightful piece of impressionist work; nothing but paint, looked at too closely, but resolving itself, when seen from the hearthrug, into a bit of real river-by-night in which Philip saw something new every time he looked. This masterpiece was flanked on either side by a delicate water-colour; the one on the left a slight sketch of the Medway at Rochester (so Philip thought, but he was not quite sure about it). There was a foreground of mud in light greens and browns; a strip of pale-yellow river in the middle distance; and an indication in the background of high rising hillside with a square tower atop. A black boat, lying lengthwise on the mud, under a clear yellow-white sunset sky, held together the somewhat loose details of the picture. The water-colour on the right was much more solidly painted; a rustic church nestled among a cluster of summer trees, seen across a meadow on which lay scattered sheep. There was an evening sky here, too, —full of fleecy cloudlets showing roseate hues here and there. Thus, though Philip had never remarked it, night was dominant on this principal wall-space. These three pictures were well above the line of the eye; on the line were three long photo frames all in a row; the middle one held six cartes-de-visite and the other two held six cabinets; all of the photographs were of boys. Philip often went right through them one by one, saying the names and bestowing a passing thought on each. He did so on this Saturday night. Beginning at the left they ran thus: (1) Gilbert, aged thirteen, full-length, standing outdoors beside a rustic chair on which sat a fox-terrier, with the boy's left hand round the dog's neck. A sturdy, mischievous-looking boy, dressed in cord riding breeches with three buttons at the knee, a little unbuttoned round jacket, and a cap with a white badge. (2) Charlie, aged twelve; a half-length of a dark round-faced little fellow in an Eton jacket, one arm resting on an ornamental table, the thumb of the other hand in his trouser-pocket. Rather deep-set eyes; the shadow of an amused smile on firm, well-closed mouth. (3) Willie, aged sixteen; a half-length, sitting down with folded arms, enlarged by Philip on smooth bromide paper out of a group; the surrounding portions of other people's anatomies ruthlessly pencilled over, and the outlines of the shoulders helped a little by a pencil line. A bright, honest face, with a cap worn well back on the head; a stand-up collar with points turned-over, and a big sailors-knot necktie. Jacket open, and handkerchief hanging out of breast pocket. (4) Ernest, aged thirteen; head and shoulders only of a pale, delicate boy, with fat cheeks, languid eyes, and pretty curving lips. Hair parted on right and brushed very smooth. Wearing a high-cut jacket, closely buttoned-up. A soupçon of seriousness — not to say sullenness — in his expression. (5) Frank, aged fourteen; a handsome boy in Eton jacket, with a large expressive mouth, showing his front teeth in a rather broad smile; hair cropped very short, making his ears look prominent. (6) Jack, aged fifteen; full-length, standing in front of an ivy-covered wall, one hand in trouser-pocket. A pretty but weak face; stand-up collar with a cross-bow; thick watch-chain right across waistcoat.

Then came the smaller photographs, as follows: (1) Bertie, aged fifteen; head and shoulders of a bonny, square-built lad, with very fair hair, frank, wide-open eyes, and very round chin; lines indicative of fat under the eyes, and a little upward curl on the full, well-arched upper lip. Broad turn-down collar with jacket worn outside it. (2) Same Jack again, rather younger, about fourteen; taken by Philip with a small camera indoors. A pianoforte, open, for the background, looking ludicrously small though only a foot or two behind the figure. The boy is wearing trousers and a turn-down collar; left hand on left hip, and right foot on music-stool, making an ungainly space between the two legs. Right elbow on right knee, and the right hand supporting the pretty, but yielding and complacent face: hair in utter confusion (he'd been bathing). (3) Alec, aged twelve; a sweet, serious little face, with dark eyes that looked you through and through; chubby cheeks and rounded chin; resolute mouth; a profusion of dark hair falling over a high broad forehead. A head and shoulders only visible; Eton jacket, broad lapels, and big sheeny black tie. (4) A different Jack, aged sixteen; clean-cut delicate features, and intellectual, alert face, with wide-awake eyes; an expression of power and self-restraint and fearlessness; high all-round collar, and big knotted white necktie. (5) Wilfred, aged twelve; full-length out-of-doors under a leafy hedge. Philip photographed him; a demure, plump little chap in Norfolk jacket and knickers, his stockings turned down over the continuations. Left thumb in waistband; right hand hanging down with a superfluity of white cuff falling over it. A circular face, with a set look and puckered little eyes, under a wavy coronal of fluffy fair hair. (6) Sidney, aged fourteen; another of Philip's attempts at portraiture, printed on a smooth bromide. A fine, dark, impudent face, with rather thick lips and a tangled mass of black hair; bright eyes, and well-marked brows. Head finely poised; low collar, and jacket with top button fastened.

Last came the set of larger portraits to the right of these: (1) Otho, aged thirteen; full-length in cassock and surplice; one hand on a chair, a book in the other. A wonderfully handsome little choir-boy, with bold black eyes and a defiant mouth. (2) Gilbert, again, aged fifteen. Nearly full-length; sitting on a low settee, with both hands steadying himself. Norfolk jacket, with the buttons undone but the belt fastened; riding breeches as before. Quiet, penetrating expression; fair hair brushed up high off the forehead. (3) Henry, aged fourteen; another choir-boy, taken by Philip, full-length, in a garden, with a glass door for background, in which the trees are reflected. A bright gentlemanly little lad, looking rather troubled, with his two hands loosely clasped in front of his short surplice. (4) Another Ernest — distinct from the former one — aged twelve; a slightly-built, aristocratic child, in a suit of black velveteen, with tunic buttoned all the way up. Three-quarter length only, so no legs visible. Pretty wavy well-brushed hair; rather sleepy expression; small, delicate mouth, with a deep dimple under the lower lip. Leaning against a table, left hand in pocket of knickers; right hand hanging loose, and painfully large owing to its prominence. (5) Tom, aged eleven; a large head of a strikingly handsome boy, with great light eyes in a dark oval face; a tuft of hair growing down over a low forehead, a rosebud of a mouth, rather big ears. Jacket buttoned, and over the top-button two white geranium blossoms with three leaves. (6) Alec, again, aged sixteen; enlarged, not too clearly, out of a football group; in a dark shirt, with a collar, and white buttons; same serious eyes looking straight out from under low brows; lips closely compressed, chin grown more determined, luxuriant mane tumbling anyhow over forehead. What at first might be taken for a curtain behind the head resolving itself, upon inspection, into the wrinkled folds of some other boy's footer bags!

All these eighteen portraits, then, made a long line of boyish forms and faces along the wall, level with the eye, — or a little below the level of Philip's eye, which was not less than five feet six inches up the wall. "Your harem," Lorey had said one morning, as he passed them all in review, much as Philip was doing now. Philip could afford to smile at this witticism which completely missed the mark. Gerrard called them, respectively, *The Joyful, The Sorrowful* and *The Glorious Mysteries*, and always declared it was just like Philip's extravagance to have had one too many of each!

Over the door was an enlargement, bought by Philip out of the annual Dudley Gallery Show; a piece of the broadest impressionism. It represented a boy, seen from behind, batting in a cricket-net in the last light of a summer's eve; a well-knit, broad-shouldered lad with uplifted bat; dressed in ordinary clothes, minus his jacket. Between the eye and the figure came the wavy lines of net-work, quite out of focus. The figure was fairly sharp, but beyond it everything was dependent on the observer's imagination; a few hazy ghost-like forms might be the bowler or bowlers, and one or two fieldsmen; the background might or might not be hillside with a splash of evening sky crowning it. At twelve feet distance you could see in it almost anything you cared to see. Gerrard called it, "Portrait of a cricket-bat supporting a shirt-sleeve." The original title bestowed on it by its perpetrator was, "Just One More!"

On the wall opposite the window were five large framed photographic groups, — football and cricket teams, choir-groups and undergraduate-groups; Philip figured in them all. High up in the central position was a charming idyllic enlargement of a nude boy of about thirteen, standing among the boughs of a low-growing leafy pear-tree, with a shepherd's pipe at his lips and both hands laid upon it. He had fluffy hair upon which the sunlight fell, and his shapely rounded form was patched here and there by leaves and leaf-shadows and broad flecks of sunshine. Philip saw a good bit of Teddy in the face and figure; several of his friends refused to believe the truthful assertion that it was not Teddy himself.

Between the corner of this wall and the fire-place stood the high bookcase, with five glass-fronted shelves, and a cupboard underneath them. Two whole shelves were filled with volumes of verse; the middle one contained fiction; the two lowest, *belles-lettres* and theology. Philip was very eclectic in his modest library; he was wont to say that a book could only figure in it on one of two pleas, — either surpassing merit or surpassing interest; on the latter count he included a number of presentation copies of works by his personal acquaintances. A catalogue of our friend's literary treasures, it strikes me here very forcibly, would sum up Philip's tastes, tendencies and ideals for my reader as no amount of delineation could possibly do. But, for fear of incurring that reader's possible wrath, the strong temptation to make such a list must be avoided; and I will content myself with saying that the poetry ranged from Tennyson and Rossetti to Philip's own slim volume, — "A Garland of Southernwood," — and a similar one by his college-chum Balsham; the fiction from George Meredith's "Richard Feverel" to Ouida's "Signa"; the essays from Emerson to Alice Meynell; the theology from "Lux Mundi" to Drummond. Vainly the ghost of Philip's maternal grandfather (a highly-cultured country rector of the Early Victorian period) might have sought a familiar title throughout the five shelves! Philip was hopelessly modern in his tastes.

On the mantelpiece, among countless nic-nacs, there were two framed photographs. One was his mother. The other was Teddy, aged twelve and a half, taken in the garden of Philip's Chalk End home. The boy was lolling, — without hat, coat or waistcoat, and with the sleeves of his cricket-shirt turned back above his elbows, — in a hammock-chair; both hands were behind his head; his eyes were half-closed; everything below the belt was vignetted off, as he had been taken full-face, and Philip's hand-camera had so exaggerated the legs and feet (in which Nature unaided had been fairly bountiful!) that they were unpresentable. This photo was known to them as *The Dolce Far Niente Teddy*. Philip held it very dear, and Teddy had accidentally cracked the negative one day in the dark-room, which enhanced the value of the few good prints extant.

Between the fire-place and the next corner stood the piano-forte; on it was Teddy in his "choir-suit," in a heavy elaborate gilt frame. Over the piano hung a sketch in oils by an Associate, an artist *de la première force* in his particular line; a slight study of the back of a naked boy in a boat, bending over a pole or an oar which he dipped into a translucent green sea; a sunlight effect, with wonderful pinks and blues in the flesh treatment; face seen in profile over the right shoulder, bright yellow hair, exquisite curves of back and arms.

Then on the left of the window was a Hollyer photograph of Rossetti's "Ecce Ancilla Domini," matching the companion picture on the right.

And now the clock chimed twelve, and Philip, as his custom was, put out the gas and retired. Getting undressed he speculated on what Teddy had been doing that evening, and — a matter less problematic — what he was doing at that moment. He tried to banish the little prick out of his now serene mood, though it stabbed him now and again; he did so want to enter into all his boy's plans and achievements, — not to be left in complete ignorance of his Saturday amusements and adventures! But he successfully combated this grievance, telling himself that certainly Teddy had been happily enjoying himself whatever or wherever the adventure had been. Therefore it behooved him, Philip, to be happy, too. Teddy often said, "I *do wish* you'd enjoy things without me! I can't always be with you; and you can't expect me to have much interest in many things which you can enjoy. You are not to give up your own employments and amusements, you'll be such a loser by doing that. And I'm not going to drag you into all my little affairs. Always imagine me having a good time when I'm away from you; and let me think the same about you." As Philip turned in he thought of this, and knew Teddy was right; he also remembered his wise colleague's quaint remark: "Keep him happy, then; so shall you have much joy!" How easily he could spoil the contentment of that affectionate little heart! But he resolved never to do so; he would be to Teddy like God was, and like Nature was: showering love and help and blessings on his life, but not making exigent demands in return: being satisfied with the spontaneous love and confidence of a child's heart: finding his chief reward in seeing how simply and unquestioningly the sweet disposition accepted all its benefits, and how splendidly the little bud was developing and thriving and opening out under helpful and loving influences.

Before he fell asleep he went back to the little "Daisy Chain" lyric, and tried to imagine Teddy standing on a flower-bedecked platform, in a room blazing with gas lights, dressed in his Eton suit, with white gloves and perhaps a white flower in his buttonhole, singing in the quartette; he secured a good mental image of it all, and could almost hear the fresh, sweet, flute-like voice in "Thank you very much indeed!"

Then his thoughts took a backward turn, and reverted to some other occasions on which Teddy's voice had stirred his heartstrings. There was the evening of Ascension Day, only a few months ago. Philip had been paying a visit in Town, — a Town of vivid green parks and crowded picture-exhibitions, — and went to Festal Evensong at St. Saviour's mainly to see his protégé; the fact of there being a Colonial Bishop as preacher did not weigh very much with him. There was a processional hymn at both ends of the service, and the second one was "Hail the day that sees Him rise." It made an indelible impression on Philip; he could quite easily bring it back mentally. There was the gathering of the banners at the Chancel-steps; the vesting of the bishop by the two handsome acolytes, in their scarlet cassocks and skull-caps; the fat-cheeked thurifer bringing in the censer from the vestry, followed by his tiny satellite, and two boys bearing the lights. While these preparations were in progress Lorey was improvising; getting gradually out of the key of the offertory-hymn into that of the next one, and giving already vague hints of forth-coming melody; while the big Cross, held by a stalwart, white-gloved, gir-dled crucifer, waited to head the procession. At last came the "Let us proceed in peace," answered by "In the name of Christ," and then at one note from the organ, the whole apparatus was set in motion. The hymn rang out, strong and joyful; the thurifer led the way down the narrow south aisle, the censer swinging out before him in rhythmic mechanical motion, sending out at the top of every swing its little cloud of incense-smoke, that went floating up among the dark pillars and rafters, leaving its pungent savour circling and spreading through the church. The demure little boat-boy paced on his left. Then came the lights and the Cross, be-fore which the heads of worshippers went bowing down like growing corn before the summer breezes. There was scarcely room down this narrow side-aisle for two abreast: the tiny children who headed the choir were not inconvenienced, but the bigger men were, and until they turned at the west end to come up the centre-aisle the two small cope-bearers had to keep well in front of the gigantic priest, — portly enough without the added width of the gorgeous vestment; it required some skill on their part to keep out of the way of his feet, as he shuffled along in his mitre, his eyes gazing straight before him and his jewelled hands held in front of his breast. Teddy was almost last of the boy-choristers, walking with a dark serious-looking boy; he was revelling in the hymn, but he had known where to look for his friend, and had not forgotten to give him a smile in passing. Philip could pick out the voice he loved among all the rest; and in every verse, when it came to the pause on the E, at the end of the last line, Teddy sent it ringing out like a bugle-note, hanging on to it till it vibrated through and through the whole building. As he came abreast of Philip, who sat high up near the south aisle, the hymn had advanced to the second verse, and the young man (he wasn't ordained at that time) marked how careful his protégé was not to make the old mistake over "waits" and "gates"; in fact, he was making "weets" and "geets" of them, in his anxiety to avoid the Chalk End fashion. One Sunday night, after Evensong, Philip heard Teddy remark to some other boy just outside the vestry door, "Whoy, that ryne!" Without endless pains Teddy would have sung "*There for 'Im 'oigh troiumph wytes.*" The memory of that hymn was flavoured even now with the emotions of that bygone moment; the soft Spring evening which had darkened during the service, till all the deep crimsons and violets and blues of the south windows had gradually faded, as Philip watched them, into dull lifeless black; the strangeness of the church to him, who had never been there before on a week-day, contrasting with the familiarity of it to the boy, who had been singing there for twelve months; the pride of hearing the lovely voice so perfectly produced, so splendidly under control; the vague uneasiness and regret assailing his heart, as he grudged so much of Teddy's company and intercourse and training to any but himself; and, as an undercurrent, flowing below all these things, the religious emotion evoked by the underlying thought of the hymn and the sermon and the whole service, penetrated and intensified to an aesthetic soul like Philip's by the elaborate dignified ritual.

During the sermon he had been impressed by the nearest wall-decoration; a panel in monotone between two of the windows on the south side. A dignified but sorrowful Figure held out His hands in blessing; from beneath His feet crushed grapes sent forth their juice. Below ran the passage, "*I have trodden the winepress alone.*"

But perhaps there was a more piquant flavour in the memories of some of the boy's triumphs in his native place. Philip began to think of one Sunday evening in August, when at Chalk End Teddy had electrified them by his singing as the anthem, "Angels ever bright and fair." Philip had read the Lessons, leaving Cecil Vickers to divide his attention between the organ and the pulpit, and old Mr. Vickers to mumble out the prayers. He recalled the breathless calm of the hot summer evening; he stood at the lectern, and looked down the dim church; half of the west door was opened, and he could see the churchyard outside, — the green grass, the gravel path, the tomb-stones, the trees listlessly swaying in the light breeze, the long shadows which the low sun was throwing right up to the porch. On the upland meadow, beyond the wall, a white hen was parading her brood of chicks. The birds were still twittering, the smell of mignonette was blown about the musty old pews, the candles on the lectern flickered. The dust of a vicar of long ago reposed almost under his feet. Scarcely legible now were the letters on the flat much-worn stone, but Philip knew the inscription well, and for him there was glamour in the old figures 1793, and the Latin that had puzzled him in childhood, *In die novissima gaudebit.* Dreamy, drowsy, odorous was the atmosphere; and listless, stupefied, somnolent was the congregation. But, though it was half-asleep upon its knees while the Vicar droned and mumbled "Lighten our darkness," it woke up the next minute, compelled to attention by young Faircloth's penetrating soprano. First came the few bars of Handel's symphonic prelude on the inadequate organ, whose pipes emitted windy notes; then the flute-like voice piercing the heavy air, throbbing and beating through the scented dusk, creating a keen poignant ecstasy of delight in the musical souls, and a sensation of supreme amazement in the uncultured ones. The choir-boys gaped with open mouth, staring at this quondam fellow-mortal who had become metamorphosed in twelve months into a perfect musical instrument. Teddy sang the *notes* well enough, certainly; his time, tune and voice-production were wonderful; but there was something more, — the actual rendering of the *music*, the spirit of the composition, the thought, the idea of the composer; one could scarcely understand whence it came, — this power of translating melody into sentiment, but undoubtedly Teddy had it. But the deep underlying aspiration of the music did not prevent Philip from appreciating the technical excellence of the solo; for instance, he enjoyed the good accent of the passages — time-accent and word-accent alike. He contrasted his little friend's vowel-sounds of the past with the way in which he now controlled the word "care," as he held it out steadily on its very long note. The feeble accompaniment enhanced the beauty of the boy's voice, as they took alternate possession of the melodious phrasing; the voice seemed to be, for a time, tolerating, yielding to the interruption of the less capable instrument, in order that it might re-assert later its own vast superiority; might ultimately burst out again in full irresistible flood. To Philip a curious comparison had presented itself vividly: — The building was like a glass vessel full of colourless fluid, and the voice was a bright stream of red aniline dye, slowly and sinuously penetrating the mass, forcing its way among the molecules, and tinging the whole very gradually, while still preserving its own identity as it sank down to the bottom of the vessel following the wavy line of least resistance. This idea, originated on that Sunday evening, had been present to his mind on a good many subsequent occasions when he had heard Teddy sing solos; but it never came to him when the boy was merely holding his own in a balanced quartet, or joining in a hymn or a chorus. Perhaps it was the organ-accompaniment which suggested the volume of colourless liquid, filling the containing vessel so fully that the colouring matter could scarce find space for itself therein. And with the idea invariably came the impression of glimmering windows in the dusk; plain square glass panes, out of which the cross-like divisions seemed to emerge more and more clearly as the fading light grew slowly less and less.

Then just one other reminiscence cropped up in Philip's drowsy consciousness. A Sunday morning in a suburban London church; a bright, cold, wintry atmosphere; a hymn being sung by the congregation on their knees at the conclusion of High Celebration. Teddy was kneeling in the pew at his side, and singing "And now, O, Father, mindful of the love"; possibly a good many other voices were singing it, too, but that escaped Philip's notice! When they got to the third verse, the celebrant gave the signal of readiness to recede, and they rose to their feet to sing:

> *"And then for those, our dearest and our best,*
> *By this prevailing Presence we appeal."*

Philip had the divine and the earthly love so intricately interwoven in his thoughts just then that they seemed to be but one. And, as he glanced from Teddy at his side to the Crucifix on the pillar beside the pulpit, a noontide gleam of sunshine shot down through the narrow lancet window on the south side of the Sanctuary, and lit up the eddying incense-wreaths that were hanging about the Chancel, and floating up towards the light.

But now all thoughts, all memories, all ideas blended into the haze of sleepiness, and when Philip woke it was morning.

{1905}

WILLA CATHER
{1873–1947}

From early on, Willa Cather cut her hair short, often dressed in men's clothes, and sometimes signed her name "William Cather, Jr." She never married, and, after an early relationship with Isabelle McClung ended, moved to New York. There she lived until her death with Edith Lewis. Among her many admirers, perhaps the most vocal was the effeminate aesthete and former "bright young thing" Stephen Tennant, who revered her novels and made a point of visiting her whenever he went to New York.

Truman Capote offers an interesting recollection of Cather in an unreliable self-interview that he published in *Interview* magazine in the late seventies:

> She was full of surprises. For one thing, she and her lifelong friend, Miss Lewis, lived in a spacious, charmingly furnished Park Avenue apartment — somehow, the notion of Miss Cather living in an apartment on Park Avenue seemed incongruous with her Nebraska upbringing, with the simple, rather elegiac nature of her novels. Secondly, her principal interest was not literature, but music. She went to concerts constantly, and almost all her closest friends were musical personalities, particularly [the violinist] Yehudi Menuhin and his sister Hepzibah.

Though she wrote no explicitly lesbian fiction, two of the stories in Cather's first collection, *The Troll Garden,* introduce a homosexual type that has become almost iconic: the isolated, artistic young man who dreams of fleeing his impoverished childhood for the glittering mecca of the city. In "Paul's Case," this suffering hero, a boy from Pittsburgh, steals money and runs away to New York. There he checks in at the Waldorf, spends an evening with a "wild San Francisco boy, a freshman at Yale," is chased down by his father, and finally — like another despairing heroine, Anna Karenina — throws himself under a train. In "The Sculptor's Funeral," Harvey Merrick has already fled his Kansas hometown, made a success of himself in New York, and died. Now it is up to Steavens, his disciple (and possibly his lover), not only to deliver his body back home, but to make sense of the "raw, biting ugliness" in which Merrick, "whose tastes were refined beyond the limits of the reasonable," grew up. ❧

FROM *The Troll Garden*

The Sculptor's Funeral

A GROUP OF the townspeople stood on the station siding of a little Kansas town, awaiting the coming of the night train, which was already twenty minutes overdue. The snow had fallen thick over everything; in the pale starlight the line of bluffs across the wide, white meadows south of the town made soft, smoke-coloured curves against the clear sky. The men on the siding stood first on one foot and then on the other, their hands thrust deep into their trousers pockets, their overcoats open, their shoulders screwed up with the cold; and they glanced from time to time toward the southeast, where the railroad track wound along the river shore. They conversed in low tones and moved about restlessly, seeming uncertain as to what was expected of them. There was but one of the company who looked as though he knew exactly why he was there; and he kept conspicuously apart; walking to the far end of the platform, returning to the station door, then pacing up the track again, his chin sunk in the high collar of his overcoat, his burly shoulders drooping forward, his gait heavy and dogged. Presently he was approached by a tall, spare, grizzled man clad in a faded Grand Army suit, who shuffled out from the group and advanced with a certain deference, craning his neck forward until his back made the angle of a jack-knife three-quarters open.

"I reckon she's a-goin' to be pretty late agin to-night, Jim," he remarked in a squeaky falsetto. "S'pose it's the snow?"

"I don't know," responded the other man with a shade of annoyance, speaking from out an astonishing cataract of red beard that grew fiercely and thickly in all directions.

The spare man shifted the quill toothpick he was chewing to the other side of his mouth. "It ain't likely that anybody from the East will come with the corpse, I s'pose," he went on reflectively.

"I don't know," responded the other, more curtly than before.

"It's too bad he didn't belong to some lodge or other. I like an order funeral myself. They seem more appropriate for people of some reputation," the spare man continued, with an ingratiating concession in his shrill voice, as he carefully placed his toothpick in his vest pocket. He always carried the flag at the G. A. R. funerals in the town.

The heavy man turned on his heel, without replying, and walked up the siding. The spare man shuffled back to the uneasy group. "Jim's ez full ez a tick, ez ushel," he commented commiseratingly.

Just then a distant whistle sounded, and there was a shuffling of feet on the platform. A number of lanky boys of all ages appeared as suddenly and slimily as eels wakened by the crack of thunder; some came from the waiting-room, where they had been warming themselves by the red stove, or half asleep on the slat benches; others uncoiled themselves from baggage trucks or slid out of express wagons. Two clambered down from the driver's seat of a hearse that stood backed up against the siding. They straightened their stooping shoulders and lifted their heads, and a flash of momentary animation kindled their dull eyes at that cold, vibrant scream, the worldwide call for men. It stirred them like the note of a trumpet; just as it had often stirred the man who was coming home tonight, in his boyhood.

The night express shot, red as a rocket, from out the eastward marsh lands and wound along the river shore under the long lines of shivering poplars that sentinelled the meadows, the escaping steam hanging in grey masses against the pale sky and blotting out the Milky Way. In a moment the red glare from the headlight streamed up the snow-covered track before the siding and glittered on the wet, black rails. The burly man with the dishevelled red beard walked swiftly up the platform toward the approaching train, uncovering his head as he went. The group of men behind him hesitated, glanced questioningly at one another, and awkwardly followed his example. The train stopped, and the crowd shuffled up to the express car just as the door was thrown open, the spare man in the G. A. R. suit thrusting his head forward with curiosity. The express messenger appeared in the doorway, accompanied by a young man in a long ulster and travelling cap.

"Are Mr. Merrick's friends here?" inquired the young man.

The group on the platform swayed and shuffled uneasily. Philip Phelps, the banker, responded with dignity: "We have come to take charge of the body. Mr. Merrick's father is very feeble and can't be about."

"Send the agent out here," growled the express messenger, "and tell the operator to lend a hand."

The coffin was got out of its rough box and down on the snowy platform. The townspeople drew back enough to make room for it and then formed a close semicircle about it, looking curiously at the palm leaf which lay across the black cover. No one said anything. The baggage man stood by his truck, waiting to get at the trunks. The engine panted heavily, and the fireman dodged in and out among the wheels with his yellow torch and long oil-can, snapping the spindle boxes. The young Bostonian, one of the dead sculptor's pupils who had come with the body, looked about him help-lessly. He turned to the banker, the only one of that black, uneasy, stoop-shouldered group who seemed enough of an individual to be addressed.

"None of Mr. Merrick's brothers are here?" he asked uncertainly.

The man with the red beard for the first time stepped up and joined the group. "No, they have not come yet; the family is scattered. The body will be taken directly to the house." He stooped and took hold of one of the handles of the coffin.

"Take the long hill road up, Thompson, it will be easier on the horses," called the liveryman as the undertaker snapped the door of the hearse and prepared to mount to the driver's seat.

Laird, the red-bearded lawyer, turned again to the stranger: "We didn't know whether there would be any one with him or not," he explained. "It's a long walk, so you'd better go up in the hack." He pointed to a single battered conveyance, but the young man replied stiffly: "Thank you, but I think I will go up with the hearse. If you don't object," turning to the undertaker, "I'll ride with you."

They clambered up over the wheels and drove off in the starlight up the long, white hill toward the town. The lamps in the still village were shining from under the low, snow-burdened roofs; and beyond, on every side, the plains reached out into emptiness, peaceful and wide as the soft sky itself, and wrapped in a tangible, white silence.

When the hearse backed up to a wooden sidewalk before a naked, weather-beaten frame house, the same composite, ill-defined group that had stood upon the station siding was huddled about the gate. The front yard was an icy swamp, and a couple of warped planks, extending from the side-walk to the door, made a sort of rickety footbridge. The gate hung on one hinge, and was opened wide with difficulty. Steavens, the young stranger, noticed that something black was tied to the knob of the front door.

The grating sound made by the casket, as it was drawn from the hearse, was answered by a scream from the house; the front door was wrenched open, and a tall, corpulent woman rushed out bareheaded into the snow and flung herself upon the coffin, shrieking: "My boy, my boy! And this is how you've come home to me!"

As Steavens turned away and closed his eyes with a shudder of unut-terable repulsion, another woman, also tall, but flat and angular, dressed entirely in black, darted out of the house and caught Mrs. Merrick by the shoulders, crying sharply: "Come, come, mother; you mustn't go on like this!" Her tone changed to one of obsequious solemnity as she turned to the banker: "The parlour is ready, Mr. Phelps."

The bearers carried the coffin along the narrow boards, while the undertaker ran ahead with the coffin-rests. They bore it into a large, unheated room that smelled of dampness and disuse and furniture polish, and set it down under a hanging lamp ornamented with jingling glass prisms and before a "Rogers group" of John Alden and Priscilla, wreathed with smilax. Henry Steavens stared about him with the sickening conviction that there had been some horrible mistake, and that he had somehow arrived at the wrong destination. He looked painfully about over the clover-green Brussels, the fat plush upholstery; among the hand-painted china placques and panels, and vases, for some mark of identification, for something that might once conceivably have belonged to Harvey Merrick. It was not until he recognized his friend in the crayon portrait of a little boy in kilts and curls hanging above the piano, that he felt willing to let any of these people approach the coffin.

"Take the lid off, Mr. Thompson; let me see my boy's face," wailed the elder woman between her sobs. This time Steavens looked fearfully, almost beseechingly into her face, red and swollen under its masses of strong, black, shiny hair. He flushed, dropped his eyes, and then, almost incredulously, looked again. There was a kind of power about her face — a kind of brutal handsomeness, even, but it was scarred and furrowed by violence, and so coloured and coarsened by fiercer passions that grief seemed never to have laid a gentle finger there. The long nose was distended and knobbed at the end, and there were deep lines on either side of it; her heavy, black brows almost met across her forehead, her teeth were large and square, and set far apart — teeth that could tear. She filled the room; the men were obliterated, seemed tossed about like twigs in an angry water, and even Steavens felt himself being drawn into the whirlpool.

The daughter — the tall, raw-boned woman in crêpe, with a mourning comb in her hair which curiously lengthened her long face — sat stiffly upon the sofa, her hands, conspicuous for their large knuckles, folded in her lap, her mouth and eyes drawn down, solemnly awaiting the opening of the coffin. Near the door stood a mulatto woman, evidently a servant in the house, with a timid bearing and an emaciated face pitifully sad and gentle. She was weeping silently, the corner of her calico apron lifted to her eyes, occasionally suppressing a long, quivering sob. Steavens walked over and stood beside her.

Feeble steps were heard on the stairs, and an old man, tall and frail, odorous of pipe smoke, with shaggy, unkept grey hair and a dingy beard, tobacco stained about the mouth, entered uncertainly. He went slowly up to the coffin and stood rolling a blue cotton handkerchief between his hands, seeming so pained and embarrassed by his wife's orgy of grief that he had no consciousness of anything else.

"There, there, Annie, dear, don't take on so," he quavered timidly, putting out a shaking hand and awkwardly patting her elbow. She turned with a cry, and sank upon his shoulder with such violence that he tottered a little. He did not even glance toward the coffin, but continued to look at her with a dull, frightened, appealing expression, as a spaniel looks at the whip. His sunken cheeks slowly reddened and burned with miserable shame. When his wife rushed from the room, her daughter strode after her with set lips. The servant stole up to the coffin, bent over it for a moment, and then slipped away to the kitchen, leaving Steavens, the lawyer and the father to themselves. The old man stood trembling and looking down at his dead son's face. The sculptor's splendid head seemed even more noble in its rigid stillness than in life. The dark hair had crept down upon the wide forehead; the face seemed strangely long, but in it there was not that beautiful and chaste repose which we expect to find in the faces of the dead. The brows were so drawn that there were two deep lines above the beaked nose, and the chin was thrust forward defiantly. It was as though the strain of life had been so sharp and bitter that death could not at once wholly relax the tension and smooth the countenance into perfect peace — as though he were still guarding something precious and holy, which might even yet be wrested from him.

The old man's lips were working under his stained beard. He turned to the lawyer with timid deference: "Phelps and the rest are comin' back to set up with Harve, ain't they?" he asked. "Thank 'ee, Jim, thank 'ee." He brushed the hair back gently from his son's forehead. "He was a good boy, Jim; always a good boy. He was ez gentle ez a child and the kindest of 'em all — only we didn't none of us ever onderstand him." The tears trickled slowly down his beard and dropped upon the sculptor's coat.

"Martin, Martin. Oh, Martin! come here," his wife wailed from the top of the stairs. The old man started timorously: "Yes, Annie, I'm coming." He turned away, hesitated, stood for a moment in miserable indecision; then reached back and patted the dead man's hair softly, and stumbled from the room.

"Poor old man, I didn't think he had any tears left. Seems as if his eyes would have gone dry long ago. At his age nothing cuts very deep," remarked the lawyer.

Something in his tone made Steavens glance up. While the mother had been in the room, the young man had scarcely seen any one else; but now, from the moment he first glanced into Jim Laird's florid face and blood-shot eyes, he knew that he had found what he had been heartsick at not finding before — the feeling, the understanding, that must exist in some one, even here.

The man was red as his beard, with features swollen and blurred by dissipation, and a hot, blazing blue eye. His face was strained — that of a man who is controlling himself with difficulty — and he kept plucking at his beard with a sort of fierce resentment. Steavens, sitting by the window, watched him turn down the glaring lamp, still its jangling pendants with an angry gesture, and then stand with his hands locked behind him, staring down into the master's face. He could not help wondering what link there could have been between the porcelain vessel and so sooty a lump of potter's clay.

From the kitchen an uproar was sounding; when the dining-room door opened, the import of it was clear. The mother was abusing the maid for having forgotten to make the dressing for the chicken salad which had been prepared for the watchers. Steavens had never heard anything in the least like it; it was injured, emotional, dramatic abuse, unique and masterly in its excruciating cruelty, as violent and unrestrained as had been her grief of twenty minutes before. With a shudder of disgust the lawyer went into the dining-room and closed the door into the kitchen.

"Poor Roxy's getting it now," he remarked when he came back. "The Merricks took her out of the poor-house years ago; and if her loyalty would let her, I guess the poor old thing could tell tales that would curdle your blood. She's the mulatto woman who was standing in here a while ago, with her apron to her eyes. The old woman is a fury; there never was anybody like her for demonstrative piety and ingenious cruelty. She made Harvey's life a hell for him when he lived at home; he was so sick ashamed of it. I never could see how he kept himself so sweet."

"He was wonderful," said Steavens slowly, "wonderful; but until to-night I have never known how wonderful."

"That is the true and eternal wonder of it, anyway; that it can come even from such a dung heap as this," the lawyer cried, with a sweeping gesture which seemed to indicate much more than the four walls within which they stood.

"I think I'll see whether I can get a little air. The room is so close I am beginning to feel rather faint," murmured Steavens, struggling with one of the windows. The sash was stuck, however, and would not yield, so he sat down dejectedly and began pulling at his collar. The lawyer came over, loosened the sash with one blow of his red fist and sent the window up a few inches. Steavens thanked him, but the nausea which had been gradually climbing into his throat for the last half hour left him with but one desire — a desperate feeling that he must get away from this place with what was left of Harvey Merrick. Oh, he comprehended well enough now the quiet bitterness of the smile that he had seen so often on his master's lips!

He remembered that once, when Merrick returned from a visit home, he brought with him a singularly feeling and suggestive bas-relief of a thin, faded old woman, sitting and sewing something pinned to her knee; while a full-lipped, full-blooded little urchin, his trousers held up by a single gallows, stood beside her, impatiently twitching her gown to call her attention to a butterfly he had caught. Steavens, impressed by the tender and delicate modelling of the thin, tired face, had asked him if it were his mother. He remembered the dull flush that had burned up in the sculptor's face.

The lawyer was sitting in a rocking-chair beside the coffin, his head thrown back and his eyes closed. Steavens looked at him earnestly, puzzled at the line of the chin, and wondering why a man should conceal a feature of such distinction under that disfiguring shock of beard. Suddenly, as though he felt the young sculptor's keen glance, he opened his eyes.

"Was he always a good deal of an oyster?" he asked abruptly. "He was terribly shy as a boy."

"Yes, he was an oyster, since you put it so," rejoined Steavens. "Although he could be very fond of people, he always gave one the impression of being detached. He disliked violent emotion; he was reflective, and rather distrustful of himself — except, of course, as regarded his work. He was surefooted enough there. He distrusted men pretty thoroughly and women even more, yet somehow without believing ill of them. He was determined, indeed, to believe the best, but he seemed afraid to investigate."

"A burnt dog dreads the fire," said the lawyer grimly, and closed his eyes.

Steavens went on and on, reconstructing that whole miserable boyhood. All this raw, biting ugliness had been the portion of the man whose tastes were refined beyond the limits of the reasonable — whose mind was an exhaustless gallery of beautiful impressions, and so sensitive that the mere shadow of a poplar leaf flickering against a sunny wall would be etched and held there forever. Surely, if ever a man had the magic word in his finger tips, it was Merrick. Whatever he touched, he revealed its holiest secret; liberated it from enchantment and restored it to its pristine loveliness, like the Arabian prince who fought the enchantress spell for spell. Upon whatever he had come in contact with, he had left a beautiful record of the experience — a sort of ethereal signature; a scent, a sound, a colour that was his own.

Steavens understood now the real tragedy of his master's life; neither love nor wine, as many had conjectured; but a blow which had fallen earlier and cut deeper than these could have done — a shame not his, and yet so unescapably his, to hide in his heart from his very boyhood. And without — the frontier warfare; the yearning of a boy, cast ashore upon a desert of newness and ugliness and sordidness, for all that is chastened and old, and noble with traditions.

At eleven o'clock the tall, flat woman in black crêpe entered and announced that the watchers were arriving, and asked them "to step into the dining-room." As Steavens rose, the lawyer said dryly: "You go on — it'll be a good experience for you, doubtless; as for me, I'm not equal to that crowd tonight; I've had twenty years of them."

As Steavens closed the door after him he glanced back at the lawyer, sitting by the coffin in the dim light, with his chin resting on his hand.

The same misty group that had stood before the door of the express car shuffled into the dining-room. In the light of the kerosene lamp they separated and became individuals. The minister, a pale, feeble-looking man with white hair and blond chin-whiskers, took his seat beside a small side table and placed his Bible upon it. The Grand Army man sat down behind the stove and tilted his chair back comfortably against the wall, fishing his quill toothpick from his waistcoat pocket. The two bankers, Phelps and Elder, sat off in a corner behind the dinner-table, where they could finish their discussion of the new usury law and its effect on chattel security loans. The real estate agent, an old man with a smiling, hypocritical face, soon joined them. The coal and lumber dealer and the cattle shipper sat on opposite sides of the hard coal-burner, their feet on the nickelwork. Steavens took a book from his pocket and began to read. The talk around him ranged through various topics of local interest while the house was quieting down. When it was clear that the members of the family were in bed, the Grand Army man hitched his shoulders and, untangling his long legs, caught his heels on the rounds of his chair.

"S'pose there'll be a will, Phelps?" he queried in his weak falsetto.

The banker laughed disagreeably, and began trimming his nails with a pearl-handled pocket-knife.

"There'll scarcely be any need for one, will there?" he queried in his turn.

The restless Grand Army man shifted his position again, getting his knees still nearer his chin. "Why, the ole man says Harve's done right well lately," he chirped.

The other banker spoke up. "I reckon he means by that Harve ain't asked him to mortgage any more farms lately, so as he could go on with his education."

"Seems like my mind don't reach back to a time when Harve wasn't bein' edycated," tittered the Grand Army man.

There was a general chuckle. The minister took out his handkerchief and blew his nose sonorously. Banker Phelps closed his knife with a snap.

"It's too bad the old man's sons didn't turn out better," he remarked with reflective authority. "They never hung together. He spent money enough on Harve to stock a dozen cattle-farms and he might as well have poured it into Sand Creek. If Harve had stayed at home and helped nurse what little they had, and gone into stock on the old man's bottom farm, they might all have been well fixed. But the old man had to trust everything to tenants and was cheated right and left."

"Harve never could have handled stock none," interposed the cattle-man. "He hadn't it in him to be sharp. Do you remember when he bought Sander's mules for eight-year olds, when everybody in town knew that Sander's father-in-law give 'em to his wife for a wedding present eighteen years before, an' they was full-grown mules then."

Every one chuckled, and the Grand Army man rubbed his knees with a spasm of childish delight.

"Harve never was much account for anything practical, and he shore was never fond of work," began the coal and lumber dealer. "I mind the last time he was home; the day he left, when the old man was out to the barn helpin' his hand hitch up to take Harve to the train, and Cal Moots was patchin' up the fence, Harve, he come out on the step and sings out, in his ladylike voice: 'Cal Moots, Cal Moots! please come cord my trunk.' "

"That's Harve for you," approved the Grand Army man gleefully. "I kin hear him howlin' yet when he was a big feller in long pants and his mother used to whale him with a rawhide in the barn for lettin' the cows git foundered in the cornfield when he was drivin' 'em home from pasture. He killed a cow of mine that-a-way onct — a pure Jersey and the best milker I had, an' the ole man had to put up for her. Harve, he was watchin' the sun set acrost the marshes when the anamile got away; he argued that sunset was oncommon fine."

"Where the old man made his mistake was in sending the boy East to school," said Phelps, stroking his goatee and speaking in a deliberate, judicial tone. "There was where he got his head full of trapseing to Paris and all such folly. What Harve needed, of all people, was a course in some first-class Kansas City business college."

The letters were swimming before Steavens's eyes. Was it possible that these men did not understand, that the palm on the coffin meant nothing to them? The very name of their town would have remained forever buried in the postal guide had it not been now and again mentioned in the world in connection with Harvey Merrick's. He remembered what his master had said to him on the day of his death, after the congestion of both lungs had shut off any probability of recovery, and the sculptor had asked his pupil to send his body home. "It's not a pleasant place to be lying while the world is moving and doing and bettering," he had said with a feeble smile, "but it rather seems as though we ought to go back to the place we came from in the end. The townspeople will come in for a look at me; and after they have had their say I shan't have much to fear from the judgment of God. The wings of the Victory, in there" — with a weak gesture toward his studio — "will not shelter me."

The cattleman took up the comment. "Forty's young for a Merrick to cash in; they usually hang on pretty well. Probably he helped it along with whisky."

"His mother's people were not long lived, and Harvey never had a robust constitution," said the minister mildly. He would have liked to say more. He had been the boy's Sunday-school teacher, and had been fond of him; but he felt that he was not in a position to speak. His own sons had turned out badly, and it was not a year since one of them had made his last trip home in the express car, shot in a gambling-house in the Black Hills.

"Nevertheless, there is no disputin' that Harve frequently looked upon the wine when it was red, also variegated, and it shore made an oncommon fool of him," moralized the cattleman.

Just then the door leading into the parlour rattled loudly and every one started involuntarily, looking relieved when only Jim Laird came out. His red face was convulsed with anger, and the Grand Army man ducked his head when he saw the spark in his blue, blood-shot eye. They were all afraid of Jim; he was a drunkard, but he could twist the law to suit his client's needs as no other man in all western Kansas could do; and there were many who tried. The lawyer closed the door gently behind him, leaned back against it and folded his arms, cocking his head a little to one side. When he assumed this attitude in the court-room, ears were always pricked up, as it usually foretold a flood of withering sarcasm.

"I've been with you gentlemen before," he began in a dry, even tone, "when you've sat by the coffins of boys born and raised in this town; and, if I remember rightly, you were never any too well satisfied when you checked them up. What's the matter, anyhow? Why is it that reputable young men are as scarce as millionaires in Sand City? It might almost seem to a stranger that there was some way something the matter with your progressive town. Why did Ruben Sayer, the brightest young lawyer you ever turned out, after he had come home from the university as straight as a die, take to drinking and forge a check and shoot himself? Why did Bill Merrit's son die of the shakes in a saloon in Omaha? Why was Mr. Thomas's son, here, shot in a gambling-house? Why did young Adams burn his mill to beat the insurance companies and go to the pen?"

The lawyer paused and unfolded his arms, laying one clenched fist quietly on the table. "I'll tell you why. Because you drummed nothing but money and knavery into their ears from the time they wore knickerbockers; because you carped away at them as you've been carping here tonight, holding our friends Phelps and Elder up to them for their models, as our grandfathers held up George Washington and John Adams. But the boys, worse luck, were young, and raw at the business you put them to; and how could they match coppers with such artists as Phelps and Elder? You wanted them to be successful rascals; they were only unsuccessful ones — that's all the difference. There was only one boy ever raised in this borderland between ruffianism and civilization, who didn't come to grief, and you hated Harvey Merrick more for winning out than you hated all the other boys who got under the wheels. Lord, Lord, how you did hate him! Phelps, here, is fond of saying that he could buy and sell us all out any time he's a mind to; but he knew Harve wouldn't have given a tinker's damn for his bank and all his cattle-farms put together; and a lack of appreciation, that way, goes hard with Phelps.

"Old Nimrod, here, thinks Harve drank too much; and this from such as Nimrod and me!

"Brother Elder says Harve was too free with the old man's money — fell short in filial consideration, maybe. Well, we can all remember the very tone in which brother Elder swore his own father was a liar, in the county court; and we all know that the old man came out of that partnership with his son as bare as a sheared lamb. But maybe I'm getting personal, and I'd better be driving ahead at what I want to say."

The lawyer paused a moment, squared his heavy shoulders, and went on: "Harvey Merrick and I went to school together, back East. We were dead in earnest, and we wanted you all to be proud of us some day. We meant to be great men. Even I, and I haven't lost my sense of humour, gentlemen, I meant to be a great man. I came back here to practise, and I found you didn't in the least want me to be a great man. You wanted me to be a shrewd lawyer — oh, yes! Our veteran here wanted me to get him an increase of pension, because he had dyspepsia; Phelps wanted a new county survey that would put the widow Wilson's little bottom farm inside his south line; Elder wanted to lend money at 5 per cent a month, and get it collected; old Stark here wanted to wheedle old women up in Vermont into investing their annuities in real-estate mortgages that are not worth the paper they are written on. Oh, you needed me hard enough, and you'll go on needing me; and that's why I'm not afraid to plug the truth home to you this once.

"Well, I came back here and became the damned shyster you wanted me to be. You pretend to have some sort of respect for me; and yet you'll stand up and throw mud at Harvey Merrick, whose soul you couldn't dirty and whose hands you couldn't tie. Oh, you're a discriminating lot of Christians! There have been times when the sight of Harvey's name in some Eastern paper has made me hang my head like a whipped dog; and, again, times when I liked to think of him off there in the world, away from all this hog-wallow, doing his great work and climbing the big, clean upgrade he'd set for himself.

"And we? Now that we've fought and lied and sweated and stolen, and hated as only the disappointed strugglers in a bitter, dead little Western town know how to do, what have we got to show for it? Harvey Merrick wouldn't have given one sunset over your marshes for all you've got put together, and you know it. It's not for me to say why, in the inscrutable wisdom of God, a genius should ever have been called from this place of hatred and bitter waters; but I want this Boston man to know that the drivel he's been hearing here to-night is the only tribute any truly great man could ever have from such a lot of sick, side-tracked, burnt-dog, land-poor sharks as the here-present financiers of Sand City — upon which town may God have mercy!"

The lawyer thrust out his hand to Steavens as he passed him, caught up his overcoat in the hall, and had left the house before the Grand Army man had had time to lift his ducked head and crane his long neck about at his fellows.

Next day Jim Laird was drunk and unable to attend the funeral services. Steavens called twice at his office, but was compelled to start East without seeing him. He had a presentiment that he would hear from him again, and left his address on the lawyer's table; but if Laird found it, he never acknowledged it. The thing in him that Harvey Merrick had loved must have gone under ground with Harvey Merrick's coffin; for it never spoke again, and Jim got the cold he died of driving across the Colorado mountains to defend one of Phelps's sons who had got into trouble out there by cutting government timber.

{1905}

HORACE ANNESLEY VACHELL
{1861–1955}

Of all the many novels of English public school life, Horace Annesley Vachell's *The Hill: A Romance of Friendship* (1905) is perhaps the finest, and unquestionably the gayest. Thomas Hughes's *Tom Brown's Schooldays* (1857) is the *Ur* English public school novel, but it contains only a single allusion to homosexual practices: "He was one of the miserable little pretty white-handed curly-headed boys, petted and pampered by some of the big fellows, who wrote their verses for them, taught them to drink and use bad language, and did all they could to spoil them for everything in this world and the next."

The homosexual aspect of *The Hill* is overt, but few of those who knew Vachell believed that he himself was aware of it: for him, the book was a fond story of friendship at Harrow — a friendship of which, as the author wrote in the dedication to fellow Harrovian George W. E. Russell, "Only the elect are capable." Still, to paraphrase Benedetto Croce, just because Vachell could not, or did not, recognize the campiness of the book does not mean that it is not there. The concert scene in chapter 6 is only the most extravagantly homosexual scene in *The Hill*; there are little touches, even flourishes, throughout: one of the boys decorates his part of the apartment that he shares with three other boys with "four pretty reproductions of French engravings, and with the help of three yards of velveteen and some cheap lace . . . a very passable imitation of the mantel-cover in his mother's London boudoir"; the older boys often make the younger ones (their "fags") remove their dirty football-boots, "but Lawrence, a manly youth, scorned sybaritic services." *The Hill* is, moreover, proof that the English conception of male friendship is so thoroughly homosexual that it passes detection as such. Mark Twain's Tom Sawyer and Huckleberry Finn do not interact in this way. (Lord Byron, himself a Harrovian, described the school as a place where "friendships were form'd, too/romantic to last.") ❧

FROM *The Hill: A Romance of Friendship*

A REVELATION

Upon the last Saturday of the term the School Concert took place. Few of the boys in the Manor, and none out of it, knew that John Verney had been chosen to sing the treble solo; always an attractive number of the programme. John, indeed, was painfully shy in regard to his singing, so shy that he never told Desmond that he had a voice. And the music-master, enchanted by its quality, impressed upon his pupil the expediency of silence. He wished to surprise the School.

The concerts at Harrow take place in the great Speech-room. Their characteristic note is the singing of Harrow songs. To any boy with an ear for music and a heart susceptible of emotion these songs must appeal profoundly, because both words and music seem to enshrine all that is noble and uplifting in life. And, sung by the whole School (as are most of the choruses), their message becomes curiously emphatic. The spirit of the Hill is acclaimed, gladly, triumphantly, unmistakably, by Harrovians repeating the creed of their fathers, knowing that creed will be so repeated by their sons and sons' sons. Was it happy chance or a happier sagacity which decreed that certain verses should be sung by the School Twelve, who have struggled through form after form and know (and have not yet had time to forget) the difficulties and temptations which beset all boys? They, to whom their fellows unanimously accord respect at least, and often — as in the case of a Captain of the Cricket Eleven — enthusiastic admiration and fealty; these, the gods, in a word, deliver their injunction, transmit, in turn, what has been transmitted to them, and invite their successors to receive it. To many how poignant must be the reflection that the trust they are about to resign might have been better administered! But to many there must come upon the wings of those mighty, rushing choruses the assurance that the Power which has upheld them in the past will continue to uphold them in the future. In many — would one could say in all — is quickened, for the first time, perhaps, a sense of what they owe to the Hill, the overwhelming debt which never can be discharged.

Desmond sat beside Scaife. Scaife boasted that he could not tell "God save the Queen" from "The Dead March in Saul." He confessed that the concert bored him. Desmond, on the other hand, was always touched by music, or, indeed, by anything appealing to an imagination which gilded all things and persons. He was Scaife's friend, not only (as John discovered) because Scaife had a will strong enough to desire and secure that friend-ship, but because — a subtler reason — he had never yet seen Scaife as he was, but always as he might have been.

Desmond told Scaife that he could not understand why John had bot-tled up the fact that he was chosen to sing upon such an occasion. Scaife smiled contemptuously.

"You never bottle up anything, Cæsar," said he.

"Why should I? And why should he?"

"I expect he'll make an awful ass of himself."

"Oh no, he won't," Desmond replied. "He's a clever fellow is Jonathan."

As he gave John his nickname, Desmond's charming voice softened. A boy of less quick perceptions than Scaife would have divined that the speaker liked John, liked him, perhaps, better than he knew. Scaife frowned.

"There are several Old Harrovians," he said, indicating the seats reserved for them. "It's queer to me that they come down for this cater-wauling."

Desmond glanced at him sharply, with a wrinkle between his eye-brows. For the moment he looked as if he were short-sighted, as if he were trying to define an image somewhat blurred, conscious that the image itself was clear enough, that the fault lay in the obscurity of his own vision.

"They come down because they're keen," he replied. "My governor can't leave his office, or he'd be here. I like to see 'em, don't you, Demon?"

"I could worry along without 'em," the Demon replied, half-smiling. "You see," he added, with the blend of irony and pathos which always captivated his friend, "you see, my dear old chap, I'm the first of my family at Harrow, and the sight of all your brothers and uncles and fathers makes me feel like Mark Twain's good man, rather — *lonesome.*"

At once Desmond responded, clutching Scaife's arm.

"You're going to be Captain of the cricket and footer Elevens, and School racquet-player, and a monitor; and after you leave you'll come down here, and you'll see that Harrow hasn't forgotten you, and then you'll know why these fellows cut engagements. My governor says that an hour at a School Concert is the finest tonic in the world for an Old Harrovian."

"Oh, shut up!" said Scaife; "you make me feel more of an outsider than poor Snowball." He glanced at a youth sitting close to them. Snow-ball was as black as a coal: the son of the Sultan of the Sahara. "Yes, Cæsar, you can't get away from it, I *am* an 'alien.' "

"You're a silly old ass! I say, who's the guest of honour?"

Next to the Head Master was sitting a thin man upon whose face were fixed hundreds of eyes. The School had not been told that a famous Field Marshal, the hero of a hundred fights, was coming to the concert. And, indeed, he had accepted an invitation given at the last moment — accepted it, moreover, on the understanding that his visit was to be informal. None the less, his face was familiar to all readers of illustrated papers. And, suddenly, conviction seized the boys that a conqueror was among them, an Old Etonian, making, possibly, his first visit to the Hill. Scaife whispered his name to Desmond.

"Why, of course," Desmond replied eagerly. "How splendid!"

He leaned forward, devouring the hero with his eyes, trying to pierce the bronzed skin, to read the record. From his seat upon the stage John, also, stared at the illustrious guest. John was frightfully nervous, but looking at the veteran he forgot the fear of the recruit. Both Desmond and he were wondering what "it felt like" to have done so much. And — they compared notes afterwards — each boy deplored the fact that the great man was not an Old Harrovian. There he sat, cool, calm, slightly impassive. John thought he must be rather tired, as a man ought to be tired after a life of strenuous endeavour and achievement. He had done — so John reflected — an awful lot. Even now, he remained the active, untiring servant of Queen and country. And he had taken time to come down to Harrow to hear the boys sing. And, dash it all! he, John, was going to sing to him.

At that moment Desmond was whispering to Scaife —

"I say, Demon; I'm jolly glad that I've not got to sing before *him*. I bet Jonathan is in a funk."

"A big bit of luck," replied Scaife, reflectively. Then, seeing the surprise on Desmond's face, he added, "If Jonathan can sing — and I suppose he can, or he wouldn't be chosen — this is a chance —"

"Of what?"

"Cæsar, sometimes I think you've no brains. Why, a chance of attracting the notice of a tremendous swell — a man, they say, who never forgets — never! Jonathan may want a commission in the Guards, as I do; and if he pleases the great man, he may get it."

"Jonathan's not thinking of that," said Desmond. "Shush-h-h!"

The singers stood up. They faced the Field-Marshal, and he faced them. He looked hardest at Lawrence, pointed out to him by the Head Master. Perhaps he was thinking of India; and the name of Lawrence indelibly cut upon the memories of all who fought in the Mutiny. And Lawrence, you may be sure, met his glance steadily, being fortified by it. The good fellow felt terribly distressed, because he was leaving the Hill; and, being a humble gentleman, the old songs served to remind him, not of what he had done, but of what he had left undone — the words unspoken, the actions never now to be performed. The chief caught his eye, smiled, and nodded, as if to say, "I claim your father's son as a friend."

When the song came to an end, John was seized with an almost irresistible impulse to bolt. His turn had come. He must stand up to sing before nearly six hundred boys, who would stare down with gravely critical and courteously amused eyes. And already his legs trembled as if he were seized of a palsy. John knew that he could sing. His mother, who sang gloriously, had trained him. From her he had inherited his vocal cords, and from her he drew the knowledge how to use them.

When he stood up, pale and trembling, the silence fell upon his sensibilities as if it were a dense, yellow fog. This silence, as John knew, was an unwritten law. The small boy selected to sing to the School, as the representative of the School, must have every chance. Let his voice be heard! The master playing the accompaniment paused and glanced at his pupil. John, however, was not looking at him; he was looking within at a John he despised — a poltroon, a deserter about to run from his first engagement. He knew that the introduction to the song was being played a second time, and he saw the Head Master whispering to his guest. Paralysed with terror, John's intuition told him that the Head Master was murmuring, "That's the nephew of John Verney. Of course you know him?" And the Field Marshal nodded. And then he looked at John, as John had seen him look at Lawrence, with the same flare of recognition in the steel-grey eyes. Out of the confused welter of faces shone that pair of eyes — twin beacons flashing their message of encouragement and salvation to a fellow-creature in peril — at least, so John interpreted that piercing glance. It seemed to say, far plainer than words, "I have stood alone as you stand; I have felt my knees as wax; I have wished to run away. But — *I didn't*. Nor must you. Open your mouth and sing!"

So John opened his mouth and sang. The first verse of the lyric went haltingly.

Scaife growled to Desmond, "He *is* going to make an ass of himself."

And Desmond, meeting Scaife's eyes, half thought that the speaker wished that John would fail — that he grudged him a triumph. None the less, the first verse, sung feebly, with wrong phrasing and imperfect articulation, revealed the quality of the boy's voice; and this quality Desmond recognised, as he would have recognised a fine painting or a bit of perfect porcelain. All his short life his father had trained him to look for and acclaim quality, whether in things animate or inanimate. He caught hold of Scaife's arm.

"Make an ass of himself!" he whispered back. "Not he. But he may make an ass of me."

Even as he spoke he was aware that tears were horribly near his eyes. Some catch in John's voice, some subtle inflection, had smitten his heart, even as the prophet smote the rock.

"Rot!" said Scaife, angrily.

He was angry, furiously angry, because he saw that Cæsar was beyond his reach, whirled innumerable leagues away by the sound of another's voice. John had begun the second verse. He stared, as if hypnotised, straight into the face of the great soldier, who in turn stared as steadily at John; and John was singing like a lark, with a lark's spontaneous delight in singing, with an ease and self-abandonment which charmed eye almost as much as ear. Higher and higher rose the clear, sexless notes, till two of them met and mingled in a triumphant trill. To Desmond, that trill was the answer to the quavering, troubled cadences of the first verse; the vindication of the spirit soaring upwards unfettered by the flesh — the pure spirit, not released from the pitiful human clay without a fierce struggle. At that moment Desmond loved the singer — the singer who called to him out of heaven, who summoned his friend to join him, to see what he saw — "the vision splendid."

John began the third and last verse. The famous soldier covered his face with his hand, releasing John's eyes, which ascended, like his voice, till they met joyfully the eyes of Desmond. At last he was singing to his friend — *and his friend knew it.* John saw Desmond's radiant smile, and across that ocean of faces he smiled back. Then, knowing that he was nearer to his friend than he had ever been before, he gathered together his energies for the last line of the song — a line to be repeated three times, loudly at first, then more softly, diminishing to the merest whisper of sound, the voice celestial melting away in the ear of earth-bound mortals. The master knew well the supreme difficulty of producing properly this last attenuated note; but he knew also that John's lungs were strong, that the vocal cords had never been strained. Still, if the boy's breath failed; if anything — a smile, a frown, a cough — distracted his attention, the end would be — weakness, failure. He wondered why John was staring so fixedly in one direction.

Now — now!

The piano crashed out the last line; but far above it, dominating it, floated John's flute-like notes. The master played the same bars for the second time. He was still able to sustain, if it were necessary, a quavering, imperfect phrase. But John delivered the second repetition without a mistake, singing easily from the chest. The master put his foot upon the soft pedal.

Nobody was watching him. Had anyone done so, he would have seen the perspiration break upon the musician's forehead. The piano purred its accompaniment. Then, in the middle of the phrase, the master lifted his hands and held them poised above the instrument. John had to sing three notes unsupported. He was smiling and staring at Desmond. The first note came like a question from the heart of a child; the second, higher up, might have been interpreted as an echo to the innocent interrogation of the first, the head no wiser than the heart; but the third and last note had nothing in it of interrogation: it was an answer, all-satisfying — sublime! Nor did it seem to come from John at all, but from above, falling like a snowflake out of the sky.

And then, for one immeasurable moment — *silence.*

John slipped back to his seat, crimson with bashfulness, while the School thundered applause. The Field Marshal shouted "Encore!" as loudly as any fag; but the Head Master whispered —

"We don't encourage *encores.* A small boy's head is easily turned."

"Not his," the hero replied.

Two numbers followed, and then the School stood up, and with them all Old Harrovians, to sing the famous National Anthem of Harrow, "Forty Years on." Only the guests and the masters remained seated.

> "Forty years on, growing older and older,
>   Shorter in wind, as in memory long,
> Feeble of foot and rheumatic of shoulder,
>   What will it help you that once you were strong?
> God give us bases to guard or beleaguer,
>   Games to play out, whether earnest or fun;
> Fights for the fearless and goals for the eager,
>   Twenty, and thirty, and forty years on!
> Follow up! Follow up! Follow up! Follow up!
>   Till the field ring again and again,
>   With the tramp of the twenty-two men.
>   Follow — up!"

As the hundreds of voices, past and present indissolubly linked together, imposed the mandate, *"Follow up!"* the Head Master glanced at his guest, but left unsaid the words about to be uttered. Tears were trickling down the cheeks of the man who, forty years before, had won his Sovereign's Cross — For Valour.

After the concert, but before he left the Speech-room, the Field Marshal asked the Head Master to introduce Lawrence and John, and, of course, the Head of the School. When John came up, there was a twinkle in the veteran's eye.

"Ha — ha!" said he; "you were in a precious funk, John Verney."

"I was, sir," said John.

"Gad! Don't I know the feeling? Well, well," he chuckled, smiling at John, "you climbed up higher than I've ever been in my life. What was it — hey? 'F' in 'alt?' "

" 'G,' sir."

"You sang delightfully. Tell your uncle to bring you to see me next time you are in town. You must consider me a friend," he chuckled again — "an old friend. And look ye here," his pleasant voice sank to a whisper, "I daren't tip these tremendous swells, but I feel that I can take such a liberty with you. Shush-h-h! Good-bye."

John scurried away, bursting with pride, feeling to the core the strong grip of the strong man, hearing the thrill of his voice, the thrill which had vibrated in thousands of soldier-hearts. Outside, Fluff was awaiting him.

"Oh, Jonathan, you can sing, and no mistake!"

"Five — six — seven mistakes," John answered.

The boys laughed.

John told Fluff what the hero had said to him, and showed the piece of gold.

"What ho! The Creameries! Come on, Esmé!"

At the Creameries several boys congratulated John, and the Caterpillar said —

"You astonished us, Jonathan; 'pon my soul you did! Have a 'dringer' with me? And Fluff too? By the way, be sure to keep your hair clipped close. These singing fellows with manes may be lions in their own estimation, but the world looks upon 'em as asses."

"That's not bad for you, Caterpillar," said a boy in the Fifth.

"Not my own," said the Caterpillar, solemnly — "my father's. I take from him all the good things I can get hold of."

John polished off his "dringer," listening to the chaff, but his thoughts were with Desmond. He had an intuition that Desmond would have something to say to him. As soon as possible he returned to the Manor.

There he found his room empty. John shut the door and sat down, looking about him half-absently. The Duffer had not contributed much to the mural decoration, saying, loftily, that he preferred bare walls to rubbishy engravings and Japanese fans. But, with curious inconsistency (for he was the least vain of mortals), he had bought at a "leaving auction" a three-sided mirror — once the property of a great buck in the Sixth. The Duffer had got it cheap, but he never used it. The lower boys remarked to each other that Duff didn't dare to look in it, because what he would see must not only break his heart but shatter the glass. Generally, it hung, folded up, close to the window, and the Duffer said that it would come in handy when he took to shaving.

John's eye rested on this mirror, vacantly at first, then with gathering intensity. Presently he got up, crossed the room, opened the two folding panels, and examined himself attentively, pursing up his lips and frowning. He could see John Verney full face, three-quarter face, and half face. And he could see the back of his head, where an obstinate lock of hair stuck out like a drake's tail. John was so occupied in taking stock of his personal disadvantages that a ringing laugh quite startled him.

"Why, Jonathan! Giving yourself a treat — eh?"

John turned a solemn face to Desmond. "I think my head is hideous," he said ruefully.

"What do you mean?"

"It's too long," John explained. "I like a nice round head like yours, Cæsar. I wish I wasn't so ugly."

Desmond laughed. John always amused him. Cæsar was easily amused, saw the funny side of things, and contrasts tickled his fancy agreeably. But he stopped laughing when he realised that John was hurt. Then, quickly, impulsively, he said —

"Your head is all right, old Jonathan. And your voice is beautiful." He spoke seriously, staring at John as he had stared in the Speech-room when John began to sing. "I came here to tell you that. I felt queer when you were singing — quite weepsy, you know. You like me, old Jonathan, don't you?"

"Awfully," said John.

"Why did you look at me when you sang that last verse? Did you know that you were looking at me?"

"Yes."

"You looked at me because — well, because — bar chaff — you — liked — me?"

"Yes."

"You — you like me better than any other fellow in the school?"

"Yes; better than any other fellow in the world."

"Is it possible?"

"I have always felt that way since — yes — since the very first minute I saw you."

"How rum! I've forgotten just where we did meet — for the first time."

"I shall never forget," said John, in the same slow, deliberate fashion, never taking his eyes from Desmond's face. Ever since he had sung, he had known that this moment was coming. "I shall never forget it," he repeated — "never. You were standing near the Chapel. I was poking about alone, trying to find the shop where we buy our straws. And I was feeling as all new boys feel, only more so, because I didn't know a soul."

"Yes," said Desmond, gravely; "you told me that. I remember now; I mistook you for young Hardacre."

"You smiled at me, Cæsar. It warmed me through and through. I suppose that when a fellow is starving he never forgets the first meal after it."

"I say. Go on; this is awfully interesting."

"I can remember what you wore. One of your bootlaces had burst —"

"Well; I'm —"

"I had a wild sort of wish to run off and buy you a new lace —"

"Of all the queer starts I —"

"Afterwards," John continued, "I tried to suck-up. I asked you to come and have some 'food.' Do you remember?"

"I'll bet I came, Jonathan."

"No; you didn't. You said 'No.'"

"Dash it all! I certainly said, 'No, thanks.'"

"I daresay. The 'No' hurt awfully because I did feel that it was cheek asking you."

"Jonathan, you funny old buster, I'll never say 'No' again. 'Pon my word, I won't. So I said 'No.' That's odd, because it's not easy for me to say 'No.' The governor pointed that out last hols. Somehow, I can't say 'No,' particularly if there's any excitement in saying 'Yes.' And my beastly 'No' hurt, did it? Well, I'm very, *very* sorry."

He held out his hand, which John took. Then, for a moment, there was a pause before Desmond continued awkwardly —

"You know, Jonathan, that the Demon is my pal. You like him better than you did, don't you?"

John had the tact not to speak; but he shook his head dolefully.

"And I couldn't chuck him, even if I wanted to, which I don't — which I don't," he repeated, with an air of satisfying himself rather than John. And John divined that Scaife's hold upon Desmond's affections was not so strong as he had deemed it to be. Desmond continued, "But I want you, too, old Jonathan, and if — if —"

"All right," said John, nobly. He perceived that Desmond's loyalty to Scaife made him hesitate and flush. "I understand, Cæsar, and if I can't be first, let me be second; only, remember, with me you're first, rain or shine."

Desmond looked uneasy. "Isn't that a case of 'heads I win, tails you lose?'"

John considered; then he smiled cheerfully, "You know you are a winner, Cæsar. You're cut out for a winner; you can win whatever you want to win."

"Oh, that's all rot," said Desmond. He looked very grave, and in his eyes lay shadows which John had never seen before.

And so ended John's first year at Harrow.

{1905}

CHARLES KENNETH SCOTT-MONCRIEFF
{1889–1930}

At the age of eighteen, Charles Kenneth Scott-Moncrieff (later to translate Marcel Proust's *À la recherche du temps perdu* into English) included his story "Evensong and Morwe Song" in the pageant issue of *New Field*, the literary magazine of which he was editor at Winchester School. This accomplished piece of fiction revealed a young writer years ahead of his time; in contrast to most of his elders, Scott-Moncrieff was not only willing to write openly about homosexuality, but to publish the work under his own name. Nor was this decision without its consequences; indeed, the story caused such a scandal at Winchester that the magazine was immediately suppressed, and its editor expelled. ("Evensong and Morwe Song" was republished in the twenties by Francis Edward Murray, in a limited edition — none of which were for sale.) At Winchester, Scott-Moncrieff's reading included E. F. Benson's *The Challoners* (he thought it "*very* good"), Horace Vachell's *The Hill*, and Henry James. (This information is given in his posthumously published *Memories and Letters*, which evades mention of the debacle by reporting simply that "The summer of 1908 brought Winchester School life to an end for Scott Moncrieff.")

Later, as Timothy d'Arch Smith records in *Love in Earnest* (1970), Scott-Moncrieff was the dedicatee of a verse-play entitled *Achilles in Scyros*, written by a Cambridge undergraduate, Philip Gillespie Bainbrigge, and published by the Cayme Press, an organ of the Uranian poets. In the preface, Bainbrigge addresses Scott-Moncrieff as follows:

> Here Aphrodite is not: Eros boy-like
> Plays his boy's games among the leaves so green,
> Bare-breeched; no decent tendril hides his toy (like
> Some curious peach) that nestles warm between
> His dainty rosy thighs — the toy that's been
> A deadlier shaft to pierce the scholar's marrow
> Than his more widely celebrated arrow.

In the twenties, Scott-Moncrieff moved to Florence, where he became part of an expatriate literary community among whose members were Reginald Turner, Norman Douglas, Ronald Firbank, Vernon Lee, Radclyffe Hall, and the Uranian poet Lord Henry Somerset (who had had to leave England some years back after his wife had caught him *in fla-*

grante delicto with a boy called Henry Smith). Florence at that time had a reputation as a haven for homosexual expatriates; a place where, as Harold Acton wrote in *Memoirs of an Aesthete* (1948), "One was continually hearing that certain men . . . were queer, not that it made much difference to their popularity: on the contrary! The queerer the dearer." It also had a reputation as a city whose boys maintained a very relaxed attitude toward sex with other men. (As early as the sixteenth century, a German dictionary was defining "Florenzer" as "buggerer," and the verb "Florenzen" as "to bugger.")

In his privately printed *Adventures of a Bookseller*, Pino Orioli described Scott-Moncrieff as

> not what I should call a lovable creature; on the contrary, nobody was more prone to take offense . . . His foot had been wounded during the War. This gave him some pain and a limp and may have made him more irritable than he need have been. He also thought that his merits as a translator were sadly underestimated by the public; it was a perennial grievance to him. . . .
>
> We sometimes walked about the pine woods at Viareggio where I had an opportunity of seeing how he did his work. He carried in his left hand the French volume he was translating, read a few lines of it, interrupted his reading in order to talk to me, and then took a notebook out of his pocket and wrote in English the few lines he had just read, leaning against a pine tree. Then the reading would begin again, then the talk, then the translation into English.

Perhaps the character of the translator's Tuscan life can best be intuited from this remark by Evelyn Waugh, who at one time tried to become Scott-Moncrieff's secretary. When the chance fell through, the youthful novelist mourned his lost fantasy of "drinking Chianti under olive trees and listening to discussions of all the most iniquitous outcasts of Europe." As is common in English responses to Italy, iniquity, for Waugh, had a distinct veneer of glamour.

Scott-Moncrieff died in Rome at the age of forty, where Norman Douglas, visiting him on his deathbed, described him as "shrivelled into a monkey, and not recognisable." He was buried in the Verano cemetery, but because his bones were later transferred to the communal ossuary he no longer has a grave. A fitting, if ironic, epitaph to his memory is his own poem "Growing Old Early" (1920):

Lovely were all my days of Spring
    With colour, fragrance, song and light;

And each slow Summer evening
    Passed, lovely-fair, to night.

Yet now, in Autumn's granary, pent
    From splitting frost and scattering wind,
Security in banishment,
    Rest after growth I find.

Evensong and Morwe Song

"If Evensong and Morwe-song accorde"
— CHAUCER, *Prologue to the Canterbury Tales,* I, 380.

I.

.... "And if we are found out?" asked Maurice. He was still on his knees in the thicket, and, as he looked up to where his companion stood in an awkward fumbling attitude, his face seemed even more than usually pale and meagre in the grey broken light. It was with rather forced nonchalance that Carruthers answered "O, the sack, I suppose" — and he stopped aghast at the other's expression. Then as only at one other time in a long and well-rewarded life did he feel that a millstone round his neck might perhaps be less offensive than the picture of those small, startled features hung for all eternity before his eyes.

But all went well. Each returned to his house (they were at school at Gainsborough — this in the early eighties) without let or hindrance. When in the next autumn but one Carruthers went up to Oxford I doubt if he remembered his debt to the Creator of the soul of Edward Hilary Maurice. "After all, had he been so scrupulous?" he argued, "I am no worse than a dozen others and Maurice no better. Indeed, Maurice is getting quite a reputation. How dreadful all that sort of thing is!" And whatever he may have remembered at Oxford, we may be certain that when with his charming nonchalance he knelt before a golfer-bishop of no mean hysterical attractions to receive deacon's orders, he presented himself as a pure, sincere, and fragrant vessel, capable of containing any amount of truth.

II.

William Carruthers turned a trifle uneasily in his stiff, new revolving chair as his victims entered. It was the last day of October. For a little more than a month he had occupied the headmaster's study at Cheddar, a school for which as a pious Gainsburgher he retained a profound contempt. This contempt was hardly diminished (to do him justice his salary was but moderate) by his having already to deal with one of those painful incidents which occur in second-rate schools almost as frequently as in the sacred Nine.

What he said to them is not our province. His weighty arguments (mainly borrowed from the boys' housemaster), his ears deaf to excuse or contradiction, his flaying sarcasm and his pessimistic prophecies drew great salt tears from the younger boy's eyes on to the gaudy new magisterial carpet before that unfortunate was sent away heavily warned against further outbreaks, and he was left free to damn the other in this world and disparage him in the next. He eyed him witheringly for some minutes, and then whispered: "Ah, Hilary! It were better for thee that a millstone were hanged about thy neck, and thou cast into the sea, than that thou shouldest offend one of these little ones." He had previously consulted a concordance, and in variously impressive tones rehearsed this and the parallel passages. Chance or inspiration might have prompted Hilary, whose whole life was being ruined to correct his first offence, to cite the following verses (read in Chapel an evening or two before) which enjoin that seven offences on the same day should be balanced by the offender's penitence. But he was silent. Carruthers, supposing him unrepentant and inveterate, lashed him with abuse that ranged from ribaldry to a little less than rhetoric; and finally dismissed him to remove his effects from his house and from Cheddar, whither he might, if well behaved, return in ten years' time.

These effectual workings over, the headmaster turned to the second part of the expulsion office — the letter to parent or guardian. It was then that he remembered his ignorance of the boy's address, and with some repugnance turned to a gaudy volume inscribed *Ordo Cheddarensis* in gold upon a red, blue and green back and sides, which had appeared there synchronically with himself. In the index he was faintly surprised to find: "Hilary, see Maurice, J. E. H."; and he was annoyed at the consequent delay. At last he found the reference, laid down the book (which crackled cheerily in its stiff, cheap binding), and read up his man:

> "Maurice, James Edward Hilary (now J.E.H. Hilary). Born 13 Sept., 18 —. Only son of Edward Hilary Maurice (now E.H. Hilary), of Leafsleigh, Co. Southampton, who on succeeding to that estate assumed the name of Hilary in lieu of that of Maurice. Addresses: 13 Worcester Gate Terrace, W.; Leafsleigh, Christchurch Road, R. S. O., Hants."

As he was transcribing the address this most consummate of headmasters received an unpleasant shock. Its pages released, the book crackled inexpensively and closed itself. In its place lay or floated a picture of two boys in a thicket; of the one's charming nonchalance; of terror sickening the other, a child that had just lost its soul. When at Oxford Carruthers had received a letter in which Maurice said: "It is not altogether because I must leave Gainsborough that I curse you now. But I can never send my sons there, nor to any decent school. Shorncliffe must receive them, or Milk-manthaite or even Cheddar — some hole that we have thought hardly worth our scorn. Because my sons will inherit the shame which you implanted, I now for the last time call you. . . ." Carruthers' fine British reserve had elided the next words from his memory.

Before his ordination he had prayed for spiritual armour, and had received a coat of self-satisfaction which had so far held out against all assaults of man or woman. Now it felt rusty. Rather half-heartedly he rang and told the butler to send someone to Mr. Herbertson's house to tell Mr. Hilary that the headmaster wanted him again and at once. Then he picked up the sheet of tremendously coat-armoured school notepaper, upon which a laboured and almost illegible "My dear Sir" was begun. On it he drew obscene figures for half-an-hour. Then the messenger returned. "Please sir," reported the butler, "James that I sent up, sir, says he couldn't find no one in Mr. Herbertson's house for him to speak to, leastways but Mrs. Wrenn, the housekeeper. She said, sir, as how Mr. Hilary had just gone off to the station in a fly with all his luggage."

The Headmaster of Cheddar took up his mortarboard and went out, swearing indiscriminately.

{1908}

SAKI
(pseudonym of Hector Hugh Munro)
{1870–1916}

Saki was the nom de plume of Hector Hugh Munro, a refined subverter of the English upper classes. Although he wrote three novels and three plays, his métier was the short story: he published six collections — *Reginald* (1904), *Reginald in Russia* (1910), *The Chronicles of Clovis* (1911), *Beasts and Super-Beasts* (1914), *The Toys of Peace* (1919), and *The Square Egg* (1924) — and in them made a claim to a minor but durable position in English literature. The homosexual element in his work sometimes passes so swiftly, so deftly, that one can almost miss it. But it is, most emphatically, there.

Noël Coward was among the admirers of Saki's work, and he wrote an introduction for *The Complete Saki* (1967). Therefrom:

> His satire was based primarily on the assumption of a fixed social status quo which, although at the time he was writing may have been wobbling a bit, outwardly at least, betrayed few signs of its imminent collapse. His articulate duchesses sipping China tea on their impeccable lawns, his witty, effete young heroes Reginald, Clovis Sangrail, Comus Bassington, with their gaily irreverent persiflage and their preoccupation with oysters, caviar and personal adornment, finally disappeared in the gunsmoke of 1914.

Though making a claim on nostalgia, Coward neglected to articulate a most important point: Saki himself fired more than one salvo at the "fixed social status quo" long before the advent of the Great War. Through such characters as Tobermory, a truly singular cat whose indiscretions get him killed by a piece of "rough trade," Saki showed that the civilization that came to an end in 1914 would have come to an end even if there had been no war: it had become too feckless.

FROM *The Chronicles of Clovis*

Tobermory

IT WAS A CHILL, rain-washed afternoon of a late August day, that indefinite season when partridges are still in security or cold storage, and there is nothing to hunt — unless one is bounded on the north by the Bristol Channel, in which case one may lawfully gallop after fat red stags. Lady Blemley's house-party was not bounded on the north by the Bristol Channel, hence there was a full gathering of her guests round the tea-table on this particular afternoon. And, in spite of the blankness of the season and the triteness of the occasion, there was no trace in the company of that fatigued restlessness which means a dread of the pianola and a subdued hankering for auction bridge. The undisguised open-mouthed attention of the entire party was fixed on the homely negative personality of Mr. Cornelius Appin. Of all her guests, he was the one who had come to Lady Blemley with the vaguest reputation. Some one had said he was "clever," and he had got his invitation in the moderate expectation, on the part of his hostess, that some portion at least of his cleverness would be contributed to the general entertainment. Until tea-time that day she had been unable to discover in what direction, if any, his cleverness lay. He was neither a wit nor a croquet champion, a hypnotic force nor a begetter of amateur theatricals. Neither did his exterior suggest the sort of man in whom women are willing to pardon a generous measure of mental deficiency. He had subsided into mere Mr. Appin, and the Cornelius seemed a piece of transparent baptismal bluff. And now he was claiming to have launched on the world a discovery beside which the invention of gunpowder, of the printing-press, and of steam locomotion were inconsiderable trifles. Science had made bewildering strides in many directions during recent decades, but this thing seemed to belong to the domain of miracle rather than to scientific achievement.

"And do you really ask us to believe," Sir Wilfrid was saying, "that you have discovered a means for instructing animals in the art of human speech, and that dear old Tobermory has proved your first successful pupil?"

"It is a problem at which I have worked for the last seventeen years," said Mr. Appin, "but only during the last eight or nine months have I been rewarded with glimmerings of success. Of course I have experimented with thousands of animals, but latterly only with cats, those wonderful creatures which have assimilated themselves so marvellously with our civilization while retaining all their highly developed feral instincts. Here and there among cats one comes across an outstanding superior intellect, just as one does among the ruck of human beings, and when I made the acquaintance of Tobermory a week ago I saw at once that I was in contact with a 'Beyond-cat' of extraordinary intelligence. I had gone far along the road to success in recent experiments; with Tobermory, as you call him, I have reached the goal."

Mr. Appin concluded his remarkable statement in a voice which he strove to divest of a triumphant inflection. No one said "Rats," though Clovis's lips moved in a monosyllabic contortion which probably invoked those rodents of disbelief.

"And do you mean to say," asked Miss Resker, after a slight pause, "that you have taught Tobermory to say and understand easy sentences of one syllable?"

"My dear Miss Resker," said the wonder-worker patiently, "one teaches little children and savages and backward adults in that piecemeal fashion; when one has once solved the problem of making a beginning with an animal of highly developed intelligence one has no need for those halting methods. Tobermory can speak our language with perfect correctness."

This time Clovis very distinctly said, "Beyond-rats!" Sir Wilfrid was more polite, but equally sceptical.

"Hadn't we better have the cat in and judge for ourselves?" suggested Lady Blemley.

Sir Wilfrid went in search of the animal, and the company settled themselves down to the languid expectation of witnessing some more or less adroit drawing-room ventriloquism.

In a minute Sir Wilfrid was back in the room, his face white beneath its tan and his eyes dilated with excitement.

"By Gad, it's true!"

His agitation was unmistakably genuine, and his hearers started forward in a thrill of awakened interest.

Collapsing into an armchair he continued breathlessly: "I found him dozing in the smoking-room and called out to him to come for his tea. He blinked at me in his usual way, and I said, 'Come on, Toby; don't keep us waiting'; and, by Gad! he drawled out in a most horribly natural voice that he'd come when he dashed well pleased! I nearly jumped out of my skin!"

Appin had preached to absolutely incredulous hearers; Sir Wilfrid's statement carried instant conviction. A Babel-like chorus of startled exclamation arose, amid which the scientist sat mutely enjoying the first fruit of his stupendous discovery.

In the midst of the clamour Tobermory entered the room and made his way with velvet tread and studied unconcern across to the group seated round the tea-table.

A sudden hush of awkwardness and constraint fell on the company. Somehow there seemed an element of embarrassment in addressing on equal terms a domestic cat of acknowledged dental ability.

"Will you have some milk, Tobermory?" asked Lady Blemley in a rather strained voice.

"I don't mind if I do," was the response, couched in a tone of even indifference. A shiver of suppressed excitement went through the listeners, and Lady Blemley might be excused for pouring out the saucerful of milk rather unsteadily.

"I'm afraid I've spilt a good deal of it," she said apologetically.

"After all, it's not my Axminster," was Tobermory's rejoinder.

Another silence fell on the group, and then Miss Resker, in her best district-visitor manner, asked if the human language had been difficult to learn. Tobermory looked squarely at her for a moment and then fixed his gaze serenely on the middle distance. It was obvious that boring questions lay outside his scheme of life.

"What do you think of human intelligence?" asked Mavis Pellington lamely.

"Of whose intelligence in particular?" asked Tobermory coldly.

"Oh, well, mine for instance," said Mavis, with a feeble laugh.

"You put me in an embarrassing position," said Tobermory, whose tone and attitude certainly did not suggest a shred of embarrassment. "When your inclusion in this house-party was suggested Sir Wilfrid protested that you were the most brainless woman of his acquaintance, and that there was a wide distinction between hospitality and the care of the feeble-minded. Lady Blemley replied that your lack of brain-power was the precise quality which had earned you your invitation, as you were the only person she could think of who might be idiotic enough to buy their old car. You know, the one they call 'The Envy of Sisyphus,' because it goes quite nicely up-hill if you push it."

Lady Blemley's protestations would have had greater effect if she had not casually suggested to Mavis only that morning that the car in question would be just the thing for her down at her Devonshire home.

Major Barfield plunged in heavily to effect a diversion.

"How about your carryings-on with the tortoise-shell puss up at the stables, eh?"

The moment he had said it every one realized the blunder.

"One does not usually discuss these matters in public," said Tobermory frigidly. "From a slight observation of your ways since you've been in this house I should imagine you'd find it inconvenient if I were to shift the conversation on to your own little affairs."

The panic which ensued was not confined to the Major.

"Would you like to go and see if cook has got your dinner ready?" suggested Lady Blemley hurriedly, affecting to ignore the fact that it wanted at least two hours to Tobermory's dinner-time.

"Thanks," said Tobermory, "not quite so soon after my tea. I don't want to die of indigestion."

"Cats have nine lives, you know," said Sir Wilfrid heartily.

"Possibly," answered Tobermory; "but only one liver."

"Adelaide!" said Mrs. Cornett, "do you mean to encourage that cat to go out and gossip about us in the servants' hall?"

The panic had indeed become general. A narrow ornamental balustrade ran in front of most of the bedroom windows at the Towers, and it was recalled with dismay that this had formed a favourite promenade for Tobermory at all hours, whence he could watch the pigeons — and heaven knew what else besides. If he intended to become reminiscent in his present outspoken strain the effect would be something more than disconcerting. Mrs. Cornett, who spent much time at her toilet table, and whose complexion was reputed to be of a nomadic though punctual disposition, looked as ill at ease as the Major. Miss Scrawen, who wrote fiercely sensuous poetry and led a blameless life, merely displayed irritation; if you are methodical and virtuous in private you don't necessarily want every one to know it. Bertie van Tahn, who was so depraved at seventeen that he had long ago given up trying to be any worse, turned a dull shade of gardenia white, but he did not commit the error of dashing out of the room like Odo Finsberry, a young gentleman who was understood to be reading for the Church and who was possibly disturbed at the thought of scandals he might hear concerning other people. Clovis had the presence of mind to maintain a composed exterior; privately he was calculating how long it would take to procure a box of fancy mice through the agency of the *Exchange and Mart* as a species of hush-money.

Even in a delicate situation like the present, Agnes Resker could not endure to remain too long in the background.

"Why did I ever come down here?" she asked dramatically.

Tobermory immediately accepted the opening.

"Judging by what you said to Mrs. Cornett on the croquet-lawn yesterday, you were out for food. You described the Blemleys as the dullest people to stay with that you knew, but said they were clever enough to employ a first-rate cook; otherwise they'd find it difficult to get any one to come down a second time."

"There's not a word of truth in it! I appeal to Mrs. Cornett —" exclaimed the discomfited Agnes.

"Mrs. Cornett repeated your remark afterwards to Bertie van Tahn," continued Tobermory, "and said, 'That woman is a regular Hunger Marcher; she'd go anywhere for four square meals a day,' and Bertie van Tahn said —"

At this point the chronicle mercifully ceased. Tobermory had caught a glimpse of the big yellow Tom from the Rectory working his way through the shrubbery towards the stable wing. In a flash he had vanished through the open French window.

With the disappearance of his too brilliant pupil Cornelius Appin found himself beset by a hurricane of bitter upbraiding, anxious inquiry, and frightened entreaty. The responsibility for the situation lay with him, and he must prevent matters from becoming worse. Could Tobermory impart his dangerous gift to other cats? was the first question he had to answer. It was possible, he replied, that he might have initiated his intimate friend the stable puss into his new accomplishment, but it was unlikely that his teaching could have taken a wider range as yet.

"Then," said Mrs. Cornett, "Tobermory may be a valuable cat and a great pet; but I'm sure you'll agree, Adelaide, that both he and the stable cat must be done away with without delay."

"You don't suppose I've enjoyed the last quarter of an hour, do you?" said Lady Blemley bitterly. "My husband and I are very fond of Tobermory — at least, we were before this horrible accomplishment was infused into him; but now, of course, the only thing is to have him destroyed as soon as possible."

"We can put some strychnine in the scraps he always gets at dinner-time," said Sir Wilfrid, "and I will go and drown the stable cat myself. The coachman will be very sore at losing his pet, but I'll say a very catching form of mange has broken out in both cats and we're afraid of its spreading to the kennels."

"But my great discovery!" expostulated Mr. Appin; "after all my years of research and experiment —"

"You can go and experiment on the short-horns at the farm, who are under proper control," said Mrs. Cornett, "or the elephants at the Zoological Gardens. They're said to be highly intelligent, and they have this recommendation, that they don't come creeping about our bedrooms and under chairs, and so forth."

An archangel ecstatically proclaiming the Millennium, and then finding that it clashed unpardonably with Henley and would have to be indefinitely postponed, could hardly have felt more crestfallen than Cornelius Appin at the reception of his wonderful achievement. Public opinion, however, was against him — in fact, had the general voice been consulted on the subject it is probable that a strong minority vote would have been in favour of including him in the strychnine diet.

Defective train arrangements and a nervous desire to see matters brought to a finish prevented an immediate dispersal of the party, but dinner that evening was not a social success. Sir Wilfrid had had rather a trying time with the stable cat and subsequently with the coachman. Agnes Resker ostentatiously limited her repast to a morsel of dry toast, which she bit as though it were a personal enemy; while Mavis Pellington maintained a vindictive silence throughout the meal. Lady Blemley kept up a flow of what she hoped was conversation, but her attention was fixed on the doorway. A plateful of carefully dosed fish scraps was in readiness on the sideboard, but sweets and savoury and dessert went their way, and no Tobermory appeared either in the dining-room or kitchen.

The sepulchral dinner was cheerful compared with the subsequent vigil in the smoking-room. Eating and drinking had at least supplied a distraction and cloak to the prevailing embarrassment. Bridge was out of the question in the general tension of nerves and tempers, and after Odo Finsberry had given a lugubrious rendering of "Mélisande in the Wood" to a frigid audience, music was tacitly avoided. At eleven the servants went to bed, announcing that the small window in the pantry had been left open as usual for Tobermory's private use. The guests read steadily through the current batch of magazines, and fell back gradually on the "Badminton Library" and bound volumes of *Punch*. Lady Blemley made periodic visits to the pantry, returning each time with an expression of listless depression which forestalled questioning.

At two o'clock Clovis broke the dominating silence.

"He won't turn up tonight. He's probably in the local newspaper office at the present moment, dictating the first instalment of his reminiscences. Lady What's-her-name's book won't be in it. It will be the event of the day."

Having made this contribution to the general cheerfulness, Clovis went to bed. At long intervals the various members of the house-party followed his example.

The servants taking round the early tea made a uniform announcement in reply to a uniform question. Tobermory had not returned.

Breakfast was, if anything, a more unpleasant function than dinner had been, but before its conclusion the situation was relieved. Tobermory's corpse was brought in from the shrubbery, where a gardener had just discovered it. From the bites on his throat and the yellow fur which coated his claws it was evident that he had fallen in unequal combat with the big Tom from the Rectory.

By midday most of the guests had quitted the Towers, and after lunch Lady Blemley had sufficiently recovered her spirits to write an extremely nasty letter to the Rectory about the loss of her valuable pet.

Tobermory had been Appin's one successful pupil, and he was destined to have no successor. A few weeks later an elephant in the Dresden Zoological Garden, which had shown no previous signs of irritability, broke loose and killed an Englishman who had apparently been teasing it. The victim's name was variously reported in the papers as Oppin and Eppelin, but his front name was faithfully rendered Cornelius.

"If he was trying German irregular verbs on the poor beast," said Clovis, "he deserved all he got."

{1911}

LOUIS UMFREVILLE WILKINSON
{1881–1966}

Louis Umfreville Wilkinson (the pseudonymous Louis Marlow) began his literary career when, while still a schoolboy at Radley, he struck up a correspondence with Oscar Wilde. His first letter to Wilde was a request to dramatize *The Picture of Dorian Gray*; Wilde granted permission in a letter from the Hôtel d'Alsace postmarked December 14, 1898. The production never came to pass, however, because the request was merely an excuse to write to Wilde. Two years later, from the same hotel, Wilde responded to Wilkinson's announcement of his intention to travel abroad: "I think it is an admirable idea. Radley had nothing left to teach you, though you could have taught it much: did so, I doubt not."

An expert parodist (not only of Henry James, but of John Cowper Powys, for example), Wilkinson also wrote, among other things, a school novel (*Puppet's Dallying*, 1905), a book of reminiscences (*Swan's Milk*, 1934), and a sort of autobiography (*Seven Friends*, 1953), in which he reprinted many of his letters from Wilde, whom he never met.

"The Better End: Conclusion of a chapter from the unpublished novel, What Percy Knew, by H*nr* J*m*s," written circa 1912, was published in 1969 in an edition of two hundred copies for presentation only. Ten copies, lettered A through J, were printed on handmade paper; the others, numbered 11 through 200, on cartridge paper. ❧

*The Better End: Conclusion of a chapter from the unpublished novel, What Percy Knew, by H*nr* J*m*s*

[The scene is a Gentleman's Library. A small company, select, is assembled. One gentleman, somewhat elderly, stands bending near the fire, his head parallel to his knees. Another gentleman, younger, stands behind him, unbent. The trousers of both gentlemen lie gathered about their ankles.]

It was, the advance to that target, heralded by a preamble somewhat more deferring than he, the bender, would, we might suppose, himself have chosen, though he was not — most indubitably he was not — one to be, on any occasion even remotely imaginable, figured as betraying an eagerness that could emerge, in the least discernibly as "vulgar." He reflected, indeed, how fine, after a manner, this choice of method — of style and mode — was: and how engaging — how really and perfectly, one might even call it, whimsical — was the way of his friend to rearward, who, while he so bristled, stiffly enough, he safely trusted, to satisfy, most admirably, their common great intent, yet with a kind of reluctant — or, it might be, even coy — patience, stretching tangents, he conceived, unexpectedly this way and unexpectedly that, held so strangely aloof, in the very aloofness none the less conveying the sense of an, at any rate not far from, almost vertiginous precipitancy. Ray Lester had, as the phrase is, the horn; but it strained, this nervous pointer, for him, under what was, in a fashion, an intellectual — could it be? — subjugation: those alert anticipatory fibres, with the quite visible quiver that they had — or indeed, if one were brought to the point of admitting it, the swelling and throbbing — hinted, and more than hinted, at some subtle variation, hardly definable, of a tragic mental tensity; while they submitted none the less — indeed, all the more — to the nicest conditions of some remoter and blander — in a way — influence: or perhaps we may conceive of them, in a more romantic view, enskied, as it were, in some far blue extraordinary recess, where vapours curl thinly, too tenuous — hardly that, though — but quite exquisitely communicative in their slender — should we say? — smoke-coils and delicate films of mist. This tensity, then, held, under a certain exterior grossness of mere appearance, a quality definable, after all, as frail; something, indeed, quite undeniably shy and sweet, while with a felicity — how rare this was! — it interrelated aether with lowly matter, and revealed — almost you might believe — the secrets — some at least — of such an interrelation, so magically penetrative, and more than a little likely — in fact, "not half," as they say, "bloody likely" — to pass beyond the reach of any interpreting that one could, in the usual "set terms," express. The older man sustained his posture, cherished his — ah! — anticipations; nor did even the indifferent warmth of that slowly dying fire prove, so far as any of the little party assembled could opine, an affliction to the forbearance that he, so incomparably, guarded.

The, as some might have supposed it, dilatoriness of Ray Lester was, rather, a test to him, to the bender, of the fine endurance, the supremely extensive restraint, that he was able — how magnificently well! — to summon and to stand — how beautifully completely! — by; and it brought about, into the, so to speak, bargain, a superlative emergence, unexpected — oh, "a bit"! — of hidden values, the patency of which was quite blithely vivifying, and therefore welcome utterly, at all tangible points, for the assurance that it, in so luminous an enlightenment, conveyed.

Nor did the fact that, in the end, little would seem to have come of it all, break the real, the unquestioned — unquestionable, even — beauty of this "preparedness" that they had had between them, this perfectly outlined preoccupation, either for Lester or for — more strangely, perhaps? or less? — the other. It could not, this especial situation, this lovely little particular phase of theirs, go on, they knew, for ever; and if that devolvulent blanching stain now perceivable upon the space of carpet dividing, yet, the two — Lester had "come," as they say, "off" — may have furnished a consummation that they could not too enthusiastically greet as the most appropriate and, wholly, satisfying that might have been looked for, at least they could recognize it as one worthy — and why not? — of their acceptance; one, indeed, to be — you understand? — bowed to.

"Ah, well, my dear," said the elder, turning and straightening, a little, and glancing forth, as he spoke, the most incalculable of comprehending eye-beams towards his — could one say "companion"? "— ah, well, my dear, so there, you see, we are!"

{circa 1912}

EDWARD IRENAEUS PRIME-STEVENSON
{1868–1942}

"The author or publisher of a homosexual book, even if scientific, not to speak of a belles-lettres work, will not readily escape troublesome consequences. Even psychiatric works from medical publishers are hedged about with conditions as to their publication and sale. Nevertheless, similisexualism is far from being an unknown note in American belles-lettres, and has even achieved its classics." So writes Edward Irenaeus Prime-Stevenson ("Xavier Mayne") in his privately printed study *The Intersexes: A History of Similisexualism as a Problem in Social Life* (1908). He names several similisexual American belles-lettres works — poetry by Walt Whitman and George E. Woodberry; prose by Alan Dale and Charles Warren Stoddard. Typical of the "psychiatric works" to which he refers was Claude Hartland's *The Story of a Life*, published in St. Louis in 1901 "for the consideration of the Medical Fraternity" (reprinted by Grey Fox Press, San Francisco, in 1985) and described by its author as "the history of a being who has the beard and the well-developed sexual organs of a man, but who is, from almost every other point of view, a woman. . . . In this little volume he offers to the medical world the strange story of his own life, hoping that it may be a means by which other similar sufferers may be reached and relieved."

Prime-Stevenson published his own "similisexual" writings privately. A wealthy American expatriate, he had already established a modest literary reputation both as E. Irenaeus Stevenson, whose stories appeared in *Harper's Weekly* and *Harper's Monthly*, and as "E. I. Stevenson," author of the boy's novels *White Cockades* (1887) and *Left to Themselves: Being the Ordeal of Gerald and Philip* (1891), by the time he wrote *Imre: A Memorandum* (1906) and *The Intersexes*. He hired The English Book-Press, R. Rispoli in Naples — where the typesetters could not read English — to bring out the two pseudonymous books.

In *Dayneford's Library: American Homosexual Writing, 1900–1913* (1995), James Gifford offers a superb analysis both of Prime-Stevenson's career and the relationship between his different literary "selves." After he moved permanently to Europe at the turn of the century, Prime-Stevenson added to his list of identities that of "Edward Prime-Stevenson," under which name he published a collection of short stories titled *Her Enemy, Some Friends and Other Personages* (Florence: Obsner, 1913). The second page of this work carries this notice: "The extremely limited edition of this volume will restrict its being obtainable except by addressing certain Continental book-sellers: including the 'Librairie Kündig,' No. 11, Corraterie, Geneva, Switzerland; H. Jaffe, No. 54, Briennerstrasse, Munich, Bavaria; Succes-sori B. Seeber, No. 20, Via Tornabuoni, Florence, Italy" — bookstores, Gifford surmises, that "catered to homosexual clientele, serving as bases for the dissemination of homosexual literature." Prime-Stevenson de-scribes "Out of the Sun" as an excerpt from a longer work, *Into the Sun,* which has not been traced.

Imre, Prime-Stevenson's story of an Englishman's love for a Hungar-ian soldier (a nationality exploited in *Teleny* as well), is no doubt his most important book. Originally published in an edition of at least five hundred copies, *Imre* was not reprinted until 1975, when the Arno Press brought it out in its Series on Homosexuality. In 1992 Badboy Books published a $4.95 paperback of a spurious 1908 edition of the novel with interpolated pornographic passages, and attributed authorship to "Anonymous"; an undisclosed, even immoral abuse of a literary text. ⚹

FROM *Her Enemy, Some Friends — and Other Personages: Stories & Studies Mostly of Human Hearts*

Out of the Sun

(to Evariste Sorrande-Lauzun)

DAYNEFORD laid down the short, last letter, finished; shut it carefully into the envelope and sealed it. With a steady hand he wrote the address, "The Honourable Frederick Frene, The Brasses. Godalming, Surrey, England." Italian posts are deliberate; but his cousin would have the letter by the week's end. In any case there was no hurry; all business-affairs always had been kept in precise adjustment, year in year out, during Dayneford's solitary and errant life. He was keen on saving post-mortem bother to the few persons concerned in his existence or rather in its ending-up, even if they were neither particularly near or dear. Besides Freddy — dear old chap! — knew the whys and wherefores of any matters to be left in his discreet care. The thought came now to Dayneford, though not for the first time, "What a good thing that Freddy and I have always been such pals! That I've never had any secrets from Freddy, no matter what sorts for the rest of the world! . . . Funny to think of it — but it's because I've always been so willing to speak the truth to Freddy about everything, that Freddy will know now just exactly how best to lie for me! . . . Ah, Freddy's one in a million for this kind of a situation!"

He got up slowly, as if very tired, and stood a moment looking around the darkening room. It had only northern windows. All the heaven, from over Ischia-way, high above Naples and the Punto di Sorrento, as well as the sea beyond the Rocks of the Sirens, were dark with cloud; though sunshine from the other direction had still a word to say in the atmosphere. The library was a pleasant place on such dull, variable afternoons. As would have been expected by at least some of Dayneford's friends, the walls were tinted in the significant green; a soft yet warm nuance, with a few details of dull red to vivify. On the pianoforte, with its broad scarf of garnet raw-silk stuff, embroidered in green and copper with a quatrain in arabic — an acclaim from Abu Nuwas to music and love — lay two big orchestral scores — "Parsifal" and Goldmark's "Die Königin von Saba." Beside them rested a well-worn volume of Beethoven's sonatas, with a bit of emerald-colored silk slipped in at the beginning of "Opus III."

Dayneford's glance moved on. But it rested again on the great heap of burned papers, crowded into the cold hearth. That heap was a sombre witness to what had been his principal occupation ever since last midnight when he had — decided. Irritating little Italian apology for a decent fireplace! How it had annoyed him, and how Gino had laughed down the annoyance, while they were beginning their domestic installation in this peaceful Capri retreat! Gino had vowed that chimney was capacious enough "to keep a whole regiment warm" — if one knew how. What fun Gino had made, when the fire was eternally burning-out, instead of behaving itself like a well-conducted English institution! Ah, those had been the weeks when their new life together often had seemed a sort of serious, beautiful jest to them; though perhaps not so disinterestedly charming to Gino as to him, Dayneford, in view of all the later insights that this evening's state of affairs summarized and compressed definitively.

Dayneford walked to the hearth once more, to turn over that blackened heap of letters, photographs, journals and what not else, that he had done well to destroy carefully. No, there were really no legible fragments! All was dust and ashes; just as, it now seemed to him, his life, and his soul had become dust and ashes, having arrived at this last short hour of — so far as he knew — his possession of either soul or life!

He came toward the great intarsia table. All was neatly arranged, quite as usual, minus only the *plein-air* carbon-study of Gino nude, sitting on the rock below the Villa of Tiberius. That portrait was charred to nothingness, across the room.

Once more he looked about the library. Never had it seemed more perfected in its atmosphere of cultured repose, though by only those quite simple and improvised conditions that he had been able to bring together. The pictures, all low-hung and well-lighted, were mostly photogravures. They were not many: but they were all subtly expressive of something to him — each a symbol of a certain current, constructively or destructively most potential in his psychology and his daily life — as that life had been *always*. . . . There was the Rembrandt etching, the little Japanese landscape by Teisai Hokuba, the two ineffable Madonnas by Coreggio, in the Dresden Zwinger; the lovely "Lampadiforo" of the Terme, in Rome, Andrea del Sarto's young San Giovanni, Bazzi's San Sebastiano, the engraving of Jupiter and Cupid, by Raimondi, after Raphael. In a farther corner, beyond his writing-table, and on a corner of the bookcase, stood a fine marble copy of the Hermes of Praxiteles. On a little gueridon was listening, in his perpetual youth and absorption, the Narcisso of the Naples Museum.

Ah, his books! The library of almost every man of like making-up, whose life has been largely solitary, so concentratedly from the inside, is companioned from youth up by innermost literary sympathies of his type. Dayneford stood now before his bookcase, reading over mechanically the titles of a special group of volumes — mostly small ones. They were crowded into a few lower shelves, as if they sought to avoid other literary society, to keep themselves to themselves, to shun all unsympathetic observation. Tibullus, Propertius and the Greek Antologists pressed against Al Nafsaweh and Chakani and Hafiz. A little further along stood Shakespeare's Sonnets, and those by Buonarrotti; along with Tennyson's "In Memoriam," Woodberry's "The North-Shore Watch," and Walt Whitman. Back of Platen's bulky "Tagebuch" lay his poems. Next to them came Wilbrandt's "Fridolins Heimliche Ehe," beside Rachilde's "Les Hors-Nature;" then Pernauhm's "Die Infamen," Emil Vacano's "Humbug," and a group of psychologic works by Krafft-Ebing and Ellis and Moll. There was a thin book in which were bound together, in a richly-decorated arabesque cover, some six or seven stories from Mardrus' French translation of "The Thousand Nights And A Night" — remorsely separated from their original companions. On a lower shelf, rested David Christie Murray's "Val Strange" and one or two other old novels; along with Dickens' "David Copperfield," the anonymous "Tim," and Vachell's "The Hill," companioned by Mayne's "Intersexes," "Imre" and "Sebastian au Plus Bel Age." The latter little book was lying flat on its face, just where Dayneford had laid it down three nights ago, when he had sprung up from the sofa — to tear open feverishly, fearfully, hopefully — yes, even then a very little hopefully! — Gino's long-expected telegram. Was it only three nights ago . . . ? Dayneford had lived much since then! Absently Dayneford took up "Sebastian" and re-read a page which his own pencil had marked, sometime or other; a passage that in English would run somewhat thus:

> . . . "But Bernard could never become quite sure of his recovery — of his immunity. He had sharp examples of that fact. One evening he was strolling home, that is to say, returning to his hotel, through a quiet residence-street, when there happened to pass him quickly a slender, graceful lad, perhaps of seventeen. The boy was tall, of an oval face, with dark, eager eyes. He called out in a high, clear voice, a voice like a wood-bird, some casual words of adieu to a companion just turning away. The personal resemblance may have been vaguer than Bernard fancied; but that made no difference — its type-mischief was instant and complete. The full psychic apparition of Sebastian flashed once more upon Bernard's soul. All the peace of the quiet afternoon, of the week, of the month was over! Again was Bernard's heart embittered and quivering with old retro-

spects, old torments. The knife had recommenced its turning in the wound, the unhealed sore was again chafing in bleeding rawness . . . Oh, nothing had *cured* him yet! Nothing seemed likely to cure him — ever! The punishment for his mystic folly, for the second folly of its sort in Bernard's life, was still cruelly upon him! It seemed now greater than he could bear . . . "That cursed boy! . . . That cursed boy!" — he cried out aloud in his anger and agony, repeating the words over and over. But somehow the accent of his reiterations became gentler, ever gentler; till at last Bernard's voice quite broke, speaking them softly. The tears stood in his eyes; and the rough phrase was no longer a malediction but a caress — "That cursed boy! — That cursed boy!" . . .

Dayneford put down the little book, unstirred now by its message. He looked up and around slowly. One would hardly suppose that here was a man making calmly what was his farewell survey, as proprietor of so much comfort and simple elegance. "Yes — it's odd to realise *that!*" Dayneford murmured, squaring his stalwart shoulders. He laid the letter to Freddy on the post-box, where very early next morning old Elena would look for it. By it he set a lira, to pay for the *raccommandare*, then placed, likewise most carefully, an envelope with a hundred lire in it, for Elena's first exigencies — *after*. Then when he had locked a window, he realized that there was really nothing more to do in his own house, so well was it set in order.

He was ready! It did seem curious that he — so well, so strong, a type of whatever speaks outwardly to the admiring world of vigorous manliness — of perfect health — he, untroubled by any vulgar worriments — that *he* should have done, or should be doing, for so few moments longer, these commonplace little things. All, all for his last time! Yet somehow that ultimate aspect did not lend the actions much dignity. Besides, great things, small things, nothing mattered now, nor had many emotional meanings! He was conscious, in these instants chiefly of feeling so tired — so inexpressibly tired! Of longing for Nothingness and (oh, it surely must be so!) for a swift and immutable Rest!

The hall of the villa was dusking into violets and browns and blacks, as Dayneford came out from the library. Only the long garden, seen beyond the glass-doors, was still sunshiny. ". . . But it's not 'into the sun' for me — this time!" Dayneford said to himself, as he came along. "It's *out* of the sun! . . . Into the Shade — for good and all!"

He took up his hat, then laid it down again. He would not need a hat . . . As he did so, he caught sight of a tightly-rolled pair of gloves in a corner of the hall. He picked the gloves up. Yes, the identical pair of gloves that Gino had worn that miserable Sunday! — when he, Dayneford, had tried to find out whether Gino really had been lying to him, was capable of lying to him! — had fabricated that history about whose gloves they really were, — about had been the reason of that long afternoon's engagement over in Naples. Oh, well — any such incidents made a clear and stale chronicle now! All lies and what not else, had culminated in yesterday's sailing of the *Krishna*, with Gino and Stephen Crome tranquilly bound for Colombo . . . If he had not been such a blind ass, how many weeks of doubt, of torture, he could have spared himself! So much of these recent days and nights of a death-fight between passion and conviction, between fire of heart and ice of evidence! So very large a part — perhaps? — of the war between "No, no! — I will *not* believe!" and the inevitable "I must believe!"

Dayneford found the sweat coming out on his forehead all at once, as retrospects and queries began attacking, enveloping, asphyxiating him, so to say; disturbing that glacial tranquility that he felt was now his supreme good. He exclaimed like King Lear, "Oh, that way madness lies!" — and struck at the gloves; dashing them away into some dim corner forever, with all the story whereof they were part, so far as he was concerned. As he put his hand back into his pocket, he felt the rustling of a crumpled paper. He pulled it out. It was not a thing to quiet the nerves in such a supreme mood and hour! But Dayneford re-read Gino's despatch calmly, perhaps for the hundredth time since it had arrived, two nights earlier:

"Impossibile venire, molto occupato avanti partenza domenica. Inutile per tutti due. Preferisco vietare altre scene melodrammatiche e penose. Scriveró da Alessandria o Cairo. Saluti ottimi. — Gino."

Verily, that was a characteristic telegram! Most characteristic, as Dayneford to-day understood Gino's cynical insincerity, Gino's lazy egotism, Gino's feminine hatred of those recent "melodramatic scenes," in which pride, contempt and sudden misery had made Dayneford's sufferings sharply articulate. But now Dayneford only curled his lip a little, as he ran his eye once more over the unkind lines. He was past being much moved by them. He tore the telegram into minute fragments, disposed of them carefully, and then passed out into the garden, locking the door after him. He went rather swiftly down the long walk toward the broken wall, the cliff, and to whatever was beyond them; beyond this world of mirage and disappointment for so many such as he! . . .

Autumn roses were still plentiful in the garden. Against the wall of the small green-house, the violet-red bougainvillia was a gorgeous mass of colour, in the last orange-red light. The sea was opal, blazing off to tones of fire, where it met the sunset. "My last Capri sunset!" Dayneford said softly to himself. He picked a rose (it was a yellow rose, lovely emblem of regard which is jealousy!) from the bush which Gino once had insisted was "a little bit too tall," and accordingly had nearly annihilated, in his drastic notions of pruning. Gino, as he had looked that morning, rose into Dayneford's memory — the symmetrical, boyish, barefooted figure, gliding so lightly about the rose-tree; every movement filled with an italic-hellenic grace; the lad's smiling beauty of face under his dark hair; his laugh that echoed around the garden, like the sound of a bar of silver, as he disputed ideas of horticulture with old Niccolo. But as Dayneford turned toward the broad south wall, by the cactus-hedge, he recalled Gino, not less beautiful, at an hour when that sinister *other* side — the real side, as it seemed now — of Gino's nature, had so startled and terrified; that sunny noon when Gino had been discovered, stretched out lazily, half-naked, on the wall, slowly cutting into thinnest pieces, inch by inch, the big green lizard; still alive — and writhing in agony under Gino's sharp pocket-knife! The boy's half-curious, half-voluptuous smile! — as he cut and sliced by millimetres the wretched, bleeding little beast, apparently with the pleasure — no, doubtless with far more! — that a human creature so young and beautiful as Gino might be expected to take in plucking a handful of roses! Well, Dayneford had now no poetical illusions as to Gino's possessing particular tenderness of temperament toward the sufferings of anything or anybody — alive or dying or dead! At the same time recurred to Dayneford's thought, those contemptuous sentences that Karl Collingwood had uttered on another morning, in just that same spot in the rose-garden, when the news had come to the three of them of the suicide, in Spezia, of Maurice Vayre: "Yes, we're a queer lot, most of us, I'll admit!" had exclaimed Collingwood. "Generally we're bound to be unhappy, right and left, into the bargain . . . I expect I know about as much of some so-called heart-breaking sides of it all, as do most of the Race. But that even a damned unlucky fool like Vayre should ever kill himself for *that!* It's a bit too — too — well, too hellenic! . . . Too much the classic thing for *me*, I must say! . . . But Vayre was quite mad of course. Don't you think so?"

Dayneford remembered now that he had assented, in a way, to Collingwood's scornful confession of unfaith. But he had said what he had said, not able to foresee Stephen Crome's advent to Naples, the *Krishna*, at anchor off the Immacolata, Crome's careless introduction to Gino at the Nautico; and thence the fatadic, tortuous, torturing history — even then not far ahead. ". . . That a man should be such a damned fool as to kill himself for *that!* . . ." Well then, he, Dayneford, must be another such "damned fool"? Or mad? Or perhaps both? Certainly time was ripe for Dayneford to guess, to know — himself! Or rather, no! — it was too late to bother!

He leaped the wall, without even glancing once more at his house and garden. He crossed the little strip of broken ground developing quickly into the abrupt, sloping path — down to the cliff's veritable edge. Attaining the head of the path, he sat down on the long stone seat beneath the old statue. The statue itself was softly rose-yellow this evening, in that magical light. Dayneford looked up at it, in a final and calm admiration. In such a transfiguring radiance, the statue was indeed wonderfully like Gino, though only through an odd coincidence; for surely it had been carved, by its now unknown sculptor, not later than the Hadrianic epoch. Yet — good God! — how like it was! . . . There was the same smile as Gino's — that smile of Leonardo da Vinci's "Madonna delle Rocche," or of Luini's "Virgin in the Rose-Arbour." Karl Collingwood had once pointed out the likeness, in a moment when "sentimental;" what Karl called "sentimental" — that is to say, not sneering about a matter of which he knew much, but reserved more; including experiences known to be of profoundly personal unhappiness.

The statue was wonderfully vivid this evening, against its background of rock and laurels, myrtles and other rambling greenery. The dead Marchese Spinalba had been lucky to find such a treasure. He had known admirably how to place it. The marble eyes of the youth seemed to be overlooking, in a Lydian serenity, the frightful precipices leaping down to the sea, the sea itself, the sunset. One might fancy the survey as absorbing all the world of life — of love — of death. "Of death!" thought Dayneford, half-apostrophising the statue, as he sat below it " — even death some men choose when they kill themselves for *that!* For that terrible other illusion, that supremely bewildering chaos of one's emotional Being — that rejection of our visible Ego, in our remediless dissidence from a whole world, to right and to left about us! . . . When one is quite fool — or mad . . ."

How long Dayneford sat there beneath the statue, I do not know. It must have been fully through two hours, or even more. At length he suddenly roused himself less from reverie than from a stupor of profound mental weariness. The statue was no longer yellow. It stood out pallid-white, against the now much-deepened twilight. The sun had quite set. Clouds and darkness were over the sea westward. One single horizontal stripe of dull ochre lingeringly marked the point whence had passed away all the glory of the evening's world. The hour was already dusky and chill and still. An owl flitted past the statue and Dayneford. Beyond the bench, stretched down — half-traceable — the final twenty or thirty yards of the aweful little path, steep and smooth, that came to end only at absolutely the last centimetre of the cliff. Beyond that threshold of death (to any live thing not winged) lay a gulf of profound emptiness, now seen — felt — as merely a brown-blue void, a space terrifying even to thought, because of its hideous finality! Terrifying, that is to say, if one had no errand exactly to its terrors . . .

Yes, yes! . . . One would have only to begin running as fast as possible, and to keep on running so, straight down that path, just as if playing some sort of game with Gino, in the rose-alley of the garden! Not checking one-self at all — a thing that in fact would be difficult from the first bound . . . How easy it was to be! Did others find such a business hard? Not so would he find it! . . . The sombre finality of such an evening-hour and errand was indeed in key with the themes of incredulity and of its rebuke, in Daudet's "L'Arlesienne" — "Say now, if you dare, that nobody kills himself for love! . . ." Was Dayneford wandering a little in his mind, which seemed to him so clear and tranquil? — or was somebody, maybe a supernatural or-chestra somewhere, playing softly, with all the despairing melancholy which pervades every measure of it, the "Adagietto" in Bizet's music to the drama of the luckless Frédéri's ruined desire to live any longer? Over and over again, Dayneford seemed to hear it — that Adagietto of such infinite sadness — renunciation — elegy!

In any case, the time had come "to do it," the moment had really ar-rived for accepting the consummation which Gino had brought upon him — mad? — or only as another "damned unlucky fool," sanely willing in his turn "to kill himself for *that?* . . ."

For that! . . . After all, what a stupid, blind, dull-witted world, a world of ignorant, credulous men and women it was — is! Obtuse world, no mat-ter how discerning it tries to pass for being! Oh, those other people every-where, who seem not even to guess "why" such or such a man's life can be-gin and can be led, as the predestined, sole reason for the tragedy of such a death! How many histories even he, one single individual, knew! . . . Why, there was Billy Gilderoy — Gilderoy still young — just in the middle of his brilliant professional successes — Gilderoy rich, manly, so good-looking, so admired and loved by a thousand good friends; envied by other men for his unlimited popularity among women; the hero of *racontars* enough to give him the reputation of a sort of Crichton-Don Juan. At a little hotel in Paris had come the interruption of all that situation, in the way of a bullet in Gilderoy's heart — "an absolutely inexplicable suicide" . . . There was Harry Alvanley — brave young soldier, gallant gentleman, the pet of the smartest drawing-rooms in town; engaged to as pretty and charming a girl as London or any other place could have held for a fellow to marry. One week before the wedding, had come Alvanley's "mysterious" suicide, in his own quiet place in Berks; where indeed they had found him dead, with only a big, black heap of burned papers — to tell no tales. There was Trayford the banker, jolly, busy Trayford, that long-headed, shrewd, successful prince of his financial circle. Daily he had seemed to grow more unwell, more of nervous aspect, plainly less interested in any sort of joyous social life; till on a certain Sunday night, Trayford had been found in his little photographic cabinet, the cyanide wilfully swallowed for *that* reason. So a letter to Dayneford — the only letter Trayford left — had told. Everybody, except Dayneford and two or three other men, had emitted the usual exclamations of bewilderment at "so wholly incomprehensible an event" — "of course, a sudden attack of neurasthenic madness" — and so on! And what about Ayre-Oram? — Ayre-Oram, the great irrigation engineer, the man spoken of right and left, as "the finest mathematical intellect of his profession" — what had happened to Ayre-Oram? Dayneford, and sundry others, could have thrown some light on Ayre-Oram's disappearance from activities during that winter in the States; as well as on the murder which was followed by Ayre-Oram's taking his own life; though that story would have been bitterly challenged by many men and women who were sure that they knew "quite everything" in the tragedy — knew Ayre-Oram as intimately as they knew themselves . . . Ah, the stupid, stupid, great world! Yet after all, likely there was an advantage that the world in general should be just so stupid, forever on wrong tracks of explanations or sympathy. Appearances were saved; and so the secret of *that* vast and multi-coloured and limitless Freemasonry of a mystic Sex — Intersex — remained just that much more its own property, *in saecula saeculorum — amen!*

. . . Therewith Dayneford got up. He was not trembling, he was not cold, he was not frightened, he was not troubled in any way. Nothing at this moment was in his confused, weary mind so much as the memory of Gino psychically; the passionate sense of a wasted idealism; of a man's heart abused and bruised; of the shipwreck, utter and complete, of all that which insidiously, beautifully and now terribly had become life to Laurence Dayneford, as any kind of existence worth his while . . . Oh, the pity of it! If it only might not have been! . . . That vain outcry against fate for a moment possessed Dayneford's sad soul . . . But it passed; again there was left only his yearning to get away for ever, to Somewhere or to Nowhere; if thought, sentience, thereby could cease to recur as vehicles of pain!

So Dayneford turned to the statue, shimmering in the violet twilight. He plucked a spray of myrtle — the flower that Gino liked. He leaned, and laid his throbbing forehead to the marble.

"Good-night — good-bye! . . ." he murmured; not to the statue. "Buona notte, buona notte! — addio, addio! . . . You brought me into the sun for a while! I am going out of it now, and away from it — and from you, for good! . . . Good-bye!"

He pulled off his coat and waistcoat, and dropped them at the foot of the statue. It was a gesture quite unconsciously symbolic. In letting fall the garments, he half-remembered what Gilderoy had often asserted — that some mystic part of our psychic selves becomes inevitably attached to whatever we wear or carry habitually. If so, at least a vague, final aura of himself perhaps would be left with what glimmered there beside him, as if representing Gino! . . . Who could prove the contrary?

Dayneford straightened himself with a quiet, manly movement. Then he began running with increasing speed and momentum, down the steep white path, straight to the top of the cliff . . . He did not make any baulk, as he neared the edge. On the contrary, when within a yard or so of that awful limit of life for him, he sprang boldly, without a cry or other sound — upward and out, in the full curve of a diver from a spring-board. Out, out and down — into the night and the abyss.

{1913}

DAVID HERBERT LAWRENCE
{1885-1930}

Although his tempestuous marriage to Frieda von Richthofen defined, if not fulfilled, D. H. Lawrence's erotic life, his work was not without a strong homosexual component. In the 1922 novel *Aaron's Rod*, the eponymous hero, arriving in Florence, nearly swoons at the sight of the David, "white and stripped in the wet, white against the dark, warm-dark cliff of the building — and near, the heavy naked men of Bandinelli," one of them "a great naked man of marble, with a heavy back, and strong naked flanks over which the water was trickling." Florence impresses Aaron as a place where "men had been at their intensest, most naked pitch, here, at the end of the old world and the beginning of the new . . . But men! Men! A town of men, in spite of everything."

Lawrence's friend, the composer and writer Cecil Gray, wrote of him in *Musical Chairs* (1948): "The man who achieves complete and satisfying sexual experience in life is never obsessed with sex to the extent to which Lawrence was in his writings. Your strong, vital, satisfied male does not rapturously hymn the act of the flesh in his work — very much to the contrary, he is generally very quiet about it. The concupiscent, insatiable Tolstoi preaches austerity and asceticism; it is the Swinburnes and Nietzsches and Lawrences who persistently glorify and magnify the joys they have never really experienced in all their fullness, if at all."

"The Prussian Officer" (1914), in its erotic sadism, recalls Robert Musil's novel of military school life, *Young Törless* (1901), and prefigures the bizarre chapter in Gore Vidal's *Myra Breckinridge* (1968) wherein Myra humiliates Rusty during a "medical exam." ❧

The Prussian Officer

I

They had marched more than thirty kilometres since dawn, along the white, hot road where occasional thickets of trees threw a moment of shade, then out into the glare again. On either hand, the valley, wide and shallow, glittered with heat; dark-green patches of rye, pale young corn, fallow and meadow and black pine woods spread in a dull, hot diagram under a glistening sky. But right in front of the mountains ranged across, pale blue and very still, snow gleaming gently out of the deep atmosphere. And towards the mountains, on and on, the regiment marched between the rye-fields and the meadows, between the scraggy fruit trees set regularly on either side the high road. The burnished, dark-green rye threw off a suffocating heat, the mountains drew gradually nearer and more distinct. While the feet of the soldiers grew hotter, sweat ran through their hair under their helmets, and their knapsacks could burn no more in contact with their shoulders, but seemed instead to give off a cold, prickly sensation.

He walked on and on in silence, staring at the mountains ahead, that rose sheer out of the land, and stood fold behind fold, half earth, half heaven, the heaven, the barrier with slits of soft snow, in the pale, bluish peaks.

He could now walk almost without pain. At the start, he had determined not to limp. It had made him sick to take the first steps, and during the first mile or so, he had compressed his breath, and the cold drops of sweat had stood on his forehead. But he had walked it off. What were they after all but bruises! He had looked at them, as he was getting up: deep bruises on the backs of his thighs. And since he had made his first step in the morning, he had been conscious of them, till now he had a tight, hot place in his chest, with suppressing the pain, and holding himself in. There seemed no air when he breathed. But he walked almost lightly.

The Captain's hand had trembled at taking his coffee at dawn: his orderly saw it again. And he saw the fine figure of the Captain wheeling on horseback at the farmhouse ahead, a handsome figure in pale-blue uniform with facings of scarlet, and the metal gleaming on the black helmet and the sword-scabbard, and dark streaks of sweat coming on the silky bay horse. The orderly felt he was connected with that figure moving so suddenly on horseback: he followed it like a shadow, mute and inevitable and damned by it. And the officer was always aware of the tramp of the company behind, the march of his orderly among the men.

The Captain was a tall man of about forty, grey at the temples. He had a handsome, finely-knit figure, and was one of the best horsemen in the West. His orderly, having to rub him down, admired the amazing riding-muscles of his loins.

For the rest, the orderly scarcely noticed the officer any more than he noticed himself. It was rarely he saw his master's face: he did not look at it. The Captain had reddish-brown, stiff hair, that he wore short upon his skull. His moustache was also cut short and bristly over a full, brutal mouth. His face was rather rugged, the cheeks thin. Perhaps the man was the more handsome for the deep lines in his face, the irritable tension of his brow, which gave him the look of a man who fights with life. His fair eyebrows stood bushy over light-blue eyes that were always flashing with cold fire.

He was a Prussian aristocrat, haughty and overbearing. But his mother had been a Polish countess. Having made too many gambling debts when he was young, he had ruined his prospects in the Army, and remained an infantry captain. He had never married: his position did not allow of it, and no woman had ever moved him to it. His time he spent riding — occasionally he rode one of his own horses at the races — and at the officers' club. Now and then he took himself a mistress. But after such an event, he returned to duty with his brow still more tense, his eyes still more hostile and irritable. With the men, however, he was merely impersonal, though a devil when roused; so that, on the whole, they feared him, but had no great aversion from him. They accepted him as the inevitable.

To his orderly he was at first cold and just and indifferent: he did not fuss over trifles. So that his servant knew practically nothing about him, except just what orders he would give, and how he wanted them obeyed. That was quite simple. Then the change gradually came.

The orderly was a youth of about twenty-two, of medium height, and well built. He had strong, heavy limbs, was swarthy, with a soft, black, young moustache. There was something altogether warm and young about him. He had firmly marked eyebrows over dark, expressionless eyes, that seemed never to have thought, only to have received life direct through his senses, and acted straight from instinct.

Gradually the officer had become aware of his servant's young vigorous, unconscious presence about him. He could not get away from the sense of the youth's person, while he was in attendance. It was like a warm flame upon the older man's tense, rigid body, that had become almost unliving, fixed. There was something so free and self-contained about him, and something in the young fellow's movement, that made the officer aware of him. And this irritated the Prussian. He did not choose to be touched into life by his servant. He might easily have changed his man, but he did not. He now very rarely looked direct at his orderly, but kept his face averted, as if to avoid seeing him. And yet as the young soldier moved unthinking about the apartment, the elder watched him, and would notice the movement of his strong young shoulders under the blue cloth, the bend of his neck. And it irritated him. To see the soldier's young, brown, shapely peasant's hand grasp the loaf or the wine-bottle sent a flash of hate or of anger through the elder man's blood. It was not that the youth was clumsy: it was rather the blind, instinctive sureness of movement of an un-hampered young animal that irritated the officer to such a degree.

Once, when a bottle of wine had gone over, and the red gushed out on to the tablecloth, the officer had started up with an oath, and his eyes, bluey like fire, had held those of the confused youth for a moment. It was a shock for the young soldier. He felt something sink deeper, deeper into his soul, where nothing had ever gone before. It left him rather blank and wondering. Some of his natural completeness in himself was gone, a little uneasiness took its place. And from that time an undiscovered feeling had held between the two men.

Henceforward the orderly was afraid of really meeting his master. His subconsciousness remembered those steely blue eyes and the harsh brows, and did not intend to meet them again. So he always stared past his mas-ter, and avoided him. Also, in a little anxiety, he waited for the three months to have gone, when his time would be up. He began to feel a con-straint in the Captain's presence, and the soldier even more than the offi-cer wanted to be left alone, in his neutrality as servant.

He had served the Captain for more than a year, and knew his duty. This he performed easily, as if it were natural to him. The officer and his commands he took for granted, as he took the sun and the rain, and he served as a matter of course. It did not implicate him personally.

But now if he were going to be forced into a personal interchange with his master he would be like a wild thing caught, he felt he must get away.

But the influence of the young soldier's being had penetrated through the officer's stiffened discipline, and perturbed the man in him. He, how-ever, was a gentleman, with long, fine hands and cultivated movements, and was not going to allow such a thing as the stirring of his innate self. He was a man of passionate temper, who had always kept himself suppressed. Occasionally there had been a duel, an outburst before the soldiers. He knew himself to be always on the point of breaking out. But he kept himself hard to the idea of the Service. Whereas the young soldier seemed to live out his warm, full nature, to give it off in his very movements, which had a certain zest, such as wild animals have in free movement. And this irritated the officer more and more.

In spite of himself, the Captain could not regain his neutrality of feeling towards his orderly. Nor could he leave the man alone. In spite of himself, he watched him, gave him sharp orders, tried to take up as much of his time as possible. Sometimes he flew into a rage with the young soldier, and bullied him. Then the orderly shut himself off, as it were out of earshot, and waited, with sullen, flushed face, for the end of the noise. The words never pierced to his intelligence, he made himself, protectively, impervious to the feelings of his master.

He had a scar on his left thumb, a deep seam going across the knuckle. The officer had long suffered from it, and wanted to do something to it. Still it was there, ugly and brutal on the young, brown hand. At last the Captain's reserve gave way. One day, as the orderly was smoothing out the tablecloth, the officer pinned down his thumb with a pencil, asking:

"How did you come by that?"

The young man winced and drew back at attention.

"A wood axe, Herr Hauptmann," he answered.

The officer waited for further explanation. None came. The orderly went about his duties. The elder man was sullenly angry. His servant avoided him. And the next day he had to use all his will-power to avoid seeing the scarred thumb. He wanted to get hold of it and — A hot flame ran in his blood.

He knew his servant would soon be free, and would be glad. As yet, the soldier had held himself off from the elder man. The Captain grew madly irritable. He could not rest when the soldier was away, and when he was present, he glared at him with tormented eyes. He hated those fine, black brows over the unmeaning, dark eyes, he was infuriated by the free movement of the handsome limbs, which no military discipline could make stiff. And he became harsh and cruelly bullying, using contempt and satire. The young soldier only grew more mute and expressionless.

"What cattle were you bred by, that you can't keep straight eyes? Look me in the eyes when I speak to you."

And the soldier turned his dark eyes to the other's face, but there was no sight in them: he stared with the slightest possible cast, holding back his sight, perceiving the blue of his master's eyes, but receiving no look from them. And the elder man went pale, and his reddish eyebrows twitched. He gave his order, barrenly.

Once he flung a heavy military glove into the young soldier's face. Then he had the satisfaction of seeing the black eyes flare up into his own, like a blaze when straw is thrown on a fire. And he had laughed with a little tremor and a sneer.

But there were only two months more. The youth instinctively tried to keep himself intact: he tried to serve the officer as if the latter were an abstract authority and not a man. All his instinct was to avoid personal contact, even definite hate. But in spite of himself the hate grew, responsive to the officer's passion. However, he put it in the background. When he had left the Army he could dare acknowledge it. By nature he was active, and had many friends. He thought what amazing good fellows they were. But, without knowing it, he was alone. Now this solitariness was intensified. It would carry him through his term. But the officer seemed to be going irritably insane, and the youth was deeply frightened.

The soldier had a sweetheart, a girl from the mountains, independent and primitive. The two walked together, rather silently. He went with her, not to talk, but to have his arm round her, and for the physical contact. This eased him, made it easier for him to ignore the Captain; for he could rest with her held fast against his chest. And she, in some unspoken fashion, was there for him. They loved each other.

The Captain perceived it, and was mad with irritation. He kept the young man engaged all the evenings long, and took pleasure in the dark look that came on his face. Occasionally, the eyes of the two men met, those of the younger sullen and dark, doggedly unalterable, those of the elder sneering with restless contempt.

The officer tried hard not to admit the passion that had got hold of him. He would not know that his feeling for his orderly was anything but that of a man incensed by his stupid, perverse servant. So, keeping quite justified and conventional in his consciousness, he let the other thing run on. His nerves, however, were suffering. At last he slung the end of a belt in his servant's face. When he saw the youth start back, the pain-tears in his eyes and the blood on his mouth, he had felt at once a thrill of deep pleasure and of shame.

But this, he acknowledged to himself, was a thing he had never done before. The fellow was too exasperating. His own nerves must be going to pieces. He went away for some days with a woman.

It was a mockery of pleasure. He simply did not want the woman. But he stayed on for his time. At the end of it, he came back in an agony of irritation, torment, and misery. He rode all the evening, then came straight in to supper. His orderly was out. The officer sat with his long, fine hands lying on the table, perfectly still, and all his blood seemed to be corroding.

At last his servant entered. He watched the strong, easy young figure, the fine eyebrows, the thick black hair. In a week's time the youth had got back his old well-being. The hands of the officer twitched and seemed to be full of mad flame. The young man stood at attention, unmoving, shut off.

The meal went in silence. But the orderly seemed eager. He made a clatter with the dishes.

"Are you in a hurry?" asked the officer, watching the intent, warm face of his servant. The other did not reply.

"Will you answer my question?" said the Captain.

"Yes, sir," replied the orderly, standing with his pile of deep Army plates. The Captain waited, looked at him, then asked again:

"Are you in a hurry?"

"Yes, sir," came the answer, that sent a flash through the listener.

"For what?"

"I was going out, sir."

"I want you this evening."

There was a moment's hesitation. The officer had a curious stiffness of countenance.

"Yes, sir," replied the servant, in his throat.

"I want you to-morrow evening also — in fact you may consider your evenings occupied, unless I give you leave."

The mouth with the young moustache set close.

"Yes, sir," answered the orderly, loosening his lips for a moment.

He again turned to the door.

"And why have you a piece of pencil in your ear?"

The orderly hesitated, then continued on his way without answering. He set the plates in a pile outside the door, took the stump of pencil from his ear, and put it in his pocket. He had been copying a verse for his sweetheart's birthday card. He returned to finish clearing the table. The officer's eyes were dancing, he had a little, eager smile.

"Why have you a piece of pencil in your ear?" he asked.

The orderly took his hands full of dishes. His master was standing near the great green stove, a little smile on his face, his chin thrust forward. When the young soldier saw him his heart suddenly ran hot. He felt blind. Instead of answering, he turned dazedly to the door. As he was crouching to set down the dishes, he was pitched forward by a kick from behind. The pots went in a stream down the stairs, he clung to the pillar of the banisters. And as he was rising he was kicked heavily again and again, so that he clung sickly to the post for some moments. His master had gone swiftly into the room and closed the door. The maid-servant downstairs looked up the staircase and made a mocking face at the crockery disaster.

The officer's heart was plunging. He poured himself a glass of wine, part of which he spilled on the floor, and gulped the remainder, leaning against the cool, green stove. He heard his man collecting the dishes from the stairs. Pale, as if intoxicated, he waited. The servant entered again. The Captain's heart gave a pang, as of pleasure, seeing the young fellow bewildered and uncertain on his feet with pain.

"Schöner!" he said.

The soldier was a little slower in coming to attention.

"Yes, sir!"

The youth stood before him, with pathetic young moustache, and fine eyebrows very distinct on his forehead of dark marble.

"I asked you a question."

"Yes, sir."

The officer's tone bit like acid.

"Why had you a pencil in your ear?"

Again the servant's heart ran hot, and he could not breathe. With dark, strained eyes, he looked at the officer, as if fascinated. And he stood there sturdily planted, unconscious. The withering smile came into the Captain's eyes, and he lifted his foot.

"I forgot it — sir," panted the soldier, his dark eyes fixed on the other man's dancing blue ones.

"What was it doing there?"

He saw the young man's breast heaving as he made an effort for words.

"I had been writing."

"Writing what?"

Again the soldier looked him up and down. The officer could hear him panting. The smile came into the blue eyes. The soldier worked his dry throat, but could not speak. Suddenly the smile lit like a flame on the officer's face, and a kick came heavily against the orderly's thigh. The youth moved sideways. His face went dead, with two black, staring eyes.

"Well?" said the officer.

The orderly's mouth had gone dry, and his tongue rubbed in it as on dry brown-paper. He worked his throat. The officer raised his foot. The servant went stiff.

"Some poetry, sir," came the crackling, unrecognisable sound of his voice.

"Poetry, what poetry?" asked the Captain, with a sickly smile.

Again there was the working in the throat. The Captain's heart had suddenly gone down heavily, and he stood sick and tired.

"For my girl, sir," he heard the dry, inhuman sound.

"Oh!" he said, turning away. "Clear the table."

"Click!" went the soldier's throat; then again, "click!" and then the half-articulate:

"Yes, sir."

The young soldier was gone, looking old, and walking heavily.

The officer, left alone, held himself rigid, to prevent himself from thinking. His instinct warned him that he must not think. Deep inside him was the intense gratification of his passion, still working powerfully. Then there was a counter-action, a horrible breaking down of something inside him, a whole agony of reaction. He stood there for an hour motionless, a chaos of sensations, but rigid with a will to keep blank his consciousness, to prevent his mind grasping. And he held himself so until the worst of the stress had passed, when he began to drink, drank himself to an intoxication, till he slept obliterated. When he woke in the morning he was shaken to the base of his nature. But he had fought off the realisation of what he had done. He had prevented his mind from taking it in, had suppressed it along with his instincts, and the conscious man had nothing to do with it. He felt only as after a bout of intoxication, weak, but the affair itself all dim and not to be recovered. Of the drunkenness of his passion he successfully refused remembrance. And when his orderly appeared with coffee, the officer assumed the same self he had had the morning before. He refused the event of the past night — denied it had ever been — and was successful in his denial. He had not done any such thing — not he himself. Whatever there might be lay at the door of a stupid insubordinate servant.

The orderly had gone about in a stupor all the evening. He drank some beer because he was parched, but not much, the alcohol made his feeling come back, and he could not bear it. He was dulled, as if nine-tenths of the ordinary man in him were inert. He crawled about disfigured. Still, when he thought of the kicks, he went sick, and when he thought of the threat of more kicking, in the room afterwards, his heart went hot and faint, and he panted, remembering the one that had come. He had been forced to say: "For my girl." He was much too done even to want to cry. His mouth hung slightly open, like an idiot's. He felt vacant, and wasted. So, he wandered at his work, painfully, and very slowly and clumsily, fumbling blindly with the brushes, and finding it difficult, when he sat down, to summon the energy to move again. His limbs, his jaw, were slack and nerveless. But he was very tired. He got to bed at last, and slept inert, relaxed, in a sleep that was rather stupor than slumber, a dead night of stupefaction shot through with gleams of anguish.

In the morning were the manœuvres. But he woke even before the bugle sounded. The painful ache in his chest, the dryness of his throat, the awful steady feeling of misery made his eyes come awake and dreary at once. He knew, without thinking, what had happened. And he knew that the day had come again, when he must go on with his round. The last bit of darkness was being pushed out of the room. He would have to move his inert body and go on. He was so young, and had known so little trouble, that he was bewildered. He only wished it would stay night, so that he could lie still, covered up by the darkness. And yet nothing would prevent the day from coming, nothing would save him from having to get up and saddle the Captain's horse, and make the Captain's coffee. It was there, inevitable. And then, he thought, it was impossible. Yet they would not leave him free. He must go and take the coffee to the Captain. He was too stunned to understand it. He only knew it was inevitable — inevitable, however long he lay inert.

At last, after heaving at himself, for he seemed to be a mass of inertia, he got up. But he had to force every one of his movements from behind, with his will. He felt lost, and dazed, and helpless. Then he clutched hold of the bed, the pain was so keen. And looking at his thighs he saw the darker bruises on his swarthy flesh, and he knew that if he pressed one of his fingers on one of the bruises, he should faint. But he did not want to faint — he did not want anybody to know. No one should ever know. It was between him and the Captain. There were only the two people in the world now — himself and the Captain.

Slowly, economically, he got dressed and forced himself to walk. Everything was obscure, except just what he had his hands on. But he managed to get through his work. The very pain revived his dull senses. The worst remained yet. He took the tray and went up to the Captain's room. The officer, pale and heavy, sat at the table. The orderly, as he saluted, felt himself put out of existence. He stood still for a moment submitting to his own nullification — then he gathered himself, seemed to regain himself, and then the Captain began to grow vague, unreal, and the younger soldier's heart beat up. He clung to this situation — that the Captain did not exist — so that he himself might live. But when he saw his officer's hand tremble as he took the coffee, he felt everything falling shattered. And he went away, feeling as if he himself were coming to pieces, disintegrated. And when the Captain was there on horseback, giving orders, while he himself stood, with rifle and knapsack, sick with pain, he felt as if he must shut his eyes — as if he must shut his eyes on everything. It was only the long agony of marching with a parched throat that filled him with one single, sleep-heavy intention: to save himself.

II

He was getting used even to his parched throat. That the snowy peaks were radiant among the sky, that the whity-green glacier-river twisted through its pale shoals, in the valley below, seemed almost supernatural. But he was going mad with fever and thirst. He plodded on uncomplaining. He did not want to speak, not to anybody. There were two gulls, like flakes of water and snow, over the river. The scent of green rye soaked in sunshine came like a sickness. And the march continued, monotonously, almost like a bad sleep.

At the next farmhouse, which stood low and broad near the high road, tubs of water had been put out. The soldiers clustered round to drink. They took off their helmets, and the steam mounted from their wet hair. The Captain sat on horseback, watching. He needed to see his orderly. His helmet threw a dark shadow over his light, fierce eyes, but his moustache and mouth and chin were distinct in the sunshine. The orderly must move under the presence of the figure of the horseman. It was not that he was afraid, or cowed. It was as if he was disembowelled, made empty, like an empty shell. He felt himself as nothing, a shadow creeping under the sunshine. And, thirsty as he was, he could scarcely drink, feeling the Captain near him. He would not take off his helmet to wipe his wet hair. He wanted to stay in shadow, not to be forced into consciousness. Starting, he saw the light heel of the officer prick the belly of the horse; the Captain cantered away, and he himself could relapse into vacancy.

Nothing, however, could give him back his living place in the hot, bright morning. He felt like a gap among it all. Whereas the Captain was prouder, overriding. A hot flash went through the young servant's body. The Captain was firmer and prouder with life, he himself was empty as a shadow. Again the flash went through him, dazing him out. But his heart ran a little firmer.

The company turned up the hill, to make a loop for the return. Below, from among the trees, the farm-bell clanged. He saw the labourers, mowing bare-foot at the thick grass, leave off their work and go downhill, their scythes hanging over their shoulders, like long, bright claws curving down behind them. They seemed like dream-people, as if they had no relation to himself. He felt as in a blackish dream: as if all the other things were there and had form, but he himself was only a consciousness, a gap that could think and perceive.

The soldiers were tramping silently up the glaring hill-side. Gradually his head began to revolve, slowly, rhythmically. Sometimes it was dark before his eyes, as if he saw this world through a smoked glass, frail shadows and unreal. It gave him a pain in his head to walk.

The air was too scented, it gave no breath. All the lush green-stuff seemed to be issuing its sap, till the air was deathly, sickly with the smell of greenness. There was the perfume of clover, like pure honey and bees. Then there grew a faint acrid tang — they were near the beeches; and then a queer clattering noise, and a suffocating, hideous smell; they were passing a flock of sheep, a shepherd in a black smock, holding his crook. Why should the sheep huddle together under this fierce sun? He felt that the shepherd would not see him, though he could see the shepherd.

At last there was the halt. They stacked rifles in a conical stack, put down their kit in a scattered circle around it, and dispersed a little, sitting on a small knoll high on the hill-side. The chatter began. The soldiers were steaming with heat, but were lively. He sat still, seeing the blue mountains rising upon the land, twenty kilometres away. There was a blue fold in the ranges, then out of that, at the foot, the broad, pale bed of the river, stretches of whity-green water between pinkish-grey shoals among the dark pine woods. There it was, spread out a long way off. And it seemed to come downhill, the river. There was a raft being steered, a mile away. It was a strange country. Nearer, a red-roofed, broad farm with white base and square dots of windows crouched beside the wall of beech foliage on the wood's edge. There were long strips of rye and clover and pale green corn. And just at his feet, below the knoll, was a darkish bog, where globe flowers stood breathless still on their slim stalks. And some of the pale gold bubbles were burst, and a broken fragment hung in the air. He thought he was going to sleep.

Suddenly something moved into this coloured mirage before his eyes. The Captain, a small, light-blue and scarlet figure, was trotting evenly between the strips of corn, along the level brow of the hill. And the man making flag-signals was coming on. Proud and sure moved the horseman's figure, the quick, bright thing, in which was concentrated all the light of this morning, which for the rest lay fragile, shining shadow. Submissive, apathetic, the young soldier sat and stared. But as the horse slowed to a walk, coming up the last steep path, the great flash flared over the body and soul of the orderly. He sat waiting. The back of his head felt as if it were weighted with a heavy piece of fire. He did not want to eat. His hands trembled slightly as he moved them. Meanwhile the officer on horseback was approaching slowly and proudly. The tension grew in the orderly's soul. Then again, seeing the Captain ease himself on the saddle, the flash blazed through him.

The Captain looked at the patch of light blue and scarlet, and dark head, scattered closely on the hill-side. It pleased him. The command pleased him. And he was feeling proud. His orderly was among them in common subjection. The officer rose a little on his stirrups to look. The young soldier sat with averted, dumb face. The Captain relaxed on his seat. His slim-legged, beautiful horse, brown as a beech nut, walked proudly uphill. The Captain passed into the zone of the company's atmosphere: a hot smell of men, of sweat, of leather. He knew it very well. After a word with the lieutenant, he went a few paces higher, and sat there, a dominant figure, his sweat-marked horse swishing its tail, while he looked down on his men, on his orderly, a nonentity among the crowd.

The young soldier's heart was like fire in his chest, and he breathed with difficulty. The officer, looking downhill, saw three of the young soldiers, two pails of water between them, staggering across a sunny green field. A table had been set up under a tree, and there the slim lieutenant stood, importantly busy. Then the Captain summoned himself to an act of courage. He called his orderly.

The flame leapt into the young soldier's throat as he heard the command, and he rose blindly, stifled. He saluted, standing below the officer. He did not look up. But there was the flicker in the Captain's voice.

"Go to the inn and fetch me . . ." the officer gave his commands. "Quick!" he added.

At the last word, the heart of the servant leapt with a flash, and he felt the strength come over his body. But he turned in mechanical obedience, and set off at a heavy run downhill, looking almost like a bear, his trousers bagging over his military boots. And the officer watched this blind, plunging run all the way.

But it was only the outside of the orderly's body that was obeying so humbly and mechanically. Inside had gradually accumulated a core into which all the energy of that young life was compact and concentrated. He executed his commission, and plodded quickly back uphill. There was a pain in his head as he walked that made him twist his features unknowingly. But hard there in the centre of his chest was himself, himself, firm, and not to be plucked to pieces.

The Captain had gone up into the wood. The orderly plodded through the hot, powerfully smelling zone of the company's atmosphere. He had a curious mass of energy inside him now. The Captain was less real than himself. He approached the green entrance to the wood. There, in the half-shade, he saw the horse standing, the sunshine and the flickering shadow of leaves dancing over his brown body. There was a clearing where timber had lately been felled. Here, in the gold-green shade beside the brilliant cup of sunshine, stood two figures, blue and pink, the bits of pink showing out plainly. The Captain was talking to his lieutenant.

The orderly stood on the edge of the bright clearing, where great trunks of trees, stripped and glistening, lay stretched like naked, brown-skinned bodies. Chips of wood littered the trampled floor, like splashed light, and the bases of the felled trees stood here and there, with their raw, level tops. Beyond was the brilliant, sunlit green of a beech.

"Then I will ride forward," the orderly heard his Captain say. The lieutenant saluted and strode away. He himself went forward. A hot flash passed through his belly, as he tramped towards his officer.

The Captain watched the rather heavy figure of the young soldier stumble forward, and his veins, too, ran hot. This was to be man to man between them. He yielded before the solid, stumbling figure with bent head. The orderly stooped and put the food on a level-sawn tree-base. The Captain watched the glistening, sun-inflamed, naked hands. He wanted to speak to the young soldier, but could not. The servant propped a bottle against his thigh, pressed open the cork, and poured out the beer into the mug. He kept his head bent. The Captain accepted the mug.

"Hot!" he said, as if amiably.

The flame sprang out of the orderly's heart, nearly suffocating him.

"Yes, sir," he replied, between shut teeth.

And he heard the sound of the Captain's drinking, and he clenched his fists, such a strong torment came into his wrists. Then came the faint clang of the closing of the pot-lid. He looked up. The Captain was watching him. He glanced swiftly away. Then he saw the officer stoop and take a piece of bread from the tree-base. Again the flash of flame went through the young soldier, seeing the stiff body stoop beneath him, and his hands jerked. He looked away. He could feel the officer was nervous. The bread fell as it was being broken. The officer ate the other piece. The two men stood tense and still, the master laboriously chewing his bread, the servant staring with averted face, his fist clenched.

Then the young soldier started. The officer had pressed open the lid of the mug again. The orderly watched the lip of the mug, and the white hand that clenched the handle, as if he were fascinated. It was raised. The youth followed it with his eyes. And then he saw the thin, strong throat of the elder man moving up and down as he drank, the strong jaw working. And the instinct which had been jerking at the young man's wrists suddenly jerked free. He jumped, feeling as if it were rent in two by a strong flame.

The spur of the officer caught in a tree root, he went down backwards with a crash, the middle of his back thudding sickeningly against a sharp-

edged tree-base, the pot flying away. And in a second the orderly, with serious, earnest young face, and underlip between his teeth, had got his knee
in the officer's chest and was pressing the chin backward over the farther
edge of the tree-stump, pressing, with all his heart behind in a passion of
relief, the tension of his wrists exquisite with relief. And with the base of his
palms he shoved at the chin, with all his might. And it was pleasant, too, to
have that chin, that hard jaw already slightly rough with beard, in his
hands. He did not relax one hair's breadth, but, all the force of all his
blood exulting in his thrust, he shoved back the head of the other man, till
there was a little "cluck" and a crunching sensation. Then he felt as if his
head went to vapour. Heavy convulsions shook the body of the officer,
frightening and horrifying the young soldier. Yet it pleased him, too, to re-
press them. It pleased him to keep his hands pressing back the chin, to feel
the chest of the other man yield in expiration to the weight of his strong,
young knees, to feel the hard twitchings of the prostrate body jerking his
own whole frame, which was pressed down on it.

But it went still. He could look into the nostrils of the other man, the
eyes he could scarcely see. How curiously the mouth was pushed out, ex-
aggerating the full lips, and the moustache bristling up from them. Then,
with a start, he noticed the nostrils gradually filled with blood. The red
brimmed, hesitated, ran over, and went in a thin trickle down the face to
the eyes.

It shocked and distressed him. Slowly, he got up. The body twitched
and sprawled there, inert. He stood and looked at it in silence. It was a pity
it was broken. It represented more than the thing which had kicked and
bullied him. He was afraid to look at the eyes. They were hideous now,
only the whites showing, and the blood running to them. The face of the
orderly was drawn with horror at the sight. Well, it was so. In his heart he
was satisfied. He had hated the face of the Captain. It was extinguished
now. There was a heavy relief in the orderly's soul. That was as it should
be. But he could not bear to see the long, military body lying broken over
the tree-base, the fine fingers crisped. He wanted to hide it away.

Quickly, busily, he gathered it up and pushed it under the felled tree
trunks, which rested their beautiful, smooth length either end on the logs.
The face was horrible with blood. He covered it with the helmet. Then he
pushed the limbs straight and decent, and brushed the dead leaves off the
fine cloth of the uniform. So, it lay quite still in the shadow under there. A
little strip of sunshine ran along the breast, from a chink between the logs.
The orderly sat by it for a few moments. Here his own life also ended.

Then, through his daze, he heard the lieutenant, in a loud voice, explaining to the men outside the wood, that they were to suppose the bridge on the river below was held by the enemy. Now they were to march to the attack in such and such a manner. The lieutenant had no gift of expression. The orderly, listening from habit, got muddled. And when the lieutenant began it all again he ceased to hear.

He knew he must go. He stood up. It surprised him that the leaves were glittering in the sun, and the chips of wood reflecting white from the ground. For him a change had come over the world. But for the rest it had not — all seemed the same. Only he had left it. And he could not go back. It was his duty to return with the beer-pot and the bottle. He could not. He had left all that. The lieutenant was still hoarsely explaining. He must go, or they would overtake him. And he could not bear contact with anyone now.

He drew his fingers over his eyes, trying to find out where he was. Then he turned away. He saw the horse standing in the path. He went up to it and mounted. It hurt him to sit in the saddle. The pain of keeping his seat occupied him as they cantered through the wood. He would not have minded anything, but he could not get away from the sense of being divided from the others. The path led out of the trees. On the edge of the wood he pulled up and stood watching. There in the spacious sunshine of the valley soldiers were moving in a little swarm. Every now and then, a man harrowing on a strip of fallow shouted to his oxen, at the turn. The village and the white-towered church was small in the sunshine. And he no longer belonged to it — he sat there, beyond, like a man outside in the dark. He had gone out from everyday life into the unknown and he could not, he even did not want to go back.

Turning from the sun-blazing valley, he rode deep into the wood. Tree trunks, like people standing grey and still, took no notice as he went. A doe, herself a moving bit of sunshine and shadow, went running through the flecked shade. There were bright green rents in the foliage. Then it was all pine wood, dark and cool. And he was sick with pain, and had an intolerable great pulse in his head, and he was sick. He had never been ill in his life. He felt lost, quite dazed with all this.

Trying to get down from the horse, he fell, astonished at the pain and his lack of balance. The horse shifted uneasily. He jerked its bridle and sent it cantering jerkily away. It was his last connection with the rest of things.

But he only wanted to lie down and not be disturbed. Stumbling through the trees, he came on a quiet place where beeches and pine trees grew on a slope. Immediately he had lain down and closed his eyes, his consciousness went racing on without him. A big pulse of sickness beat in him as if it throbbed through the whole earth. He was burning with dry heat. But he was too busy, too tearingly active in the incoherent race of delirium to observe.

III

He came to with a start. His mouth was dry and hard, his heart beat heavily, but he had not the energy to get up. His heart beat heavily. Where was he? — the barracks — at home? There was something knocking. And, making an effort, he looked round — trees, and litter of greenery, and reddish, bright, still pieces of sunshine on the floor. He did not believe he was himself, he did not believe what he saw. Something was knocking. He made a struggle towards consciousness, but relapsed. Then he struggled again. And gradually his surroundings fell into relationship with himself. He knew, and a great pang of fear went through his heart. Somebody was knocking. He could see the heavy, black rags of a fir tree overhead. Then everything went black. Yet he did not believe he had closed his eyes. He had not. Out of the blackness sight slowly emerged again. And someone was knocking. Quickly, he saw the blood-disfigured face of his Captain, which he hated. And he held himself still with horror. Yet, deep inside him, he knew that it was so, the Captain should be dead. But the physical delirium got hold of him. Someone was knocking. He lay perfectly still, as if dead, with fear. And he went unconscious.

When he opened his eyes again he started, seeing something creeping swiftly up a tree trunk. It was a little bird. And the bird was whistling overhead. Tap-tap-tap — it was the small, quick bird rapping the tree trunk with its beak, as if its head were a little round hammer. He watched it curiously. It shifted sharply, in its creeping fashion. Then, like a mouse, it slid down the bare trunk. Its swift creeping sent a flash of revulsion through him. He raised his head. It felt a great weight. Then, the little bird ran out of the shadow across a still patch of sunshine, its little head bobbing swiftly, its white legs twinkling brightly for a moment. How neat it was in its build, so compact, with piece of white on its wings. There were several of them. They were so pretty — but they crept like swift, erratic mice, running here and there among the beech-mast.

He lay down again exhausted, and his consciousness lapsed. He had a horror of the little creeping birds. All his blood seemed to be darting and creeping in his head. And yet he could not move.

He came to with a further ache of exhaustion. There was the pain in his head, and the horrible sickness, and his inability to move. He had never been ill in his life. He did not know where he was or what he was. Probably he had got sunstroke. Or what else? — he had silenced the Captain for ever — some time ago — oh, a long time ago. There had been blood on his face, and his eyes had turned upwards. It was all right, somehow. It was peace. But now he had got beyond himself. He had never been here before. Was it life, or not life? He was by himself. They were in a big, bright place, those others, and he was outside. The town, all the country, a big bright place of light: and he was outside, here, in the darkened open beyond, where each thing existed alone. But they would all have to come out there sometime, those others. Little, and left behind him, they all were. There had been father and mother and sweetheart. What did they all matter? This was the open land.

He sat up. Something scuffled. It was a little brown squirrel running in lovely undulating bounds over the floor, its red tail completing the undulation of its body — and then, as it sat up, furling and unfurling. He watched it, pleased. It ran on again, friskily, enjoying itself. It flew wildly at another squirrel, and they were chasing each other, and making little scolding, chattering noises. The soldier wanted to speak to them. But only a hoarse sound came out of his throat. The squirrels burst away — they flew up the trees. And then he saw the one peeping round at him, half-way up a tree trunk. A start of fear went through him, though in so far as he was conscious, he was amused. It still stayed, its little keen face staring at him halfway up the tree trunk, its little ears pricked up, its clawey little hands clinging to the bark, its white breast reared. He started from it in panic.

Struggling to his feet, he lurched away. He went on walking, walking, looking for something — for a drink. His brain felt hot and inflamed for want of water. He stumbled on. Then he did not know anything. He went unconscious as he walked. Yet he stumbled on, his mouth open.

When, to his dumb wonder, he opened his eyes on the world again, he no longer tried to remember what it was. There was thick, golden light behind golden-green glitterings, and tall, grey-purple shafts, and darknesses farther off, surrounding him, growing deeper. He was conscious of a sense of arrival. He was amid the reality, on the real, dark bottom. But there was the thirst burning in his brain. He felt lighter, not so heavy. He supposed it was newness. The air was muttering with thunder. He thought he was walking wonderfully swiftly and was coming straight to relief — or was it to water?

Suddenly he stood still with fear. There was a tremendous flare of gold, immense — just a few dark trunks like bars between him and it. All the young level wheat was burnished gold glaring on its silky green. A woman, full-skirted, a black cloth on her head for head-dress, was passing like a block of shadow through the glistening, green corn, into the full glare. There was a farm, too, pale blue in shadow, and the timber black. And there was a church spire, nearly fused away in the gold. The woman moved on, away from him. He had no language with which to speak to her. She was the bright, solid unreality. She would make a noise of words that would confuse him, and her eyes would look at him without seeing him. She was crossing there to the other side. He stood against a tree.

When at last he turned, looking down the long, bare grove whose flat bed was already filling dark, he saw the mountains in a wonder-light, not far away, and radiant. Behind the soft, grey ridge of the nearest range the farther mountains stood golden and pale grey, the snow all radiant like pure, soft gold. So still, gleaming in the sky, fashioned pure out of the ore of the sky, they shone in their silence. He stood and looked at them, his face illuminated. And like the golden, lustrous gleaming of the snow he felt his own thirst bright in him. He stood and gazed, leaning against a tree. And then everything slid away into space.

During the night the lightning fluttered perpetually, making the whole sky white. He must have walked again. The world hung livid round him for moments, fields a level sheen of grey-green light, trees in dark bulk, and the range of clouds black across a white sky. Then the darkness fell like a shutter, and the night was whole. A faint flutter of a half-revealed world, that could not quite leap out of the darkness! — Then there again stood a sweep of pallor for the land, dark shapes looming, a range of clouds hanging overhead. The world was a ghostly shadow, thrown for a moment upon the pure darkness, which returned ever whole and complete.

And the mere delirium of sickness and fever went on inside him — his brain opening and shutting like the night — then sometimes convulsions of terror from something with great eyes that stared round a tree — then the long agony of the march, and the sun decomposing his blood — then the pang of hate for the Captain, followed by a pang of tenderness and ease. But everything was distorted, born of an ache and resolving into an ache.

In the morning he came definitely awake. Then his brain flamed with the sole horror of thirstiness! The sun was on his face, the dew was steaming from his wet clothes. Like one possessed, he got up. There, straight in front of him, blue and cool and tender, the mountains ranged across the pale edge of the morning sky. He wanted them — he wanted them alone — he wanted to leave himself and be identified with them. They did not move, they were still and soft, with white, gentle markings of snow. He stood still, mad with suffering, his hands crisping and clutching. Then he was twisting in a paroxysm on the grass.

He lay still, in a kind of dream of anguish. His thirst seemed to have separated itself from him, and to stand apart, a single demand. Then the pain he felt was another single self. Then there was the clog of his body, another separate thing. He was divided among all kinds of separate things. There was some strange, agonised connection between them, but they were drawing farther apart. Then they would all split. The sun, drilling down on him, was drilling through the bond. Then they would all fall, fall through the everlasting lapse of space. Then again, his consciousness reasserted itself. He roused on to his elbow and stared at the gleaming mountains. There they ranked, all still and wonderful between earth and heaven. He stared till his eyes went black, and the mountains, as they stood in their beauty, so clean and cool, seemed to have it, that which was lost in him.

IV

When the soldiers found him, three hours later, he was lying with his face over his arm, his black hair giving off heat under the sun. But he was still alive. Seeing the open, black mouth the young soldiers dropped him in horror.

He died in the hospital at night, without having seen again.

The doctors saw the bruises on his legs, behind, and were silent.

The bodies of the two men lay together, side by side, in the mortuary, the one white and slender, but laid rigidly at rest, the other looking as if every moment it must rouse into life again, so young and unused, from a slumber.

{1914}

PATRICK WESTON
(pseudonym of Gerald Bernard Francis Hamilton)
{1888–1970}

The model for Mr. Norris — the antihero of Christopher Isherwood's novel *Mr. Norris Changes Trains* (1935) — Gerald Hamilton published *Desert Dreamers* in 1914 under "The Sign of the Tiger Lily" (and under the pseudonym Patrick Weston). As Isherwood writes in *Christopher and His Kind* (1976), the two first met in 1930, when Hamilton was working in Berlin as a sales representative for the *Times* (London) — a job he had managed to obtain despite having spent time in prison both during the Great War, when he had "openly expressed pro-German and anti-British sentiments," and the twenties, when he was "charged with swindling a Milanese jeweler out of a pearl necklace," an accusation he dismissed as a "technicality." (Hamilton titled his 1956 autobiography *Mr. Norris and I.*)

Like the vastly superior *Maurice*, completed the same year, *Desert Dreamers* not only portrays a homosexual affair with forthrightness, but confronts the perils homosexual men often faced at that time. Thus, into the central story of Julian Thelluson's passion for his handsome Arab guide, Hamilton inserts a would-be blackmailer named Hoxton. In the England of 1914, blackmail was a real and serious threat as a consequence of Henry Labouchere's notorious 1885 "blackmailer's charter," which criminalized acts of "gross indecency" committed either in public or private between adult males. What is surprising here is that Hamilton, through the agency of a mystical French doctor, turns the tables on Hoxton (and Labouchere) — enacting a revenge fantasy nursed by many Englishmen of the period.

The Guild Press republished *Desert Dreamers*, with an introduction by Isherwood, in 1966. Today even this edition is difficult to find. Here, those epigraphs to the individual chapters that were originally written in languages other than English have been translated. Also, the back of the dust jacket features a caricature of the author as "Sister Hamilton" by Ronald Searle. The caption reads, "I did make some plans for going clandestinely across the Irish Sea disguised as a nun . . ." 🕮

FROM *Desert Dreamers*

CHAPTER 7

> Clothe not the truth with vanity, neither conceal the truth
> against you over knowledge.
> — *Koran*

All that day — long, endless day, Julian saw nothing of Tayeb. Where could he be? Exhaustive inquiries from the stoical Ibrahim elicited the fact that Tayeb had other duties to perform. His father being dead, he had a mother and sister to take care of. He was the head of the family.

That evening, as he was descending the steps from the room of the hotel, where he had been admiring the sunset, he heard a voice at his elbow.

"Monsieur like also the beautiful things?"

"Tayeb, Tayeb, where have you been? I have looked for you all day. I have inquired —"

The boy raised his delicately arched eyebrows.

"Monsieur is kind — too kind. I also have thought of Monsieur. We will go out after dinner to-night, eh?"

"Yes, Tayeb, we will go out together and see what the night has to say to us — but not again to the dancing-girls."

"No-o-o," laughed the Arab. "Monsieur likes not ze girls!"

Julian strode towards his room to dress for dinner. Now he realised that this son of the desert had some fascination, attraction, influence — call it what you will — that no one had ever possessed before for him, which he hoped no one would ever possess again. He thought of his mother sunning herself at Hyères, or at Cannes, dividing her time between abusing the other visitors to the amiable Miss Mackenzie, the maid-companion whom she took with her wherever she went, and abusing the same Miss Mackenzie to the visitors whom she chanced to meet. What did his mother know or care about the inner meaning of life? The increase per pound of the price of butter or the exact reason why "that *odious* Mrs. So-and-So" left the hotel so hurriedly, absorbed all that lady's interest. Julian was young; but, at the same time, under the subtle, all-pervading influence of the desert he had attempted some sort of self-analysis — always a dangerous task. He had analysed his own soul — in his bath, it is true — still he quite thought he had analysed it sufficiently. He had weighed it in the balance and found it wanting. Wanting what? If something had not occurred to disturb the trend of his thoughts he might have been able to supply the answer. He wanted sympathy and understanding; he wanted friendship and love; he wanted life and laughter; and all these things one person and one alone seemed able to offer him. That person was Tayeb ben Mahmud. If Julian did not realise it then he realised it later.

Dinner over, Julian hurried to the hall, but no Tayeb was there waiting for him as he had expected.

Julian felt a keen sense of disappointment and anger. He strolled into the bureau and chatted with the manager.

"Monsieur has not had his coffee."

He turned round and saw Tayeb beside him.

"By Jove! No, I hav'n't. Why are you late, Tayeb?"

"Tayeb is not late. If Monsieur had remembered his coffee he would have found Tayeb awaiting him."

Julian looked at the Arab. Those wonderful eyes, so bright, so brown, fascinated, compelled him. When Tayeb was present he felt as one in a dream from which he would soon wake up. A desire to prick himself continually assailed him.

"*Allons!*" he said.

"To-night Monsieur will visit the Casino?"

"Heavens, Tayeb, is there a casino here? I came to be in the desert! Still, by all means, let us visit the Casino."

A few steps brought them to the low, white building which served as casino and Casino-Hotel. A kinematograph performance attracted some of the scanty visitors. The bar or the *boule* tables occupied the rest.

Tayeb strolled towards the tables, rolling a cigarette. Soon the gambling fever caught him and he began to lose franc after franc. Julian, who had been drinking a liqueur at the bar, joined him at the tables.

"Tayeb, why lose your money thus?" he began.

"And why not, Monsieur, if I wish to?"

The Arab's beautiful mouth melted into a smile that discovered a row of teeth such as no one ever had before. The sting of the gentle rebuke was cancelled at once.

"Come, Tayeb, I do not wish to stay."

"Monsieur commands. I am but his servant."

Tayeb swung his burnous more closely round him and, with a grace and dignity which surprised the few loafers round the door, he preceded Julian out of the Casino. As he descended the steps he threw away the end of his cigarette. Julian, who had been struggling into his overcoat, followed. With a sudden determination he stooped and picked up the cigarette end, popping it quickly into his cigarette case.

Tayeb had turned round to see if his master was following, and noticed Julian's strange action. He clenched his hand, opened it and clenched it more firmly than ever.

"Where shall we go, Tayeb?"

"Where Monsieur wills."

"Oh, anywhere! Let us take a walk. The Casino stifled me."

Tayeb walked on ahead with a swinging gait, humming to himself some Sahara love-song:

> The heart of a lion,
> The grace of a gazelle,
> The temper of a camel:
> All these has my love.
> Yet my soul is full of sorrow and my cup of bitterness.

"Tayeb, Tayeb, what a melancholy theme," said Julian.

"It is a song of life, Monsieur."

"Of life, Tayeb? Or of love?"

"Of both, Monsieur. They are the same."

"And is life so unhappy, then?"

"*Mais, oui, Monsieur!* If life was otherwise, how then should we have any pleasures?"

Julian was silent. It seemed as if he had stepped over from the world in which he had lived into another world, a world as different as black is from white, as joy is from sorrow, as an Arab is from a European.

All about them hung the purple blackness of the African night, full of mystery, full of charm, ponderous yet subtle. A faint breeze wafted the scent of mimosa from a clump of shrubs close by. The great moon shed a white, delicate light on the scene. Yes, indeed, Julian felt himself to be in another world.

On the two strolled together, till suddenly Tayeb changed from the melancholy sounds of his desert songs to a tune which was familiar to Julian, yet seemed strangely bizarre in his present surroundings.

> Au clair de la lune,
> Mon ami, Pierrot!

Tayeb began.

Julian joined in, his voice sounding harsh and loud compared to the gentle tones of his companion: —

> Prêtez-moi ta plume
> Pour écrire un jot —

> Ma chandelle est morte;
> Donnez-moi du feu;
> Ouvrez-vous la porte
> Pour l'amour de Dieu!

"*Pour l'amour de Dieu!*" repeated Tayeb, "*pour l'amour de Dieu!*"

They had now reached a dark part of the road with tall palm trees on either side. Julian could scarcely see Tayeb, but he felt the warmth of his fragrant breath on his cheek, the boy's breath, fragrant with the scent of a hundred flowers, fragrant with the perfume of jasmine and musk.

"Tayeb, Tayeb, let us return! I don't feel well. I feel afraid — of the night, of you, of myself. Let us return!"

Tayeb did not answer.

"Quick, Tayeb, let us return before it is too late."

"Will Monsieur deign to give his servant a cigarette?"

Tayeb had suddenly become the Arab guide again, obsequious, flattering.

"Of course — of course! but let us return," said Julian, proffering his case.

A low laugh, musical, infectious, tinkled like a bell in his ear. It seemed to echo and re-echo through his head. His brain was on fire. He felt he was losing control of himself. He looked at his companion. There stood Tayeb, proud and upright, the cigarette case flashing in the moon, empty but for the stump which Julian had picked up in the Casino gardens.

There was no need for words. The situation explained itself.

Tayeb stretched out his hand and took Julian by the arm. The latter felt the boy's warm body passionately vibrating with the force of life. His own body seemed to reply, as one bell sets another tingling.

"Too late!" murmured Julian; but the cry was hardly heard in the intensity of the moment.

The scent of mimosa was everywhere. Mimosa!

In after years Julian never allowed any one to bring that scent into his house. But upstairs a little shrine was always decorated with mimosa blossom.

Too late! He had gone down the dangerous path and had crossed — crossed to the other side.

Too late!

The bark of a desert dog brought him for a moment to his senses, but only for a moment.

The warm body at his side, the fire in his heart, set his pulses tingling. The blood coursed like fire through his veins.

With a cry of resignation to fate, with a cry of joy or rather of sorrow ended, he drew Tayeb to him; and, as there is a God in heaven, those two souls became united in that one sacred moment.

And all about them, all around them, hung the stillness of the desert.

CHAPTER 8

> He said "My name is Love."
> Then straight the first did turn himself to me
> And cried, "He lieth, for his name is Shame,
> But I am Love, and I was wont to be
> Alone in this fair garden, till he came
> Unasked by night; I am true Love, I fill
> The hearts of boy and girl with mutual flame."
> Then, sighing, said the other, "Have thy will,
> I am the Love that dare not speak its name."
> — LORD ALFRED DOUGLAS

The line that separated Arab from European, master from servant, had been rudely snapped. Julian and Tayeb became as one.

No longer did the Arab wait among the guides in the porch of the hotel. He went straight to Julian's room, chatted to him as he dressed, fingered his different toilet things, and asked innumerable questions. Sometimes, as Julian's room was on the ground floor, he would walk over the stretch of sand and tap at the window, thus avoiding the porter and the other Arabs at the doorway. Tayeb was proud of being an Arab, just as he was proud of his friendship with Julian. On the whole, he had a dislike and contempt for Europeans; but he knew that Julian was as different from most Europeans as he himself was different from other Arabs.

One morning on entering Julian's room, he said:

"We will visit the Jardin de Landon."

"Yes," assented Julian. "I have heard so much about it. With you, my Tayeb, I do not mind where I go."

They set out for the famous garden and, on reaching it, they wandered aimlessly, happily, down the shady paths and through the olive groves.

"I have never lived until now," exclaimed Julian with enthusiasm. "What glorious sunshine and what wonderful plants!"

Soon they came to a little square white house used by the owner of the garden as a smoke-room. Tired after their wanderings, the two stretched themselves upon the Eastern rugs and told stories. Then Tayeb took out a flute made of reeds and the haunting melody which he produced seemed to hover over them like a cloud of incense.

At last Tayeb ceased, and Julian, stretching out his hand, drew the boy towards him, till their lips met in a strange ecstasy. Outside, amidst the riot of flowers, bees droned an eternal chant. Then it seemed as if the light was eclipsed and the little room became full of shadows. Julian looked up. Tayeb, like a startled faun, clung to the arm of his master.

There, looking in through the square opening in the wall, was Joseph Hoxton. His face was a study. Critical as the moment was, Julian could not help a smile of amusement at the blank and utter surprise which was written on the face of the other.

"I heard a noise, so I came here," he began, awkwardly.

"Come in, by all means, Hoxton," said Julian, with forced cheerfulness. "Tayeb and I were just fooling about. Come round!"

But the Englishman made no movement. He looked again from one to the other of the two occupants of the weird Eastern room. Julian forgot that he was still clasping Tayeb's hand, and Tayeb returned that startled look. Very slowly, almost ponderously, the expression on Hoxton's face changed from one of surprise to one of horror.

"Good God, Thelluson! To think that you — And an Arab, too!"

He came round to the door.

"I can put only one construction on this strange intimacy of yours with that Arab boy. I think you are a dirty swine, and the sooner you clear out of here the better. Don't address yourself to me, sir, or I shall speak to the manager and tell him what kind of person you are. As for you, you dirty little Arab — be off! No wonder, Thelluson, you didn't care to stay with the dancing-girls that evening. Too superior, weren't you? You low hound! Bah!"

Joseph Hoxton stalked off, leaving Julian and Tayeb with a look of blankest amazement on their faces, compared to which Hoxton's former look of surprise was nothing.

Dimly, gradually, Julian began to realise what Hoxton meant. Of course, in the eyes of the world, he must seem diabolically vicious, a maniac, a worse criminal than a thief or a forger. He deserved to be cut by all "decent" society. Worthy fellows still wrangled as to whether a prison or a lunatic asylum was the better place for people with such tendencies. Joseph Hoxton, who at every opportunity dabbled in a loathsomeness which actually was revolting to the fine delicacy of one of Julian's temperament, was in comparison pure.

Julian gave vent to a loud burst of laughter. His thoughts caused him endless merriment. Tayeb, joining in the infectious mirth, produced his flute again, till at length the shadows had quite gone from his dear master's face.

Julian resolved to pay not the least attention to Hoxton's remarks. The man would be leaving Biskra soon. Julian decided to do nothing more than avoid him.

"Come, Tayeb," he said, presently, "I want to go out from this garden to a greater garden — the garden of oblivion."

"Whither, Looly?"

"Take me to the desert, Tayeb. There at least will be peace; there at least one may forget the littleness of man."

They returned first to the hotel, where they procured two fast Arab horses.

"We will go to the sand dunes; and, if there is time, we will return by Sidi-Okbar."

For a long time the two rode on without saying a word. Down the long, sandy road they went, past the Arab cemetery, through old Biskra, until it seemed that they were quite alone, alone in the wide world.

They reached the sand-dunes while the sun was still high in the heavens. Then, dismounting, they walked about, hand in hand. In front of them, behind them, all round them, stretched the desert, infinite, pitiless.

"Do you believe in God, Tayeb?" Julian suddenly inquired.

"But, of course, Looly," replied the boy. "I am not a fool."

True, indeed, thought Julian. All those absurd atheists, with their poisonous platitudes, their cheap cynicism, their disgusting doubt! He would have liked to have brought them all to that spot and there to have asked them the question which he had put to Tayeb. Then, if any one of them could honestly answer otherwise, why he would be inclined himself to disbelieve in God.

It is only in such places and at such times that God is truly manifest. Julian felt His presence on all sides.

"Tayeb, does God condemn our love?" he asked.

Tayeb did not answer. He motioned Julian to remount his horse, and they rode on in silence farther into the desert. Soon, in the distance, Julian noticed a clump of palm trees and a still pool of clear water.

"An oasis! Do you see, Tayeb?"

Still Tayeb kept silent.

They approached the oasis, yet it came no nearer. At last they reached the palm trees, but the delicious pool of water was nowhere to be seen.

A word tugged at Julian's heart.

"Mirage! Mirage!" exclaimed Julian.

"God's like a mirage," Tayeb softly replied, his gentle voice soothing Julian's overstrung nerves. "God appears to order this and to forbid that; and then — then we find it is quite otherwise. God is in our hearts. Each of us must judge for himself. I know if what I do is wrong or right."

"And, Tayeb, when you love me, is that wrong or right?"

"I never do what I know to be wrong," replied the Arab with simple sincerity. "Allah Al-lah el akbar: God is God: there is no God but God."

They rode homewards by the village of Sidi-Okbar, passing the famous mosque just as the muezzin was calling the faithful to prayer. Tayeb, without the least trace of awkwardness, dismounted from his horse, and, turning his face toward Mecca, bent his head in prayer.

Julian waited in an attitude of reverence.

God was surely present at that strange scene.

On reaching the hotel Julian was informed by the porter that Mr. Hoxton had left suddenly for England. Julian could scarcely disguise the sign of unmistakable relief with which he greeted the announcement.

That night, leaning out of his window, he drank in the perfume of the African night.

Very faintly, away in the distance, the sound of tom-toms and music told him that Biskra was alive with human beings. Otherwise his isolation was complete.

Suddenly he noticed a white form in the distance. Dreamily he watched it approaching nearer and nearer. The form was strangely familiar.

"Tayeb!" he whispered.

"Master!" answered the boy. "I felt afraid. I needed you. I —"

And Julian helped him into his room.

CHAPTER 9

> Angel of ecstasy, do you really know sorrow?
> Do you know shame, remorse, tears, boredom,
> And the hidden panic of sleepless nights when
> My heart is broken up like paper? Tell me,
> Angel of ecstasy? Have you ever known sorrow?
>   — CHARLES BAUDELAIRE

The days seemed to grow a little longer. The sun became more fierce; the tourists were fewer than before. March was well advanced. Then something happened. Something utter, cataclysmic, soul-destroying. Tayeb fell ill. Quite suddenly, without any warning, a fever seized him.

It came about thus:

One evening Julian was sitting in his room attempting to read an English newspaper. Every now and then he glanced anxiously at his watch, for he was expecting Tayeb.

Time went on: the bustle of the hotel became less and less obvious; the occasional footsteps past his door ceased altogether; the noise of the Arab cafes was over; the silence of the long corridor mocked at him.

Eleven o'clock: eleven-thirty: twelve — and Tayeb, Tayeb, who was never late and never too early, had promised to come at ten.

The possibility of his not being able to come never entered Julian's head as a serious contingency. Tayeb always came: never once had he failed. For the hundredth time Julian arose and looked longingly out of the window. The moon seemed to laugh at him, and he imagined that he saw a ghostly figure in white coming towards him. Then the palm-trees would rustle in the night-breeze and the figure would disappear.

Twelve o'clock! Two hours late! It seemed impossible, unheard of. Eventually the chill wind blew into his room, and Julian, sitting in an attitude of alertness, felt his bones shivering and his eyes growing dim.

Slowly, in an attitude of despair, he closed the window and prepared for the night of sorrow, the first night since the beginning of his love that he had been other than happy.

Morning came, and with it bad news. It was hardly seven when Ibrahim knocked at Julian's door and, entering, announced that Tayeb was sick of a bad fever, and was continually calling for his friend.

Scarcely noticing the clothes which he put on, Julian dressed himself and accompanied Ibrahim to Tayeb's house.

A low building, little better than a mud hut, situated in old Biskra, was where his love had been born and lived. Tayeb's mother opened the wooden door and, with many apologies for her unworthiness, implored the English lord to bless her house and to enter.

Without a word, as if he did not see the woman, Julian walked quickly to the low bed in a corner of the room on which, stretched out in an attitude of delirium, lay the body of his beloved.

Julian knew little of illness. Tayeb's continued and delirious chatter frightened him, though he distinctly heard his name mentioned over and over again.

"Ibrahim, you must get a doctor. Bring the best doctor here at once. Go quickly! Why do you delay?"

Ibrahim was entering into a long and heated argument with Tayeb's mother who, hitherto more a shadow than a human being, suddenly became assertive.

"Monsieur," said Ibrahim, "Tayeb's mother, she a stupid woman. No like French medicine man. Marabout, he come soon."

"Ibrahim, do at once what I tell you. Take no notice of her. Oh, go, for God's sake!"

By this time Julian had worked himself into a positive frenzy. He pulled out his pocket-case and thrust a hundred-franc note into the astonished Arab woman's hand. She had never in her life seen so much money before, and probably had never spent that amount in all her long years.

"Now tell her," Julian continued, "that I will give her another as soon as the doctor is here."

Ibrahim, showing a new interest in the matter now that money was concerned, spoke again to the woman, who now appeared more placid.

Meanwhile an idea, like a ray of sunny hope, struck Julian. The little French doctor of the Café d'Apollon at Algiers! He had always been so kind and sympathetic! Surely he would — understand! Julian, cautious even in his distress, began to wonder what the little doctor would think of the situation.

He pulled out a piece of paper and wrote on it hurriedly: "Can you come at once? I have urgent need of you." And he added the name and address of his friend at Algiers.

"Don't go for a doctor, Ibrahim, but take this telegram to the post-office. Run all the way!"

Ibrahim withdrew at once.

All that day Julian remained by the bedside of his love. Haunted by a thousand fears he refused to eat or drink. What if Tayeb should die? Die? The very thought was impossible. If Tayeb were to die, Julian would kill himself and leave instructions that they should be buried together.

As evening grew into night, Julian had perforce to leave. A telegram might be waiting for him at his hotel.

Through the shadows he stumbled on his way home, down the road with the tram-lines, past the spot where he and Tayeb had first discovered their love, past the tamarisk trees and the Casino.

As he entered the hotel the group of Arab guides, squatting in the doorway, became silent and looked at one another with meaning glances; but Julian noticed nothing. He went up to the porter and asked if there was a telegram for him.

"Monsieur Thelluson?" said the porter, as he proceeded, with appalling deliberation, to look in Julian's letter-rack. "*Mais, oui; le voilà; ceci vient d'arriver.*"

Julian tore it open and read: "For two months I have awaited such a telegram. I arrive to-morrow at afternoon."

There was no signature, nor was there need of any. Julian's heart went out in boundless gratitude to the friend who seemed so thoroughly to understand him.

That night Julian slept soundly, dreamlessly.

CHAPTER 10

> Many a time
> I have been half in love with easeful Death,
> Call'd him soft names in many a mused rhyme,
> To take into the air my quiet breath;
> Now more than ever seems it rich to die,
> To cease upon the midnight with no pain.
>
> — JOHN KEATS

Morning brought the news that Tayeb's condition was worse; but Julian was consoled by the thought that the doctor would soon arrive from Algiers.

In a dream he went to the station, and in a dream he conducted the doctor (tired though he was) straight to the little mud hut, there to battle for the life of Tayeb ben Mahmud.

The doctor installed himself at the Royal Hotel as Julian's guest, and before many days had passed his patient was under the same roof. Then, slowly, slowly, but very surely, Tayeb began to recover.

The early April sun, which had emptied the hotel of its visitors, filled Julian's heart with joy during those balmy days of Tayeb's convalescence. He would sit on the low balcony for hours together, absorbed in his own thoughts, supremely happy with the knowledge that his dear one was close to him, happy and nearly well. He enjoyed also the delightful companionship of the quaint little doctor. Briefly, he was too happy.

Then, as is always the way, IT happened.

Julian realised that his happiness could not continue long unpaid for; but he little anticipated such a dire and drastic ending.

He came in one day after a long walk in the desert. He walked with an easy, happy gait into the lounge, noticing no one, when suddenly a word reached him like the deathknell of all his hopes and all his happiness.

"Julian!"

He could not mistake his mother's voice, and the tone with which she pronounced his name made the word into a battle-cry. Instinctively he realised that his mother *knew*. He paused for a second, and then, fearfully, turned his head.

There sat his mother, very important, very prim, obviously angry. By her side sat her maid-companion, that poor creature who had to drive through Paris with the blinds down lest her purity should be outraged by the wickedness of the city.

But it was not at his mother, nor at her maid, that Julian looked so fiercely.

As he caught sight of Joseph Hoxton, sitting on one side of his mother,

Julian saw a look of challenge in his eyes. He saw it all. Joseph Hoxton's strange departure and strange silence: he had not bothered to heed about either; but now he saw that there was reason for both.

There sat the great Hoxton, a sad expression on his hypocritical face, the very embodiment of British respectability.

"Julian," commanded his mother, "come upstairs to my room. I wish to speak to you."

Then the devil rose in Julian, who was usually the most docile of children. And a voice, which was not his, spoke words over which he had no control.

"No, mother," he said quietly. "If you have anything to say to me, say it now before all."

At that moment the doctor passed through the corridor, and Julian called to him.

"May I introduce my mother?" he said. "Mother, this is Dr. Maisnon, who — who has been very kind to me."

Lady Evelyn Thelluson raised her lorgnettes and bowed stiffly to the doctor who, for his part, was almost too much astonished to speak.

"Madame will excuse me — I have a patient!" he managed to exclaim.

"No, sir!" thundered Lady Evelyn. "Perhaps you may be able to give some explanation of my son's extraordinary conduct."

"Madame?"

"Let us go on to the balcony, then, mother," said Julian, hurriedly, "and have tea."

Slowly they went upstairs.

"Will you introduce me to your friend?" said the doctor to Julian. "I have seen him in Algiers."

"Not my friend — my mother's," Julian corrected in a loud voice.

"Oh! oh!" whispered the little doctor, who was not slow-witted, but was extremely distressed and puzzled by this scene. "As I said, I have seen your friend in Algiers — at other places besides the Governor's parties," he added, leaving Julian to wonder what the enigmatic statement was meant to imply.

"Will Madame allow a few moments' conversation?" asked the doctor, politely. Then, turning to Julian, he said, "Go to Tayeb — quickly."

Julian hastened away.

What actually took place between his mother and the doctor, Julian never knew. But after dinner the doctor came into his room and, closing the door, looked fixedly at him. Then (how hot the night was, thought Julian) he began to speak of strange things. Gradually Julian fell into a kind of doze, a dreamy doze, the very opposite of a nightmare.

He dreamed that he was in a kind of Moslem Paradise, such as Tayeb had once described to him. On all sides were beauteous maids, who tempted him with rare fruits, their lascivious movements all the while being intended to excite his passions. In his dream the colours were vivid — that pleased him — and when he awoke that was all he remembered.

"My dear doctor, do excuse me," he laughed. "Awfully rude of me, but I was so tired. I must have slept. I had such a wonderful dream." Then he stopped abruptly, noticing the strange excited light that shone in the doctor's usually expressionless eyes.

"Yes, yes," said the doctor, thickly, "go on, go on."

"It seems to interest you, but really I don't remember much about my dream. How's Tayeb? That's more important."

The doctor jumped up and waved his hands excitedly, all the while muttering to himself.

"Good heavens, doctor, what is the matter?" asked Julian, by this time seriously alarmed.

"Nothing — or rather everything, my son. Some day, very soon, I will tell you. Go now to Tayeb. It is fated."

Julian found Tayeb not so well again.

"So the mother of my lord has come to the desert, all the way to the desert, because her son loves Tayeb. Am I so *vairy* important?"

"Tayeb, Tayeb, don't talk like that! My mother is a woman; she cannot understand our love. At any rate nothing, nothing in the world shall part us. Speak to me, Tayeb, and forgive my mother."

Once again their lips met. When Julian turned he found the doctor standing by him, a happy, almost paternal look of benevolence on his face. He looked as if he were going to say, "Be happy, my children; make the most of the present."

After a little while Julian took his farewell of Tayeb, and the doctor opened the door for him as he said goodnight.

A quick step was heard down the passage — it sounded louder in the silence. In a flash the doctor disappeared. Julian followed.

"So, Monsieur Hoxton, you like to listen at the doors," said the doctor, threateningly. "Very well! A little telegram will bring here to me one Bayo ben Salim, from Algiers, who would do anything for me. Ah, I see you know him! A guide, is he not? Yes, yes! Well, with what he could tell about you and from evidence collected here, I think we could convince *cette chère madame* — yes? Perhaps it would be as well if your business recalled you to London to-morrow!"

And in the morning, sure enough, Joseph Hoxton left, to the frantic regret of Lady Evelyn and apparently also of the doctor.

{1914}

EDWARD MORGAN FORSTER

{1879–1970}

In a letter to Forster, whom he had met in 1929 at one of Virginia Woolf's parties, William Plomer wrote:

> I can't understand anybody thinking *Maurice* ought to have a tragic ending. The happy ending seems to me in a sense the whole point of the book, and the way it is led up to is magnificent. In actual technique the book seems to me marvellous — I don't know anybody who produces so well the feeling of life without fishy realism. I think in some ways your own private magic is at its very best in this book. If I had read it when I was seventeen I should have made a better job of my life in the succeeding ten years or bust in the attempt. It would have been something to steer by.

Maurice was completed in 1914, but not published until 1971. Even at that relatively late date, much of the critical response to the novel was homophobic. Cynthia Ozick, in a review titled "Morgan and Maurice: A Fairy Tale" (published first in *Commentary*, then included in her collections *Art and Ardor* and *What Henry James Knew*), displayed a willful obtuseness. *Maurice*, for her, is a fairy tale because it is about "make-believe," because "the wish for lasting homoerotic bliss is allowed to come true." But this claim, like Freud's analysis of the origins of Leonardo da Vinci's homosexuality, is based upon a misreading. That Maurice and Alec live in love "for the ever that fiction allows" is declared only in the "Terminal Note" written almost half a century after the novel itself. This "Terminal Note" was, no doubt, a mistake, insofar as it has been used to give the novel a program. As it is, nothing in *Maurice* itself promises the "happily ever after" of the classical fairy tale. All that Forster has given Maurice and Alec is a chance; "though loyalty cannot be counted on it can always be hoped for and be worked towards and may flourish in the most unlikely soil."

And yet, even if Forster had allowed the two men to live "happily ever after," why would Ozick call *Maurice* a "fairy tale"? Is a story a fairy tale just because two people find happiness in each other? Forster had before him more than one example of male couples who spent most of their lives together: Benjamin Britten and Peter Pears, William Plomer and Charles Erdmann, Edward Carpenter and George Merrill — the last of whom, in touching Forster's backside, produced a sensation that "seemed to go straight through the small of my back into my ideas, without involving my thoughts."

And thus bubbled forth the first, and perhaps still greatest, of all homosexual novels. ❧

FROM *Maurice*

CHAPTER 6

All that day and the next Maurice was planning how he could see this queer fish again. The chances were bad. He did not like to call on a senior-year man, and they were at different colleges. Risley, he gathered, was well known at the Union, and he went to the Tuesday debate in the hope of hearing him: perhaps he would be easier to understand in public. He was not attracted to the man in the sense that he wanted him for a friend, but he did feel he might help him — how, he didn't formulate. It was all very obscure, for the mountains still overshadowed Maurice. Risley, surely capering on the summit, might stretch him a helping hand.

Having failed at the Union, he had a reaction. He didn't want anyone's help; he was all right. Besides, none of his friends would stand Risley, and he must stick to his friends. But the reaction soon passed, and he longed to see him more than ever. Since Risley was so odd, might he not be odd too, and break all the undergraduate conventions by calling? One "ought to be human," and it was a human sort of thing to call. Much struck by the discovery, Maurice decided to be Bohemian also, and to enter the room making a witty speech in Risley's own style. "You've bargained for more than you've gained" occurred to him. It didn't sound very good, but Risley had been clever at not letting him feel a fool, so he would fire it off if inspired to nothing better, and leave the rest to luck.

For it had become an adventure. This man who said one ought to "talk, talk" had stirred Maurice incomprehensibly. One night, just before ten o'clock, he slipped into Trinity and waited in the Great Court until the gates were shut behind him. Looking up, he noticed the night. He was indifferent to beauty as a rule, but "what a show of stars!" he thought. And how the fountain splashed when the chimes died away, and the gates and doors all over Cambridge had been fastened up. Trinity men were around him — all of enormous intellect and culture. Maurice's set had laughed at Trinity, but they could not ignore its disdainful radiance, or deny the superiority it scarcely troubles to affirm. He had come to it without their knowledge, humbly, to ask its help. His witty speech faded in its atmosphere; and his heart beat violently. He was ashamed and afraid.

Risley's rooms were at the end of a short passage, which since it contained no obstacle was unlighted, and visitors slid along the wall until

they hit the door. Maurice hit it sooner than he expected — a most awful whack — and exclaimed "Oh damnation" loudly, while the panels
quivered.

"Come in," said a voice. Disappointment awaited him. The speaker
was a man of his own college, by name Durham. Risley was out.

"Do you want Mr Risley? Hullo, Hall!"

"Hullo! Where's Risley?"

"I don't know."

"Oh, it's nothing. I'll go."

"Are you going back into college?" asked Durham without looking up:
he was kneeling over a castle of pianola records on the floor.

"I suppose so, as he isn't here. It wasn't anything particular."

"Wait a sec, and I'll come too. I'm sorting out the Pathetic Sym-
phony."

Maurice examined Risley's room and wondered what would have
been said in it, and then sat on the table and looked at Durham. He was a
small man — very small — with simple manners and a fair face, which
had flushed when Maurice blundered in. In the college he had a reputation for brains and also for exclusiveness. Almost the only thing Maurice
had heard about him was that he "went out too much," and this meeting
in Trinity confirmed it.

"I can't find the March," he said. "Sorry."

"All right."

"I'm borrowing them to play on Fetherstonhaugh's pianola."

"Under me."

"Have you come into college, Hall?"

"Yes, I'm beginning my second year."

"Oh yes, of course, I'm third."

He spoke without arrogance, and Maurice, forgetting due honour
to seniority, said, "You look more like a fresher than a third-year man, I
must say."

"I may do, but I feel like an M.A."

Maurice regarded him attentively.

"Risley's an amazing chap," he continued.

Maurice did not reply.

"But all the same a little of him goes a long way."

"Still you don't mind borrowing his things."

He looked up again. "Oughtn't I to?" he asked.

"I'm only ragging, of course," said Maurice, slipping off the table.
"Have you found that music yet?"

"No."

"Because I must be going;" he was in no hurry, but his heart, which had never stopped beating quickly, impelled him to say this.

"Oh. All right."

This was not what Maurice had intended. "What is it you want?" he asked, advancing.

"The March out of the Pathétique —"

"That means nothing to me. So you like this style of music."

"I do."

"A good waltz is more my style."

"Mine too," said Durham, meeting his eye. As a rule Maurice shifted, but he held firm on this occasion. Then Durham said, "The other movement may be in that pile over by the window. I must look. I shan't be long." Maurice said resolutely, "I must go now."

"All right, I'll stop."

Beaten and lonely, Maurice went. The stars blurred, the night had turned towards rain. But while the porter was getting the keys at the gate he heard quick footsteps behind him.

"Got your March?"

"No, I thought I'd come along with you instead."

Maurice walked a few steps in silence, then said, "Here, give me some of those things to carry."

"I've got them safe."

"Give," he said roughly, and jerked the records from under Durham's arm. No other conversation passed. On reaching their own college they went straight to Fetherstonhaugh's room, for there was time to try a little music over before eleven o'clock. Durham sat down at the pianola. Maurice knelt beside him.

"Didn't know you were in the aesthetic push, Hall," said the host.

"I'm not — I want to hear what they're up to."

Durham began, then desisted, saying he would start with the 5/4 instead.

"Why?"

"It's nearer waltzes."

"Oh, never mind that. Play what you like. Don't go shifting — it wastes time."

But he could not get his way this time. When he put his hand on the roller Durham said, "You'll tear it, let go," and fixed the 5/4 instead.

Maurice listened carefully to the music. He rather liked it.

"You ought to be this end," said Fetherstonhaugh, who was working by the fire. "You should get away from the machine as far as you can."

"I think so — Would you mind playing it again if Fetherstonhaugh doesn't mind?"

"Yes, do, Durham. It is a jolly thing."

Durham refused. Maurice saw that he was not pliable. He said, "A movement isn't like a separate piece — you can't repeat it" — an unintelligible excuse, but apparently valid. He played the Largo, which was far from jolly, and then eleven struck and Fetherstonhaugh made them tea. He and Durham were in for the same Tripos, and talked shop, while Maurice listened. His excitement had never ceased. He saw that Durham was not only clever, but had a tranquil and orderly brain. He knew what he wanted to read, where he was weak and how far the officials could help him. He had neither the blind faith in tutors and lectures that was held by Maurice and his set nor the contempt professed by Fetherstonhaugh. "You can always learn something from an older man, even if he hasn't read the latest Germans." They argued a little about Sophocles, then in low water Durham said it was a pose in "us undergraduates" to ignore him and advised Fetherstonhaugh to re-read the *Ajax* with his eye on the characters rather than the author; he would learn more that way, both about Greek grammar and life.

Maurice regretted all this. He had somehow hoped to find the man unbalanced. Fetherstonhaugh was a great person, both in brain and brawn, and had a trenchant and copious manner. But Durham listened unmoved, shook out the falsities and approved the rest. What hope for Maurice who was nothing but falsities? A stab of anger went through him. Jumping up, he said good night, to regret his haste as soon as he was outside the door. He settled to wait, not on the staircase itself, for this struck him as absurd, but somewhere between its foot and Durham's own room. Going out into the court, he located the latter, even knocking at the door, though he knew the owner was absent, and looking in he studied furniture and pictures in the firelight. Then he took his stand on a sort of bridge in the courtyard. Unfortunately it was not a real bridge: it only spanned a slight depression in the ground, which the architect had tried to utilize in his effect. To stand on it was to feel in a photographic studio, and the parapet was too low to lean upon. Still, with a pipe in his mouth, Maurice looked fairly natural, and hoped it wouldn't rain.

The lights were out, except in Fetherstonhaugh's room. Twelve struck, then a quarter past. For a whole hour he might have been watching for Durham. Presently there was a noise on the staircase and the neat little figure ran out with a gown round its throat and books in its hand. It was the moment for which he had waited, but he found himself strolling away. Durham went to his rooms behind him. The opportunity was passing.

"Good night," he screamed; his voice was going out of gear, and startling them both.

"Who's that? Good night, Hall. Taking a stroll before bed?"

"I generally do. You don't want any more tea, I suppose?"

"Do I? No, perhaps it's a bit late for tea." Rather tepidly he added, "Like some whisky though?"

"Have you a drop?" leaped from Maurice.

"Yes — come in. Here I keep: ground floor."

"Oh, here!" Durham turned on the light. The fire was nearly out now. He told Maurice to sit down and brought up a table with glasses.

"Say when?"

"Thanks — most awfully, most awfully."

"Soda or plain?" he asked, yawning.

"Soda," said Maurice. But it was impossible to stop, for the man was tired and had only invited him out of civility. He drank and returned to his own room, where he provided himself with plenty of tobacco and went into the court again.

It was absolutely quiet now, and absolutely dark. Maurice walked to and fro on the hallowed grass, himself noiseless, his heart glowing. The rest of him fell asleep, bit by bit, and first of all his brain, his weakest organ. His body followed, then his feet carried him upstairs to escape the dawn. But his heart had lit never to be quenched again, and one thing in him at last was real.

Next morning he was calmer. He had a cold for one thing, the rain having soaked him unnoticed, and for another he had overslept to the extent of missing a chapel and two lectures. It was impossible to get his life straight. After lunch he changed for football, and being in good time flung himself on his sofa to sleep till tea. But he was not hungry. Refusing an invitation, he strolled out into the town and, meeting a Turkish bath, had one. It cured his cold, but made him late for another lecture. When Hall came, he felt he could not face the mass of Old Sunningtonians, and, though he had not signed off, absented himself, and dined alone at the Union. He saw Risley there, but with indifference. Then the evening began again, and he found to his surprise that he was very clear-headed, and could do six hours' work in three. He went to bed at his usual time, and woke up healthy and very happy. Some instinct, deep below his consciousness, had advised him to let Durham and his thoughts about Durham have a twenty-four hours' rest.

They began to see a little of one another. Durham asked him to lunch, and Maurice asked him back, but not too soon. A caution alien to his nature was at work. He had always been cautious pettily, but this was on a large scale. He became alert, and all his actions that October term might be described in the language of battle. He would not venture onto difficult ground. He spied out Durham's weaknesses as well as his strength. And above all he exercised and cleaned his powers.

If obliged to ask himself, "What's all this?" he would have replied, "Durham is another of those boys in whom I was interested at school," but he was obliged to ask nothing, and merely went ahead with his mouth and his mind shut. Each day with its contradictions slipped into the abyss, and he knew that he was gaining ground. Nothing else mattered. If he worked well and was nice socially, it was only a by-product, to which he had devoted no care. To ascend, to stretch a hand up the mountainside until a hand catches it, was the end for which he had been born. He forgot the hysteria of his first night and his stranger recovery. They were steps which he kicked behind him. He never even thought of tenderness and emotion; his considerations about Durham remained cold. Durham didn't dislike him, he was sure. That was all he wanted. One thing at a time. He didn't so much as have hopes, for hope distracts, and he had a great deal to see to.

CHAPTER 7

Next term they were intimate at once.

"Hall, I nearly wrote a letter to you in the vac," said Durham, plunging into a conversation.

"That so?"

"But an awful screed. I'd been having a rotten time."

His voice was not very serious, and Maurice said, "What went wrong? Couldn't you keep down the Christmas pudding?"

It presently appeared that the pudding was allegorical; there had been a big family row.

"I don't know what you'll say — I'd rather like your opinion on what happened if it doesn't bore you."

"Not a bit," said Maurice.

"We've had a bust up on the religious question."

At that moment they were interrupted by Chapman.

"I'm sorry, we're fixing something," Maurice told him.

Chapman withdrew.

"You needn't have done that, any time would do for my rot," Durham protested. He went on more earnestly.

"Hall, I don't want to worry you with my beliefs, or rather with their absence, but to explain the situation I must just tell you that I'm unorthodox. I'm not a Christian."

Maurice held unorthodoxy to be bad form and had remarked last term in a college debate that if a man had doubts he might have the grace to keep them to himself. But he only said to Durham that it was a difficult question and a wide one.

"I know — it isn't about that. Leave it aside." He looked for a little into the fire. "It is about the way my mother took it. I told her six months ago — in the summer — and she didn't mind. She made some foolish joke, as she does, but that was all. It just passed over. I was thankful, for it had been on my mind for years. I had never believed since I found something that did me better, quite as a kid, and when I came to know Risley and his crew it seemed imperative to speak out. You know what a point they make of that — it's really their main point. So I spoke out. She said, 'Oh yes, you'll be wiser when you are as old as me': the mildest form of the thing conceivable, and I went away rejoicing. Now it's all come up again."

"Why?"

"Why? On account of Christmas. I didn't want to communicate. You're supposed to receive it three times a year —"

"Yes, I know. Holy Communion."

"— and at Christmas it came round. I said I wouldn't. Mother wheedled me in a way quite unlike her, asked me to do it this once to please her — then got cross, said I would damage her reputation as well as my own — we're the local squires and the neighbourhood's uncivilized. But what I couldn't stand was the end. She said I was wicked. I could have honoured her if she had said that six months before, but now! now to drag in holy words like wickedness and goodness in order to make me do what I disbelieved. I told her I have my own communions. 'If I went to them as you and the girls are doing to yours my gods would kill me!' I suppose that was too strong."

Maurice, not well understanding, said, "So did you go?"

"Where?"

"To the church."

Durham sprang up. His face was disgusted. Then he bit his lip and began to smile.

"No, I didn't go to church, Hall. I thought that was plain."

"I'm sorry — I wish you'd sit down. I didn't mean to offend you. I'm rather slow at catching."

Durham squatted on the rug close to Maurice's chair. "Have you known Chapman long?" he asked after a pause.

"Here and at school, five years."

"Oh." He seemed to reflect. "Give me a cigarette. Put it in my mouth. Thanks." Maurice supposed the talk was over, but after the swirl he went on. "You see — you mentioned you had a mother and two sisters, which is exactly my own allowance, and all through the row I was wondering what you would have done in my position."

"Your mother must be very different to mine."

"What is yours like?"

"She never makes a row about anything."

"Because you've never yet done anything she wouldn't approve, I expect — and never will."

"Oh no, she wouldn't fag herself."

"You can't tell, Hall, especially with women. I'm sick with her. That's my real trouble that I want your help about."

"She'll come round."

"Exactly, my dear chap, but shall I? I must have been pretending to like her. This row has shattered my lie. I did think I had stopped building lies. I despise her character, I am disgusted with her. There, I have told you what no one else in the world knows."

Maurice clenched his fist and hit Durham lightly on the head with it. "Hard luck," he breathed.

"Tell me about your home life."

"There's nothing to tell. We just go on."

"Lucky devils."

"Oh, I don't know. Are you ragging, or was your vac really beastly, Durham?"

"Absolute Hell, misery and Hell."

Maurice's fist unclenched to reform with a handful of hair in its grasp.

"Waou, that hurts!" cried the other joyously.

"What did your sisters say about Holy Communion?"

"One's married a clerg — No, that hurts."

"Absolute Hell, eh?"

"Hall, I never knew you were a fool —" he possessed himself of Maurice's hand — "and the other's engaged to Archibald London, Esquire, of the — Waou! Ee! Shut up, I'm going." He fell between Maurice's knees.

"Well, why don't you go if you're going?"

"Because I can't go."

It was the first time he had dared to play with Durham. Religion and relatives faded into the background, as he rolled him up in the hearth rug and fitted his head into the waste-paper basket. Hearing the noise, Fetherstonhaugh ran up and helped. There was nothing but ragging for many days after that, Durham becoming quite as silly as himself. Wherever they met, which was everywhere, they would butt and spar and embroil their friends. At last Durham got tired. Being the weaker he was hurt sometimes, and his chairs had been broken. Maurice felt the change at once. His coltishness passed, but they had become demonstrative during it. They walked arm in arm or arm around shoulder now. When they sat it was nearly always in the same position — Maurice in a chair, and Durham at his feet, leaning against him. In the world of their friends this attracted no notice. Maurice would stroke Durham's hair.

And their range increased elsewhere. During this Lent term Maurice came out as a theologian. It was not humbug entirely. He believed that he believed, and felt genuine pain when anything he was accustomed to met criticism — the pain that masquerades among the middle classes as Faith. It was not Faith, being inactive. It gave him no support, no wider outlook. It didn't exist till opposition touched it, when it ached like a useless nerve. They all had these nerves at home, and regarded them as divine, though neither the Bible nor the Prayer Book nor the Sacraments nor Christian ethics nor anything spiritual were alive to them. "But how can people?" they exclaimed, when anything was attacked, and subscribed to Defence Societies. Maurice's father was becoming a pillar of Church and Society when he died, and other things being alike Maurice would have stiffened too.

But other things were not to be alike. He had this overwhelming desire to impress Durham. He wanted to show his friend that he had something besides brute strength, and where his father would have kept canny silence he began to talk, talk. "You think I don't think, but I can tell you I do." Very often Durham made no reply and Maurice would be terrified lest he was losing him. He had heard it said, "Durham's all right as long as you amuse him, then he drops you," and feared lest by exhibiting his orthodoxy he was bringing on what he tried to avoid. But he could not stop. The craving for notice grew overwhelming, so he talked, talked.

One day Durham said, "Hall, why this thusness?"

"Religion means a lot to me," bluffed Maurice. "Because I say so little you think I don't feel. I care a lot."

"In that case come to coffee after hall."

They were just going in. Durham, being a scholar, had to read grace, and there was cynicism in his accent. During the meal they looked at each other. They sat at different tables, but Maurice had contrived to move his seat so that he could glance at his friend. The phase of bread pellets was over. Durham looked severe this evening and was not speaking to his neighbours. Maurice knew that he was thoughtful and wondered what about.

"You wanted to get it and you're going to," said Durham, sporting the door.

Maurice went cold and then crimson. But Durham's voice, when he next heard it, was attacking his opinions on the Trinity. He thought he minded about the Trinity, yet it seemed unimportant, beside the fires of his terror. He sprawled in an armchair, all the strength out of him, with sweat on his forehead and hands. Durham moved about getting the coffee ready and saying, "I knew you wouldn't like this, but you have brought it on yourself. You can't expect me to bottle myself up indefinitely. I must let out sometimes."

"Go on," said Maurice, clearing his throat.

"I never meant to talk, for I respect people's opinions too much to laugh at them, but it doesn't seem to me that you have any opinions to respect. They're all second-hand tags — no, tenth-hand."

Maurice, who was recovering, remarked that this was pretty strong.

"You're always saying, 'I care a lot.' "

"And what right have you to assume that I don't?"

"You do care a lot about something, Hall, but it obviously isn't the Trinity."

"What is it then?"

"Rugger."

Maurice had another attack. His hands shook and he spilt the coffee on the arm of the chair. "You're a bit unfair," he heard himself saying. "You might at least have the grace to suggest that I care about people."

Durham looked surprised, but said, "You care nothing about the Trinity, anyway."

"Oh, damn the Trinity."

He burst with laughter. "Exactly, exactly. We will now pass on to my next point."

"I don't see the use, and I've a rotten head any way — I mean a headache. Nothing's gained by — all this. No doubt I can't prove the thing — I mean the arrangement of Three Gods in One and One in Three. But it means a lot to millions of people, whatever you may say, and we aren't going to give it up. We feel about it very deeply. God is good. That is the main point. Why go off on a side track?"

"Why feel so deeply about a side track?"

"What?"

Durham tidied up his remarks for him.

"Well, the whole show all hangs together."

"So that if the Trinity went wrong it would invalidate the whole show?"

"I don't see that. Not at all."

He was doing badly, but his head really did ache, and when he wiped the sweat off it re-formed.

"No doubt I can't explain well, as I care for nothing but rugger."

Durham came and sat humorously on the edge of his chair.

"Look out — you've gone into the coffee now."

"Blast — so I have."

While he cleaned himself, Maurice unsported and looked out into the court. It seemed years since he had left it. He felt disinclined to be longer alone with Durham and called to some men to join them. A coffee of the usual type ensued, but when they left Maurice felt equally disinclined to leave with them. He flourished the Trinity again. "It's a mystery," he argued.

"It isn't a mystery to me. But I honour anyone to whom it really is."

Maurice felt uncomfortable and looked at his own thick brown hands. Was the Trinity really a mystery to him? Except at his confirmation had he given the institution five minutes' thought? The arrival of the other men had cleared his head, and, no longer emotional, he glanced at his mind. It appeared like his hands — serviceable, no doubt, and healthy, and capable of development. But it lacked refinement, it had never touched mysteries, nor a good deal else. It was thick and brown.

"My position's this," he announced after a pause. "I don't believe in the Trinity, I give in there, but on the other hand I was wrong when I said everything hangs together. It doesn't, and because I don't believe in the Trinity it doesn't mean I am not a Christian."

"What do you believe in?" said Durham, unchecked.

"The — the essentials."

"As?"

In a low voice Maurice said, "The Redemption." He had never spoken the words out of church before and thrilled with emotion. But he did not believe in them any more than in the Trinity, and knew that Durham would detect this. The Redemption was the highest card in the suit, but that suit wasn't trumps, and his friend could capture it with some miserable two.

All that Durham said at the time was, "Dante did believe in the Trinity," and going to the shelf found the concluding passage of the *Paradiso*. He read to Maurice about the three rainbow circles that intersect, and between their junctions is enshadowed a human face. Poetry bored Maurice, but towards the close he cried, "Whose face was it?"

"God's, don't you see?"

"But isn't that poem supposed to be a dream?"

Hall was a muddle-headed fellow, and Durham did not try to make sense of this, nor knew that Maurice was thinking of a dream of his own at school, and of the voice that had said, "That is your friend."

"Dante would have called it an awakening, not a dream."

"Then you think that sort of stuff's all right?"

"Belief's always right," replied Durham, putting back the book. "It's all right and it's also unmistakable. Every man has somewhere about him some belief for which he'd die. Only isn't it improbable that your parents and guardians told it to you? If there is one won't it be part of your own flesh and spirit? Show me that. Don't go hawking out tags like 'The Redemption' or 'The Trinity'."

"I've given up the Trinity."

"The Redemption, then."

"You're beastly hard," said Maurice. "I always knew I was stupid, it's no news. The Risley set are more your sort and you had better talk to them."

Durham looked awkward. He was nonplussed for a reply at last, and let Maurice slouch off without protest. Next day they met as usual. It had not been a tiff but a sudden gradient, and they travelled all the quicker after the rise. They talked theology again, Maurice defending the Redemption. He lost. He realized that he had no sense of Christ's existence or of His goodness, and should be positively sorry if there was such a person. His dislike of Christianity grew and became profound. In ten days he gave up communicating, in three weeks he cut out all the chapels he dared. Durham was puzzled by the rapidity. They were both puzzled, and Maurice, although he had lost and yielded all his opinions, had a queer feeling that he was really winning and carrying on a campaign that he had begun last term.

For Durham wasn't bored with him now. Durham couldn't do without him, and would be found at all hours curled up in his room and spoiling to argue. It was so unlike the man, who was reserved and no great dialectician. He gave as his reason for attacking Maurice's opinions that "They are so rotten, Hall, everyone else up here believes respectably." Was this the whole truth? Was there not something else behind his new manner and furious iconoclasm? Maurice thought there was. Outwardly in retreat, he thought that his Faith was a pawn well lost; for in capturing it Durham had exposed his heart.

Towards the end of term they touched upon a yet more delicate subject. They attended the Dean's translation class, and when one of the men was forging quietly ahead Mr Cornwallis observed in a flat toneless voice: "Omit: a reference to the unspeakable vice of the Greeks." Durham observed afterwards that he ought to lose his fellowship for such hypocrisy.

Maurice laughed.

"I regard it as a point of pure scholarship. The Greeks, or most of them, were that way inclined, and to omit it is to omit the mainstay of Athenian society."

"Is that so?"

"You've read the *Symposium*?"

Maurice had not, and did not add that he had explored Martial.

"It's all in there — not meat for babes, of course, but you ought to read it. Read it this vac."

No more was said at the time, but he was free of another subject, and one that he had never mentioned to any living soul. He hadn't known it could be mentioned, and when Durham did so in the middle of the sunlit court a breath of liberty touched him.

CHAPTER 8

On reaching home he talked about Durham until the fact that he had a friend penetrated into the minds of his family. Ada wondered whether it was brother to a certain Miss Durham — not but what she was an only child — while Mrs Hall confused it with a don named Cumberland. Maurice was deeply wounded. One strong feeling arouses another, and a profound irritation against his womenkind set in. His relations with them hitherto had been trivial but stable, but it seemed iniquitous that anyone should mispronounce the name of the man who was more to him than all the world. Home emasculated everything.

It was the same with his atheism. No one felt as deeply as he expected. With the crudity of youth he drew his mother apart and said that he should always respect her religious prejudices and those of the girls, but that his own conscience permitted him to attend church no longer. She said it was a great misfortune.

"I knew you would be upset. I cannot help it, mother dearest. I am made that way and it is no good arguing."

"Your poor father always went to church."

"I'm not my father."

"Morrie, Morrie, what a thing to say."

"Well, he isn't," said Kitty in her perky way. "Really, mother, come."

"Kitty, dear, you here," cried Mrs Hall, feeling that disapproval was due and unwilling to bestow it on her son. "We were talking about things not suited, and you are perfectly wrong besides, for Maurice is the image of his father — Dr Barry said so."

"Well, Dr Barry doesn't go to church himself," said Maurice, falling into the family habit of talking all over the shop.

"He is a most clever man," said Mrs Hall with finality, "and Mrs Barry's the same."

This slip of their mother's convulsed Ada and Kitty. They would not stop laughing at the idea of Mrs Barry's being a man, and Maurice's atheism was forgotten. He did not communicate on Easter Sunday, and supposed the row would come then, as in Durham's case. But no one took any notice, for the suburbs no longer exact Christianity. This disgusted him; it made him look at society with new eyes. Did society, while professing to be so moral and sensitive, really mind anything?

He wrote often to Durham — long letters trying carefully to express shades of feeling. Durham made little of them and said so. His replies were equally long. Maurice never let them out of his pocket, changing them from suit to suit and even pinning them in his pyjamas when he went to bed. He would wake up and touch them and, watching the reflections from the street lamp, remember how he used to feel afraid as a little boy.

Episode of Gladys Olcott.

Miss Olcott was one of their infrequent guests. She had been good to Mrs Hall and Ada in some hydro, and, receiving an invitation, had followed it up. She was charming — at least the women said so, and male callers told the son of the house he was a lucky dog. He laughed, they laughed, and having ignored her at first he took to paying her attentions.

Now Maurice, though he did not know it, had become an attractive young man. Much exercise had tamed his clumsiness. He was heavy but alert, and his face seemed following the example of his body. Mrs Hall put it down to his moustache — "Maurice's moustache will be the making of him" — a remark more profound than she realized. Certainly the little black line of it did pull his face together, and show up his teeth when he smiled, and his clothes suited him also: by Durham's advice he kept to flannel trousers, even on Sunday.

He turned his smile on Miss Olcott — it seemed the proper thing to do. She responded. He put his muscles at her service by taking her out in his new side-car. He sprawled at her feet. Finding she smoked, he persuaded her to stop behind with him in the dining-room and to look between his eyes. Blue vapour quivered and shredded and built dissolving walls, and Maurice's thoughts voyaged with it, to vanish as soon as a window was opened for fresh air. He saw that she was pleased, and his family, servants and all, intrigued; he determined to go further.

Something went wrong at once. Maurice paid her compliments, said that her hair etc. was ripping. She tried to stop him, but he was insensitive, and did not know that he had annoyed her. He had read that girls always pretended to stop men who complimented them. He haunted her. When she excused herself from riding with him on the last day he played the domineering male. She was his guest, she came, and having taken her to some scenery that he considered romantic he pressed her little hand between his own.

It was not that Miss Olcott objected to having her hand pressed. Others had done it and Maurice could have done it had he guessed how. But she knew something was wrong. His touch revolted her. It was a corpse's. Springing up she cried, "Mr Hall, don't be silly. I mean *don't* be silly. I am not saying it to make you sillier."

"Miss Olcott — Gladys — I'd rather die than offend —" growled the boy, trying to keep it up.

"I must go back by train," she said, crying a little. "I must, I'm awfully sorry." She arrived home before him with a sensible little story about a headache and dust in her eyes, but his family also knew that something had gone wrong.

Except for this episode the vac passed pleasantly. Maurice did some reading, following his friend's advice rather than his tutor's, and he asserted in one or two ways his belief that he was grown up. At his instigation his mother dismissed the Howells who had long paralysed the outdoor department, and set up a motor-car instead of a carriage. Everyone was impressed, including the Howells. He also called upon his father's old partner. He had inherited some business aptitude and some money, and it was settled that when he left Cambridge he should enter the firm as an unauthorized clerk; Hill and Hall, Stock Brokers. Maurice was stepping into the niche that England had prepared for him. ·

CHAPTER 9

During the previous term he had reached an unusual level mentally, but the vac pulled him back towards public-schoolishness. He was less alert, he again behaved as he supposed he was supposed to behave — a perilous feat for one who is not dowered with imagination. His mind, not obscured totally, was often crossed by clouds, and though Miss Olcott had passed, the insincerity that led him to her remained. His family were the main cause of this. He had yet to realize that they were stronger than he and influenced him incalculably. Three weeks in their company left him untidy, sloppy, victorious in every item, yet defeated on the whole. He came back thinking, and even speaking, like his mother or Ada.

Till Durham arrived he had not noticed the deterioration. Durham had not been well, and came up a few days late. When his face, paler than usual, peered round the door, Maurice had a spasm of despair, and tried to recollect where they stood last term, and to gather up the threads of the campaign. He felt himself slack, and afraid of action. The worst part of him rose to the surface, and urged him to prefer comfort to joy.

"Hullo, old man," he said awkwardly.

Durham slipped in without speaking.

"What's wrong?"

"Nothing;" and Maurice knew that he had lost touch. Last term he would have understood this silent entrance.

"Anyhow, take a pew."

Durham sat upon the floor beyond his reach. It was late afternoon. The sounds of the May term, the scents of the Cambridge year in flower, floated in through the window and said to Maurice, "You are unworthy of us." He knew that he was three parts dead, an alien, a yokel in Athens. He had no business here, nor with such a friend.

"I say, Durham —"

Durham came nearer. Maurice stretched out a hand and felt the head nestle against it. He forgot what he was going to say. The sounds and scents whispered, "You are we, we are youth." Very gently he stroked the hair and ran his fingers down into it as if to caress the brain.

"I say, Durham, have you been all right?"

"Have you?"

"No."

"You wrote you were."

"I wasn't."

The truth in his own voice made him tremble. "A rotten vac and I never knew it," and wondered how long he should know it. The mist would lower again, he felt sure, and with an unhappy sigh he pulled Durham's head against his knee, as though it was a talisman for clear living. It lay there, and he had accomplished a new tenderness — stroked it steadily from temple to throat. Then, removing both hands, he dropped them on either side of him and sat sighing.

"Hall."

Maurice looked.

"Is there some trouble?"

He caressed and again withdrew. It seemed as certain that he hadn't as that he had a friend.

"Anything to do with that girl?"

"No."

"You wrote you liked her."

"I didn't — don't."

Deeper sighs broke from him. They rattled in his throat, turning to groans. His head fell back, and he forgot the pressure of Durham on his knee, forgot that Durham was watching his turbid agony. He stared at the ceiling with wrinkled mouth and eyes, understanding nothing except that man has been created to feel pain and loneliness without help from heaven.

Now Durham stretched up to him, stroked his hair. They clasped one another. They were lying breast against breast soon, head was on shoulder, but just as their cheeks met someone called "Hall" from the court, and he answered: he always had answered when people called. Both started violently, and Durham sprang to the mantelpiece where he leant his head on his arm. Absurd people came thundering up the stairs. They wanted tea. Maurice pointed to it, then was drawn into their conversation, and scarcely noticed his friend's departure. It had been an ordinary talk, he told himself, but too sentimental, and he cultivated a breeziness against their next meeting.

This took place soon enough. With half a dozen others he was starting for the theatre after hall when Durham called him.

"I knew you read the *Symposium* in the vac," he said in a low voice.

Maurice felt uneasy.

"Then you understand — without me saying more —"

"How do you mean?"

Durham could not wait. People were all around them, but with eyes that had gone intensely blue he whispered, "I love you."

Maurice was scandalized, horrified. He was shocked to the bottom of his suburban soul, and exclaimed, "Oh, rot!" The words, the manner, were out of him before he could recall them. "Durham, you're an Englishman. I'm another. Don't talk nonsense. I'm not offended, because I know you don't mean it, but it's the only subject absolutely beyond the limit as you know, it's the worst crime in the calendar, and you must never mention it again. Durham! a rotten notion really —"

But his friend was gone, gone without a word, flying across the court, the bang of his door heard through the sounds of spring.

CHAPTER 10

A slow nature such as Maurice's appears insensitive, for it needs time even to feel. Its instinct is to assume that nothing either for good or evil has happened, and to resist the invader. Once gripped, it feels acutely, and its sensations in love are particularly profound. Given time, it can know and impart ecstasy; given time, it can sink to the heart of Hell. Thus it was that his agony began as a slight regret; sleepless nights and lonely days must intensify it into a frenzy that consumed him. It worked inwards, till it touched the root whence body and soul both spring, the "I" that he had been trained to obscure, and, realized at last, doubled its power and grew superhuman. For it might have been joy. New worlds broke loose in him at this, and he saw from the vastness of the ruin what ecstasy he had lost, what a communion.

They did not speak again for two days. Durham would have made it longer, but most of their friends were now in common, and they were bound to meet. Realizing this, he wrote Maurice an icy note suggesting that it would be a public convenience if they behaved as if nothing had happened. He added, "I shall be obliged if you will not mention my criminal morbidity to anyone. I am sure you will do this from the sensible way in which you took the news." Maurice did not reply, but first put the note with the letters he had received during the vac and afterwards burnt them all.

He supposed the climax of agony had come. But he was fresh to real suffering as to reality of any kind. They had yet to meet. On the second afternoon they found themselves in the same four at tennis and the pain grew excruciating. He could scarcely stand or see; if he returned Durham's service the ball sent a throb up his arm. Then they were made to be partners; once they jostled, Durham winced, but managed to laugh in the old fashion.

Moreover, it proved convenient that he should come back to college in Maurice's side-car. He got in without demur. Maurice, who had not been to bed for two nights, went light-headed, turned the machine into a bylane and travelled top speed. There was a wagon in front, full of women. He drove straight at them, but when they screamed stuck on his brakes, and just avoided disaster. Durham made no comment. As he indicated in his note, he only spoke when others were present. All other intercourse was to end.

That evening Maurice went to bed as usual. But as he laid his head on the pillows a flood of tears oozed from it. He was horrified. A man crying! Fetherstonhaugh might hear him. He wept stifled in the sheets, he sprang about kissing, then struck his head against the wall and smashed the crockery. Someone did come up the stairs. He grew quiet at once and did not recommence when the footsteps died away. Lighting a candle, he looked with surprise at his torn pyjamas and trembling limbs. He continued to cry, for he could not stop, but the suicidal point had been passed, and, remaking the bed, he lay down. His gyp was clearing away the ruins when he opened his eyes. It seemed queer to Maurice that a gyp should have been dragged in. He wondered whether the man suspected anything, then slept again. On waking the second time he found letters on the floor — one from old Mr Grace, his grandfather, about the party that was to be given when he came of age, another from a don's wife asking him to lunch ("Mr Durham is coming too, so you won't be shy"), another from Ada with mention of Gladys Olcott. Yet again he fell asleep.

Madness is not for everyone, but Maurice's proved the thunderbolt that dispels the clouds. The storm had been working up not for three days as he supposed, but for six years. It had brewed in the obscurities of being where no eye pierces, his surroundings had thickened it. It had burst and he had not died. The brilliancy of day was around him, he stood upon the mountain range that overshadows youth, he saw.

Most of the day he sat with open eyes, as if looking into the Valley he had left. It was all so plain now. He had lied. He phrased it "been fed upon lies," but lies are the natural food of boyhood, and he had eaten greedily. His first resolve was to be more careful in the future. He would live straight, not because it mattered to anyone now, but for the sake of the game. He would not deceive himself so much. He would not — and this was the test — pretend to care about women when the only sex that attracted him was his own. He loved men and always had loved them. He longed to embrace them and mingle his being with theirs. Now that the man who returned his love had been lost, he admitted this.

{1914}